To Patricia and Rosella Anderson for
their love, understanding, and support

—JCA

To Grace, Ryan, and Jeffrey Narus ... thank you for
your inspiration, patience, and humor during this project

—JAN

Contents

PREFACE

The state-of-knowledge and state-of-best-practice in business markets have advanced considerably since the publication of our first edition. The second edition of *Business Market Management* interprets and integrates these advances within the framework that our first edition established. It also strongly reflects the changes in our views of business markets and what firms need to do to prosper. Two significant developments in the second edition are especially noteworthy.

We now provide detailed discussion of *customer value management* as a progressive, practical approach to delivering superior value to targeted market segments and customer firms, and getting an equitable return on the value delivered. Customer value management relies on building customer value models to gain an understanding of customer requirements and preferences, and what it is worth in monetary terms to fulfill them. Leading suppliers leverage the knowledge they gain from customer value models to create value-based sales tools that enable them to persuasively demonstrate and document the superior value their marketing offerings deliver. In our second edition, we relate the best practices of these leading suppliers. Complementing this discussion, we describe in detail an approach to customer value management and building customer value models that we have developed and refined while working with numerous firms in diverse industries over the past several years.

Brands and brand building are concepts that are of growing interest in business markets. Establishing and building their brands are goals that managers in business markets increasingly seek to accomplish. They believe that by adapting the concepts and practices of their counterparts in consumer markets to the business-to-business setting, they can build brand equity and benefit from it. In our second edition, we provide extended consideration of *brands in business markets*. New sections are devoted to brands as resources, building brands and brand equity in business markets, positioning in business markets and crafting persuasive value propositions, branding market offerings, and global branding. Each of these sections is reinforced and enlivened with best practice company examples.

Our second edition retains the framework for understanding, creating, and delivering value established in our first edition. Chapters are devoted to each of the business market processes in this framework, such as Crafting Market Strategy, Managing Market Offerings, and Sustaining Customer Relationships. The same four guiding principles of business market management still recur throughout the second edition:

- Regard Value as the Cornerstone
- Focus on Business Market Processes
- Stress Doing Business Across Borders
- Accentuate Working Relationships and Business Networks

Our second edition continues with our first edition title of *Business Market Management* instead of *Business Marketing*. Although our book is about business marketing, our choice of title reflects our recognition that marketing work processes, such as segmentation, targeting and positioning, increasingly take place *within* business market processes such as crafting market strategy and managing market offerings. Business market processes cut across functional areas and depend upon seamless cross-functional cooperation for marketplace success. Thus, business market management requires significant participation from many functional areas, not just marketing, to decide what market segments and customer firms are of primary interest (i.e., targeting) and how to deliver superior value to them (i.e., positioning). We think that *business market management* better conveys this broader responsibility for the market, and this perspective makes our book not only of greater interest to those in a marketing functional area, but also to those in related functional areas and general management.

To formulate, test, and refine our thinking, as well as to gather best practice illustrations throughout our book, we continue to conduct extensive management practice research with leading European and North American companies. We also have studied and provide examples from the best practices of some leading Asian companies operating in Europe and the Americas. These leading-edge firms serve a variety of business markets, providing offerings as diverse as bearings, air cargo service, enterprise software, and commercial banking services. Our primary research enables us to generate illustrations and examples that offer greater texture and richness than do examples that come from secondary sources. Because this research is conducted with firms that excel at value-based market management, the illustrations and examples that come from them provide insight into how the models, frameworks, and concepts we present can be put into practice. Reflecting this continuing commitment, our second edition contains 24 new breakout boxes, most of which resulted from primary management practice research. Of course, we also continue to supplement the illustrations generated from our management practice research with numerous examples from secondary sources.

The intent of our second edition is to provide the most progressive managerial approach to business marketing and business markets. Whether readers are students with limited experience or seasoned managers, they will find the second edition a valuable resource, containing concepts, frameworks, and best practices that will stir up and advance their thinking. We think that our second edition delivers superior value in return for the time readers invest in it, and we believe that after reading it, you will agree.

ACKNOWLEDGMENTS

In writing the second edition, we interpreted and integrated significant developments in the state-of-knowledge and state-of-best-practice in business markets that have occurred since our first edition. Although writing the second edition was easier than the first, we have received significant support from a number of individuals and organizations to enable us to accomplish this. We begin by acknowledging this support for the second edition and then reprint the acknowledgments from the first edition, which provided us with the strong foundation and framework.

SECOND EDITION

Many individuals and organizations have provided support and contributions to enable us to complete our second edition. While we are grateful to them all, we single out some of them here to explicitly acknowledge their support and contributions.

The Institute for the Study of Business Markets (ISBM), located at Penn State University, continued to support our research and the preparation of the second edition. Without their generous financial support of our work, we would have been unable to produce the revision we envisioned. We are thankful to Ralph Oliva, the Executive Director of ISBM, Gary Lilien, the Research Director of ISBM, and David Wilson, the Managing Director at ISBM, for believing in us and our work over the years.

We thank the many managers who so graciously took time out of their overfull schedules to meet and talk with us. The best practices that these managers shared with us made an enormous contribution. In particular, we single out a number of managers for their exemplary support and assistance: Marla Berry, Bank of America; Andrew Burtis, Siebel Systems; Lance Dixon, Bose; Jan Ekonomy, Sprint; Leonard Fuld, Fuld & Company; Johan Godemont and Bart Huysmans, SEGHERS group; Phoebe Johnson, EMBREX; David Kaplan, Eli Lilly; Michael Lawrence, Honeywell; Mark McElhinny and Joseph Razum, Rockwell Automation; André Mulder, KLM Cargo; Wolfgang Platzer and Louise Gorman, ABN-AMRO Bank; Frank Schuringa, OTRA; Todd Snelgrove, SKF; and Guy Wolff, Infineon Technologies.

Completing a revision requires many tasks to be completed and contributions to be made. Over the course of this revision, we greatly benefited from the capable support and assistance of a number of Research Associates at the Kellogg School. We thank Arnaud Melin, Pankaj Tibrewal, Ketan Shah, and, especially, Florent Carbonneau and Amy Walls for their wonderful contributions to this revision.

We are grateful for the support and assistance we have received from the following editors at Prentice Hall: Suzanne Grappi, Bruce Kaplan, Melissa Pellerano, John Roberts, and Katie Stevens. We also are grateful to Michelle O'Brien of Prentice Hall for her help in marketing our book and to Jennifer Welsch of BookMasters for her project management of our second edition.

Finally, we gratefully acknowledge a number of individuals in Amsterdam and the Netherlands, which has become our "home away from home" in conducting our management practice research in Europe. Professors Arjan van Weele and Finn Wynstra continue to significantly influence our thinking on purchasing and understanding firms as customers. Fred Tromer, recently retired from Heineken, has become a gracious mentor and "gezellig" friend. We again thank the artists and their friends at Verbeelding b.v. for the evenings of thought-provoking conversation and wonderful fellowship. Gerard Gooiker and our late friend, Eddy Agelink, have been a source of inspiration for us, and we are indebted to them. We also gratefully acknowledge Gerard for his evocative watercolor, *Upon Arrival*, which graces the cover of our second edition.

FIRST EDITION

Writing this book would not have been possible without the contributions and support of a number of individuals and organizations. Words fall far short of the gratitude that we feel for their contributions and support. But, as a small measure of our appreciation for what they have done for us, we acknowledge them here.

The Institute for the Study of Business Markets (ISBM), located at Penn State University, has been instrumental in the completion of this book. Without their generous financial support of our field research, we would have been unable to produce the book we envisioned. We are thankful to Irwin Gross, the founding Executive Director of ISBM, Gary Lilien, the Research Director of ISBM, and David Wilson, the Managing Director at ISBM, for believing in us and our work over the years. We are especially indebted to Irv Gross, who was also our former manager in the corporate marketing research and consulting group at DuPont Company. It is Irv who imparted to us the philosophy of doing business based on value in business markets and who has acted as a mentor to us over the years. And, it was a number of businesses at DuPont that first provided us with real-world demonstrations that value-based business market management can succeed.

We thank the many managers that so graciously took time out of their overfull schedules to meet and talk with us. The best practices that these managers shared with us made an enormous contribution. In particular, we single out several managers for their exemplary support and assistance: William Babtie, Dresner Kleinwort Benson; Donald Bielinski, W. W. Grainger; Arne Bennborn, ABB; Steven Dehmlow, GLS; Terry Mulligan, Baxter; Wolfgang Platzer and Hanno van Veen, ABN-AMRO Bank; and Fred Tromer, Heineken.

Writing a book is a complicated undertaking, requiring many tasks to be completed and contributions to be made. Over the course of this project, we have greatly benefited from the capable support and assistance of a number of Research Associates at the Kellogg School. We thank Nicole Avril, Ellen Carr, Sandra Diaz, Robin Dodge, Laura Farrelly, Heather Funke, and Pamela Jo Platt for their wonderful support in making this book a reality.

Although we have written a number of articles, this is our first book. We are grateful that we have been able to rely on Philip Kotler, the Prentice Hall International

Marketing Series Editor, for his guidance and advice throughout this project. There is no one better to turn to for counsel and advice on writing a textbook than Phil. We are also grateful for the support and assistance we have received from the various editors at Prentice Hall: Whitney Blake, David Borkowsky, Gabrielle Dudnyk, Linda DeLorenzo, Aileen Mason, and Audrey Regan.

We want to express our appreciation to a number of individuals for reading drafts and offering comments. Professors Björn Axelsson, Wesley Johnston, Gary Lilien, Jacqueline Pels, Robert Spekman, and David Wilson each helped us strengthen our manuscript. Dr. Eugene Lieb of Custom Decision Support read our manuscript and graciously provided some material to us. Two students made noteworthy contributions: James Nelles read Chapter 3 and offered many useful suggestions, and Samuel Bachman read Chapter 6 and contributed two boxes on concurrent engineering.

James Anderson acknowledges Dean Donald P. Jacobs and his colleagues at the Kellogg Graduate School of Management. Without Don Jacobs' generous support, this book could not have been completed. Moreover, Jim Anderson gratefully thanks Don for believing in him throughout his career at Kellogg, and for Don's willingness to break conventions that benefited Jim. Jim Anderson wants to express his appreciation to Jeanne Brett for her support and encouragement, and her insights on culture and cross-cultural negotiations. He is deeply indebted to his colleagues in the Marketing Department. Working with a group of such smart, motivated, and accomplished scholars provides a phenomenal setting for learning. He especially thanks Anand Bodhapati, Gregory Carpenter, Sachin Gupta, Dipak Jain, Philip Kotler, and Mohanbir Sawhney for their many helpful comments and suggestions on earlier drafts. Finally, he is greatly appreciative of his relationships with Philip Kotler and Louis Stern, who have generously given their time and been mentors to him over the years.

James Narus thanks the Babcock Graduate School of Management for providing partial financial support during one summer of this project. He expresses his appreciation to Babcock School colleagues, Rick Harris and Ram Baliga, for suggesting topics from managerial economics and commenting on a chapter draft, respectively. Jim Narus also acknowledges the prompt and diligent assistance of the Babcock School's head librarian, Bob Hebert, in locating and retrieving books, articles, and monographs.

Finally, we both gratefully acknowledge a number of individuals in Amsterdam, which has become our "home away from home" in conducting our field research in Europe. We thank Kathryn Wentzel of Home Abroad for her assistance in arranging a comfortable apartment and work space for us. Ariane von Raesfeld joined us for a number of lively, insightful discussions. Arjan van Weele and Finn Wijnstra greatly shaped our thinking on purchasing and understanding firms as customers. We thank the artists and their friends at Verbeelding b.v. for the evenings of thought-provoking conversation and wonderful fellowship. Eddy Agelink and Gerard Gooiker have been a source of inspiration for us, and we are indebted to them. We also gratefully acknowledge Gerard for the marvelous lithograph that graces the cover of our book.

James C. Anderson
James A. Narus
Amsterdam, The Netherlands

Research funding for this book has been graciously provided by:

About the Authors

James C. Anderson

James C. Anderson is the William L. Ford Distinguished Professor of Marketing and Wholesale Distribution, and Professor of Behavioral Science in Management at the Kellogg School of Management, Northwestern University. Professor Anderson joined the faculty of the Kellogg School in 1984 as an assistant professor of marketing. In 1987 he was named the first to hold the Kellogg School's newly-endowed William L. Ford Distinguished Chair in Marketing and Wholesale Distribution.

Professor Anderson teaches graduate-level courses in business marketing. He is a faculty member of the Executive Master's Program and teaches in a number of executive development programs at the James L. Allen Center. He is the program director of the Business Marketing Strategy executive program. He has consulted and provided seminars for a number of companies in North America and Europe, such as ARCADIS, AT&T, bioMérieux, Dow Chemical, FEMSA Empaque, G.E. Capital Services, International Paper, Johnson & Johnson, 3M, PPG Industries, Pharmacia, and Solutia.

Professor Anderson's research interests are in constructing persuasive value propositions in business markets, measurement approaches for demonstrating and documenting the value of market offerings, and working relationships between firms in business markets. He has written more than 30 journal articles, including several published in *Harvard Business Review*. He is a member of the editorial boards of the *International Journal of Research in Marketing, Journal of Business-to-Business Marketing,* and *Journal of Strategic Marketing,* and has served on the editorial boards of the *Journal of Applied Psychology* and *Journal of Marketing Research*. He is a Fellow of the American Psychological Association.

Professor Anderson is the Irwin Gross Distinguished ISBM Research Fellow at the Institute for the Study of Business Markets and a member of its advisory board. He also is a visiting research professor at the School of Technology and Management, University of Twente, The Netherlands. He has been a visiting research professor at Eindhoven University of Technology, the Netherlands, and at Uppsala University and Stockholm School of Economics, Sweden. He also has been vice president of the business marketing division of the American Marketing Association (AMA) and a member of the board of directors of the AMA.

Professor Anderson came to Kellogg after three years as a member of the marketing faculty of the University of Texas at Austin. Prior to that, from 1978 to 1981, he worked as a senior research psychologist in the corporate marketing research division of E.I. duPont de Nemours and Company, Inc. He earned his doctorate in psychology from Michigan State University in 1978.

James A. Narus

James A. Narus is Professor of Business Marketing at the Babcock Graduate School of Management, Wake Forest University in Charlotte, North Carolina. He joined the faculty in 1988. Professor Narus's teaching, research, and consulting interests include value-based marketing, the management of market offerings, distribution channel design and management, and partnerships and networks within business markets.

Professor Narus routinely teaches courses on business-to-business marketing and marketing management in the Babcock School's full-time, evening, executive, and Charlotte MBA programs. His teaching portfolio includes such courses as marketing channel management, strategic account management, sales management, marketing strategy and policy, brand management, and advertising management. Over the years, Professor Narus has taught in executive development programs at Northwestern University, Pennsylvania State University, the University of Texas at Austin, and Texas A&M University, as well as in international management seminars at the Universidad Torcuato Di Tella (Argentina), Copenhagen Business School (Denmark), Bordeaux School of Management (France), University College Dublin (Ireland), and Twente University (The Netherlands).

Professor Narus has written numerous articles and research papers on business market management topics. These articles have appeared in the *Harvard Business Review*, *Sloan Management Review*, *California Management Review*, and the *Journal of Marketing*, among other journals.

Professor Narus is a member of the editorial review boards of the *Journal of Business-to-Business Marketing* and the *Journal of Marketing Channels*, as well as an ad hoc reviewer for several other publications. He is a longstanding member of the American Marketing Association. For seven years, he served as the coordinator of its Business-to-Business Marketing Special Interest Group. Professor Narus belongs to the NAPM–Carolinas and Virginia, an affiliate of the Institute for Supply Management, and is a member of the Charlotte North Rotary Club.

Professor Narus has provided management consulting expertise or executive training seminars for numerous corporations including the Allen-Bradley Company, DuPont, Eastman Chemicals, Gardner-Denver Corporation, General Motors, S. C. Johnson, McKinsey & Company, Merck, Pacific Technologies, Parker-Hannifin Corporation, Rockwell Automation, and the Toronto Dominion Bank. Prior to his academic career, Professor Narus worked as a market research analyst and fellow in the corporate marketing research division of E.I. duPont de Nemours and Company, Inc. There, he conducted studies on a variety of issues related to distribution channel management. He earned his doctorate in marketing management from Syracuse University in 1981.

Section I

Introduction and Overview

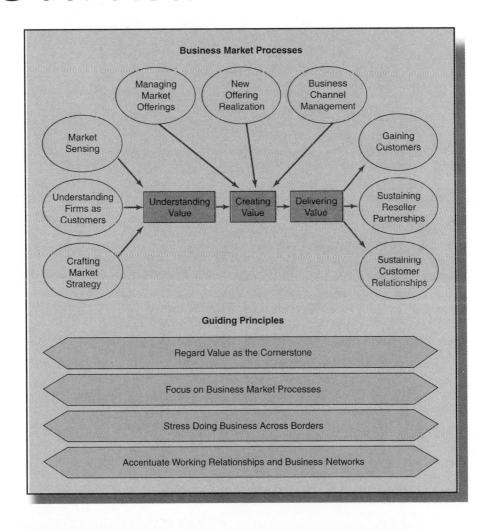

Business Market Processes

- Managing Market Offerings
- New Offering Realization
- Business Channel Management

- Market Sensing
- Understanding Firms as Customers
- Crafting Market Strategy

Understanding Value → Creating Value → Delivering Value

- Gaining Customers
- Sustaining Reseller Partnerships
- Sustaining Customer Relationships

Guiding Principles

- Regard Value as the Cornerstone
- Focus on Business Market Processes
- Stress Doing Business Across Borders
- Accentuate Working Relationships and Business Networks

Chapter 1

Business Market Management: Guiding Principles

OVERVIEW

Much attention in recent years has been given to value and its provision to customers. However, remarkably few firms have the knowledge and capability to actually assess value in practice and gain an equitable return for the value they deliver to customers. Although many supplier firm managers tout the value their market offerings provide customers, those managers have little to say when pressed for specifics on what their market offerings are actually worth to customers. One firm's stationery and business cards boast: "Delivering Superior Value with *Alpha* and *Beta* Brands."[1] Yet, when senior management was asked what actual assessments had been done to understand the value of their firm's offerings, they answered that the firm had not done any. Perhaps the firm was delivering superior value. What is more in doubt is whether the firm was receiving an equitable return, or if it was simply giving value away.

Because a large percentage of the typical firm's revenues go to pay for goods and services it acquires from suppliers, firms increasingly focus on their purchasing practices to improve profitability. Widespread quality management in production and greater availability of comparable market offerings from international sources has led firms to pressure their suppliers to reduce prices and provide discounts.[2] As a result, suppliers in many industries find that, although their sales revenues are growing, it is often at the expense of profitability. To persuade customer managers to focus on total costs rather than simply on acquisition price, suppliers must have an accurate understanding of what the customer firm values and *would* value.

3

For a moment, put yourself in the role of a commercial grower. Two suppliers are offering you mulch film, which is a thin plastic sheet that commercial growers place on the ground to hold in moisture, prevent weed growth, and allow closer planting of vegetables and melons. One supplier comes to you with the proposition, "Trust us, our mulch film will lower your cost." The other supplier, Sonoco Products Company, comes to you with the proposition, "Sonoco just lowered the cost of your mulch film by $16.83 per acre," and it offers to show you exactly how. Which supplier's proposition do you find most persuasive?

Business market management is the process of understanding, creating, and delivering value to targeted business markets and customers. Business market management provides a means of gaining an equitable return on the value delivered and of enhancing a supplier firm's present and future profitability. It is a progressive way of thinking about business markets and what supplier firms are attempting to accomplish in them. **Business markets** are firms, institutions, or governments that acquire goods and services either for their own use, to incorporate into the products or services that they produce, or for resale along with other products and services to other firms, institutions, or governments. By this definition, a professional painter's purchase of paint brushes from a mass merchant such as Home Depot would be a business market transaction, whereas a homeowner's purchase of the same paint brushes from the same mass merchant, to paint his own home, would be a consumer market transaction.

This chapter provides an overview of business market management. In doing so, it also provides an overview for this book, which is organized around nine constituent processes of business market management. Some fundamental ideas recur throughout this book. We think of these ideas as defining or guiding principles of business market management:

- Regard value as the *cornerstone* of business market management
- Focus on business market processes
- Stress doing business across borders
- Accentuate working relationships and business networks

We sketch the business market processes and guiding principles of business market management in Figure 1.1. The figure organizes the business market processes, which constitute business market management, into three groups, based on whether they are a part of understanding, creating, or delivering value. We devote a chapter to each business market process. In the following sections of this chapter, we discuss each guiding principle.

VALUE AS THE CORNERSTONE OF BUSINESS MARKET MANAGEMENT

One distinction between business markets and consumer markets is that customers in business markets predominantly focus on functionality or performance, whereas

Figure 1.1 Business Market Management

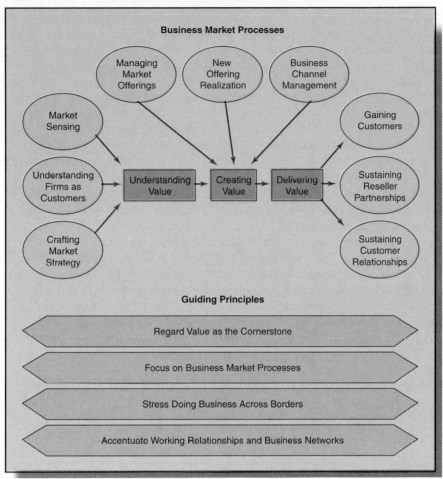

customers in consumer markets predominantly focus on aesthetics or taste. In each case, most decisions are driven predominantly, but not exclusively, by these considerations.[3] For example, it would be difficult to imagine a plant manager saying, "I bought the machine tool from Supplier X, rather than Supplier Y, because I wanted green instead of blue." However, if the plant manager judged the performance of the two machine tools in her particular application to be the same in all significant respects, then she might choose on the basis of aesthetics or taste.

We use **value** to express in monetary terms the functionality or performance of a market offering in a given customer application.[4] We regard value as the cornerstone of business market management because of the predominant role that functionality or performance plays in business markets. We first discuss exactly what value is in business markets, and then, how business market management crucially relies on the assessment of value.

What Is Value in Business Markets?

More formally, **value in business markets** is the worth in monetary terms of the economic, technical, service, and social benefits a customer firm receives in exchange for the price it pays for a market offering.[5] We want to elaborate on some aspects of this definition.

First, we express value in monetary terms, such as dollars per unit, euros per liter, or kronor per hour. Economists may care about "utils," but we have never met a manager who did.

Second, we can conceptually represent any market offering as a set of economic, technical, service, and social benefits a customer firm receives. By benefits, we mean *net* benefits, where any costs a customer incurs in obtaining the desired benefits, except for purchase price, are also included.

Third, value is what a customer firm gets in exchange for the price it pays. Therefore, we conceptually view a market offering as having two elemental characteristics: value and price.

Finally, considerations of value take place within some context. Even when no direct, in-kind market offerings exist, there is always a competitive alternative. In business markets, one competitive alternative may be that the customer firm decides to make the product itself rather than purchase it from outside suppliers.

We can capture the essence of the concepts in our definition of value in a **fundamental value equation**:

$$(\text{Value}_f - \text{Price}_f) > (\text{Value}_a - \text{Price}_a) \tag{1.1}$$

where Value_f and Price_f are the value and price of a particular firm's market offering (Offering$_f$), and Value_a and Price_a are the value and price of the next-best-alternative market offering (Offering$_a$). This equation will prove useful at a number of points in this book, such as when we consider value-based pricing in Chapter 5.

Note that we have not specified a particular perspective in our definition of value, such as the customer firm's point of view, because we regard value in business markets as a construct, similar to market share. Because it is a construct, in practice, we can only *estimate* value, just as we can only estimate market share. For example, the supplier may *overestimate* the value of a given market offering to a customer, while the customer may *underestimate* the value. The supplier may have a significantly different perception from the customer of the technical, economic, service, and social benefits that the customer firm actually receives from a market offering, or of what specific benefits are actually worth in monetary terms to the customer.

Value changes occur in two fundamental ways.[6] First, a market offering could provide the same functionality or performance while its cost to the customer changes. Remember, price is *not* considered in this cost. Thus, the technical, service, and social benefits remain constant while the economic benefits change. For example, one product has higher value than another product because it has lower conversion costs and has the same performance specifications. Second, value changes whenever the functionality or performance provided changes while cost remains the same (again, price is not a part of this cost). For example, a redesigned component part now provides longer usage until failure for the customer's customer, yet its acquisition and conversion costs to the customer remain the same. Finally, even if functionality or performance of a product is lowered, it may still meet, or even exceed, a customer's specified minimum requirement. More is better for some, but not all, customer requirements. Exceeding minimum requirements continues to deliver benefits to the customer, even though the customer deems a lesser level to be acceptable. For example, lowering the melting point of a plastic resin beyond a specified temperature requirement continues to lower the customer's energy costs and to reduce the time it takes to convert the resin into a molded plastic part.

Finally, notice that in our definition, value is the expression in monetary terms of what the customer firm receives in exchange for the price it pays for a market offering. Because make-versus-buy decisions are possible in business markets, the value provided must exceed the price paid. This difference between value and price is the **customer incentive to purchase**.[7] In this concept of value in business markets, raising or lowering the price of an offering does not change the value that offering provides to a customer firm. Rather, it changes the customer's incentive to purchase that offering.

Assessing Value in Practice

In contrast to the supplier of Alpha and Beta brands, business market management critically relies upon actual assessment of value in the marketplace. Having an accurate assessment of value provides a solid foundation for supplier firm efforts to create and deliver value to targeted market segments and customers. The recognition that the value of a given market offering can vary by market segment and by customer characteristics is a significant underpinning of business market management. Business market management strives to both understand and capitalize on this variation.

Customer firms often do not have an accurate understanding of what suppliers' market offerings are actually worth to them. Certainly, customers may understand their own requirements, but they do not necessarily know what the fulfillment of these requirements is worth to them, how differing ways of meeting these requirements affect their costs, or what changes in their requirements would be worth to them. As Irwin Gross, a business marketing expert, sagely observed:

> The vendor can't assume the customer accurately perceives or understands the value being offered. For a customer to buy a product, he or she needs to perceive only that the value exceeds the price, but not necessarily by how much.[8]

This lack of understanding requires business market managers to further develop the ability to be customer- or market-oriented in business markets. Most business market managers now understand that their firms need to translate features to benefits for their present and prospective customers. In making this translation, a supplier firm takes the customer's point of view. However, this translation is no longer adequate. Business market managers need to go beyond this point and further translate what the benefits are worth in the customer's own setting. That is, a supplier must persuasively demonstrate the value that its market offering provides to the customer. In doing so, a supplier firm not only takes the customer's viewpoint, it makes the customer firm managers' task of deciding upon a supplier easier. In an era when managers are being asked to perform a greater amount of work with fewer resources, what customer firm managers wouldn't appreciate a supplier that provides them with a more accurate understanding of what they ought to acquire? Box 1.1 elaborates on this translation.

In Chapter 2, "Market Sensing: Generating and Using Knowledge About the Marketplace," we first present a number of methods for customer value assessment in business markets. We then present a comprehensive, practical approach for demonstrating and documenting the value of present and prospective market offerings, **customer value management**. Here, we say simply that value assessment is not always easy, but it is essential. Without a specific knowledge of the value provided, discussions

BOX 1.1
Demonstrating and Documenting Value: "Green Money Versus Gray Money"

Senior executives at most firms in business markets have come to realize that if they can cut the cost of acquired goods and services, those savings will fall right to the bottom line as improved profitability. Thus, they establish goals for purchasing that are typically expressed as total cost reductions. These goals might be expressed as a targeted cost reduction amount, such as reducing the cost of acquired goods and services by $5 billion in three years, as one oil company did, or as a yearly percentage reduction, such as reducing the costs by 10%, 5%, and 5% in three consecutive years, as one automotive manufacturer did. Because purchasing management is pressed for time and may not have adequate measurement capability, the translation of these goals into purchasing practice leads to a bias that one purchasing director captured with the expression "Green money versus gray money." What did he mean?

Green money (the color of all U.S. currency) refers to cost savings that purchasing managers can readily claim, whereas gray money refers to cost savings that are difficult for them to claim. Getting three bids, picking the lowest one, and then negotiating a further reduction is green money. It reflects directly on purchasing's contribution to the goal that senior management has set. Acquiring an offering that provides a lower total cost of ownership but has a higher purchase price is

gray money. Because of limited time and measurement capability, a purchasing manager may not be able to document that she has actually received the cost savings that the supplier assured her firm. As a purchasing manager, what color money would you prefer?

It doesn't have to be that way. A manufacturer of controls for automating manufacturing lines has its salespeople spend time at prospective customers gathering data on what controls would be required, what the total cost of those controls would be (not just purchase price, but all costs such as installation and training), and what the payback period would be if the customer were to purchase the controls. The salesperson pulls this research together into a report that demonstrates the potential savings, which he then provides to the prospective customer. Whose name appears on the cover of the report? The purchasing manager's! The supplier salesperson's name appears nowhere on the cover of the report. Now, the purchasing manager can take this report to his senior management and say, "Look, I have been doing some research in conjunction with this supplier, and this is how we can save some money." What has this supplier done? Enabled the purchasing manager to turn "gray" money into "green" money. It also has provided a social benefit by allowing the purchasing manager to leverage his time, which is in short supply.

with customers largely center on price. Examining our fundamental value equation supports why. Without knowledge of $Value_f$ and $Value_a$, making them absent, what's left in the equation? Knowledge of $Value_f$ and $Value_a$ also enables business market managers to persuasively counter claims that the two market offerings are equivalent.

Finally, customer firms themselves may assess the value of alternative suppliers' offerings through **value analysis**. A value analysis is conducted by a cross-functional team within the customer firm, typically with representatives from engineering, manufacturing, R&D, and purchasing. Supplier representatives may contribute to the team's analysis as well. The team assesses a market offering's attributes in terms of their functionality or performance, calculates the total costs associated with providing this specific functionality or performance, and attempts to identify lower-cost alternatives. The use of value analyses appears to be increasing, even though customer firms do not perform them often.[9]

MANAGING BUSINESS MARKET PROCESSES

Business market management is an overarching business process composed of a series of related, interdependent business market processes. A **business process** is "a collection of activities that takes one or more kinds of input and creates an output that is of value to the customer."[10] Because this definition explicitly gives creating value for customers as the purpose of a business process, it reinforces the guiding principle of value as the cornerstone of business market management.

Business market management takes a process orientation to the business unit, viewing it as a value-generating enterprise. Allaire elaborates on three different kinds of processes, each operating at a different level of the enterprise:

> At the highest level, there are **management processes**—how the CEO runs the company, how management interacts with employees, how decisions get made, and how communication takes place. Those processes set the organizational context and style of working, like "the IBM way." Then there are **business processes**, which are the focus of reengineering efforts. Business processes are large, crosscutting collections of activities, like product design, order fulfillment, and customer service. Finally, there are **work processes**, which are the basic building blocks of business processes. Work processes are focused and operational; they are how the work actually gets done. Examples include such activities as prototype development, finished-goods warehousing, and purchasing.[11]

Therefore, in our consideration of business market processes, we must also be mindful of management processes and work processes. For example, because work processes still take place largely within functional areas or departments of a business unit, adopting a business process orientation directs greater attention to mechanisms for gaining cross-functional cooperation.

In this section, we first consider shareholder value, core business processes, and the role of marketing. We then outline the specific, constituent business market processes in business market management, and articulate what the role of business marketing is within business market management.

Shareholder Value, Business Processes, and Marketing

Shareholder value is a concept that a growing number of senior executives have adopted as the ultimate criterion for evaluating business performance. Simply put, a business creates **shareholder value** when the economic returns generated from realizing its business strategy exceed the cost of capital employed to realize it. Shareholder value is reflected in the shareholder returns of dividends and appreciation in share price. Shareholder value analysis draws on estimates of a set of **value drivers**—sales growth rate, operating profit margin, income tax rate, working capital investment, fixed capital investment, cost of capital, and forecast period—to calculate the present value of forecasted cash flows and the residual value of the business after the forecast period. Although providing accurate estimates for these value drivers can challenge the expertise and forecasting capabilities of managers, and assumptions are required to estimate the residual value of a business, advocates of shareholder value stress that discounted cash flows are superior to other measures for evaluating business performance, such as earnings and return on investment.[12]

How is shareholder value related to our core concept of customer value? Al Rappaport, a pioneer and leading advocate of shareholder value, provides an insightful answer:

> Even the most persistent advocate of shareholder value understands that without customer value there can be no shareholder value. The source of a company's long-term cash flow is its satisfied customers. On the other hand, providing customer satisfaction does not automatically translate into shareholder value. Providing a comparable product at a lower cost than competitors, or providing superior value to the customer through higher quality, special features, or postsales services, are not genuine advantages if the total long-term cost, including the cost of capital, is greater than the cash generated by the sale. A business that provides more value than customers are willing to pay for is hardly competitive—and may not even be viable.[13]

Thus, translating customer value into shareholder value critically depends on a business being able to claim an equitable return on the value it delivers to customers. We contend that by persuasively demonstrating and documenting the superior value it delivers to customers, a business will be better equipped to successfully accomplish this translation.

What are the core business processes for shareholder value and customer value creation, and what contributions can marketing make to each of them?

Core Business Processes

Srivastava, Shervani, and Fahey recently argued that three core business processes are essential to customer value creation, and in turn, shareholder value creation:

product development management, supply chain management, and customer relationship management. **Product development management** (PDM) is the process of understanding customer requirements and preferences, anticipating how they will change, and then responsively constructing solutions to fulfill those requirements and preferences in a way that customers are willing to pay for. **Supply chain management** (SCM) is the process that "incorporates acquisition of all physical (and increasingly informational) inputs, as well as the efficiency and effectiveness with which they are transformed into customer solutions." Finally, **customer relationship management** (CRM) is the process that "addresses all aspects of identifying customers, creating customer knowledge, building customer relationships, and shaping their perceptions of the organization and its products."[14] Notice how each of these core business processes extend beyond the firm to its suppliers, customers, and other strategic partners.[15]

Contributions of Marketing

Srivastava, Shervani, and Fahey contend that infusing each of these core business processes with marketing capability is crucial to the creation of customer value and that marketing activities can positively affect the cash flows that underlie shareholder value. A marketing perspective can bring about a shift in each core business process:

- The change to a market-driven PDM process entails shifting from an emphasis on designing the most technically superior product to creating a solution that enables customers to experience the maximum value and benefit from its use.
- The change to a market-driven SCM process entails shifting from a focus on obtaining the functionally best inputs at the cheapest possible prices to designing, managing, and integrating the firm's own supply chain with that of both suppliers and customers.
- The change to a market-driven CRM process entails shifting from a modus operandi that views customer relationships as solely the means to sell, deliver, and service a product to one that regards them as means to learn about customers' needs and wants and how best to create, satisfy, and sustain them.[16]

Marketing's contribution to making these core business processes more market-driven has positive effects on the cash flows for a business. Marketing can contribute to the acceleration of cash flows through involving customers earlier in the PDM process, focusing new offering realization efforts to reduce the time to market; and through persuasively demonstrating and documenting the new offering's value, gaining earlier adoption from targeted customers. Marketing can contribute to the enhancement of cash flows by creating value-based sales tools that enable the sales force to capture a greater portion of the superior value delivered. Through superior demonstration and documentation of the value customers receive, marketing can assist customer purchasing managers in turning gray money into green money, and at the same time, not have to give as much value away as incentive to purchase. Marketing can contribute to reducing the volatility and vulnerability of cash flows through superior monitoring of competitors, accurately gauging their resources, capabilities and intentions, so as to minimize marketplace surprises that undercut forecast sales and profits of the business' market offerings. Finally, marketing can contribute to the residual value of the business through increasing the number of profitable customers and creating customer expectations that the business will continue to deliver superior value because of its superior anticipation of changing customer requirements and preferences.[17]

Business Market Management and Business Marketing

We have purposely chosen *Business Market Management* rather than *Business Marketing* for the title of our book. Why? Isn't this a book about business marketing? Yes, it is a book about business marketing, but we recognize that the nature of marketing practice in business markets is changing.[18] A growing requirement for marketplace success is that marketing work processes, such as segmentation, targeting, and positioning, take place *within* business market processes such as market sensing and managing the market offering. Business market processes cut across functional areas and depend upon seamless cross-functional cooperation for marketplace success. Therefore, business market management requires significant participation from many functional areas, not just marketing, to decide what market segments and customer firms are of primary interest (i.e., targeting) and how to deliver superior value to them (i.e., positioning).[19] We think that business market management better conveys this broader responsibility for the marketplace, and this perspective makes our book not only of greater interest to those in a marketing functional area, but also to those in related functional areas and general management. What are the constituent business market processes of business market management and what role does business marketing play?

Business Market Processes

As we mentioned earlier and depict in Figure 1.1, the business market processes that constitute business market management can be organized into three groups, based on whether they are a part of understanding, creating, or delivering value. Because a number of market initiatives are underway at any given time, the firm will be engaged in most or all of these business market processes concurrently.

Market sensing, understanding firms as customers, and crafting market strategy are the component business market processes for understanding value. **Market sensing** is the process of generating knowledge about the marketplace that individuals in the firm use to inform and guide their decision making. It is a market-driven process of learning about present and prospective customers and competitors, as well as other actors that affect them and the firm, such as resellers and regulatory agencies. The substantive facets of market sensing are defining the market, monitoring competition, assessing customer value, and gaining customer feedback. **Understanding firms as customers** is the process of learning how companies rely on a network of suppliers to add value to their offerings, integrate purchasing activities with those of other functional areas and outside firms, and make purchase decisions. **Crafting market strategy** is the process of studying how to exploit a firm's resources to achieve short-term and long-term marketplace success, deciding upon a course of action, and flexibly updating it as learning occurs during implementation. We discuss these business market processes in Chapters 2, 3, and 4, respectively.

Managing market offerings, new offering realization, and business channel management are the component business market processes of creating value. **Managing**

market offerings is the process of putting products, services, programs, and systems together in ways that create the greatest value for targeted market segments and customer firms. **New offering realization** is the process of developing new core products or services, augmenting them to construct market offerings, and bringing them to market. Realization encompasses all of the activities a firm does to transform an idea into a market offering that it commercializes. **Business channel management** is the process of designing a set of marketing and distribution arrangements that create superior customer value for targeted market segments and customers, and executing those arrangements either directly through supplier firm sales forces and logistics systems or indirectly through resellers and third-party service providers. We devote Chapters 5, 6, and 7, respectively, to these business market processes.

The component business market processes for each of the first two sets come together for the firm to understand and create value, respectively. In contrast, the firm delivers value in three distinct ways. We indicate this in Figure 1.1 by the direction of the arrows linking the business market processes to the metaprocesses of understanding, creating, and delivering value.

Gaining customers, sustaining reseller partnerships, and sustaining customer relationships are the business market processes for delivering value. **Gaining customers** is the process of prospecting for new business relationships, assessing the mutual fit between prospective customer requirements and supplier offerings and priorities, making the initial sale, and fulfilling the initial order to the customer's complete satisfaction. **Sustaining reseller partnerships** is the process of a supplier and its resellers fulfilling commitments they have made to deliver value to customer firms, strengthening this delivered value, and working progressively together to continue to fulfill changing marketplace requirements. **Sustaining customer relationships** is the process of fulfilling mutually agreed-upon customer requirements in a superior way over time, and selectively pursuing continuity and growth through building mutual self-interest. We discuss these business market processes in Chapters 8, 9, and 10, respectively.

Business Marketing

In the philosophy and practice of business market management, what is the role of business marketing? The essential undertaking of **business marketing** remains what it has been conceptually for many years: Understand what the customer does, and would, value. Management guru Peter Drucker voiced this point in 1980, "The true meaning of marketing [is] knowing what is value for the customer."[20] What is changing slowly is the practice of business marketing, with emerging recognition of what advances in marketing work processes and marketing relationships are needed to realize and profit from this understanding of value.

The marketing work process of customer value assessment is crucial to understanding value. Neglected or absent in most firms in business markets, customer value assessment is a work process in need of the greatest advancement. Customer value assessment can be a business marketing capability that gives a firm a marketplace advantage over its competitors. In conducting value assessments and building customer value models, a firm not only gains detailed knowledge of what customers value, but also has some capacity to shape how customers view their own requirements. Further, by gaining an understanding of what the customer would value, now or in the foreseeable future, business marketers significantly affect their own firm's business market processes, such as managing market offerings and new offering realization.

Segmentation, targeting, and positioning are the fundamental building blocks of business marketing, and having value as the cornerstone of business market management affects each of these work processes. Value-based segmentation moves beyond the conventional bases of partitioning markets, such as product market or size of customer firm, to examine product application, customer capabilities, and usage situation as potential ways for the supplier firm to further segment the market and gain some leverage. Value-based targeting compels the supplier to decide which market segments and customer firms have requirements that most closely match what the supplier does relatively well (i.e., its distinctive competencies and capabilities).[21]

Value-based positioning orients and updates each of the "four Ps":

- *Product*. Business marketers construct flexible market offerings that consist of naked solutions—only those product and service elements that *all* segment members value—wrapped with options that *some*, but not all, segment members value. In this way, the supplier's offerings are responsive to the residual variation in customer requirements and preferences that remains, no matter how finely the market is segmented.
- *Pricing*. Pricing is based on what a market offering is worth to the customer, rather than its cost to the supplier or simply matching a competitor's price.
- *Promotion*. Marketing communications are more focused, tailored to varying requirements for gaining customers or sustaining relationships with customers and resellers, and shape and reinforce the supplier's value proposition to each constituency.
- *Place*. Business marketers design distribution channels that are customer-driven. They also provide channel offerings that build marketplace equity, and implement cooperative channel arrangements that are adaptive to customer requirements, which sometimes can change from order to order.

Business marketers, along with the sales force, have had primary responsibility in the past for managing marketplace relationships—with present and prospective customers, with the firm's resellers, and with the firm's competitors. With the emphasis on relationships and networks in business market management, the role of business marketing in managing relationships expands significantly. As suppliers engage in closer, more collaborative relationships with selected customers and resellers, business marketers need to strengthen their relationship management knowledge and skills, particularly in the areas of communication and negotiations. Business marketers also increasingly need to employ these in defining and refining areas of collaboration and competition with competitors.[22]

In addition to strengthening external relationships, business market management demands that business marketers strengthen their internal relationships with other functional areas. Business marketing should act as the catalyst in helping other functional areas understand how the firm generates value in its market offerings and how this value varies across defined market segments and customer characteristics. To do this, business marketers need to continually communicate what they are learning from the marketplace, and wherever possible, to involve managers from other functional areas in learning firsthand. Customer visits, observation of focus group discussions with customers, and participation in reseller advisory councils are ways for managers in other functional areas to deepen and broaden their understanding. McKenna nicely articulates the growing demands on marketers in contributing to and managing relationships: "The marketer must be the integrator, both internally—synthesizing technological capability with market needs—and externally—bringing the customer into the company as a participant in the development and adaptation of goods and services."[23]

DOING BUSINESS ACROSS BORDERS

Because business markets are predominantly concerned about functionality and performance, business market management stresses doing business across international borders. Customers in country markets in the Americas, Asia, and Europe are seeking essentially the same functionality and performance from business market offerings in such industries as machine tools, computer software, chemicals, and management consulting. In contrast, because aesthetics and tastes tend to vary, often dramatically, across country markets, firms in consumer markets have greater difficulty doing business across borders. Consider, for example, the fuss created by the European Commission when it attempted to define the requirements for cheese within the European Community.[24] Relative to offerings for consumer markets, offerings for business markets require much less adaptation for suppliers to sell them across borders.

A number of developments help suppliers of business market offerings in doing business across borders. The ongoing reduction and elimination of trade barriers and tariffs is leveling the playing field for foreign suppliers to compete with domestic suppliers in their home-country markets. Innovation in logistics and transportation, such as containerization of cargo and use of intermodal transportation, enable firms to reach foreign markets more efficiently and cheaply. Advances in communication technologies, ranging from telecommunications to Internet commerce, continue to erode the barrier of geographical distance between suppliers and prospective customers in other country markets.[25]

These changes make it easier for firms to do business across borders, but firms also have strategic reasons to stress doing business across borders. Foreign markets provide firms with a means for profitable growth, because they can leverage comparative advantages that they have developed in their home-country markets. This source of growth is preferable to pursuing business from prospective customers in the home market that have requirements and preferences different from what the firm does well.[26] Another strategic reason is that the experience and learning firms gain in doing business across borders better prepare them to withstand foreign competition in their home-country markets.

Some readers may believe that doing business across borders is something that only large firms in business markets can do successfully. As the accompanying Box 1.2 on Germany's Mittelstand companies illustrates, medium and small firms can be worldwide market-share leaders. A number of medium and small firms in the

BOX 1.2
Mittelstand: German Midsize Companies that Grew Big by Thinking Small

Germany's 300,000 small and midsize companies, collectively known as the **Mittelstand**, are considered to be the backbone of the country's economy. These businesses, each with fewer than 500 employees, produce two-thirds of Germany's gross national product, train 9 out of every 10 apprentices, and employ 4 out of every 5 German workers. Among these firms are many of Germany's most powerful exporters, which successfully compete with Asia's and America's best. They collectively generate 30% of German exports, and often have world market shares of 70–90%. More than three-quarters of Mittelstand companies are family owned or closely held, and nearly two-thirds are managed by their owners.

The critical factors in the Mittelstand companies' success are

1. *Combining product focus with geographic diversity.* Mittelstand companies pursue a focus or niche market strategy to narrowly define the product markets in which they compete, but strive to be market leaders in them worldwide. Thus, they achieve sufficient scale to recover R&D expenses and keep their costs competitive. For example, Heidenhain, the world market leader in measurement and control instruments for lengths and angles, earns more than 50% of its revenues from exports.

2. *Ensuring superiority in the areas customers value most.* Mittelstand companies strive to provide products with superior performance, responsive service, and punctual delivery. Reliability and closeness to customers are vital to their success. They spend a large portion of their revenues on R&D to create technological breakthroughs that customers value. G. W. Barth, a producer of roaster machines, developed a technology that narrowed the variance in cocoa bean roasting temperatures, which gave customers such as Hershey Foods added control over the taste of their chocolate. This capability allowed Barth to obtain 70% of the global market, up from 25% 10 years ago.

3. *Plentiful government support.* The Germans' export infrastructure greatly assists smaller companies in doing business across borders. Embassies, banks, trade associations, and chambers of commerce in dozens of countries alert Mittelstand companies to potential export deals via newsletters and databases at no cost. They also help with documentation, translation, and legal and shipping services, and allow German companies to use their in-country offices when negotiating deals, especially in places where the infrastructure is lacking. Deutsche Bank, for example, offered G. W. Barth use of an office and secretary while prospecting for business in Indonesia, Nigeria, and Russia. Specialized banks or Mittelstand departments of large commercial banks, which are sensitive to the needs of the exporters, also provide export finance, and arrange credit and political risk insurance, although some recent tightening of this bank credit and raising of interest rates on Mittlestand bank loans has occurred.

Contributed by Research Associate Sandra Z. Diaz, J. L. Kellogg Graduate School of Management, Northwestern University. *Sources*: Gail Schares et al., "Think Small: The Export Lessons to Be Learned from Germany's Midsize Companies," *Business Week*, 4 November 1991, 58–65; Hermann Simon, "Lessons from Germany's Midsize Giants," *Harvard Business Review* (March–April 1992): 115–123; "German Lessons," *The Economist*, 13 July 1996, 59; and "Germany's Middlestand: Slipped Disc," *The Economist*, 15 December 2001, 54–55.

United States are significantly increasing their sales abroad, often with the assistance of local, state, and national government agencies, such as the U.S. Department of Commerce.[27]

The Commerce Department's Gold Key Service, for example, greatly assists small and medium-sized businesses in doing business in other countries. As a start, embassy officials distribute company literature to various contacts. U.S. Commercial Service personnel, posted at the embassies and missions in 84 countries, next arrange meetings with key executives at targeted companies, and then accompany representatives of U.S. firms as advisers and interpreters of both language and business customs for a low fee. The Video Gold Key Service of the U.S. Commerce Department is similar in intent to the Gold Key Service, except that the U.S. companies meet prequalified overseas customers, distributors, agents or international experts in video conferences, saving the time and expense involved in traveling abroad. Finally, the U.S. Commercial Service has introduced a new e-marketplace, BuyUSA.com, which links together its network of more than 260 offices located in the United States and abroad, U.S. suppliers seeking business in international markets, and qualified customers and potential business partners around the world.[28]

Regardless of their size, firms in business markets do face some additional considerations in doing business across borders. In this section, we discuss language and culture, cross-border negotiation and dispute resolution, and currency exchange and payment risk.

Language and Culture

Doing business across borders does not always mean that the language and culture of managers from the supplier and customer firms will be different, just as doing business within the same country does not always mean that the culture and language will be the same. For example, Argentina and Uruguay have essentially the same culture and language, and both countries are members of the Mercosur free trade area, which further facilitates doing business across their border.[29] Yet, the Flanders and Wallonia regions of Belgium have different languages and cultures. Most often, though, the language and culture of managers from supplier firms and customer firms located in different countries will be different.

A first step in doing business across borders is to determine what language to use. English is regarded as the language of international business, because it is the most frequently used.[30] The language that businesspeople are most likely to know other than their native language is English. Even in circumstances where managers from one country do know the language of their counterparts' country, they may prefer to speak English. French and German managers, for example, may conduct business discussions in English, because it does not give either side an advantage.

Alternatives to using English are to use the language of one of the parties, use another language that both parties are willing to use, or rely on interpreters. When the supplier and customer managers do not have a common language that they are comfortable using for business discussions, one or both parties need to employ interpreters. Use of interpreters, however, can lengthen the time needed for the business discussions, change the "atmosphere" of the discussions, increase the costs of the discussions, or increase the chances for misunderstandings.[31] Nevertheless, doing business through interpreters is sometimes the only viable alternative.

The meaning that managers attach to the words and actions of their counterparts in a business discussion depends in part on the culture of the managers. Culture is an abstract and imprecise concept; it broadly refers to the bundle of characteristics that uniquely define members of a particular group. A particular group's distinctive language, its social customs, the specific artifacts and art forms it produces, and the legal and economic structures that govern it collectively convey its culture. Culture also comprises a set of assumptions, values, beliefs, and norms that are socially instilled in members of the group, which serve as a guide to appropriate behavior and to understanding the words and actions of others.[32]

It is difficult to say how much influence culture has on doing business across borders in business markets. Broad definitions of culture tend to neglect the influences of ideology and personality, which cut across national cultures. Ideology refers to an organized set of values and beliefs that individuals hold about how life should be lived and the means for accomplishing this lifestyle. Personality refers to the traits or behavioral predispositions, such as extroversion-introversion, that a person manifests to a greater or lesser extent and which collectively define that person's character. Commonalities and differences in ideology and personality may exert greater influence on how managers from different countries relate to one another than do their national cultures.[33] In its review of cultural explanations, *The Economist* concluded, "Culture is so imprecise and changeable a phenomenon that it explains less than most people realize. . . . And within the overall mix of what influences people's behavior, culture's role may well be declining, rather than rising, squeezed between the greedy expansion of the government on one side, and globalization on the other."[34]

Still, business market managers must be perceptive about any cultural influences, so they can tailor the social elements of a market offering to enhance its value to managers in firms within that culture. A useful start is for the managers to think through the influence of their own culture on their behavior and their assumptions about how to behave. Before doing business across borders, managers should also gain some understanding of the culture of their business counterparts. Managers should especially learn about the characteristic ways of doing business in that culture, such as the meaning and timing of business entertainment, and how to show respect. The managers also should seek to understand the company culture of their business counterparts and how this reinforces or contradicts the country culture.[35] Finally, although managers need to be culturally aware, they need to regard their business counterparts first as individuals and resist cultural stereotyping.

Cross-Border Negotiation and Dispute Resolution

When supplier firms consider doing business across borders, they need to decide how flexible they will be with the policies and practices they use to conduct business in their home-country market. That is, to what extent are they willing to negotiate ways of doing business across borders that are different from how they do business in the home-country market? Also, to what extent are they willing to negotiate ways of doing business that vary across different foreign country markets? A supplier firm's willingness to negotiate depends on a number of considerations, such as the profitability of the business to be gained, the perceived benefits of a relationship with the prospective customer firm, and any anticipated consequences of the negotiated deal on the supplier's business in other country markets.

Cross-Border Negotiations

Cross-border negotiations can differ from domestic negotiations in eight critical respects: (1) culture, (2) unfamiliar and uncomfortable settings, (3) the influence of ideology, (4) greater involvement of government in business, (5) defining which country's laws govern the business transaction, (6) instability and sudden change in the foreign market, (7) dispute resolution, and (8) foreign currencies.[36] The culture of each negotiator (or, often, negotiations team) affects his interests and priorities as well as the strategies that he will employ in the negotiation. The complementarity between the interests and priorities of each negotiator will enable them to trade them off in ways that generate value-creating or integrative agreements. The strategies of each negotiator will affect the interaction patterns in the negotiation, which can facilitate or hinder reaching an integrative agreement. The negotiation strategies that each side pursues also will be shaped by its expectations of who on the other side is involved in the negotiation, what roles they play, what the informal influences are, and what process the other side engages in to reach an accord, such as top-down, consensus, and multistage coalition building.[37]

Although supplier managers might prefer to negotiate with the prospective customer firm within their own country, the supplier often has to travel to the customer's country, which may impose difficulties. It may lack the amenities to which the business traveler is accustomed. The time difference from that of the home country may be significant, leading to jet lag. Outside the actual negotiations, communicating with local people in their own language or the traveler's native language (or some combination) may be a struggle. The physical surroundings and climate may be dramatically different. Also, the support services readily available at home may be difficult to find or otherwise problematic. These potential difficulties contribute to the psychological and economic costs of doing business across borders, and lessen the chance of successfully negotiating an equitable deal.

Supplier managers may find they have significant ideological differences with their counterparts in cross-border negotiations. Private investment, profit, and individual rights are three principal areas where ideological differences may arise.[38] Whenever possible, managers should downplay ideological differences and seek ways to accommodate the prospective customer, which may require imagination and pursuing creative alternatives. For example, a principle codified under *Sharia*, Islam's holy law, is the proscription of interest payments on loans. To respect this principle, a foreign supplier working with a bank may employ the Islamic financial instrument of *murabaha*, or markup, where "instead of lending to a customer which buys goods with the money lent and pays interest on the loan, the financial institution buys the goods and sells them to the company at a higher price at a later date."[39]

Governments in country markets vary significantly in the extent to which they control or actively participate in commercial activities. Thus, government officials may simply need to be apprised of ongoing business discussions, their approval of any business deal may be required, or they may even be the main participants in the cross-border negotiations. Separate from the extent of government control is the issue of which country's laws—the supplier firm's or the customer firm's—will govern the business transaction. "Virtually all international business contracts contain a clause stating that the law of a particular country, to the exclusion of all other laws, will apply to a transaction and to any disputes that may arise between the parties."[40]

The taxes applicable under each country's laws can be a determinant factor in this decision.

Firms routinely use country risk assessments to understand and manage their exposure in doing business in a particular country, and often factor this evaluation into the pricing for negotiated deals as risk premiums.[41] Paiton Energy Co., a consortium led by subsidiaries of Edison Mission Energy Co. and General Electric Co. of the United States and Mitsui & Co. of Japan, negotiated an agreement in 1994 to build a power plant in East Java, Indonesia, at a total investment of U.S. $2.5 billion. The state electricity company, PT Perusahaan Listrik Negara (PLN), agreed to buy power from Paiton Energy at a cost of 8.47 U.S. cents per kilowatt. After the Suharto government was overthrown in 1998, the PLN told Mission-GE (Paiton) that it would not buy any electricity from the plant once it went online in 1999. PLN, with the backing of the ruling government, filed a lawsuit against Paiton to nullify the 30-year Power Purchase Agreement (PPA). In 1999, with another government taking power, renegotiations were initiated, but no substantial outcome was reached. Finally in 2002, with yet another government in power—the fourth since the PPA was signed— Paiton and PLN reached an agreement under which PLN will pay a tariff of 4.93 U.S. cents per kilowatt.[42]

Cross-Border Dispute Resolution

A crucial issue to negotiate before doing business across borders is how to resolve any disputes that may arise. International commercial arbitration as a preagreed dispute resolution mechanism not only avoids the greater costs of litigation, it also provides additional motivation to the two parties to work out disagreements themselves. "Most international contracts today contain a clause that should a dispute arise between the parties (even if one of the parties is a government or state corporation), they will not go to court, but will refer the matter to an arbitrator or arbitrators, usually located in a third country, to hear the matter and make a decision."[43] Whenever possible, the two parties should specify a particular arbitration institution, such as the International Chamber of Commerce, the American Arbitration Association, or the London Court of Arbitration, to which they will submit any disputes. Firms can gain enforcement of arbitration decisions by these institutions in the courts of countries that have signed the treaty: the United Nations Convention on the Recognition and Enforcement of Foreign Arbitral Awards.[44]

Finally, in the next section, we consider how firms doing business across borders resolve the problem of foreign currencies.

Currency Exchange and Payment Risk

When a firm in one country wants to do business with a firm in another country, one term that the two firms must specify is the currency for the transaction: the supplier firm's country currency, the customer firm's country currency, or some third country's currency (e.g., U.S. dollars, Japanese yen). Depending on the currency chosen, one or both firms will need foreign currency exchange service.[45] Further, if either firm perceives significant risk in doing business with the other, a letter of credit may be required to enable the transaction to take place. A **letter of credit** (LC) is an irrevocable commitment that the customer firm's bank issues specifying the conditions under which payment for the transaction will be made to the supplier firm (e.g., when the bank is presented with an acceptable bill of lading and packing list for the products). Finally, when the supplier also believes that significant risk is associated with the issuing bank, it may require its bank or some other bank to **confirm** the letter of credit, which is an irrevocable guarantee by the confirming bank that payment will be made when the specified conditions have been satisfactorily met.

Foreign currency exchange, letters of credit and their confirmations, and other services that enable firms to do business across borders are provided by the correspondent banking units (CBUs) of commercial banks. These CBUs are responsible for managing a set of relationships with banks in other countries, referred to as correspondent banks, that provide agreed-upon banking services (e.g., confirming letters of credit) to one another. Without these correspondent banking relationships, it would be virtually impossible for companies to conduct any cross-border trade. Correspondent banks provide account and trade services to each other that facilitate the efficient movement of payments across borders, and provide protection to both the sellers and buyers doing business across borders. ABN-AMRO (AA), the large Dutch bank, provides an instructive example of how correspondent banking works.

AA has branch offices in about 70 countries, yet it does business in more than 100 countries. The Correspondent Banking Group (CBG), with its head office in Amsterdam, has correspondent bankers in 40 countries in which AA has branch offices. In countries where it has no local branch, AA relies on its correspondent banks. In countries where AA has a local branch, some competition naturally occurs between the branch network and the correspondent banks for the same business (e.g., payment traffic, LCs), and this is especially so for the 40 branches where there is a local correspondent banker. In these circumstances, AA CBG has to strike a delicate balance between directing business to its correspondent banks and targeting corporate customers to take direct through the AA (branch) network. Sustaining cooperative relations with the correspondent banks is essential because the local AA branch is dependent on domestic banks for funding and, often, foreign exchange clearing.

Correspondent banking units not only do business across borders themselves; more important, they enable their corporate clients to do so.

WORKING RELATIONSHIPS AND BUSINESS NETWORKS

A firm's success in business markets depends directly on its working relationships. The working relationships themselves are embedded in business networks comprised of connected relationships. These relationships and business networks enable firms to attain outcomes, such as profitability and marketplace success, that they could not achieve acting alone. Hence, the final guiding principle of business market management is that firms should accentuate working relationships and business networks.

Working relationships and business networks are complex phenomena that exist at multiple levels. We can think about them at the level of the individuals who participate in them as part of their work activities. We can also think about them at the level of the functional areas or subunits that relate to one another, such as the relationship between marketing and manufacturing within a business unit. At this level, the relationships may be within the same firm or across firms, as in the relationship between marketing in a supplier firm and purchasing in a customer firm. Finally, we can think about them at the business unit level, where the actors are firms engaged in working relationships, such as a customer firm and supplier firm working relationship; a distributor firm and manufacturer firm working partnership; or a customer firm, distributor firm, and manufacturer firm business network.

In this section, we first consider work teams, which capture working relationships and work networks of individuals. We then move to working relationships between firms in business markets. We end by broadening our consideration to the embedded context in which working relationships occur: business networks.

Work Teams

Work teams have become the primary mechanism for accomplishing working relationship goals within and across functional areas, other business units, and firms. A **work team**, or simply a **team**, "is a small number of people with complementary skills who are committed to a common purpose, set of performance goals, and approach for which they hold themselves mutually accountable."[46] Katzenbach and Smith distinguish teams from other forms of working groups in terms of performance results:

> A working group's performance is a function of what its members do as individuals. A team's performance includes both individual results and what we call "collective work-products." A collective work-product is what two or more members must work on together, such as interviews, surveys, or experiments. Whatever it is, a collective work-product reflects the joint, real contribution of team members.[47]

Significantly, teams create value in their collective work-products that could not be produced outside of the team setting.

How do teams accomplish this? Through synergy, which comes from the Greek word *synergos*, which means working together. Yet, creating value through synergy requires that the individuals on the team possess the blend of skills needed to achieve the team's purpose.[48] Three broad categories of skill requirements are technical or functional expertise, problem-solving and decision-making skills, and interpersonal skills. Somewhat paradoxically, the last category may be the most critical skill set and the most difficult to find. "Common understanding and purpose cannot arise without effective communication and constructive conflict, which in turn depend on interpersonal skills. These include risk taking, helpful criticism, objectivity, active listening, giving the benefit of the doubt, and recognizing the interests and achievements of others."[49] Senior management should not overlook the process aspects of teamwork, with the corresponding need to train individuals on how to work together as a team and develop their interpersonal skills.

Many firms have trouble with teams.[50] What are the characteristics of effective teams that will help business market managers steer clear of potential troubles? Baxter International, Inc., a leading, worldwide supplier of state-of-the-art health-care products, systems, and services, has found that there are eight characteristics which we outline in Box 1.3. Individuals coalesce into a team through the process of translating *a clear, elevating goal* into specific performance goals for which they are mutually accountable (*a results-driven structure*). A *collaborative environment* is crucial for the team to produce collective work-products. Trouble occurs when team members are not able to "check their egos at the door," or attempt to advance their own (or their functional area's) agenda over the team agenda. Further, any violation of team members' trust in one another produces a diminishing return of trust: After a disappointment, trust can be rebuilt, but never to its prior level. A final problem occurs when team members talk past one another ("You're talking so loudly I can't hear you!").

BOX 1.3
Eight Characteristics of Effective Teams at Baxter International, Inc.

1. *A clear, elevating goal*. Team members need to understand what they are trying to accomplish and why it is important to the company. The goal should give the team the opportunity to excel.

2. *A results-driven structure*. Each team member should know what is his or her role and what results are expected of him or her. Team members should view feedback as a gift that only people who care about them give.

3. *Competent team members*. Everyone on the team has to be able to do his or her part *and* be a team player.

4. *Unified commitment*. Each member has a strong desire to contribute *and* a sense of team spirit where each member expects team success.

5. *A collaborative environment*. The team strives for collaboration over compromise, which has the connotation of giving up something. The team individually, and as a whole, protects an open and supportive process that makes it safe to address the real issues respectfully. To do this, team members employ a Baxter process called "getting connected" to raise and resolve issues.

6. *Standards of excellence*. Each team member is driven by his or her own standard of excellence that exceeds team standards or expectations. Each team member has the attitude: "I want them to name a street after me at Baxter someday."

7. *External support and recognition*. Compensation is specifically tied to team performance. Teams also need to be revered. Baxter teamwork excellence award winners gain recognition by presenting to the corporate officers at an annual event.

8. *Principled leadership*. The leader needs to create a clear elevating goal that is inspiring (and continually arouse the morale of the team members), help to create and reinforce the collaborative environment, control personal ego needs, and manage performance issues. The leader needs to be able to give as well as receive honest and open "no-kidding-around" feedback (e.g., "You're a great individual contributor, but you're killing me on this team!"). Leaders need to be generous in sharing credit with the team.

Source: Terry Mulligan, Group Vice President, Baxter International, Inc., presentation at the Kellogg Graduate School of Management, 5 March 1996.

Notice in Box 1.3 that *external support and recognition* refers to both monetary compensation and social recognition. Taken together, they are complementary and mutually reinforcing. Firms may need to change existing measurement and compensation systems to accurately measure and reward team-based performance. Some management thinkers, though, do not support monetary compensation specifically tied to team performance.[51] Reflecting the necessary, but not sufficient character of monetary compensation, a senior manager wryly observed, "It's not the money, it's the money!" Finally, a key aspect of *principled leadership* is the "180 feedback" that Baxter managers get anonymously from their direct reports once a year. This feedback is critical for managers to understand how they are perceived and what interpersonal skills they need to develop further.

Box 1.4 describes a program Baxter used to promote and reinforce teamwork in managing its working relationships with hospital customers.

Working Relationships

All customer and supplier firms that do business together have some sort of working relationship. After all, people in business markets do not buy from people they do not know. Most firms have a policy that purchases can be made only from approved vendors, where some effort has been made to understand the quality and reliability of the vendor's offering. Moreover, a working relationship between a customer firm and a supplier firm can range along a continuum:

BOX 1.4
Baxter Reinforces Teamwork to Better Serve Hospital Customers

Baxter International's Team Excellence Award Program provides an instructive example of the use of teams to manage working relationships with customers. The objective of this program was to promote and reinforce teamwork among salespeople who called on the same hospital customer in Baxter's corporate relationship program. Each of 30 account executives for the corporate relationship program identified three teamwork accounts (for a total of 90 targeted teamwork accounts). Teams were composed of the Baxter salespeople responsible for the account, ranging from 10 to 31 individuals. (At the time, Baxter was organized in divisions around major product lines, each having its own sales force, with no motivation to cooperate with one another.) Senior management specified criteria for judging success in the areas of meeting customer requirements, effective internal teamwork, execution of the account strategy, and financial results.

At the end of the program year, each of the nine area vice presidents selected a finalist team, which then made a presentation to a board of corporate officers (a board officer also visited the account for its feedback). One team was selected as the overall winner. Each of the nine finalist teams received 1,200 shares of Baxter stock, and the overall winning team received an additional 1,200 shares. An intriguing aspect of the program was that the team members decided among themselves how to allocate the shares. This teamwork program was so successful that Baxter extended it to multihospital systems, where a part of each salesperson's bonus was tied to cooperation and team performance for the entire hospital network.

Purely **transactional relationships**, where the customer and the supplier focus upon the timely exchange of basic products for highly competitive prices, anchor one end. Purely **collaborative relationships**, or partnerships, anchor the other end. This latter kind of relationship comes about through **partnering**, which is a process where a customer firm and supplier firm form strong and extensive social, economic, service, and technical ties over time, with the intent of lowering total costs and/or increasing value, thereby achieving mutual benefit.[52]

The working relationship between a customer firm and supplier firm depends upon their mutual interest in working together. Because the relationship takes place within some industry context, it will depend in part on marketplace norms, which vary by industry. We discuss a supplier firm's relationship strategy and implementation at length in Chapter 10, "Sustaining Customer Relationships." Here, we want to discuss what prospective partner firms need to agree upon when they begin a collaborative relationship and the development of such relationships.

Collaborative Relationship Agreements

A collaborative relationship between two firms is a kind of **strategic alliance**, which is simply a commercial agreement between two (or more) parties to work together in some mutually defined ways.[53] Because of the natural misunderstandings that can occur in communication between firms, we recommend that this agreement be written. While the detail, length, and formality of alliance or partnering agreements vary widely in practice, we recommend that firms specify three basic considerations: **"gives & gets"**, **time horizon**, and a **preagreed dispute-resolution mechanism**.

"Gives" capture the specific investments and resources each firm contributes, such as knowledge, personnel, fixed assets, and money; whereas, "gets" capture the specific gains each firm receives, such as greater expertise, enhanced capabilities, or additional profits. Prospective partner firms often do not have a clear understanding of each other's gives & gets. Disconnects often occur here: What one firm thinks it is giving to its partner firm is significantly different from what the partner perceives that it is getting. Each firm needs to comprehensively list both its own gives & gets and those of its partner. Exchanging these lists allows the firms to discover any discrepancies that exist in perception of the gives & gets. They can then negotiate changes to attain equity. After agreement is reached on an equitable set of gives & gets, the partner firms need to specify a process for handling unanticipated changes in the gives & gets as well as unforeseen gives & gets that may arise. Gives & gets provides a mechanism for defining the scope of the cooperation between firms, the specific resources and activities each firm will contribute, and the specific outcomes of the cooperation that the firms anticipate.

Time horizon specifies the period of time the firms agree to work together. When the time for collaboration is lengthy, intermediate partnership reviews may also be specified, most likely corresponding to scheduled completion of defined milestones that chart progress in the collaboration. At the end of the time horizon, the firms agree to mutually review the relationship and determine their willingness to continue in the collaborative relationship.

A preagreed dispute resolution mechanism specifies how the two firms will handle any disagreements they cannot resolve themselves. Options include negotiation, mediation, and arbitration, and two or more dispute resolution procedures may be used in sequence.[54] It is crucial that the firms specify a mechanism at the outset of the collaboration. One of our sayings is, "It's hard to dance smoothly when your pants are on fire!" In fact, two marketing scholars from Australia offered business dancing as an intriguing metaphor for collaborative relationships.[55] Firms with a preagreed dispute resolution mechanism find that they not only avoid costly litigation, but are also motivated to find a way to work out disagreements themselves. Thus, it not only lowers the cost of conflict, it fosters productive resolution of the conflict that does occur.

Collaborative Relationship Development

Most firms in business markets now realize that to prosper they must have close, collaborative relationships with selected suppliers, customers, and value-added resellers.[56] A crucial question then is: How do collaborative relationships develop over time? We contend that the participating firms in a relationship experience and manage that development as a series of **exchange episodes**.

Relationship development begins with a partner selection stage. Even when two firms have been doing business together on a transactional basis, they will need an initial exchange episode where the defined purpose becomes more collaborative. Often, this episode takes the form of a pilot program in which each firm gains a better understanding of what collaborative exchange between them might mean. For example, a supplier firm and customer firm might experiment with single-sourcing at one plant in the customer's manufacturing network.

Each exchange episode is composed of four sequentially related events, which are "critical incidents when parties engage in actions related to the development of their relationship."[57] The events are defining purpose, setting relationship boundaries, creating value (and claiming value), and evaluating exchange outcomes. Through information sharing and negotiation, the two firms mutually define the nature of their collaboration as well as establish its limits. Creating value through joint action (that could not be created by each firm acting independently) is the raison d'être of collaborative relationships. Expectation of future collaboration, where working together will enable the creation of more value, has a strong influence on each firm's willingness to share the created value. Each firm evaluates its outcomes from the exchange episode against its expectations and against outcomes it perceives it could have obtained from collaborating with others instead.

At the conclusion of each exchange episode, each firm decides whether to continue the relationship at the same level, to broaden it, or to curtail it. The collaboration may be broadened through expanded scale or scope. As the collaborative relationship progresses, the two firms may be engaged in a number of concurrent exchange episodes, with overlapping beginnings and endings, and some with no apparent common coordination.

We regard each of these exchange episodes as a business strand of the collaborative relationship between the two firms. The same actors within each firm may engage in several overlapping exchange episodes, and distinctly different groups of other actors may engage in different exchange episodes. More likely is a mixture of common and distinct actors engaged across the set of exchange episodes occurring at a given point in time. In our view, the numerous business strands become "interwoven" through conscious coordination (mutual strategy) by the partner firms and repeated social interaction between the actors.

The partner firms continuing to engage in collaborative exchange episodes together constitute a relationship maintenance stage. In addition to renewing sequentially related exchange episodes, such as a single-source, just-in-time supply arrangement, the partner firms may initiate other exchange episodes that broaden the collaborative relationship. Conversely, when an exchange episode comes to an end, the partner firms may mutually decide not to renew this strand of collaborative exchange. It may be that this strand has reached its natural conclusion between the partners, such as in a customer's material substitution where the supplier does not have capability in the new material. Alternatively, because of changing self-interest, one or the other partner firm may unilaterally decide to terminate this strand of collaborative exchange (in extreme circumstances, it may occur even partway through an exchange episode).

Ongoing collaborative relationships may be broadened in some respects, curtailed in others. In this way, relationship maintenance is a more overarching, organic stage that captures the ebb and flow in the collaboration between the customer and supplier firms over time. Rather than being a separate stage, we consider relationship dissolution as simply the ultimate conclusion (or termination) of the relationship maintenance stage.

Business Networks

As firms build a number of close, collaborative relationships, or alliances, the inevitable next step is understanding how to better interrelate the set of relationships. A **business network** is a set of two or more connected business relationships. *Connected* means the extent to which "exchange in one relation is contingent upon exchange (or non-exchange) in the other relation."[58] Moreover, two connected relationships of interest can themselves be both directly and indirectly connected with other relationships that have some bearing on them, as part of a larger business network. As illustrated in Figure 1.2, a focal relationship is connected to several different relationships that either the supplier or the customer has, some of which are with the same third parties.[59]

Figure 1.2   Connected Relations for Firms in a Dyadic Relationship

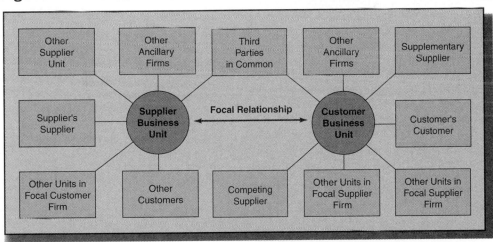

Source: James C. Anderson, Håkan Håkansson, and Jan Johanson, "Dyadic Relationships Within a Business Network Context," *Journal of Marketing* (October 1994), 3.

A type of business network of particular interest to business market managers is the **alliance network**, which is a clique of interrelated and coordinated business relationships.[60] Firms engage in alliance networks to create new markets, to bring together resources that are beyond any two firms, to gain consensus on a "dominant design" that will speed the adoption of an innovation, and to spread risk across a greater number of firms. We begin with a case study of building and managing an alliance network. This study of the Joint Strike Fighter (JSF) business network, which we present in Box 1.5 and depict in Figure 1.3, both motivates our discussion of analyzing business networks and serves as a source of examples.

Business Network Characteristics

The JSF business network aptly illustrates three characteristics increasingly found in business networks, particularly alliance networks. First, it is organized around developing and realizing an envisioned market opportunity. The relationships depicted in the JSF business network are connected to other relationships not depicted, just as other nondepicted relationships between the depicted firms are organized around other market opportunities. As an example, Northrop Grumman is a major subcontractor on the F/A-18 fighter, which competes against the Lockheed

BOX 1.5
Joint Strike Fighter (JSF) Alliance Network

The Joint Strike Fighter (JSF) program nicely illustrates how firms collaborate in an alliance network to fulfill a market opportunity with the U.S. government as a primary customer. In October 2001, Lockheed Martin beat Boeing in a winner-take-all contract from the U.S. Defense Department. Under this contract, Lockheed would supply the United States, Great Britain, and other countries, such as the Netherlands and Italy, with a fighter jet beginning in about 2008 and continuing for many years after. The award, which could be worth more than $200 billion to Lockheed, its alliance partners, and subcontractors, is the richest Pentagon contract ever awarded. The JSF, or F-35 as it is designated, will be a significant advance in technical and performance prowess for the U.S. military and its allied partners, as the F-35 will combine stealth (radar avoiding) and supersonic capabilities in an affordable, multi-role fighter that fulfills the various operating requirements of the U.S. military and its allies.

The contract award announcement gives the Lockheed Martin, Northrop Grumman, and BAE Systems (the former British Aerospace Co.) team the go-ahead to begin the program's System Design and Development (SDD) phase to produce 22 test aircraft. This part of the contract is worth about $19 billion, and Lockheed Martin will get about 66% of the contract value. Northrop Grumman and BAE Systems will get 20% and 14%, respectively. Led by Lockheed Martin, these three companies form a matchless team, each with more than 50 years of experience in designing and producing fighter and attack aircraft.

The uniqueness of the Lockheed Martin's JSF program lies in the fact that it smoothly integrates various resources and technologies it owns, while leveraging the distinctive capabilities and resources of its two alliance partners. It draws on the low-cost, rapid-prototyping, and advanced technology experience from its Palmdale facility; the integrated product team structure, critical stealth technologies, and firsthand knowledge gained from its F-22 fighter program based in Marietta; and the total systems integration and world-class, lean production capability of its Fort Worth facility. Lockheed Martin also will depend on

BOX 1.5
Continued

its two alliance partners to realize the JSF. On its part, Northrop Grumman contributes a vast experience in tactical aircraft integration, carrier suitability, stealth technologies, sensors, and avionics systems integration. Finally, BAE Systems contributes its unique expertise and background with short takeoff and vertical landing technology, subcontract management and lean manufacturing, and also will produce many of the electronic warfare components the fighter will possess.

Geographical separation doesn't prevent virtual integration. State-of-the-art technology enables the alliance partners to create virtual workplaces, enabling rapid and real-time exchange of information. Lockheed Martin's Fort Worth plant will be responsible for the final assembly. Northrop Grumman's El Segundo, California, plant and BAE Systems' facility at Samlesbury, England, will be in charge of the major subassemblies. Each partner also has contributed members to the JSF program team, which is based at Lockheed's Fort Worth facility. Thus, it is not unusual to be walking down the hall and hear a serious conversation that involves a Texas drawl on one side and a clipped English accent on the other!

Another major beneficiary of the contract is Pratt & Whitney (P&W), a division of United Technologies Inc., which captured a $4 billion deal to develop the F-35 propulsion system (i.e., the engine) for JSF. This contract will cover ground and flight testing, and production qualification of the Pratt & Whitney propulsion system. A key aspect of the JSF acquisition strategy is the development of two parallel propulsion systems. Thus, the Pratt & Whitney system will compete with the joint team of General Electric (GE) and Rolls Royce (RR). An essential requirement for these two systems is that the engines P&W and GE/RR each develop will be physically and functionally interchangeable in both the aircraft and support systems. Either engine must be able to be used in all JSF aircraft variants.

Northrop and Raytheon will work on developing the plane's radar systems, and Goodrich Corporation will provide the landing gear. In addition to these high-profile companies, Lockheed and Pratt & Whitney will subcontract work on the plane's systems with potentially hundreds of lesser-known firms. For example, Netherlands-based Stork will develop the moving wing and tail components, wing and tail tips, doors and hatches, and the engine cable system. Urenco Nederland BV will contribute its expertise in developing and manufacturing engine subsystems as it works closely with Rolls Royce and Pratt & Whitney.

Finally, competitive rivalry is not the only relation that Lockheed and Boeing have with one another. Boeing is working together with Lockheed on the F-22 fighter project Lockheed was awarded, where Boeing receives one-third of the contract award for F-22 production. Thus, rivalry and collaboration coexist between two major players in this huge business market—defense procurement.

Sources: "Lockheed Martin Team Wins Joint Strike Fighter Competition, Pledges Full Commitment to this Cornerstone of Future Defense Capability," press release, *http://www.lockheedmartin.com*; "The Lockheed Martin JSF Team," *http://www.lmaeronautics.com*; " JSF Contractor Award," U.S. Department of Defense news release, *http://www.defenselink.mil/news*; "Defense Industry Boost," CNN Money, *http://money.cnn.com*; James Fallows, "Uncle Sam Buys an Airplane," *The Atlantic Monthly*, June 2002, 62–75; Anne Marie Squeo, "Fighter-Jet Contract Adds Crucial Thrust to Lockheed Rebound," *The Wall Street Journal*, October 29, 2001, A1, A14; and interview with John Kent of the JSF communication team.

Martin F-16 fighter in world markets. From a business market management perspective, a meaningful way to delimit a network is around a defined market opportunity.

Second, the relationships between firms may not be simple ones, but **multiplex relations**, where the firms are potentially suppliers, customers, and competitors to

Figure 1.3 Joint Strike Fighter (JSF) Alliance Network

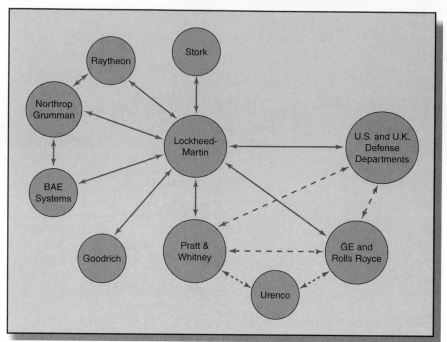

one another for the same market opportunity. For example, BAE Systems is one of the partners in the Typhoon Eurofighter program, which is a direct competitor to the JSF. Third, business networks are increasingly international in composition, unlike business networks such as the Japanese *keiretsu* or the Korean *chaebol*, which are domestic business networks.[61]

Analyzing Business Networks

We can analyze business networks using a model with three components: actors, activities, and resources.[62] **Actors** are firms, such as customers and suppliers, or other organizations, such as regulatory agencies, that perform activities and control resources. Actors perform **activities** such as transactions (e.g., order management cycle) and create value through transforming resources. **Resources** refer to anything that actors explicitly value, such as technical know-how, equipment, personnel, or capital, which they can use to generate greater value for themselves and others. Even though a firm may possess a given resource, for strategic purposes, it may instead look to other firms to collaboratively develop the resource.

Three pivotal concepts help us analyze business networks: network horizon, network context, and network identity. Let's analyze each in terms of actors, activities, and resources. **Network horizon** refers to how extended an actor's view of the network is. It depends on the actor's experience as well as on the structural network features, such as the connectedness of relationships. A firm may engage banks, consultants, or export management companies as "scouts" to extend its network horizon.

For example, Standard Chartered, the British merchant bank, ran a series of ads touting its international networking capability in China, where it can provide its clients with "market studies, introductions, and joint-venture assistance."[63]

The part of the network within the horizon is the actor's **network context**. The network context is structured in terms of the three earlier components: the actors, who they are and how they are related to each other; the activities, what activities are performed and the ways in which they are linked together; and the resources, what resources are used and the pattern of adaptation between them. The contexts are partially shared by the network actors, at least by those close to each other. Yet, because of differential knowledge and experience, every actor has a different network context. Consider, for example, how the network context for Boeing, which has a commercial aircraft unit as well its military aircraft unit, would be different from Lockheed Martin's, which does not have a commercial aircraft unit.

In this ambiguous, complex, and fluid configuration of firms that constitute a network, in which the relations between firms have such importance, the actors develop **network identities**. Such an identity refers to how the firms see themselves in the network and how they are seen by other network actors. Network identity captures the uniqueness of each firm in its set of relationships. As such, it is time dependent and context related. For example, Netherlands-based Stork made such an impression on Boeing in its preliminary collaborations on the JSF work that it is now getting orders from Boeing for commercial aircraft.[64] Network identity communicates a certain orientation toward others, such as being positively connected, having a multiplex relationship, or having no relationship. It conveys a certain competence in terms of an actor's perceived capability to perform certain activities, and it has a certain power content.

For business networks to possess advantages beyond the sum of the involved dyadic relationships, consideration must take place within those relationships about their connectedness with other relationships. A firm needs to consider how generalizable or incompatible a relationship with its partner firm will be viewed by other actors in the network. Through a relationship, a firm can signal other actors about its availability and willingness to have relationships with them. Conversely, having a relationship can make a firm repulsive to other actors, even though the firm may desire a relationship with them. For example, Mitsubishi has been reluctant to engage in collaborative relations with Daimler-Benz because Mitsubishi has a strong supplier relationship with Boeing, while Daimler-Benz is part of the Airbus consortium, an ardent rival to Boeing.[65] A firm needs to consider how complementary and irreconcilable the activities it undertakes with its partner firm are with its activities in other connected relationships. Finally, a firm needs to consider how transferable resources developed with its partner firm are to other connected relationships and how particular they are to that single relationship. For example, some of the technical know-how that Stork develops in its participation in the JSF alliance network may well be transferable to its new supply relationship with Boeing in commercial aircraft.

A final aspect of analyzing and managing business networks is network roles. Snow, Miles, and Coleman argue that in constructing business networks, certain managers operate as brokers, creatively marshaling resources that other actors control.[66]

They sketch out three broker roles that significantly contribute to the success of business networks: the architect, who facilitates the building of specific networks, yet seldom has a complete grasp or understanding of the network that ultimately emerges; the lead operator, who formally connects specific actors into an ongoing network; and the caretaker, who focuses on activities that enhance network performance and needs to have a broader network horizon. These network roles may be more apparent in some business networks, such as alliance networks, than in others. In Box 1.6, the decentralization of the ABN-AMRO Correspondent Banking Group provides an illustration of these network roles in practice.

BOX 1.6
ABN-AMRO Correspondent Banking Group: Decentralizing the Network

Recently, the Correspondent Banking Group (CBG) of ABN-AMRO (AA), the large Dutch bank, moved to decentralize its correspondent banking relationships from the head office to the bank's own network of local branches. Prior to this change, AA CBG Amsterdam had responsibility for managing correspondent banking relationships with 4,300 banks. These responsibilities included providing product coverage (e.g., credit lines, trade services) for services sold to these banks, as well as conducting due diligence on credit limits that AA extended to 3,000 of the correspondent banks.

Clearly, the situation was unworkable. Simply too many bank customers needed the attention of too few CBG relationship managers. Relationship managers were geographically too far away from their correspondent bank customers, which led to communication barriers and prevented building close relationships. As a result, client contact was too infrequent. To find a better way to conduct business, AA senior management looked to where in the AA (branch) network correspondent banking was exemplary. The United States seemed to be working well, so they sought to understand why it was working there and what could be generalized to other parts of the network.

To change the network, AA senior management tapped Wolf Platzer for the role of network **architect**. Platzer was running the correspondent banking unit for European American Bank, an AA U.S. subsidiary. In this assignment, he had become aware that AA was missing out on opportunities for its correspondent banking business due to infrequent contact with bank customers and uncoordinated business development efforts of the local AA CBG units. Platzer began to work out policies and procedures that were more flexible to accommodate the needs of AA's correspondent bank customers, and in turn, their corporate clients that were doing business across borders. The more efficient these correspondent relationships could become (e.g., lower processing cost and higher execution speed), the more banks' corporate clients could benefit as well. His vision was of a correspondent banking unit network comprising a head office correspondent banking unit, regional correspondent banking units, and local correspondent banking units, each with defined primary and support responsibilities.

In this decentralized network, three senior relationship managers occupy the role of **caretaker**: one responsible for the Americas, one for Asia, and one for Europe, the Middle East, and Africa. These managers have the functional responsibility for correspondent banking in their sectors. Hans Duijn, Senior Vice President and Head of Correspondent Banking, acts as the **lead operator** for the decentralized network. Business cases are made by AA branch managers for adding a local correspondent banking unit, or Duijn may approach a country manager or regional manager, wanting more correspondent banking presence there. Duijn

BOX 1.6
Continued

expects to be consulted on all correspondent banking appointments made at the local AA branch, and the head office is sometimes asked to do "head-hunting."

Implementation of the network change has been done in a practical way, as the capabilities of the local and regional CB units improve (e.g., building regional infrastructure in terms of technology and creation of a regional credit committee). Funding for the needed training and development comes out of several pockets, depending on the resource needed: products, marketing materials, or training.

SUMMARY

This chapter provided an overview of business market management. In so doing, it also provided an overview for this book, which is organized around the constituent processes of business market management. Four fundamental ideas that recur throughout this book are the defining or guiding principles of business market management: (1) regard value as the cornerstone of business market management; (2) focus on business market processes; (3) stress doing business across borders; and (4) accentuate working relationships and business networks.

Value is the monetary worth of all a market offering provides to a customer firm. Although value in business markets is a construct, business market management relies upon assessment of value in the marketplace. Translating customer value into shareholder value depends on a business being able to claim an equitable return on the value it delivers to customers. We contend that through persuasively demonstrating and documenting the superior value it delivers to customers, a business will be better equipped to successfully accomplish this translation.

Business market management is a business process that is itself composed of a series of related, interdependent business processes. Each of these business market processes is the subject of a chapter in this book. The essential undertaking of business marketing remains what it has conceptually been for many years: Understand what the customer does, and would, value.

Because business markets are predominantly concerned about functionality and performance, their offerings are valued similarly across borders more than is the case for consumer market offerings, where aesthetics and taste predominate. Nonetheless, business market managers doing business across borders will likely have to resolve complications arising from language and culture, cross-border negotiation and dispute resolution, and currency exchange and payment risk. Finally, a firm's marketplace success in business markets is directly dependent upon its working relationships and, because these relationships are connected to other relationships of interest, its business networks. Thus, business market managers must be adept at analyzing, understanding, building, and playing an active part in work teams, working relationships, and business networks.

1. To disguise the firm's identity, we have not used its actual brand names.

2. Howard Gleckman, with Gary McWilliams, "Ask and It Shall Be Discounted," *Business Week*, 6 (October 1997): 116, 118.

3. Of course, we recognize in stating a generality that exceptions do occur, such as when a firm purchases art for display on the walls of its corporate headquarters or when a consumer purchases power tools for home repairs.

4. By **market offering**, we mean the core product or service that a supplier offers, augmented with its supplementary services, programs, and systems. We define market offering in greater detail in Chapter 5. Although usage varies across business markets, functionality most often refers to what specifically the core product or service does, such as a white pigment providing whitening, brightening, and opacifying when it is added to a coating. Performance most often more broadly refers to all that a market offering provides to a customer firm and includes consideration of the costs a customer incurs in obtaining the functionality.

5. James C. Anderson, Dipak Jain, and Pradeep Chintagunta, "Customer Value Assessment in Business Markets: A State-of-Practice Study," *Journal of Business-to-Business Marketing*, 1, no. 1 (1993): 3–29.

6. Lawrence D. Miles, *Techniques of Value Analysis and Engineering*, 3d ed. (Washington, DC: Lawrence D. Miles Value Foundation, 1989).

7. Economists refer to this difference as "consumer surplus" (cf. Robert S. Pindyck and David L. Rubinfeld, *Microeconomics* [New York: Macmillan, 1989]). This expression is doubly inapt in business markets because our focus is on customers, not consumers, and in our context, this difference is not a "surplus," but an absolutely necessary inducement for customers to purchase a supplier's offering.

8. Irwin Gross, "C-ing Customer Value," *Marketplace: The ISBM Review* (Spring 1992): 4.

9. Miles, *Techniques of Value Analysis*; Lawrence Miles, "Value Analysis: Buying Is a Spirited Game," *Purchasing World* (September 1984): 46; Hamid Noori and Russell Radford, *Production and Operations Management: Total Quality and Responsiveness* (New York: McGraw-Hill, 1995). Value analysis is sometimes referred to as value engineering; see Louis De Rose, *Value Selling* (Chicago: Amacom, American Management Association, 1989).

10. Michael Hammer and James Champy, *Reengineering the Corporation* (New York: Harper Business Press, 1993), p. 35.

11. David A. Garvin, "Leveraging Processes for Strategic Advantage: A Roundtable with Xerox's Allaire, USAA's Herres, SmithKline Beecham's Leschly, and Pepsi's Weatherup," *Harvard Business Review* (September–October 1995): 89 [emphases added].

12. In this section, we draw on the classic source: Alfred Rappaport, *Creating Shareholder Value*, rev. ed. (New York: The Free Press, 1998). For an extended treatment of the implications for shareholder value on marketing, see: Peter Doyle, *Value-Based Marketing: Marketing Strategies for Corporate Growth and Shareholder Value* (Chichester, England: Wiley, 2000).

13. Rappaport, *Creating Shareholder Value*, p. 8.

14. Rajendra K. Srivastava, Tasadduq A. Shervani, and Liam Fahey, "Marketing, Business Processes, and Shareholder Value: An Organizationally Embedded View of Marketing Activities and the Discipline of Marketing," *Journal of Marketing* (Special issue 1999): 168–179. Both quotes are taken from p. 169.

15. Michael Hammer, "The Superefficient Company," *Harvard Business Review* (September 2001): 82–91.

16. Srivastava, Shervani, and Fahey, "Marketing, Business Processes." The three quotes are taken from pp. 170 and 172.

17. Srivastava, Shervani, and Fahey, "Marketing, Business Processes;" and Rajendra K. Srivastava, Tasadduq A. Shervani, and

Liam Fahey, "Market-Based Assets and Shareholder Value: A Framework for Analysis," *Journal of Marketing* (January 1998): 2–18.

18. For an extended treatment of the changing marketing concept and its implementation, see a pair of articles by Frederick E. Webster, Jr.: "Defining the New Marketing Concept," *Marketing Management*, 2, no. 4 (1994): 22–31; and "Executing the New Marketing Concept," *Marketing Management*, 3, no. 1 (1994): 9–16.

19. Benson P. Shapiro, "What the Hell Is 'Market Oriented'?" *Harvard Business Review* (November–December 1988): 119–125.

20. Peter F. Drucker, "Learning from Foreign Management," *The Wall Street Journal*, 4 June 1980, 24.

21. Webster, "Defining the New Marketing Concept"; Webster, "Executing the New Marketing Concept"; and Gary Hamel and C. K. Prahalad, "Strategy as Stretch and Leverage," *Harvard Business Review* (March–April 1993): 75–84.

22. Max H. Bazerman and Margaret A. Neale, *Negotiating Rationally* (New York: The Free Press, 1992); Max H. Bazerman and Margaret A. Neale, "Negotiating Rationally," *Business Week Advance Executive Brief*, vol. 1 (New York: McGraw-Hill, 1992), 1–22; Adam M. Brandenburger and Barry J. Nalebuff, "The Right Game: Use Game Theory to Shape Strategy," *Harvard Business Review* (July–August 1995): 57–71; and Gary Hamel, Yves L. Doz, and C. K. Prahalad, "Collaborate with Your Competitors—And Win," *Harvard Business Review* (January–February 1989): 133–139.

23. Regis McKenna, "Marketing Is Everything," *Harvard Business Review* (January–February 1991): 65–79.

24. Marlise Simons, "The Message to Europe: Don't Mess with Cheese," *The New York Times*, 29 November 1991, A4; and "Why Brussels Sprouts," *The Economist*, 26 December–8 January 1993, 70–72. For a similar fuss about defining sausages in the European Community, see: "Even the Lowly Bratwurst Gains a Starring Role in Euro-ization," *The Wall Street Journal*, 26 October 1993, B2.

25. "Trade Winds," *The Economist*, 8 November 1997, 85–86; "Delivering the Goods," *The Economist*, 15 November 1997, 85–86; "When Trade and Security Clash," *The Economist*, 6 April 2002, 59–62. For an example of how Japan Airlines is using the Internet to attract new, foreign sources of supply, see "Webbed Flight," *The Economist*, 8 February 1997, 66.

26. For further discussion of the strategic advantages of pursuing growth in foreign markets, see Michael Porter, "What Is Strategy?" *Harvard Business Review* (November–December 1996): 61–78.

27. Richard T. Hise, "Globe Trotting," *Marketing Management* (Fall 1997): 50–58; and Gene Fox, "Systran Creates Niche Through Export Sales," *Dayton Business Reporter*, 4, no. 11 (August 1995): Sec A, 10.

28. Mark Wells, Julia Vanover, and Debbie Dirr, "Making a Group Effort," *Export America*, August 2001, 8–9; and Doug Barry and Joel Reynoso, "Welcome to BuyUSA.com: New E-Marketplace Offers Clicks, Mortar and Plenty of Buyers," *Export America* (June 2001): 22–25. For discussions of potential downsides of having governments involved in international trade, see "Don't Be Salesmen," *The Economist*, 1 February 1997, 17–18; and "Governments and Exports: Thoroughly Modern Mercantilists," *The Economist*, 1 February 1997, 23–25.

29. "The Grand Illusion," *The Economist*, 26 November 1994, 17.

30. "Sharp Tongues: The Nordics' Pragmatic Choice is English," *The Economist*, 14 June 2003, 9; "Cultural Explanations: The Man in the Baghdad Café," *The Economist*, 9 November 1996, 23–26; Jeswald W. Salacuse, *Making Global Deals* (New York: Times Books, 1991).

31. Salacuse, *Making Global Deals*.

32. Jean-Claude Usunier, *Marketing Across Cultures*, 2d ed. (London: Prentice Hall Europe, 1996); "Cultural Explanations," *The Economist*.

33. Jack D. Wood, "Culture Is Not Enough," in *Mastering Management*, George Bickerstaffe, ed. (London: Pitman Publishing, 1997), 414–418.

34. "Cultural Explanations," *The Economist,* 23, 26.

35. Geert Hoftstede, "The Interaction Between National and Organizational Value Systems," *Journal of Management Studies* (July 1985): 347–357. As mentioned earlier, the country may be multicultural in which case the specific cultural group of the business counterparts needs to be understood.

36. Adapted from Salacuse, *Making Global Deals,* 7.

37. Jeanne M. Brett, *Negotiating Globally* (San Francisco: Jossey-Bass, 2001); James K. Sebenius, "The Hidden Challenge of Cross-Border Negotiations," *Harvard Business Review* (March 2002): 76–85.

38. Salacuse, *Making Global Deals.*

39. Nigel Wilkins, *The Correspondent Banking Handbook* (London: Euromoney Books, 1993), 28. See also "Islamic Finance: Turning the Prophet's Profits," *The Economist,* 24 August 1996, 58–59; and "Islamic Banking: Forced Devotion," *The Economist,* 17 February 2001, 76–77.

40. Salacuse, *Making Global Deals,* 122.

41. "Business in Difficult Places: Risky Returns," *The Economist,* 20 May 2000, 85–88; "The Worm That Never Dies," *The Economist,* 2 March 2002, 12; "The Short Arm of the Law," *The Economist,* 2 March 2002, 63–65; and "Everything for a Price," *World Press Review,* October 2001, 6–15.

42. A'an Suryana, "Government, PT Paiton Reach Power Deal," *The Jakarta Post Archives,* 5 July 2002.

43. Salacuse, *Making Global Deals,* 128.

44. Salacuse, *Making Global Deals.* See also "Happy Endings Not Guaranteed," *Business Week,* 20 November 2002, 69–73.

45. We limit our discussion to the more common occurrences of currency exchange and payment risk in doing business across borders. Firms may employ hedging to protect themselves against large foreign currency exchange fluctuations; see, for example, Stephen D. Makar and Stephen P. Huffman, "Foreign Currency Risk Management Practices in U.S. Multinationals," *Journal of Applied Business Research* (Spring 1997): 73–86. Foreign currencies that are nonconvertible provide additional problems to resolve; see, for example, Ben Craig, "Competing Currencies: Back to the Future?" *Economic Commentary* (Federal Reserve Bank of Cleveland), 15 October 1996; and "World Wire: Prague, Russia Set Up Barter," *The Wall Street Journal,* 21 March 1991, A15.

46. Jon R. Katzenbach and Douglas K. Smith, "The Discipline of Teams," *Harvard Business Review* (March–April 1993): 112.

47. Katzenbach and Smith, "The Discipline of Teams," 112.

48. Some management thinkers recommend that senior managers acquire knowledge of the informal networks of relationships that individuals have across functions and divisions, and factor this into decisions about team composition. See David Krackhardt and Jeffrey R. Hanson, "Informal Networks: The Company Behind the Chart," *Harvard Business Review* (July–August 1993): 104–111.

49. Katzenbach and Smith, "The Discipline of Teams," 115.

50. "The Trouble with Teams," *The Economist,* 14 January 1995, 69. For a recent best practice example, see Amy Edmondson, Richard Bohmer, and Gary Pisano, "Speeding Up Team Learning," *Harvard Business Review,* October 2001, 125–132.

51. Christopher Meyer, "How the Right Measures Help Teams Excel," *Harvard Business Review* (May–June 1994): 95–103; Alfie Kohn, "Why Incentive Plans Cannot Work," *Harvard Business Review* (September–October 1993): 54–56, 58, 60, 62–63; "Rethinking Rewards," *Harvard Business Review* (November–December 1993): 37–39, 42–45, 48–49; and "Just Desserts," *The Economist,* 29 January 1994, 69.

52. James C. Anderson and James A. Narus, "Partnering as a Focused Market Strategy," *California Management Review* (Spring 1991): 95–113.

53. For a review on alliance management, see Robert E. Spekman, Theodore M. Forbes III, Lynn A. Isabella, and Thomas C. MacAvoy, "Alliance Management: A View from the Past and a Look to the Future," *Marketing Science Institute Working Paper,* Report No. 95-119 (December 1995): 1–32.

54. Jeanne M. Brett, Stephen B. Goldberg, and William L. Ury, "Managing Conflict: The Strategy of Dispute Systems Design," *Business Week Advance Executive Brief,* vol. 6 (New York: McGraw-Hill, 1994), 1–26; see also Todd B. Carver and Albert A. Vondra, "Alternative Dispute Resolution: Why It Doesn't Work and Why It Does," *Harvard Business Review* (May–June 1994): 120–130.

55. Ian F. Wilkinson and Louise C. Young, "Business Dancing: The Nature and Role of Interfirm Relationships in Business Strategy," *Asia-Australia Marketing Journal,* 2, no. 1 (1994): 67–79.

56. This section draws heavily on James C. Anderson, "Relationships in Business Markets: Exchange Episodes, Value Creation, and Their Empirical Assessment," *Journal of the Academy of Marketing Science* (Fall 1995): 346–350. See also David T. Wilson, "An Integrated Model of Buyer-Seller Relationships," *Journal of the Academy of Marketing Science* (Fall 1995): 335–345.

57. Peter Smith Ring and Andrew Van de Ven, "Developmental Processes of Cooperative Interorganizational Relationships," *Academy of Management Review* (January 1994): 112.

58. Karen S. Cook and Richard M. Emerson, "Power, Equity, Commitment in Exchange Networks," *American Sociological Review* (October 1978): 725. For consideration of how customer and supplier firms create value through their commitment to business network relationships, coordinating their activities with those of their business partners in connected relationships, see Desirée Blankenburg Holm, Kent Eriksson, and Jan Johanson, "Creating Value Through Mutual Commitment to Business Network Relationships," *Strategic Management Journal,* 20 (1999): 467–486.

59. Alajoutsijärvi, Möller, and Rosenbröijer have defined this set of connected relationships with the focal relationship as the *focal business net* to delineate it from the broader business network in which these relationships are embedded. See Kimmo Alajoutsijärvi, Kristian Möller, and Carl-Johan Rosenbröijer, "Relevance of Focal Nets in Understanding the Dynamics of Business Relationships," *Journal of Business-to-Business Marketing,* 6, no. 3 (1999): 3–35.

60. Ranjay Gulati, "Social Structure and Alliance Formation Patterns: A Longitudinal Analysis," *Administrative Science Quarterly* (December 1995): 619–652; and Benjamin Gomes-Casseres, "Group Versus Group: How Alliance Networks Compete," *Harvard Business Review* (July–August 1994): 62–66, 70, 72–74.

61. Kenichi Ohmae, "The Global Logic of Strategic Alliances," *Harvard Business Review* (March–April 1989): 143–154.

62. This section draws upon James C. Anderson, Håkan Håkansson, and Jan Johanson, "Dyadic Relationships Within a Business Network Context," *Journal of Marketing* (October 1994): 1–15.

63. "International Networking," Standard Chartered Advertisement, *The Economist,* 23 April 1994, 1–2.

64. Monique van Nieuwenhuizen, "Joint Strike Fighter Will Boost Dutch Economy," *Holland Horizon,* December 2002, 6–9.

65. Steven Brull and Brandon Mitchener, "The Alliance Demands Patience: Five Years On, Daimler and Mitsubishi Are Still Talking," *International Herald Tribune,* 15 December 1993, 11, 15.

66. Charles C. Snow, Raymond E. Miles, and Henry J. Coleman, Jr., "Managing 21st Century Network Organizations," *Organizational Dynamics* (Winter 1992): 5–19.

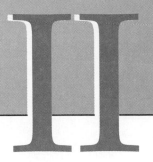

Understanding Value

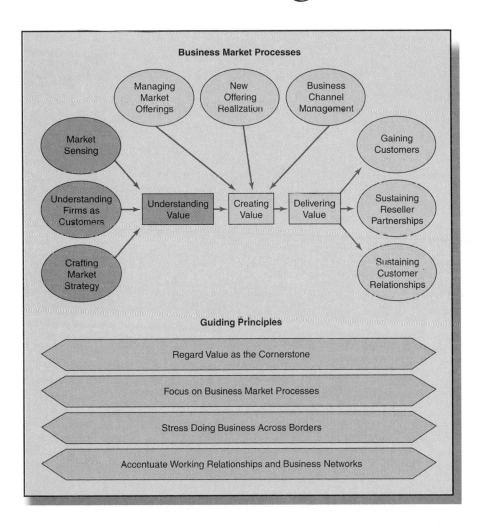

Chapter 2

Market Sensing

Generating and Using Knowledge About the Market

OVERVIEW

Market-driven firms are distinguished by an ability to sense events and trends in their markets ahead of their competitors. They can anticipate more accurately the responses to actions designed to retain or attract customers, improve channel relations, or thwart competitors. They can act on information in a timely, coherent manner because the assumptions about the market are broadly shared. This anticipatory capability is based on superiority in each step of the process. It is achieved through open-minded inquiry, synergistic information distribution, mutually informed interpretations, and accessible memories.[1]

*D*ay calls this distinctive capability of market-driven organizations *market sensing*. He also has sketched out a market sensing process, which is shown in Figure 2.1. Market sensing can provide a firm with an edge over its competitors, yet most firms do not recognize this. We have never seen a firm that was in trouble because it had too much knowledge about its market, yet we routinely encounter firms in trouble because they have faulty or inadequate knowledge about their markets.

Figure 2.1   Market Sensing: Process for Learning About Markets

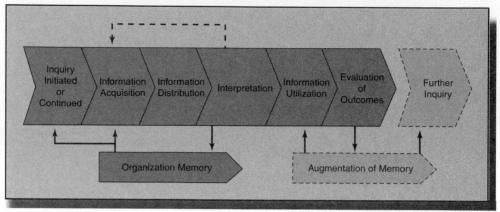

Source: George S. Day, "The Capabilities of Market-Driven Organizations," *Journal of Marketing* (October 1994): 43.

Market sensing is the process of generating knowledge about the marketplace that individuals in the firm, such as business market managers, salespersons, or senior executives, use to inform and guide their decision making. Market sensing is a market-driven process of learning about present and prospective customers and competitors, as well as about other actors that affect them and the firm, such as resellers and regulatory agencies. Market sensing enables business market managers and others in the firm to formulate, test, revise, update, and refine their **market views**, which are simplified representations of the marketplace and how it works. Market sensing greatly contributes to the value of these mental models by providing a way to test assumptions about customers, competitors, and the firm's own resources and capabilities that often are largely implicit. It also advances decision rules and heuristics that supplier managers use to interpret and act upon changes in the marketplace.[2]

This chapter is organized around four substantive facets of market sensing: defining the market, monitoring competition, assessing customer value, and gaining customer feedback. To attain a distinctive capability in market sensing, the firm should strive to be superior to its competitors in each of these facets, particularly in assessing value, because value is the cornerstone of business market management. Figure 2.2 provides an overview not only of these substantive facets of market sensing but also of the chapter. Before we discuss each substantive facet, though, let's briefly consider some requirements for market sensing as a business market management process.

Market sensing encompasses market research, which is a crucial business marketing process for generating knowledge about the marketplace, but it is broader than that. Marketplace knowledge is generated in other ways; for example, when supplier engineers have discussions with customer engineers about customer development projects at an

Figure 2.2 Substantive Facets of Market Sensing

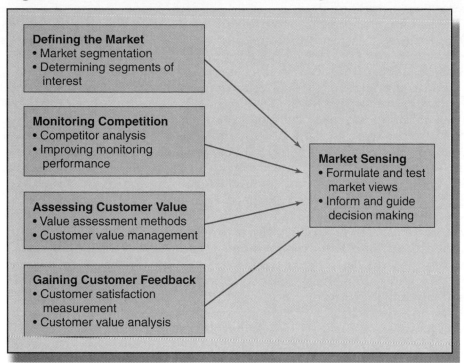

industry or professional association meeting, or when manufacturing managers talk with equipment suppliers about new equipment and learn that competitors have purchased it. Moreover, use of the generated knowledge by individuals in the firm to inform and guide their decision making is a crucial part of market sensing. Thus, the generated knowledge must be accessible and individuals must be willing to use it.[3]

The generated knowledge may be tacit, where the individuals possessing it have difficulty expressing it or putting it in an explicit form that others can use. Seasoned salespeople may develop routines and practices, such as subtle variations in their sales presentations that enhance their performance, but which they may not be able to readily articulate. Based on trial-and-error learning, production workers may make subtle, minor adjustments to the component materials "recipe" or to equipment to make products that perform better in particular customer applications. Individuals can use metaphors, analogies, and conceptual models as tools to transform their tacit knowledge to explicit knowledge that is valuable to others in the firm.[4]

Firms have great difficulty realizing what they *do* know. Individuals in one part of the firm may have generated knowledge that could inform and guide the decision making of individuals in another part of the firm, yet each is unaware of this knowledge and its availability. It is a challenge for a firm to pull together all it knows about the marketplace and to make this knowledge available to relevant individuals in a meaningful way. Firms traditionally have used reports, plans, written policies and procedures, and manuals to provide a collective or **organization memory**. Progressive firms increasingly employ sophisticated information technology to create relational databases, link disparate databases, and provide decision-support tools, such as expert systems and decision calculus models. In an ever-changing marketplace, it is essential for firms to refresh, update, and assess the continued accuracy of the information in the organization's memory.[5]

An old saying in German business is "If Siemens only knew what Siemens knows." This paradoxical saying captures the difficulties that large, multinational firms, such as the conglomerate Siemens, have in knowledge management. **Knowledge management** refers to the processes and supporting systems that enable a firm to gather know-how, best practices, and learning that potentially have value elsewhere in the firm, convert them into a form that can be readily found and understood, and then make them accessible for reuse more broadly within the firm. To make progress against this saying, Siemens recently made a substantial investment in a "sharenet," which is an intranet system on which knowledge is posted for use throughout the firm. In preparing its bid for a high-speed data network linking Kuala Lumpur with its new airport, Siemens Malaysia found itself lacking some necessary know-how. A search on the sharenet revealed that Siemens was already working on a similar project in Denmark. Adapting what had been done there to its own setting, Siemens Malaysia was able to leverage this knowledge gained from Denmark to win an order for a pilot project.[6]

Even when it is accessible, generated knowledge about the marketplace has little value if individuals are not willing to use it. A user's trust in the individual who generates the market knowledge, or market research, significantly predicts willingness to use the market research. The user's perception of the researcher's integrity and willingness to reduce research uncertainty (through the provision of explanations for research results) are significant antecedents of the user's trust in the research provider.[7] Further, a complementary blend of formal and informal communications between providers and users in different functional areas significantly contributes to the users' perceptions of the quality of the market intelligence. In turn, this perception of quality significantly affects their use of that market intelligence. Formal dissemination of market intelligence itself is a significant, direct antecedent of its use. "Although informal communications may provide greater openness and clarification opportunities, formal communications tend to be more credible and verifiable, thereby encouraging the use of intelligence, particularly if it is contrary to receivers' prior beliefs."[8]

More broadly, individuals' willingness to use knowledge management systems depends on their perception that doing so provides worthwhile assistance to them, which depends, in part on the process the firm pursues to make contributions to its knowledge database. Customer service representatives at Xerox share insights they gain when fixing Xerox machines through a process that ensures that what finally makes it into their Web-based, knowledge management system, known as the Eureka database, is relevant, accurate, and easily understood. Reps submit suggestions or tips to local experts, who work together with the rep to screen and refine them. Tips that pass this initial screen are submitted to a centralized review process, where the relevant business unit screens the tips, eliminates redundancies, and further refines the tips, contributing any deeper technical expertise needed. Tips that ultimately are placed in the Eureka database have the contributing rep's name attached to them, providing social recognition. Interestingly, in the pilot program to design this system, Xerox found that the reps preferred this social recognition to financial incentives for contributing tips, which they felt might subvert the process.[9]

DEFINING THE MARKET

In **defining the market**, business market managers choose descriptors that characterize and delimit a market, with the intent of pinpointing groups of firms that are of greater interest to the supplier firm. The descriptors chosen significantly affect the way a firm views a market, what its prospects are, and the courses of action it subsequently pursues. Market segmentation and determining market segments of interest are fundamental to defining the market.

Market Segmentation

"If you're not thinking segments, you're not thinking."[10] Levitt made this provocative observation a number of years ago, and it is even more true now, as markets have become more diverse and dynamic. **Market segmentation** is the process of partitioning a market into groupings of firms that have relatively similar requirements and preferences for market offerings. When segmenting markets, business market managers look for descriptors that capture significant differences in requirements and preferences for market offerings or how prospective customers will respond to marketing initiatives. Different descriptors can provide dramatically different views of the market and provide insights to gain competitive advantage.

Significantly, irrespective of which descriptors a firm chooses, any market segmentation requires empirical support to validate the market view it suggests. Otherwise, the firm may overlook some subtle, yet critical, distinctions that exist. As an example, a manufacturer of downhole drills initially grouped strip mines and quarries together into a single segment, thinking they were similar. Mines and quarries both use downhole drills to create blastholes in which workers place explosives to blow the "face" off the production wall to extract material such as iron ore or limestone. The manufacturer developed a new downhole drill that was capable of drilling significantly more feet per hour, which would provide users with time savings and lower cost. In its subsequent market research, the manufacturer discovered that a faster drill would provide significantly greater value in strip mines than it would in quarries. An additional step in the quarries' production process was the cause of this difference. Unlike strip mines, quarries perform a crushing operation on the extracted material. It turns out that the crushing equipment that reduces the blasted rock to a smaller, more uniform size creates a "bottleneck" in the typical quarry's production process. One blast each day extracts enough material to keep the crushing equipment running at full capacity. In contrast, a faster drill that shortens the drill-blast-clear cycle significantly improves a strip mine's productivity.

Business market managers use a variety of ways, or bases, to segment markets. Often, they rely on several bases in conjunction to further segment or subsegment markets. We first discuss conventional bases of segmentation, then more progressive bases of segmentation. Whatever bases of segmentation business market managers decide on, they should apply the following four criteria to judge validity of their proposed segmentation scheme:[11]

1. *Measurable*: Can the size, growth, and market potential of a segment be measured?
2. *Profitable*: How profitable is the marketing effort likely to be? What is the payoff from each segment?
3. *Accessible*: Can segments be identified and reached successfully?
4. *Actionable*: Can effective marketing and sales programs be formulated for attracting and serving the segments?

Conventional Bases of Segmentation

Industry, customer size, customer behavior, and geography are customary ways of segmenting business markets. Finding **industries** that use (or might use) a supplier firm's market offering is a first step in segmentation. In North America, business market managers often use the North American Industry Classification System (NAICS) codes, which succeeded the U.S. Standard Industrial Classification (SIC) codes, to segment an industry.[12] As an example of the successively finer industry classifications that four-digit versus six-digit NAICS codes provide, ship and boat building has the four-digit code of 3366, whereas boat building itself has the six-digit code of 336612. One problem that business market managers find with using NAICS codes is that the classification may still not be precise enough for their needs. For instance, a supplier of fiberglass resin for structural applications such as boat hulls would find the 336612 code insufficient, in that it also includes manufacturers of boats with aluminum hulls, which are not potential customers.

Business market managers segment by **customer size** when they believe that firm size is a strong proxy for customer demand for their firm's market offerings. Specific measures of customer size, which often come from secondary sources, are total sales, number of employees, and number of establishments (locations). **Customer behavior** captures a number of actions that firms take. Doing business with the supplier is a basic one, resulting in four segments: firms that are purchasing the supplier's market offering for the first time; firms that have purchased the supplier's market offering previously and currently are purchasing it; firms that have not purchased the supplier's market offering; and firms that have previously purchased the supplier's market offering, but no longer are purchasing it. Business market managers may further segment present customers' purchase behavior based on their extent of usage of a market offering—light, medium, or heavy.

Finally, business market managers segment by **geography** when they believe that customer location has a significant effect on doing business. Many firms implicitly use a basic geographic segmentation: the home-country market versus "the rest of the world." Most of these firms only do business in their home-country market. When the home-country market is large, firms may segment further and pursue business only on a local or regional basis.

Progressive Bases of Segmentation

Many business market managers are finding that the conventional bases of segmentation no longer have the vitality that they once had. Even though they may provide a useful start, they are not enough to pinpoint groups of customers with sufficiently similar requirements and preferences. To gain a more detailed understanding of how customer requirements and preferences vary, business market managers use more progressive bases of segmentation, such as application, customer capabilities and business priorities, usage situation, and customer profitability.

Business market managers segment by **application** because firms that use the supplier's core product or service in the same way or for the same purpose tend to derive value from it similarly. As an example, Glen Raven Mills, a manufacturer of acrylic woven fabrics, found two different applications for its products within the marine market: outside the boat as boat covers and canopies and inside the boat as seat covers.[13] Customers had distinct requirements and preferences for each application. Another often-occurring application segmentation is between sales to original equipment manufacturers (OEMs) and replacement (aftermarket) sales for maintenance, repair, and operating (MRO) applications.

Customer capabilities can be a worthwhile basis of segmentation when customers vary significantly in what competencies they possess, and what knowledge and skills they want suppliers to provide. Many firms now focus on their core competencies and strategic capabilities, and rely on outside firms to provide the rest.[14] Some customer firms, for example, may possess technical know-how and problem-solving capability, while others do not and expect their suppliers to provide these aspects. **Customer business priorities** strongly guide which capabilities customer firms seek to possess as sources of competitive advantage, and they also provide a progressive basis of segmentation themselves. Eli Lilly and Company has used customer business priorities as a basis of market segmentation with success, which we relate in Box 2.1

Customers may use a core product or service in the same application, but may have markedly different requirements and preferences for it across **usage situations**. For example, truck fleet owners have different time and price sensitivities for truck parts that they purchase for scheduled maintenance versus those for emergency repairs of roadside breakdowns. Another instance of usage situation segmentation is a distributor that segmented its customers based on the number of lines on the order: Customers that were using the distributor for "fill-in" orders paid a higher price than "full-order" customers.

BOX 2.1
Lilly Segments the Managed Care Market Based on Customer Business Priorities

Eli Lilly and Company is a leading innovation-driven pharmaceutical company. Historically, the pharmaceutical industry focused its marketing efforts on influencing physician prescribing. In the early 1990s, managed care organizations began to exert a growing influence over physician prescribing decisions. In response, Lilly created a special division to gain a deeper understanding of this kind of customer, so that it could customize value propositions to them.

Lilly considers segmentation extremely important to its marketing strategy for the managed care business. Initial efforts at segmentation focused on the size of the managed care organization (enrollment), control level (ability to influence physician prescribing), and the organization's business model (e.g., staff model HMO, Pharmacy Benefit Management Company). This early segmentation schema was highly actionable because segments were readily identifiable. Conversely, this segmentation also ignored critical differences in the key business requirements and preferences of these customers. More sophisticated market segmentation would be needed to better understand these critical differences. This knowledge would enable Lilly to customize its marketing approaches and apply its marketing resources more efficiently and effectively. Lilly undertook an extensive segmentation project to accomplish this task.

A cross-functional group was formed to develop an actionable segmentation scheme. The internal team included market research, strategic planning, brand marketing, account managers, and pricing. The first critical step of the team was gaining alignment on the objectives of the project and how the results would be used. This initial step was critically important to the success of the project and guided future decisions the group made. The team also formed an initial hypothesis on how the market might be segmented, based on their practical experience

with this group of customers. This hypothesis helped Lilly direct the market research more efficiently.

The research first included focus groups and exploratory in-depth, one-on-one interviews with senior executives (CEO and COO) and department heads (Pharmacy Director and Medical Director) of managed care organizations. The purpose of this initial step was to deeply understand their decision-making process for determining how drugs are reimbursed by their organizations, and their key business requirements and priorities.

The results of this preliminary research were used to develop a quantitative survey that measured customer responses across multiple dimensions, including drug selection decision-making processes, business priorities, and perceptions of pharmaceutical companies. The completed survey data was then analyzed using several analytical techniques, such as cluster analysis and factor analysis, to find discrete groups of customers with similarities across these parameters. Lilly ultimately decided to drive the segmentation based on customer's business priorities and requirements. The team felt this segmentation schema would give the greatest insights and be most actionable.

Several logical customer segments emerged from the analysis:

- *Enrollment Expanders*: Greater focus on enrollment growth and market share attainment.
- *Low-Cost Providers*: Higher priority on reducing their cost structure and becoming a low-cost health-care provider.
- *Quality Seekers*: More oriented toward clinical quality and less focused on being the low-cost health-care provider.
- *Patient Empowermenters*: Organizations focused more on enabling consumer choice of medical care, while simultaneously shifting costs to the patient.

BOX 2.1
Continued

The process helped Lilly identify customer segments and customer requirements using a common conceptual framework and common language. However, one challenge with a segmentation based on business priorities was not being able to readily identify which customers would fall into which segment. Customer business priorities and requirements are nearly impossible to predict using existing secondary data. Therefore, Lilly created a survey tool that enabled its account executives to quantify the business priorities and requirements of their key customers in a real-time interaction. This 5-minute, laptop PC-based survey asked customers to prioritize a variety of potential business priorities and requirements. Customer responses could then be compared with national norms calculated from the segmentation research. These segmentation results were immediately available upon completion of the survey.

An unexpected and beneficial side effect of this survey process was the positive interactions account executives had with their customers while conducting the survey. They engaged in deep, extensive conversations with customers about their strategies and requirements. Discussions shifted from being product-focused to being customer-oriented. This interaction allowed Lilly account executives to discuss programs that would truly meet the varying requirements of the managed care organizations. Ultimately, the segmentation assisted Lilly in creating a process to more fully understand a customer's business priorities and to more efficiently deliver those programs and services that are most meaningful to customers—truly a win-win situation.

Segmentation based on customer behavior has advanced from simple purchase behavior to more sophisticated analyses of doing business with customers. Progressive business market managers, as an example, segment on **contribution to profitability**; that is, how much profit does the supplier earn from doing business with a particular customer? They use measures such as the cost to serve a customer and the customer's willingness to pay for offerings to gain estimates of contribution to profitability. On the horizon for firms in business markets is gaining estimates of customer equity, which assesses the expected profits from doing business with a customer for as long as the relationship lasts.[15] Sprint Business provides an outstanding example of a firm that segments its market on the value of customers to Sprint Business *and* the value of Sprint offerings to customers, which we recount in Box 2.2.

Finally, progressive business market managers update geographic segmentation to take advantage of doing business across borders. They segment firms based on those firms' requirements and preferences, where this segmentation is across country markets. Segments with relatively similar requirements and preferences may actually be composed of customers located in several country markets. In this way, suppliers can standardize by providing the same market offering in a number of country markets, and customize by providing more than one offering in each country market.[16]

Determining Market Segments of Interest

Whatever market-segmentation approach business market managers pursue, as part of their research they need to assess which markets—and segments within them—are of greater interest to the firm. This approach enables the firm to pinpoint which

A few years ago, senior management at Sprint Business gave a challenging segmentation charter to its Market Insights (MI) group: "Find an actionable segmentation approach that will enable Sprint Business to support efficient, customer-focused revenue acquisition, retention, and growth. The methodology chosen must be able to be implemented successfully and supported across the organization." Recognizing that cross-functional support would be crucial for the success of any segmentation initiative, MI managers formed a team with representation from internal communications, market development, market research, marketing information systems, product management, and sales.

The effort began with a best practices assessment. The segmentation team reviewed past segmentation efforts at Sprint Business, which had employed firmographics (e.g., industry, location, size by number of employees) and usage behaviors (e.g., products purchased, revenue/spend). It found that the traditional segmentation frameworks fell short of answering important market questions, such as: "Why will the prospect purchase our products and services over the competitors?" The team next examined refinements on the traditional approaches, as well as segmenting on the value of the customer, and customer requirements, preferences, and actions. As part of this effort, the team conducted interviews with thought leaders on the topic of market segmentation.

After in-depth discussions on state-of-the-art segmentation approaches, the segmentation team decided on a two-stage segmentation approach. Sprint Business first would segment customers or prospects on their present or potential value to Sprint, and then subsegment on the attractiveness or perceived value of Sprint's offerings to those customers or prospects. This approach best met the criteria that the team had established for a segmentation approach at Sprint Business, such as supporting prioritization, prediction

of future behavior, and relatable to known business descriptors.

Segmentation is progressing as Sprint Business is able to use more sophisticated measures. The MI group, which is responsible for ongoing segmentation development, is working toward segmenting prospects and customers on their value to Sprint Business, using a formula composed of business factors, such as cost to serve. Using sophisticated predictive modeling, it estimates the dollar value of each business location to Sprint business. After defining a number of segments based on their value to Sprint, it next estimates the attractiveness or perceived value of Sprint offerings to each segment, based on customer requirements, preferences, and likelihood of actions profiles. These profiles are constructed from weighted measures in the customer/prospect areas of strategic business and operational requirements or decision drivers; functional-level requirements and preferences for technology and communications services; current and expected usage/demand for specific products and services; and current and expected use of specific channels and sources of information.

MI managers emphasize that market segmentation at Sprint Business is an ongoing process, not a research project at one point in time. Implementation of this segmentation program has entailed creating products, tools, and infrastructure for Sprint Business managers. Segment profiles and "success stories" are product examples; predictive models and a proprietary Web-based research panel are examples of tools; whereas Mindshare, an intranet marketing portal to go to for segmentation updates (a knowledge management system), is an example of supporting infrastructure.

Most critical to its success is that the segmentation program has enabled Sprint Business to significantly improve its targeting and prospecting efficiency. For example, prioritizing leads by predicted attractiveness

BOX 2.2
Continued

of Sprint offerings increased "good" leads (i.e., those receptive to receiving additional information and contact) by more than 100 percent. As another example, Sprint Business found that it required more than 45 percent greater sales costs to close a sale with a prospect in those customer segments indicated as not the best prospects from the segmentation research. As a result, Sprint Business reduced its investment in pursuing these prospects and redirected it to higher potential prospect segments, thereby significantly increasing its marketing return on investment.

groups of customers it should pursue, and as importantly, what groups it should not. As Chuck Lillis, former CEO of U S WEST Media Group, once observed perceptively: "I will know when our businesses are doing a good job of market segmentation when they can articulate who we should *not* sell to."[17] Gaining an understanding of market segments of interest occurs in two related steps: (1) obtaining estimates of each defined market segment's size and growth, and (2) assessing its sales and profit potential.[18]

Market Segment Size and Growth

Business market managers would like to know how many prospective customers are in each segment, how much of the defined offering category they will purchase, and how each of these factors will change over time. Two concepts that provide these figures are market potential and total market demand. **Market potential** "identifies the maximum units of a defined product or service capable of being purchased within a designated geographic area, during a designated time period, when supported by a realistic level of marketing activity." In contrast, **total market demand**, which tends to have a shorter time focus, is a prediction of the actual number of units that will be purchased.[19]

Business market managers can use three approaches for estimating the market potential for a segment: the buildup method, the chain ratio method, and the index method. The buildup method is simply taking market potential estimates from subsegments, using available secondary research or conducting primary research, and combining them to reach an estimate for the segment. The chain ratio method starts with a large number of prospective customers as identified by the business market manager, perhaps from using NAICS codes. This number is then multiplied by a series of percentages (ratios) that correspond to the assumptions made, such as the percentage of potential customers that use a certain technology, to arrive at a final estimate. The index method ties the estimate to a single factor affecting the market, such as the number of new housing starts, or to multiple factors, which the business market manager might obtain from an econometric forecasting service. By their nature, these approaches cannot provide precise estimates, and their accuracy is heavily dependent on the validity of the assumptions that a business market manager makes.[20]

Business market managers would like to know which market segments will have the largest growth in total market demand over some time horizon of interest, such as the next year, three years, or five years. Barnett describes the four basic steps needed in any forecast of total market demand:[21]

1. Define the market.
2. Divide total industry demand into its main components.
3. Forecast the drivers of demand in each segment and project how they are likely to change.
4. Conduct sensitivity analyses to understand the most critical assumptions and to gauge risks to the baseline forecast.

At the outset, the business market manager should define the market broadly, such as by the basic functionality that prospective customers are seeking. The second step is market segmentation, using the progressive bases of application, customer capabilities, and usage situation. The drivers of demand most often are macroeconomic variables and industry-specific developments, which the business market manager might ask a number of industry experts to predict. Finally, rather than putting these numbers together to produce a single estimate of future demand, business market managers should construct several scenarios. Each scenario is built around a set of internally consistent assumptions, with the set of scenarios spanning a set of plausible outcomes.[22]

Naturally, forecasting market potential or total market demand for new categories of market offerings or for embryonic markets is especially challenging. As an example, consider Univac, which pioneered commercial computers:

> In 1950 Univac's market research predicted that by the year 2000 there would be one thousand computers in use. Its initial forecast called for sales of about a dozen large mainframes to the Census Bureau, Bell Laboratories, the Atomic Energy Commission, and similar large-scale users. . . . The forecast failed because it was based on the mistaken assumption that the market for computers was for advanced scientific purposes. Univac did not foresee the extensive, but mundane, business applications to which those wonderful machines were mostly put. IBM's success was due to its focus on business customers rather than scientists.[23]

In these situations, business market managers should use multiple methods to produce a combined forecast, which likely will be more accurate than the forecast from any single method. They need to be aware of their assumptions and challenge each one. An assessment of the value of an innovation relative to existing alternatives should be a crucial input to any forecast. How does the innovation provide superior functionality or performance over existing alternatives, or how does it provide equivalent functionality or performance at a lower price? Finally, business market managers might build scenarios to produce a set of plausible demand estimates.[24]

Sales and Profit Potential

Business market managers also would like to know what the potential is for their firms' market offerings in each market segment. **Sales potential** "identifies what one particular firm could sell if it applied maximum marketing effort."[25] In contrast, a **sales forecast**, which tends to have a shorter time focus, is a prediction of the actual number of units that a firm will sell with defined commitments of marketing and sales resources.

Supplier firms often use sales force composites or regression analyses to estimate sales potential and a sales forecast for each market segment.[26] With a sales force composite, the business market manager asks each salesperson to predict how much of each market offering he or she will sell, and then combines the predictions to produce the firm's overall sales potential or sales forecast. With regression analysis, the manager uses past years' sales, often along with particular macroeconomic variables and industry drivers, to predict future years' sales. The sales forecast and predicted total market demand, taken together, provide a prediction of the supplier's market share for each segment.

For market segments that the firm presently serves, business market managers should strongly consider building up their sales and profit forecasts from estimates of their **share of each customer's business**.[27] At the broadest level, a supplier's share would be defined as the percentage it supplies of the customer's total purchase requirements for all product offerings that the supplier would be able to supply. In short, what percentage of the total business that a supplier and customer could potentially do together are they doing?

Knowing the share of total customer requirements supplied, though, provides no understanding of where the most profitable prospects for growth are. To determine the best prospects for profitable growth with customers, which may come from discovering possibilities of doing more business in a different way, a supplier needs a more fine-gauged understanding of its shares of each customer's business. Understanding the share of the customer's business for each product category supplied provides a more insightful picture. When the customer has multiple locations, further insight comes from understanding how the supplier's business is spread across locations. Thus, if a customer has 10 plants in its manufacturing network, what percentage of each plant's purchase requirements does each of the supplier's offerings account for? A supplier can find that the percentage of a given offering it supplies can vary dramatically across customer locations, from being single source to supplying nothing at all. The cost to serve a customer and the customer's own total cost of ownership can each vary significantly, depending on how the same amount of supplier business is spread across locations.

Most firms rely upon their sales forces to gather the data to estimate shares of customers' business. To gain initial acceptance and sustain the data gathering effort over time, supplier management must have persuasive answers to the questions "Why should the sales force cooperate in this task?" and "Why should the customers cooperate in this task?" Each must clearly understand why it is beneficial to them to participate. Technische Unie, the leading distributor in the Netherlands for electrical, plumbing, and heating supply, provides an outstanding example of how to manage this process. As the Technische Unie case in Box 2.3 exemplifies, progressive firms not only gain accurate share estimates, they use other (independent) sources to validate their share estimates, and they build a customer share database to pull together and leverage the value of this gathered data.

Business market managers typically derive profit potential and predicted profit from the sales potential and sales forecast by making additional assumptions. As an example, the business market manager might multiply the sales forecast in units by the past year's contribution margin to provide the predicted gross profit dollars for each market segment. More sophisticated analyses take into account more subtle differences in customers and market segments, such as the cost to serve or the willingness to pay for augmenting services.

BOX 2.3
Technische Unie Estimates Its Share of Its Customers' Business

Technische Unie (TU) is the leading distributor in the Netherlands for the electrical, plumbing, and heating product segments to the housing, commercial/institutional, and industrial plant (both OEM and MRO) application segments. Spurred on by an economic downturn, TU formulated a business strategy for profitable growth based on selective growth in its shares of its customers' business. It provides an outstanding case of minimizing the data-gathering burden for salespeople and customers while providing significant benefits to both in participating in its customer-share assessments.

To gain a fine-grained understanding of its share of each of its customers' business, TU employs two full-time persons who conduct field interviews with customers. They go to a TU branch, select a random sample of 30 customers, stratified by customer size, and then visit these customers to collect data. Stratification is by the number of mechanics that a customer employs: small (less than 10 mechanics); medium (between 10 and 50 mechanics); and large (more than 50 mechanics). These visits are seen as customer reviews. Every six weeks, each of these researchers visits another branch. In total, TU conducts about 500 in-depth interviews per year, each lasting about 2 hours. There are 35 TU branches in the Netherlands, so TU calibrates the information about every two years. TU additionally uses the information collected to allow the branches to benchmark one another.

Customers cooperate because they believe that TU will use the information to improve its business with them. For instance, customers use these interviews to argue for TU to add specific products to its assortment (TU's goal is to provide 70 percent of the market requirements). They discuss other issues as well, such as electronic ordering. As part of this interview, the customer relates the total amount of material purchased in each product segment (and within product segment, by major product families, such as porcelain and piping) and the number of mechanics working in that area (i.e., electrical, plumbing, heating), which enables calculation of the amount of material used per mechanic over the year. The customer also relates the percentage of material bought from wholesalers versus direct. TU also cooperates closely with the Association of Electrical Installation Firms and the counterpart associations for plumbing and heating to gain independent estimates for comparisons.

To provide share estimates for each customer firm, TU has a related initiative that its sales force performs. Twice a year, TU sales reps (about 100 in number) interview each customer to ask about changes in the number of mechanics that the customer has working in each product area. These data enable TU to make comparisons of sales history by product category for each account compared to similar others. Thus, for example, TU knows that while it is getting its targeted share of the customer's porcelain business, it is not getting the piping business, all within the plumbing product segment.

To gain cooperation from the sales force, TU needed the sales reps' confidence that the information would not be used for individual blame, but for management discussion. TU also has one person check on the validity of the data provided by the sales reps. TU developed KIS (Klanten Informatie System), a proprietary laptop program for tracking development, sales by order, margin, and share of customer's business for each customer. The program provides benchmark information by product group to the salesperson, who can use KIS to guide his or her inquiries with the customers about their purchases.

The TU branch manager and the sale reps jointly develop prospects for growth. The market consists of 4,500 electrical installation firms and 9,000–10,000 installer firms in total. Thus, TU must be selective in its targeting. To guide these decisions, TU performs a customer

BOX 2.3
Continued

contribution analysis. TU knows its acquisition costs per product group. To this information, it adds the cost of sales calls on the customer, the logistics cost, the handling cost, the credit cost, and the year-end bonus paid to the customer to determine the true profit margin. Thus, the net result for each customer is known. TU can then leverage this customer knowledge to identify the best prospects for profitable growth.

Source: Adapted from James C. Anderson and James A. Narus, "Selectively Pursuing More of Your Customer's Business, *MIT Sloan Management Review* (Spring 2003): 42–49.

MONITORING COMPETITION

Business market management is the process of understanding, creating, and delivering value to targeted market segments and customers. Business market managers have a goal of gaining knowledge about present and prospective customer requirements and preferences as their principal concern. However, because customer judgments about the value of the firm's market offerings take place within the context of market offerings from other firms, business market managers also need knowledge about their competitors. They use knowledge about competitors in crafting their own firm's market strategy, anticipating competitors' reactions to it, and deciding what reactions to make in response to competitors' actions in the marketplace.

How do business market managers determine which set of firms to monitor? They look at the other market offerings that present and prospective customers consider as alternatives to their firms' market offerings. The firms providing them are their competitors. Much the same is done for market segments that the firm is considering entering: What firms currently are supplying market offerings that are most closely related to the firm's anticipated market offering? It is more difficult to determine which firms to monitor that may become competitors. These firms are not currently doing business in a market segment of interest, but may be entering it in the near future. In these instances, business market managers rely on their research-and-development colleagues to monitor advances in technologies from outside the industry that have the potential, with further innovation, to provide entry for firms employing the new technology in their market offerings.[28] Business market managers especially need to monitor merger and acquisition activity in related industries that could produce business units that are formidable, potential competitors. Although firms typically spend most, if not all, of their monitoring resources on present competitors, business history suggests that firms should devote a greater proportion to potential and new competitors.[29]

We next discuss a framework for competitor analysis. Business market managers can use this framework to synthesize a comprehensive understanding of each of their competitors. We then suggest some ways to improve monitoring performance.

A Framework for Competitor Analysis

Porter provided a good framework for competitor analysis.[30] This framework consists of four diagnostic components: future goals, assumptions, current strategy, and capabilities. Pulling together knowledge of these areas provides a comprehensive understanding of each competitor.

Future Goals

Understanding what a competitor wants to accomplish in the market provides insight into what actions it will take and how it will react to the firm's actions. Competitors have financial goals, such as increasing profitability or reducing the cost of sales. They also have market performance goals, such as growing market share or increasing the percentage of sales from recently introduced products. Goals exist at the corporate level and the business unit level as well. Gaining an understanding of the compensation plans of senior management, business market managers, and the sales force often will reveal these goals. Learning that a competitor is embarking on a companywide or business-unit-wide training program can signal a shift in its goals, such as when Dupont Company educated its workforce on being market oriented.[31]

Assumptions

Understanding what assumptions a competitor makes about itself, other firms in the industry, and in its market view are critical for predicting what it will do. Significantly, the competitor itself may not be explicitly aware of some of its assumptions. Identifying biases or blind spots of a competitor's managers suggest areas a firm can exploit. **Blind spots** "are areas where a competitor will either not see the significance of events (such as a strategic move) at all, will perceive them incorrectly, or will perceive them only very slowly."[32]

Marketplace success may cause senior management to have blind spots. Perhaps due to its great success with VAX minicomputers using proprietary systems, the former Digital Equipment Corporation (DEC) was slow to comprehend the industry's movement to open systems. Even though DEC founder and former CEO Kenneth Olsen was regarded as a visionary, he did not adjust well to an evolving business environment. In 1991, for example, he stated, "You can be sure our plan was perfect; it's just that the assumptions were wrong."[33]

Current Strategy

A competitor's current market strategy guides its actions in the marketplace, as well as suggesting its likely reaction to the firm's actions. The firm should understand a competitor's market strategy in terms of its three basic components: the competitor's selected target markets, the competitor's positioning of its market offerings, and the marketing mix that it is implementing in support of its market strategy.[34] The firm usually has little difficulty understanding what segments a competitor is targeting. Finding out what industry and trade publications a competitor has selected for advertising and studying the content of its ads should indicate which market segments it is pursuing. A firm's sales force can also learn what sales force promotions a competitor is running. To learn about the positioning of a competitor's market offerings, a firm can study the content of the competitor's ads and the editorial statements it makes about its offerings, obtain its sales literature, visit its Web site on the Internet, and visit its booth at trade shows.

The firm should also have little difficulty gaining knowledge about a competitor's marketing mix, with pricing perhaps being the exception. In gaining an understanding of a competitor's target markets and positioning, the firm will already have studied the competitor's promotion element of the marketing mix. Whenever possible, the firm should purchase and analyze a competitor's market offering to better understand its product element. The firm should learn from its sales force which channels of distribution a competitor is using, especially any new channels. Gaining an accurate understanding of a competitor's pricing is often difficult because of problems in determining comparability.[35]

Capabilities

To gauge its strengths and weaknesses relative to a competitor, the firm needs to know the core competencies and strategic capabilities of that competitor. Specifically, the firm should investigate a competitor's capability to conceive and design, produce, market, finance, and manage. In the process, the firm also should examine a competitor's recent history to estimate how well that competitor is able to adapt to change and how quickly it is able to respond to actions of its competitors.[36]

Finally, the firm needs to gauge a competitor's strength of will or commitment to compete in each market segment.[37] What significance does each of the competitor's market offerings and segments hold for it? For market offerings or market segments that the competitor regards as crucial, it will make strong retaliations to the firm's marketing actions. At times, a competitor's commitment may be emotionally driven, so that what it does is not rational in terms of overall or long-term profitability. As an example, senior executives may have sentimental attachments to particular offerings or market segments that launched them to success in their careers with the firm.

Improving Monitoring Performance

With some persistence, creativity, consistency of effort, and a reasonable investment of resources, managers can gain sufficient knowledge about competitors to inform and guide their decision making. However, monitoring competitors in many firms falls short, with the firms having a sketchy understanding of their competitors. How can firms improve their monitoring performance? They need to have competitor intelligence systems in place, and they need to practice seeking out disconfirming as well as confirming evidence in building knowledge about competitors.

Competitor Intelligence Systems

To improve monitoring performance, firms need to implement an organized approach for seeking, gathering, analyzing, and interpreting competitor data, and for disseminating the resulting information to guide decisions. An outstanding framework for accomplishing these tasks is the Fuld Intelligence Pyramid™ constructed by Fuld & Company, a leading firm in competitive intelligence consulting. We reproduce this framework in Figure 2.3. Let's consider how businesses would use this framework to strengthen their competitive intelligence.[38]

As preparation prior to working through the Intelligence Pyramid, businesses must decide which competitive issues are critical to address and frame them in a set of questions whose answers are sought. In a business culture where time is increasingly a scarce resource, focus is essential to motivate and direct the assistance of those working throughout the business. The competitive questions for which

Figure 2.3 The Intelligence Pyramid

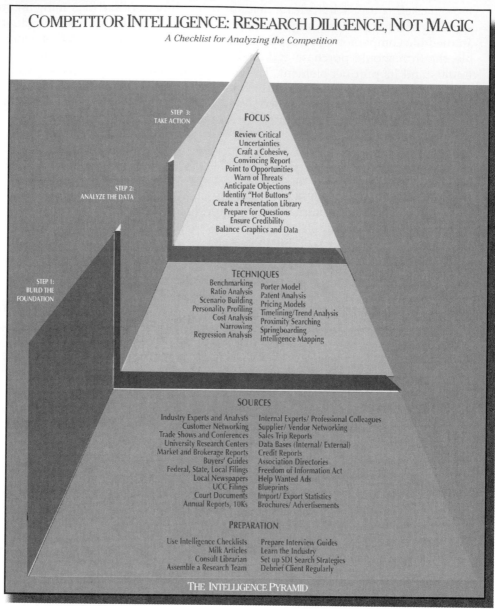

COMPETITOR INTELLIGENCE: RESEARCH DILIGENCE, NOT MAGIC

A Checklist for Analyzing the Competition

STEP 3:
TAKE ACTION

FOCUS

Review Critical
Uncertainties
Craft a Cohesive,
Convincing Report
Point to Opportunities
Warn of Threats
Anticipate Objections
Identify "Hot Buttons"
Create a Presentation Library
Prepare for Questions
Ensure Credibility
Balance Graphics and Data

STEP 2:
ANALYZE THE DATA

TECHNIQUES

Benchmarking   Porter Model
Ratio Analysis   Patent Analysis
Scenario Building   Pricing Models
Personality Profiling   Timelining/Trend Analysis
Cost Analysis   Proximity Searching
Narrowing   Springboarding
Regression Analysis   Intelligence Mapping

STEP 1:
BUILD THE
FOUNDATION

SOURCES

Industry Experts and Analysts   Internal Experts/ Professional Colleagues
Customer Networking   Supplier/ Vendor Networking
Trade Shows and Conferences   Sales Trip Reports
University Research Centers   Data Bases (Internal/ External)
Market and Brokerage Reports   Credit Reports
Buyers' Guides   Association Directories
Federal, State, Local Filings   Freedom of Information Act
Local Newspapers   Help Wanted Ads
UCC Filings   Blueprints
Court Documents   Import/ Export Statistics
Annual Reports, 10Ks   Brochures/ Advertisements

PREPARATION

Use Intelligence Checklists   Prepare Interview Guides
Milk Articles   Learn the Industry
Consult Librarian   Set up SDI Search Strategies
Assemble a Research Team   Debrief Client Regularly

THE INTELLIGENCE PYRAMID

answers are sought should be accompanied by compelling rationales for what is needed and why, to gain the needed support. The business also should provide social recognition, which may be preferable to monetary rewards, to individuals providing critical competitor information. As an example, the general manager of a bearings distributor gave up his parking spot, which was right next to the building entrance, and awarded it each month to the salesperson who contributed the most valuable piece of competitive information.

The managers with primary responsibility for competitive intelligence function as catalysts for the whole process. To use a circus metaphor, they act as "ringmasters," directing and sequencing the activities going on around them. For example, they should contact others in the business who will be attending a trade show to alert them to seek out critical competitor information. After (or even during) the show, the manager contacts the attendees again to debrief them on what has been learned.

Progressive businesses also use group productivity software in conjunction with internal computer networks (intranets) to create competitor intelligence systems that are readily accessible and useful. Ceregen, the biotechnology unit of Monsanto Company, uses Lotus Notes on its intranet to continuously update competitor (and customer) profiles from public news sources, field sales reports, attendees' notes from industry conferences and conventions, and so forth. This database is accessible online to all its employees, wherever they are in the world, at any time of the day. [39]

As Figure 2.3 depicts, *building the foundation* is the first step. To find the answers to the critical competitive questions, the business often will form a competitive intelligence research team, whose members may be competitive analysts, market analysts, business development managers, or sales representatives. The team begins with background research culled from a variety of traditional and untraditional sources. Searching the Internet and traditional databases is just the beginning. Help wanted advertising, court documents, and the underside of corrugated boxes are the less traditional—but potentially revealing—documents in the universe of potential secondary sources. The information gained from these secondary sources guides the team's research to primary sources—who to contact and what to ask them. The team seeks to independently corroborate what it learns from one source with another.

Analyze the data is the second step, and probably the most critical. Rarely can the team expect to find all the data it might want. What's more, even if team could collect it all, it would take so much time to collect that the business would miss the competitive opportunity it was seeking in the first place. Astute and clever use of analysis techniques allows the team to make more out of less. It gives the team a perspective on a situation where it has less than perfect data. The team uses competitive intelligence analytical tools, such as benchmarking, timelining, and scenario analysis, to extrapolate or predict a rival's moves or a market's shift.

Benchmarking "is the art of finding out, in a perfectly legal and aboveboard way, how others do something better than you do so you can imitate—and perhaps improve upon—their techniques." Progressive firms engage in benchmarking their competitors (as well as noncompetitors that represent best practice). To satisfy confidentiality concerns among competitors, a number of consulting firms, such as A. T. Kearney and Towers Perrin, facilitate benchmarking efforts among the firms. The consulting firms first assist in setting up groups of companies that will benchmark one another. They then act as intermediaries, collecting the individual company benchmarking information and reporting the best practices to member companies without revealing the sources.[40]

Timelining is a technique to predict how the very near future will unfold, by drawing on knowledge of the steps inherent in some process and how long it typically takes to perform each one. Experts within a business, supplemented perhaps by outside consultants, can lay out the milestones to track the progress of a competitor in activities such as opening a new plant or introducing a new product to the market.

Timelining enables a business to make the most of incomplete data to generate a fairly accurate understanding of its competitors' moves.

Take action is the third step, corresponding to the highest level, and pinnacle of the pyramid, which is *focus*. Here, the team pulls together all it has learned from the analysis, reducing all the charts and interview transcriptions, all the observations to a few pithy conclusions that create opportunities through decision. Businesses at this level benefit from these early warnings to give their managements opportunities to stay ahead of the market and the competition. An essential characteristic of the focus level is acting on these generated insights expediently, while few other businesses know about them.

Seek Disconfirming as Well as Confirming Evidence

Individuals who have primary responsibility for monitoring competitors have dual tasks to perform in generating accurate knowledge about competitors. They seek *convergence* of data from more than one source to increase their confidence in its meaning about a competitor. For example, they might confirm a salesperson's report of competitor price cutting of a market offering by seeking other instances where this has happened. Market research from an outside firm might be used to further improve confidence in an inference made about a competitor's price cutting.

At the same time, though, the monitor has the task of seeking out *disconfirming* evidence. Continuing with the example, how many instances can be cited where the competitor did *not* cut the price of the market offering? A common bias in managerial decision making is seeking out confirming evidence to support an inference, while not seeking out disconfirming evidence that would invalidate the inference.[41] Individuals who have primary responsibility for monitoring competitors need to be mindful of this potential bias and must pursue both kinds of information to provide the most accurate knowledge about competitors.

ASSESSING CUSTOMER VALUE

"Everything is worth what its purchaser will pay for it."
—Publilius Syrus, first century, B.C.

Although this maxim is old, actually assessing what some present or potential market offering is worth to present or prospective customers remains a challenging task for business market managers. Because assessing value in monetary terms initially appears to be such a daunting task, most firms in business markets do not even try to do it. Yet, the few but growing number of progressive firms that excel at customer value assessment find that the more value assessments they do, the easier they become. That is, through experience and learning, they develop this business marketing capability. They also uniformly find that value assessment provides them with superior knowledge about the marketplace that they are able to convert to superior market performance.

As stated in Chapter 1, customer firms often do not have an accurate understanding of what suppliers' market offerings actually are worth to them. Even some government customers are realizing this inadequacy and are looking to potential suppliers to show them how they can add value or reduce the total cost of government.[42] As part of their proposals, though, governments increasingly want suppliers to guarantee results, something that suppliers cannot do knowledgeably without value assessment. Moreover, irrespective of whether the customer is in the public or private sector, value assessment provides better understanding of the customer's business to both the customer and the supplier. Without value assessment, business market managers make decisions based on a sketchy and often inaccurate understanding of not only how alternative suppliers' differing ways of meeting the customer's requirements affect its costs but also what changes in the customer's requirements would be worth.

We first discuss a number of methods that firms in business markets have used to assess value. We then present customer value management, which is a comprehensive, practical approach for demonstrating and documenting the value of present and prospective market offerings in business markets.

Value Assessment Methods[43]

Value assessment is the work process of obtaining an estimate of the worth in monetary terms of some present or proposed market offering or elements of it. Business market managers have employed a number of methods to provide estimates of value. These methods vary significantly in the extent to which they rely upon customer perceptions of worth versus supplier assessment of the functionality or performance of an offering and its worth (i.e., gathering empirical data).

Internal Engineering Assessment

With this method, scientists or engineers within the supplier's own firm conduct laboratory tests on a product to provide an estimate of its value. Application of this method depends on detailed knowledge of the customer's usage system. As an example, if the supplier's product is a component part of the customer's product, the supplier needs to have a detailed understanding of the customer's production process and how the supplier's market offering affects all other costs incurred in making that product. To provide a value estimate, the supplier typically makes some assumptions about the way in which results from lab tests will generalize to the customer's actual use of the product.

Field Value-in-Use Assessment

With this method, supplier personnel (or their consultants) conduct interviews and often gather data at customer firm(s) to provide a comprehensive listing of benefit and cost elements associated with usage of the supplier's market offering compared with the incumbent or next-best-alternative offering. Making explicit assumptions, they assign monetary amounts to these elements to provide an overall value estimate of its market offering in that application. In contrast with internal engineering assessment, field value-in-use assessment requires considerable customer firm cooperation and active participation to arrive at an estimate of customer value.

Supplier firms sometimes do process mapping in field value-in-use assessment to be certain that they have captured all of an offering's benefit and cost elements. Grainger Consulting Services (GCS), a unit of the industrial supply distributor W. W. Grainger, uses process mapping to study the total costs a client incurs in acquiring maintenance, repair, and operating (MRO) items. In numerous engagements, GCS mapped out processes such as inventory replenishment and unplanned purchases, as well as subprocesses, such as issuing a purchase order and MRO credit card payment. GCS charts the activity flows in a process using Post-it® notes on a large sheet of paper, where the functional areas are the rows and the detailed steps in the process are the columns. GCS also gains estimates of the time it takes to perform each step and the total compensation costs of individuals performing the step. After the process has been delineated adequately, GCS transfers the data to spreadsheet software to portray the process in a compact way and to calculate its costs. Armed with this knowledge, W. W. Grainger can show the customer how its distribution system can lower the customer's total acquisition costs by greatly reducing the number of emergency purchases and lowering the cost per purchase order for the remaining ones.

Indirect Survey Questions

Participants in a field research study act as informants for their firms and answer questions on what the effects of one or more changes in a presently used market offering would be on certain aspects of their firm's operations. From these answers, typically combined in some way with other known information, supplier analysts can derive estimates of the worth in monetary terms of each change in the market offering. This method enables a supplier firm to fill critical gaps in its knowledge of the customer firm's usage system as it relates to the supplier's market offering. Note that a critical assumption of this method is that the customer has an accurate perception of the effects of the studied changes upon its usage system.

Focus Group Value Assessment

Within a focus group setting, participants are shown potential product offerings or product concepts and then asked what the value of these offerings or concepts would be to their firms. This method is a qualitative approach to gaining a better understanding of the perceptions and reactions of participants. In doing so, the research analyst also generates estimates of value. The participants typically are knowledgeable individuals within customer firms that are targets for the studied market offering, although a supplier firm also may be interested in the reactions of industry consultants or pundits.

A telecommunications firm employed focus group value assessment to understand the worth of a number of advanced intelligent network (AI-Net) services, such as single-number reach. Single-number reach is provided from a central office switch and seeks out an individual a caller is trying to reach at a sequence of different telephone numbers the individual has previously programmed. Single-number reach also provides the option of voice mail. (The recipient of the call has the option of putting the caller into voice mail without the caller ever knowing the recipient was reached.) As an initial target market segment, the firm conducted focus groups with itinerant, Generation-X professionals, some of whom had six telephone numbers on their business cards!

At the beginning of each focus group, the moderator demonstrated the single-number reach service, using a specially arranged prototype. The moderator then asked focus group participants to write down their first impressions of the service and how much they would be willing to pay per month for the service. The participants then engaged in a discussion of the service, how they would most likely use it, and so on. At the conclusion of the approximately hour-long discussion, the moderator asked the participants to write down their interest in the service, using a 10-point scale, and again, how much they would be willing to pay per month for the service.

Although the firm was interested in the actual monetary amounts given at the beginning and at the end, it was more interested in any pattern of differences between the specified amounts. An ominous pattern would be significant declines from the initial amounts to the ending amounts, indicating that the participants were initially intrigued with the service, but upon further consideration, concluded that the service would actually provide them little value. No significant change between the initial amounts and ending amounts would be a preferable pattern, provided the specified amounts were sufficiently large for the service to be profitable. The final pattern, significant increases from the initial amounts to the ending amounts, would indicate that when the participants thought about the service, they came to recognize its greater value to them. This pattern would suggest the crucial role of business marketing communications in conveying the value of using the service to prospective customers.

Direct Survey Questions

In a field research survey, participants are given a description of a potential market offering or product concept, and then are asked what its value would be to their firms. Participants might be asked, "What would your firm be willing to pay for this offering?" Participants may be unwilling to answer candidly, or they may lack adequate knowledge of their own usage systems and the offering's effect on it to answer accurately. The extent to which either of these occurs will affect the validity of the value estimate. A series of follow-up questions would be asked to gain an understanding of how parts of an offering contribute to its overall perceived value.

Conjoint Analysis

Conjoint analysis is a family of methods for statistically transforming a research participant's judgments about potential market offerings into estimates of the value the participant places on those offerings' constituent attributes and the alternative levels of those attributes.[44] We limit our consideration to the most commonly used conjoint analysis method: the full-profile approach employing ordinary least squares (OLS) estimation. In a field personal interview or a combination telephone-mail-telephone research methodology, research participants are asked to evaluate a set of potential market offerings. Each offering typically appears on a separate card, which lists the set of attributes the supplier is studying, along with the specific level of each attribute that the offering possesses. For example, in a conjoint study of titanium dioxide, a white pigment used as a primary component in coatings, the supplier studied four attributes: dispersability, gloss, hiding power/tinting strength, and price. The attribute of dispersability, for example, had two levels: 10 minutes and 30 minutes time required to attain 7 Hegman fineness units in a Cowles high-speed disperser.[45] The levels of the attributes the supplier is studying are systematically varied within the set of offerings.

Participants provide a purchase preference rating for each offering. The research analyst then uses OLS regression analysis to decompose the ratings into estimated **part-worths** or values for each level of each attribute. The range of these part-worths for each attribute provides an estimate of the relative value of the attributes themselves. Price should be included as an attribute in the design so that the part-worths can be scaled in monetary terms.

Benchmarks

In a field research survey, participants are given a description of a market offering, typically the present industry standard, that serves as a **benchmark offering**. They then are asked how much more their firm would be willing to pay for selected additions (or increases) in attributes or features to this benchmark offering. Likewise, they might be asked how much less their firm would expect to pay for selected reductions in attributes or features from the benchmark offering. The benchmark method trades off some of the methodological rigor and breadth of value estimates that conjoint analysis provides in favor of lower cost and ease of use.

Compositional Approach

The compositional approach is also sometimes called the **self-explicated approach** because research participants are asked to directly express the value they place on each of a number of attributes and their selected levels. As an example, participants might be asked to provide the value in Norwegian kronor per unit for each of three alternative levels of a particular attribute, where all other attributes of the market offering were the same (held constant). When this assessment is done for each attribute, the values given for the attribute levels then can be added to provide estimates of the value of various market offerings to the participant's firm. Although the composition approach has the strength of being relatively easy to use, it does have some potential shortcomings, such as finding that the sum of the values for the component attribute levels is greater than the value the participant actually places on the offering as a whole.

Some research in marketing, though, has found that a self-explicated approach that places some constraints on how research participants generate their estimates provides a surprisingly good prediction of actual choice.[46] This approach has three steps in gathering participant perceptions. First, the research participants indicate any attribute levels that are totally unacceptable; that is, they would reject any potential offering containing that attribute level, no matter how attractive the other attribute levels of the offering might be. Second, for the remaining levels, the participants designate the most-preferred and least-preferred levels of each attribute as 10 and 0, respectively, and then indicate a value within this range for any other levels on each attribute. Finally, the participants designate the attribute where the change from the least-preferred to the most-preferred level is most valuable as 10, and then rates the other attributes relative to it from 0 to 10.

Practitioners have also made advances in the use of constrained, self-explicated approaches. Business & Market Research Ltd., an English market research firm specializing in business market research, developed an approach that is relatively easy for research participants to complete, yet also provides estimates of value in monetary terms. Business & Market Research's approach appears in Box 2.4.

Importance Ratings

In a field research survey, participants are given a set of attributes of a market offering and then are asked to rate them on importance to their firm. The participants also are asked to rate each of a number of supplier firms with respect to their performance on each of the attributes. Multiplying each supplier's performance rating on each attribute by that attribute's importance rating and summing them across attributes produces a competitor analysis of the relative value each supplier's market offering provides. A significant shortcoming of importance ratings as a method of customer value assessment is that they do not provide an estimate of the worth in monetary terms of the market offering or its elements. Importance ratings also do not provide an estimate of a customer firm's relative value for a change in the level of performance on one attribute versus another.[47]

BOX 2.4
Measuring Customer Value at Business & Market Research Ltd.

Business & Market Research Ltd. (B&MR) has conducted many studies to understand what end-users perceive as the total market offering and how they value the different components. This is a particularly important exercise in undifferentiated markets, such as electricity, where customers perceive the core products of alternative suppliers to be almost identical. The winners in these markets are those who augment their core products with the right combination of added-value components, such as special tariffs, superior service back-up, and easily understood billing.

To optimize the bundle of attributes that is added to the core product, B&MR must isolate the value that customers attach to each attribute. Having established the relative worth of an attribute, B&MR must then determine at what level it should be delivered. B&MR's constrained, self-explicated approach uses initial exploratory research to develop a *Customer Service Grid*. This grid lists all the attributes that augment the generic core product. For each attribute, a scale from poor to good is defined using the customers' own language. A limited example is shown here, although in reality B&MR typically might have 20 to 30 different attributes, with up to eight levels for each.

The numeric points in the grid correspond to the approximate relative costs of providing the service levels, thereby conveying to the research participant that the costs for providing the different levels of the different services can vary greatly. B&MR determines these relative costs of provision in consultation with senior management at the client firm. Thus, in the example, to always have a named contact available is five times

CUSTOMER SERVICE GRID					
Attributes	Level of Delivery				
Speed of answering the phone	Is often not answered and I call back	Is answered in at least 10 rings	Is answered in 7–10 rings	Is answered in 4 rings	Is answered in 3 rings
	0	3	6	8	12
Availability of contact person	Never anyone available and I leave messages	Somebody available, though not a named contact	Named contact usually available and if not, calls back same day	Named contact always available	
	0	5	15	25	
Knowledge of contact person	Person I contact can only answer a few questions and I have to recontact someone else for the rest	Person I contact can answer most questions and I have to recontact someone else for the rest	Person I contact can answer most questions, and if necessary, will contact someone else to get me the answer	Person I contact can answer all questions	
	0	10	15	25	

(continued)

BOX 2.4
Continued

more expensive than simply having somebody available. Note that each basic level of service delivery starts at zero, because the client is concerned about the additional costs of adding to its basic product.

Once B&MR has developed the customer service grid, it can use it in a number of ways to understand value. Participants might be asked to indicate where a current provider was across all attributes, and then be given a certain number of points to spend (typically 30 to 50 across 20 or more attributes) and asked how they would spend them to improve the offering. B&MR calculates for each project the specific number of points that participants are given to spend, based on the total points on the grid and the client's inclination to make changes (i.e., do they want to make wholesale changes or small-scale improvements). Essentially, the number must be high enough so that participants can afford the most expensive improvement if they want it, yet it must be low enough so that they cannot afford to improve the offering to the best possible level on each line. Thus, the

participants have to make choices, revealing the levels of service for each attribute that they value most, given those levels' costs. Once all data are gathered, B&MR can model them to identify the optimum service offering (i.e., which would appeal to the most respondents) and examine the impact of not meeting certain criteria (i.e., underspecifying the offer). Finally, with a sufficiently large sample, B&MR's approach will normally identify segments that value different overall products, with an indication of the relative price differential between them.

B&MR has used this approach in many different markets. In both financial services and public utilities, it has helped clients define meaningful customer service standards that give customers what they value. In mature industrial markets, it has identified the optimum market offering. Getting the add-ons right in these markets is particularly important because core products can be identical (e.g., chemicals) and service enhancements (e.g., on-site technical backup) very expensive.

Customer Value Management[48]

Customer value management is a progressive, practical approach that, in its essence, has two basic goals:

- Deliver superior value to targeted market segments and customer firms.
- Get an equitable return on the value delivered.

Customer value management relies upon *customer value assessment* to gain an understanding of customer requirements and preferences, and what it is worth in monetary terms to fulfill them. Although firms may be able to accomplish the first goal without any formal assessment of customer value, it is unlikely that they will be able to accomplish the second goal—getting an equitable return on the value delivered—without it. Simply put, to gain an equitable or fair return on the value their offerings deliver, suppliers must be able to persuasively demonstrate and document the value they provide customers relative to the next-best alternative for those customers. As we recount in Box 2.5, when suppliers do not spend the time and money on customer value management, they are unaware of how much *not* doing it is costing them.

An essential undertaking in customer value management is building **customer value models**, which are data-driven estimates of what a present or prospective market offering is worth in monetary terms to targeted customers relative to the

BOX 2.5
Can Suppliers Afford *Not* to Build Customer Value Models?

An electronics engineer was leading his firm's development effort for a next-generation, electronic control device, which was projected to have a total cost of about $7. An important component of this device was a power factor correction (PFC) integrated circuit (IC). This engineer had narrowed down the potential suppliers for these PFC ICs to two: Supplier A, which was quoting a price of 45 cents per IC, and Supplier B, which was quoting a price of 35 cents per IC. The firm anticipated purchasing 5 million of these PFC ICs for the new control devices.

This electronics engineer happened to be enrolled in a part-time, evening MBA program where he was taking a graduate course in business marketing. Having learned in this course that customer firms should focus on total value of ownership rather than simply purchase price, he decided to build a customer value model, to fulfill part of his course requirements and to determine which of the two suppliers would provide the greater value to his firm.

Pulling together the data and building the customer value model, the engineer estimated that Supplier A's offering was worth 15.9 cents more per PFC IC than Supplier B's. Two value elements emerged as the most critical points of difference between the two suppliers. Supplier A provided *earlier access to product samples*, which significantly shortened the time to market for the new devices. Because of the competitive nature of the customer firm's own market, getting to market earlier with new devices affected both the revenue and profit it earned. Supplier A also provided superior *technical engineering support*, which provided design expertise and was a supplementary engineering resource that the customer firm would otherwise have to supply itself. There also were several other points of difference that were of lesser monetary value.

Drawing on the customer value model results, the engineer's recommendation to purchasing was that, even though Supplier A's price was 10 cents more expensive than Supplier B's, the firm should purchase the PCF ICs from Supplier A because of the superior value that its offering provided. In delivering this report to the purchasing manager who was supporting his development project, the engineer related the outcome of his research to the purchasing manager. "That's interesting to learn," replied the purchasing manager with a smile, "But I think that you will be interested to learn that in the meantime, I have negotiated a price reduction with Supplier A from 45 cents to 35 cents per IC!"

Think for a moment about what occurred. By not standing firm on its price in the negotiation, how much incremental profit had Supplier A just given away? $500,000—on one transaction with one customer. Yet Supplier A's salesperson is not the culprit here. His firm is. Supplier A had done no customer value research, built no customer value models, and constructed no value-based sales tools to enable the salesperson to persuasively demonstrate and document the superior value of his offering relative to Supplier B's.

Interestingly, as part of his research, the engineer interviewed the salespersons from Supplier A and Supplier B, and asked each of them what they thought was the source of their offering's superior value was relative to the other. The salesperson from Supplier A did not name either of the two value elements that provided the greatest differential value. Apparently, he was unaware of the extent of the differences between his offering and Supplier B's on these elements. Instead, he stated that he believed that his offering was worth more, attributing it to his dedicated and superior servicing of the account. His superior service was worth something: .2 cents per IC in the engineer's customer value model!

Perhaps sensing that this superior service was not worth the 10-cent price difference between quotes, when push came to shove,

(continued)

BOX 2.5
Continued

Supplier A's salesperson reduced the price to match Supplier B's lower price. Now, even with a value-based sales tool that enabled him to persuasively demonstrate his offering's superior value, as part of the give-and-take of negotiation, he might have reduced the price somewhat and perhaps even split the price difference with the purchasing manager. Even in this latter scenario, though, Supplier A still would have retained $250,000 in incremental profit.

This case study brings to life a choice that most often remains implicit for suppliers and, as such, one that they cannot fully know the consequences of implicitly making. They can spend the time and money upfront to persuasively demonstrate and document the superior value that their offerings deliver and capture a more equitable portion of this delivered value. Or, they can choose not to, and give value away unknowingly as price reductions, just as Supplier A did in this case study. Either way, suppliers are going to pay. As this case study amply reveals, can suppliers afford *not* to build customer value models?

next-best-alternative offering for those customers. Some suppliers have built what they regard as customer value models, but which have the character of being "data light" and "assumption heavy." Quite naturally, customers are skeptical of such models, claiming that they do not accurately reflect their businesses. In contrast, customer value management stresses building customer value models that are "data heavy" and "assumption light." Wherever possible, suppliers gather data to minimize the number of assumptions made and to ensure that the assumptions that are made are reasonable.

Drawing on experience in working with firms over the past several years, we briefly discuss the process of customer value management. This process can be viewed as five phases: (1) translating business issues into projects, (2) customer value workshop, (3) customer value research, (4) constructing a business case for change, and (5) value realization.

Translating Business Issues into Projects

In the initial phase, senior managers think through significant issues that the business is facing, where greater knowledge of customer value would enable them to make more profitable decisions. Customer value management has been used to inform and guide a variety of management decisions, such as which potential product developments and modifications to make; which augmenting services, programs, and systems to offer as standard or for-fee options; setting pricing strategy and tactics; and which market segment(s) to target. Because customer value management costs both time and money, with time becoming a scarcer resource, it should be applied to business issues that are significant for the business unit.

To give a broader experience and understanding of customer value management and what its potential is, we counsel firms to engage in a pilot program where they tackle three to five business issues. A project is defined for each issue, where decisions are made about the scope of the project, the definition of success, and the composition of the team that will carry out the customer value research to address the issue.

The scope of each project needs to be sufficiently defined so that the customer value research can be conducted over a three- or four-month period. When the business issue is complex, aspects or facets of it can be addressed with successive projects over time. It is unwise to overwhelm teams with projects that demand more time than is reasonably available, or to have projects last more than four months. When the nature of the business issue is sufficiently broad or complicated, it is better to conceptualize it as a series of phases, each of which will take three or four months to complete.

Senior management must define at the outset what its expectations of success are for each project. A business case for change that results in $1 million of incremental profitability within 12 months has been most often defined as the principal goal of each project undertaken. This result represents a relatively quick and attractive financial return on the resources that a business commits to each pilot project, while also gaining the knowledge and skills to practice customer value management. It also ensures that the projects are addressing business issues of sufficient magnitude, yet can be accomplished within the established timeframe.

The composition of each customer value research team will vary, depending on the nature of the project, but often includes someone who most often spends time at the customers solving problems (e.g., field technical rep, field applications engineer), someone from the product marketing or development functional area, and two or three progressive salespersons. Having salespersons involved at the start is crucial. They provide needed expertise on the customer and its use of the offering, and they have knowledge of and relationships with customers that would be willing to cooperate in customer value research. Being part of a customer value management initiative from the outset also builds support for the approach with those salespeople, who then can persuasively relate their experiences to others in the sales force.

Each team should have a leader selected by senior management prior to the start of the project. The team leader should be someone with superior project management and interpersonal skills. We recommend that the manager with primary responsibility for implementing the business case for change *not* be the team leader. For example, although the product manager for a new offering who has to decide which market segment to enter initially will be a significant contributor to the team, it is preferable to have another more "objective" manager assume primary responsibility for the project management and process aspects of teamwork. Customer value assessments are an intensive analytical effort, which may require up to a half-time commitment by the project leader. Other team members will spend varying amounts of time on the project, with a quarter-time commitment being typical.

For customer value research projects to succeed, the active support of senior management is crucial. Most often, a senior manager serves as the sponsor or champion of each team, which should be decided before the start of the projects. Even though senior managers should communicate to the teams the importance of the pilot program to the business, they make a more visible statement through how they spend their own time. Making the commitment to attend at least the opening morning of the customer value workshop, monitor the progress of their team, and attend the presentation day for the business cases sends a strong signal to the teams.

Customer Value Workshop

The teams come together for a Customer Value Workshop, which is a two- or three-day session where they gain the requisite knowledge and skills to build customer value models, and plan and launch their projects. During this workshop, they practice building customer value models using one or more case studies written for that purpose. In breakout sessions, each team begins to define the value elements for their project, determine the next-best alternative to their market offering, decide which customers to invite to participate in the customer value research, and create their work plans for accomplishing the project. Coaching support is provided throughout each breakout session to reinforce the concepts that the participants have learned and to work through the unforeseen issues that the teams inevitably encounter.

Each team begins by listing all the value elements for the market offering under consideration. Value elements define in a comprehensive and elemental way how the offering reduces customer costs or adds value to what the customer is trying to accomplish, and capture the technical, economic, service, and social benefits that customers receive from the offering. Teams generally find it easier to consider the value elements for the core product or service, and then the value elements for the supplementary services, programs, and systems that augment the core offering. A fundamental consideration here is to be *comprehensive* and *elemental*.

Leaving out elements—particularly if they are unfavorable for the supplier's market offering relative to the next-best-alternative offering—compromises the effort and undermines its credibility with customers that detect the missing elements. By being as elemental as possible, the supplier firm is able to more accurately gauge the differences in functionality and performance its offering provides relative to the next-best alternative. Customer managers may find it easier to answer broadly stated questions, such as the cost of an hour of downtime in the customer's plant. However, their answers often will leave out effects on the customer's usage system, producing less valid estimates of worth.

Teams are advised to write out this list of the value elements, which can be lengthy, in relatively quick fashion, drawing on their collective experience. Each team next hypothesizes what kinds of customers would receive the greatest value from the offering and what kinds of customers would receive the least value. Team members determine what customer characteristics, such as application or customer capabilities, best capture these hypothesized differences in value received and could be used to segment (or further segment) the market. The team uses these customer descriptors to define two market (sub)segments that would be of most interest to study in the customer value research.

Each team next considers what would be the next-best-alternative offering in the minds of customers in each segment. The team selects the next-best-alternative offering and the firm providing it for each segment (the next-best-alternative offering may vary between selected segments, and on rare occasions, teams may choose to study two next-best-alternative offerings within a segment). The team then revisits its list of value elements, with this next-best alternative in mind.

While firms are doing many wonderful things for their customers, the reality in most business markets is that so, too, are the competitors supplying the next-best-alternative offering doing many wonderful things. So, to focus the customer value research and make it more manageable, we take advantage of a rearrangement of the fundamental value equation from Chapter 1:

$$(\text{Value}_f - \text{Price}_f) > (\text{Value}_a - \text{Price}_a) \qquad \textbf{(2.1)}$$
$$(\text{Value}_f - \text{Value}_a) > (\text{Price}_f - \text{Price}_a) \qquad \textbf{(2.2)}$$
$$\Delta\,\text{Value}_{f,\,a} > (\text{Price}_f - \text{Price}_a) \qquad \textbf{(2.3)}$$

where Value$_f$ and Price$_f$ are the value and price of the focal firm's market offering (Offering$_f$), Value$_a$ and Price$_a$ are the value and price of the next-best-alternative market offering (Offering$_a$), and Δ denotes the difference in value between Offering$_f$ and Offering$_a$. Thus, what really matters is not the value of each offering but the *difference* in value between the two offerings relative to the difference in their prices.

For each value element on its list, the team decides whether there is a difference on its offering's functionality or performance on that element relative to the next-best alternative. Teams are encouraged to be candid in their appraisals. If the team is honest with itself, out of a lengthy list, the team typically will decide only a handful of value elements are differences between offerings. Most of these differences will be in favor of the team's offering, yet some will be differences favoring the next-best-alternative offering. Value elements on which the team believes that there are no differences between the two offerings are termed **points of parity**. Value elements on which the team believes that there are differences are termed **points of difference**. The team constructs an initial **word equation** for each point of difference, which expresses in words how to assess the differences in functionality and performance on the element and what those differences are worth in monetary terms. Accompanying each word equation are the assumptions that the team makes about the value element and how its monetary value can be assessed. It is crucial to be *explicit* in all assumptions made.

The teams focus their customer value research on the points of difference, setting the points of parity aside.[49] In initial meetings to invite customers to participate in the customer value research, team members relate the list of value elements and which elements they regard as points of parity and points of difference. Team members then share the initial word equations for the hypothesized points of difference. If the team has been honest with itself, the customers will largely agree with them. Inevitably, though, on some value elements they will disagree with the team's assessment. For example, the customer might regard a point of parity as a point of difference favoring the next-best alternative. Value elements on which disagreements occur are termed **points of contention**. Such disagreements should not be regarded as bad because they provide further motivation to the customers to participate in research and gather data to resolve the point of contention. We elaborate on points of difference, points of contention, and word equations in Box 2.6.

Customer Value Research

The customer value research that each team conducts proceeds in three steps: (1) gaining initial customer cooperation, (2) gathering the data, and (3) analyzing the data. These steps are considered next.

Prior to contacting any present or prospective customers to participate in the research, the team has some tasks to perform. First, it must decide on present or prospective customers that are of most interest to have as research participants in each subsegment. Although the number of research participants sought will depend on the market, typically the team seeks the participation of six to eight customers from each subsegment. The team next thinks through why the customers should cooperate in the research. In our experience, customers cooperate in customer value research for one or more of four basic kinds of reasons: a low-cost resource to better understand their business, an opportunity to benchmark, earlier access to some new product or service, or the desire for a meaningfully lower price.

Customer value research focuses on the points of difference and points of contention between the studied market offering and the next-best-alternative offering. Together, these capture the prospective differences in value between offerings and what they are worth in monetary terms. The intent of the supplier is to demonstrate and document these differences so that customer managers can easily grasp them, understand precisely how the supplier has assessed them, and find the results persuasive. To assist in accomplishing this task, we have created the concept of word equations.

A word equation expresses in words precisely how to assess the differences in functionality and performance between the studied offerings for a value element and how those differences are converted into worth in monetary terms. One is constructed for each point of difference and point of contention, where the value element, expressed as either cost savings or incremental profit, is on the left side of the equal sign and the components defining the differences in functionality or performance and what these are worth are on the right side. Word equations were invented to counter a rampant problem in business markets: "spreadsheet mania." By spreadsheet mania, we mean the construction of overly complicated, difficult-to-understand spreadsheets. In many businesses, technically minded individuals take pride in their capabilities with spreadsheet software, such as Microsoft Excel®. This skill unfortunately often manifests itself as densely packed, number-laden spreadsheets with minimal-to-nonexistent explanations of what the numbers mean. When questioned about their contents, even their creators sometimes have difficulty reconstructing what is meant.

In contrast, customer value research teams first construct a word equation for each point of difference and point of contention. These word equations make clear to the teams and the customers participating in the research what data need to be gathered and how those data will be combined to provide value estimates. After the data have been gathered, in presentations of the results, each word equation first is presented. Then, the data are substituted in each equation to calculate the estimate in monetary terms for each value element. These results are then collected in a value summary, which we refer to as the customer value model. As an example, a point of difference between two large-format document reproduction systems (denoted as B and next-best-alternative A) was the number of paper jams a customer would experience each day. The word equation for this point of difference was expressed as:

$$\text{Paper Jam Cost Savings}_{B,A} =$$
$$[(\text{paper jams per day} \times$$
$$\text{minutes to fix jam})_A - (\text{paper jams}$$
$$\text{per day} \times \text{minutes to fix jam})_B] /$$
$$60 \text{ minutes per hour} \times \text{operator}$$
$$\text{wages per hour} \times \text{annual work}$$
$$\text{days}$$

Substituting in the gathered data, an estimate for this value element then was calculated as:

$$\text{Paper Jam Cost Savings}_{B,A} =$$
$$[(3 \times 10)_A - (1 \times 10)_B] / 60 \times \text{€}31.82$$
$$\times 240 = \text{€}2,545.60$$

Thus, the estimate for this value element was €2,545.60 annually for system B relative to system A.

Accompanying each word equation are the assumptions that the team is making about the value element and how its monetary value is assessed. In all customer value research, some assumptions will be needed to complete the analysis. The assumptions might be about the functionality or performance the market offering actually provides in the customer's specific setting, particularly for aspects that are extraordinarily difficult or costly to measure. Alternatively, assumptions might be made in assigning worth in monetary

BOX 2.6
Continued

terms to measured differences in performance an offering provides in the customer's setting. Continuing with the example, an explicit assumption made was that if operator hours could be reduced, the Engineering Department would reassign him or her to other value-adding tasks.

It is crucial that the supplier be *explicit* in the assumptions it makes. When a customer firm catches the supplier in one or more implicit assumptions, particularly ones that are dubious, it has a devastating effect on the credibility of the whole analysis. In contrast, when all assumptions are made explicit, customer management simply can disagree with them. When disagreement happens, the astute supplier invites customer managers to share the rationales underlying their alternative assumptions. Depending on how plausible their rationales seem, the supplier can either adopt the alternative assumptions for the analysis or suggest that the supplier and customer engage in some joint research to mutually discover the most appropriate assumptions for the customer's specific setting.

The team next considers what managers at the customer firm the team would like to meet with. It contacts the salesperson responsible for each customer that the team wants to participate in the research, explains the purpose of research, and gains the salesperson's support. The salesperson provides names and contact information for managers to invite for the initial meeting.

Having completed these tasks, the team is now prepared to contact customer managers to arrange an initial meeting to explain the purpose of the research and gain their cooperation. Depending on company protocol, the salesperson responsible for each customer may accompany the team members to the initial meeting. It must be stressed, though, that this meeting is *not* a sales call. At least two team members should visit each customer.

In the initial meeting, the team members explain the purpose of the research and what the customer can expect to gain from participation. They discuss the hypothesized points of parity and points of difference, gain customer agreement, and discover any points of contention. They then reach agreement on word equations that capture each point of difference and point of contention. Revisiting the points of difference and points of contention, they discuss what sources of data that the customer presently generates or would be able to generate to provide an estimate of each point of difference and point of contention. They discuss timing and resource requirements for data collection. Finally, they discuss what sources of data outside the customer firm (e.g., industry association studies) might be worthwhile to pursue.

In doing the research, wherever possible, the team prefers to gather data rather than simply rely on customer perception. If the customer volunteers to generate or collect the data, the team should inquire into the method that will be used. Wherever possible, team members should offer to work with the customer to generate or gather these data.

The team needs to be creative, using other sources where desirable or necessary. Independent industry consultants or knowledgeable personnel within the supplier firm can be sources of initial estimates. In some instances, retired customer personnel may be a resource. Where the provision of a service element mitigates a risk the customer would otherwise have, supplier firms sometimes employ actuarial consultants to estimate what the cost of that risk would be. QUALCOMM drew upon American Trucking Association research studies to provide ranges for some of the elements in its value model for its OmniTRACS® mobile communication system.[50]

When the data have been gathered, the team analyzes them to estimate what each value element that is a point of difference or a point of contention is worth in monetary terms. It also calculates the mean and the variance (or standard deviation) for each. It then conducts comparisons between the two studied subsegments to understand how the estimate for each value element varies across the two. The team next collects these value element results in a value summary—the customer value model. The team should be certain to list any assumptions made in assigning monetary amounts to each element.

To gain a deeper understanding of the results, the team performs sensitivity analyses, using the information on the variances around each element. It considers what characteristics might drive the variation in value and whether that variation warrants a new segmentation approach. It identifies which customers are the most attractive prospects.

The team finally considers the **value placeholders**, which are value elements where measurement is either too difficult or too costly. Relying on customer perception, what is each qualitatively worth? How might proxy estimates be obtained? When no other source than customer perception is available, framing the worth of the element in the customer's mind is critical. What seems reasonable? Although QUALCOMM assigns no monetary amounts to some less tangible elements, it still includes them in its analysis as value placeholders. In this way, QUALCOMM conveys that it believes those elements are worth something to the customer, and leaves open the possibility that some specific amount might be ascertained in the future.

Constructing a Business Case for Change

Based on the knowledge of value that the team gains from its research, what does it recommend that the business do differently? The business case for change should address:

1. What specific actions does the team recommend based on its customer value research?
2. What resources would be needed to accomplish the recommended change in doing business?
3. What are the specific concerns in implementing the business case?
4. What milestones can be specified to chart the progress in accomplishing the change?
5. What would be the profitability impact if the business case for change were approved?

These business cases are presented to senior managers who have served as project sponsors and the top management of the business unit. The business case should be viewed as a prospective commitment: If senior management provides the requested resources, the business will deliver the specified results, especially the estimated incremental profitability.

Value Realization

The period following the presentations of business cases for change to senior management is a critical phase for realizing the value, and incremental profitability, identified in the business cases. The teams may need to gather additional data to refine or extend the customer value models presented to senior management. Further work likely will be needed on the action plans, particularly in addressing implementation issues. Value-based sales tools need to be created, and training devised to give the sales force practical experience using them. Supporting changes in performance review and compensation may be needed. A method of feedback should be put in place to document the value that customers actually experience relative to what was promised to them. Finally, a system for tracking the incremental profitability actually realized should be put in place.

After building the initial value model, the supplier needs to validate it by conducting additional assessments with other customers. Conducting multiple value assessments enables the supplier to refine its values estimates and to better understand how the value of its market offering varies across market segments defined by customer descriptors such as application, customer capabilities, and usage situation. In conducting the additional assessments, the supplier also records the customer's status on the descriptors that it hypothesized are related to differences in value. The supplier builds a database that contains the value estimates and the customer descriptors. After conducting a sufficient number of value assessments, the supplier uses regression analysis to determine which descriptors significantly predict differences in estimated value for the market offering. This evaluation enables the supplier to target market segments and customers where its offering provides superior value relative to competitors' offerings.

Suppliers not only use customer value models to inform and guide their own decision making, they also use them to create value-based sales tools that better enable their sales forces to persuasively convey the superior value their firms' offerings provide. These tools tend to take one of two forms: value case histories and value assessment as a value-adding, consultative selling tool. **Value case histories** are written accounts that document the cost savings or added value a customer firm actually received from its use of a supplier's market offering. Sonoco Product Company's Protective Packaging Division (SPPD), for example, audits actual cost savings that implementation of its total packaging solution proposals produce. At the end of the first year, SPPD constructs a cost-of-use case study and reports the findings to customer management. SPPD maintains a database of these cost-of-use case studies, which SPPD salespersons draw on when making proposals to other prospects. These case studies persuasively convey the cost savings that the prospects themselves would likely realize.

Value assessment itself can become a value-adding service that suppliers offer as part of a consultative selling approach. They develop customer value assessment tools, which we term **value calculators**, as spreadsheet software applications that salespeople or value specialists conduct on laptop computers to demonstrate the value that customers would receive from their offerings. Although these value calculators are typically quite user-friendly, they may require input data that the customer does not have readily available. To facilitate gathering the required input, the supplier may develop a worksheet that pulls together the necessary input data. The *BT Compass* Logistics Planning System developed by BT Products AB of Sweden (which is a member of Toyota Industries Corporation) serves as an outstanding example. We reproduce the *BT Compass* data collection worksheet in Box 2.7 and give a case example of how *BT Compass* is used as part of a value-adding, consultative approach to selling in Box 2.8.

BOX 2.7
BT Compass Value Assessment Worksheet

BT Compass data collection

Customer:	Date:
Comments:	

Machinery	Alternative 1	Alternative 2	Alternative 3
Type of truck/crane			

Wire guidance	Radio shuttle	Select conveyer

Load dimension

	Number of different unit widths				Number of different unit heights for selected unit width		
Unit no.	Width	Depth	No./bay	Height	No of units	Weight in kg	
1.							
2.							
3.							
4.							

Customize

Building height	Building length	Number of aisles	Sprinkler	Aisle width if not standard	Pallet per channel	Upright width	Vertical pitch

	Rear transfer aisle for order picking	Type of high-level picking truck
	Low order picking truck	Type of low-level picking truck

Capacity:

Pallet handling		Order picking	
Pallet movement/day		No. of orders/day	
Number of shifts/day		No. of orderlines/order	
Working time/shift		No. of items/orderline	
Double cycles in %		No. of orders/picking round	
Max. utilization in %		No. of shifts/day	
No. of cycles/transfer		Working time/shift in hours	
No. of cycles/channel change		Prep. time/pick. round in sec	
Admin. time/cycle in sec		Prep. time/orderline in sec.	
P and D located outside store, in %		Picking time/item in sec.	
Dist. in meters to that position		Replenishment	
No. of 90-degree curves		Pos. time/orderline 1st level	
Battery capacity in Ab		Pos. time/orderline 2nd level	
Relocations in % (cranes)		% of picking 2nd level	
No. of relocations/cycle (cranes)		Picking from 2nd level	
		Effective working time in %	

Commercial overview
Depreciation time in years

		Picking height in mm	
Building		No. of picking aisles	
Racking		Battery capacity in Ah	
Trucks			
Cranes		Operational cost	
Conveyors		Heating/m3 and year	
Others		Personnel incl. social/year	
Interest in %			

BOX 2.8
BT Compass *Logistics Planning System*

BT Lifters, a Division of BT Products AB (which is a member of Toyota Industries Corporation), based in Sweden, has created *BT Compass*, which is a logistics planning system, to help customers make a significant difference in the profitability of their businesses through lowering the total cost of the handling process. The *BT Compass* system is an advanced software package that provides:

- A full analysis of the customer's operational requirements
- A fast comparison of different pallet handling and order picking solutions
- Optimum warehouse layout
- Accurate calculations of handling capacities
- A complete analysis of projected life cycle costs

The *BT Compass* system has been developed to work in seven languages, and all inputs and outputs can be translated to any language with a single keystroke. It displays different layout options by using high-quality color graphics, and all plans can be printed quickly using a printer or plotter.

BT Lifters uses *Compass* when a customer is contemplating a change in materials handling or is adding a new facility. About 75 percent of the applications are for making changes in existing facilities, with about 25 percent of the applications for new facilities or "green field" sites. *Compass* is used about 50 percent of the time for new customers and 50 percent for existing customers. *Compass* provides BT Lifters a means of demonstrating its expertise as a material handling solutions supplier to new customers.

Compass provides a layout of the warehouse. It optimizes interactions such as aisle width with the dimensional requirements for a counterbalance truck. It calculates the layout and equipment requirements to meet peak hour needs in pallets per hour. The calculations include performance specifications, such as the number of 90° turns. BT Lifters measures the actual performance of its competitor's equipment, often buying the equipment to test it. Thus, it knows the actual performance on critical measures that customers use to judge lift trucks. A detailed, accurate understanding of the customer's usage system also is critical. A number of customers provide functional specifications and ask the lift truck suppliers to respond with the number and type of trucks required to provide the functional performance. If the performance is not met, the selected supplier has to provide additional trucks at no cost!

The data necessary as input for using *Compass* require some competence on the customer's part. Some customers know the required data well, others do not. BT Lifter's most senior salespeople serve as internal materials handling champions for the customers, and work with them in using *Compass* and doing the analysis. They even will provide "hands-on" data collection as needed at the customer's facility.

Although some customers use logistics consultants to help them in facilities planning, the advantage of working with BT Lifters and using *Compass* is that it provides a combination of planning the warehouse and specification of the kind and number of trucks needed to optimize warehouse performance. A recent case example illustrates this advantage. Birkenstock, a German manufacturer of health shoes, decided to build a new warehouse in Asbach, Germany. An in-house consultant responsible for the procurement process for this new warehouse had made a layout that indicated three lift trucks would be necessary to handle the pallet movements per hour. By using *Compass*, BT Lifters was able to demonstrate how an alternative layout in conjunction with its high-performance trucks required only two trucks—one less truck and also one less operator. According to

(continued)

BOX 2.8
Continued

BT Lifter's management, without *Compass*, they would never have been able to find this new solution and see the detailed performance results for their trucks. In addition, they believed that they would not have been able to convince Birkenstock management that their solution was correct without the *Compass* assessment.

Suppliers that practice customer value management understand that they must not only *demonstrate* the value that their offerings would deliver to customers, but that they must *document* the cost savings and incremental profits their offerings actually deliver to customers purchasing them. Thus, they work with customers to define the measures on which they will track the cost savings or incremental profit produced, and then after a suitable period of time, work with customer managers to document what the actual results have been. They use these tools, which we term **value documenters**, to further refine their customer value models, create value case histories, enable the customer managers to turn "gray" money into "green" money (i.e., cost savings for which they will get credit), and enhance the credibility of the demonstrated value of their offerings, because customer managers know that the supplier is willing to return to document the actual value received. W. W. Grainger's practice of customer value management with Pharma Labs (a disguised name) provides an outstanding case of the significant benefits to each firm, which we relate in Box 2.9.

GAINING CUSTOMER FEEDBACK

Gaining knowledge of how well the supplier firm has met its customers' requirements and preferences is a crucial facet of market sensing. Based upon its knowledge of what targeted market segments and customer firms value and would value, the supplier constructs its market offerings. In marketing these offerings, the supplier, in essence, makes a promise that its offerings will satisfy the customer's requirements and preferences. Gaining customer feedback enables the firm to know how well it has fulfilled its promises to customers. Customer feedback can tell the supplier where its offerings provided the functionality and performance customers expected, and where they did not. Thus, customer feedback provides the supplier with a chance to remedy problems that occur and to retain a customer's business. It also gives the supplier an early warning of changing customer requirements and preferences.

Although many supplier firms draw no distinctions and simply seek feedback from present customers, they can benefit from gaining customer feedback from three distinct kinds of customers. New customers provide valuable feedback on the initial experiences a firm has in doing business with the supplier and knowledge about converting new customers to established customers. Established customers provide essential feedback on how well the supplier sustains its relationships with customers and how the supplier's share of the customer's total purchase requirements is likely to change. Finally, customers that recently have stopped doing business with the supplier provide critical feedback on how the offering fell short of what was

BOX 2.9
Customer Value Management Benefits Grainger and Its Customers

Pharma Labs (a disguised name) is a rapidly growing pharmaceuticals manufacturer. At one of its largest plants—a facility with 380 employees—purchasing managers were questioning whether to outsource their MRO procurement and inventory management processes. During a routine sales call, the W. W. Grainger account manager learned of the managers' concerns and arranged a half-day meeting with the vice president of operations, the purchasing manager, and the maintenance manager at that facility. He asked two Grainger Consulting Services (GCS) managers to attend this meeting, thinking that GCS might be of assistance.

Following the meeting, GCS proposed that it perform what it calls a *baseline assessment*, which documents the total costs of MRO supplies management and then, following that assessment, offer Pharma managers some strategic recommendations about how they could improve their operations. GCS told Pharma Labs that the assessment and the strategy development would take 6 to 12 weeks to complete and would cost $45,000. Pharma Labs management agreed to the proposal, hiring GCS in January 1997.

To begin, GCS put together a case team, which consisted of a consulting manager, a consultant, and a business analyst. Pharma Labs formed a steering committee and a project team. The steering committee comprised the relevant department heads, such as maintenance, purchasing, manufacturing, inventory management, management information systems, and finance, and was responsible for project oversight and strategy development. The project team was a smaller cross-functional group with representatives from each of the departments on the steering committee and was responsible for working with the GCS case team.

Generally, GCS looks for the elements of its customer value models in four primary areas: processes (from how the need for items is identified to payment of invoices), products

(product price, usage factors, brand standardization, and application), inventory (on-hand value and carrying costs), and suppliers (performance, consolidation, and value-adding services provided). In each area, GCS defines value and cost-saving elements (such as freight and courier charges and the cost of overtime), specifies the measures for the elements (such as procurement cost per purchase order, number of suppliers, and inventory accuracy), collects the data and analyzes them, and specifies measures for monitoring performance. At Pharma Labs, the measures for monitoring performance included supply expenditures, number of suppliers, and transaction volume.

In a baseline assessment, GCS uses process mapping and activity-based costing to build customer value models, drawing on proprietary databases that the company has built from its findings in past engagements. At Pharma Labs, GCS applied an activity-based costing approach to identify procurement costs across all typical functional areas: purchasing, maintenance, receiving, and accounts payable. These identified costs were generally in line with costs tracked in the GCS databases.

In any analysis, GCS attempts to use the customer's electronic data whenever possible. The team usually attempts to get one year's worth of data. Early on, the case team makes a site visit to examine the customer's data and to assess how accurate and complete they are. In the case of Pharma Labs, GCS analyzed two years' worth of purchasing and accounts payable data, as well as six months of procurement card data. The data provided GCS and Pharma with insights about the potential for consolidating the number of products Pharma purchased regularly from various suppliers. It also suggested how Pharma might consolidate its purchases in return for lower prices and greater value-adding services from its remaining suppliers.

(continued)

BOX 2.9
Continued

At Pharma Labs, as in most GCS engagements, the case team also had to do an invoice analysis—actually inspecting past invoices to gather usable data—to validate the electronic data and to provide additional line-item product detail when available. The level of detail that the customer has is usually not adequate. The customer's system may contain only aggregated purchase order information, showing only how much was paid in total. Complicating the task further, invoices themselves often have incomplete item descriptions that make it difficult to determine exactly what was purchased.

The GCS team also found from its inventory analysis that Pharma Labs had no records of the amount of inventory on hand or its usage. Inventory levels were extremely high—the team later found that Pharma had more then $1 million worth of slow-moving inventory—but no actual record of this inventory was maintained in a system to track and manage its items.

The GCS case team supplemented its analyses by interviewing the Pharma project team members. In these interviews, GCS shared its preliminary findings, tried to uncover anything that they might have overlooked, and learned what the Pharma managers themselves perceived to be potential areas of improvement. The interviews were, in fact, fruitful, alerting GCS and Pharma managers to at least one significant finding in the procurement area. It turned out that Pharma lab technicians played an unusually large role in the procurement process, handling some routine purchasing, maintaining detailed, handwritten logs of all transactions, receiving the items into inventory, and managing that inventory. The GCS value model showed that Pharma Labs was spending 30 percent of its procurement costs—or the equivalent of nearly three full-time positions—on lab technicians who could be redeployed

from this purchasing function to more value-adding activities in their intended function. Pharma Labs eventually signed a supply agreement with another company, which, in return, put one of its people on site to manage this procurement process.

After GCS completes a baseline assessment, it then tries to specify improvements that the customer can make in 6 to 12 months. It also works with the customer to formulate changes in the MRO-supplies-management strategy.

At Pharma, GCS identified at least $327,000 in total cost savings on the $6.1 million Pharma was spending yearly on MRO supplies, including the costs of acquiring and managing them. These projected cost savings came about through consolidation of suppliers and product-spending reductions ($165,000), inventory reduction ($72,000), and process improvements ($90,000). For example, GCS recommended that Pharma Labs dramatically consolidate its MRO supplies purchases. Pharma Labs agreed and initiated a national account agreement with Grainger in June 1997. In return, Grainger provided Pharma Labs with an on-site Grainger representative to manage the purchase and inventory processes at the company. This allowed a Pharma Labs maintenance technician who had been spending 100 percent of his time purchasing MRO supplies to return to performing value-adding maintenance activities.

What were the ultimate results of Grainger's work with Pharma Labs? In December 1997, GCS and Pharma Labs jointly conducted an audit of achieved cost savings, which were found to be $387,000 during the first six months. What's more, for the whole of 1997, W. W. Grainger sales to Pharma Labs increased sevenfold, from $50,000 to $350,000. The next year, sales nearly doubled, to $650,000. Clearly, a better understating of value created substantial benefits for each company.

Source: Adapted from James C. Anderson and James A. Narus, "Business Marketing: Understand What Customers Value," *Harvard Business Review* (November–December 1998): 53–65.

promised, the adequacy of the supplier's service recovery processes, and potential problems in the supplier's targeting and customer selection strategies.[51]

We consider two related kinds of customer feedback: customer satisfaction measurement and customer value analysis.

Customer Satisfaction Measurement

Customer satisfaction measurement experienced the kind of fervent adoption by the business community in the 1990s that total quality management (TQM) received in the 1980s. Although the fervor for customer satisfaction measurement appears to be dwindling in recent years, most firms in business markets still are using customer satisfaction measurement in some form to monitor how well they are doing with their customers. A number of firms still even have customer satisfaction ratings linked to compensation for salespeople and others within the firm.

We first discuss a superior approach to customer satisfaction measurement and then consider some issues in what customer satisfaction results mean for the supplier.

American Customer Satisfaction Index (ACSI)

Fornell and his colleagues have provided the most comprehensive and methodologically rigorous approach to customer satisfaction measurement.[52] They recognize that no matter how carefully a researcher crafts a measure of customer satisfaction, in addition to assessing customer satisfaction, it also will likely measure other factors not of interest, as well as contain random measurement error. To overcome this problem, Fornell and his colleagues use multiple measures of customer satisfaction, which enables them to converge on the underlying concept of interest. They also embed the concept of customer satisfaction in a model that specifies its critical antecedents and consequences. They then use a sophisticated statistical analysis, partial least squares, to estimate the relationships between the measures and their intended underlying concepts, such as customer satisfaction, and the relationships among the concepts themselves, such as the relationship between customer satisfaction and customer loyalty. This approach produces results that demonstrate greater reliability and validity and provides supplier firms with a broader understanding of customer satisfaction.

We reproduce the American Customer Satisfaction Index (ACSI) model in Figure 2.4. **Overall customer satisfaction** "represents a cumulative evaluation of a firm's market offering, rather than a person's evaluation of a specific transaction."[53] The three measures of overall customer satisfaction include an overall satisfaction measure, a measure of the extent to which an offering's performance falls short or exceeds expectations, and a measure of the offering's performance relative to the customer's ideal product or service in the category. Customer expectations, perceived quality, and perceived value are antecedents of overall customer satisfaction. Note that customer expectations not only affect customer satisfaction directly, but also indirectly through their effects on perceived quality and perceived value. Customer complaints and customer loyalty are consequences of overall customer satisfaction. Two measures define customer loyalty: a rating of repurchase likelihood and a composite measure that assesses how increases in price and decreases in price would change the customer's purchase decision. Notice that the effect of customer complaints on customer

Figure 2.4 The American Customer Satisfaction Index

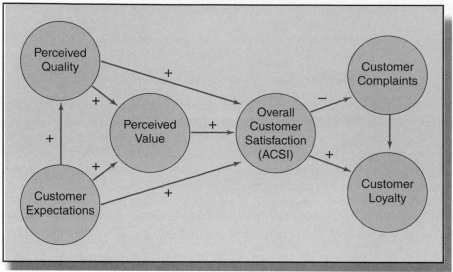

Source: Claes Fornell, Michael D. Johnson, Eugene W. Anderson, Jaesung Cha, and Barbara Everitt Bryant, "The American Customer Satisfaction Index: Nature, Purpose, and Findings," *Journal of Marketing* (October 1994): 8.

loyalty is not specified in advance because it depends on whether a supplier resolves complaints in a way that either builds or damages customer loyalty.

The ACSI model builds on earlier work that Fornell did in Sweden, where he constructed a national customer satisfaction "barometer" to assess how well Swedish industry was doing. Fornell and his colleagues started similar indices in other countries besides Sweden and the United States, such as New Zealand. Their model of overall customer satisfaction can be applied to study customers at the level of a nation, an industry level, or a single supplier firm. At the level of the firm, Anderson, Fornell, and Lehman found that overall customer satisfaction is a significant predictor of economic returns to the firm, such as return on investment (ROI).[54]

What Customer Satisfaction Results Mean

Even with reliable and valid measurement of customer satisfaction, supplier firm management still needs to understand what the results mean. What does the difference between customers that are satisfied and customers that are completely satisfied—the difference between a "4" and a "5" response on a five-point customer satisfaction measure—mean for the firm? Jones and Sasser researched the relationship between customer satisfaction and loyalty, studying 30 firms in five industries that include both consumer and business markets.[55] By **customer loyalty**, they mean:

> Broadly speaking, customer loyalty is the feeling of attachment to or affection for a company's people, products, or services. These feelings manifest themselves in many forms of customer behavior. The ultimate measure of loyalty, of course, is share of purchases in the category.[56]

Note that Jones and Sasser's ultimate measure of customer loyalty is the same as the earlier concept, **supplier's share of customer's business**; that is, the percent of a customer's total purchase requirement for a market offering that the supplier obtains. In their research, though, Jones and Sasser used an intention to repurchase measure as a proxy for customer loyalty. Their results show that the relationship between customer satisfaction and repurchase intention is not a simple, linear relationship, but one where completely satisfied customers are loyal to a much greater extent. A case example from Xerox that they report illustrates this finding: Totally satisfied customers were six times more likely to repurchase Xerox products over the next 18 months than were satisfied customers.

Recent research suggests that suppliers should not mistake customer tenure (i.e., the length of time the supplier has done business with a customer) with customer loyalty. Just because customers have been doing business with a supplier for a long time does not mean that they will be less costly to serve, that they will pay more for the supplier's offerings, or that they will engage in positive word-of-mouth communication about the supplier with others—all actions ascribed to loyal customers. Instead, suppliers are advised to assess customer loyalty by the extent of their customers' agreement with statements such as, "This supplier has earned my loyalty."[57]

Value is an essential antecedent of customer satisfaction and loyalty. Jones and Sasser observe: "Even in markets with relatively little competition, providing customers with outstanding value may be the only reliable way to achieve sustained customer satisfaction and loyalty."[58] Perceived value is an antecedent of overall customer satisfaction in the ACSI model, too. Understanding the pivotal role that value plays, a senior executive at DuPont Company once commented: "I am not out to delight my customers. . . . I just want to become indispensable to them, so that they can't live without me."[59]

The preceding quote alludes to what a number of suppliers state that they are pursuing—**customer delight**, which means to exceed rather than simply meet customer requirements and preferences. For example, one supplier's expressed goal is 100 percent customer delight. Businesses should rethink their unqualified pursuit of this goal, though. First, increasing performance levels is most often more costly, so supplier management must understand customers' willingness to pay for this performance and how much it will reduce profitability. Second, exceeding expectations tends to raise customers' expectation levels, so suppliers should pursue customer delight only to accomplish some strategic purpose, such as collaborative relationships with customers that afford the supplier a superior means of learning about changing market requirements. Lacking this purpose, completely satisfying customer requirements and preferences is sufficient.

Finally, suppliers should recognize that they may not be able to delight or even completely satisfy certain customers. It may well be that the supplier's market offering cannot deliver superior value against that customer's specific requirements and preferences, and to do so would be extraordinarily difficult or costly. This realization underscores the critical nature of selection strategies in determining which market segments and customers to serve, as well as the need to recognize mistakes in account selection.[60]

Customer Value Analysis

Gale proposed customer value analysis to remedy two shortcomings that he sees in customer satisfaction measurement programs.[61] Often, these programs do not survey noncustomers that are purchasing the offerings of competitors. They also do not provide a market assessment for supplier firms of how well they are doing relative to their competitors. Even though a supplier's performance is improving and customers report that they are satisfied, if a competitor's performance is improving faster, the "satisfied" customers will eventually defect.

Gale recommends that suppliers construct a **market-perceived quality profile** to pull together customer (and noncustomer) feedback.[62] Renee Karson, Director of Customer Value Measurement at US WEST Communications, provided a hypothetical illustration shown in Table 2.1.[63] Research participants first allocated 100 points across a set of attributes important in their purchase decisions (quality drivers), such as voice reliability, to reflect their relative importance. They then rated the performance of each service provider on each quality attribute, using an 11-point rating, where 0 is poor, 5 is acceptable, and 10 is outstanding. Multiplying each provider's average perceived quality on each attribute by the average importance weight, summing these products, and dividing by 100 produced the customer satisfaction score for the supplier firm and its competitors. From the illustration in the table, we see that US WEST had a customer satisfaction score of 8.0, while its primary competitor had a score of 8.1. Dividing the supplier firm's average score on each attribute by that of a primary competitor (or the average of all other competitors), multiplying each ratio by its associated importance weight, and then summing produced a **market-perceived quality ratio**. In the illustration, US WEST fell slightly below its primary competitor with a ratio of 99.9.

Table 2.1 A Hypothetical Illustration of a Market-Perceived Quality Profile for US WEST Communications: Small Business Customer Segment

| | OVERALL QUALITY DRIVERS | | | | |
CATEGORY	IMPORTANCE	US WEST SCORE	PRIMARY COMPETITOR SCORE	US WEST RATIO	BEST IN CLASS
Voice Reliability	30.0	9.0	9.0	1.00	Company A
Repair Service	20.0	8.0	8.5	.94	Company B
Data Reliability	20.0	8.0	7.0	1.14	US WEST
Account Relationship	10.0	7.2	8.5	.85	Company C
Installation Service	10.0	7.0	7.5	.93	Company C
Billing Service	10.0	6.8	6.5	1.05	Company A
Customer Satisfaction Score:		8.0	8.1		
Market Perceived Quality Ratio:				99.9	

Source: Renee Karson, formerly Director Customer Value Measurement, Market Intelligence and Decision Support, US WEST Communications.

As part of its customer value measurement program, US WEST augmented the market-perceived quality profiles with additional analyses. Research participants provided an overall price rating, an overall quality rating, and a value score ("Thinking about both quality and price, how would you rate US WEST on what you get for what you pay?"). To understand the relative contribution of quality and price to perceptions of value, US WEST regressed the overall value score on the overall quality and overall price measures. US WEST also measured nine specific price attributes, such as installation charges, which enabled it to regress the overall price rating on the specific price attributes to statistically determine the relative contributions of each to overall perceptions of price. Customer value measurement as practiced at US WEST provided an ongoing assessment to alert business units to emerging opportunities or threats. It can lead to "spin-off" market research studies that could provide value assessments expressed in monetary terms, using approaches such as conjoint analysis.

SUMMARY

Market sensing is the process of generating knowledge about the marketplace that individuals in the firm use to inform and guide their decision making. It is a market-driven process of learning about present and prospective customers and competitors, as well as other actors that affect the firm, such as resellers and regulatory agencies. Market sensing enables business market managers and other relevant individuals to formulate, test, revise, update, and refine their market views, which are simplified representations of the marketplace and how it works. We organized this chapter around four substantive facets of market sensing: defining the market, monitoring competition, assessing customer value, and gaining customer feedback.

In defining the market, business market managers choose descriptors that characterize and delimit a market, with the intent of pinpointing groups of firms that are of greater interest to the supplier firm. Market segmentation and determining market segments of interest are fundamental to defining the market. Market segmentation is the process of partitioning a market into groupings of firms that have relatively similar requirements and preferences for market offerings. Business market managers gain an understanding of which market segments are of greater interest by obtaining estimates of each defined market segment's size and growth, and its sales and profit potential.

Because customer judgments about the value of the firm's market offerings take place within the context of market offerings of other firms, business market managers also need knowledge about their competitors. We discussed Porter's framework for competitor analysis, which consists of four diagnostic components: future goals, assumptions, current strategy, and capabilities. To improve monitoring performance, supplier firms must have competitor intelligence systems, such as the Fuld Intelligence Pyramid™, and seek disconfirming as well as confirming evidence about competitors.

Customer value assessment is the work process of obtaining an estimate of the worth in monetary terms of some present or proposed market offering, or elements of it. Business market managers have employed nine methods to provide estimates of value. Customer value management is a comprehensive, practical approach for demonstrating and documenting the worth in monetary terms of what a supplier is doing, or could do, for defined market segments and customer firms. An essential undertaking in customer value management is building customer value models, which are data-driven estimates of what a present or prospective market offering is worth in monetary terms to targeted customers relative to the next-best-alternative offering for those customers.

Gaining knowledge of how well the supplier firm has met its customers' requirements and preferences is a crucial facet of market sensing. Gaining customer feedback tells the firm how well it has fulfilled its promises to customers and provides the supplier with a chance to remedy problems and retain a customer. We considered two related kinds of customer feedback: customer satisfaction measurement and customer value analysis.

ENDNOTES

1. George S. Day, "The Capabilities of Market-Driven Organizations," *Journal of Marketing* (October 1994): 44.
2. George S. Day, "The Capabilities of Market-Driven Organizations," 37–52; George S. Day, "Learning About Markets," *Marketing Science Institute Report No. 91–117* (June 1991): 1–23; Berend Wierenga and Gerrit H. van Bruggen, "The Integration of Marketing Problem-Solving Modes and Marketing Management Support Systems," *Journal of Marketing* (July 1997): 21–37; and Gerald Zaltman, "Rethinking Market Research: Putting People Back In," *Journal of Marketing Research* (November 1997): 424–437.
3. Simply put, *data* are codified observations; *information* is data that have been interpreted or put into context using some decision framework; *intelligence* results from making judgments or inferences about the meaning of the information; and *knowledge* is intelligence about which there is greater certainty and acceptance. For more discussion of data, information, intelligence, and knowledge and how they can be considered as an ordered progression in their worth to the firm, see Vincent P. Barabba and Gerald Zaltman, *Hearing the Voice of the Market* (Boston, MA: Harvard Business School Press, 1991), pp. 45–46 and Chapter 6.
4. Zaltman, "Rethinking Market Research"; and Ikujiro Nonaka, "The Knowledge-Creating Company," *Harvard Business Review* (November–December 1991): 2–9.
5. Day, "Learning About Markets"; and Wierenga and van Bruggen, "The Integration of Marketing Problem-Solving Modes." It is crucial that a firm periodically test the validity of the knowledge in its organization memory, such as recorded insights drawn from past analyses, and heuristics about the meaning of marketplace relationships.
6. "Electronic Glue," *The Economist*, 2 June 2001, 77–78. The quote is from p. 77.
7. Christine Moorman, Rohit Deshpandé, and Gerald Zaltman, "Factors Affecting Trust in Market Research Relationships," *Journal of Marketing* (January 1993): 81–101.
8. Elliot Maltz and Ajay Kohli, "Market Intelligence Dissemination Across Functional Boundaries," *Journal of Marketing Research* (February 1996): 57–58.
9. John Seely Brown and Paul Duguid, "Balancing Act: How to Capture Knowledge Without Killing It," *Harvard Business Review* (May–June 2000): 73–80.

10. Theodore Levitt, *The Marketing Imagination* (New York: The Free Press, 1983), p. 128.

11. Thomas S. Robertson and Howard Barich, "A Successful Approach to Segmenting Industrial Markets," *Planning Review* (November–December 1992): 6 [emphasis in original].

12. NAICS codes can be obtained at *http://www.naics.com*. This Web site also matches the NAICS codes to their corresponding old SIC codes.

13. James C. Anderson and James A. Narus, "Partnering as a Focused Market Strategy," *California Management Review* (Spring 1991): 95–113.

14. C. K. Prahalad and Gary Hamel, "The Core Competence of the Corporation," *Harvard Business Review* (May–June 1990): 79–91; and George Stalk, Philip Evans, and Lawrence E. Schulman, "Competing on Capabilities: The New Rules of Corporate Strategy," *Harvard Business Review* (March–April 1992): 57–69.

15. Das Narayandas, "Note on Customer Management," *Harvard Business School Note* 9-502-073 (Boston, MA: Harvard Business School Publishing, 2002); Robert S. Kaplan and V. G. Narayanan, "Measuring and Managing Customer Profitability," *Journal of Cost Management* (September–October 2001): 5–15; and Robert C. Blattberg, Gary Getz, and Jacquelyn S. Thomas, *Customer Equity* (Boston, MA: Harvard Business School Press, 2001).

16. Imad B. Baalbaki and Naresh K. Malhotra, "Marketing Management Bases for International Market Segmentation: An Alternate Look at the Standardization/Customization Debate," *International Marketing Review*, 10, no. 1 (1993): 19–44. Finally, for a worthwhile resource on segmentation in business markets, see Grahame, Dowling, Gary L Lilien, Arvind Rangaswamy, and Robert J. Thomas, *Harvesting Customer Value: Understanding and Applying Customer Value Based Segmentation (2003)*, available at: *www.marketingIQ.com*.

17. Roger J. Best, *Market-Based Management: Strategies for Growing Customer Value and Profitability*, 3rd ed. (Upper Saddle River, NJ: Prentice Hall, 2004), p. 120 [emphasis in original].

18. When market segments correspond to different country markets, country risk can be an additional factor that supplier firms assess in determining which segments are of interest. See, for example, "Business in Difficult Places: Risky Returns," *The Economist*, 20 May 2000, 85–88.

19. George J. Kress and John Snyder, *Forecasting and Market Analysis Techniques: A Practical Approach* (Westport, CT: Quorum Books, 1994); and F. William Barnett, "Four Steps to Forecast Total Market Demand," *Harvard Business Review* (July–August 1988): 28. The quote is drawn from Kress and Snyder, *Forecasting and Market Analysis Techniques: A Practical Approach*, p. 224.

20. Kress and Snyder. See the discussion in Chapter 13.

21. Barnett, "Four Steps to Forecast Total Market Demand," p. 28.

22. Kress and Snyder. We discuss constructing scenarios in Chapter 4.

23. Steven P. Schnaars, *Megamistakes: Forecasting and the Myth of Rapid Technological Change* (New York: The Free Press, 1989), pp. 134–135.

24. Kress and Snyder. See the discussion in Chapters 10 and 11.

25. Kress and Snyder, p. 219.

26. Kress and Snyder, p. 219.

27. James C. Anderson and James A. Narus, "Selectively Pursuing More of Your Customer's Business," *MIT Sloan Management Review* (Spring 2003): 42–49.

28. We discuss this further in Chapter 6, as part of creating market-oriented realization.

29. Schnaars, "Megamistakes."

30. Michael E. Porter, *Competitive Strategy* (New York: The Free Press, 1980). We draw on Chapter 3 of *Competitive Strategy* for this section, and adapt it where necessary to the business market management context. Professor Porter also makes the point that the firm should apply this framework to study *itself*, as a means to better understand what conclusions competitors are likely to draw about the firm.

31. Donald R. Lehmann and Russell S. Winer, *Analysis for Marketing Planning*, 5th ed. (Burr Ridge, IL: McGraw Hill/Irwin, 2001).

32. Porter, *Competitive Strategy*, p. 59.

33. Kenneth Labich, "Why Companies Fail," *Fortune*, 14 November 1994, 60. Digital Equipment Corporation was acquired by Compaq Computer Corporation in June 1998, which merged with Hewlett-Packard Company in May 2002.

34. Lehman and Winer, "Analysis for Marketing Planning." We discuss positioning in business markets in Chapter 4.

35. Michael V. Marn and Robert L. Rosiello, "Managing Price, Gaining Profit," *Harvard Business Review* (September–October 1992): 84–94.

36. Prahalad and Hamel, "Core Competence"; Stalk, Evans, and Schulman, "Competing on Capabilities"; and Lehman and Winer, "Analysis for Marketing Planning."

37. Lehman and Winer, "Analysis for Marketing Planning."

38. We are grateful to Leonard Fuld, founder and president of Fuld & Company, for his generous assistance with this section. For further information on competitive intelligence, see Stephen D. Solomon, "Spies Like You," *Fortune Small Business* (June 2001): 76–82.

39. Thomas A. Stewart, with David C. Kaufman, "Getting Real About Brainpower," *Fortune* (27 November 1995): 201–203.

40. Jeremy Main, "How to Steal the Best Ideas Around," *Fortune* (19 October 1992): 102–106. The quote on benchmarking is drawn from p. 102.

41. Max H. Bazerman, *Judgment in Managerial Decision Making*, 3d ed. (New York: John Wiley & Sons, 1994).

42. Stephen Goldsmith, "Can Business Really Do Business with Government," *Harvard Business Review* (May–June 1997): 110–121.

43. This section draws heavily from James C. Anderson, Dipak C. Jain, and Pradeep K. Chintagunta, "Customer Value Assessment in Business Markets: A State-of-Practice Study," *Journal of Business-to-Business Marketing*, 1, no. 1 (1993): 3–29.

44. For a basic exposition of conjoint analysis, see Chapter 21 of Naresh K. Maholtra, *Marketing Research: An Applied Orientation*, 3rd ed. (Upper Saddle River, NJ: Prentice Hall, 1999). For a discussion of recent advances, see J. Douglas Carroll and Paul E. Green, "Psychometric Methods in Marketing Research: Part I, Conjoint Analysis," *Journal of Marketing Research* (November 1995): 385–391. For discussions of the practical considerations in applying conjoint analysis, see Joseph Curry, "After the Basics," *Marketing Research* (Spring 1997): 6–11; and Susan Auty, "Using Conjoint Analysis in Industrial Marketing," *Industrial Marketing Management* (June 1995): 191–206.

45. Notice the amount of technical detail that is provided to ensure that the supplier and the participants have the same understanding of what exactly the attribute levels are and what they mean.

46. V. Srinivasan and Chan Su Park, "Surprising Robustness of the Self-Explicated Approach to Customer Preference Measurement," *Journal of Marketing Research* (May 1997): 286–291.

47. David B. Montgomery, "Conjoint Calibration in the Customer/Competitor Interface in Industrial Markets," in *Industrial Marketing: A German-American Perspective*, eds. K. Backhaus and D. Wilson (Berlin: Springer-Verlag, Inc., 1986), pp. 297–319.

48. This section draws heavily from James C. Anderson, *Customer Value Management* (Wilmette, IL: James C. Anderson LLC, 2003).

49. Once in a while, a team might pursue a point of parity that represents a *nuisance* to customers. Nuisances are points of parity where, if a supplier could make a difference, it would have a significant effect on the value the customers receive and it also would deliver a social benefit of ending or reducing the "pain" customers experience.

50. We discuss the OmniTRACS mobile communication system and how QUALCOMM conducts value assessments for it in Box 8.5.

51. Frederick F. Reichheld, "Learning from Customer Defections," *Harvard Business Review* (March–April 1996): 56–69.

52. Claes Fornell, "A National Customer Satisfaction Barometer: The Swedish

Experience," *Journal of Marketing* (January 1992): 6–21; Eugene W. Anderson, Claes Fornell, and Donald R. Lehman, "Customer Satisfaction, Market Share, and Profitability: Findings from Sweden," *Journal of Marketing* (July 1994): 53–66; Claes Fornell, Michael D. Johnson, Eugene W. Anderson, Jaesung Cha, and Barbara Everitt Bryant, "The American Customer Satisfaction Index: Nature, Purpose, and Findings," *Journal of Marketing* (October 1996): 7–18.

53. Fornell et al., "The American Customer Satisfaction Index," p. 8.

54. Anderson et al., "Customer Satisfaction, Market Share, and Profitability."

55. Thomas O. Jones and W. Earl Sasser, Jr., "Why Satisfied Customers Defect," *Harvard Business Review* (November–December 1995): 88–99.

56. Jones and Sasser, p. 94.

57. Frederick F. Reichheld, "Lead for Loyalty," *Harvard Business Review* (July–August 2001): 76–84; Werner Reinartz and V. Kumar, "The Mismanagement of Customer Loyalty," *Harvard Business Review* (July 2002): 86–94; and "Letters to the Editor: The Mismanagement of Customer Loyalty," *Harvard Business Review* (November 2002): 125–129. The Loyalty Acid Test for customers and employees can be found at *www.loyaltyrules.com*. Recent research has found that business unit employee satisfaction-loyalty shows a substantial relationship with customer satisfaction-loyalty and business unit profitability. See: James K. Harter, Frank L. Schmidt, and Theodore L. Hayes, "Business-Unit-Level Relationship Between Employee Satisfaction, Employee Engagement, and Business Outcomes: A Meta-Analysis," *Journal of Applied Psychology* (April 2002): 268–279.

58. Jones and Sasser, "Why Satisfied Customers Defect," p. 90 [emphasis in original omitted].

59. Joseph Weber, with Linda Bernier and Edith Updike, "For DuPont, Christmas in April," *Business Week*, 24 April 1995, 130.

60. For more on cautions in customer satisfaction, see Dawn Iacobucci, Kent Grayson, and Amy Ostrom, "Customer Satisfaction Fables," *Sloan Management Review* (Summer 1994): 93–96; Jones and Sasser, "Why Satisfied Customers Defect"; and Wilton Woods, "After All You've Done for Your Customers, Why Are They Still NOT HAPPY?" *Fortune* (11 December 1995): 178–180, 182.

61. Bradley T. Gale with Robert Chapman Wood, *Managing Customer Value* (New York: The Free Press, 1994); and Bradley T. Gale, *How Much Is Your Product Really Worth?* (Boston, MA: Bradley T. Gale, 2002). For an approach that uses customer value analysis in conjunction with a measure of customer loyalty to derive a loyalty index that captures the nature of the satisfaction-loyalty relationship, see Madhav Srinivasan, "New Insights into Switching Behavior," *Marketing Research: A Magazine of Management & Applications* (Fall 1996): 27–33.

62. A potential problem with grouping data from customers and noncustomers together is that they may have significantly different perceptions of the importance of different attributes in a market offering and the alternative suppliers' performances on them. Because of this potential discrepancy, we would recommend first performing the analyses separately to assess any differences before combining the two subsamples in a single analysis.

63. Renee Karson headed a customer value measurement group at US WEST. In her group were six Customer Value Managers who worked closely with the market/business units to identify, define, monitor, and analyze customer value perceptions of US WEST and its competitors. US WEST did not follow Gale's exact approach in practice. Instead, it tailored the approach to its specific needs for understanding its industry. US WEST merged with Qwest Communications International in 2000, where Karson now is Senior Director of Marketing.

3

Understanding Firms as Customers

OVERVIEW

A detailed understanding of customer requirements, prefer-ences, and purchasing processes enables supplier managers to know where their resources and capabilities have the greatest potential to create and deliver customer value. Supplier managers use this knowledge to guide decisions about which market seg-ments and customer firms to target. Moreover, these insights serve as a beacon, directing a supplier firm's new offering realiza-tion and market offering management activities. On a more tactical level, detailed understanding of firms as customers allows a sup-plier to focus efforts on those customer managers who matter the most in a purchase decision, to tailor its information to the prefer-ences of those managers, and to persuasively demonstrate why the supplier's market offerings deliver superior customer value.

Understanding firms as customers is the process of learn-ing how companies rely on a network of suppliers to add value to their offerings, integrate purchasing activities with those of other functional areas and outside firms, and make purchase decisions. In this chapter, we examine each aspect of the process. We begin by discussing how progressive firms recon-figure the task of securing external resources—from executing transactions to managing supply. We introduce three purchas-ing orientations—buying, procurement, and supply manage-ment—and investigate their defining themes, concepts, and practices.

Figure 3.1 Understanding Firms as Customers

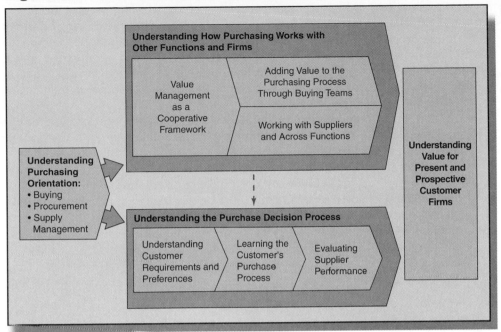

Next, we explore such initiatives as cross-functional buying teams and early supplier involvement programs that progressive firms increasingly employ to make more productive use of their resources. Finally, we describe how companies make actual resource acquisition decisions. Among the major issues we address are how business market managers gain a better understanding of customer firm requirements and purchase decision processes, and how customer firms evaluate supplier performance. We depict the process of understanding firms as customers in Figure 3.1.

UNDERSTANDING PURCHASING ORIENTATION

Broadly speaking, **purchasing** is the process of acquiring resources and capabilities for the firm from outside providers. **Purchasing orientation**, on the other hand, is the philosophy that guides managers who make purchasing-related decisions and delineates their domain and span of influence. Seasoned business market managers know that all customer firms do not share the same purchasing orientation. They are aware that shrewd customer firms may even embrace several at once, deliberately matching each orientation with a specific category of acquired products or services. When business market managers understand a customer firm's purchasing orientation, they can more knowledgeably decide such things as whether to serve the account, how to adapt the market offering to better meet the customer firm's requirements and preferences, and how to craft pertinent, persuasive sales presentations.

In practice, customer firms commonly select from three purchasing orientations—buying, procurement, or supply management.[1] Figure 3.2 illustrates the scope of the three purchasing orientations from the perspective of a customer firm, a final assembly manufacturer. The icons and arrows represent the **value network**, or set of organizations that perform portions of business processes designed to create economic, technical, service, and social benefits, and then equitably share those resulting benefits. The diagram indicates that as the manufacturer's purchasing orientation progresses from buying to procurement to supply management, the domain and span of influence of purchasing broadens.[2]

Our fundamental value equation 1.1 from Chapter 1 helps distinguish the thrusts of the three orientations. With a buying orientation, a customer manager's efforts focus solely on minimizing the price paid in a given transaction commonly for a single product or service. Breaking down value in the equation into benefits minus any costs incurred to achieve them, shows the intent of procurement and supply management. With a procurement orientation, a customer manager strives to reduce the total costs of ownership of an offering, which is often comprised of a bundle of products and/or services or a total solution. With a supply management orientation,

Figure 3.2 Purchasing Orientations and the Value Network

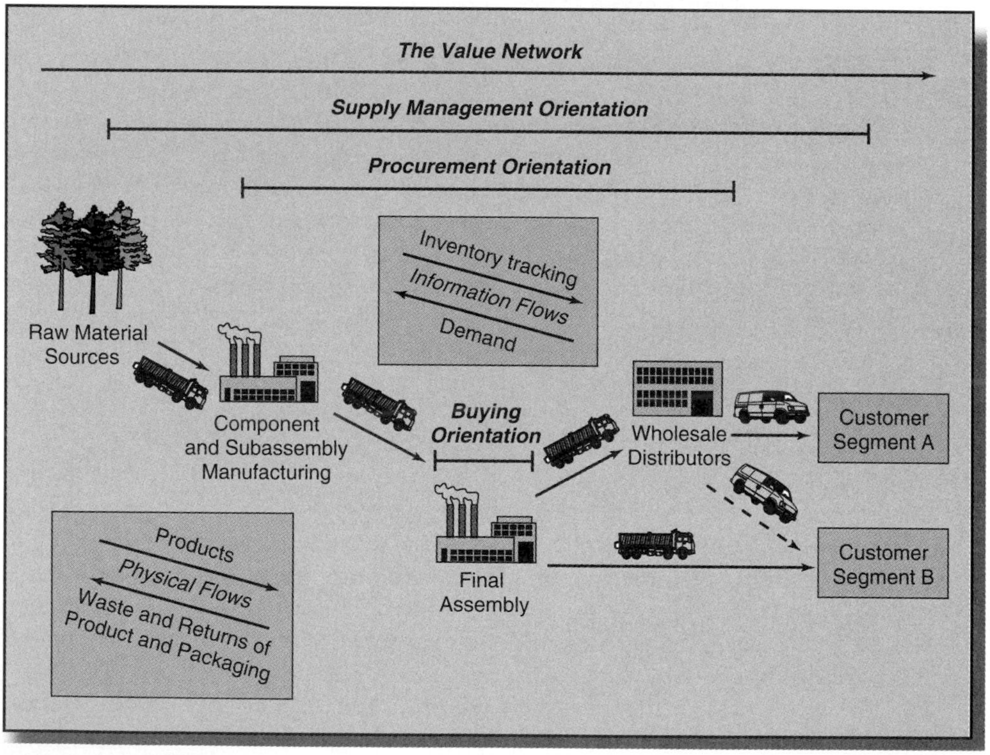

Source: Adapted from a chart by Professor Sunil Chopra, J.L. Kellogg Graduate School of Management, Northwestern University, 1999.

a customer manager seeks to obtain the greatest value relative to price from a close working relationship with a supplier.

The Buying Orientation

It is essential that business market managers recognize which prospective customer firms have a buying orientation, because these firms afford managers the fewest degrees of freedom for creating and sharing value. As shown in Figure 3.2, buying is the most narrowly focused purchasing orientation. **Buying** concerns executing discrete transactions, often for a single item at a time, with suppliers. A buying organization's prime objective is to reduce its annual **total spend** or the monetary amount of acquisitions in a given year. Buyers maintain arm's-length, often adversarial relationships with vendors. Buying practices are tactical and short term in nature. Under this orientation, buyers often have little if any input concerning what to acquire, in what quantity, and when. Firms commonly reward buyers for reducing prices paid to suppliers and for lowering the total spend from the previous year.

The central pursuits of the buying orientation are:

- Obtain the best deal in terms of price, quality, and availability from suppliers.
- Maximize power over suppliers.
- Avoid risk wherever possible.

Obtaining the Best Deal

When given a purchase request by another functional group, the buyer searches potential vendors for the best combination of price, quality, and availability. The buyer treats quality and availability as "order qualifiers" when evaluating competitive offerings. That is, they are necessary for a supplier to be considered but not sufficient to gain the order. Initially, buyers use price as an order qualifier too. As Ross points out, customer firms rarely consider a vendor's offering unless its price falls within the acceptable price band for that product or service class. A price band represents the range of acceptable prices around the average price paid for a product or service. In many industries, the price band is ±3 percent of this average. Under a buying orientation, the customer firm then usually selects the lowest-price vendor offering. Thus, price is the sole "order winner".[3]

How do buyers get the best deal? To understand these dynamics fully, let's assess buying as a form of distributive negotiations. In **distributive negotiations**, the customer and supplier assume that the "value pie" is fixed in size. Both firms see the situation as win-lose with one gaining more pie only at the expense of the other. Customer and supplier haggle over one thing—price. To gain the best price, both firms resort to gamesmanship and persuasion, while withholding critical information.

To bolster their negotiating position and lower the minimum price the supplier is willing to accept, buyers draw on two tools—price analysis and supplier cost analysis. In a price analysis, the buyer compares a seller's price proposal (bid) to the prices charged (or bid) by other possible vendors. Technological innovations, such as shared information systems and the comparison agents on the Internet, bring greater price transparency, making it far easier for buyers to conduct price analyses. Armed with price comparison data, the buyer is obviously in a better position to demand price concessions.[4]

Supplier cost analysis entails a review of actual or estimated cost data for a potential vendor. To conduct a supplier cost analysis, the buyer obtains all information possible on supplier costs directly from supplier personnel. Then, industrial engineers from the buyer's firm estimate the remaining supplier costs using published data on materials usage, labor rates, and equipment utilization. The buyer then adds on a "reasonable" profit margin to arrive at a "fair" price, which is demanded during negotiations. Typically, buyers use the supplier's overall corporate profit margin gleaned from annual reports as an estimate of reasonable profit. Of course, such analyses are based upon two pivotal assumptions. First, they presume a buyer has a better understanding of efficient production processes. Second, they assume the overall corporate profit margin accurately reflects the profit margin on the offering that the customer purchases and that the customer has the right to determine what constitutes a "reasonable" profit margin for the supplier firm.[5]

Maximizing Power over Suppliers

Power is the ability of one firm to get another firm to undertake actions it wouldn't undertake on its own. In a given transaction, the firm that has the power advantage or leverage can force the weaker firm to make price concessions. Thus, if the customer firm has the power advantage, it can secure a lower price from the supplier.[6]

How can a customer firm gain power over suppliers? When buyers do act to gain power, they often turn to two related tactics—commoditization and multisourcing. Through **commoditization**, buyers eliminate or downplay any points of difference between the value elements of competing offerings. For example, a buyer might contend that one supplier's technical support services are equivalent to another supplier's service. In essence, the buyer tries to equalize and remove $Value_f$ and $Value_a$ from the fundamental value equation 1.1, leaving competing vendors with reducing price as their only means for gaining an advantage and thus the sale. Through **multisourcing**, the customer firm requests price quotations from and places orders with a number of suppliers, playing one off against the other. To get more business, each supplier cuts price, triggering a downward price spiral.

As corollaries to multisourcing, buyers avoid sole-sourcing and single-sourcing because they would make the customer firm too dependent on one supplier. Buyer concern may be somewhat justified because of the possibilities of catastrophic events such as labor strikes, raw materials shortages, and plant explosions. In a **sole-sourcing** situation, only one supplier produces a needed product or service. Examples might include rare raw materials, patented product innovations, and new technologies. To avoid sole-sourcing, the buyer postpones acquisition of an offering until competitors emerge. In a **single-sourcing** situation, the buyer purchases the firm's total requirement from one vendor even though alternatives exist. Historically, buyers refrain from this practice "to keep vendors honest."

Critically, buyers are careful not to "squeeze" suppliers too much on price. If the customer firm does not allow a supplier a measure of profit, the supplier might go out of business or stop producing the needed offering. This event would reduce the number of potential suppliers, increasing the power of the remaining suppliers and ultimately, prices. Thus, buyers engage in an intricate "dance" with suppliers, relentlessly seeking price reductions yet stopping short of bankrupting them.

Avoiding Risk

Most managers try to minimize their exposure to risk, but buyers have a penchant for avoiding risk altogether. They use two tactics for avoiding risk—follow established procedures and rely on proven vendors. Research has demonstrated that buyers tend to use time-honored decision rules or heuristics when buying products and services such as the following. Seek quotes from at least three competing vendors. Divide an order among several suppliers with the greatest share going to the lowest bidder. Consider new vendors only if their bid is 10 percent less than that of lowest-priced incumbent supplier.[7]

Buyers also seek to avoid risk by relying on proven vendors. Often, buyers even give these preferred suppliers breaks during the purchasing process. For example, buyers frequently afford incumbent suppliers the right to "meet or release", which means that whenever an incumbent supplier's bid is significantly higher than that of a new supplier, the buyer allows the incumbent to revise its quotation downward. The buyer accepts the new supplier's bid only if the incumbent refuses to lower its bid. Importantly, the buyer does not extend the same courtesy to new suppliers.

Developments in Buying

It is important to emphasize that the practice of buying is evolving. An increasingly popular practice is that of **target pricing**. This approach is commonly used in the Japanese automobile industry. Target pricing works as follows. Through market research, buyers determine the target price for their product or service among their firm's customers. For instance, they might conclude that a given car model must sell for $20,000. Next, managers divide the car into systems and estimate what portion of the car's price should come from each system. They "drill" downward to subsystems and eventually to parts. Thus, buyers might conclude that in order to market a $20,000 car, they cannot pay more than $20 for a door handle. When entering into negotiations with prospective suppliers, buyers demand a $20 or less door handle.[8]

Another trend in buying is **global sourcing**. As the world becomes smaller because of breakthroughs in communication and transportation, buyers are increasingly able to take advantage of international marketplaces. Moreover, international suppliers often feature reduced prices, increased quality, and new technologies. Most important, buyers use global sourcing to broaden the customer firm's portfolio of suppliers, and in turn, enhance the firm's purchasing power.

Electronic networks, including the public Internet and private extranets, now enable customer firms to simultaneously reap the price reduction benefits of multi-sourcing and global sourcing through **e-sourcing** or online purchasing. Among the e-sourcing tools that buyers have begun to use in earnest are comparison agents, online reverse auctions, and e-RFQs. Comparison agents or "shopping bots" are software programs that enable a firm to search the Internet for suppliers of specific products or services, rank order those vendors from lowest price to highest, and place orders with the lowest-priced supplier. A firm can rely on internal comparison agent software or contract for the services of a third-party application service provider. Comparison agents are most useful for buying widely available, standardized or branded commodity items.[9]

In an online reverse auction, two or more suppliers bid against one another electronically to secure an order from a customer firm. Participants place bids anonymously in a Dutch auction format (i.e., descending monetary amounts), with the lowest bidder most often winning the entire order (i.e., if the lowest bidder does not meet specifications, the customer firm may select another bidder). Depending on the nature of the products and services being exchanged and bidding rules, an online auction can last from five minutes to several hours.

Although online reverse auction service and software providers (e.g., Ariba, Commerce One, and FreeMarkets, Inc.) claim that price savings commonly range between 10 percent and 50 percent, managers at GXS (formerly GE Global eXchange Services), which has conducted more than 32,000 auction events from 2000 through early 2002, are more sanguine, citing average price savings between 7 percent and 9 percent. Some customer firms publicly tout millions of dollars in total price savings from online reverse auctions. Others privately lament that such savings have come at the expense of product quality, timely delivery, support service, and long-term collaboration with trusted suppliers. Research suggests that online reverse auctions are most beneficial to buyers when securing low-tech commodities, used equipment, and surplus or distressed merchandise.[10]

For a fee or commission on a transaction, a customer firm can post an electronic request for quotation (eRFQ) on a third party moderated Web site (e.g., GXS) or on a business-to-business (B2B) exchange (e.g., Covisint, ChemConnect, eSteel, Exostar). Suppliers from around the world can then electronically submit quotes for the order. In a sealed bid format, the customer firm automatically selects the lowest bidder. In an eRFQ plus negotiations process, customer managers identify the lowest bidder and then follow up with direct contacts to negotiate an even lower price.[11]

Purchasing experts cite overspecification as a major cause of needlessly high-priced goods and services. An overspecified offering contains "bells and whistles" that are not needed to meet a customer's requirements in a given application. Through **defeaturing** or **cooperative pricing**, customer and supplier managers work together to identify superflous features, attributes, and performance specifications that can be eliminated or relaxed in exchange for lower price. For example, a customer firm may trade longer lead times, fewer product variations, fewer delivery locations, or less-technical support for reduced prices. Importantly, defeaturing can yield win-win outcomes in that the customer gains the offering it truly requires at a lower price, while the supplier sustains a reasonable profit margin.[12]

The Procurement Orientation

Although the buying orientation still remains predominant, progressive customer firms have adapted their thinking, often in response to two related observations. They realize that for the typical firm, the costs of goods and services purchased account for about 60 percent of net sales and that a $1 reduction in total costs has the same impact on net profits as a $6 increase in revenues. The $1 reduction drops right to the bottom line, whereas only $1 of every $6 in revenue typically does. With so much at stake, a customer firm cannot afford to make shortsighted, strategic acquisition decisions. For the supplier firm, this insight makes all the difference in the world, in that they can work closely with the customer firm to create and share additional value.[13]

As diagrammed in Figure 3.2, **procurement** entails broadening the domain and span of influence of purchasing. The firm doggedly pursues quality improvements and cost reductions through the integration of procurement activities such as order processing with such other functions as materials handling, logistics, and physical distribution, and through more cooperative relationships with suppliers. The procurement group becomes strategic in its thinking and proactive in its efforts. Its highly trained professionals evolve from buyers into managers of external resources. Increasingly, they focus on acquiring total solutions or offerings comprised not only of products and services but also technology and knowledge.[14]

With a procurement orientation, a firm seeks to increase its productivity through the following:

- Improving quality
- Reducing total cost of ownership
- Cooperating with suppliers

Improving Quality

Firms that adopt a procurement orientation are deeply committed to producing high-quality offerings. Instead of relying on abstract notions of goodness or aesthetics, these firms define **quality** as "conformance to specifications that result in a product which meets customers' expectations." **Specifications**, in turn, describe the offering that the firm is seeking. In contrast to buyers, procurement managers are actively involved in writing specifications as participants in, or even as the leaders of, cross-functional teams. Written specifications come in several forms. Functional specifications delineate what an offering does, technical or materials specifications describe the physical properties of the acquired product, process specifications describe how the offering is to be produced, and performance specifications tell what outputs the customer firm will get from using the offering.[15]

The advantage to defining quality in this manner is that procurement managers can readily measure it by comparing an offering's specifications to company requirements. The consistently closer the offering is to customer requirements, the higher the quality. Procurement managers classify products and services that fail to meet company requirements as **underspecified** and those that provide far more features than necessary as **overspecified**. Under a procurement orientation, the purchasing manager's seeks "perfect" quality in the form of offerings that precisely meet company requirements.

To achieve higher quality, procurement-oriented firms practice total quality management (TQM). The International Standardization Organization (ISO) describes TQM as "a management approach to an organization centered on quality, based on the participation of all its members and aiming at long-term success through customer satisfaction, and benefits to the members of the organization and society." TQM alters procurement thinking and practices. Procurement managers realize that they must work closely with other functional areas to better define the firm's product and service requirements and to coordinate the acquisition and flow of these products and services throughout the organization. And they understand that they are responsible for sustaining the quality of acquired goods.[16]

Reducing Total Cost of Ownership

Procurement managers apply strategic cost management, making purchasing decisions based on the goal of minimizing total cost of ownership rather than just reducing supplier prices. We define the **total cost of ownership (TCO)** as the sum of purchase price plus all expenses incurred during the productive lifetime of a product or service minus its salvage or resale price. Such expenses fall into three categories: acquisition, conversion, and disposal.[17]

Acquisition costs are those associated with securing an offering and include search costs, processing orders, and delivery charges. W. W. Grainger dramatizes these costs and proposes an innovative solution in a series of advertisements, one of which we present in Figure 3.3. Firms incur conversion costs when using an offering. They include warehousing and handling, inventory storage, materials processing, installation and maintenance, repair, operating supply costs, as well as the cost of poor quality. Corrective actions that a customer must take in response to quality problems also are a part of conversion costs. Disposal costs encompass recycling, environmental protection, and waste management expenses.

To estimate these costs, procurement managers regularly perform TCO analyses. **TCO analysis** applies activity-based costing (ABC) concepts and methods to quantify all expenses related to the use of a product or service apart from price. "Although TCO and ABC both are costing systems, TCO is focused on a firm's interfaces with suppliers to support decisions related to sourcing strategy, while internal activities are the scope of ABC systems." In contrast to customer value assessment, which we describe in Chapter 2, TCO analysis focuses on expenditures and does not consider revenue-generating opportunities an offering might afford.[18]

Through a TCO analysis, procurement managers identify the firm's major **cost drivers** or those factors that influence the nature and level of a major expenditure category. They summarize findings in the form of a TCO model on an interactive spreadsheet. With a TCO model, procurement managers can readily evaluate numerous sourcing scenarios, quantifying trade-offs among cost drivers and developing comprehensive sourcing strategies in order to reduce and avoid unnecessary costs.

By using a comprehensive TCO model, they avoid the so-called "seesaw effect" that blindsides managers who only consider price or a single cost when making a purchasing decision. The seesaw effect characterizes situations where an action intended to lower one cost unintentionally causes other costs to rise. The net result is to negate potential cost savings or to even increase overall costs. For example, in the recent rush to acquire customer relationship management (CRM) systems, firms that based their decisions solely on the purchase price of basic CRM software or on the opportunity to reduce customer data collection costs reportedly were dumbfounded months later to discover that they had to spend four to six times more for necessary auxiliary software, hire consultants to write customized programs to link it to legacy systems, and wait 6–18 months for the system to be fully operational.[19]

TCO analyses often reveal opportunities to eliminate costs. For example, the Grainger research illustrated in Figure 3.3 enlightened firms to the fact that acquisition costs often exceeded the price of an item, particularly in the case of maintenance, repair, and operating supplies (MRO). This realization prompted companies to seek new ways to reduce these costs. One simple yet effective solution is the use of corporate purchasing cards. A **corporate purchasing card** is a company credit card with

Figure 3.3

Source: Advertisement courtesy of W.W. Grainger, Inc.

predefined spending limits issued to authorized personnel for the acquisition of MRO items, personal computers and related equipment, and office supplies. By streamlining costly and timely paperwork associated with purchase approvals, a corporate credit card saves time and money. Research shows that purchasing cards have reduced average transaction costs from $91 per order to less than $15 while cutting order fulfillment time from an average of 9.1 days to virtually zero.[20]

TCO analyses also demonstrated that the key long-term benefit from e-sourcing comes in the form of cost rather than price savings. Researchers discovered, for example, that firms gain spectacular price savings the first time they use a reverse auction for an item. As they run additional auctions for that item, firms observe that price savings decrease and bottom out and that prices may actually increase as the number of participating suppliers falls. At the same time, they find that costs savings related to better specifications and standardized RFQs, more accurate requirement forecasting, reduced safety inventories, the elimination of manual and paper-based order processing, and global sourcing remain stable if not grow. This potential prompted leading reverse auction suppliers such as FreeMarkets and GXS to offer a greater variety of cost savings services. Surviving B2B marketplaces such as Covisint and Elemica report similar findings and new services.[21]

In order to achieve TCO reductions, procurement managers strive to integrate their efforts with other functions in their own firms, such as manufacturing, materials handling, and logistics. They increasingly rely on enterprise resource planning (ERP) systems. **ERP systems** are server- or Internet-based software applications that warehouse, manage, and report cross-functional accounting, financial, inventory and order processing, payroll transactions, and data from a centralized location. SAP, ORACLE, J. D. Edwards, Peoplesoft, and Baan have emerged as the key global suppliers of ERP systems.[22]

Serving as the foundation "back office" data processing software, ERP systems often host major "front office" applications including supply chain management (e.g., e-sourcing, order tracking), enterprise relationship management (i.e., personnel files), customer relationship management, and partner relationship management (i.e., channels and strategic alliance data) software. In recent years, ERP systems incorporated materials requirement planning (MRP I) and manufacturing resource planning (MRP II) software designed to determine the quantity and timing requirements of materials used in the manufacturing operation and provide the user with simulation capability to analyze alternative production scenarios.

Cooperating with Suppliers

With a procurement orientation, managers must draw upon resources of suppliers to gain significant quality improvements and cost reductions. For example, they may call upon a supplier to codesign products. To lower delivery and inventory costs, they may integrate their logistics function with those of suppliers. For these kinds of things to happen, age-old adversarial relationships must give way to those where there is greater cooperation.

Through cooperative relationships with suppliers, customer firm managers attempt to expand the value pie for both firms. This effort requires a new form of bargaining—integrative negotiation. **Integrative negotiation** is based upon the assumption that resources can be expanded to benefit both parties. The process entails identifying shared interests and goals, freely exchanging information, emphasizing commonalities and minimizing differences between parties, and seeking creative and nonobvious solutions that meet the goals of both sides. Agreement is accomplished by first prioritizing the interests of both sides and then by trading off less important interests for critical interests so that both firms achieve their primary goals. For example, a major paint company wanted to gain 100 percent share of a customer firm's annual requirement for coatings. The customer firm wanted to reduce the total cost of coating the parts it produced by 10 percent. Rather than haggling over price per liter of coating, the customer firm agreed to give the vendor 100 percent of its requirement if the vendor could meet the customer's cost savings goal.[23]

Customer managers actively work with suppliers to improve the quality in two important ways. The first is standardization of requirements. Dobler and Burt define **standardization** as "the process of establishing agreement on uniform identifications for definite characteristics of quality, design, performance, quantity, service, and so on." Standardization applies not only to physical characteristics but also to operating practices, procedures, and systems. Progressive firms require their suppliers to meet international standards, such as ISO 9000, before they are approved as potential vendors. In a second approach, procurement managers help suppliers establish their own quality assurance programs. Quality assurance entails methods and procedures for production, such as statistical process control, product testing, defect prevention, and process inspections.[24]

Another way to cooperate is target costing. **Target costing** differs fundamentally from target pricing in that its focus is on reducing TCO, not simply price. Customer managers begin by setting a target price for their product. Then they determine a target cost that would enable the firm to profitably market the product at that price. Let's use the automobile example again and say that company managers conclude that a target price of $20,000 is desirable and that the total costs for a given model cannot exceed $18,000. At this point, they evaluate the TCO of various systems, subsystems, and components that comprise the automobile. Customer managers conclude that the TCO the firm can incur on one door handle including price and installation costs is $40 and ask the door handle supplier to provide a solution that does not exceed that amount. Here, the supplier has the flexibility to respond in two different ways. The supplier can lower the price of a door handle appropriately so that it meets the $40 target cost. Alternatively, the supplier can propose creative cost reduction programs to achieve the $40 target. As contrasted with target pricing, target costing requires customer and supplier to work together, sharing technical, process, and cost information.

The Supply Management Orientation

Firms migrate to a supply management orientation when managers realize that the fate of their organization is inextricably linked to other companies in the value network depicted in Figure 3.2. Moreover, they recognize that they are not just acquiring a product or solution from a supplier, they are building a long-term relationship. Thus, **supply management** entails the integration and coordination of purchasing with other functions within the organization as well as with other firms in the value network, such as customers, customers' customers, resellers, suppliers, and suppliers' suppliers. Under supply management, the business market manager views purchasing "not just as a department, but as a series of value-adding activities." Supply managers, highly trained middle- and upper-level managers, become so involved with strategic planning and dealing with key suppliers that they may no longer do any buying![25]

Supply management has four central tenets:

- Focus all of the firm's efforts on delivering value to end users,
- Craft a sourcing strategy around the the firm's core competencies and resources,

- Build a supply network that efficiently completes required business processes, and
- Sustain highly collaborative relationships with select supplier and subsupplier firms.[26]

Focus on End-Users

Traditional corporate strategy seeks demand largely through technology push—sell what you can make. Reflecting this strategy, buying and procurement strive to meet the specifications of manufacturing and the forecasts of sales. Advocates of supply management turn this thinking on its head. Relying upon demand pull—make what you can sell—supply management proactively directs the entire supply network to meet the requirements of end-users. Their primary goal is to efficiently deliver the greatest value possible to end-users.

To better understand the end-user, supply managers participate in market research projects, customer advisory councils, and personnel exchange programs. Taking a supply network perspective, managers learn about the worth of their firm's market offering not only to immediate customers but also to their customers' customers. They relay value assessment results to their own product and service development group and to key suppliers, suggesting changes in respective offerings. Once market offerings have been redesigned, supply managers then use market research findings to help reengineer business processes across the entire supply network to deliver superior value to end users.

Craft a Sourcing Strategy

Supply managers act as catalysts in formulating and administering a **sourcing strategy**. The overall process has several steps, depicted in Figure 3.4. First, senior management, with the assistance of supply managers, identifies the core competencies of the firm. Although the concept is widely used in management circles, many firms have difficulty articulating their own core competencies. Quinn and Hilmer describe core competencies as skills or knowledge, not products or functions. They are flexible, long-term platforms capable of adaptation or evolution. Core competencies are limited in number. They provide unique sources of value network leverage in areas where the company can dominate. Finally, they are important to customers in the long run. In Chapter 4, we describe and provide examples of core competencies.[27]

Second, managers divide the firm's products and services into systems, subsystems, and components. Next, they categorize systems, or subsystems if systems are too broad, as strategic or nonstrategic. Wherever feasible, firms outsource nonstrategic systems or subsystems—those that involve mature technologies and have many qualified vendors.

Companies also outsource strategic systems or subsystems whose internal design and production capabilities have eroded to the point of noncompetitiveness. Firms gain outsourcing results not only on a transactional basis but also through a variety of long-term partnering arrangements, such as codevelopment, technology licensing, and joint ventures. The firm then makes a concerted effort to improve production processes for marginally competitive strategic systems and subsystems. After a prespecified time period, managers reevaluate these systems and subsystems. If they remain marginally competitive, they are also outsourced.

Figure 3.4 The Strategic Sourcing Process

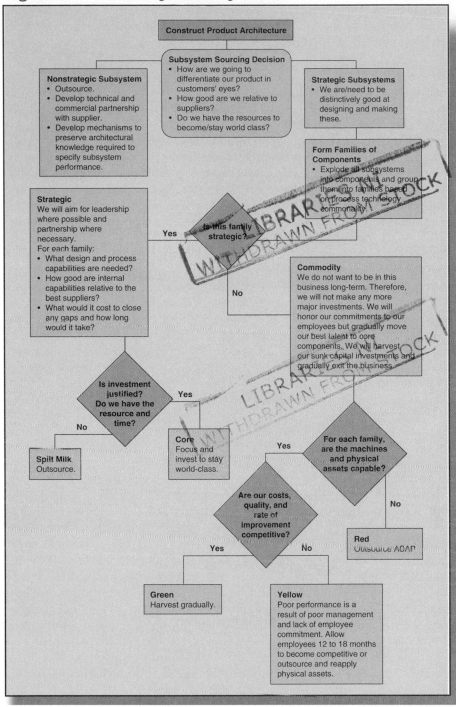

Source: Ravi Venkatesan, "Strategic Outsourcing: To Make or Not to Make," *Harvard Business Review* (November–December 1992): 103.

Finally, the firm insources, or produces itself, the remaining strategic systems and subsystems. Why? The company has superior expertise and stands to gain a high rate of improvement and major technological advancements from their continued production.

Build a Supply Network

Managers establish a vision for a supply network and set goals using the concept of the lean enterprise. According to Womack and Jones,

> The **lean enterprise** is a group of individuals, functions, and legally separate but operationally synchronized companies. The notion of the value stream defines the lean enterprise. The lean group's mission is collectively to analyze and focus a value stream so that it does everything involved in supplying a good or service (from development and production to sales and maintenance) in a way that provides maximum value to the customer.[28]

Under the lean enterprise concept, purchasing becomes a center of expertise within the firm. Supply managers rotate jobs, working within the supply management group on strategic purchasing tasks and on cross-functional teams completing broader company tasks. Based upon experiences on teams or assignments in other divisions, supply managers identify problems the firm faces in purchasing policies, procedures, and practices. When they return to a functional area assignment, they locate the best purchasing practices within the firm, conduct research, and benchmark other industries to find state-of-the-art solutions. The purchasing department becomes a repository for knowledge of best practice. When assigned to new cross-functional teams, supply managers disseminate their findings to colleagues across the company.

In a lean enterprise, firms rely on a network of direct suppliers and a larger number of second- and third-tier suppliers, share critical information across functions within and between firms, practice just-in-time management, and participate in codesign projects. In Box 3.1 and Figure 3.5, we demonstrate how Nike manages a supply network. To build an operational supply network, managers first select a overall supply network strategy and then rely upon the techniques of business process engineering to specify value-adding activities, identify partner firms, and chart the flows of activities across firms in the form of a supply network model.[29]

Supply network strategies trace their origins back to the classic marketing strategies of postponement and speculation. When the key customer value driver pivots around highly tailored, flexible, and timely offerings, supply managers advocate postponement. With a **postponement strategy**, a supplier delays final changes to an offering's form until the last possible moment through the use of local assemblers, fabricators, or other value-adding resellers. Conversely, when low price is the sole driver in the customer's decision, supply managers propose speculation. With a **speculation strategy**, a supplier produces standardized products in large lots and stores inventory in a central location in anticipation of orders.[30]

Academics and consultants identify two intermediate supply network strategies. When the central customer value driver is timely delivery, supply managers turn to **logistics speculation** whereby a vendor produces standardized products and either

BOX 3.1
Nike's Supply Management Network

Nike, the world's largest supplier of athletic shoes, has created a demand-driven supply network that allows the company a high degree of flexibility in the dynamic and global sneaker market. Subcontractors, or "production partners" in Nike's parlance, manufacture virtually 100 percent of the company's product. Rather than contributing identically, each production partner occupies one of three tiers in Nike's supply network and serves a distinct role, as shown in Figure 3.5 (page 106). Nike functions as the network architect and lead operator—identifying market trends, designing new products, scheduling production, assigning production responsibilities, and managing distribution and marketing.

First-tier production partners assemble finished products. Developed partners, located in Taiwan and South Korea, produce Nike's latest and most expensive "statement products." These firms produce in lower volumes, codevelop products, and coinvest along with Nike in new technologies. Volume producers are above average in size, manufacture a specific type of footwear, such as basketball shoes, and are vertically integrated. Nike does limited development work with them because each may work simultaneously for several sneaker companies. Nike also uses exclusive developing sources, which

are often situated in Thailand, Indonesia, and China, to capitalize on low labor costs and to diversify assembly locations. To enable developing partners to improve their capabilities, Nike has established technology exchanges through a "tutelage program," and encouraged joint ventures between developing and developed partners.

Second-tier production partners manufacture components and subassemblies for first-tier subcontractors and supply them with a variety of processed materials. Most second-tier partners are independently owned and operate in the same country as the first-tier partners they supply. Some of Nike's developed partners invest in the machinery required for second-tier suppliers to manufacture components specific to Nike. Nike plays an important central role in selecting second-tier production partners and integrating their activities with those of first-tier partners.

Third-tier production partners, specialty components manufacturers, produce the more specialized and technical components, such as Nike Air Soles, that are used by second-tier partners. Nike sometimes owns these firms. For example, Nike acquired Tetra Plastics Inc., the sole supplier of the polyurethane film used in the manufacture of Nike's patented air-cushioning components.

Sources: Contributed by Research Associate Nicole Avril, J. L. Kellogg Graduate School of Management, Northwestern University. Michael T. Conaghu and Richard Bariff, "Nike Just Did It: International Subcontracting and Flexibility in Athletic Footwear Production," *Regional Studies* (December 1990): 537–552; James Brian Quinn and Frederick G. Hilmer, "Strategic Outsourcing," *Sloan Management Review* (Summer 1994): 43; and Meg Rottmann, "Nike to Aquire Tetra Plastics," *Footwear News* (December 17, 1990): 4.

stocks inventory in local distribution centers or relies on overnight delivery services such as FedEx or UPS. When customers demand low price yet require minor adjustments to offerings, supply managers draw upon **manufacturing speculation** whereby a vendor produces large quantities of modules or components and delays assembly to some point downstream in the value chain, perhaps at a distribution center or wholesaler's location.[31]

Figure 3.5 Nike's Supply Management Network

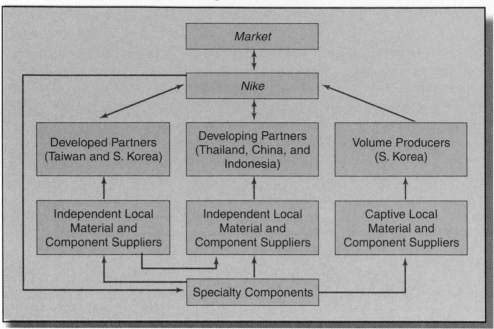

Source: Adapted from Michael T. Donaghu and Richard Bariff, "Nike Just Did It: International Subcontracting and Flexibility in Athletic Footware Production," *Regional Studies* (December 1990): 537–552.

Once they select a strategy, managers formulate a supply network model. A **supply network model** traces the value-adding steps needed to produce a desired market offering from the ultimate customer backward through a variety of first-, second-, and third-tier suppliers.[32] Numerous supply network models are documented and illustrated in the operations research literature. The models determine the optimal number of members, ideal amounts and locations of inventory, and delivery routing.[33]

For example, when securing predictable quantities of MRO items, supply managers commonly design a **make-to-stock model** featuring manufacturers that produce standardized products to demand forecasts, lengthy distribution channels, and local dealers that provide one-stop shopping, local delivery, and credit services. When acquiring personal computers (PCs) in a large one-time transaction, supply managers might select a **build-to-order model**, directly purchasing the PCs from a vendor such as Dell Computers. A build-to-order model utilizes mass customization and flexible manufacturing, features rapid delivery, and encourages substitution of new technology in product designs.

In the case of essential spare parts, supply managers might choose a **continuous replenishment model** or **efficient customer response (ECR) system**. In an ECR system, a single vendor manages a customer's entire plant inventories, immediately replacing out-of-stock items through an electronic data interchange (EDI) based logics network. To obtain access to next-generation technology, supply managers might recommend a **design-to-build model** whereby customer and supplier R&D personnel jointly develop a new product. In turn, the supplier would produce the one-of-a-kind product in a single batch.[34]

Sustain Highly Collaborative Relationships with Select Suppliers

Supply managers learn to collaborate with key suppliers in even more creative ways. For example, in Box 3.2 we describe how the Bose Corporation and its major suppliers improved quality and reduced costs through the JIT II® Program. Other firms create password-protected extranets to permit supplier firms to exchange proprietary data and collaborate on joint cost-reduction or in new offering realization programs. Chapter 10 explores such partnering opportunities in greater detail.

With a supply management orientation, customer and supplier firms strive to equitably share delivered value. Increasingly, they employ value-in-use and value-in-use price as yardsticks for evaluating the superior value of the supplier's offering and for agreeing upon a fair price. **Value-in-use** (VIU) represents the superior value minus price that a supplier's offering (Offering$_f$) provides a customer firm relative to a competitive offering (Offering$_a$). VIU is a useful benchmark in that it captures an offering's value proposition in monetary terms.[35] Using our fundamental value equation 1.1, we calculate it as follows:

$$VIU_{fa} = (Value_f - Value_a) - (Price_f - Price_a) \tag{3.1}$$

Value-in-use price (VIU price) or the indifference price is the monetary amount at which the customer has no preference between the supplier's offering (Offering$_f$) and the next-best-alternative supplier's offering (Offering$_a$). Supply managers, as well as business market managers, calculate the VIU price because it approximates the maximum price a customer firm should pay for a market offering and thus can serve as a critical upper bound in price negotiations.[36] Algebraically manipulating the fundamental value equation 1.1, we state the VIU price of Offering$_f$ relative to Offering$_a$ as follows.

$$VIU\ price_f = Price_a + (Value_f - Value_a) \tag{3.2}$$

Apply Purchasing Portfolio Management

Noting that firms purchased a wide variety of products and services, consultant Peter Kraljic argued in a now classic article that a company may have to adopt multiple sourcing strategies, build unique supply networks, and sustain diverse relationships with suppliers as a function of the supply situations it faces. Kraljic proposed that a firm's purchasing approaches could be summarized and managed via a **purchasing portfolio** or **supplier segmentation model**. Popular among scholars and managers in Europe, the Kraljic approach spawned variations that take a commodity perspective in focusing on the nature of products and services being acquired. [37]

In Figure 3.6, we synthesize the various versions of the Kraljic-inspired models. The rows capture the customer value and the columns the customer risk associated with purchasing and using a given offering. Following value assessments and risk analyses, supply managers categorize acquired offerings as either **generics** (e.g.,

BOX 3.2
The BOSE Corporation's JIT II® Program

With annual sales in excess of $600 million, the BOSE Corporation is a leading manufacturer and global marketer of top-end loudspeakers, noise-canceling headsets, and professional sound systems. For more than a decade, the firm has invited select supplier partners to assign one or more employees to work full-time at BOSE plants across the world as participants in its celebrated JIT II Program. To participate, a supplier must be one of BOSE's best vendors in terms of consistent quality, on-time delivery, and competitive prices and be willing to sign a long-term JIT II contract.

BOSE management refers to these supplier representatives as *inplants*. As part of JIT II, they furnish inplants with unprecedented access, resources, and insights into BOSE operations. For example, BOSE gives inplants a 24-hour access card to BOSE facilities, an office, the ability to log on to certain BOSE information systems, and even allows them to print their own BOSE business cards. Inplants can formally or informally meet with BOSE manufacturing, engineering, marketing, and senior managers, and attend planning meetings. In exchange, inplants electronically place orders for their firm's products at prespecified standard prices, ensure that these parts are delivered to the right BOSE plants on time and in conformance to specifications, and provide trouble-shooting assistance.

Through JIT II, suppliers increase their share of BOSE business, improve their profitability, dramatically reduce operations costs, and develop new products. Here is how they do it. With access to BOSE's production planning system, supplier firms better synchronize their manufacturing and delivery schedules with BOSE requirements. Furthermore, they identify additional products to cross-sell to BOSE. By openly and frequently communicating with BOSE sales and marketing personnel as well as with BOSE customers, inplants gain timely and strategic insights on market conditions and trends. Inplants routinely participate in concurrent engineering and codesign projects with BOSE's research and development (R&D) group. As a result, they "get the jump" on the competition when it comes to technology advancements and new product development. By being able to freely walk around BOSE facilities and interact with managers and workers, inplants gain a better understanding of BOSE operations, contribute value to BOSE efforts, and earn the respect and friendship of BOSE employees. Over time, inplants become highly valued and not easily replaced resources for BOSE.

What does BOSE get in return? For starters, BOSE gains full-time purchasing, production planning, and order fulfillment personnel at no charge. Moreover, they see lower order-processing, inventory holding and handling, and delivery costs. BOSE R&D receives supplier technical expertise and market intelligence. In recent years, BOSE and its suppliers have established electronic links via the Internet and private extranets. Two emerging applications of these information technologies are electronic collaborative design through which BOSE and supplier engineers continuously exchange new product development drawings, and real-time shipment tracking through which Bose can track incoming and outgoing inventory movements. Inplants are continuously involved in cost-reduction, quality-improvement, and value-analysis projects. Design and delivery cycle times are reduced significantly. Suppliers provide not only BOSE but also BOSE customers with more rapid technical problem-solving assistance. And the "icing on the cake" for BOSE comes from the fact that they have achieved all of these benefits while holding the line on supplier price increases!

The JIT II concept has been so successful in its implementation at BOSE that a number of other major corporations, such as AT&T, Gulfstream Aerospace, IBM, Intel, Motorola, Siemens, and Sun Microsystems have adopted it in their purchasing and logistics.

BOX 3.2
Continued

BOSE also licenses qualified supplier firms as "certified JIT II vendors." Licensees can promote JIT II certification to current and prospective customers. Deloitte & Touche, Roadway Express, SGS-Thomson, and TAC Worldwide Companies among other firms, actively use their JIT II vendor certification in this manner.

MRO items), **leverage items** (e.g., raw materials), **bottleneck items** (e.g., essential spare parts), or **criticals** (e.g., new technology). Then they pursue two overall goals: (1) add value through functionality-cost management, service, effective administration, and the sourcing and integration of innovation; and (2) reduce risk through quality, availability, assurance, agile responsiveness, and sourcing activities. Kraljic and others recommend distinctive tactics to accomplish these ends for each of the four offering groups.

As with other portfolio approaches, academics and consultants urge supply managers to strive for advantage and balance by taking steps to move offerings across the matrix into more beneficial categories. Professor Arjan van Weele articulates one of the most elaborate approaches. He argues that the customer firm's ultimate objective should be to shift as many offerings to the leverage grouping as is possible. Why? Because in leverage circumstance, the customer firm governs the relationship and garners the greatest share of value created.[38]

To cultivate a greater number of leverage items, van Weele urges supply managers to initiate a variety of actions. At some point in time, most firms require criticals and must forge strategic partnerships with important vendors. In these alliances, the customer firm seeks to lower the cost of performance through such things as early supplier involvement, codevelopment, and codesign programs. Long term, van Weele counsels supply managers to reduce dependence on these vendors by standardizing and simplifying specifications and cultivating alternate suppliers. When successful, managers transform these criticals into leverage items. In the case of bottleneck items, supply managers must seek to lower the costs of operations. As with criticals, supply managers can relocate them to the leverage category through standardization and simplification. Alternatively they can attempt to convert them into

Figure 3.6 Purchasing Portfolio Matrix

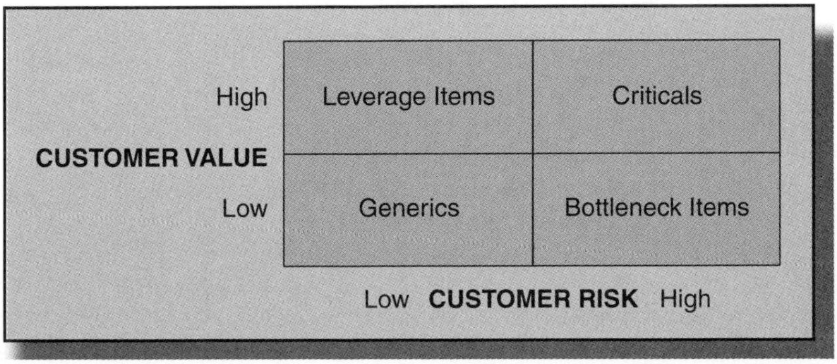

generics by keeping emergency stocks on hand, hedging, Internet buying, relaxing standards, modularization, and/or pooling requirements.

For generics, van Weele urges customer firms to pursue lower acquisition costs. Customers do so by reducing the number of buys and by consolidating orders through techniques such as blanket or systems contracts, facilities management, and outsourcing. When successful, customer managers change them into leverage items. Lastly, in the ideal case of leverage items, van Weele recommends that customer firms enhance their purchasing power by reducing the number of suppliers and then using that superior power to secure lower prices and force suppliers to assist in lowering the customer firm's conversion costs.

Putting Knowledge of Purchasing Orientation to Use

Business market managers gain significant insights from understanding a customer firm's purchasing orientation. Knowing whether a firm embraces buying, procurement, supply management, or several orientations simultaneously says a great deal about how a supplier will be able to create and deliver value to that customer. For example, a customer firm with a buying orientation largely constrains a supplier to focus on reducing its own costs and pass them along to the customer in the form of lower price. Although the supplier may understand how a higher-priced material would lower the customer's conversion costs, the supplier may be unable to persuade the customer even to consider making changes in its production process. Instead, the buyer simply tells the supplier to "Quote the spec" if it wants to do business.

Certainly, an understanding of a firm's purchasing orientation ought to significantly affect a supplier's customer selection strategy. Depending on how they create and deliver value, suppliers might focus on firms that are seeking the lowest purchase price, the lowest total cost, or the greatest value. For example, an offshore supplier with lower labor costs, but no in-country inventory or technical support, may focus on selling container loads to firms with a buying orientation.

Looking internally at their own firms, business market managers recognize that they too are customers. A better understanding of how their firm's purchasing strategies and activities contribute to or hinder the completion of business processes helps business market managers pinpoint ways to improve their organization's ability to create and deliver value to the marketplace. In Box 3.3 and Figure 3.7 (page 112), we provide an example of how Shell International used the concept of purchasing orientation over the years to improve the purchasing practices of its many subsidiaries.

BOX 3.3
Shell International Uses Purchasing Orientation Internally

Several years ago, the Board of Directors of Shell International came to the company's corporate Contracting & Procurement (C&P) group, directed by Roger White at the time, with an urgent directive. With annual sales in the multibillions of dollars, Shell International is a holding company for approximately 174 partially and wholly owned subsidiaries that operate in 105 countries around the world. The Board requested that C&P find ways to

BOX 3.3
Continued

reduce the total costs of the purchase and use of acquired goods and services across Shell by $2 billion in two years and by 30 percent over the next decade.

White and his group began work on the project by estimating the savings Shell would achieve by placing extreme pressure on all its suppliers to cut prices to a minimum. They quickly learned that across-the-board price cuts would not lower Shell's total costs enough to meet the short- and long-term goals. Moreover, C&P concluded that such heavy-handed tactics would enrage and alienate suppliers to the extent that they would refuse to contribute cost-savings ideas to Shell. Turning to more advanced purchasing concepts and strategies, the C&P group determined that if Shell could educate and convince its subsidiaries to use supply management, Shell could meet the short-term goal as well as exceed the long-term total cost-savings goal.

To implement supply management across Shell subsidiaries, C&P first articulated five purchasing orientations or levels of purchasing sophistication. In Figure 3.7, we present these orientations in a simplified version of a chart that Roger White provided. The first column of the chart identifies what Shell calls purchasing stages and we refer to as purchasing orientations. The second column, milestone activities, lists purchasing practices that are characteristic of firms that practice each purchasing orientation. The third column, results, identifies the outcomes Shell expects when a group uses a given orientation. Next, the C&P group plotted each of Shell's 174 subsidiaries according to their respective purchasing orientations. With a map of the state of purchasing across Shell, C&P has begun efforts with each subsidiary to raise their level of purchasing sophistication across each of the five orientations. To date, White reports significant progress toward the Board's short- and long-term goals.

Understanding How Purchasing Works with Other Functions and Firms

We next examine how purchasing provides greater value to end users by working closely with other functions as well as other firms. We begin by discussing value management, which provides a comprehensive framework for cross-functional and interfirm cooperative activities. Then we examine the buying team as the major tool for cross-functional coordination. In the process, we discuss the roles of buying team members, the various buying situations teams confront, and team tasks. We conclude the section by showing how purchasing expertise can add value in the new offering realization or existing offering modification processes.

Value Management as a Cooperative Framework[39]

Value management (VM) entails the systematic use of value techniques for a general problem-solving method in business, research, and administration. The two aspects of value management occur at different levels. At the strategic level, all executives learn to manage by value. That is, they systematically and routinely take into account the concepts of function and performance when making important decisions. At the

Figure 3.7 Purchasing Orientations at Shell International

Stages	Milestone Activites	Results
1. Basic Supply Operations	• Cost/spend analysis • Quality/cost teams • Supplier quality focus (TQM) • Volume leverage • Supplier base consolidation • Transaction benchmarking	• Quality assurance • Local leverage • Efficient supply operations
2. Differentiated Supply Tactics	• Regional sourcing • Cross-location teams • Supplier base optimization • Procurement plans established • Commodity family focus • Nontraditional (indirect) purchasing • Ad hoc alliances • Cost benchmarking	• Regional leverage • Clear procurement strategy • Focused use of resources by benefit/cost ratio • Life cycle cost improvement
3. Supply Chain Improvement	• Global sourcing • Optimum use of industry standards • Dock to stock pull systems • Early supplier involvement • Strategic alliances • Cross-functional supply teams • Process benchmarking	• Global leverage • Reduced cycle time and capital employed • Reduced total costs of operations • Best practices
4. Integrated Supply Chains	• Proactive outsourcing • Cross-enterprise decisions • Supplier key strengths analysis • Supply chain core competencies • Market intelligence • Global SCM into major markets	• World-class supply chain links • Alliances unleash creativity • Improved value to customer
5. Optimum Value Chains	• Differentiated users/stakeholders • Customer value driver analysis • "Value" optimization • High value add position for operating unit	• New customers/new products • Maximum value/cost ratio and optimum value chains

Source: Adapted from a chart contributed by Roger White, Corporate Contracting & Purchasing, Shell International, 1998.

tactical level, all personnel focus on the management of value by completing projects designed to sustain or enhance the value of their market offerings. The use of value management allows a firm to better focus and efficiently manage its operations, to gain a clearer understanding of the needs and priorities of its customers, and to deliver optimal value to the customer with trade-offs between performance and cost.

The pioneering work of Lawrence Miles at General Electric during the 1960s on the techniques of value analysis (VA) provides the foundation for value management.[40] **Value analysis** (or value engineering) is a method of value assessment that customer firms use to evaluate supplier offerings. A consortium led by the French Association of Value Analysis (AFAV) and the Association of German Engineers (VDI Zentrum Wertanalyse) explored, developed, and articulated the value management

Figure 3.8 Value Management (VM)

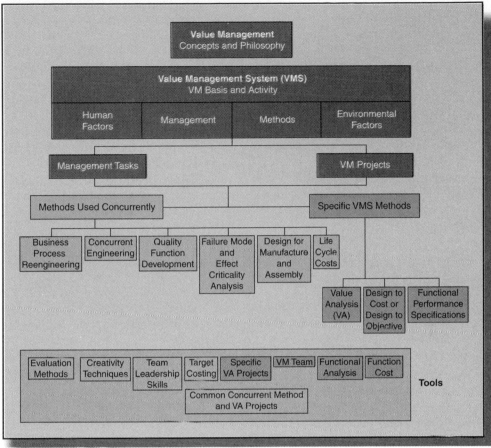

Source: Adapted from European Commission, *Value Management Handbook* (Luxembourg: Office for Official Publications of the European Communities, 1995), p. 89.

approach for the European Union. We present their framework for value management in Figure 3.8.

The consortium began with VA, which is project focused, and "exploded it" outward, deliberately making value management more strategic in its thrust. As depicted in Figure 3.8, value management activities take place at four levels. At the top are the concepts and philosophy of value management. Central among these, as is the case with our approach, is the goal of achieving optimal value, which is the best possible ratio of quality to total cost delivered to customer firms. Three of the four guiding principles of business market management—value is the cornerstone of business management, focus on business processes, and place emphasis on working relationships and business networks—closely correspond to those of VM.

After adopting value management, a company sets into place a value management system (VMS), the second level of Figure 3.8. The VMS is composed of an operating structure, management, and methods that are responsive to the external environment.

Often the operating structure takes the form of cross-functional teams, task forces, and councils. In turn, the VMS undertakes two sets of actions, the third level of VM. As contrasted with traditional VA efforts, the VMS completes strategic and far-ranging corporate initiatives referred to as management tasks, which emphasize such diverse activities as strategic planning, new product realization, new plant design, and product positioning. At the same time, managers conduct highly focused and more traditional VM projects. For example, a value team might search for ways to reduce the TCO of a critical component in one of the firm's market offerings.

The fourth level of Figure 3.8 shows the methods that managers use to complete VMS tasks. Proponents of other management approaches have devised methods used concurrently. They include many of the other techniques such as business process reengineering and quality function deployment. Advocates of VM, on the other hand, have created specific VMS methods. Obviously, when confronted with a task, a cross-functional team chooses the method or combination of methods from both categories that are best suited to the problem at hand. The box in Figure 3.8 lists specific VMS tools.

Adding Value to the Purchasing Process Through Buying Teams

The **buying team** or buying center "refers to all those members of an organization who become involved in the buying process for a particular product or service." Business market managers must consider three aspects of buying teams: member roles, buying situations, and tasks.[41]

Team Member Roles

Roles are the responsibilities of buying team members. The job title of the manager who performs these roles will likely vary from one organization to the next. Let's examine a simple buying team task—hiring a service vendor to repair a piece of equipment. The initiator is the person within the firm who realizes the acquisition of a product or service can solve or avoid a problem. For example, a production worker watches a piece of equipment erratically produce defective parts and concludes that it needs to be repaired. The worker-initiator alerts the shop manager to the problem. In turn, the manager contacts purchasing. The gatekeeper controls the flow of information in and out of a firm and provides vendors access to key personnel. Thus, the purchasing manager forwards a list of certified vendors to the shop manager for consideration.

The influencer guides the selection process by expressing preferences or recommending vendors or offerings. For instance, the production worker prefers and lobbies for a particular service contractor because its technicians are easier to work with and more personable. The decider has ultimate responsibility for determining which product or service will be purchased and for choosing the supplier. In our example, the shop manager selects the service contractor and is therefore the decider.

The buyer is the individual who negotiates with the vendor and formally executes the purchase or acquisition. Thus, the purchasing manager issues a formal work order and arranges a service contractor call. Finally, the user is the individual who employs the acquired product or service. In our example, the production worker returns to the job following the repair of the equipment.

With a VM philosophy, the buying team operates beyond the transaction—team members attempt to add value to the process. In our example, team members practice the Japanese method of kaizen or continuous improvement. As the contractor repairs the equipment, the production worker ponders, "How can I use the equipment more effectively to avoid breakdowns?" The purchasing manager seeks out and evaluates information on more reliable equipment and on alternative service vendors. The shop manager, in turn, examines the equipment in the context of overall production flow and proposes a preventive maintenance schedule and the redesign of parts of the manufacturing process. Lastly, the purchasing manager reduces costs by shifting to a long-term service contract.

Successful business market managers gain a deep understanding of the distribution and performance of buying roles within each customer firm. They use this knowledge to craft and disseminate customized promotional messages, as well as to gather intelligence. To begin with, they learn if the buying team is a nominal group in which members operate independently, or a formal group in which members meet face-to-face to make decisions. In our example, the buying team is a nominal group because members do not work together. Next, managers identify key players within a customer firm who perform these roles. These role assignments vary from firm to firm and within firms over time. For instance, a classic mistake for a sales representative is to call on a purchasing manager over a period of months, only to then learn that the shop manager ultimately makes the purchase decision.

Lastly, business market managers must learn whether all members of the buying team are aware of the total value of the supplier's offering. In certain instances, particularly when the buying team is a nominal group, individual members are only aware of the specific value elements that benefit their particular functional areas of the customer firm. In this case, one of the major promotional tasks confronting the business market manager will be to inform each buying team member how the offering benefits all other functional areas and the customer firm as a whole. In doing so, supplier managers not only increase the potency of their value proposition but also the likelihood they can gain a price premium. Professor Das Narayandas describes this task as "building the value stack."[42]

Buying Situations

Business market managers also study customer firm buying situations. The distribution and performance of team roles is often a function of purchase situations. Scholars have identified three recurring purchase situations: straight rebuy, modified rebuy, and new task. These three situations represent a "newness" continuum of the purchasing tasks customers encounter. We characterize the three purchase situations by the customer's knowledge of its functional and technical specifications. In a new task buying situation, the firm confronts a novel requirement. Managers do not know what the functional or technical specifications of the offering should be. With a VM philosophy, if the new task requires innovation, the firm charters a cross-functional team that uses techniques such as process reengineering to create "lean" procedures for purchasing the item.[43]

In a modified rebuy, the customer firm has had experience securing the product or service, but managers need to reevaluate alternatives. Perhaps, for instance, users are dissatisfied with the current supplier or product. Alternatively, managers know the functional specs but are uncertain as to what the technical specifications should be. To solve the problem, the firm assembles a quality circle to suggest a new product, vendor, or substitute materials.

In a straight rebuy situation, the company has considerable buying experience and requires little or no new information about the offering. Functional and technical specifications are well documented, and the buyer only needs to learn price and availability. As a solution, the firm reorders the item from a preferred vendor. With VM philosophy, the buying team also explores how the reorder process might be simplified, such as with an automated inventory replenishment system.

Buying Team Tasks

Today, buying teams perform both strategic and tactical tasks. Commodity procurement strategy (CPS) teams develop a comprehensive strategy for the acquisition of entire product or service categories, assemble and cultivate a supplier base for the category, and identify suppliers that can solve difficult technical problems related to the category. For example, Hewlett-Packard (HP) created CPS teams for each major category of its products and services. Team members come from R&D, manufacturing, quality assurance and control, and purchasing. They evaluate suppliers on the basis of such things as technology, quality, cost, responsiveness, and delivery. They also determine which supplier gets what proportion of HP's business, and they negotiate long-term supply contracts with these vendors.

Companies deploy a variety of buying teams to address tactical issues. Supplier certification teams help selected suppliers reach desired levels of quality, reduce costs, improve service, and increase delivery reliability. Specification teams select and then write appropriate functional, technical, and process specifications for goods and services to be acquired. Supplier performance evaluation teams monitor their activity and performance data and rate vendors.

Working with Suppliers and Across Functions

Business market managers integrate purchasing activities with those of suppliers and other functions to develop supply resources, improve existing offerings, and contribute to new offering realization.

Developing Supply Resources

Managers in diverse functional areas can assist with the performance of purchasing activities in several key ways. Based on their contacts and experience, they can help purchasing managers find and qualify new suppliers from around the world. Technical people from operations and R&D can work side by side with suppliers to improve vendor's capabilities. Often, customer firms even make financial investments in supplier firms to ensure the flow of materials and new technologies. Lastly, technical service personnel can provide consulting and training to strengthen supplier service.

Improving Existing Offerings

Progressive customer firms collaborate with suppliers to improve existing offerings. They conduct joint value or TCO assessments to find process improvements and materials substitutions. They determine the most economic lot-sizing for supplier production and establish long-term contracts for dedicated production lines to meet specific customer firm requirements. And, they rethink and reallocate tasks from supplier firm to customer firm, or vice versa. The following example from General Motors (GM) demonstrates how such a collaborative approach can streamline inbound logistics and materials handling and benefit both supplier and customer firms.

To improve its performance and lower costs, GM revamped the inbound logistics and materials handling of parts to its 26 assembly plants across the United States, Canada, and Mexico. Previously, decentralized purchasing, transportation, materials handling, and production personnel at each plant independently handled parts for their respective operations. This practice led to inefficiencies, backlogs, and cost overruns. GM called in long-time supplier Penske's Leaseway Auto Carriers to set up and operate a system to manage the inbound logistics and materials handling operations for each of GM's 26 plants. Now, Leaseway or subcontractors ship all parts directly to a Leaseway warehouse in Cleveland, where they are sorted by GM plant and then shipped out in a timely fashion via truck or air.

Counterintuitively, GM's outsourcing strategy has not resulted in layoffs and has improved the status of both purchasing and materials handling personnel. Relieved of the burdens and headaches associated with the management of inbound parts, these groups focus on building better cars. For instance, purchasing spends more time in parts supplier selection and relationship-building efforts. Materials handling personnel concurrently spend greater time planning outbound movements of cars. GM has seen the amount of paperwork decline as payments are consolidated. The bottom line has been lower costs and higher-quality cars.[44]

Contributing to New Offering Realization

Operations experts claim that about 80 percent of a product's or service's total costs are "locked in" prior to commercial production.[45] Once production begins, the costs associated with changing product or service specifications become extremely high. Firms intent on reducing their total costs carefully scrutinize the product design process. To make it more efficient, these firms partner with vendors through early supplier involvement (ESI) programs and include purchasing personnel in the design process via early purchasing involvement programs. Often, ESI programs entail joint value engineering projects to codevelop and codesign supplier components and materials. Box 3.4 relates Sun Microsystems' noteworthy use of an ESI program.[46]

Increasingly, firms are involving purchasing personnel in the new offering realization process as active members of cross-functional development teams. Pundits commonly refer to such initiatives as early purchasing involvement (EPI) programs. Researchers in Europe identified potential purchasing contributions to the process. Among the most important of these contributions are helping senior management craft corporate strategy by identifying the firm's core competencies, funneling new technologies from suppliers to appropriate managers within the firm, selecting leading-edge suppliers for partnerships and alliances, and recommending sourcing options.[47]

During the crafting of corporate strategy and design of supply networks, purchasing managers serve as technology "matchmakers" between the firm and its suppliers. Because such matchmaking requires technical discussions, firms are

BOX 3.4
Early Supplier Involvement in New Offering Realization at Sun Microsystems

Sun Microsystems' comprehensive early supplier involvement (ESI) programs, championed by its supply management group, have given it a competitive edge in the top-end computing workstation marketplace. To begin the initiative, Sun's vice president of supplier management wrote a letter to all Sun suppliers asking, "What is Sun doing that is driving up the cost of your product? What are we doing that is prohibiting your flexibility? Are we asking for too much 'Sunness' in our specifications? How can we work together to reduce our costs?" Based upon supplier responses, Sun took several actions. Most importantly, Sun began to involve suppliers as early as possible in the concept stage of new product development to help the firm write better specifications. As part of this effort, Sun invited key vendors to participate in a resident supplier program in which vendor representatives work in Sun factories directly with Sun counterparts. These representatives also develop product acquisition schedules, place purchase orders, and even do their own performance scorecards.

To ensure that Sun has early access to the latest and best technologies, Sun uses cross-functional commodity teams consisting of purchasing managers and engineers to evaluate the technology road maps of suppliers in such areas as memory, mass storage, displays, and integrated circuits. A technology road map charts the direction that innovations are expected to take over time and the position the firm hopes to have on it at any one point in time. Teams use the road maps to identify prospective suppliers as well as to encourage existing suppliers to migrate to new technologies. Perhaps more importantly, Sun uses the road maps to share technology breakthroughs with its vendors, to learn of gaps that must be filled, and as guidelines for the new product development process.

Taking ESI one step further, Sun created a Supplier Council composed of its top five suppliers. The council continues to work with Sun task forces in a major reengineering effort, called Business Process Simplification (BPS), to redesign the way Sun does its business with vendors. It has the goals of utilizing fewer suppliers, creating closer supplier relationships, outsourcing activities outside Sun's core competencies, and initiating more joint efforts with suppliers.

And the results of ESI? Sun has seen new product cycle time reduced dramatically, product delivery reliability and accuracy improved significantly, and time to volume shrunk considerably. Sun introduces new technology far more rapidly than many of its competitors. Suppliers, on the other hand, gain a greater share of Sun's business, reduced costs, and knowledge of new technologies.

Source: James Carbone, "Sun Shines by Taking Out Time," *Purchasing*, 19 September 1996, 34–45.

increasingly hiring engineers to work within the purchasing department. For instance, IBM assigns procurement development engineers to design teams and R&D labs. These engineers scour the market for sources of new technology and help IBM form alliances with competent new vendors.

When relationships with individual suppliers are to be forged, purchasing managers provide a "reality check" concerning part costs and the capabilities of potential vendors. For example, at AT&T, purchasing managers reside in R&D laboratories and participate on cross-functional design teams in the Cost-Effective Product Introduction (CEPI) program. For major parts and components, purchasing managers scrutinize the process, alert engineers when they are about to specify high-cost, long lead-time, and overly customized parts, and recommend standard parts as alternatives. They identify and advocate suppliers with proven records for reliable delivery, quality, and capacity utilization. AT&T says that CEPI has reduced development costs, cycle time, and time to volume.

During single projects, purchasing managers keep designers "grounded" in the nature of operating costs. At Cisco Systems, a leading supplier of switches and routers on the Internet, purchasing managers serve as watchdogs for expensive and overengineered parts, and provide detailed cost estimates that help designers better forecast the total costs and profitability of new products. Finally, in the area of non-technical service projects, purchasing managers serve as "catalysts." They take the lead in the service design process. Purchasing managers may even provide creative ideas behind the new service and help to map out procedures for its provision.

UNDERSTANDING THE PURCHASE DECISION PROCESS

In the final section of this chapter, we examine how firms secure products and services, technology, and knowledge from other organizations. With knowledge of the customer firm's purchasing process, business market managers are in a far better position to develop marketing strategies, sales presentations, and promotional efforts that can successfully inform and influence purchasing decisions. We start by discussing how supplier firms identify customer requirements as well as map activity and value cycles. Next, we use the BuyGrid Framework to describe the typical purchasing processes customers use. Finally, we investigate the procedures firms commonly use when evaluating supplier performance.

Understanding Customer Requirements and Preferences

Customer requirements and preferences serve as an essential guidepost for all business market management efforts. Over the years, scholars and consultants proposed a variety of frameworks and methods for surveying these guideposts. For example, Michael Porter outlined an approach that business market managers can use to first determine a customer's use criteria or specifications and then to rank them based upon their worth to that customer. He proposed that supplier managers organize use criteria into a 2×2 matrix. One dimension of the matrix is whether worth of the use criteria can be readily measured or is difficult to measure. The other dimension is whether the use criteria produce increased customer benefits or reduced the customer's total costs.[48]

Porter takes pains to point out that although a supplier can readily measure the worth of some use criteria, it may be difficult, if not impossible, to accurately measure the worth of others. When the worths of use criteria are difficult to measure, he recommends that firms investigate signaling criteria or those activities, attributes, promotions, and reputation of a supplier firm that indicate to a customer that the supplier's offering, in fact, delivers value.

As with Porter, Håkansson, Johanson, and Wootz suggest three sources of uncertainty that make it difficult for a customer firm to understand its own requirements and preferences. Need uncertainty refers to difficulties customers have in interpreting the exact nature and importance of goods and services that their firms require. For example, managers may have a tough time predicting how often a piece of machinery will break down and the severity of consequences. Market uncertainty reflects the buyer's inability to predict how many alternate suppliers will be available and what quality of goods and services will be forthcoming when a need arises. The fewer the suppliers offering high-quality solutions, the more the buyer will be willing to pay. Transaction uncertainty is inversely related to the customer's confidence that suppliers have easy-to-use procedures for doing business, processing orders accurately, and providing reliable and timely deliveries. Rather than ignore these uncertainties, Håkansson, Johanson, and Wootz encourage managers to evaluate them thoroughly when investigating customer requirements and preferences.[49]

Triangulate on Customer Requirements

Rather than relying on one technique to understand customer requirements and assess the worth of market offerings, progressive business market managers use multiple methods concurrently. In effect, they triangulate on the customer's actual requirements. In doing so, they realize that in some instances customer personnel have a better understanding of their own requirements, while in others the supplier has superior knowledge. Customers use the product or service and are often in a better position to define their requirements in terms of functionality and performance in specific applications. They have a better grasp of their firm's capabilities. At the same time, suppliers often know more about the offering's technology and can better match solutions to problems customers don't anticipate.

To triangulate on customer requirements, business market managers think in terms of a 2×2 **requirements matrix** where the rows and columns capture the extent of knowledge that the supplier firm and customer firm possess, respectively.[50] Then they conceive and initiate various research projects designed to yield insights from the perspective of each cell. When they complete the projects, business market managers aggregate findings into one comprehensive profile of customer requirements. In Figure 3.9 and Box 3.5, we present an illustration and explanation of the requirements matrix the customer support service group of Microsoft Corporation has designed and uses to triangulate on customer service requirements.

Map Customer Activity and Value Cycles

Some managers assume that the value of an offering remains stable over its lifetime. For some products and services, particularly those that are time-sensitive, reusable, or acutely sensitive to the market forces of supply and demand, worth may actually ebb and flow. This fluctuation is due in part to the fact that benefits and costs accrue in different amounts and at distinct points in time in concert with the offering's activity cycle. The **activity cycle** refers to the steps required to produce, productively use, recycle, and dispose an offering while the **value cycle** captures the changes in worth across these steps.[51]

Business market managers can map both cycles with the tools of business process engineering and value assessment. It is critical that they understand the

Figure 3.9 Microsoft Customer Support Requirements Matrix

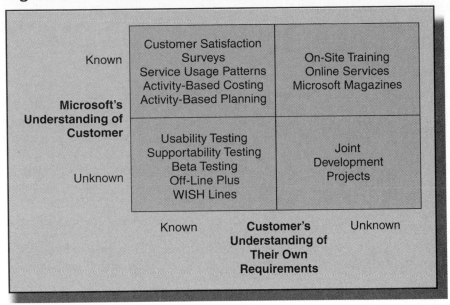

BOX 3.5
Microsoft Triangulates on Customer Support Services Requirements

Long ago, managers of the support services group of the Microsoft Corporation realized the complexity of their customer firms' information systems and the diversity of their technical support service requirements. Rather than using one method for probing customer needs, Microsoft managers devised the requirements matrix in Figure 3.9 and implemented a variety of ongoing research activities. The columns in the matrix capture requirements that the customer firm either knows or doesn't know. The rows, on the other hand, represent customer needs that Microsoft either knows or doesn't know.

To better understand requirements that are known to both firms, Microsoft managers periodically conduct customer satisfaction surveys and monitor service usage patterns, among other things. To learn about requirements customers are aware of but Microsoft isn't, managers test new software at customer locations through usability and beta testing. They use the Internet and special telephone numbers, Off-Line Plus and WISH Lines respectively, to gather suggestions on service improvements.

Microsoft educates customers to make them aware of the benefits of using Microsoft products and services. They use on-site training, online services, and several Microsoft magazines. In the final cell of the matrix, neither the customer nor Microsoft has a clear understanding of certain customer requirements. To come to grips with such needs, Microsoft initiates joint development projects with select customers. The partners then draw upon the customer's understanding of applications and Microsoft's knowledge of technology. Microsoft managers find that even though none of the techniques in the matrix provide full information, taken together they furnish a sharper image of the complete array of customer requirements.

activity and value cycles for their offerings in that these cycles may reveal sources for new and profitable, augmenting products and services. Figure 3.10 contains an illustration of the activity cycle for industrial containers. In Box 3.6, we discuss how Greif Incorporated used an understanding of the activity and value cycles to create a new service: trip leasing.

Learning the Customer's Purchase Process

Many companies follow a structured and orderly process for acquiring goods. Scholars summarized this process in the **BuyGrid Framework**. The purchase decision process begins with problem recognition, when someone within the firm identifies an opportunity or threat to address. For example, a production worker notices that stocks of a repair part are running low and need to be reordered. At this point, the employee provides a written general need description. This statement clearly identifies the problem or opportunity at hand and suggests a general solution. A purchasing manager then translates this need into product specifications. For instance, the purchasing manager takes the production worker's description of the repair part needed and describes it in terms of functional and technical specifications.[52]

Once specifications are known, purchasing managers conduct a supplier search to identify potential sources of the repair part. They begin with the firm's certified

Figure 3.10 Activity Cycle for Industrial Containers

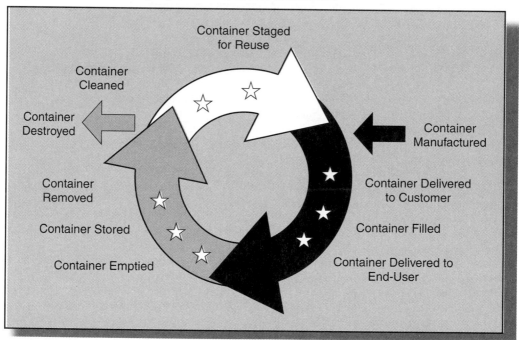

Source: Adapted from Gregory F. Wall, "Creating Customer Value: Greif Brothers Packaging Services," Presentation at Institute for Study of Business Markets Conference (January 2000).

BOX 3.6
Greif Incorporated Introduces Trip Leasing

With annual sales of $1.5 billion, Greif Incorporated is a leading supplier of total packaging solutions including shipping containers, corrugated products, and packaging-operations management, as well as inventory and logistics services. During the mid-1990s, Greif managers recognized that the firm's principal products—steel and plastic drums and intermediate bulk containers—had reached commodity status as price competition intensified. To regain profitable growth, managers decided to reposition the firm as a value-added service provider.

They began the process by mapping the activity cycle for industrial containers (see Figure 3.10). Managers soon recognized that containers had a distinctive value cycle for customer firms. When newly manufactured drums are delivered to the customer's facility, they have potential value yet they incur not only opportunity costs in that they are unused assets but also acquisition and storage expenses. As the drums are filled, transported, and stored, they yield significant realized value to the customer firm. Once the contents are removed, the drums have significant negative value. At a minimum, they must be removed and placed in a storage yard, consuming valuable space. If they are cleaned, recycled, or disposed the customer firm has significant expenses. Disposal also entails significant risks in that the customer firm may be held accountable for any drums

that leach hazardous chemical residues into the ground at landfills. Failure to comply with related environmental protection rules and regulations can bring costly fines and lawsuits. Lastly, once drums have been cleaned and reconditioned, they again have potential value. Reviewing the activity and value cycles, Greif managers came to an important conclusion: customer firms don't really want to buy the drums, they just want to transport materials from point a to point b.

With significant input from customer firms, managers developed a comprehensive value model encompassing each step in the activity cycle. They discovered a tremendous opportunity to profitably add value beyond the supply of newly manufactured drums. In turn, managers created a set of value-added services including drum filling, container leasing, on-site warehousing, and inventory management, among others. Perhaps more importantly, they hit on the idea of trip leasing. Rather than purchasing drums, customer firms would lease them for a trip. Greif would serve as a system integrator, assembling an end-to-end solution. In doing so, Greif would perform some of the tasks and outsource the rest to partner firms. Today, Greif gives customer firms a choice. They can buy drums or they can contract for some or all of the services associated with a trip lease. In this way, Greif converted a low-margin commodity into a profitable total solution.

Sources: Adapted from Gregory F. Wall, "Creating Customer Value: Greif Brothers Packaging Services," presentation at Institute for Study of Business Markets Conference (January 2000); *Greif Incorporated 2001 Annual Report* (Delaware, OH: Greif Incorporated, 2002); and Greif Incorporated [Internet] (Delaware, OH: Greif Incorporated, September 10, 2002), available at *http://www.greif.com*.

---

vendor list, then seek other vendors if necessary. The next stage is proposal solicitation. Purchasing managers send out written requests for quotations (RFQs) to certified vendors. With returned RFQs in hand, purchasing managers go through the supplier selection process. Depending on the purchasing orientation of the firm, purchasing managers select the supplier or suppliers that best meet company requirements. In the order-routine specification phase, the purchasing manager and vendor set up procedures for processing invoices and paperwork and receiving deliveries. Finally, the purchasing manager conducts a formal performance review of the supplier.

The BuyGrid Framework implies that the purchase process will vary across purchase situations. In a straight rebuy, a customer that has a track record of purchasing a given product from a given vendor can avoid many steps. In the new task situation, on the other hand, the customer has no experience purchasing the good or service. As a result, the customer must go through the entire process. We argue that a third dimension should be added to the BuyGrid Framework—ongoing versus new working relationships. In an ongoing relationship as with a straight rebuy situation, the customer may be able to eliminate some of the steps from the process. In a new relationship, the customer may have to go through a lengthier process.

One question frequently arises: "Is the purchasing process for services the same as that for physical products?" According to a market research study the Institute for Supply Management (formerly the National Association of Purchasing Managers) conducted in the United States among its members, the processes of purchasing a product and service are fairly similar. Only three significant differences stood out in the ISM study. First, managers have a more difficult time writing specifications for services because of their ambiguous nature. As a result, purchasing managers report encountering problems when it comes to acquiring services and evaluating vendor performance. Second, firms often have a tough time forecasting when they will need services. For example, a firm may not be able to predict precisely when it will need legal services and the nature of those legal services. Third, companies do not have sophisticated planning systems for services, such as ERP, MRP I, and MRP II. Scholars and practitioners have yet to develop them.[53]

Evaluating Supplier Performance

To make more productive use of external resources, firms are spending more time and effort evaluating supplier performance. Best practice companies are employing balanced scorecards, which assess performance using a set of pertinent measures. Furthermore, they are turning to quantifiable performance measures whenever possible. However, as the Dilbert cartoon in Figure 3.11 illustrates, although supplier evaluations may be quantitative, the numbers come from subjective judgements that can be influenced by social or personal considerations. Supplier performance evaluation systems tend to vary by purchasing orientation.[54]

Reviewing Price, Quality, and Availability

Companies that subscribe to the buying orientation evaluate suppliers largely in terms of realized price, quality, and availability. They draw on four types of analyses. In a subjective categorical summary, purchasing managers examine suppliers on several dimensions such as price, quality, and availability. To do so, they construct a survey instrument that features several questions for each performance category. The questionnaire is subjective in that respondents are asked to rate a given supplier on a scale ranging from poor to excellent. Managers from relevant functional areas within

Figure 3.11 DILBERT

DILBERT reprinted by permission of United Feature Syndicates, Inc.

the firm complete the questionnaire. Buyers report results for each supplier in the form of averages for each question, then compare category performance across suppliers and across time periods.

Other firms summarize category results in the form of a single subjective index. For example, if managers believe that all the questions are of equal value, they might simply report the grand mean as an overall index of supplier performance. On the other hand, if managers believe that certain categories are more important than others, they might report a weighted grand mean. Thus, if they felt price represents 50 percent of performance, quality 30 percent, and availability 20 percent, they would multiply a supplier's price, quality, and availability ratings by .5, .3, and .2, respectively.

To be less judgmental, some firms replace the subjective questions with operational measures. However, managers still exercise considerable discretion in selecting categories. These are reported as objective categorical summaries. As an illustration, purchasing managers might subtract actual purchase price paid for a supplier's product this period from the purchase price paid last period and report it as an indicator of a supplier's performance on price. Concurrently, the firm might track the number of defective products delivered or the percentage rejection rate on products delivered as a measure of a supplier's quality. Managers might record reliability as percent of orders delivered on time or delivery accuracy in terms of the percent of items ordered that were delivered.

To convert these items into a single objective index of performance, managers would allocate a certain number of points for meeting acceptable performance standards for each price, quality, and availability measure; calculate; and then report the grand mean as the supplier's performance index. Alternatively, if managers believe that certain criteria are worth more than others, they can assign weights to each category and report the weighted grand mean. Even in more objective performance evaluations, managers exercise some judgment by choosing categories and weights.

Scrutinizing Total Costs

As firms migrate to a procurement orientation, they create performance measures that focus on TCO. Two cost-based supplier evaluation approaches have emerged. In the first approach, companies review the costs associated with supplier nonperformance. For example, Monczka and Trecha created a supplier performance index (SPI) that recognizes cost attributed to supplier nonperformance on delivery, materials quality, and prices.[55] The SPI formula is

$$SPI_{(item)} = \frac{\text{extended purchase price} + \text{nonperformance costs}}{\text{extended purchase price}}$$

Extended purchase price represents the net price the customer firm pays after deducting discounts and allowances. Nonperformance costs are additional costs the customer firm incurs to correct mistakes the supplier made during a relevant time period, such as a year. Such costs might cover additional quality inspections, shipping defective parts back to the vendor, production downtime attributed to stockouts, and emergency shipments, among others.

Monczka and Trecha recommend that firms create and monitor SPI indices for each category of item purchased from each competing supplier. Procurement managers then use the resulting indices as indicators of the quality of alternate vendors. Customer firms can also multiply the resulting indices by the respective unit prices paid to each supplier to determine the costs per unit. They argue that using costs per unit rather than unit price is a superior means of comparing vendors.

In the second approach, customers audit and then calculate the TCO for a product or service during a prespecified time period. Procurement managers use results to determine how much each supplier has reduced the firm's total costs.

Tracking Supplier Value

Contrary to what many believe, supply managers conduct the most thorough and demanding evaluations of suppliers. Why? Because they expect more from suppliers. They also have fewer suppliers to review. These managers gather performance data from the techniques described previously. However, they take their analyses further. Utilizing the tools of value assessment and our fundamental value equation, supply managers evaluate vendors in terms of the value each contributes to their firm's market offering. Specifically, they estimate the benefits, total costs, and prices paid to each vendor. Some estimates will be qualitative in nature, such as the extent to which suppliers contributed to innovations achieved by the customer firm.

Consistent with the supply management orientation, these firms supplement direct vendor evaluations with studies of their own customers' satisfaction. Supply managers draw upon methods of gaining customer feedback we described in Chapter 2. The goal is to assess the impact of supplier contributions on end-user satisfaction. In this way, supply managers can better focus or redirect the efforts of the entire supply network toward the delivery of superior value to end-users.

SUMMARY

In this chapter, we examined how firms secure resources from the external environment and integrate them with their internal operations. Understanding firms as customers is the process of learning how companies rely on a network of suppliers to add value to their offerings, integrate purchasing activities with those of other functional areas and outside firms, and make purchase decisions. Business market managers must be familiar with the ways that both customer firms and their own firms handle this process. By understanding firms as customers, the business market manager is better able to craft responsive market strategies. By better comprehending one's own firm, the business market manager is in a better position to coordinate cross-functional efforts designed to deliver greater value to customers.

We began the chapter by exploring three purchasing orientations firms use in business markets. With a buying orientation, firms strive to obtain the best deal in terms of price, quality, and availability; maximize power over suppliers; and avoid risks wherever possible. As firms become more strategic, they tend to adopt a procurement orientation. Procurement managers work to improve quality of goods and services acquired, reduce TCO, and coordinate and integrate the activities of diverse functions not only within the firm but also with suppliers. Best practice organizations adhere to a value-based supply management orientation. Supply managers are actively involved with the integration and coordination of the value-adding activities not only among the diverse functions of their own firms but also with their customers, customers' customers, suppliers, and suppliers' suppliers.

We also looked at the ways progressive firms are working to integrate purchasing activities with those of other functions. Value management is an overarching framework for doing so. Firms that adopt a value management philosophy often turn to cross-functional groups such as buying teams to acquire goods and services, certify vendors, and conduct value analyses.

We concluded this chapter by reviewing the purchase decision process. First, we examined how managers gain a better understanding of the requirements and preferences of customer firms. Next, we described the purchase decision process using the BuyGrid Framework. The eight steps in the process range from problem identification to performance evaluation. Firms vary the extent of these activities as a function of the buying situation. Finally, we discussed alternate methods of supplier performance evaluation. We illustrated how firms rely upon a balanced scorecard of measures to more accurately assess supplier performance.

ENDNOTES

1. We chose buying, procurement, and supply management in order to be consistent with the work of Donald W. Dobler and David N. Burt, *Purchasing and Supply Management*, 6th ed. (New York: McGraw-Hill, 1996), xix.

2. We use the phrase *value network* instead of *value chain* to capture the diversity of relationships in business markets. For example, suppliers may buy from customers, firms may cooperate with direct competitors, and

resellers may perform manufacturing operations.

3. Elliott R. Ross, "Making Money with Proactive Pricing," *Harvard Business Review* (November–December 1984): 148.

4. Ross, "Making Money," 305.

5. Dobler and Burt, *Purchasing and Supply Management*, 315; and Richard G. Newman and John M. McKeller, "Target Pricing—A Challenge for Purchasing," *International Journal of Purchasing and Materials Management* (Summer 1995): 16.

6. Anne T. Coughlin, Erin Anderson, Louis W. Stern, and Adel I. El-Ansary, *Marketing Channels*, 6th ed. (Upper Saddle River, NJ: Prentice Hall, 2001).

7. Niren Vyas and Arch G. Woodside, "An Inductive Model of Industrial Supplier Choice Processes," *Journal of Marketing Research* (Winter 1984): 30–45.

8. Newman and McKeller, "Target Pricing," 14.

9. David Ford, et al., *The Business Marketing Course* (Chichester, UK: John Wiley & Sons, Ltd., 2002); Rob Rosenthal and Richard Villars, "The Online Sourcing Advantage," *IDC White Paper* (Framingham, MA: IDC, 2002).

10. Pierre Mitchell, "E-Sourcing Tools Can Improve Strategic Sourcing Processes, but Proceed with Caution," *Inside Supply Management* (March 2002): 46–52; Sari Kalin, "Reversal of Fortune," *Darwin* (February 2002): 12; Robert E. Hall, *Digital Dealing* (New York: W. W. Norton & Company, 2001); "GE GSN, The World's Largest Private Supplier Marketplace," GE Global eXchange Services (Gaithersburg, MD: GXS, cited August 2002), available at *http://www.gxs.com*.

11. Hall, *Digital Dealing*, 71.

12. Arjan J. van Weele, *Purchasing and Supply Chain Management* (London: Thompson Learning, 2002).

13. Dobler and Burt, *Purchasing and Supply Management*, 24–30.

14. J.Y.F. Wynstra, "Purchasing's Development Role, The Internal and External Integration of Purchasing in Technological Development Processes," *Intermediate Report I, EUT/Bdk/73* (Eindhoven, The Netherlands: Eindhoven University of Technology Faculty of Technology Management & Uppsala University Department of Business Studies, 1995), 5.

15. Dobler and Burt, *Purchasing and Supply Management*, 182.

16. Dobler and Burt, *Purchasing and Supply Management*, 452.

17. *Total cost* is an alternate term for the life cycle cost of a product or service.

18. Carolyn Pye Sostrom, "Strategic Cost Management Programs: What's the Plan to Follow?" *Purchasing Today* (September 2000): 42; and Marc Wouters, James C. Anderson, and Finn Wynstra, "The Adoption of Total Cost of Ownership for Sourcing Decisions—A Structural Equations Analysis," *Eindhoven University of Technology Working Paper* (August 2002): 3.

19. Susan Kuchinskas, "One-to-(N)one?" *Business 2.0* (September 12, 2000): 141–148.

20. Richard J. Palmer, "Survey Shows How Purchase Cards Save Time, Money," *Journal of Accountancy* (May 2000): 18–19.

21. Hall, *Digital Dealing*, 103; and Eric Young, "Web Marketplaces that Really Work," *Fortune* (Winter 2002): 78–84.

22. Philip B. Schary and Tage Skjøtt-Larsen, *Managing the Global Supply Chain* (Copenhagen: Copenhagen Business School Press, 2001).

23. James A. Narus and James C. Anderson, "Using Teams to Manage Collaborative Relationships in Business Markets," *Journal of Business-to-Business Marketing*, 3 (1995): 26.

24. Dobler and Burt, *Purchasing and Supply Management*, 179; and van Weele, *Purchasing and Supply Chain Management*, 192.

25. Virginia T. Freeman and Joseph L. Cavinato, "Fitting Purchasing to the Strategic Firm: Frameworks, Processes, and Values," *Journal of Purchasing and Materials Management* (Winter 1990): 9; and Peter Hines, "Purchasing for Lean Production: The New Strategic Agenda," *International Journal of Purchasing and Materials Management* (January 1996): 6–7.

26. Wynstra, "Purchasing's Development Role," II–XI; and James Brian Quinn and Frederick G. Hilmer, "Strategic Outsourcing," *Sloan Management Review* (Summer 1994): 43.

27. Ravi Venkatesan, "Strategic Outsourcing: To Make or Not to Make," *Harvard Business Review* (November–December 1992): 98; and Quinn and Hilmer, "Strategic Outsourcing," *Sloan Management Review*, 45–47.

28. James P. Womack and Daniel T. Jones, "From Lean Production to the Lean Enterprise," *Harvard Business Review* (March–April 1994): 94.

29. Michael Hammer and James Champy, *Reengineering the Corporation* (New York: HarperBusiness, 1993).

30. Louis P. Bucklin, "Postponement, Speculation, and the Structure of Distribution Channels," *Journal of Marketing Research* (February 1965): 26–31.

31. Schary and Skjøtt-Larsen, *Managing the Global Supply Chain*, 69.

32. Supply network models are also referred to as supply chain models.

33. Candace Arai Yano, "IIE Transactions Special Issue on Planning and Coordination of Supply Chains with Outsourcing," *IIE Transactions* (August 2002): IV–VIII.

34. Other popular supply network models include order-to-delivery, locate-to-order, and build-only-against-customer-order.

35. Adam Smith, *An Inquiry into the Nature and Causes of The Wealth of Nations* (1776) appearing in *Masterworks of Economics*, Volume 1 (New York: McGraw-Hill Book Company, 1946): 74.

36. Philip Kotler, *Marketing Management*, 11th ed. (Upper Saddle River, NJ: Prentice Hall, 2003): 482.

37. Peter Kraljic, "Purchasing Must Become Supply Management," *Harvard Business Review* (September–October 1983): 109–117; Schary and Skjøtt-Larsen, *Managing the Global Supply Chain*, 193–199; M. Bensaou, "Portfolios of Buyer-Supplier Relationships," *Sloan Management Review* (Summer 1999): 35–44; and Jan B. Heide, "Interorganizational Governance in Marketing Channels," *Journal of Marketing* (January 1994): 71–85.

38. van Weele, *Purchasing and Supply Chain Management*, 145–149; and Cees J. Gelderman and Arjan J. van Weele, "Strategic Direction Through Purchasing Portfolio Management: A Case Study," *Journal of Supply Chain Management* (Spring 2002): 30–37.

39. Much of this discussion is based on Commission of the European Communities Directorate General XIII Telecommunications, Information Market and Exploitation of Research, *Value Management Handbook* (Luxembourg: Office for Official Publications of the European Communities, 1995).

40. Lawrence D. Miles, *Techniques of Value Analysis and Engineering*, 3rd ed. (Washington, DC: Lawrence D. Miles Value Foundation, 1989).

41. Wesley J. Johnston and Thomas V. Bonoma, "The Buying Center: Structure and Interaction Patterns," *Journal of Marketing* (Summer 1981): 143–156. Although the term *buying center* has been widely used in academic literature, we prefer to use the word *team*, which has wider acceptance among practitioners. Furthermore, we believe that *team* is more appropriate because it conveys the key characteristics of a common orientation, mutual goals, and coordinated efforts. Finally, we use the word *buying* because of its widespread usage in this context, rather than to refer to any particular purchasing orientation.

42. Das Naryandas, *Note on Customer Management* (Boston, MA: Harvard Business School Publishing, 2002).

43. Patrick J. Robinson and Charles W. Faris with Yoram Wind, *Industrial Buying and Creative Marketing* (Boston, MA: Allyn and Bacon, 1967).

44. Tim Minahan, "GM Looks Outside to Fuel Internal JIT Initiatives," *Purchasing*, 5 September 1996, 40–41.

45. van Weele, *Purchasing and Supply Chain Management*, 186.

46. James Carbone, "Sun Shines by Taking Out Time," *Purchasing*, 19 September 1996, 34–45.

47. Company examples in this section come from James Carbone, "A Buyer's Place Is in the Design Lab," *Purchasing*, 7 March 1996, 59–63; and Wynstra, "Purchasing's Development Role," 46–62.

48. Michael E. Porter, *Competitive Advantage* (New York: The Free Press, 1985), 146–150.

49. Håkan Håkansson, Jan Johanson, and Bart Wootz, "Influence Tactics in Buyer-Seller

Processes," *Industrial Marketing Management*, 4 (1976): 319–332.

50. We attribute the design of this 2×2 matrix to Ron Kegarise, formerly of the ALCOA Corporation.

51. Mohanbir Sawhney, "Services-Led Growth Strategies for Difficult Economic Times," presented at Institute for the Study of Business Markets Conference (August 2002); and Robert G. Cross, *Revenue Management* (New York: Broadway Books, 1997).

52. Robinson and Faris, *Industrial Buying*, 14.

53. Carolyn Pye, "An Open Mike for Service-Industry Purchasers," *Purchasing Today* (December 1996): 24–26.

54. Robert S. Kaplan and David P. Norton, "The Balanced Scorecard—Measures that Drive Performance," *Harvard Business Review* (January–February 1992): 71–79.

55. Robert M. Monczka, Robert B. Handfield, and Robert J. Trent, *Purchasing and Supply Chain Management* (Cincinnati, OH: South-Western College Publishing, 2001); and Robert M. Monczka and Steven J. Trecha, "Cost-Based Supplier Performance Evaluation," *Journal of Purchasing and Materials Management* (Spring 1988): 2–7.

Chapter 4

Crafting Market Strategy

OVERVIEW

*T*he business market processes of market sensing and understanding firms as customers provide supplier managers with an understanding of what particular market segments and customer firms value. These managers understand that the variation in requirements and preferences across market segments and customer firms means their firm will not be able to serve all segments and customers equally well. In the last business market process for understanding value—crafting market strategy—supplier managers integrate their market and customer firm knowledge with an understanding of their firm's resources to make decisions about where and how to create and deliver value.

Crafting market strategy is the process of studying how to exploit a firm's resources to achieve short-term and long-term marketplace success, deciding on a course of action to pursue, and flexibly updating it as learning occurs during implementation. Studying how to exploit a firm's resources draws on market sensing and understanding customer firms, yet involves more than just analysis. Studying also means contemplating the information and knowledge the firm generates through market sensing and understanding firms as customers, and creatively thinking through its implications. Crafting market strategy is also more than simply making a plan and following it. It recognizes real-world complexity and the interplay between **deliberate strategy**, where the firm decides on a course of action to pursue, and **emergent strategy**, where marketplace activities have a pattern to them that the firm recognizes and acts upon in a coordinated way.[1]

Crafting market strategy requires significant participation from many functional areas besides marketing to decide what market segments and customer firms to pursue and how to deliver superior value to them. In an article titled, "What the Hell Is 'Market Oriented'?" Shapiro stresses that a firm's most important strategic decision is to choose its relatively important customers. He also stresses that collaboration among the firm's various functions is essential when pinpointing the market segments and customers that the firm will target.[2]

Because business market management regards value as its cornerstone, crafting market strategy is about understanding how the firm can be meaningfully different in ways that targeted market segments and customer firms value. This task requires understanding what the firm does, or is capable of doing, that would fulfill the requirements and preferences of targeted market segments and customer firms in a superior way—that is, better than the customer firms themselves or the supplier firm's competitors could do. At the same time, the firm must understand what it needs to do now to put itself in position to have market success in the foreseeable future. What resources will the firm have to invest in within and across its constituent functional areas to be able to deliver superior value over the long term?

We portray the process of crafting market strategy in Figure 4.1. This chapter parallels the flow of Figure 4.1.[3] We begin by considering business strategy as the context for market strategy. The firm first understands what resources it has, and how it can best exploit them in one or more fundamental value-based business strategies. As we will see, the delineation between business strategy and market strategy has

Figure 4.1 Crafting Market Strategy

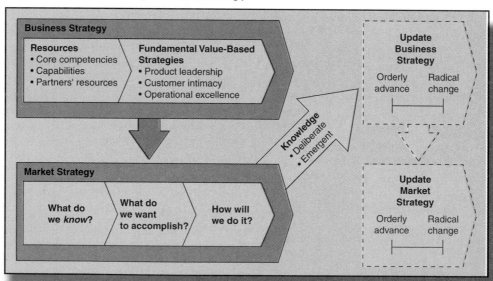

blurred somewhat. We next consider how the firm plans its market strategy. We organize our discussion of market strategy around three fundamental questions that firms must meaningfully answer. Planning the market strategy and implementing it provide the firm with gains in deliberate as well as emergent knowledge. The firm uses this knowledge to update its business and market strategies. Although business strategy often is seen as setting the constraints for market strategy, so too should market strategy inform and significantly influence business strategy. The nature of the changes in the updated strategies can range from orderly advances to radical change.

BUSINESS STRATEGY AS THE CONTEXT FOR MARKET STRATEGY

Strategy is written about more than any other topic in management practice. Advocates tout various prescriptive approaches for senior management to embrace. These approaches range from strategy as something that management designs and deliberately pursues to strategy as rapid learning and adapting from mistakes, experiments, and chance happenings in the marketplace.[4] Some strategy thinkers contend that senior management needs to move beyond strategy to defining an engaging purpose for the firm that workers will find fulfillment in accomplishing. One strategy expert even concludes that "strategic thinking is a necessary but overrated element of business success."[5]

In an article titled "What Is Strategy?" Porter contends that many firms fail to distinguish between operational effectiveness and strategy. **Operational effectiveness** "means performing similar activities *better* than rivals perform them." Firms that unwittingly pursue operational effectiveness as strategy find themselves in a continual race against competitors to extend the productivity frontier, with the differences among firms narrowing rapidly. Benchmarking each other's activities and the same set of best practice firms outside the industry, these firms become undifferentiated in the marketplace. In contrast, Porter says **strategy** "is the creation of a unique and valuable position, involving a different set of activities." **Strategic positioning** "means performing *different* activities from rivals' or performing similar activities in *different ways*." Significantly, strategy is about pursuing a course of action different from competitors and providing superior value to particular market segments. It is about making choices of what to do, and perhaps more importantly, what the firm will *not* do. Strategy is about putting together activities that generate superior value in complementary or synergistic ways. Because a strategic position is a fundamental course of action that a firm commits itself to pursuing, Porter contends that it should provide a competitive advantage for at least 10 years.[6]

We can think of business strategy as the overarching strategy that brings together sourcing strategy, technology strategy, and market strategy in ways that reinforce one another. **Sourcing strategy**, which we discussed in Chapter 3, specifies what the firm should acquire from others and what it will produce itself. **Technology strategy**, which we discuss further in Chapter 6, concerns the design knowledge and process know-how that transforms inputs to outputs of greater value. Business strategy provides the context for a dialogue among these constituent strategies, with the intent of harmonizing them. Business strategy influences each of them and is itself influenced by each of them. Further, the distinction between business strategy, or simply strategy, and market strategy has blurred somewhat. As an example, consider this statement by Porter: "Deciding which target group of customers, varieties, and needs the company should serve is fundamental to developing a strategy."[7]

We focus our discussion on business strategy as it relates to business market management, which views the firm as a value-generating enterprise. Resources provide the capacity to produce offerings that fulfill particular market requirements and preferences in a superior way, thereby creating value. Consequently, we take a resource-based view of the firm, and then discuss some fundamental value-based strategies. We conclude by examining some alternative perspectives on strategy making.

A Resource-Based View of the Firm

The resource-based view of the firm "sees companies as very different collections of physical and intangible assets and capabilities. No two companies are alike because no two companies have had the same set of experiences, acquired the same assets and skills, or built the same organizational cultures."[8] As discussed in Chapter 1, **resources** are anything that firms (as collective actors) explicitly value, such as technical know-how, equipment, personnel, or capital, that can generate greater value for themselves and others. The resource-based view combines and builds upon the internal perspective of the firm, associated with concepts like core competencies and capabilities, and the external perspective of the firm, associated with Porter's five-forces framework of industry analysis and more recent work on market-based assets.[9]

Resources are the building blocks for strategy. To be a source of competitive advantage, a resource must pass five external market tests of its value. The first test is *inimitability*, which is how difficult the resource is to copy or the length of time it will take for a competitor to replicate the resource. The second test is *durability*, which is how long a resource will last in providing value before it is overtaken by innovation either within the industry or outside of it. The third test is *appropriability*, which is the extent to which other firms or individuals can capture the value that the resource creates. The fourth test is *substitutability*, which is the ability of a different resource to provide similar functionality or performance at the same or lower cost. The fifth test is *competitive superiority*, which refers to a market assessment of how a resource compares to those of the firm's competitors. Management applies these tests to resources using empirical assessments in the marketplace, such as customer value assessment.[10]

Core competencies and capabilities are resources that are complementary building blocks of a value-generating strategy that provides competitive advantage. Brands represent a special resource through which suppliers can gain competitive advantage. Finally, the firm need not own all of the resources it requires to actualize its strategy, though. It may decide instead to engage those resources through alliances with partner firms.

Core Competencies

A **core competence** is "a complex harmonization of individual technologies and production skills."[11] As an example, 3M Company has core competencies in substrates, coatings, and adhesives that it has brought together in distinct ways to create a number of successful businesses. How can a firm sort out what are its core competencies?

> At least three tests can be applied to identify core competencies in a company. First, a core competence provides a potential access to a wide variety of markets. . . . Second, a core competence should make a significant contribution to the perceived customer benefits of the end-product. . . . Finally, a core competence should be difficult for competitors to imitate.[12]

Notice that these tests partly overlap those for resources. Reflecting the differences, though, some strategy thinkers draw a distinction between a core competence as something that the firm does particularly well and a **distinctive competence**, which is something that the firm does better than its competitors.[13]

Another strategy thinker, Peter Drucker, recommends that to measure and manage core competencies, a firm should carefully track its own and competitors' performances, looking particularly for unexpected successes and unexpected poor performances. He believes that these are revealing of what the market regards as core competencies in the firms, and changing market perceptions of them. Finally, he contends that innovation is one core competence that every organization must have, and that to appraise this, a business should study the record of innovation in its entire field during a given period.[14]

Capabilities

A **capability** is "a set of business processes strategically understood."[15] Product replenishment at Wal-Mart is an example of a capability, which closely coordinates business processes of Wal-Mart and its strategic suppliers to provide superior inventory turns. Although some strategy thinkers use the terms *core competencies* and *capabilities* interchangeably, others regard them as useful complements:

> Both concepts emphasize "behavioral" aspects of strategy in contrast to the traditional structural model. But whereas core competence emphasizes technological and production expertise at specific points along the value chain, capabilities are more broadly based, encompassing the entire value chain. In this respect, capabilities are visible to the customer in a way that core competencies rarely are.[16]

Day regards capabilities as "complex bundles of skills and collective learning, exercised through organizational processes, that ensure superior coordination of functional activities."[17] He recognizes that firms have numerous capabilities, not all of which they perform well, and uses **distinctive capabilities** to mean those the firm surpasses its competitors in performing. "The most defensible test of the distinctiveness of a capability is whether it makes a disproportionate contribution to the provision of superior customer value—as defined from the customer's perspective—or permits the business to deliver value to customers in an appreciably more cost-effective way."[18] He contends that market-driven organizations characteristically excel at *market sensing, customer linking*, and *channel bonding* capabilities. We considered market sensing as a business market process in Chapter 2. Customer linking refers to building and sustaining collaborative relations with customers, which we consider in detail in Chapter 10. *Channel bonding* refers to building and sustaining partnerships with resellers, which we consider in detail in Chapter 9.

Brands as Resources

Brands and brand building are concepts that are of growing interest and significance in business markets. A **brand** is a means of identifying a particular supplier and its market offerings as well as differentiating them from other suppliers and their offerings. To accomplish this, a brand draws on visual and verbal elements such as a name, logo, symbol, design, packaging, slogan, or some combination of these. A brand serves as a shorthand descriptor of the technical, economic, service, and social benefits that a particular supplier's market offering delivers to targeted market segments and customer firms.[19]

In business markets, brand elements may have no inherent meaning; instead, they become endowed with meaning through the performance of the supplier and its market offering over time. For example, at DuPont Company, brand names most often are generated as two-syllable, nonsense words, which are pronounceable. Well-known examples are Dacron®, Teflon®, Lycra®, and Kevlar®. Through their association with offerings that consistently deliver superior functionality and performance, brand elements such as brand names become a valuable resource themselves for suppliers.

Brand equity is a concept that is meant to capture the value of a brand and refers to how customers regard a brand relative to offerings of other competing suppliers (or an offering of a unnamed supplier), based on those customers' knowledge from experience with and learning about the brand. Brand equity is reflected in the following kinds of preferential actions or responses of present or prospective customers:

- Greater willingness to sample or trial the offering
- Reduction in time to close the sale of the offering
- Greater likelihood of purchasing the offering
- Willingness to award a larger share of purchase requirement
- Willingness to pay a higher price
- Greater unwillingness to switch to competitor offerings after price increases
- Less willingness to sample or trial competitor offerings

Suppliers build brand equity for their market offerings through the superior functionality and performance of those offerings, but also through the branding strategy that they pursue.

"A *branding strategy* for a firm identifies which brand elements a firm chooses to apply across the various products it sells." In business markets, the most significant aspect of branding strategy is deciding on the brand hierarchy to pursue. "A *brand hierarchy* is a means of summarizing the branding strategy by displaying the number and nature of common and distinctive brand elements across the firm's products, revealing the explicit ordering of brand elements. . . . Because certain brand elements are used to make more than one brand, a hierarchy can be constructed to represent how (if at all) products are nested with other products because of their common brand elements." The potential levels of a brand hierarchy, from highest to lowest, would be corporate brand, family brand, individual brand, and modifier. An example of this brand hierarchy would be *IBM ThinkPad X30*. *IBM* is the corporate brand, *ThinkPad* is the family brand for all notebook computers (as contrasted with desktop computers), *X Series* is the individual brand that refers to extra-light, extra-small, and ultra-portable notebooks, and *30* is the modifier that refers to the Ethernet connection models (as contrasted with wireless network connection models, *31*).[20]

Properly understood and implemented, the brand hierarchy positions brands as resources enabling a supplier to leverage previous investments in brand building. The investment required to successfully gain awareness and purchase of the *IBM Thinkpad G* Series is much less because of the previous brand-building for the *IBM* corporate brand and *Thinkpad* family brand. Brand equity that has been built in one offering category can be leveraged to launch a brand extension in another offering category. The brand equity 3M Company has established for its Post-it® Notes was a resource to enable 3M to enter the market for flip-chart pads with its Post-it Self-Stick Easel Pads.

That a supplier's brands are valuable resources also is reflected in the acquisition prices paid by firms in business markets. Citigroup acquired Grupo Financiero Banamex-Accival in 2001 for $12.5 billion, the largest ever U.S.–Mexican corporate merger. Less than six months later, an integrated Citibank Mexico and Banamex began operating under the *Banamex* brand name. The acquiring firm must adroitly manage the newly acquired brands, deciding how best to fit them within the existing brands, brand hierarchy, and brand architecture of the firm. GE, which has extensive experience in this brand management, provides a noteworthy case, which we relate in Box 4.1.[21]

Reliance on Outside Partners for Resources

Firms use collaborative relationships with other firms to gain access to resources and to leverage their own resources. In rapidly changing, technology-driven markets, no one firm will possess all of the resources needed to create innovative products. Business relationships and business networks form to focus on specific market opportunities. The Joint Strike Fighter business network that we discussed in Chapter 1 is an instance of this focus. Chapter 6 discusses the roles that outside development relationships and networks can play in a new offering realization strategy.[22]

Firms increasingly rely on the resources of outside logistics and transportation providers, such as United Parcel Service (UPS) or FedEx, to realize their business strategies. For example, Dell Computer restructured its order fulfillment process to leverage outside partnerships. In the past, the suppliers would ship the monitors first to Dell, which would in turn ship them on to the customer. Now, when Dell is ready to ship a computer, it sends an electronic mail (e-mail) message to its shipping partner, which coordinates the arrival of Dell's computer with the arrival of the ordered monitor from its supplier, and then delivers the complete order at the same time to the customer.[23]

A firm with an underutilized resource, such as an exceptionally proficient sales force or field service engineers, may seek out other firms that would value this resource *in exchange* for another. Two firms with complementary product lines may

BOX 4.1
How GE Manages Hundreds of Acquired Brands a Year

In 2000 and 2001, GE acquired 200 companies each year, a pace of about four acquisitions a week. In order to have a coherent approach to managing this brand portfolio, GE applies its proprietary "acquired affiliate-naming scheme," which is part of GE's Identity Program.

Because GE's overall brand strategy is technically "monolithic"—focusing on "GE" as the only core identity—this process encourages linking GE with its acquisitions, but it also considers the external variables that influence the degree to which a particular acquisition should be associated with GE. Therefore, the objective of this five-level naming scheme is twofold: to protect the equity of the GE brand and to leverage the brand equity of the acquired company, where appropriate. The five levels are:

- *Naming Level 1* represents the highest level of identification and the strongest association with GE. The acquired company's name becomes a combination of "GE" and a succinct generic name describing the business. A noteworthy example of this level would be Thomson CGR, which became GE Medical Systems Europe in 1987.
- *Naming Level 2* associates GE with the proper or communicative name of the acquisition, when highlighting the acquired name is beneficial and a lesser degree of association with GE is desirable. For example, because Fanuc had strong brand equity in the industrial automation market, the company was named GE Fanuc. At GE Medical Systems, for acquired brands such as "OEC" (surgical C-arms) and "Lunar" (bone densitometry) that had significant brand equity, their names were placed below the GE Medical Systems' name in the GE logo format (called a "graphic signature").

- *Naming Level 3* corresponds to a logo endorsement, where only a strong visual association is desirable. The acquired brand name is used in the GE logo format. Such is the case with Employers Reinsurance, which currently uses the GE Monogram without any GE prefix to their name. When GE's Medical Systems' business acquired Marquette Medical Systems in 1998, the brand had such recognition in the cardiology market that the existing Marquette logo was transitionally incorporated into the GE logo format.
- *Naming Level 4* represents a verbal endorsement when only a verbal association is desirable. The existing name and logo of the acquired company are kept (i.e., the GE logo format is not used) and are combined with a reference to GE in a tag line, such as with Transportation International Pool, a GE Capital Company.
- *Naming Level 5* keeps GE invisible, because no benefit comes from associating GE with the acquired brand, such as is the case with NBC, which has retained its own separate identity.

GE determines the appropriate naming level for an acquired business by considering three types of issues, each requiring subjective judgment.

- *Business issues* focus on management control (Does GE control the company?) and commitment (Does GE have a long-term commitment to this company?).
- *Industry issues* deal with the image value of the industry (Is the industry perceived to be dynamic and innovative?) and performance expectations (How well is GE expected to perform in this industry?).

BOX 4.1
Continued

- *Identity issues* are tied to the equity of the existing brand (Is it strong?) and the impact on GE (What is the impact when the new brand is associated with the parent company?).

GE uses these kinds of questions as sequential steps of a decision tree to determine the best naming strategy.

The scheme as described is designed to integrate and manage *newly* acquired brands. With time, brands evolve and may move up the ladder of association with GE after a transitional period. The "Marquette" example mentioned earlier illustrates this point. In 2000, approximately two years after the acquisition of Marquette (when the Marquette logo was integrated into the GE logo format), the company was renamed "GE Medical Systems Information Technologies" and given a new logo. The "Marquette" name no longer appeared as part of the name of the company or in its logo. Instead, it was transitioned to be an umbrella product brand. Recently, it was phased out completely.

GE's acquired affiliate-naming scheme provides branding guidance that can be applied consistently across a firm as vast and diversified as GE. The structured alternatives enable GE to protect and build its brand equity, yet leverage the existing equity of acquired brands, gaining the greatest return on this resource.

Sources: Richard Costello (Brand Management), GE Corporate; Karen Grishaber (Brand Management), Mohit S. Kathuria (Global Business Development), GE Medical Systems; and *http://www.ge.com/identity*.

agree to comarket each other's product line. This approach can leverage the resources of each firm, particularly when the firms primarily operate in different country markets. In this way, each firm can offer and service a broader product line and achieve geographical diversity in its sales. For example, Delta Airlines offers service between Atlanta and Zürich, with a stop in Paris. The Atlanta-Paris leg is operated by Delta, while the Paris-Zürich leg is operated by code-sharing partner Air France. However, when business travelers purchase a ticket from Atlanta to Zürich from Delta, their tickets list only Delta as the operating carrier, with two Delta flight numbers for the entire route. In the same way, a business traveler purchasing a ticket from Air France for the Zürich to Atlanta route via Paris would find two Air France flight numbers listed.

A firm may look to *pool* its resources with those of one or more other firms so they all can pursue a strategy that none could do alone. The chemical distribution industry, for example, is consolidating to a few large players that offer worldwide distribution to chemical producers and customers. One medium-sized, privately held chemical distributor in the United States is talking with similar firms in Germany and Japan about a strategic alliance. Working together, the three firms would offer producers and customers worldwide distribution coverage and the superior flexibility and responsiveness of dealing with smaller, family-run businesses.

Relying upon outside partners for resources is a strategic decision, one where senior management must contemplate the long-term as well as short-term benefits and consequences. What knowledge will be transferred between partner firms and what learning will take place? What resources will be expended, which will be replenished, and what new resources will result from working with the partner firm? Research indicates that alliances are most successful when firms carefully decide which resources will come from outside partners, select partners with which they are compatible, and engage in alliances where each firm contributes significant resources and treats the other as an equal.[24]

Fundamental Value-Based Strategies

At the core of every successful strategy is understanding what targeted market segments and firms regard as superior value and how to provide it to them. Not all markets nor firms within them value the same things, though, which means that a firm may provide superior value in multiple ways. Although prescriptions for fundamental strategies based on value vary somewhat, we consolidate them into three for discussion: product leadership, customer intimacy, and operational excellence. These basic value strategies are not mutually exclusive, and a firm that surpasses its competitors on two of them will have an extraordinary advantage.[25] Figure 4.2 outlines how several firms pursue product leadership, customer intimacy, or operational excellence, and the following sections describe these fundamental value-based strategies.

Product Leadership

Product leadership "means offering customers leading-edge products and services that consistently enhance the customer's use or application of the product, thereby making rivals' goods obsolete."[26] A firm that builds its strategy around product leadership pursues innovation relentlessly. It broadly seeks out technologies from other industries that it might creatively adapt to solve problems or further enhance its offerings' performance. Not content to have market offerings that deliver the best performance in an industry, it seeks to obsolete its own products before its competitors can. The firm uses its experience and learning to both speed up the realization process and lower its costs. Hewlett-Packard relies heavily on innovation and product obsolescence in its business strategy. More than half of its annual sales come from products introduced within the last two years.[27]

A firm might accomplish a product leadership strategy with **variety-based positioning**, which focuses on a subset of products or services that its industry offers. The firm concentrates its resources on producing a focused range of products that are outstanding for particular customer requirements or preferences. For particular applications, for customers with certain capabilities, or for specific usage situations, the firm's market offerings surpass those of any competitor. The Vanguard Group appears to pursue variety-based positioning with its index funds, which offer customers consistently good performance relative to their target indices, in part because their extraordinarily low expenses boost investor return.

Customer Intimacy

Customer intimacy "means segmenting and targeting markets precisely and then tailoring offerings to match exactly the demands of those niches."[28] A firm that builds its strategy around customer intimacy recognizes that when it retains customers over

Figure 4.2 How Firms Pursue Product Leadership, Customer Intimacy, and Operational Excellence

Product Leadership	Customer Intimacy	Operational Excellence
Microsoft:	**Airborne Express:**	**Federal Express:**
• Innovative Microsoft Office product enables users to automatically update changes across multiple applications using *Paste* link function.	• Functions as the shipping department for one customer, enabling it to take orders until 1:00 A.M. for packages that Airborne Express delivers later that morning.	• To make use of idle aircraft capacity, FedEx sought partnership with LL Bean to use FedEx planes during the day as LL Bean's sole shipping method.
Kadant:	• Customized delivery times ranging from 8:00 A.M. to 9:30 A.M. to better meet the requirements of Xerox's copy machine service business.	• Utilizes information technology to coordinate package movement and delivery.
• Created a method of extracting printer's ink from used paper, which allows paper producers to make clean, white paper stock from recycled paper products.	**Cable & Wireless:**	**GE Appliances:**
	• Develops profession-specific services, such as tracking features for the legal profession that facilitate call billing to clients.	• Created *Direct Connect* "virtual inventory" system, which reduced GE's inventory requirements while improving service to small appliance retailers.
Intel:	**Intel:**	**Dell:**
• CEO's mandate is to "double machine performance at every price point every year."	• Maintains active dialogue not only with its PC manufacturer customers, but also with end-use customers to improve Intel product development.	• Low-cost, direct marketing and sales method is the cornerstone of a strategy to provide customers with extraordinary service and choice for extremely competitive prices.
• Extraordinary investment in R&D enables Intel to rapidly introduce next-generation products, as well as extend existing products, such as its line of Pentium chips.	• "Intel Inside" and other targeted marketing campaigns educate end-use customers about new product performance capabilities.	

Source: Contributed by Research Associate Ellen Carr, Kellogg School of Management, Northwestern University. Developed from Michael Treacy and Fred Wiersema, *The Discipline of Market Leaders* (Reading, MA: Addison-Wesley Publishing Company, 1995).

time, it tends to gain more profits from them. This greater profitability comes from a deep understanding of the customers' requirements and preferences, and how the firm can adapt its market offerings to fulfill them in ways that are worth more or that lower total cost. When a firm pursues close relationships with its customers, it can better anticipate changes in requirements and preferences, which enables it to sustain its superior value. The supplier firm and its customers might work together to discover how they can make advantageous changes in requirements as well as processes for doing business together. Grainger Consulting Services' use of process mapping, which we discussed in Chapter 2, is an example. A worthwhile complement to these market sensing activities is for senior management to spend a day in the life of selected customers, gaining a firsthand understanding of their experiences and problems.[29]

Needs-based positioning, where the firm tailors a set of activities to provide superior value to targeted market segments and firms, is closely related to customer intimacy. For example, a supplier might develop a field engineering staff thoroughly trained in customer applications that can offer field problem-solving assistance to customers that have limited technical capability in-house. Critical to this positioning is the notion that this set of activities must be significantly different from ones that provide superior value to other segments. Thus, the firm organizes its activities to specifically fulfill targeted customers' requirements and preferences.

Supplier's share of the customer's business is a critical measure for gauging the success of a customer intimacy strategy. Gaining a deep understanding of customers' requirements and preferences takes greater time and other resources. This effort is worthwhile only when the supplier receives a large share of their business. A supplier pursuing a customer intimacy strategy should also measure additional business in complementary areas that it gains from fulfilling its customers' needs in other related areas. After all, a deep understanding of targeted customers' needs should suggest some possibilities for the firm to broaden its business with those customers.

Operational Excellence

Operational excellence means "providing customers with reliable products or services at competitive prices and delivered with minimal difficulty or inconvenience."[30] A firm that builds its strategy around operational excellence organizes itself to provide market offerings that fulfill a defined set of customer requirements and preferences at the lowest cost. Such firms are creative in the design and implementation of their business processes, and continually search for ways to eliminate redundant activities that do not contribute to customer value. Dell Computer is an example of a firm that has pursued operational excellence. "By selling to customers directly, building to order rather than to inventory, and creating a disciplined, extremely low-cost culture, Dell has been able to undercut Compaq and other PC makers in price yet provide high-quality products and service."[31]

How does operational excellence differ from operational effectiveness, which we discussed earlier? Operational effectiveness means performing *similar* activities better than the firm's competitors. In contrast, operational excellence stems from performing *different* activities from competitors that enable the firm to provide comparable offerings at a lower total cost.

Strategy Making

How firms should develop a strategy is a topic of keen interest to senior management, business market managers, and strategy thinkers. The conventional view of strategy making is that senior management charts a course of action where the fit between the firm's resources and the requirements of markets it elects to serve is best. Some strategy thinkers challenge this view, and instead advocate a view of strategy making as radical change. However, although a radical view of strategy making has some merit, it neglects the fact that firms do pursue strategies over time and often achieve success with methodical progress. We attempt a balance in discussing who makes strategy, defining purpose, and strategy as orderly advances punctuated by radical change.

Who Makes Strategy?

The conventional view is that top management makes strategy. This view is reinforced by the business press, which regularly writes about senior executives who pioneered "Killer Strategies That Make Shareholders Rich."[32] Other firms claim to use a top-down, bottom-up process for strategy making where the more financially driven view of senior management informs and is informed by the view of lower management, which is closer to and more knowledgeable about the marketplace. Middle management traditionally transmits the views and mediates the disparities that occur between the financial results that senior management wants and the marketplace results that lower management believes it can produce. This critical intermediary role has become impoverished in many firms with the reduction of middle management.[33]

Recent management practice research has found that middle managers play critical, yet undervalued roles in strategy making and its successful implementation. The four primary findings of this research were:

> First, middle managers often have value-adding entrepreneurial ideas that they are able and willing to realize—if only they can get a hearing. Second, they're far better than most senior executives are at leveraging the informal networks at a company that make substantive, lasting change possible. Third, they stay attuned to employees' moods and emotional needs, thereby ensuring that the change initiative's momentum is maintained. And finally, they manage the tension between continuity and change—they keep the organization from falling into extreme inertia, on the one hand, or extreme chaos, on the other.[34]

An iconoclastic view is that in order to create innovative strategies, firms need to rely less on senior management, and instead, promote broader involvement of managers throughout the firm. This emergent view of strategy contends that imaginative thinking exists in many places within a firm as a result of experiments, mistakes, and learning. The challenge for the firm is to pull together and capitalize on this strategy-making resource. It requires a more democratic process for strategy making, where senior management encourages and actively seeks out revolutionary thinkers—wherever they are—in the firm. Three constituencies that are typically underrepresented in strategy making can have a disproportionate influence: employees who have youthful perspectives (not necessarily the same as young employees); employees at the geographic periphery of the firm (e.g., those in local country markets far removed from the corporate headquarters); and newcomers to the industry, who tend to a have a fresh perspective. Each of these constituencies can contribute thinking that challenges industry and firm beliefs, and produces strategy-making insight.[35]

Defining Purpose

The cornerstone of strategy making is defining the purpose of the firm. A firm may express its purpose in a **mission statement** or **vision statement**, which sets out a broad strategic charter for the course of action that the firm will pursue. As an example, consider the mission statement for R. R. Donnelley & Sons Company, whose traditional business has been printing: "It is the mission of R. R. Donnelley & Sons Company to be a preeminent worldwide provider of printing and related information and value-added services and products for owners, publishers, and users of information." This mission statement appears on a plaque near the elevators on the ground floor of corporate headquarters (and at other places throughout the building) to continually reinforce the firm's purpose. Notice that the statement suggests a strategic direction that broadens the business beyond printing. Reflecting this intention, R.R. Donnelley is pursuing business in related areas, such as database management, direct marketing, and mapping services.[36]

Hamel and Prahalad advocated that a firm define its purpose in a statement of **strategic intent**, which expresses "a desired leadership position and establishes the criterion the organization will use to chart its progress."[37] Komatsu, a Japanese manufacturer of bulldozers and construction equipment, expressed its strategic intent as "Encircle Caterpillar," the industry leader. Strategic intent also provides a bridge to strategy making by having the firm broadly specify the path to achieving its strategic intent, including establishing intermediate milestones and review mechanisms to track progress.

Other strategy thinkers contend that strategic intent can produce an obsessive focus on a competitor that makes the firm myopic to other strategic options for profitable growth. Komatsu's senior management was concerned that its strategic intent of "Surround Caterpillar" was causing its managers to become fixated on trying to surpass what Caterpillar was doing and overlook emerging growth markets, such as hydraulic excavators. In place of strategic intent, senior management should define the **purpose of the firm** as an ambition that engages its employees to develop, refine, and renew that ambition. So, Komatsu defined its purpose as "Growth, Global, Groupwide" to spur its managers' thinking on ways to grow through expanding geographically and leveraging the group's resources.[38]

The challenge for the firm is to define its purpose in a way that broadly guides strategy making, yet is still meaningful and motivating to employees. Most firms find this dual task difficult to do well. Thus, mission statements tend to have a dulling, generic sameness about them, which employees justifiably regard cynically. The firm improves its chances of having a meaningful and motivating definition of purpose by having a broad cross-section of employees participate in its creation, and then having senior management discuss the meaning of the purpose in dialogues with groups of employees throughout the firm. As part of these dialogues, senior management should sincerely solicit employees' thoughts on how the firm can realize its purpose.

Strategy as Orderly Advances Punctuated by Radical Change

Reacting to firms that pursue operational effectiveness as strategy, Hamel proposed the metaphor of "strategy as revolution." In this notion of strategy, firms pursue strategies that represent radical change in their industries. These revolutionary strategies break the established rules of competition within an industry. In implementing its strategy, the firm enacts new ones that give it unique advantages.[39]

This concept of strategy as revolution builds upon Hamel and Prahalad's earlier concept of "strategy as stretch and leverage." Firms that embrace this concept establish a strategic intent that is extraordinarily ambitious and that the firm cannot accomplish with conventional thinking. This situation spurs managers to creatively pursue ways to leverage their limited resources to attain the firm's strategic intent. Hamel and Prahalad outline five basic ways in which a firm can leverage its resources. First, it can *concentrate* its resources through astutely pursuing its strategic intent over time and focusing at any given time to accomplish more with limited resources. For example, Intel Corporation made a strategic decision in the early 1980s to concentrate its resources on developing its emerging microprocessor business, moving away from its past core business of dynamic random access memory (DRAM) chips. Second, it can *accumulate* resources through superior extracting of learning from its experiences and "borrowing" the resources of alliance partners. Third, a firm can *complement* resources, blending its resources in a superior way or balancing them to get the best return from the set of resources. Fourth, it can *conserve* resources in ways such as recycling them, coopting other firms to pursue a common objective, and shielding them from direct confrontations with entrenched competitors. Finally, the firm can *recover* resources by quickly generating revenue from them or otherwise making them available for redeployment.[40]

Although strategy making as the pursuit of radical change appears compelling in some respects, it does leave some unanswered questions. How frequently should a firm "revolutionize" its strategy? For what duration are individuals in a firm capable of pursuing (and going through themselves) dramatic changes before those changes become dysfunctional to the firm's performance? Is strategy making as revolution really just a search for dramatically different ways to enact the fundamental value-based strategies we discussed earlier? When multiple firms within an industry pursue strategy making as revolution, does this produce greater differentiation and industry profitability, or hypercompetition that is potentially damaging to the industry and its customers?

Progressive firms recognize the strengths and weaknesses of each kind of strategy making and alternate using them when each best suits their needs. The result is longer periods of strategy making as orderly advances punctuated by shorter periods of strategy making as radical change.[41] Mintzberg has found from his research on organizations over time that "clear periods of stability and change can usually be distinguished in any organization: while it is true that particular strategies may always be changing marginally, it seem equally true that major shifts in strategic orientation occur only rarely."[42] Further, he finds that more creative organizations, such as Canada's National Film Board, experience a more balanced pattern of stability and change, perhaps due to their willingness to experiment and their sensitivity and openness to external events that precipitate change.

The impetus for radical change may come from within the firm, such as bringing innovations to the market. It may come from the market, such as competitors or major customers enacting strategy as revolution. It may come from interaction between internal and external events, such as when a firm preoccupied with internal affairs becomes increasingly disconnected with changing market requirements and preferences. In any event, to prosper, the firm must pursue dramatically different ways to enact a fundamental value-based strategy. After the firm has settled on a strategy to pursue, a period of orderly advances ensues as the firm works to improve the fit among its activities to more fully realize its strategic positioning.

PLANNING MARKET STRATEGY IN BUSINESS MARKETS

"Chance favors the prepared mind."

The preceding quote by Louis Pasteur captures the essence of what the firm attempts to accomplish with planning market strategy. Planning is a mechanism for learning. It should afford managers the time to validate their **market views**—the mental models that are simplified representations of the market and how it works. Planning also provides a way for the firm to build its **institutional learning**, "which is the process whereby management teams change their shared mental models of their company, their markets, and their competitors."[43] Through planning, members of the management team compare, revise, and update their individual market views, with the intent of having them converge on a shared market view, which serves as the basis for discussing alternative courses of action for the firm to pursue.

In many firms, though, planning as practiced has little to do with learning. Pressed for time and with little or no market research results to draw on, managers produce plans that are uninspired, straight-line extensions of the previous year's plan. In many cases, the plans are little more than the financial performance targets for the upcoming year. Devoid of market insights, such plans contribute little to running the business or reacting to changes that inevitably occur.

Fortunately, recognition of the need for meaningful planning of strategy is growing.[44] A number of firms have reinvigorated their strategic planning to chart ways to grow their businesses and improve their profitability. Mintzberg contends that strategic planning is misnamed and should instead be called **strategic programming**:

> In more formal language, strategic programming involves three steps: codification, elaboration, and conversion of strategies. Codification means clarifying and expressing the strategies in terms sufficiently clear to render them formally operational, so that their consequences can be worked out in detail. . . . Elaboration means breaking down the codified strategies into substrategies and ad hoc programs as well as overall action plans specifying

what must be done to realize each strategy. . . . And conversion means considering the effects of changes on the organization's operations.[45]

Although we agree with the content of strategic programming that Professor Mintzberg outlines, for familiarity, we will continue to use planning market strategy in this section.

Firms employ many different planning processes and plan formats in their strategic planning efforts. The particular planning process and plan format are not what is important, though; it is the thinking that goes into the plan and the learning that results. We organize our presentation of planning market strategy in business markets around three fundamental questions:

- What do we know?
- What do we want to accomplish?
- How will we do it?

Regardless of planning process and plan format, firms that can *meaningfully* answer these three questions will have constructed a market strategy that is worth pursuing.

What Do We *Know*?

We want to emphasize the word *know* in this question. To construct a market strategy, managers must distinguish between what they know, what they believe, and what they want to believe. Moreover, they must be willing to challenge what they think they know and ask themselves how they know it. Is this knowledge accurate and supported by data from internal assessments and market sensing? As Benjamin Disraeli perceptively observed, "To be conscious that you are ignorant is a great step to knowledge."

To answer what do we know, the management team should review recent performance, gather essential market information, and when there is considerable uncertainty, construct scenarios.

Review Recent Performance

As a start, managers should review recent performance to see how it compares with prior plan objectives. Share of customer's business and sales of new products by market segments are examples of informative measures of market performance, and segment contribution (segment total sales minus total variable costs and assignable fixed costs) and customer contribution to profitability are examples of informative measures of financial performance. Divergence between planned and achieved results signals faulty assumptions, such as how well a market offering fulfills particular customer requirements and preferences.

Accurate explanation of past performance requires that managers have skill in **thinking backward**.[46] That is, to construct valid explanations for past performance, they must find relevant variables, put them in a causal sequence, and assess the plausibility of the causal sequence occurring. To improve their backward thinking, managers should take several steps:

- They should experiment with several metaphors as explanations, each of which might add to their understanding.

- They should recognize that an event or outcome may have more than one cause.
- Because a defining characteristic of insights is that they take us by surprise, the manager should go against what appear to be more probable causes to consider their opposites.
- Managers should assess candidate causal chains by the number and strength of their links; longer chains generally are less probable.
- Finally, managers should generate and test alternative explanations rather than simply settling on the first or seemingly most likely one.

Each of these steps can strengthen causal reasoning, enabling managers to learn more from past performance.

Reviewing past performance also connects planning market strategy with performance review. It establishes accountability for accomplishing the course of action in the prior market plan. Managers should provide explanations, supported by data, for significant variances between planned and achieved results. Reviewing past performance can also pinpoint problematic goal or objective setting and resource allocation. Overly ambitious goals or objectives that managers continually miss can cause dispirited performance and a growing disregard for taking goals or objectives seriously. Rather than working together to devise an ambitious, yet achievable course of action, successive layers of management instead engage in game playing that wastes a valuable but often unaccounted-for resource: management time.

Gather Essential Market Information

To build knowledge and reduce uncertainty, supplier firms must gather market information. Because managers' market views significantly affect the kinds of information they seek and use, they must challenge their market views using a variety of market information to forestall becoming market myopic.[47] We outline what we regard as essential market information for planning market strategy in business markets in Box 4.2. This market information would seem vital for meaningful discussions

BOX 4.2
Market Information Essentials for Strategic Market Planning in Business Markets

1. Alternative ways of segmenting the market that give the firm some leverage

2. Estimates of the size and growth of each market segment presently and potentially served

3. The distribution of estimates of the firm's share of customer's business for each market segment

4. Estimates of the value of the product offering and the value of the augmenting services for each market segment

5. Two or three strengths and two or three weaknesses where actionable improvements would significantly affect customer's perceptions of the firm's performance

6. Knowledge of the firm's most- and least-profitable products, and most- and least-profitable customer groups

of alternative courses of actions to pursue, yet most firms lack some of this information. Certainly additional kinds of market information would be useful to know, such as the identification of **lead-users** and **leap-froggers**—progressive firms whose present strong needs will become widespread in a marketplace months or years in the future.[48]

We discussed gathering the kinds of market information in Box 4.2 in Chapter 2 as part of market sensing. We build on this earlier discussion here with a few comments related to crafting market strategy. Gaining estimates of the supplier's share of customer's business may not be easy, yet with some persistence and imagination it can be done. Box 4.3 recounts the experience of MASER LTDA, a small distributor of laboratory equipment and supplies in Colombia, and how share of customer's business can produce insights for market strategy.

BOX 4.3
MASER LTDA Researches Its Share of Customer's Business

MASER LTDA is a small distributor of laboratory equipment and supplies located in Cali, Colombia. It represents companies such as VWR Scientific Products in its local area. MASER achieved tremendous growth based on a broad product and industry focus. However, its sales became stagnant due to low sales effectiveness, aggravated by the political and economic instability in Colombia. MASER's low sales effectiveness was due in large part to its lack of focus, which created a large number of requests for quotes. Responding to these requests took so much of its few employees' time that they had little remaining time to follow up on the quotes provided and convert them into sales. To remedy this problem, management began to formulate a market strategy.

To analyze the firm's market performance, management researched share of customer's business. It reasoned that this indicator would provide some understanding of where the firm was successful, and suggest where it might focus its limited resources. When it began assessing its share of customer's business, management encountered several measurement challenges, the most important one being the difficulty of obtaining data at the product level. Customer accounting systems did not isolate the particular products purchased, and so customers were reluctant to provide detailed information due to the effort needed to retrieve past records. MASER tackled the issue by cross-referencing the data customers did provide against the company's own quotations and invoices. To simplify matters, management grouped its product lines into four categories based on their list prices and degree of complexity: laboratory supplies, basic laboratory equipment (e.g., balances and microscopes), analytical instruments (e.g., spectrophotometers and chromatographs), and spare parts. These categories also reflected differences in the time and approval levels required in the purchase decision.

To supplement its knowledge about its estimated shares of customer total purchase requirements for these categories, MASER conducted in-depth interviews with key customers to better understand the drivers of share of customer's business, and especially, what caused the variation in shares per customer from year to year. The interviews revealed three issues that MASER management needed to consider in developing a market strategy to grow its share of customer total purchase requirements with targeted customers:

1. Although purchase requirements for supplies were uniform and predictable from year to year, customer purchase requirements for the remaining categories were not and depended largely on

(continued)

BOX 4.3
Continued

laboratory application. For example, because service laboratories performed many more routine analyses on the same equipment (e.g., quality control at a water utility company) than did R&D laboratories, their equipment tended to wear out more frequently.

2. Public sector customers differed from private sector customers. "Transparency" laws governing the public sector forbid single-supplier agreements, thereby proscribing MASER from gaining a 100 percent share of these customers' total purchase requirements. Significantly, the majority of company sales came from the public sector. Another difference was that the source of budgets affected the likelihood and regularity of purchase. Public sector purchases were guaranteed by government development plans, while private sector purchases occurred mainly

in December, because their budgets were affected by planned-versus-actual sales and profit performance.

3. Customers selected providers of laboratory supplies without much thought, simply focusing on brand names at low price. In contrast, technical expertise, local postsale service, direct distribution of the brands offered, and maintaining local inventory made a firm the supplier of choice for basic laboratory equipment and analytical instruments. Importantly, because laboratory personnel played a key role in the purchase decision for equipment as it becomes more complex, MASER discovered that it could increase its share of customer total purchase requirements by providing assistance to laboratory personnel in constructing economic justifications for equipment purchases to customer senior management.

Source: Contributed by Research Associate Sandra Diaz, Kellogg School of Management, Northwestern University.

Understanding strengths as well as weaknesses is critical for making changes consistent with different market strategies. Business marketing sage Irwin Gross contended, "Firms buy from you for what you are good at, and despite what you are bad at; for firms that do not buy from you, it is exactly the reverse." So, suppliers that pursue a **defensive market strategy**—one aimed at retaining present customers—may choose to strengthen what are already strengths. In contrast, suppliers that pursue an **offensive market strategy**—one aimed at gaining new customers—must remedy weaknesses that have kept firms from doing business with them. Of course, the firm also may craft a market strategy that represents a composite of both.

Profitability of market offerings and customer groups is something that most firms find difficult to know. It requires accurate tracking of the actual price the firm realizes from each market offering and customer transaction. It also requires an activity-based costing system that accurately conveys the costs of producing and providing the products and augmenting services, programs and systems to particular customers.[49] Yet, even when the firm has this market information, it will need further research to understand the market strategy implications. It needs to understand what firms are purchasing the least-profitable and most-profitable market offerings, and for what applications they are using them. Isolating applications of most-profitable customers can suggest targeting of other firms with that application and comparable customer characteristics. Least-profitable products may be providing completeness of product line, which resellers and customers value overall, and that prevent potential competitor inroads.

Supplier firms that are in dynamic markets may argue that they do not have the time to gather much market information because it will slow their decision making. It is natural for these firms to be concerned about "paralysis by analysis," yet they must balance it against "extinction by instinct"![50] Interestingly, management practice research on firms in dynamic markets has found that fast-decision-making firms use as much or more information as their slow-decision-making counterparts.[51] The crucial difference is in the kind of information:

> Slow decision makers rely on planning and futuristic information. They spend time tracking the likely path of technologies, markets, or competitor actions, and then develop plans. In contrast, the fast decision makers look to real time information—that is, information about current operations and current environment which is reported with little or no time lag. . . . They prefer indicators such as bookings, backlog, margins, engineering milestones, cash, scrap, and work-in-progress to more refined, accounting-based measures such as profitability. . . . Fast decision makers also relay to each other external real time information such as new product introductions by competitors, competition at key accounts, and technical developments within the industry.[52]

So, it appears that fast decision makers use internal and market information to construct more elaborate market views, which they update frequently. This practice enables them to react quickly to changing events in the market.

Many firms use a **situation assessment** as a mechanism for pulling together market information and internal knowledge. Situation assessments typically consider the marketplace (customers and environment), competitors, and internal resources and capabilities. A critical aspect is for a firm to recognize the assumptions it implicitly makes about each of these areas. Comparisons of internal resources and capabilities with those of competitors define strengths and weaknesses, and comparisons of competitors with the marketplace define opportunities and threats. Situation assessments must be based upon market data and information, not simply managers' beliefs and opinions, to be worthwhile.

Construct Scenarios

When firms have considerable uncertainty about their markets, they find scenario analysis more useful than traditional forecasting.[53] A **scenario** is a plausible representation of a firm's possible future, where the pertinent factors basic to the representation relate to one another in a consistent way. A scenario analysis consists of multiple scenarios that portray provocatively different futures that, taken together, compel managers to contemplate the main forces driving the market, their interrelationships, and the crucial uncertainties. To keep from overwhelming managers, the number of scenarios should be limited to four or fewer.

When Los Alamos National Laboratory in the United States was forced to reinvent itself in the postnuclear era, its management constructed five scenarios to help it envision different end states for the Lab. For example, in one scenario, Los Alamos would become a "nuclear factory" for the disassembly of nuclear weapons and materials; in another, it would dedicate itself to civilian purposes, such as environmental research.

Ultimately, management drew upon the five scenarios to formulate a coherent strategy and related set of short-term tactics for the Lab to pursue. The Lab's management reported that the scenario analysis enabled it to escape its existing (and potentially limiting) perceptions of the Lab's core competencies, capabilities, and the current environment.[54]

Scenario analysis should cause managers to challenge their market views. In thinking through the set of scenarios, they should attempt to specify critical **milestones** or **signposts**, that signal whether a given scenario likely will, or will not, occur. The Royal Dutch/Shell Group has used scenario analysis to spur institutional learning. It provides scenarios as written cases in management games, where it challenges groups of managers to explore the question: "What will we do if this happens?" Shell has found that such games significantly accelerate institutional learning.

What Do We Want to *Accomplish*?

We want to emphasize the word *accomplish* in this question. We mean this not only in the sense of what the business wants to attain, but that if it does, it will provide a sense of accomplishment or fulfillment for the individuals responsible for achieving it. And, when the business prospers, the individuals who have collectively worked to produce it feel that they, not just senior management, will share in it.[55]

The length of time that firms consider in answering, "What do we want to accomplish?" will vary. A three- or five-year planning horizon for a market strategy is the most common. Often, the firm updates the plan yearly, with the first year of the plan serving as the firm's operating plan. In rapidly changing markets, such a long planning horizon may make little sense. The chief executive of a software firm once remarked that the market window—from idea to commercialization—for a new software program in his segment was six months. In such situations, answering the question "What do we want to accomplish?" might have a one-year horizon, with the firm revisiting the question each quarter.

The firm has more than one course of action that it might pursue. Business market managers should act as catalysts in structuring the market strategy alternatives and engaging the management team and their respective functional areas in a dialogue about them. Figure 4.3 shows how a management team can argue the alternatives, yet still get along. Rather than considering alternatives sequentially, the firm should work through multiple alternatives simultaneously. This approach promotes faster decision making, as comparative analysis sharpens preferences, builds confidence that a superior alternative has not been overlooked, and provides a better fallback position when the first alternative does not work out. By basing their arguments on market knowledge rather than opinion, the management team minimizes interpersonal conflict, which motivates team members to contribute ideas more freely. In reaching a decision on the market strategy alternative to pursue, the firm should use **consensus with qualification**, which means the management team attempts to reach a shared agreement. When agreement is not possible, the general manager and the senior marketing manager make the choice.[56]

The market strategy that the firm wants to accomplish begins with targeting. After selecting target market segments and customer firms to focus on, the firm's

Figure 4.3 How Teams Argue but Still Get Along

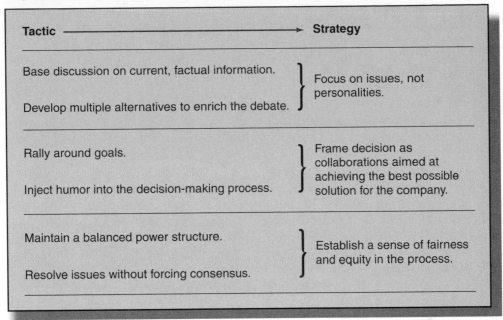

Tactic ⟶ Strategy

Base discussion on current, factual information.

Develop multiple alternatives to enrich the debate.

⎫ Focus on issues, not
⎬ personalities.
⎭

Rally around goals.

Inject humor into the decision-making process.

⎫ Frame decision as
⎪ collaborations aimed at
⎬ achieving the best possible
⎭ solution for the company.

Maintain a balanced power structure.

Resolve issues without forcing consensus.

⎫ Establish a sense of fairness
⎬ and equity in the process.
⎭

Source: Kathleen M. Eisenhardt, Jean L. Kahwajy, and L. H. Bourgeois III, "How Management Teams Can Have a Good Fight," *Harvard Business Review* (July–August 1997): 82.

establish goals and objectives. Management also thinks through positioning and, increasingly, brand building to decide what the firm wants to accomplish.

Targeting

Targeting refers to selecting particular market segments and customer firms that the supplier firm will focus its resources on serving. That is not to say that the firm will not sell to other market segments or customer firms, but instead, targeting specifies which segments and customer firms are of particular interest. As we mentioned in the chapter overview, collaboration among the various functions is essential when pinpointing the market segments and customers that the firm will target. As part of this targeting activity, each functional area should decide what constitutes its ordinary performance, and what it is prepared to do as extraordinary performance. Then, with the business market manager acting as a catalyst, the functional areas should collectively decide under what circumstances and for what customer firms they will provide each, and what they expect in return. For example, extraordinary performance may be extended to relatively important customers as standard in return for a larger share of the customer's business. For other customers, the firm may offer this extraordinary performance as an option and charge for it.

A firm may target particular market segments or customer firms for different reasons. Firms with a business-market management perspective will focus on segments and customers where value assessments demonstrate that their offerings provide superior value. They also target promising country markets for market development efforts. Expanding abroad allows a firm to leverage and deepen its strategic position.[57] As we discussed in Chapter 1, German Mittelstand companies target narrow product markets and achieve leverage by serving many country markets. Firms also prefer to target growing segments and customer firms, as "a high tide raises all ships."

Finally, firms might target segments and customers for purposes of learning. That is, serving these markets or customers will build the firms' knowledge and capabilities in ways that are valuable elsewhere. As an example, Boeing Company's participation in the military aircraft segment enables it to develop cutting-edge design and production knowledge and know-how, which it then can use to sustain its market leadership in the commercial aircraft segment.

Setting Goals and Objectives

We use **goals** to refer to the longer-term, strategic directions that the firm pursues, which often are imprecisely stated or qualitative. In contrast, we use **objectives** to refer to the near-term, more measurable standards that a firm uses to judge whether it achieved what it wanted to accomplish during a specific time period. In this way, objectives serve as milestones that enable the firm to chart its progress in attaining its goals. A firm pursues its strategic intent in this way, by broadly specifying the path to achieving it, and then establishing intermediate milestones and review mechanisms to track progress.

The business must specify measures that correspond to its objectives (and goals) or that signal the extent to which the firm has accomplished the market and financial performance it envisioned. Examples of informative measures of market performance include increased share of customer's total requirements by market segment (supplier share of customer's business), number of new customers by market segment, and sales of new products by market segment. Examples of informative measures of financial performance include segment contribution, customer contribution to profitability, and incremental revenues from optional, value-adding services.

Progressive firms should look at cash flow as a measure that bridges market performance and financial performance. Marketplace initiatives can accelerate and enhance cash flows, reduce their volatility and vulnerability, and enhance their long-term residual value. Cash flow is a critical measure of financial performance for a firm, as financial markets often use the net present value of cash flows as an indicator of shareholder value. Related to this, senior management at Siemens, for example, is compensated largely on the basis of accomplishing Economic Value Added (EVA®) objectives, which reflect the extent to which net operating profits after tax exceed the cost of capital employed.[58]

Successive layers of management translate the business's market goals and objectives into group and individual goals and objectives. Some firms use the **balanced scorecard**, which assesses customer, financial, internal business process, and learning and growth performance, as a mechanism to accomplish this.[59] Research has found that one of the best ways to gain superior cross-functional cooperation is to have some objectives, and rewards for accomplishing them, at the broader level of the cross-functional unit.[60] Even within the marketing and sales functional area, shared objectives and rewards significantly improve coordination. Baxter's Team Excellence Award Program, which we discussed in Chapter 1, is an example. Also, senior management must prioritize and consider linkage implications among the objectives that the firm sets. For example, gaining new customers and lowering the cost of sales as a percentage of total sales most often have a negative linkage because getting new customers typically requires a number of sales calls before the first sale.

Often, significant slippage or disconnects occur between stated objectives and the measures that the firm uses for performance review and reward. Predictably, individuals in the workforce seek to excel on these measures, with business performance on the objectives falling short. This situation was captured in the title of a classic management article, "On the Folly of Rewarding A, While Hoping for B."[61] An often-occurring example in business markets is the folly of rewarding salespeople on revenue or volume, while hoping for profitability. Even in instances where some measure of offering or customer profitability is a part of the salesperson review and reward system, its weighting relative to revenue or volume measures often is insufficient to focus salesperson actions on profitability over volume or revenue. To remedy this problem, tighter linkages are needed between what senior management wants to happen and the measures that they put in place to evaluate the performance of the individuals who are responsible for accomplishing those objectives.

Finally, the firm should set goals and objectives for learning about the marketplace. For example, a goal the firm might want to accomplish is to become and remain the industry leader in knowledge about customer requirements and preferences, and how they are changing. Setting learning goals and objectives should trigger the commitment of resources and specification of mechanisms for learning. The firm might increase the number of customer value assessments and market experiments that it conducts. Having goals and objectives for market learning also causes the firm to rethink the meaning of, and how it regards, failure. Even though initiatives fall short of their financial or market objectives, they might be strong contributors to the firm's learning and subsequent market success.[62] Each time the firm engages in planning, it wants to be better equipped to answer the question, "What do we know?" than it was previously.

Positioning in Business Markets

Positioning in business markets is absolutely critical for success, because it provides the conceptual cornerstone for constructing and managing marketing offerings (the topic of Chapter 5). However, positioning is often either neglected or poorly understood by business market managers. Contributing to this, perhaps, is that no generally accepted definition of positioning exists. For our purposes, **positioning** is the process of establishing (and sustaining) an intended meaning for a market offering in the minds of targeted customers.

Writing a positioning statement is the central element of the positioning process. Although guidance varies on writing positioning statements, the critical components are target, offering concept, and value proposition. The **target** component succinctly characterizes the specific type of customers for the market offering that are of most interest to the supplier. For example, "itinerant, Generation-X professionals" might be specified as the target for some advanced, intelligent network telephone services, such as single-number reach. The **offering concept** component specifies the essential attributes of the market offering for the selected target, out of the potentially larger set of attributes that an offering might possess.

The **value proposition** component expresses the points of difference, and some-times, points of parity of the market offering relative to the next-best-alternative offering that are the most valuable to the target customer. The value proposition should be a persuasive one- or two-sentence answer to the customer question: "Why should I do business with your firm and not your competitor?" Although the results of building a customer value model may show that a larger number of value ele-ments have monetary worth, we advise business market managers to focus on the one or two points of difference that are most valuable to the target customers. These one or two points of difference may be supplemented by a point of parity when it is critical to establish that the supplier's brand has comparable performance on a value element to the next-best-alternative offering. The essence of the value proposition is that it should persuasively convey how the target customer will be more profitable by using the supplier's brand rather than the next-best alternative. Marketing com-munications of the value proposition may state this point in a provocative way. For example, Sonoco Products Company once trumpeted the value proposition: "Sonoco just lowered the cost of your mulch film by $16.83 per acre."[63]

Depending on the situation, two additional components might be included in a positioning statement: the sales and delivery approach and the claim support. The sales and delivery approach is added when channels are a significant contributor to the value of the market offering, such as Caterpillar dealers are for construction equipment because of the significance of after-sale repair and spare-part services. Claim support is needed when the selected target may be skeptical about the sup-plier's ability to deliver on the value proposition. For example, a new supplier to an industry may have to state the technical means by which its alternative technology is able to solve a problem that has plagued the industry for years.

After generating a number of candidate, alternative positioning statements, the business market manager needs to select the final positioning statement for the brand. Some criteria for assessing a positioning statement are as follows.[64] First, is it meaningful? The positioning statement should be expressed in the everyday lan-guage of target customers. Both target customers and everyone within the supplier firm should readily grasp its exact meaning. Positioning statements that contain hackneyed words or phrases, such as "highest performance," "best quality," or "world class," lose any true meaning with target customers and within the supplier's own workforce. Even experienced and knowledgeable marketers can fall prey to phrases devoid of specific meaning. Consider this example:

> This portable fatigue-o-tron provides the highest performance in a portable package for corn growers who need in-the-field metal fatigue analysis.[65]

Contrast "highest performance" with "most durable performance" or "most reliable accuracy." Each of these last two offers a different nuance, but is more specific and meaningful than "highest."

Second, does the positioning statement convey the value of the brand? Business market managers must strive to make the value proposition precise, tangible, and credible for target customers. Third, is it consonant with what the business unit as a whole is trying to accomplish? Senior management as well as other functional area managers must be willing to support the actions needed to attain that positioning in the marketplace. Finally, does it provide a foundation for creative executions of business marketing communications, such as advertisements and sales presentations?

Applied Industrial Technologies (AIT), a large distributor of specialty replacement bearings, power transmission components, fluid power products, rubber products, and a large variety of specialty items in the United States and Canada, provides a noteworthy example of value-based positioning. It uses a series of business marketing communications, which convey value case histories, to reinforce and make its positioning statement tangible: "Award winning service through documented value added savings." We reproduce two of the executions of this positioning statement in Figure 4.4.

Figure 4.4a
Value-Based Positioning for Applied Industrial Technologies

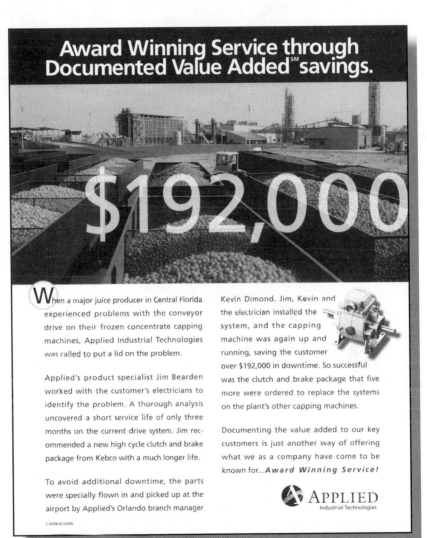

Source: Applied Industrial Technologies case history reprinted with permission from Applied Industrial Technologies.

Figure 4.4b
Continued

Source: Applied Industrial Technologies case history reprinted with permission from Applied Industrial Technologies.

Many managers think of positioning statements as just something that the marketing folks do as a basis for creating business marketing communications. We believe that positioning statements can be much more than that. By involving managers from all the relevant functional areas in the positioning process, at least to some extent, the creation and assessment of positioning statements provide a means of forging shared understanding of what the supplier is seeking to accomplish in the market.

Viewed in this way, the positioning statement can serve as a guiding beacon and touchstone for the agreed-upon market strategy, and especially as the answer to the question: "What do we want to accomplish?" It puts into sharper focus which firms the supplier regards as the relatively important customers, what the supplier wants to emphasize about the market offering, and what promise the supplier is making to customers about the value they will receive. Everyone in the supplier's workforce needs to have a good grasp on these issues. Yet, not everyone in the firm may want the greater direction and focus that positioning statements provide. For example, some may want to avoid positioning statements, or to write only vague ones, because they are afraid that customers might find out the supplier does not consider them the targets for an offering. They would rather have the customers, and their own sales force, believe that all customers are equally good prospects for an offering! This belief not only dilutes sales force efforts but can also have negative consequences when customers purchase an offering that was not designed to meet their requirements.

Finally, over time, the positioning statement can function as a touchstone or reference standard in making decisions about contemplated changes in the market offering. Are the changes congruent and reinforcing, or will they subtly shift the character of the market offering? Either may be desirable, but by actively managing change, firms can avoid blurring the firm's positioning in the marketplace.

Building Brands in Business Markets

Establishing and building their brands is something that managers in business markets increasingly seek to accomplish. They believe that by adapting the concepts and practices of their counterparts in consumer markets to the business-to-business setting, they can build brand equity and benefit from it. To guide their thinking about brand building, managers in business markets have been advised to ask, answer, and act on the following questions:

- How does the brand strategy support our business strategy?
- What is our aspirational brand identity, and what do we need to do to get there?
- What value proposition is most valuable to our customers?
- How do I align my organization to make the brand and value proposition a reality?[66]

Managers in business markets should meaningfully answer each of these questions and put responsive action plans into place prior to pursuing a brand-building initiative.

Some special considerations apply in building brands in business markets, as contrasted with consumer markets. Kevin Lane Keller, an expert in strategic brand management, offers the following additional guidelines for business markets:[67]

1. Adopt a corporate or family branding strategy and create a well-defined brand hierarchy.
2. Link non-product-related imagery associations.
3. Employ a full range of marketing communication options.
4. Leverage equity of other companies that are customers.
5. Segment markets carefully and develop tailored branding and marketing programs.

The non-product-related imagery associations refer to social benefits, such as "peace of mind" and "ease of doing business," which tend to be difficult to estimate in monetary terms. Nonetheless, they can affect customer managers' purchase decisions, especially when taken together with demonstration in monetary terms of the technical, economic, and service benefits a brand delivers. The brand also conveys other value placeholders, which contribute value but whose worth in monetary terms is not estimated in a customer value model.

Building a strong brand in business markets is critical whenever and wherever customer managers believe that formal assessments of value delivered are not worthwhile. In these instances, brand may serve as the sole basis for purchase. As an example, customer managers may feel that it is not worthwhile to conduct a formal value assessment for repositionable sticky notes and instead simply purchase 3M Post-it Notes, even if the price for them is slightly higher than lesser-known or generic brands.

The value proposition for a market offering serves as the cornerstone for brand building in business markets. What is the relationship of the value proposition to the customer value models we advocate in Chapter 2? The customer value model has the intent of estimating the worth in monetary terms of the points of difference and points of contention between the supplier's brand and the next-best-alternative offering in the minds of targeted customers. As noted in the previous discussion of value propositions, although a number of points of difference and points of contention may have positive estimates, we advise managers in business markets to focus on the one or two that have the most value to the target customer firms. And, at times when it is critical to establish comparable performance on some value element (e.g., a point of contention where prior to building the customer value model, customers believed that the next-best alternative was superior on the value element), a point of parity is added to complete the value proposition. The one or two points of difference selected to build the value proposition should be those value elements where, for the foreseeable future, improvements will be most valued by the target customers. Brand building for a market offering then would encompass devoting resources to significantly improve functionality or performance on those elements, demonstrating and documenting success in this with customer value management, and persuasively communicating this progress to target customers.

Building the corporate brand is of paramount importance in business markets in that it positions the firm or business unit in the minds of present and prospective customer firms. As we noted previously in our discussion of brands as resources, investments in building the corporate brand can provide dividends in brand building for specific market offerings. Building the corporate brand also can guide and energize the actions of the supplier's workforce in attaining the desired corporate brand identity.[68] The recent experience of Infineon Technologies® in deciding upon and then building its corporate brand, which we relate in Box 4.4, provides an outstanding case study.

How Will We Do It?

This question is about thinking through implementation of the market strategy. Firms can propose the most wonderful-sounding market strategies, but if they lack the requisite knowledge, skills, and abilities to put them into play, little will be accomplished.[69] Just as market strategy informs and guides implementation, implementation considerations should inform and guide the generation of market strategy. It is in answering the question, "How will we do it?" that the firm engages in strategic programming, as

BOX 4.4
Building the Infineon Technologies® Brand

Siemens is a Germany-based, 160-year-old giant comprised of diverse businesses such as telecommunications, appliances, computers, nuclear power plants, trains, and medical equipment. In 1999, a decision was reached to carve Siemens Semiconductor (SC) out of the group. Three reasons led to this spin-off decision: First, as a small part of the company (5 percent of Siemens' total revenues), Siemens SC did not have a separate identity and suffered from negative perceptions of Siemens as a slow-moving conglomerate. Secondly, being part of a highly centralized organization limited its flexibility dramatically. For example, Siemens SC could not compensate its employees with stock options or aggressive compensation plans as other high-tech component suppliers could. Finally, Siemens SC needed to have its own, more attractive stock to purchase start-up companies and grow through mergers and acquisitions.

To implement this decision and create an identity for the new firm, senior managers organized workshops in Europe and in the United States. They purposely selected as workshop participants younger employees in technology or sales who were close to the core activities and the customers. Workshop participants were asked to brainstorm about the attributes of the new company, based on reality as well as desire. Words like *dynamic, enthusiastic, innovative, passionate, flexible,* and *adaptable* represented the character and values that employees wanted the new brand to reflect the most.

The results of these workshops were critical in deciding upon the actual brand name. Management chose Infineon as a blend of *infinity, eternity* (*eon* in Greek), and *new* (*neon* in Greek). *Infinity* refers to the scope of the business and the fact that Infineon is a global company. *Eternity* conveys a sense of security for everyone: Infineon will be around for a long time. *New* reminds about the new start, the new culture, and the new entrepreneurial

spirit. The appropriateness of the Infineon name was thoroughly checked legally and linguistically. Management chose a tag line for the brand: "Never stop thinking." Employees found this tag line exciting and engaging because it reinforced that the company valued and encouraged their thinking.

To announce the new brand and use it as a catalyst for launching a new culture, management decided to organize a huge party at each of its sites worldwide. The 25,000 Infineon employees were invited to celebrate on March 26, 1999, when the CEO announced and explained the new name. A short advertisement was played to introduce Infineon. Management explained why the company was going public. The next day, when people came back to the office, they found huge canvasses along their buildings, displaying the images of the initial advertising campaign. Some of the messages were rather provocative. Referring to employees, one stated: "On April 1, 1999, something happened . . . and 25,644 people became completely OBSESSED." Referring to the CEO, another message gave a visionary image: "What kind of MANIAC CREATES something when NO ONE is asking for it?" A third message emphasized the new entrepreneurial culture of the global firm: "It seems that every famous high-tech company has started in a garage. Ours happens to park 24,983 cars."

A team responsible for launching the new brand identity had some daunting tasks to perform, such as insuring that within a week, all employees had new Infineon business cards. Because the new name, brand identity, and the IPO were radical changes, cultural change did not happen overnight and some employees resisted. Nevertheless, the brand has been a catalyst for a new attitude and the company has already achieved great progress.

A 12-person team is responsible for monitoring the new firm's progress toward

(*continued*)

BOX 4.4
Continued

achieving its desired brand identity. Assisted by organizational psychology consultants, the team makes a periodic, internal assessment of qualitative and quantitative changes in the firm's culture. This research charts progress on several criteria, such as the level of empowerment, internal communication, and how employees feel about the impact of their jobs on the company. The team documents its findings in a report entitled "Cultural Mirror of the Company," which is shared with all employees.

Infineon Technologies also assesses externally the progress of its brand in an annual "Brand Tracking Survey." Infineon interviews customers as well as managers at target companies to understand what they think about the brand and how their perceptions of Infineon have evolved since 1999.

Source: Interview with Guy Wolff, Senior Vice President, Corporate and Investor Communications, Infineon Technologies. Contributed by Research Associate Florent Carbonneau, Kellogg School of Management, Northwestern University.

we discussed earlier. It develops action plans, designs sales and marketing programs, takes stock of its implementation skills, and prepares for learning and adapting.

Develop an Action Plan

An **action plan** translates the market strategy into the coordinated activities and specific resources the firm will use to attain what it wants to accomplish. It spells out the set of programs the firm will implement and mechanisms for coordinating them so that the firm best leverages its resources. Central to this task is gaining input from each functional area in the construction of the programs that affect them and their collective commitment to work together to produce seamless marketplace performance. The action plan associates each objective, or set of related objectives, in the market strategy with the program (or programs) the firm will carry out to achieve it.

Coordination of the various market initiatives is a must, but in firms organized around products rather than markets, it can be haphazard. We have heard resellers exclaim that such suppliers need a "traffic cop" to keep the various product managers from launching sales and marketing programs that "collide," competing with one another for the reseller's attention and effort. Coordinating the timing and complementarity of the programs the firm enacts in the market leverages rather than dilutes the firm's efforts.

Before putting an action plan "to bed," the management team should ask a retrospective question in advance: "Six months down the road, when this strategy has failed, what will have been the cause of it?"[70] Early in the process of developing the action plan, creativity and imagination need to be encouraged, and so negativity must be suspended. After the action plan has been tentatively set, though, it benefits from intense scrutiny and questioning. By institutionalizing this question as part of the market planning process, it becomes clear to managers that it is not meant to undercut their efforts, but to help them strengthen the plan prior to its implementation. When the question is phrased in this manner, managers do a surprisingly good job at isolating the plan's shortfalls. The management team then makes changes to buttress these shortfalls, which might mean allocating additional resources or shifting resources. To accomplish this, they may combine some programs or defer others to the next year. It is critical that the management team amply fund the programs that remain in the final action plan to ensure their greatest chance of market success.

Marketing and Sales Programs

A **sales and marketing program** is a set of connected activities that consumes resources to produce results in pursuit of some objective. The actors performing these activities may come from one functional area, such as sales, but more often the activities cut across functional areas, relying on actors from them. Examples of sales and marketing programs are a new offering introduction, participation in an industry trade show, or increasing the supplier's share of customer's business in a targeted segment. Box 4.5 provides a detailed example of how MASER LTDA developed a program to increase its share of customers' business in the sugar cane segment.

Sales and marketing programs consist of two external elements "wrapped around" four internal elements. The external elements are an objective (or related objectives), which flows from the market strategy, and measures of feedback. A common problem with objectives is that they are missing or not sufficiently defined. For example, some firms do not set specific objectives for participating in a trade show, such as generating 100 percent awareness for a new equipment leasing program, gaining commitments to conduct field demos at 40 qualified prospect firms in a target segment, or learning the positioning of a competitor's new offering and specific details about the advanced technology it uses. Thus, after the show, the only things the firm's participants are in a position to evaluate are whether the Heineken® in the hospitality suite were cold or whether the jumbo shrimp were a bit mealy this year!

Simply put, measures of feedback are indispensable. They enable the firm to assess the extent to which the program accomplished its objectives. They signal needed modifications in programs to be responsive to changing marketplace conditions. They establish benchmarks, so that the firm can gauge the cost and returns on programs that are repeated over time, and have a baseline for evaluating refinements. Finally, they provide accountability of individuals who have ownership of the program or its constituent activities, and serve as a basis for performance review.

The four internal elements of a sales and marketing program are the actions to be taken, the responsibilities defined, the timing, and the budget. The individual who has ownership of the program should detail each of its major actions and indicate who has taken responsibility for each action. The initials of the individual having primary responsibility for each major action (or group of activities) should appear in parentheses following it. The timing element lays out the program's sequential timeline; it specifies the date for completing each action. Finally, budgets refer to the resources, such as money or individuals' time, that the program requires and from whose budget(s) these resources will come.

Take Stock of Implementation Skills

Four behavioral skills of managers are fundamental in implementation: interacting, allocating, monitoring, and organizing.[71] **Interaction skills** are a manager's behavioral style of relating to others within the firm and outside the firm, such as resellers and customers. Interaction skills capture how a manager works together with others, uses influence strategies, and negotiates. **Allocation skills** refer to a manager's expertise in budgeting time, people, and money. **Monitoring skills** are a manager's

Drawing on its analysis of its share of customer's business, MASER LTDA management decided to focus its efforts and target the sugar cane industry as a market segment where it could potentially achieve 100 percent of customer total purchase requirements. Three factors contributed to this decision. Several large regional firms dominate the industry, and MASER found that it had its highest shares of customer's business with four of these firms. A second factor was the sugar cane industry's considerable export business, which protects it from downturns in the Colombian economy, but at the same time exposes it to the pressures of global competition to modernize. The third factor was that the sugar cane industry was part of the private sector, making it exempt from single-source supply legal proscriptions. The main concern MASER faced when targeting this industry was its cost-cutting mentality, which traditionally accounted for its lack of capital investment.

MASER set its market strategy objective to achieve 100 percent shares of the sugar producers' total laboratory purchase requirements. Before crafting a positioning statement for this target that would guide its market strategy, MASER salespeople visited current customers to learn more about their laboratories. They found out that sugar producers are focusing on increasing yield as a way to reduce total costs. Laboratory analyses are crucial in this pursuit, in monitoring the sugar content in the cane that growers supply and in monitoring the by-products of the production process. Consequently, MASER formulated the following positioning statement: "To laboratories of sugar producers, MASER is the local distributor of equipment and supplies, providing laboratory personnel with state-of-the-art technical support to select and implement optimal solutions for monitoring the sugar content of inputs and in-process materials."

MASER next developed a sales and marketing plan designed to achieve its objective. The firm allocated a dedicated salesperson to visit all targeted companies on a weekly basis, while others served the rest of the customers in other market segments to avoid losing current sources of revenue. The objective of the visits was to increase MASER's share of the customer's mind to influence purchase decisions and to facilitate monitoring of competitor activity. MASER also used these visits to obtain information for the development of an equipment purchase economic justification model, which it could tailor to particular customers.

MASER offered supplementary services that could either be sold separately as value-adding options with the equipment, or exchanged for a greater share of the customer's business. These services included just-in-time inventory of required supplies, local availability of spare parts, technical training, preventive maintenance and repairs, and equipment loaners. The company was able to offer many of these services at reasonable cost to itself by pooling resources across similar customer requirements. Obtaining direct distribution for the equipment and supplies used in targeted applications was also key to being price competitive.

The measures of feedback in this program were the acquired share of customer total purchase requirements, and customer and target segment profitability. MASER is considering providing incentives for sugar cane customers to further consolidate their laboratory business with MASER. These incentives might entail the provision of additional services that would be justified for those customers willing to commit to 100 percent of their laboratory purchase requirements to MASER. Finally, MASER plans to utilize the application expertise it acquires to expand to other market segments, including growers, sugar cane associations, and users of sugar cane process by-products.

Source: Contributed by Research Associate Sandra Diaz, Kellogg School of Management, Northwestern University.

ability to stay informed on what matters and to recognize when to intervene in ongoing activities. **Organizing skills** capture a manager's proficiency at drawing upon, or when needed circumventing, the formal organizational structure to bring together the resources to accomplish a market task. Organizing skills reflect how adroit a manager is in connecting relationships and managing group dynamics, whereas interacting skills refer to one-on-one interaction adeptness.

Although each of these implementation skills is challenging to master, firms struggle most to strengthen the interaction skills of their managers. The increasing emphasis on working together more collaboratively, such as in closer cross-functional cooperation and partnering with customers, requires interaction skills. Significantly, when the senior management team has problems interacting with one another, cross-functional cooperation likely won't happen below them in the organization either. To align their interests and promote improved interaction, several years ago the 60 top executives of Baxter, Inc., took out personal notes to purchase, in total, $120 million of Baxter stock. The deal was structured so that the dividends on the stock would pay the interest payments for five years. At that time, a balloon payment was due. If Baxter stock had risen a certain number of points, the executives would be at break-even; if the stock price was below that level, they were personally liable for the difference; if the stock price was above that level, they would gain. A senior executive commented that cooperation among the senior management team dramatically improved. Reflecting this cooperative attitude in part, the share price of Baxter stock rose significantly above the break-even share price.

Firms generally have difficulty making a knowledgeable and unbiased appraisal of their own skills and capabilities, no doubt because they are more familiar with their own capabilities and skills than they are with competitors'. In addition, firms tend to know what they do well; they tend not to know what they do not do well. That is, they tend to overestimate the number of capabilities and skills on which they are superior. To gain a more unbiased appraisal, firms often rely on outsiders, such as management consultants. Outsiders can assist them in producing a more objective appraisal, by performing comparative analyses using internal data as well as external customer and competitor data.

Learning and Adapting

"It is a bad plan that admits of no modification." Publilius Cyrus made this statement in the first century B.C. So, although some may regard the emergent view of strategy as a recent phenomenon, the recognition that plans need to be adapted as learning occurs has existed for quite some time! At several points in this chapter, we have emphasized the criticality of learning and putting mechanisms in place to facilitate it. Here, we consider some ways to learn quickly to be able to make responsive adaptations or modifications in market strategy.

One way for firms to excel at learning and adapting is to gain early feedback, either before or just after implementing parts of the market strategy. A **customer advisory panel**, where the firm brings together a group of its leading-edge and key customers to provide reactions, advice, and counsel, provides a valuable mechanism for learning and adaptation. Box 4.6 recounts how Hitachi Data Systems learns from its customer advisory panel. Reseller councils, which we discuss in greater detail in Chapter 9, are also a potentially valuable mechanism for learning about changes in

BOX 4.6
Hitachi Data Systems Learns from Its Customer Advisory Panel

Hitachi Data Systems (HDS) is one of the first service companies to actively learn from its customers. In 1993, this $2 billion mainframe, storage device, and service company created a **customer advisory panel** (CAP) with the goal of using its best customers as market experts and teachers. The key to successfully learning from the CAP lies in careful selection of its members. According to Al Mascha, HDS's vice president of Service Operations, the best participants are outspoken customers with the most complex technological needs. These customers are lead-users, whose present requirements portend future, widespread market requirements.

Every nine months, HDS brings together 20 of these key customers for a three-day meeting to discuss service issues, technological development, and—most importantly—the customers' strategic directions. Salespeople do not attend the CAP meetings, nor are there third-party facilitators present. The goal is unfiltered, free-flowing discussion. HDS presents a loose agenda, and in the ensuing three days, participants relate their emerging strategies and what they want from HDS to help them achieve their strategies. HDS then creates delivery arrangements, training programs, and other service offerings that meet the requirements and preferences that the CAP expressed. Significantly, the CAP meetings generate benefits for both HDS and the participants; while HDS learns what its customers want, the participants learn from each others' experiences.

Source: Contributed by Research Associate Ellen Carr, Kellogg School of Management, Northwestern University. Adapted from Don Peppers, "How You Can Help Them," *Fast Company* (October–November 1997): 128–136.

the market as well as gauging reactions to proposed market initiatives. Finally, business market managers must remember that in constructing sales and marketing programs, they need to devise feedback measures that provide some early indication of how a program is doing—postprogram evaluations are not enough.

Pilot programs are a valuable way of learning by doing. The firm should design them so that, to the extent possible, they are limited in scale and scope. The firm also should think through the conditions that will promote success, so that it can pick the best chances for a pilot program becoming a "success story." To maximize learning and guard against idiosyncrasies, whenever possible, the firm should implement at least two pilot programs of the same kind. This provides some estimate of the variance in outcomes the firm can expect and provides insights on the conditions for more consistent results.

In the process of learning, business market managers must also consider the best method of disseminating what they have learned throughout the organization. At times, the medium of transmitting information can significantly influence the success and application of the learning within the firm. Pipsa-Mex, a Mexican paper company, uses a *grupo musical* (musical group) to communicate its market strategy, supplier relationships, and other critical information to its employees. The eight PIPSA musicians sing and play an assortment of folk instruments, ranging from guitars to the teeth of a donkey skull, in order to transmit information to the organization. Rather than rely upon more conventional written and spoken media, PIPSA management recognized and leveraged its employees' responsiveness to a more culturally familiar mode of learning.[72]

When firms do have success with an innovative market activity, program, or system, they often have difficulty reliably reproducing this best practice elsewhere in the firm. From their management practice research, Szulanski and Winter find:[73]

> People approach best-practice replication with the optimism and overconfidence of a neophyte stock trader out to beat the market. They try, for example, to go one better than an operation that's up and running nearly flawlessly. Or they try to piece together the best parts of a number of different practices, in hopes of creating the perfect hybrid. They assume, usually incorrectly, that the people running best-practice operations fully understand what makes them successful. As a result of this general overoptimism, people attempting to replicate a best practice are nowhere near as disciplined as they need to be.

What can business market managers do to improve their chances of successfully replicating best practices?

Although managers should consult the experts and the documentation on the best practice to be copied, these sources are not substitutes for carefully observing the best practice firsthand, to learn as much of the tacit detail as possible. They then should attempt to copy the working example in detail, as closely as they can, using it as a template to replicate. Intel developed its "Copy Exactly!" method to ensure the precise transfer of manufacturing know-how from the initial facility making a particular device to subsequent ones. Managers also should demonstrate decent results with the replicated best practice before beginning adaptations intended to improve performance. Rank Xerox requires managers first to demonstrate a comparable level of performance to that of the benchmark unit before they can initiate adaptations in the reproduced practice. Business market managers adhering to these guidelines then can use a search for discrepancies from the best practice example as a diagnostic device when implementation problems inevitably arise.

Finally, senior management must actively support a culture that values systematic market experiments. Progressive firms have at least several different market experiments underway at any time in pursuit of superior learning. To accomplish this learning and experimentation culture in large firms, senior management should practice *subsidiarity*, which means that "power belongs to the lowest possible point in the organization."[74] Subsidiarity is the opposite of the concept of empowerment, where upper management delegates power to lower levels of management and frontline workers. With subsidiarity, "power is assumed to lie at the lowest point in the organization and it can be taken away only by agreement."[75] Senior management that practices subsidiarity recognizes that most opportunities to learn occur in or close to the market. Thus, the power for imagining and conducting market experiments must be there also. For this culture to flourish, senior management must practice forgiveness and understanding for inevitable mistakes and failed experiments, provided that there is learning.

SUMMARY

Crafting market strategy is the process of studying how to exploit a firm's resources to achieve short-term and long-term marketplace success, deciding on a course of action to pursue, and flexibly updating it as learning occurs during implementation. It requires significant participation from many functional areas, not just marketing, to make decisions about what market segments and customer firms to pursue, and what needs to be done to deliver superior value to them. Crafting market strategy recognizes real-world complexity and the interplay between deliberate strategy, where the firm decides on a course of action to pursue, and emergent strategy, where marketplace activities converge into a pattern that the firm recognizes and acts upon in a coordinated way.

Business strategy provides the context for market strategy. Although business strategy is often seen as setting the constraints for market strategy, so too should market strategy inform and significantly influence business strategy. We took a resource-based view of the firm, where core competencies and capabilities are complementary building blocks of strategy that generate value and provide competitive advantage. Product leadership, customer intimacy, and operational excellence represent fundamental value-based strategies. Disparate views are held on a number of issues in making strategy, such as who makes strategy and defining the purpose of the firm. Although the view of strategy as radical change appears compelling in some respects, progressive firms recognize the strengths and weaknesses of each kind of strategy making and alternate using them when each best suits their needs. The result is longer periods of strategy making as orderly advances punctuated by shorter periods of strategy making as radical change.

Through planning market strategy, members of the management team compare, revise, and update their individual market views, with the intent of having them converge on a shared market view, which serves as the basis for discussing alternative courses of action for the firm to pursue. We organized our presentation of planning market strategy in business markets around three fundamental questions: What do we know? What do we want to accomplish? and How will we do it? Regardless of planning process and plan format, we contend that firms that can meaningfully answer these three questions will have constructed a market plan that is worth pursuing.

To construct a market plan, managers must distinguish between what they know, what they believe, and what they want to believe. Through reviewing recent performance, gathering essential market information, and in situations of considerable uncertainty, constructing scenarios, the management team answers, "What do we know?" After considering multiple alternatives, the management team selects a market strategy it wants to accomplish. It targets market segments and customer firms to focus on, sets goals and objectives, and engages in positioning to work out the implications of what the firm wants to accomplish. Brands and brand building are of growing interest and significance in business markets. In answering the question, "How will we do it?" the firm engages in strategic programming, where it develops action plans and sales and marketing programs, takes stock of its implementation skills, and prepares for learning and adapting.

ENDNOTES

1. Henry Mintzberg, "Crafting Strategy," *Harvard Business Review* (July–August 1987): 66–75.
2. Benson P. Shapiro, "What the Hell Is 'Market Oriented'?" *Harvard Business Review* (November–December 1988): 119–125.
3. Although we use the term *firm* most often, our treatment of crafting market strategy is for a single business. Alternatively, we can view it as crafting market strategy for the smaller firm or for a business unit in a larger corporation. For focus, we do not discuss corporate strategy or strategy at the group or sector level for multiple business unit corporations. For discussion of these strategies, see Michael Porter, *Competitive Advantage* (New York: The Free Press, 1985).
4. For an interesting set of exchanges on the "design" versus "emergent" schools of strategy, see Henry Mintzberg, "The 'Honda Effect' Revisited: Introduction," *California Management Review* (Summer 1996): 78–79; Richard T. Pascale, "The Honda Effect," *California Management Review* (Summer 1996): 80–91; Henry Mintzberg, "Learning 1, Planning 0," *California Management Review* (Summer 1996): 92–93; Michael Goold, "Design, Learning and Planning: A Further Observation on the Design School Debate," *California Management Review* (Summer 1996): 94–95; Henry Mintzberg, "Reply to Michael Goold," *California Management Review* (Summer 1996): 96–99; Michael Goold, "Learning, Planning, and Strategy: Extra Time," *California Management Review* (Summer 1996): 100–102; Richard P. Rumelt, "The Many Faces of Honda," *California Management Review* (Summer 1996): 103–111; and Richard T. Pascale, "Reflections on Honda," *California Management Review* (Summer 1996): 112–117.
5. Christopher A. Bartlett and Sumantra Ghoshal, "Changing the Role of Top Management: Beyond Strategy to Purpose," *Harvard Business Review* (November–December 1994): 79–88. The quote is from Rumelt, "The Many Faces of Honda," 110.
6. Michael E. Porter, "What Is Strategy?" *Harvard Business Review* (November–December 1996): 61–78. The three quotes in the paragraph are from pp. 62, 68, and 62, respectively, with the emphases in the original. See also Keith H. Hammonds, "Michael Porter's Big Ideas," *Fast Company* (March 2001): 150–156.
7. Porter, "What Is Strategy?" 77. To some extent, this statement even blurs the distinction between strategy and marketing strategy.
8. David J. Collis and Cynthia A. Montgomery, "Competing on Resources: Strategy in the 1990s," *Harvard Business Review* (July–August 1995): 119.
9. Michael E. Porter, *Competitive Advantage: Creating and Sustaining Superior Performance* (New York: Free Press, 1985); and Rajendra K. Srivastava, Liam Fahey, and H. Kurt Christensen, "The Resource-Based View and Marketing: The Role of Market-Based Assets in Gaining Competitive Advantage," *Journal of Management*, 27, no. 6 (2001): 777–802.
10. Collis and Montgomery, "Competing on Resources."
11. C. K. Prahalad and Gary Hamel, "The Core Competence of the Corporation," *Harvard Business Review* (May–June 1990): 84.
12. Prahalad and Hamel, "Core Competence," 83–84.
13. Collis and Montgomery, "Competing on Resources."
14. Peter F. Drucker, "The Information Executives Truly Need," *Harvard Business Review* (January–February 1995): 54–62.
15. George Stalk, Philip Evans, and Lawrence E. Shulman, "Competing on Capabilities: The New Rules of Corporate Strategy," *Harvard Business Review* (March–April 1992): 62.
16. Stalk, Evans, and Shulman, "Competing on Capabilities," 66; see Pascale, "Reflections on Honda," for an example of the use of core competence and capability interchangeably.

17. George S. Day, "The Capabilities of Market-Driven Organizations," *Journal of Marketing* (October 1994): 38.

18. Day, "The Capabilities of Market-Driven Organizations," 39.

19. Most research and writing on brands and branding has been based on, and focuses on, consumer markets. Drawing on this work and our experience, we adapt it for application in business markets. For a comprehensive source on brands and brand building, which we draw on in this chapter, see Kevin Lane Keller, *Strategic Brand Management: Building, Measuring, and Managing Brand Equity*, 2nd ed. (Upper Saddle River, NJ: Prentice Hall, 2003).

20. Keller, *Strategic Brand Management*, p. 563 and p. 535 for the first and second quotes, respectively.

21. For a recent exposition on the brand value chain, which begins with marketing program investment and concludes with shareholder value, see Kevin Lane Keller and Donald R. Lehman, "How Brands Create Value," *Marketing Management* (May–June 2003): 26–31.

22. Kenichi Ohmae, "The Global Logic of Strategic Alliances," *Harvard Business Review* (March–April 1989): 143–154. Gary S. Ruderman, "Collaboration Adding Strength," *Chicago Tribune*, 8 July 2000, sec. 4, 1, 4.

23. Gary McWilliams, "Whirlwind on the Web," *Business Week*, 7 April 1997, 132.

24. David Lei and John W. Slocum, Jr., "Global Strategy, Competence Building and Strategic Alliances," *California Management Review* (Fall 1992): 81–97; Louis P. Bucklin and Sanjit Sengupta, "Organizing Successful Co-Marketing Alliances," *Journal of Marketing* (April 1993): 32–46.

25. Michael Treacy and Fred Wiersema, "Customer Intimacy and Other Value Disciplines," *Harvard Business Review* (January–February 1993): 84–93; and Porter, "What Is Strategy?" We draw on both articles in this section.

26. Treacy and Wiersema, "Customer Intimacy," 85.

27. Edward Barnholt, "Fostering Business Growth with Breakthrough Innovation," *Research-Technology Management* (March–April 1997): 12–16.

28. Treacy and Wiersema, "Customer Intimacy," 84.

29. Francis J. Gouillart and Frederick D. Sturdivant, "Spend a Day in the Life of Your Customers," *Harvard Business Review* (January–February 1994): 116–125. We discuss sustaining customer relationships in greater detail in chapter 10.

30. Treacy and Wiersema, "Customer Intimacy," 84.

31. Treacy and Wiersema, "Customer Intimacy," 86.

32. Gary Hamel, "Killer Strategies That Make Shareholders Rich," *Fortune*, 23 June 1997, 70–88.

33. Henry Mintzberg, "Musings on Management," *Harvard Business Review* (July–August 1996): 61–67.

34. Quy Nguyen Huy, "In Praise of Middle Managers," *Harvard Business Review* (September 2001): 73.

35. Barlett and Ghoshal, "Changing the Role of Top Management"; Gary Hamel, "Strategy as Revolution," *Harvard Business Review* (July–August 1996): 69–82; Henry Mintzberg, "The Fall and Rise of Strategic Planning," *Harvard Business Review* (January–February 1994): 107–114.

36. James C. Anderson and James A. Narus, "Capturing the Value of Supplementary Services," *Harvard Business Review* (January–February 1995): 75–83.

37. Gary Hamel and C. K. Prahalad, "Strategic Intent," *Harvard Business Review* (May–June 1989): 64.

38. Barlett and Ghoshal, "Changing the Role of Top Management." For research on how a competitor-focused market strategy can produce lower profits for the firm, see J. Scott Armstrong and Fred Collopy, "Competitor Orientation: Effects of Objectives and Information on Managerial Decisions and Profitability," *Journal of Marketing Research* (May 1996): 188–199.

39. Hamel, "Strategy as Revolution"; and Gary Hamel, "Waking Up IBM," *Harvard Business Review* (July–August 2000): 137–146.

40. Gary Hamel and C. K. Prahalad, "Strategy as Stretch and Leverage," *Harvard Business*

Review (March–April 1993): 75–84; and Robert A. Burgelman and Andrew S. Grove, "Strategic Dissonance," *California Management Review* (Winter 1996): 8–28.

41. Mintzberg, "Crafting Strategy"; Suzy Wetlaufer, "The Business Case Against Revolution: An Interview with Nestlé's Peter Brabeck," *Harvard Business Review* (February 2001): 112–119; and Gary Hamel, "Revolution vs. Evolution: You Need Both," *Harvard Business Review* (May 2001): 150–154.

42. Mintzberg, "Crafting Strategy," 71.

43. Arie P. de Geus, "Planning as Learning," *Harvard Business Review* (March–April 1988): 70.

44. John Bryne, "Strategic Planning," *Business Week*, 26 August 1997, 48–52; Mintzberg, "The Fall and Rise of Strategic Planning."

45. Mintzberg, "The Fall and Rise of Strategic Planning," 112.

46. Hillel J. Einhorn and Robin M. Hogarth, "Decision Making: Going Forward in Reverse," *Harvard Business Review* (January–February 1987): 66–70.

47. George S. Day and Prakesh Nedungadi, "Managerial Representations of Competitive Advantage," *Journal of Marketing* (April 1994): 31–44.

48. Eric von Hippel, *The Sources of Innovation* (New York: Oxford University Press, 1988); James C. Anderson and James A. Narus, "Partnering as a Focused Market Strategy," *California Management Review* (Spring 1991): 95–113. We discuss lead-users and leap-froggers as sources of innovation that are of particular interest for a supplier firm to research in Chapter 6.

49. Michael V. Marn and Robert L. Rosiello, "Managing Price, Gaining Profit," *Harvard Business Review* (September–October 1992): 84–94; and Drucker, "The Information Executives Truly Need." We discuss monitoring transaction prices and activity-based costing in greater detail in Chapter 10.

50. Ann Langley, "Between 'Paralysis by Analysis' and 'Extinction by Instinct,'" *Sloan Management Review* (Spring 1995): 63–76.

51. Kathleen M. Eisenhardt, "Speed and Strategic Choice: How Managers Accelerate Decision Making," *California Management Review* (Spring 1990): 1–16.

52. Eisenhardt, "Speed and Strategic Choice," 3–4.

53. This section is based on de Geus, "Planning as Learning"; Paul J. H. Shoemaker, "Scenario Planning: A Tool for Strategic Thinking," *Sloan Management Review* (Winter 1995): 25–40; Pierre Wack, "Scenarios: Shooting the Rapids," *Harvard Business Review* (November–December 1985): 139–150; and Pierre Wack, "Scenarios: Uncharted Waters Ahead," *Harvard Business Review* (September–October 1985): 73–89. See also Ian Wylie, "There Is No Alternative to…," *Fast Company* (July 2002): 106–110.

54. Miriam Leuchter, "A Quantum Change at Los Alamos," *Journal of Business Strategy* (January–February 1997): 16–21.

55. Aaron Bernstein, "Sharing Prosperity," *Business Week*, 1 September 1997, 64–69; and Robert D. Hof, "Stock Options Aren't the Only Option," *Business Week*, 14 April 2003, 60.

56. Eisenhardt, "Speed and Strategic Choice"; and Kathleen M. Eisenhardt, Jean L. Kahwajy, and L. II. Bourgeois III, "How Management Teams Can Have a Good Fight," *Harvard Business Review* (July–August 1997): 77–85.

57. Porter, "What Is Strategy?"

58. Rajendra K. Srivastava, Tassadduq Λ. Shervani, and Liam Fahey, "Market-Based Assets and Shareholder Value: A Framework for Analysis," *Journal of Marketing* (January 1998): 2–18; Peter Doyle, *Value-Based Marketing* (Chichester, England: John Wiley & Sons, 2000); and Phillippe Haspeslagh, Tomo Noda, and Fares Boulos, "Managing for Value: It's Not Just About the Numbers," *Harvard Business Review* (July–August 2001): 64–73.

59. Robert S. Kaplan and David P. Norton, "Using the Balanced Scorecard as a Strategic Management System," *Harvard Business Review* (January–February 1996): 75–85.

60. Ann Majchrzak and Qianwei Wang, "Breaking the Functional Mind-Set in Process Organizations," *Harvard Business Review* (September–October 1996): 92–99.

61. Steven Kerr, "On the Folly of Rewarding A, While Hoping for B," *Academy of Management Executive* (February 1995): 7–16.

62. Gary Hamel and C. K. Prahalad, "Corporate Imagination and Expeditionary Marketing," *Harvard Business Review* (July–August 1991).

63. Kevin Lane Keller, Brian Sternthal, and Alice Tybout, "Three Questions You Need to Ask About Your Brand," *Harvard Business Review* (September 2002): 80–86.

64. George P. Dovel, "Stake It Out: Positioning Success, Step by Step," *Business Marketing* (July 1990): 43, 44, 46, 48–51.

65. Dovel, "Stake It Out."

66. Daniel P. Morrison, "B2B Branding: Avoiding the Pitfalls," *Marketing Management* (September/October 2001): 30–34.

67. Keller, *Strategic Brand Management*, 737.

68. Colin Mitchell, "Selling the Brand Inside," *Harvard Business Review* (January 2002): 99–105.

69. Jeffrey Pfeffer and Robert I. Sutton, "The Smart-Talk Trap," *Harvard Business Review* (May–June 1999): 135–142.

70. We gratefully acknowledge Joseph Durette of Kraft General Foods for suggesting this question.

71. Thomas V. Bonoma and Victoria Crittenden, "Managing Marketing Implementation," *Sloan Management Review* (Winter 1988): 7–14.

72. Eric Matson, "You Can Teach This Old Company New Tricks," *Fast Company* (October–November 1997): 44–46. Pipsa-Mex, now owned by Grupo Industrial Durango (GIDUSA), was formerly Producer and Importer of Paper S.A. (PIPSA).

73. Gabriel Szulanski and Sidney Winter, "Getting It Right the Second Time," *Harvard Business Review* (January 2002): 62–69. The quote is from p. 64.

74. Charles Handy, "Balancing Corporate Power: A New Federalist Paper," *Harvard Business Review* (November–December 1992): 64.

75. Handy, "Balancing Corporate Power," 64.

Creating Value

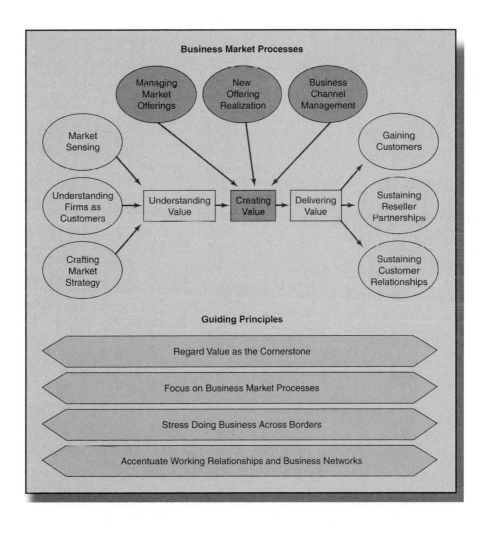

Business Market Processes

Managing Market Offerings

New Offering Realization

Business Channel Management

Market Sensing

Understanding Firms as Customers

Crafting Market Strategy

Understanding Value → Creating Value → Delivering Value

Gaining Customers

Sustaining Reseller Partnerships

Sustaining Customer Relationships

Guiding Principles

Regard Value as the Cornerstone

Focus on Business Market Processes

Stress Doing Business Across Borders

Accentuate Working Relationships and Business Networks

Chapter 5

Managing Market Offerings

OVERVIEW

*T*he business market processes of market sensing, understanding firms as customers, and crafting market strategy provide supplier firms with an understanding of value. As Figure 1.1 portrays, the firm puts this understanding of value to use in creating value for the market segments and customer firms that it has decided are of greater interest. Creating value is composed of the business market processes of managing market offerings, new offering realization, and business channel management.

Managing market offerings is the process of putting products, services, programs, and systems together in ways that create the greatest value for targeted market segments and customer firms. The challenge for business market managers is to construct offerings that uniquely leverage a business's resources to provide this value. The process involves both responsively meeting targeted segment and customer requirements, and managing their supplier expectations.

What exactly do we mean by *market offering*? To better understand this, we will unravel what in the past has been called a *product offering* and view it in several layers.[1] The **core product** is simply the fundamental, functional performance a generic product provides that solves a customer's basic problem. For example, the core product for an agricultural herbicide would be a specific chemical compound that has the ability to control particular broadleaf and grassy weeds. The **minimally augmented product** adds to this core product the least amount or number of services, programs, or systems that customers consider absolutely essential for doing business with *any* supplier. Examples of these essentials might include payment terms, delivery, and customer service for problems with the core product.

The **augmented product** adds to the core product those services, programs, and systems a supplier offers to meet a broader set of customer requirements and preferences, or to exceed the customer's expectations in ways that add value or reduce cost for the customer. Examples of augmenting services, programs, and systems offered in business markets appear in Figure 5.1. Finally, a **potential product** goes beyond the augmented product to encompass any imaginable product change or service, program, or system a supplier might create to add value or reduce cost in ways that set itself apart from others. As these potential additions are realized, they become a part of the augmented product. For example, an agrichemical supplier and dealer might consider jointly offering a "rain guarantee," whereby if the dealer applies the supplier's herbicide to the grower's fields and unexpected rain washes it away, the dealer will reapply the herbicide at no charge.

We prefer market offering to the more-often-used product offering as a way to capture these layers of meaning for three reasons. First, the core product may not be a concrete, palpable "thing" but instead may be a service, such as management consulting or building maintenance.

Figure 5.1   Examples of Augmenting Services, Programs, and Systems

Services	
Corrective or Remedial:	problem-solving, trouble-shooting, operations assistance
Fulfillment:	availability assurance, order quantity, logistics, delivery, installation, maintenance, training, returns, warranty
Programs	
Economic:	deals, terms, conditions, off-invoice, freight, co-op allowances, rebates/bonuses
Relationship:	advice and consulting, specification, co-design, process engineering, process redesign, cost reduction, responsiveness to information requests, joint marketing research, co-promotions, communication, partnering and participation in other customer programs
Systems	
Linking:	computer-to-computer ordering, shared material resource planning (MRP), information exchange (EDI)
Efficacy:	expert systems, logistics management systems, responsiveness systems

"Market" accommodates either equally well. Second, even when the core product is a concrete and tangible "thing," use of market offering emphasizes that what a supplier brings to the market is a package composed of a core product or service and a set of augmenting services, programs, and systems. The package as a whole, not simply the core product, must create value for the customer. In a number of instances, the augmenting services, programs, and systems provide the predominant part of the value over competitors' offerings. Finally, "market" reinforces an outward-focused perspective of what the supplier is trying to accomplish in the marketplace, as contrasted with "product," which can promote an inward-looking or technology-driven perspective.

In this chapter, we discuss constructing and managing market offerings. After briefly considering some conventional thinking about market offerings, we present our approach, which we call **flexible market offerings**. We then discuss value-based pricing as a means for sharing created value with customers. We conclude by considering the potential complexities of managing market offerings across international borders. We depict the process of managing marketing offerings in Figure 5.2.

Figure 5.2 Managing Market Offerings

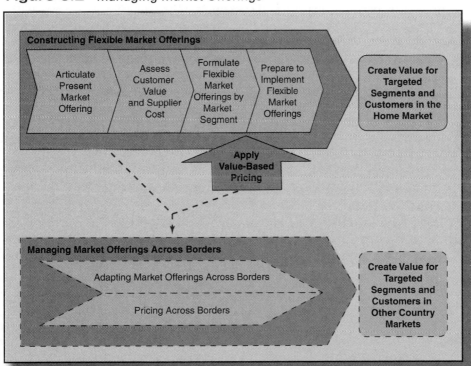

Some Conventional Thinking About Market Offerings

Because business markets change and thinking about business marketing advances, even experienced business market managers need to periodically revisit their market views. It can thus be worthwhile to reexamine conventional thinking about what suppliers should and can do in the marketplace. Here, we reevaluate two often-encountered, conventional thoughts about market offerings to separate truth from apparent fiction.

The Tunnel Vision of Commodity Markets

If you think you are in a commodity market, you're thinking too narrowly about the market you're in.

Over the years, when discussing business marketing approaches for firms to differentiate themselves from competitors, we have had a number of supplier managers respond with something to the effect of: "That is all well and good, but I'm in a commodity market!" Our response, most often, has been the preceding quote. As we saw in Chapter 3, the buying orientation tactic of **commoditization** is to convince suppliers that no differences exist among offerings. In turn, it is the responsibility of business market managers to persuasively demonstrate to customers that their offering is different in valuable ways.

Indeed, as products mature and customers gain extensive experience with them, there appears to be a routine narrowing of perceived differences among offerings in customers' minds and a corresponding unwillingness to pay anything different for them. In other words, the offerings over time tend to become undifferentiated in the minds of customers, with price becoming the sole basis for deciding among them. This is the definition of a **commodity**. The seemingly inexorable pull on a market toward commoditization has been referred to as the "commodity magnet."[2] To beat the commodity magnet, or at least to slow its pull over time, supplier managers must continually search for ways to differentiate their market offerings in ways that customers value.

In his classic article titled, "Marketing Success Through Differentiation—of Anything," Levitt begins by stating:

> There is no such thing as a commodity. All goods and services are differentiable. Though the usual presumption is that this is more true of consumer goods than of industrial goods and services, the opposite is the actual case.[3]

As support, Levitt provides a number of examples of differentiation, two of which we would like to recount. Durum is a particular variety of wheat principally used in making pasta. Many readers would regard it as a commodity, and, in fact, grain elevator operators and food processors quote standard prices for durum wheat. Yet, closer scrutiny reveals that the prices growers actually receive vary, depending on the results of tests of the wheat's more elemental properties, such as its protein, moisture, farina, and gluten content. As Levitt notes, "Premiums and discounts for quality differences in a particular year have been known to vary from the futures prices on commodity exchanges by amounts greater than the futures price fluctuations themselves during that year."[4] By carefully studying how subtle variations in the core product's characteristics provide incremental value for certain sets of customers, such as pasta manufacturers in the example, suppliers may find meaningful ways to differentiate.

In some cases, though, the core products of alternative suppliers are essentially interchangeable. Still, augmenting services, programs, and systems present various ways for suppliers to set themselves apart from one another. As Levitt relates, although commodities dealers trade in totally undifferentiated core products, such as metals, grains, and pork bellies, they differentiate their offerings on their professed distinction in their execution of the trades and supporting activities for their clients. A supplier can discover potentially valuable ways to do business differently by more broadly considering all of the activities a customer undertakes and the resources it employs in using a supplier's offering.[5]

What can suppliers do to forestall or reverse this trend toward commoditization? The initial step for suppliers to take is to understand the true extent of commoditization for their offerings, which also uncovers some possibilities for differentiation. Armed with this knowledge, suppliers can pursue several strategies to rebuild their market offerings into differentiated offerings that customers value more than those of competitors.[6]

Understanding the True Extent of Commoditization

Oftentimes, suppliers simply conclude, "We're in a commodity business," because they are thinking narrowly about the core product or service. That is, the personal computer, hospital supplies, or letter-of-credit that the customer purchases may be nearly or exactly the same across suppliers. But the market offerings that customers purchase typically are more than simply the core product or service. These market offerings contain supplementary services, programs, and systems that enhance the value of the core product (or service) and provide additional value to customers. Thus, before concluding they are in a commodity business, suppliers need to more carefully examine exactly what differences exist between their offerings and those of competitors, drawing on market and internal data. Specifically, they should gain estimates of the value that customers receive, validate their market pricing, and gain estimates of their firm's share of customer's business.

Although much attention in recent years has been given to value and its provision to customers, remarkably few firms have the knowledge and capability to assess value in practice. We discussed customer value management in Chapter 2, which has as a central undertaking building customer value models. A supplier needs a fine-grained understanding of the value that a customer receives from its market offering relative to the next-best alternative. At the same time, suppliers should investigate what potential changes in their market offerings *would* be worth to customers. Although suppliers are more conversant with the technical and economic benefits of their offerings, they should not neglect service and social benefits, which can be significant sources of value.

Consider, for example, safety glasses (protective eyewear). Safety glasses provide the technical benefit of protecting workers' eyes from infrared and ultraviolet light, and foreign substances such as chemical stray. They provide the economic benefit of fewer lost days due to on-the-job injuries and lower insurance premiums. To obtain these technical and economic benefits, however, the worker must wear the safety glasses, looking like a "dork". As a result, younger workers more concerned about how they look than about safety often do not wear them when they should. Taking a more comprehensive view of value, Dalloz Safety Products designed a line of protective eyewear that look like designer sunglasses. The glasses have contoured wrap-around frames that come in a variety of colors, with lenses in a selection of tints and colors. Now, workers actually like wearing their stylish Dalloz protective eyewear, making workplace compliance no longer a problem.

Gaining an accurate understanding of competitors' prices often is difficult in business markets. A supplier must *systematically* gather data from the field on the range of prices that customers are paying for competitor market offerings. A supplier also should investigate what supplementary services are and are not included in a competitor's quoted price for a market offering, to better understand offering comparability. Gathering these data will give the supplier a finer-grained understanding of variations in competitor pricing in the marketplace.

A supplier must also gather data about its own prices. Use of off-invoice rebates or allowances, whose percentages may depend on the amount of business that the customer has done with the supplier during the quarter or year, make it difficult for a supplier to know at the time exactly what price it is realizing from a given transaction. Monitoring transaction prices enables a supplier to learn the extent to which exceptions are being made from set pricing strategy and tactics. One supplier discovered that 67 percent of its business was done on the basis of out-of-policy requests—transaction pricing that deviated from established pricing policy.

Finally, a supplier must gain an estimate of the percentage of each customer's total purchase requirements it obtains for each market offering it provides. Although most firms in business markets have some estimate of their market share, far fewer have estimates of their shares of each customer's business in the markets they serve. Yet, **share of customer's business** is much more diagnostic in that it pinpoints customer accounts that perceive the supplier's offering as superior to those of competitors and suggests sources of differentiation.

Suppose that a supplier has a 20 percent market share. It is unlikely that each customer in the market is purchasing 20 percent of its requirement from the supplier. Rather, some customers purchase nothing from the supplier and others are purchasing more than 20 percent of their requirements from the supplier. What differentiates large-share customers from minor-share customers and what sources of differentiation are possible if the customer were to give the supplier 100 percent share?

Rebuilding Differentiation

In business markets where the core product or service is seen as a commodity, it may be extremely costly or difficult to achieve a difference in the core product or service that customers would perceive as significant. By considering more broadly how they might deliver value to customers, suppliers can identify significant sources of differentiation. Supplementary services, programs, and systems most often are more profitable sources of differentiation that can significantly change the way customers value market offerings.

Suppliers can search for knowledge that would be valuable for customers to have, yet difficult for them to gain by themselves. We refer to this as *creating knowledge banks*. One sort of knowledge is how the customer operations and ways of doing things compare with those of its competitors. Allegiance Healthcare, a leading distributor of hospital supplies, built a best practice database from the experiences of 100 leading hospitals for the 30 surgical procedures that drive 80 percent of a hospital's volume. This database details the activities performed and resources consumed for each of these surgical procedures. Armed with the knowledge this database provides, Allegiance clinical consultants work with hospital customers to identify where the hospitals deviate from best practice and assist in efforts to reduce costs and improve productivity.

Suppliers can search for problems or nuisances that a number of customers each experience, where the supplier could invest in expertise that could be shared across customers to solve or alleviate the problems. In doing so, the suppliers are able to provide superior solutions to customer problems, often at lower costs, and differentiate themselves from competitors. We refer to this as *building leveraging expertise*.

GLS Inc., a leading distributor of composite materials and elastomers, recognized that it could leverage its superior expertise in environmental, health, and safety regulatory compliance as a value-adding service for its customers, which mostly are medium and small firms. GLS monitors the *Federal Register* and writes bulletins alerting customers on regulatory changes, as well as reminding them of existing standards. It provides customers with a regulatory compliance manual, performs audits of Enviromental Protection Agency (EPA) and Occupational Safety and Health Administration (OSHA) regulatory compliance at customer locations, and assists smaller customers in preparing their annual toxic chemical release inventories and air emissions statements. Without GLS's assistance, these customers would find it difficult and costly to keep informed of regulatory changes, and what they need to do to comply. Senior management at these customers greatly appreciates GLS's support, because failure to comply now can lead to criminal prosecution.

When corporate customers purchase personal computers (PCs), they often want to install software specific to their firms in addition to software licensed from firms such as Microsoft. To do this customization, though, typically takes an hour or two, costs between $200 and $300, and is a bother to both the user and the firm's PC support staff. Dell Computer recognized that it could build some leveraging expertise that would enable it to solve this costly nuisance for its major customers. It created a high-speed, 100-megabit ethernet at its factory that can instantly download a tailored mix of software onto its major customers' PCs.[7]

Customers that focus on the core product or service tend to see only lowering price, not total cost, as a way of suppliers setting themselves apart from one another. Yet, suppliers that change the customer's frame of reference to total cost have much greater opportunities to add value, reduce costs, and differentiate themselves from competitors. We refer to this process as *changing the customer's frame of reference*. As an example, Boeing has 100,000 Dell PCs. Dell Computer has 30 employees on-site at Boeing, who work closely with Boeing managers in planning their requirements and configuring their network. Because of this arrangement, the Dell personnel are regarded more like Boeings' PC department than a PC vendor.

In exchange for 100 percent share of a customer's business, suppliers sometimes are able to change how they do business with the customer. As an example, a coatings supplier was willing to put a technician on-site to oversee the painting process and to quote a price per coated object rather than the customary price per liter of coating. And, after all, isn't price per coated object what the customer should really care about?

Finally, no matter how precisely a supplier segments a market, some residual variation in the product and service requirements of segment members will remain. That is, even though customers within a segment may be essentially the same in many of their requirements, they remain different in others. Rather than ignore residual variation, perceptive suppliers take advantage of it by *building flexibility into their market offerings*. Later in this chapter, we discuss at length constructing and managing flexible market offerings. Here, we simply mention that flexible market offerings do set a supplier apart from its competitors, which continue to offer a "standard" offering constructed for the "average" customer that "defines" each segment.

Services as Core Products in Market Offerings

Many of us are used to thinking of the core product as some tangible item. However, when the core product is a service, how does it affect our thinking about managing the market offering? Two views can be taken on this point. One is that services are fundamentally different.[8] In support of this viewpoint, four characteristics are thought to be unique to services:[9]

1. *Intangibility*. Services can't be touched but rather are experienced.
2. *Inseparability of production and consumption*. Services are consumed as they are produced.
3. *Perishability*. Following from this inseparability, services cannot be saved or stored for later use.
4. *Heterogeneity*. Because of their greater dependence on the provider, services have the potential for high variance in their performance.

The opposing view is that the differences between products and services are a matter of degree and that all market offerings can be thought of as falling along a continuum of tangibility. Further, few, if any, products or services are completely tangible or completely intangible. As Levitt notes, "Even the most tangible of products can't be *reliably* tested or experienced in advance." Based on this view, suppliers provide promises of performance satisfaction to prospective customers, which they attempt to tangibilize in their presentation.[10]

We concur with this latter view for two reasons. First, with some thought, we can identify services and products that are not consistent with the uniqueness characteristics listed previously. Cleaning services performed at night and market research studies are each produced separately and prior to their consumption or usage by customers. On the other hand, tangible products such as specialty organic chemicals are relatively perishable. Services themselves differ significantly in the tangibility of the outputs that they produce. Consider, for example, the range of tangibility for the following business services: architectural drawings, commercial banking, investment banking, tax attorney consultation, and commercial insurance. Second, in our experience, market offerings in the business marketplace are changing in ways that are moving them toward the center of the tangibility continuum. Services marketers appear to be increasingly seeking to "tangibilize" their market offerings, while product marketers appear to be increasingly wrapping their products with augmenting services.[11]

CONSTRUCTING FLEXIBLE MARKET OFFERINGS

Firms in business markets are learning that success depends upon adroitly balancing three pervasive, but often conflicting, marketplace requirements.[12] First, markets are becoming highly fragmented and customers are requesting, and getting, more customized offerings. Second, customers are uncompromising in their demands that market offerings be sold for either the lowest price or the lowest total cost. Third, due to the success of the total quality management movement, many purchasers now take quality as a given and believe that few meaningful differences separate competing products. Customer firms increasingly expect suppliers to deliver added value and differentiation in the form of an augmenting bundle of **services**, **programs**, and **systems** such as those listed earlier in Figure 5.1. Hereafter, for simplicity, we most often refer to these value-adding elements inclusively as "services."[13]

However, few firms have discovered all the implications of these requirements. Instead, most choose to add layer upon layer of services to their market offerings at prices that reflect neither customer value nor their own costs, in the hope of keeping customers satisfied and gaining some competitive advantage. As the anecdotes in Box 5.1 reveal, such efforts often produce unintended results.

How can business market managers avoid such nightmares and confront seemingly paradoxical pressures to differentiate themselves from competitors, yet keep their own costs and prices to customers down? On the product side of the market offering, flexible manufacturing, modularization, and product platform design have each been part of the solution. This paradigm shift has challenged conventional thinking that it is impossible to provide product variety and low cost.[14] On the services side of the market offering, a counterpart paradigm shift is occurring. The firms leading the way have begun to provide flexible market offerings, consisting of **naked solutions**, **with options**.

The Concept of Flexible Market Offerings

Business market managers start with the realization that no matter how precisely a firm segments a market, some residual variation in the product and service requirements of segment members will remain. That is, even though customers within a segment may be essentially the same in some of their requirements, they remain different in others. In the past, suppliers either ignored or were unable to deal with this variation, choosing instead to provide market offerings composed of "standard" bundles or packages of products and services designed to meet the needs of the "average" customer within each segment. Even worse, in many instances, suppliers

BOX 5.1
Market Offering Practice Runs Amok

A supplier of closures and terminals for copper and fiber optic cables lost a multimillion dollar contract to a renegade "bare-bones" competitor. The customer had been an account for more than 15 years, and the supplier felt that it completely understood its requirements. At contract renewal time, its sales personnel visited the customer's plant site and came away with a list of detailed product specifications and service requests. In response, the supplier developed a premium-priced, "full-service" package that completely met the customer's stated requirements.

Supplier managers were shocked when they learned they lost the account to a new competitor offering a low-priced, "no-frills" package. Not only did this competitive offer contain no support services, but the products included also fell slightly below the customer's stated specifications. When asked why they switched to the new vendor, customer managers replied that the competitor's quote was so low that even if the products failed, the firm would have enough funds available from the price difference to readily pay for a consulting engineering company to correct the problems. In retrospect, supplier management concluded that if its sales force had spent more time understanding what the customer actually valued and was willing to pay for, it might have avoided this sizable loss in sales.

In an attempt to grab market share in a stagnant commodity marketplace, a textile producer volunteered to store its products "on consignment" at the plants of a major, apparel-producing customer. In addition to keeping the inventory on its books until the customer firm used it, the textile producer agreed to lease warehouse space in the customer's plant to store the inventory; furnish an optical scanner and computer system to monitor textile consumption; and pay for insurance against inventory damage, theft, or loss. Not surprisingly, the customer immediately jumped at the opportunity to implement this innovative program.

What came as a shock to the textile producer, though, was that within one week, all three of its major competitors duplicated that program for the apparel producer. Moreover, after a short-term increase in its share of the customer's business, the textile producer saw its share and those of its competitors return to their preprogram levels. Soon, other apparel producers began to demand the same service. Taking stock at the end of the year, the textile producer discovered that the consignment program had resulted in an overall loss of several million dollars in operating profits. Its managers assumed the same was the case for its competitors. The textile producer took little solace in the fact that its customer satisfaction ratings from the apparel producer had soared to an all-time high.

---

have provided essentially the same "vanilla" offering across all segments. As a result, some customers felt that they were forced to pay for services they did not need, while others did not get the depth of service they required, even if they were willing to pay extra.

Rather than ignore residual variation, perceptive business market managers take advantage of it by building flexibility into their market offerings. They do so by first constructing **naked solutions** for each market segment—the bare minimum of products and services that all segment members uniformly value. Importantly, naked solutions are sold at the lowest profitable price. In turn, naked solutions are wrapped with **options** that some, but not all, segment members value, and are offered separately for those segment members that do value them.

Although flexible market offerings enable customers to tailor the offering to their own requirements and preferences to a greater degree, this concept is not the same as mass customization. **Mass customization** is the capability to offer individually specified products or services on a large scale. As Zipkin details:

> Mass-customization systems have three key capabilities: *elicitation* (a mechanism for interacting with the customer and obtaining specific information); *process flexibility* (production technology that fabricates the product according to the information); and *logistics* (subsequent processing stages and distribution that are able to maintain the identity of each item and to deliver the right one to the right customer). Those elements are connected by powerful communications and thereby integrated into a seamless whole.[15]

In contrast, flexible market offerings are comprised of a few well-chosen naked solutions, each of which is wrapped with well-chosen options, where the supplier makes these choices prior to offering them to customers. Thus, flexible market offerings are more akin to the concepts of modularity and commonality in product design, which we discuss in Chapter 6. Our experience concurs with the views of pundits that most firms in business markets are not able to profitability offer mass customization. Moreover, we contend that these firms can gain most, if not all, of the benefits of mass customization at a much-lower cost through flexible market offerings.[16]

Although flexible market offerings comprise both product components and services components, hereafter in this chapter we focus primarily on the services part of the market offerings. In many industries, business market managers find that services are the predominant means of creating value to differentiate their offerings from those of competitors. We discuss gaining flexibility on the product part of the market offering at lower cost in Chapter 6 as part of new offering realization.

How can suppliers move to flexible market offerings? In the following sections, we discuss how this approach is put into practice. In the process, we consider the difficulties business market managers can expect to encounter, and suggest solutions.

Articulate the Present Market Offering for Each Market Segment

To start, business market managers need to take stock of how their firm is doing business by detailing their current market offerings for each segment. As an illustration, consider the service portion of Baxter Healthcare Corporation's market offering to two segments of interest: transactional hospital customers, which do business with Baxter on an order-by-order basis, and strategic customers, which are hospitals that have made a commitment to a closer relationship with Baxter (see Figure 5.3).[17] Baxter constructed these offerings to provide ordinary and extraordinary levels of services, programs, and systems that reinforce its commitment to fulfilling strategic customers' requirements, and enhancing their medical services and financial performance. Even programs that are optional and charged for separately, such as Baxter

Figure 5.3   Baxter Healthcare's Market Offerings to Two Segments: Transactional and Strategic Hospital Customers

	Segment	
Market Offering Element	Transactional Customer	Strategic Customer
Services		
Product returns	standard	standard
Technical assistance	standard	standard
Single point-of-contact	not offered	standard
Future disease incidence forecast	not offered	option
⋮		
Programs		
Price deals	standard	standard
Corporate customer bonus (financial incentive)	not offered	standard
Executive perspectives	not offered	standard
Consolidated purchasing report summary	not offered	standard
ACCESS Program	not offered	option
Baxter Corporate Consulting	not offered	option
⋮		
Systems		
ASAP order entry system	standard	standard
COMDISCO technology assessment	not offered	standard
ValueLink stockless inventory program	option	option
COMDISCO asset management system	option	option
⋮		

Corporate Consulting, reflect this commitment because they provide value or savings that far exceed their cost to the strategic customer.

Businesses that have market offerings as well-articulated and well-managed as Baxter's are rare. More often, managers' understanding of the services, programs, and systems their firm offers within and across market segments is piecemeal, uneven, and inaccurate. For this reason, managers from all functional areas that "touch" the customers in some way should take part in a structured process to elicit the present market offerings for each segment. Meeting as a group, a facilitator systematically takes these managers through the various kinds of services, programs, and systems a business might offer. For each one, the managers are asked, "Are you doing something like this?" As a follow-up question, the managers are asked, "Are you doing this sometimes, for some customers?"

Supplier managers can gain at least three different kinds of insights from this process: the true breadth of the market offering, the arbitrary nature of charges, and lack of variation across segments.

The True Breadth of the Market Offering

Managers invariably spend more time, and have less difficulty, thinking about the product portions of their market offerings. On the other hand, most have trouble identifying the services their firms provide. Inevitably, the services portions of market offerings are found to be more extensive than managers realize.

The Arbitrary Nature of Charges

Another revelation is the lack of discipline in what is offered as "standard" at the package price, and what is marketed as an "option" for which customers pay separately. All too often, suppliers find that their sales forces are guilty of "fourth-quarter habits;" that is, the practice of giving away service options "for free" at the end of the year in order to meet their sales quotas. In doing so, they cloud customer expectations of what services are standard and what are optional. Suppliers sometimes discover that certain customers are adept in circumventing charges, perhaps through knowing who to call for a favor or special treatment.[18]

Lack of Variation Across Segments

A final insight that many suppliers gain from the examination of market offerings is the "vanilla" nature of their offerings across segments. In business markets, a number of firms still segment the market and then proceed to provide much the same, if not exactly the same, offering to each segment. As the marketing manager for a large chemical company related, "For 90 percent of our customers, we offer the identical mix of support services."

Assess Customer Value and Supplier Cost

Before supplier managers can formulate flexible market offerings for each segment, they need to gain an estimate of the value of each service and the cost to provide it. Having this knowledge would seem to be fundamental in managing market offerings. However, few businesses have undertaken any formal value or cost assessments.

Measuring Customer Value

Many business market managers seem content to rely solely on measures of customer satisfaction. As one manager observed, "Our research exclusively takes the form of 'how are we doing' surveys (i.e., customer satisfaction) rather than 'how much are they worth to you' studies (i.e., customer value assessment)." Customer satisfaction studies capture a supplier's performance against expectations about services that have been shaped by customers' past experiences with a supplier as well as with its competitors. They also capture what the customer perceives to be "fair and appropriate" in a market offering's content and price.

Because they delineate customer expectations and measure supplier performance against them, customer satisfaction measurement studies are worthwhile, but sole reliance on them can lead to serious errors in judgment. Naturally, customers will be more satisfied when they receive services for free than when they have to pay for them. After all, the supplier is giving value away. Suppliers can easily overcommit resources and overspend budgets by blindly pursuing incremental improvements in customer satisfaction.[19] Finally, if they do not assess the worth of services, marketers are ill-equipped to set market offering prices at fair levels.

How do leading-edge firms measure the value of their augmenting services? Greif Inc., which manufactures fiber and plastic drums, routinely conducts what it calls *cost-in-use* studies to document the incremental cost savings, and thus the superior value, that a customer gains by using Greif products and services rather than a competitor's. To add credibility to the results, one of Greif's technical service managers works with customer managers to complete the research. In addition to examining manufacturing, the team undertakes a series of process flow analyses in which it diagrams the customer's business operations and estimates their current costs. From these estimates, Greif managers brainstorm system solutions for the customer. For example, they might envision a complete materials handling system, including just-in-time deliveries, utilized delivery systems (e.g., placing rollers on trucks to facilitate unloading), and drum recycling. Importantly, Greif gives the customer a variety of service alternatives along with estimates of cost savings. In this way, customers can make informed purchase decisions based upon the worth of proposed system solutions to them.[20]

Coming to Grips with Service Costs

As for costs, recent strides in the development and implementation of activity-based costing (ABC) techniques would seem to facilitate the assessment of costs on a customer-by-customer basis. However, few companies appear to be using ABC in the management of their market offerings. Why? For starters, existing ABC techniques are best suited for the measurement of manufacturing and product-related costs. Little work has been done to apply ABC techniques to service, program, or system costs. Thus, many firms simply don't know how to apply ABC to services. We find that three specific factors inhibit the application of ABC techniques in managing the services portion of the market offering: services definitions are often "fuzzy"; service costs are often buried in the fixed costs of staff departments; and many companies remain organized around the products they sell rather than around market segments or customers.[21]

Overcoming inertia and systems impediments is essential, because more fully and accurately allocated costs can provide quite a different picture of how costly some services actually are. In an activity-based costing study, drug wholesalers found that the returned goods service they provided to customers cost approximately 3.7 percent of the average wholesaler's gross sales, not 1 or 2 percent as was commonly thought. This substantial disparity was due to reliance on credited dollars as a percentage of sales as a measure of service cost, which did not recognize a number of "hidden" transaction costs for wholesalers.[22]

How do progressive companies understand the services costs associated with their market offerings? To eliminate the problems associated with fuzzy services and the tendency of sales reps to bury service costs, Van Den Bergh Foods, a manufacturer of food additives and seasonings, revamped its service delivery and planning systems. For starters, the company more precisely defined its services and the levels of each it offered. Its sales force, which is composed of highly trained technical representatives, is now required to handle all minor services, such as basic problem solving. Charges for such services account for a portion of the total yearly budget allotted to each sales representative. All major services, such as detailed technical problem solving, are now offered on a project basis and delivered by technical experts from departments such as customer service. Either the customer directly pays for the project, which is preferred, or a charge is placed against the allotted, discretionary budget of its sales representative. At the beginning of each year, Van Den Bergh managers construct an annual operational plan for each major customer account that defines financial and volume targets and specifies the levels of services Van Den Bergh will provide. At the end of the year, the managers review these plans, examine service costs and account profitability, and recommend changes in level of account services for the next year.

The Payoff from Value and Cost Assessments

What results can supplier managers expect when they perform customer value assessments in conjunction with cost assessments, as we advocate? Box 5.2, which details the experience of AKZO Industrial Coatings (now AKZO NOBEL), demonstrates that the payoff can be substantial.

Understanding the value of services to customers and the cost to perform them enables business market managers to identify **value drains**, which are services that cost the supplier more to provide than they are worth to customers receiving them and have no strategic significance. A producer of chemicals for use in extracting oil from wells routinely performed a field analytic monitoring service for each of its customers

BOX 5.2
Putting Measures of Expectations, Value, and Costs to Use

About 10 years ago, spurred on by unacceptable profitability, managers at the Netherlands-based AKZO Industrial Coatings (IC) asked themselves the question, "Are we not giving more service than the customer is paying for?" To answer this, AKZO managers first developed a method based on ABC techniques, and then undertook an analysis of the contribution to profit (CTP) of each customer. Next, relying on a field value-in-use method of customer value assessment, they determined the value of each service that they provided. So, for example, when an investigating engineer was dispatched to analyze dust in a customer's paint line and identify where the dust came from, the value of this service would be quantified in terms of the effects of this problem on customer cost (e.g., downtime and scrap parts) and other performance parameters, such as the first-run OK percentage and the percentage of defects.

AKZO managers discovered that they were in fact giving away more service than many customers were paying for. Furthermore, they learned that some of their services provided little value to customers. Many of these services were offered by competing firms "for free," and customers expected to get them, even though they didn't place much value on some. AKZO managers decided to take unprecedented strategic action. First, embracing a philosophy of "growth in selected areas," they targeted those industries and market segments where AKZO products furnished the greatest customer value and thus had the greatest profit potential. Second, utilizing CTP measures, they revamped their market offerings and pricing. Price discussions were held with selected customers, where AKZO was determined to get an equitable return on the services it provided. Although AKZO IC lost some customers because they no longer got a variety of services for free, overall, its perseverance resulted in stable sales volume at significantly better profitability, even during the next recession.

to determine when, and in what amounts, they should apply its products. A salesperson visiting one of the firm's smaller, less-sophisticated customers noticed the analysis reports stacked in a corner of the production shed. When asked about their usefulness, the customer replied that he was not using the information at all, and instead just had the producer's truck driver pump a few gallons into each well whenever the truck came by. Learning this, the producer offered to discontinue the field testing, and in exchange, give the customer a 7 percent per gallon price reduction. The customer readily agreed, and, significantly, account profitability went from minus 6 percent to 32 percent! Rather than finding value drains by chance, as in this example, suppliers can use value assessment proactively in conjunction with activity-based costing analysis to detect them.

Gaining an estimate of the value of market offering elements is not always easy; having one, though, is essential. With an understanding of value, discussions with customers can focus on performance and meeting customer requirements. Without this knowledge, discussions center on price. Yet, fine-grained estimates of each element are not required. Instead, managers are seeking to make a basic, categorical judgment about the value of each element. That is, what supplier managers are trying to do is to isolate elements within a segment that are uniformly highly valued from those that are highly valued by some but not others, and those that are not highly valued by any customers.

Much the same can be said about trade-offs between precision and cost in activity-based costing analyses. AKZO managers caution against pursuing too fine a level of allocation. The goal of a realistic assessment of each business activity needs to be acceptably met. Beyond this level, resources are better directed elsewhere. To start, if supplier managers have not already done so, they should establish baselines of services usage across customers within segments.

Formulate Flexible Market Offerings by Market Segment

When formulating flexible market offerings for each market segment, business market managers can choose from three strategic alternatives for each service element: Do not market the service; market it as standard for which there is no charge; or market it as an option for which there is a charge. Each service itself has one of three statuses: The service is a new one (meaning that it has not been previously marketed by the supplier although it may have been offered by some competitor); it is an existing standard service; or it is an existing optional service. We cross service status with service strategic alternative to provide nine unique combinations. A useful way to organize these nine resulting strategies is a **flexible market offering strategy matrix**, which we show in Figure 5.4. By arranging the services in their appropriate cells, this matrix can provide a systematic picture of the nature and balance of a supplier's market offering. It also can promote further inquiry and offering strategy development, as when, for example, managers find one or more cells empty of elements. We consider, in turn, the rows of this matrix. We then discuss the pricing implications of flexible market offerings.

Reevaluating Existing Standard Services

Because the overriding philosophy is to keep the standard offering as "naked" as possible, only those service, program, and system elements that all firms within a segment highly value should be standard. The first place to start putting this philosophy

Figure 5.4 Flexible Market Offering Strategy Matrix for Services, Programs, and Systems

	SERVICE ELEMENT DEPLOYMENT		
SERVICE ELEMENT STATUS	Do Not Market	Market as "Standard"	Market as "Option"
Existing "standard" service	Prune from standard offering	Retain in standard offering	Recast as surcharge option
Existing "optional" service	Discontinue option	Enhance standard offering	Retain as value-added option
New service	Keep on shelf	Augment standard offering	Introduce as value-added option

into practice is by reevaluating the existing standard services. By discontinuing, or "pruning," some of these services and recasting others as options, business market managers retain just the subset of standard services that will serve as the base of an updated standard offering.

Suppliers are often far more reluctant to discontinue existing services than they are to add services. Nonetheless, managers need to scrutinize existing elements for pruning candidates. One source is those services that most segment members rarely use. The customers that still value the service are so few that it is not worthwhile for the supplier to continue to offer it. In the interest of these customers, though, the supplier can sometimes outsource the service, or suggest another firm that provides it.

Certain services are readily pruned. For example, value drains that provide low customer value yet incur high costs for the supplier are ideal candidates. Following detailed investigations, a chemical manufacturer learned to its chagrin that while each of its 186 services continued to incur annual fixed costs, many had not been used in the past year. Its managers responded by pruning a large number of these services. Many customers didn't even realize the services were discontinued.

Beyond the services that all firms within a segment value highly, in some circumstances a supplier retains additional services in the standard offering. The success of certain services, in terms of their value or cost, depends upon their widespread usage by customers. Web-based order placement and tracking systems and logistics management systems are examples.

Service elements that a supplier cannot readily differentiate from those of competitors are candidates for matching, and most likely, for inclusion in the standard offering. Such elements are often regarded as standard in industry market offerings and often make up a substantial part of the naked offering. The challenge in offering these parity services is to have customers perceive their value as not significantly less than competitors' comparable services, but at the same time manage their costs below those of the competitors. The rationale is that because customers typically do not place much value on these services, they do not factor into customers' decisions about changing suppliers as long as they are minimally acceptable.

Supplier managers report that recasting a standard service as a surcharge option is the most difficult of the nine strategies to implement. Customers may react angrily when told they must now pay for something they had expected to get for free. It is even more difficult when competitors continue to market the service for free as part of a standard offering. Nowhere is this issue more of a problem than in industries characterized by high levels of fixed costs, such as commodity industrial chemicals and fully integrated steel mills. In such industries, managers are hesitant to implement any scheme that may result in reduced sales volume because it may jeopardize their ability to reach profitable capacity utilization levels. As a result, they routinely add services to retain volume and rarely drop any.

Infrequently performed services that deliver value at specific points in time, such as training, installation, and retrofitting, are perhaps the best candidates for redeployment as surcharge options. By marketing these services as value-added options, suppliers retain the business of customers that still derive value from them and are willing to pay for them. Often, this approach provides a "litmus test" for services that customers claim have no value for them (or are said to be the same as those obtainable for free from other suppliers), but that suppliers believe are worth something to customers. Depending on the market response, in the next period suppliers can either continue them as value-added options or discontinue them.

Leading supplier firms use a variety of approaches to recast services as value-added options. To make the overhaul of its standard service package more palatable to its customers, one specialty chemical company implemented a variation of this strategy. Along with specialty organic chemicals, the company offers a variety of services including laboratory support, field consulting, on-site testing, and educational seminars, all of which are costly. Realizing that its customers value and use these services differently, the company offers customers a variety of levels for each service. If a customer purchases a minimum amount of products each year, it receives "basic" levels of services along with the standard offering. If that same customer wants to receive a higher level of service, it can either increase its annual purchases to a prespecified amount or pay extra. Thus, some level of each service that customers expect is available with each standard offering. Customers that place greater value on the service have the option to buy more.

As a prelude to making some previously standard services value-added options, a large computer company began listing a charge for the provided services, which was then subtracted with the notation "Do not pay this." An accompanying letter explained that the company was pleased to have been able to provide the field service and stated what it estimated this service was worth to the customer, using market-based rates for independent industry consultants. In doing so, the company established the value of its services in the minds of its customers and positioned the services as not necessarily being performed at no charge in the future. Thus, a sharp distinction can be drawn between offering an element separately, even as an invoice reduction "no charge," and simply "burying" it within the standard package.

Another alternative is to have the customer pay, in full or in part, for whatever options they value with "bonus dollars," earned from doing business with the supplier. Strategic customers accrued "Baxter dollars" based on the amount of and growth in their purchases from Baxter Healthcare, which they then applied to any of a number of optional services, programs, and systems. In this way, strategic hospital customers used a common "Baxter dollars" resource to tailor Baxter's market offering to their own individual requirements.

Reexamining Optional Services

Next, supplier managers should reexamine existing optional services to determine whether they should be discontinued, used to enhance the standard offering, or continued as options.

As is the case with the standard package, evaluation and construction of options menus should begin with a deliberate attempt to prune existing optional services. Optional services that were once good sources of revenue for the supplier but are no longer used enough to justify their fully allocated costs are pruning candidates. Similarly, services whose cost has outstripped customers' willingness to pay for them (due to changes in technology, necessary expertise, or insurance risk) are also candidates. For example, because of insurance risk, most manufacturers are unwilling to provide transportation for drums of solvents, even for an additional delivery fee. As with pruning standard services, suppliers sometimes can help customers that still need these services to outsource them from other firms.

At times, suppliers may fold into standard offerings services that they have marketed as options. Where the core product of the market offering is regarded as a "commodity," suppliers look to enhance the standard offering as a means of differentiating themselves in the market. Their underlying belief is that customers do business on the basis of which supplier has the best or most extensive set of services. Because customers within segments will vary in how they value these services, however, the supplier is often driven to offer more elements in the standard offering.

Instead, suppliers should consider trimming the standard offering to the naked solution, offering a set of options, and letting customers pay, in full or in part, for whatever options they value with "bonus dollars." The more customers concentrate their purchases with the supplier, the more bonus dollars they earn, and the more services they can purchase. Not only does this alternative allow customers to tailor the supplier's market offering to their own particular requirements, it reinforces to them that they do not have to pay for services they do not want, as is the case with the totally bundled offering. To underscore the value of the services it offers, a supplier can promise to give customers cash for any unused bonus dollars at the end of the agreement, as did Baxter Healthcare.

Building Flexibility with New Services

What are the sources of new services? Some suppliers rely on their own strengths and capabilities to identify new services to offer. Another source of ideas is to focus on the cost structures and strategic imperatives of targeted key customers. What new services can the supplier innovate that will assist these customers in their own initiatives to lower costs or improve performance?

Because they have not been offered in the past, new services do not carry the "baggage" of customer expectations about how a supplier should provide them ("Now you want us to pay extra for something we used to get for free?"). Thus, new services provide the best means to build flexibility into market offerings. Even though they should try to preserve new services as stand-alone options, at times suppliers may elect not to offer them or use them to enhance the standard offering.

Suppliers may decide to not offer a new element because of a variety of market timing issues. It may be that customers have not yet recognized an element's value, the cost of providing it is still too high, or the present element it would replace is still deemed adequate. AKZO Industrial Coatings (IC) provides an example. They anticipated greater environmental concerns about current painting technologies, and invested substantial time and resources in the technological development of a process for "water-borne" paint application. As a service to its customers, AKZO would consult with them on changing to this more environmentally benign technology. Unfortunately, although many customers were interested to learn that AKZO possessed this capability, no one was willing to pay extra for it. AKZO managers believed that customers would not value the process until environmental protection laws required a significant reduction in solvent emissions. As a result, they decided to keep the technology on the shelf until customer value increased.

Suppliers sometimes enhance the standard offerings with new services. Where suppliers segment the market by relationships, managers look for new elements that will sustain and invigorate the collaborative relationships. One way is to add new services that anticipate and are responsive to customers' changing requirements. Okuma, a Japanese builder of computer numerical control (CNC) machine tools, provides an example. In one year, it introduced a *24-Hour Parts Shipment Guarantee*, while in the next, it began to sell a *Guaranteed Trade-In Program*. Okuma management believed that in addition to being responsive to a changing marketplace, the practice forced its distributors and employees to be more efficient—they must learn how to ship parts anywhere in the United States in 24 hours. It also gave the sales force something new and interesting to discuss during sales presentations.

Shrewd suppliers also add new services to standard offerings to thwart or stymie competitors. Baxter Scientific Products' Industrial Division, for example, deliberately seeks out new services that customers value and that Baxter can perform better than the competition or at lower costs. By bundling them in with the standard offering, Baxter forces competitors to choose from a series of unpleasant alternatives. If competitors decline to offer the service altogether, Baxter can tout its unique service to customers as an extra benefit of doing business with Baxter. If competitors attempt to match Baxter and offer the service, they must incur both added costs and time delays associated with learning how to deliver the new service. New elements that also are likely candidates for inclusion in the standard offering are those for which (1) most of the costs are incurred in their initial development or deployment; (2) continuing costs are relatively invariant over the number of customers actually using the element; or (3) usage of the element in some way reduces the supplier's own costs.

Offering new elements separately provides value-added options for customers that seek them and allows suppliers to readily gauge interest in new services, programs, and systems. For example, although R.R. Donnelley Company's traditional business has focused around printing, binding, film preparation, and prepress work, its management believes that future growth and profits will come from innovative services, such as database management, consulting and training, dimensional and talking ads, direct marketing, layout systems, and mapping services. To test their viability in the marketplace, Donnelley has offered these services as value-added options.

"New" elements that a supplier can offer separately as value-added options can emerge from reconsidering services in the standard offering. For each service that is offered at a constant level, supplier managers should ask whether they can define alternate levels that would have different value for different customers. In one electrical wholesaler, an overworked inside sales force used overnight airfreight to cover mistakes in orders or delivery dates. It regarded this practice as "standard" (i.e., the sole service recovery element) when, in many instances, second-day UPS and third-day common carrier would have been viable options.

ABB's Power Transformers business has recognized that not all customers want the same level of maintenance service, nor value it the same. Traditionally, utilities required equipment maintenance. Instead of simply offering this service, as in the past, ABB now offers different levels of maintenance service as part of a service agreement. ABB draws on its experience in providing the different levels of service to customers to price these service agreements. Rather than having service on all their transformers, some customers even tell ABB what transformers to check and then ask how much ABB will charge for providing just that service.[23]

Pricing Implications

It is crucial to recognize that constructing flexible market offerings says little, if anything, about their pricing. Pricing is based on the supplier's strategy for each market segment. For example, suppliers that pursue enhancing the standard offering with additional services may alternately decide to raise the price, keep it the same, or even lower it. The market offering's price might be raised commensurate with the greater value provided, or raised less than the added value to "soften" the effects of a needed price increase due to rising costs. A supplier might keep the price the same in a stable marketplace to gain new or incremental business through superior value, or in a price-declining marketplace simply to hold price. The price might even be lowered in support of an aggressive market development or market share growth strategy.

Further, customers may value certain services offered as standard, but the only way they are affordable to a supplier is if it has all the customer's business. With single-sourcing, a supplier can take responsibility for the customer process in which its products play a principal role, such as a coatings supplier's taking responsibility for the whole painting process in a customer's paint shop. These single-source service arrangements can lead to innovative pricing, such as the customer's paying for the number of coated objects, rather than liters of paint. The supplier may even be paid more for lower rejects and rework on the coated objects.

Similarly, pruning elements has no inherent pricing implication, but again the effect depends on the segment market strategy. A supplier might lower its price equal to the cost of the discontinued services, thereby maintaining the competitive status quo. Alternatively, to improve contribution margins, a supplier might not lower the price at all, or lower the price but less than the cost of providing the service. This latter tactic has the dual advantage of improving the value of the offering to customers that did not value the pruned service, while providing an incentive for competitors that are similarly looking to improve their profitability to match the supplier's action. Suppliers might even raise prices in situations where they are pursuing a harvest strategy, taking as much profit out of the business as possible while letting it decline.[24]

Offering services separately provides flexibility not only to the customers within a segment, but to the supplier, too, in terms of pricing. Putting a price on a service (or a higher-level of a service whose base level is standard) preserves the supplier's option of charging separately for it. The supplier then is able to either charge a customer for its provision or trade its provision for a larger share or more-profitable mix of the customer's purchase requirement. One alternative is to show the service charge on an invoice and then "net out" the charge for a specific reason (e.g., initial use discount). This approach has at least three advantages. It provides a readily captured way of tracking service "giveaways." Suppliers employ it in a selective, transitory way, such as to close a deal, to blunt a competitive inroad, or to attract business in targeted new segments. For example, Mitsubishi Electric Industrial Controls offers as an option a proprietary software development tool, but to win targeted new accounts, it may provide the tool at no charge. Consulting on usage of this software tool, which it also offers separately, may initially be provided at no charge, but subsequent consulting is not. Finally, showing a charge establishes and reinforces the value of services to customers and the supplier's salespeople.[25]

Prepare to Implement Flexible Market Offerings

After constructing flexible market offerings, a supplier has several tasks to accomplish prior to implementing those offerings. The supplier needs to decide how it will present the flexible market offerings to the market. Presenting a flexible market offering as an option menu or as a tailored-value package are two basic alternatives. Branding each market offering is a means of differentiating it from other market offerings, particularly with respect to the value it delivers. A supplier must anticipate implementation problems with customers and how it will handle them. Finally, the supplier works through the issues involved in breaking away from the pack of competitors' market offerings.

Option Menu versus Tailored-Value Package

What will the customer see in making its decision: an option menu or a tailored-value package? The option menu approach makes the flexible market offering transparent to the customer by listing all optional elements. Although the salesperson may provide consultation, the customer has the primary responsibility for tailoring the market offering to its perceived requirements. Apple Computing and Microsoft each provide detailed, multiple-page menus of technical support services with pricing options, and let customers decide.

Figure 5.5 conveys the recent flexible market offerings of KLM Special Cargo (SC), a business unit of KLM Royal Dutch Airlines. By providing a base level of service and optional higher levels for its market offerings, KLM SC enables customers to tailor the service level to their own varying performance requirements. In doing so, KLM SC has been able to obtain a larger share of targeted customers' purchase requirements.[26]

Rather than treating all elements as options, suppliers often provide a standard package with a menu of options, and let the customer craft its own market offering. Certainly, in negotiated bid situations, a preferred strategy is to start with a naked offering at the lowest possible bid price, to be selected for further negotiations. The supplier then uses consultative selling efforts to "trade-up" the customer to select options that will provide value. Astute suppliers realize that if they do not have a competitively low bid price, they have no opportunity to do business, so they develop a two-part negotiations strategy.

Figure 5.5 Flexible Market Offerings of KLM Special Cargo

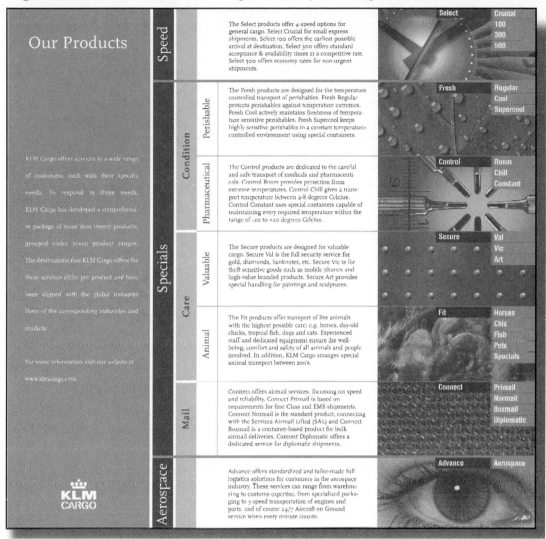

Source: Promotional price courtesy of KLM Cargo.

In contrast, the **tailored-value package** approach keeps the flexible market offerings opaque to customers. Working with the customer, the salesperson develops a list of specifications and then crafts an offering based on a menu of options that only she sees. This method places greater responsibility on the salesperson to accurately comprehend and respond to stated customer requirements. In practice, salespeople would most often respond with several packages and let the customer choose among them. Purchasing managers may request several packages in an attempt to gain an understanding of the trade-offs the supplier is implicitly offering.

Sonoco Product Company's Industrial Products Division uses both approaches. The division manufactures fiber cores around which products such as newsprint, commercial printing paper, textiles, yarns, plastic films, and aluminum foil are wrapped. Its customers select from several market offerings. For customers that want the lowest possible price, it markets a naked solution comprised of parent cores (uncut cores in standard lengths ranging from 8 to 30 feet) plus a minimum of support services. Sonoco will also sell these customers trimming equipment to cut the parent cores into usable sizes. For customers that don't want to be bothered with the tasks and investments associated with cutting cores, Sonoco markets fiber cores that match customer specifications. Along with fiber cores, Sonoco offers a variety of optional services such as process redesign of customer packaging systems. Finally, for customers located great distances from Sonoco plants and concerned that deliveries won't arrive on time, Sonoco will even set up a satellite plant near the customer's location (often in space leased in industrial parks). There, Sonoco employees will cut the cores to customer specifications. Sonoco also offers these customers the optional services.

As mentioned, Sonoco sales representatives sell these market offerings in two ways. If the customer desires, reps will provide customers with a detailed menu of all Sonoco products and services along with their respective prices. The customer can pick and choose the products and services it desires. Alternatively, Sonoco sales reps can use their expertise to assemble several tailored packages of products and services. Along with the price of each proposed package, Sonoco sales reps provide a summary of the cost savings the customer can expect to gain if it buys the package. In this way, the customer can choose an appropriate package based not only on its price, but also on its value. Sonoco managers report that since they began offering customers such extensive choices, both division sales volume and market share have increased.

Branding Market Offerings

A **brand** is a shorthand descriptor of the promised value that a market offering delivers to targeted customers and a means of differentiating this value from that of other market offerings. These other market offerings may come from the same supplier or they may come from its competitors. Branding market offerings allows suppliers to make intangible benefits tangible to targeted customers, build differentiation in near-commodity markets, achieve identity and preference with customers' customers, and differentiate market offerings that have the same or very-similar core product but are augmented with different services, programs, and systems. We briefly consider each of these purposes of branding market offerings.

A market offering may provide a social benefit to customers. Because social benefits are intangible, branding can serve to make the intangible tangible. Excelon chose to brand its environmentally preferable power as Eco-Preferred® Power to make tangible its ISO 14042 certification that this energy has a reduced impact on human health and the environment when compared with competing sources of energy that serve the same purpose. Excelon is thus able to better convey this social benefit to its commercial, government, and industrial customers that have environmental stewardship as part of their strategies.[27]

In many business markets, customers regard the offerings of competing suppliers as basically the same. Yet, through gaining a more fine-grained understanding of how subtle changes in the product can affect its performance in target customer applications, progressive suppliers can differentiate their offerings from less-astute competitors. They then persuasively communicate the significance of these subtle differences to target customers in branding initiatives to build **brand equity** for their market offerings. The experience of South Africa-based Mondi Paper Company in building and sustaining brand equity for its Rotatrim® copier paper provides an illustrative case, which we relate in Box 5.3.

When a supplier's market offering creates significant value for its customers' customers, pursuing a branding initiative enables the supplier to build identity and preference for its offering over those of competitors with the customers' customers. This is particularly the case when the presence of the supplier's product in its customer's product is not easily detectable by the customer's customers. The Intel Inside® branding initiative for its processors in personal computers is a well-known example. Pursuing an **ingredient branding strategy**, as this is sometimes called, is especially applicable when the customers' customers receiving the significant value are consumers. DuPont has pursued this strategy successfully with its STAINMAS-TER® brand of carpet protector, which it sells along with its fibers to carpet mills so that they can produce STAINMASTER carpet. In either case, brand-building efforts are focused primarily on the customers' customers.

Finally, branding market offerings enables a supplier to differentiate offerings where the core offering is essentially the same, but it has augmented the core offering with different services, programs, and systems to deliver superior value to target market segments having different requirements and preferences. The supplier then uses brand-building initiatives to reinforce the distinctive character of each brand and the value it delivers to its target customers. The experience of Germany-based BASF Corporation with its Glasurit® and R-M® brands of automotive refinish coatings provides a noteworthy case, which we relate in Box 5.4.

Anticipating Implementation Problems with Customers

Suppliers can minimize implementation problems by understanding customer requirements and shaping customer expectations, through education and persuasion, about the superior value of the flexible market offerings. Suppliers need to manage service and pricing expectations to avoid acquiring a "nickel-and-diming" reputation. By developing collateral materials and case histories, they convey that less is more, and can more easily combat the "we used to get it for free" gripes. These messages portray flexible market offerings from the perspective, "You don't have to pay for what you don't want."

Suppliers need to be relentless in communicating the value story to customers. As mentioned earlier, new services provide perhaps the best opportunity to implement flexibility in market offerings. As a rollout or phase-in, suppliers also might consider implementing flexible market offerings at the same time they make product changes or introductions.

Ross Controls, a maker of pneumatic valves, had to educate its customers about the value its new customized service offering provided. Ross's customers were used to making purchasing decisions based on price, and did not see the benefit of spending a long time working with Ross to design custom valves for their specific applications. Because of its investment in computer-aided design tools and equipment automation, however, Ross could design and produce in several days what had

BOX 5.3
Mondi Rotatrim®: Branding Initiatives in a Near-Commodity Market in South Africa

To most white-collar professionals in the world, paper is simply paper, a commodity that purchasing managers negotiate mainly on price. This assumption is not the case in South Africa, where a company, Mondi Paper Company, has been successfully branding its high-quality Mondi Rotatrim paper for almost 20 years. At the beginning of the twenty-first century, it enjoys a stable and comfortable 35 percent market share. Because of its perceived superior performance, Mondi Rotatrim has obtained a pricing premium in certain markets, while maintaining its customer share.

In the 1980s, Mondi Paper was the first company to move away from the guillotine cutting method to use precision rotary cutting. Using a guillotine cutting method can produce a curled edge on the paper as well as rough edges or burrs. These problems can lead to more frequent jams in copiers, particularly with high-speed "production" machines that produce 180 copies per minute. Rotary cutting is more precise, does not put pressure on the edge of the paper and cuts through only 4 or 5 layers of paper at a time, for greater consistency. Mondi built a strong reputation for high-quality paper, exceptionally accurate and uniform sheet size that translated into customers' benefits that include increased quality in copying, faxing and printing, and reduced machine downtime, lost time and paper waste from fewer paper jams.

In the 1990s, all major competitors moved to rotary cutting. By that time, Mondi had built a significant market share, but could no longer enjoy a technological advantage over the competition. Moreover, in 1994–1995, following political changes, South Africa began to open its markets to outside competition and several companies from Asia started offering extremely competitive paper. To compete with Mondi, local competitors relaunched their products and started to introduce lower-grade paper at a much lower price to the market. Mondi Paper executives believed that they needed to pursue a strong branding initiative for Mondi Rotatrim to fend off these anticipated foreign competitors, as well as the aggressive resistance from South African ones. In 1996, Mondi began magazine and radio advertising to support the Rotatrim brand in the market.

In 1997, Mondi achieved a new technological prowess. Rotatrim moved from an acid-based to an alkaline-based formulation. As part of this change, Mondi used precipitated calcium carbonate, which is eight times less abrasive than the ground calcium carbonate that competitors use (still). Mondi Rotatrim became a significantly more environment-friendly paper. The brand gained a new technological advantage over the competition.

The same year, a large bank in South Africa issued a tender for its paper requirement. It took the samples that prospective suppliers provided and instead of doing the testing itself, had the South African Bureau of Standards test them. Rotatrim met the standards for "B" grade, which is superior paper for business application, and was the only brand to attain such a high quality rating.

In 1999, Mondi began using television advertising to communicate the value proposition for Rotatrim. Management thought it was appropriate to do so in order to reach the myriad of potential customers, including corporate purchasing managers, government agencies, printers, retailers, Small Offices Home Offices (SOHO), and stationers. Mondi Paper executives are convinced that branding has contributed significantly to reinforcing the high-end positioning of Mondi Rotatrim. Senior management allocated significant increases in the Mondi Rotatrim marketing budget in 2001 and 2002, confirming Mondi's willingness to support the brand. According to them, supporting the brand is a key element to sustain Mondi Rotatrim's differentiation in the minds of customers.

Source: Contributed by Research Associate Florent Carbonneau, Kellogg School of Management, Northwestern University.

BOX 5.4
BASF Sustains Two Brands That Differentiate Essentially the Same Coatings in Europe

Back in the 1960s, BASF acquired a German coatings company called Glasurit. Later on, in 1986, the group acquired another brand, R-M, originally from the United States. At that time, a debate arose within the firm among those who wanted to fold the R-M brand and retain Glasurit as the unique brand and others who argued that the company should get rid of both brands and replace them with the BASF name. Some, finally, forcefully made a case for the survival of Glasurit and R-M, believing that two brands with different identities would allow the company to target two segments of customers and result in larger sales. This last group prevailed, and today, Glasurit and R-M are both strong brands.

Glasurit and R-M produce very similar coatings. The production of the paint is done with the same technology, the same molecules and the same chemical reaction. The differentiation takes place as late as possible in the production process to allow differentiation at lowest cost. Glasurit and R-M target repair shops all over Europe, which use the coatings to repaint cars and trucks. In theory, the two brands are competing with each other. To minimize the competition and reinforce their separate brand identities, each brand maintains its own distribution channel, with no distributor allowed to carry both brands.

The main difference between Glasurit and R-M is their brand identity, which comes from the marketing messages and augmenting services each provides. As a "German" brand, Glasurit has a technical and technological character. Its tag line is "The Preferred Technology Partner." In contrast, as an "American" brand, R-M is business-oriented, with the tag line: "Business Partner." BASF Coatings managers have developed and promoted these distinct characters tirelessly.

Glasurit is meant to appeal to body shop owners or managers with requirements for best-in-class paint quality. Thus, many of its customers tend to be in the high-end car repair segment. Its marketing messages emphasize technology and state-of-the-art performance. Glasurit salespeople engage repair shop managers in technical discussions, educating them about innovations and providing documentation on technical features. They assist these repair shops in "pushing the edge" of what is possible in applying coatings. In addition to this traditional sales argumentation, which has made the reputation of Glasurit, best-in-class profitability enhancement services also are offered to shop owners whose main focus is shifting now from technical to bottom-line considerations.

On the other hand, R-M is the "business partner." Its marketing messages are about productivity, profitability, and lowering costs for customers. The services that augment the R-M coatings reinforce this positioning. For example, R-M sales reps advise their customers on organizing their workshops to be more efficient and on new paint methodologies that would lower costs.

When an innovation occurs, management makes sure that Glasurit gets it in priority. For example, in keeping with it technical prowess, Glasurit first introduced waterborne paint. Later on, R-M presented waterborne paint as an innovation that would lower customers' costs.

In terms of pricing, there is a slight premium for Glasurit. The goal of having two brands is not to discriminate with price, but rather to meet the differing requirements and preferences of two segments of customers.

Source: BASF Coatings Strategic Marketing Department. Contributed by Research Associate Florent Carbonneau, Kellogg School of Management, Northwestern University.

taken up to 16 weeks in the past. To demonstrate this new service capability to design and produce custom valves quickly, Ross asked its customers to provide prototype specifications. Within a few days, Ross provided them for free an actual prototype valve, which could cost as much as $20,000. Customers were delighted with Ross's responsiveness to their prototype specifications and were even willing to pay a premium for it. As a result, Ross has experienced growth in an otherwise stagnant-to-declining industry.[28]

Breaking Away from the Pack

In our field research, a number of managers wistfully expressed a desire for change, but were concerned about what competitors would do. These managers believed their competitors were similarly looking to improve profitability, but that they wouldn't match a move to flexible market offerings. In addition, there are timing and discipline concerns. Before discussing these issues, we first consider breaking away as a means of countering competitors' dubious parity claims.

One way to break away (which also works for services included in the standard offering) is to guarantee outcomes based on the service. The larger and more complicated the list of services a firm markets, the more likely it is competitors will promise, "We can do that." When this occurs, savvy marketers respond by transforming service claims into guarantees. For instance, when Okuma's competitors began to promise rapid delivery, Okuma announced its *24-Hour Shipment Guarantee*. If a customer orders a part and it is not shipped in 24 hours, the customer gets the part for free. Greif Inc. takes the guarantee one step further. In the past few years, Greif introduced a *Guaranteed Cost Savings Program*. If a customer requests that they be given a 5 percent price cut, the division guarantees to find at least a 5 percent cost savings. This arrangement is formalized into a written contract. If the customer doesn't realize the 5 percent savings, Greif agrees to pay the difference. If more than 5 percent of savings are found, the customer gets to keep it all. To date, Greif has had no problem delivering as guaranteed. Furthermore, managers find that it is a great way to turn discussions away from price.

Knowing when to break away and unbundle is difficult. Is there an advantage to being the first, or is it better to be a rapid follower? To be an industry paradigm breaker, the first supplier must have tough resolve and be willing to "take the heat." An intermediate strategy is to pilot-test flexible market offerings in one of two ways: (1) either add two new services but offer them as options, or (2) pick two services from the present industry "standard" package and unbundle them, making them surcharge options. Going against industry standards can be the first step toward an industry paradigm shift and a market offering rule change.

Many companies refrain from implementing flexible market offerings because they fear they will lose certain customers by requiring them to pay extra for optional services. Instead, managers might adopt the philosophy of firms that have implemented flexible market offerings and found that while losing some accounts, they also gain new business because their market offerings now more closely meet customer requirements at reasonable prices. Other suppliers that have implemented flexible market offerings have found they now get a better return on their resources by focusing them on the segments and customers that value them.

Timing is always a concern. AKZO IC initiated its customer contribution to profitability approach in Europe about 10 years ago. Because revamping service offerings and pricing them to get an equitable return on the value provided was not only new to the industry, but internally controversial, AKZO IC decided to implement it first in the Netherlands and Germany, "home" markets where AKZO was strongest. It then rolled out the approach to Northern Europe. Southern Europe, the last to be converted, proved to be the most difficult markets to bring around due to sales force resistance (because of anticipated decreases in their commission incomes). Although AKZO IC lost some customers because they no longer got a variety of services for free, overall, its perseverance resulted in stable sales volume at significantly better profitability.

A final, paramount way to lead the pack is to be disciplined, operating within the imposed structures of the flexible market offerings. To maintain this discipline requires development of a most difficult-to-acquire customer skill: adroitly saying "no" to some customers. Flexible market offerings provide customers with choices from which they choose, but suppliers must be willing to say "no" to customers that want full-service packages at no-frills prices.[29] Without this skill, flexible market offerings devolve to business as usual, "giving it away." Practiced deftly, it builds a reputation for the supplier within the industry as firm, consistent, and fair.

VALUE-BASED PRICING

How do business market managers decide upon a specific price for the market offering? "In most firms prices are determined by intuition, opinions, rules of thumb, outright dogma, top management's higher wisdom, or internal power fights."[30] This quote by Hermann Simon, an expert on pricing, accurately captures our experience in business markets. Even though superior pricing capability can have a significant impact on profitability, strangely enough, few firms in business markets attempt to systematically build and leverage their pricing capability.[31]

Pricing consideration ought to take place at the strategy level, at the tactics level, and at the level of the individual transaction.[32] In any market, we find a range of prices. **Pricing strategy** focuses on where within this range to position the market offering, and how to shift the range itself and the supplier's relative position within it. In contrast, **pricing tactics** focus on shifting the supplier's position within the existing price range and are often transitory in nature. Finally, **transaction pricing** focuses on realizing the greatest net price for each individual order. Our primary focus in this section is at the strategy level. In later chapters we take up pricing at the tactic and transaction levels.

The intent of pricing strategy is to establish the basic pricing for the market offering. Some approaches or methods can be used to inform this process, yet they can only provide guidance on the range of feasible prices with respect to the existing market price range. In our experience, although elaborate rationales are sometimes constructed to explain the prices selected for market offerings, supplier managers rely on what we call (somewhat in jest) **management numerology**—the belief that certain numbers are imbued with greater meaning and significance than others and thus make for more desirable prices. So, although a rationale is put forth that may appear internally quite consistent, when scrutinized, it has one or more implicit assumptions. Even though customer value assessment provides research-based guidance, ultimately some managerial judgment is required to select the specific price.

Traditional Pricing Approaches

Although we advocate a value-based approach to pricing, we have found that most firms rely on the traditional methods of cost-plus pricing or competition-based pricing. Each of these approaches may appear to give the business market manager some comfort as a basis for setting prices, but each has some problematic aspects.[33]

Cost-Plus Pricing

In **cost-plus pricing**, based upon knowledge of their own costs, supplier managers add some percentage onto those costs to arrive at the market offering price. First, let's consider the "cost" component that serves as the base. Often, cost is narrowly defined by what the supplier can readily measure: cost of goods sold, variable costs, or full costs. This approach assumes that the supplier has an accurate understanding of these costs, something many firms lack. Even firms that have instituted activity-based costing for their production, and thus have a relatively accurate understanding of cost of goods sold, may be neglecting the costs of the supplementary services, programs, or systems. Often, these latter costs are lumped into an overhead allocation component, "sales and general administration," which is subtracted out to provide the net profit margin.

The "plus" component represents the supplier's target profit. It may be a standard percentage that senior management sets for all businesses, or it may be specific to the business unit, perhaps representing historical margins on past market offerings. Target gross margin or net profit margin percentage commonly serve as the plus component.

Cost-plus pricing assumes that the customer cares about the supplier's costs, that they are somehow relevant to what the customer should pay for the market offering. Interestingly, some business market managers have related to us that their own sales forces have this belief too. Consequently, they do not feel comfortable selling virtually the same market offerings (in cost) to different market segments at different prices. The value that the market offering provides to the customer is not considered, so the supplier risks either being uncompetitively high priced or giving away value that it does not know it provides to the customer. Although some may argue that knowledge of cost is relevant because it serves as the base for prices the supplier can charge and still make an operating profit, without knowledge of the value provided, this claim might not be true. Often, the cost numbers are based on assumptions of certain volumes being produced. If the market offering is uncompetitively high priced, the number of units actually sold may fall below these forecasted volumes, making the acquisition prices of component materials and conversion costs higher than anticipated in the original costing calculations.

Competition-Based Pricing

With **competition-based pricing**, supplier managers simply set their price in relation to what the competitors' prices are. The price may be set exactly the same as the predominant competitors, signaling commodity, or it may be slightly higher or lower because of perceived minor reputation, quality, or service differences. Price changes by competitors tend to be imitated reflexively, with perhaps slight deviations as managers attempt to capture greater volume or margins. Supplier managers who use competition-based pricing are essentially giving control of a critical aspect of their market*ing* strategy to their competitors.

The supplier with the largest market share (and likely, industry capacity share) may provide price leadership. As an example, Arcelor was created by a merger of Aceralia, Arbed, and Usinor in early 2002, making this Luxembourg-based steel producer the world's largest in flat carbon steel and long carbon steel products. In the third quarter of 2002, Arcelor announced that it would raise its prices €20 per ton for deliveries in the fourth quarter. In doing so, Arcelor not only gave its customers time to plan their purchases using this new pricing, it also exerted price leadership encouraging other steel producers to raise their prices as well, which they did.[34]

Competition-based pricing assumes that the supplier managers have an accurate understanding of competitors' prices, which may not be the case. Competitors may actively disguise their true prices through such tactics as off-invoice discounts, surcharges for services, and year-end bonuses or rebates, making exact comparisons difficult. Supplier managers may also receive misinformation about competitors' prices from customers or their own distributors. After all, each has self-interest that is better served with lower prices. For example, an already overworked field sales force may not have the time to validate all distributor requests for pricing relief to meet competitive pricing in their local markets. Unscrupulous distributors, seeking some extra margin, may invent "street prices" knowing that they will likely evade detection.

Even with an accurate understanding of competitors' prices, how many suppliers in a market can have the lowest price? One! But many suppliers are not content to accept this fact, and willingly cut price to meet a competitor's lower price. Shrewd customers can orchestrate a downward-spiraling exchange among suppliers. Just as troubling is the message it sends to the market about the supplier: "Me too!" That is, the supplier is essentially signaling that it regards its offering as no different from the competitor's. No wonder, then, that the sales force claims it can only sell on price! What's left?

Finally, just as with cost-plus pricing, without knowledge of their market offering's value, supplier managers may be giving value away. It seems less likely that their offering will be uncompetitive, because suppliers that embrace competition-based pricing may implicitly gain some coarse understanding of their offering's value by observing how pricing changes affect the volume sold. Seldom, though, is this knowledge the result of carefully planned market experiments. Rather, it is gathered piecemeal and anecdotally. Moreover, it presumes that the customer has an accurate understanding of the value of each competitor's market offering, which often may not be the case.

An Approach to Value-Based Pricing

Our philosophy is that price should be set in relation to a market offering's value, which is called **value-based pricing**. However, deciding upon a specific price is not simple, because there are other considerations. To help us understand these considerations, we next develop a framework for value-based pricing. Underpinning this framework is the **fundamental value equation** that we presented in Chapter 1:

$$(\text{Value}_f - \text{Price}_f) > (\text{Value}_a - \text{Price}_a) \qquad \textbf{(5.1)}$$

where $Value_f$ and $Price_f$ are the value and price of the firm's market offering (Offering$_f$), and $Value_a$ and $Price_a$ are the value and price of the next-best-alternative market offering (Offering$_a$). In practice, a rearrangement of this equation better captures how customer firm managers decide between offerings:

$$(Value_f - Value_a) > (Price_f - Price_a) \qquad \textbf{(5.2)}$$
$$\Delta Value_{f,a} > (Price_f - Price_a) \qquad \textbf{(5.3)}$$

Often, value analyses or customer value assessments are performed on a comparative basis, where the differences in performance and total cost are ascertained for two market offerings of interest. Then these differences are expressed in monetary terms and summed to obtain $\Delta Value_{f,a}$. Equation 5.3 also represents a natural way that customer managers decide between two offerings: "What is the difference in the worth of the two offerings to my firm, and how does it compare to the difference in their prices?"

However, understanding $Value_f$, $Value_a$, and $Price_a$ says nothing about a specific price that the firm should choose for Offering$_f$. We rearrange equation 5.3 to isolate $Price_f$ on the left side of the equation:

$$Price_f < Price_a + \Delta Value_{f,a} \qquad \textbf{(5.4)}$$

Given that $Price_a$ is known, which after some investigation is usually the case, equation 5.4 then defines the feasible range of prices the firm could charge and still maintain the inequality. Equation 5.4 also reveals an insight: Competition-based pricing is a special case of value-based pricing, when $\Delta Value_{f,a}$ is either zero, the definition of a commodity, or unknown and regarded as though it were zero.

Selecting $Price_f$ depends upon some additional considerations. To begin, let's consider Figure 5.6. Because value is expressed as the worth in monetary terms, we provide a value continuum expressed in Norwegian kronor per unit (NOK/unit). For simplicity (and without loss of generality), we assume the cost of Offering$_f$ and Offering$_a$ are the same. The difference between $Price_a$ and $Cost_a$ defines the **profit** for Offering$_a$. The difference between $Value_a$ and $Price_a$ represents the **customer incentive to purchase** Offering$_a$ (labeled as ι). Note that in business markets, the value provided will likely exceed the price or else the customer will be indifferent. And, with

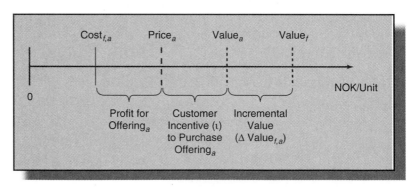

Figure 5.6
A Value-Based
Pricing Framework

the make-versus-buy consideration inherent in business markets, if the price equals the value received, the customer may be tempted to make rather than buy.[35]

Now, the difference between $Value_f$ and $Value_a$ represents the **incremental value** $Offering_f$ provides over $Offering_a$. What part of this incremental value to retain as profit and what part to share with the customer as an incentive to purchase is a strategic decision. Significantly, by sharing part of this incremental value with the customer, in essence, a supplier *creates* value for the customer.

Suppose we set $Price_f$ at $Value_a$. In this case, we would be giving all the incremental value to the customer as incentive to purchase $Offering_f$, with the relatively small remainder being the profit for the firm. Contrast this option with the alternative where we set $Price_f$ relatively close to $Value_f$, so that we are giving only enough of the incremental value as customer incentive to purchase to maintain the inequality of equation 5.3. The first alternative is sometimes called a **penetration pricing strategy**, because the firm intends to make its overall profit through selling a larger number of units at a lower profit per unit. The second alternative is sometimes called a **skimming pricing strategy**, because the firm intends to make its overall profits through selling fewer units at a higher profit per unit. A number of factors can support pursuing one or the other strategy, such as the market size and forecasted growth, the significance of any learning effects (e.g., experience curve or market knowledge), anticipated reactions by present or potential competitors, and how persuasively demonstrable the value proposition is.[36] The fundamental consideration that we want to emphasize, though, is that *pricing strategy can only be understood within the context of the business unit's market strategy for each segment.*

Furthermore, underlying the choice of a pricing strategy is the recognition that prospective customers vary in the value they place on a supplier's market offering and that this value may change over time. So, although we conceptually represent $Value_f$ and $Value_a$ as point estimates in equation 5.1 and Figure 5.6, when we broaden our consideration from a single, prospective customer firm to a market segment, these points become mean estimates of value distributions for the prospective customers in that segment. As we move $Price_f$ closer to $Value_a$, customer incentive to purchase $Offering_f$ over $Offering_a$ passes the threshold for a larger proportion of the distribution of prospective customers. That is, a greater number of those customers whose value for $Offering_f$ is less than the mean $Value_f$ will still have the inequality of equation 5.1 satisfied (using the individual $Value_f$ for their own firms).

Finally, consider the alternative where $Price_f$ is set so that the customer incentive to purchase $Offering_f$ is exactly equal to that of $Offering_a$, depicted as *ı*. Which offering will the customer choose? From equation 5.1, we might predict indifference. Yet in practice, we find that if one is the incumbent offering, say $Offering_a$, customers will continue to purchase it. Why? Generalized risk, or what might simply be called **inertia**. Even after all specific cost and value differences are accounted for in the respective value assessments, including any specific, identifiable risks in changing to $Offering_f$, a reluctance to change remains. Thus, to displace the incumbent offering, some additional portion of the incremental value must be given, a pricing tactic that we call **incentive to change**. Although the size of this incentive will vary by situation, based on some qualitative research with purchasing managers, we offer 5 to 7 percent as a rough heuristic. So, if the reduction in price (or gain in value) is less than this, purchasing managers are apparently unwilling to even investigate changing from the incumbent to another offering.

Because it is based upon what the customer is willing to pay for a market offering, value-based pricing is preferred over other approaches to pricing, and it is an essential component of a business market management philosophy. Yet, for firms to successfully implement it, some critical assumptions need to be met: (1) the supplier has an accurate understanding of either $Value_f$ and $Value_a$, or $\Delta Value_{f,a}$; and (2) the supplier has an accurate understanding of $Price_a$. To satisfy these assumptions, most often a supplier will need market sensing using the customer value assessment methods that we discussed in Chapter 2.

How do firms in business markets put value-based pricing into practice? Box 5.5 provides a disguised application of value-based pricing for a printing process monitoring system. Box 5.6 relates how Embrex Inc. prices its market offering on a per inoculated egg basis. Doing so enables Embrex to better demonstrate and document the value its proprietary Inovoject® system delivers, fulfill poultry producers' preferences for costing, and realize its own market strategy.

BOX 5.5
Value-Based Pricing for a Printing Process Monitoring System

Gutenberg Technology (a disguised name) had developed an innovative printing process monitoring system for offset lithographic printing. The business team responsible for the development of this system wanted to set its price based on the value that printing firms would receive from using the system. The team had little time to make this decision, though, because it had to launch the system in three weeks at the industry's annual trade show.

The printing process monitoring system provided three major improvements to existing print firm performance. Using it would reduce *makeready time,* which is the amount of time it takes to mount the plates on a printing press, reach acceptable inking, and obtain acceptable registration of the four colors on the paper (having them printed exactly on the right spot of the paper). Use of the system also would reduce *paper waste,* which is the amount of paper discarded initially or when mistakes develop during printing. Lastly, use of the system would reduce *print variability,* which refers to the range in the shades of color and alignment of images that occur on the printed pages.

To understand the value of these improvements in performance, the team used two customer value assessment methods: conjoint analysis and field value-in-use assessment. Suspecting that there would be significant differences in value, the team studied two printing segments: sheet-fed printing firms and web printing firms. Sheet-fed printing has shorter runs and uses higher-quality paper for applications such as art magazines and corporate annual reports. Web printing has faster throughput and uses a large roll of paper for applications such as large-circulation magazines and newspapers. Given the time constraints, the team conducted in-depth interviews with a small number of each type of printing firm.

The team found remarkable consistency between the two value assessment methods. In this instance, the value that research participants perceived their printing operations would receive from adopting the printing process monitoring system closely corresponded to the value estimates uncovered in the value-in-use assessment. As might be expected, the sheet-fed segment appeared to

BOX 5.5
Continued

place a much greater value on reducing print variability, whereas the web-fed segment placed much greater value on waste reduction. Both segments placed about the same value on reduction in makeready time. During its in-depth interviews, the team also discovered some technical requirements for the web-fed segment that would require further development of the system. So, the team focused its further consideration on determining the introductory price for the sheet-fed segment.

To arrive at a price, it was necessary to extend the research findings from the small number of firms to the total sheet-fed market segment. The team developed a market model based on the research findings, assumptions about the distributions of model parameters, and published data on the printing industry. The output this model generated was a distribution of value estimates for this market segment. The team also conducted sensitivity analyses to determine the impact of various parameters in the model generating the value estimate distribution. At the same time, the team estimated what Gutenberg's total cost would be to produce, market, and service the system.

The number of printing firms in the distribution having an estimated value greater than a given prospective price defined the potential market for the system at that price. So, progressively higher prices would lead to progressively smaller markets of prospective customers that would adopt the system. The team assumed that for a potential market of any given size, customer adoption of the system would follow an established long-term growth curve for cumulative sales of technology-based products, thus enabling the team to estimate the units sales for each year over time. The team also examined alternative life spans in years for the system. The team then estimated the net present values to Gutenberg (total earnings discounted to the present) for the system under alternative prices and life spans. Based on these analyses, the team determined that the optimum price of the print process monitoring system ranged from $40,000 to $46,000.

After some deliberation, the team selected $40,000 as the price to introduce the system to the market. The system had market acceptance at that price, particularly with printing firms that served the upper end of the printing market, such as corporate annual reports.

BOX 5.6
Embrex Charges Poultry Producers on a Price per Inoculated Egg Basis

With annual sales exceeding $44 million, Embrex Inc. (*www.embrex.com*) is an international agricultural biotechnology company based in Research Triangle Park, North Carolina. In 1993, the firm commercialized the Inovoject® system, a proprietary, automated-injection system for inoculating fertilized broiler chick eggs against the ravages of avian illnesses (e.g., Marek's disease and infectious bursal disease). The system creates significant value for poultry producers by simultaneously eliminating the need for manual vaccination of newly hatched broiler chicks and increasing the rate of vaccination to 20,000 to 50,000 eggs per hour. Today, Inovoject systems vaccinate more than 80 percent of all North American broilers and significant numbers in more than 30 countries around the world.

Rather than selling Inovoject systems outright to poultry producers, Embrex senior managers have developed a novel customer-oriented pricing method. As part of a 3- to 5-year contract, Embrex charges customers on a negotiated price per inoculated egg basis! The price not only includes Inovoject system leasing fees, but also disposable supplies (e.g.,

(continued)

BOX 5.6
Continued

needles, tubing, and replacement parts), operator and maintenance training, routine and emergency inspections and repairs, equipment upgrades, and system usage and cost reports. Although Embrex markets a limited variety of avian serums, poultry producers purchase most vaccines from pharmaceutical companies or their distributors. Intriguingly, although Embrex has the capability to monitor the usage of its system, it prefers to rely on the "honor system," allowing hatchery managers to report on monthly invoices the number of eggs their firms have inoculated with Inovoject systems.

Why does Embrex charge on a price per inoculated egg basis? According to Randall Marcuson, Embrex president and CEO, the firm works hard to be customer oriented. Back in the early 1990s, senior managers realized that the poultry industry differed from other livestock industries in that it was vertically integrated. Major poultry producers (e.g., ConAgra, Perdue Farms, and Tyson Foods) own each chicken for most of its life cycle from fertilized egg to grocer's warehouse, outsourcing some activities such as "growing out the birds" to contracted poultry farmers. Most importantly, Embrex managers understood that poultry producers do not reap the value of their efforts until they sell processed chicken meat to a wholesaler or grocery chain. As a result, poultry producers collect detailed cost and profit data and make many of their business decisions on a per chicken basis. Pricing on an inoculated egg basis has two benefits for poultry producers. First, poultry producers are able to immediately enter the cost associated with Embrex's Inovoject system into their accounting systems, evaluate and compare inoculation costs to other costs of operation, and correlate the cost with the related value they receive, and make decisions. Second, poultry producers are able to convert a potentially significant capital equipment outlay into a variable cost, dramatically improving cash flow and return on assets.

At the same time, Marcuson believes that Embrex is in a far better position to deliver and gain an equitable share of customer value because it retains ownership of the Inovoject equipment. To begin with, managers have refined Embrex's management accounting system to monitor the total cost of Inovoject ownership on an inoculated egg basis. Secondly, they have developed systems to monitor the value that the Inovoject system provides. For example, most prospective customers must perform a 60- to 120-day "side-by-side" test in which they compare the costs and profits generated by the Inovoject system relative to their incumbent inoculation system.

Over the years, Embrex managers have identified key value drivers: hatchability (i.e., the percent of fertilized eggs that hatch), mortality and/or marketability of birds (i.e., the percent of hatched birds that survive the entire processing life cycle), growth rate (i.e., the time it takes to produce a sellable bird), feed conversion (i.e., the amount of feed it takes to produce a pound of body weight), plus labor costs. Most importantly, Embrex managers have been able to link the positive impact that the Inovoject system has on these value drivers to the profits that the poultry producers gain. So, when an Embrex salesperson enters into negotiations with a new prospect or a returning customer, he or she can demonstrate the total costs relative to the value that the Inovoject system delivers.

Marcuson believes that Embrex's price per inoculated egg approach has enabled his company to convert what might have been transactional relationships with poultry producers into partnerships. Embrex owns the Inovoject systems, so it is in the firm's best interest to maintain each unit at peak productivity and to actively seek continuous cost reductions. Finally, because Embrex personnel have regular access to hatchery incubation rooms, they are in a far better position to gain insights into customer applications and then to more closely tailor the Inovoject system to meet the requirements and preferences of poultry producers.

MANAGING MARKET OFFERINGS ACROSS BORDERS

Because business markets are predominately about functionality and performance, they are inherently more global in nature than consumer markets, which are predominately about aesthetics and taste. Quite often, then, business market managers will have the responsibility of managing multiple market offerings across borders. Although regions or countries might be regarded as simply another basis of market segmentation, some considerations beyond what we've already discussed occur in managing market offerings across borders. In this section, we consider how the market offering may vary across borders and how to manage pricing strategy across borders.

Adapting Market Offerings Across Borders

The extent to which business market managers adapt their market offerings when doing business across borders typically depends on their firm's stage of international market development. When coordinating market offerings across borders is a concern, managers should consider flexible market offerings and global branding.

International Market Development

Douglas and Craig provide a framework for international market development that is useful for thinking about how managing market offerings across borders evolves as firms gain experience in international markets. Firms progress through three phases. After a preliminary phase of pre-internationalization, where the firm focuses on serving its home market, subsequent phases are: (1) initial foreign market entry, (2) local or national market expansion, and (3) global rationalization.[37]

Firms in the initial foreign market entry phase typically vary their market offering little from that of the home market. As Douglas and Craig observe, "Attention is centered on pinpointing the closest match between the firm's current offerings and market conditions overseas so that minimal adaptation of products or market strategies is required."[38] So initially, other than required changes in distribution, the market offering remains virtually the same as in the home market. In fact, firms appear to decide which national markets to enter first based on their perceived similarity to the home market. As a result, managing market offerings across borders is not a significant issue.

Firms in the local market expansion phase attempt to broaden their base of business in each country market by gaining greater market penetration of presently served segments and constructing market offerings that better meet the requirements and preferences of new segments. The focus is on tailoring the market offerings to the unique, local requirements of each country market. "The emphasis shifts from 'export' of strategy and its direction from the domestic market base, to development of strategy on a country-by-country basis."[39] Because of this shift, although firms may have multiple market offerings corresponding to the country markets in which they participate, little attention is given to managing the market offerings across borders. Instead, the supplier often manages the market offerings for each country locally, with perhaps the home office providing or supporting some common core of services, programs, and systems.

It is only when firms progress to the third phase, global rationalization, that managing market offerings across borders becomes a paramount concern for firms. "The national orientation thus disappears, and markets are viewed as a set of interrelated, interdependent entities which are becoming increasingly integrated and interlinked worldwide."[40] The growing openness of borders for international trade, overlaid with continuing developments in integrated logistics systems, challenge the business market manager to truly grasp what it means to "think global, act local."[41] To provide superior value and lower costs in local markets, firms should develop **transnational capabilities**: "The ability to manage across national boundaries, retaining local flexibility while achieving global integration."[42] Ericsson, the Swedish telecommunications firm, uses its national company boards as one mechanism to foster this process. "At least one, and often several senior corporate managers are members of each board, and subsidiary board meetings become an important means for coordinating activities and channeling local ideas and innovations across national lines."[43]

Providing Transnational Market Offerings

The underlying logic and philosophy of flexible market offerings—naked solutions with options—readily generalizes to transnational management of market offerings. A supplier can design its product offering and service offering platforms around regional or global requirements to offer them at lower cost. At the same time, it can tailor augmenting features and supporting services, programs, and systems to local market requirements to provide superior value. These product offering and service offering platforms are (much) fewer in number that the country markets served. How, though, does the firm go about deciding what will constitute its product offering and service offering platforms?

As a start in this endeavor, business market managers should adopt a genuine **equidistance of perspective**—that is, rather than having a bias toward the home market, managers instead regard each market, including the home market, as being the same distance away from the corporate center.[44] With equidistant view, managers can step back and decide which country markets are most significant and interesting to their firms. Making decisions about which subset of all the countries the firm serves are the *relatively* important markets is essential. Rather than designing a product to meet the average requirements of a regional (or global) market, business market managers can instead pursue what Nissan terms a *lead country* model: "A product carefully tailored to the dominant and distinct needs of individual national markets."[45] Within each region, the firm designates as the lead country that country market it deems most important. It designs product offering platforms that will provide the greatest value in each lead country. Then, managers in other country markets are asked whether small changes can make one of these platforms acceptable to their local markets.

So, too, are business market managers advised to construct lead country service offerings and marketing programs, which local managers in the other country markets can modify to better meet their requirements. Again, flexibility is critical for accomplishing the difficult balance between global and local. Often, "backroom operations" that are characteristic of most systems and many programs can be advantageously integrated across borders. The "face" to the customer, though, must remain local. However, this does not necessarily mean that the supplier is located locally. For example, a supplier may provide customer service in Belgium, the Netherlands, and Germany from one customer service center, staffed by nationals from each country market. Customers, dialing a local telephone number, may be completely unaware that the call is being routed to a service center in another country. Moreover, they may not even care as long as the voice on the other end is a native-speaking one. However it is accomplished in practice, the goal of the firm is to be regarded as a local company in every country market in which it participates.[46]

Global Branding

As we discussed in Chapter 1, because business markets are predominantly concerned about functionality and performance, business market management stresses doing business across international borders. Most often, customers in country markets in the Americas, Asia, and Europe are seeking essentially the same functionality and performance from market offerings. In our discussion of brands as resources and brand building in business markets in Chapter 4, we emphasized the paramount importance of corporate brands in business markets, such as 3M and IBM. Taken together, the implication is that firms in business markets should pursue global branding of their market offerings. Yet, a number of circumstances can make this sort of branding difficult to accomplish in practice, with the result being that the firm may have global brands, regional brands, or local country brands for their market offerings.[47]

When customer requirements and preferences vary across regional or country markets, suppliers may pursue regional or local country branding to reflect these variations. The overarching goal, though, should be to strive for as much consistency and standardization in the brand strategy and brand building as possible. Country managers often have a tendency to believe that their market situation is unique, and consequently global (or regional) brand-building initiatives will not work in their markets. To counter this notion, the firm must assign global responsibility for the brand strategy of a market offering to one individual, who may accomplish managing the market offering globally through leading a team comprised of regional or country brand (or marketing) managers. Senior management should require country managers to adopt global or regional brand-building efforts, unless they can persuasively document their claims of uniqueness with data from the local market.

Having different brands for the same market offering in different parts of the world also occurs through acquisition of firms that have strong corporate or family brands in particular regional or local country markets. The acquiring firm may be reluctant to change brands in this situation and may instead opt to manage the greater complexity of multiple brands for essentially the same market offering. Citigroup, opting to operate under the Banamex brand name in Mexico after it acquired Grupo Financiero Banamex-Accival (discussed in Chapter 4), is an instance of this. Finally, a firm may find that it must alter the positioning of its market offering in particular country or regional markets due to the presence of an entrenched formidable competitor. In this circumstance, the firm may choose to use an alternate brand for its market offering to avoid confusion with its positioning of the market offering in other regional or country markets, where it may be the market leader.

Launching a new brand in business markets appears to be an outstanding opportunity to use a global brand. This appears especially so for technology-driven firms and market offerings, where it is more likely that customer firms in developed markets around the world are seeking essentially the same functionality and performance. The experience of Infineon Technologies® in launching its global brand provides an instructive case, which we recount in Box 5.7.

Pricing Across Borders

Pricing market offerings within the home market is a vexing enough task for most business market managers. Pricing across borders often is even more daunting. Firms in the initial foreign market entry and local or national market expansion phases of international market development have the primary concern of pricing relative to local competitors. When firms reach the global rationalization phase, they face the added concern of harmonizing pricing across borders.

Pricing in Local Markets

An implication of equations 5.1 and 5.2 for foreign markets is that what is regarded as the next-best-alternative offering may change, depending on the local market competition. In some country markets, local competitors may provide offerings that are state-of-the-art, while in others, the local competitors are not nearly as strong as those the firm confronts in its home market.[48] The competitors in the local market may be national companies or foreign subsidiaries of firms from other countries in the region or the world at large. So, the incremental value that a firm's market offering provides likely varies across its country markets. In some, the value even may be at parity, but the prices of the local market offerings are much higher, perhaps reflecting a higher cost structure of local firms.[49] Finally, foreign suppliers may encounter difficulty, at least initially, demonstrating to potential customers in the local markets the superior value of their offerings (that is, $\Delta \text{Value}_{f,a} > 0$), and Price_a for the best local competitor may be lower than in the supplier's home market.

Perceived superior value relative to local market offerings would seem to be a critical factor in initial foreign entry decisions, yet we have not seen this issue discussed much. Moreover, firms typically have not conducted formal customer value assessments to support these decisions. Instead, firms tend to focus on price, with a subjective, and often sketchy, understanding of the relative value of the locally available competitive market offerings ($\Delta \text{Value}_{f,a}$). Apart from this, firms that employ a cost-plus approach to pricing may view foreign markets simply as a place to gain additional business, thereby improving capacity utilization. Therefore, they are willing to accept even a lower price than in the home market—a practice known as **dumping.** Finally, the incentive to change that a firm needs to offer prospective customers in the local country markets will likely be greater than in its home market. How much greater this incentive needs to be depends on the strength of the firm's reputation or corporate brand equity in that local market.[50]

BOX 5.7
Infineon Technologies® Decides upon Global Branding

On March 26, 1999, the CEO of Siemens Semiconductor announced to his employees that the company name would be changed to Infineon Technologies after carving the company out of Siemens. This new name corresponded to the desire to create a brand identity apart from Siemens, which would also serve as a catalyst for attitude and cultural change on the part of its 25,000 employees. It also signaled to present and prospective customers that Infineon Technologies would become more innovative, flexible, and passionate as a firm than it had been as a Siemens' unit. To provide one voice and one message all over the world, senior management decided to launch Infineon Technologies as a global brand.

Using the same brand worldwide provided several benefits. Among them, greater speed of implementation was key, because the company was under time pressure before its initial public offering (IPO). Infineon was able to go from concept to global launch in just six weeks. Launching its brand globally also allowed the company to run a single campaign worldwide, employing a lead advertising agency (Thompson). Finally, launching a global brand with a single campaign worldwide enabled centralization of planning and budgeting, resulting in greater control and lower total costs.

Nevertheless, launching a global brand also presented shortcomings. It took a while to verify that the Infineon name was legally available everywhere in the world. It also took some time to make sure that it would be appropriate in every language and every country. Moreover, the new brand name, which blends infinity, eternity, and new, was not accepted instantly everywhere. In the United States, people thought it resembled too much new start-up names from the Silicon Valley. In some countries of Asia, Infineon was difficult to pronounce. In China, people liked the meaning of the name so much that they instead used a Chinese translation of the words infinity, eternity, and technology! Later on, they had to move back and accept the Infineon brand as given. Another challenge was the choice of communication messages that would be appropriate all over the world. For example, Infineon management cautions against the use of word plays, which are characteristic of American advertising, because they are not always understandable in other languages.

Infineon managers learned a great deal while launching their brand globally. Based on their experience, Infineon managers would counsel other firms to insist that their agency account team has representation from each of the major cultures. In doing so, Infineon has been able to create brand messages that are consistently understood and culturally accessible beyond the United States or Europe. Further, they counsel to take the additional time and expense to pretest the brand message in each of the world's major regions, to be certain that the message is equally resonant. Doing so, a firm can build a global brand rather than simply having a brand that it advertises around the world.

Source: Interview with Guy Wolff, Senior Vice President, Corporate and Investor Communications, Infineon Technologies. Contributed by Research Associate Florent Carbonneau, Kellogg School of Management, Northwestern University.

Harmonizing Pricing Across Borders
Firms in business markets face increasing pressure to harmonize pricing across borders. More and more firms are now in the global rationalization phase. Customers that operate across borders increasingly expect unified pricing from their suppliers.

For example, companies that do business in each country within the European Union may demand pricing rationalization from their suppliers. One consequence of a single European currency is to put pressure on suppliers to move to a single European price, expressed in euros.[51]

The growing openness of borders for international trade coupled with advances in integrated logistics systems has led to a disconcerting number of instances of cross-border arbitrage. Customers purchase a product in a country where it has a lower price, transport the product themselves to another country for use, and still incur a lower total cost than had they purchased the product at the higher price in that country. This cross-border arbitrage forces suppliers to confront their widely varying prices across countries.

Yet, harmonizing pricing is a thorny undertaking. Local country managers with lower relative pricing often claim that they cannot raise prices to meet regional or global pricing targets without a significant loss of sales. This claim may have some substance in that these managers may face national competitors that sell only in their home market. Conversely, senior management is loath to lower pricing in the country markets with relatively higher pricing and thus forgo incremental profit.

One approach is to move to **pricing bandwidths**, where pricing within each country market is within an agreed-upon range around the target pricing. For example, a coatings supplier set a target price ±10 percent to create an acceptable pricing bandwidth. Subsidiary business unit managers whose local markets are outliers are asked how they plan to move within the bandwidth, and their progress is closely monitored. New products are introduced within even a smaller bandwidth. As Box 5.8 recounts, Web-based electronic commerce across borders may compel suppliers to move to a single worldwide price for an offering, and then adjust it to include local country shipping costs, taxes, and tariffs.

Finally, fluctuating currency exchange rates also add to the complexity of harmonizing pricing across borders. Movements between currencies that are relatively predictable can be built into the pricing bandwidths, whereas structural changes (currency devaluations, loss of confidence in a local market currency by the international banking community) require case-by-case market strategy adjustments.

BOX 5.8
AMP Harmonizes Its Offerings and Pricing Across Borders on the Internet

Web-based electronic commerce is an innovative marketing channel that may compel suppliers to harmonize their product offerings and pricing across borders. AMP, the world's largest manufacturer of electric connectors, was one of the first firms to recognize the potential of an Internet-based marketing and sales platform in doing business across borders. When AMP decided to use online, electronic commerce as another marketing channel to reach its then 90,000 customers in 50 countries, it began with cutting-edge technology that enabled it to generate electronic catalogs in eight different languages from a single database of its 500,000 electronic parts.

To ensure that customers in various country and industry markets would receive consistent service, AMP phased in access to its online catalog over the course of two years. During this time, AMP's advanced technology enabled

BOX 5.8
Continued

it to restrict access to customers depending on their country and industry. AMP's online catalog now serves an international customer base located in 145 countries; 15,000 customers from 80 countries access it daily. In addition to expanding AMP's global presence, the move to an online catalog also reduced its costs significantly. AMP's fax bill decreased by 20 percent, and its paper catalog costs by 40 percent.

When users access the AMP Web site for the first time, they are required to register and provide their country location. They also select one of the eight language versions of the AMP catalog to view. Upon subsequent visits, the AMP site greets the user in that language and provides that language version of the catalog. In addition to product and price information, registered users can access design drawings, test data, and product changes, about 300 of which occur daily. For greater speed and ease of use, customers can create streamlined versions of the catalog that more closely correspond to their particular interests and requirements.

With its rollout of online ordering, AMP faces the challenge of harmonizing its pricing across borders, which in the past varied considerably across country markets. AMP's solution is to move to a single, worldwide price for each product offering, which it then explicitly adjusts to include local shipping costs, taxes, and tariffs. This pricing policy blunts "gray market" activity, where customers in countries with higher prices seek out lower prices online.

AMP provides a noteworthy example of electronic commerce across borders on the Web, the potential of which is just unfolding. At this time, it is not apparent what kinds of market offerings will be purchased internationally through this marketing channel. Electronic commerce across borders may become the preferred marketing channel for customers seeking naked solutions, while customers seeking market offerings consisting of service offerings wrapped around the naked solutions may continue to rely on in-country marketing channels.

Sources: Contributed by Research Associate Ellen Carr, Kellogg School of Management, Northwestern University. Adapted from Laurie Berger, "AMP Building on Overseas Base," *Business Marketing* (January 1998): 1, 27; and Dana Blankenhorn, "AMP Online Catalog Shows Way to Support Languages," *Business Marketing* (January 1998): 26.

SUMMARY

Managing the market offering is the process of putting products, services, programs, and systems together in ways that create the greatest value for targeted segments and customers. We began by considering some conventional thinking about market offerings. Business market managers can overcome the tunnel vision of commodity markets by first understanding the true extent of commoditization and then rebuilding differentiation through strategies that focus more broadly on how to deliver value, such as creating knowledge banks and building leveraging expertise. Regarding the distinction between products and services, we prefer the view that differences between products and services are a matter of degree, and that all market offerings can be more usefully thought of as falling along a continuum of tangibility.

Further, market offerings in the business marketplace are changing in ways that are moving them toward the center of the tangibility continuum.

Recognizing the variation in customer requirements that remains no matter how finely a market is segmented, flexible market offerings provide naked solutions consisting of offering elements that all segment members highly value, augmented with optional offering elements that some, but not all, segment members value. We advocate flexible market offerings as an approach for managing market offerings. Business market managers begin by articulating the present market offering for each market segment, which most often turns out to be far greater than any manager realizes. Business market managers next assess customer value and supplier cost for each service. Armed with this knowledge, they construct flexible market offerings for each market segment, specifying which service elements will be standard, which will be options, and which services they will not offer (but which perhaps a third party will provide). We considered some implementation issues, such as whether a supplier should provide flexible market offerings as naked solutions with option menus or as tailored-value packages; how branding a market offering provides a means of differentiating it from other market offerings, particularly with respect to the the value it delivers; and how to break away from the pack to move to flexible market offerings.

Although supplier firms have traditionally relied upon cost-plus or competition-based approaches to pricing, each of these has its problems in practice. Instead, we advocate that business market managers pursue value-based pricing, where they select a price from the feasible range defined by what the customer is willing to pay for the market offering. We developed a framework for understanding how to accomplish value-based pricing, and discussed penetration pricing and skimming pricing as alternative pricing strategies.

Finally, the extent to which business market managers adapt their market offerings when doing business across borders typically depends on their firm's stage of international market development. When coordinating market offerings across borders is a concern, our approach of flexible market offerings proves useful in constructing transnational offerings. Firms in business markets should pursue global branding of their market offerings, yet a number of circumstances can make this sort of branding difficult to accomplish in practice, with the result being that the firm may have global brands, regional brands, or local country brands for their market offerings. Pricing market offerings within the home market is a vexing enough task for most business market managers, yet pricing across borders often is even more daunting. Firms in the early phases of international market development have the primary concern of pricing relative to local competitors. When firms reach the global rationalization phase, they face the added concern of harmonizing pricing across borders.

ENDNOTES

1. Theodore Levitt, "Marketing Success Through Differentiation—of Anything," *Harvard Business Review* (January–February 1980): 83–91.

2. V. Kasturi Rangan and George Brown, "Beating the Commodity Magnet," *Industrial Marketing Management,* 21 August 1992, 215–224.

3. Levitt, "Marketing Success," 83.

4. Levitt, "Marketing Success," 89.

5. Ian C. MacMillan and Rita Gunther McGrath, "Discovering New Points of Differentiation," *Harvard Business Review* (July–August 1997): 133–138, 143–145.

6. The following two subsections draw heavily on James C. Anderson and Gregory S. Carpenter, "Escaping the Commodity Trap in Business Markets," in Tim Dickson and Neville Hawcock, eds., *Mastering Marketing* (London: Pearson Education, 1999), pp. 241–246.

7. Joan Magretta, "The Power of Virtual Integration: An Interview with Dell Computer's Michael Dell," *Harvard Business Review* (March–April 1998): 72–84.

8. See, for example, A. J. Magrath, "When Marketing Services, 4Ps Are Not Enough," *Business Horizons* (May–June 1986): 44–50; or Ralph W. Jackson and Philip D. Cooper, "Unique Aspects of Marketing Industrial Services, *Industrial Marketing Management*, 17 May 1998, 111–118.

9. Valarie A. Zeithamel, A. Parasuraman, and Leonard L. Berry, "Problems and Strategies in Services Marketing," *Journal of Marketing* (Spring 1985): 33–46.

10. Theodore Levitt, "Marketing Intangible Products and Product Intangibles," *Harvard Business Review* (May–June 1981): 94–102. The quote is drawn from p. 95, with emphasis in original.

11. For some examples of the "servicization of products and the productization of services," see Regis McKenna, "Marketing Is Everything," *Harvard Business Review* (January–February 1991): 65–79

12. This sections draws heavily from the same research project as the previously published article: James C. Anderson and James A. Narus, "Capturing the Value of Supplementary Services," *Harvard Business Review* (January–February 1995): 75–83.

13. "The Secrets of the Production Line," *The Economist*, 17 October 1992, 5–6; Fay Rice, "The New Rules of Superlative Service," *Fortune* (Autumn–Winter 1993): 50–53; and Rahul Jacob, "Beyond Quality & Value," *Fortune* (Autumn–Winter 1993): 8–11.

14. Steven C. Wheelwright and Kim C. Clark, *Revolutionizing Product Development* (New York: The Free Press, 1992); B. Joseph Pine II, Bart Victor, and Andrew Boynton, "Making Mass Customization Work," *Harvard Business Review* (September–October 1993): 108–119.

15. Paul Zipkin, "The Limits of Mass Customization," *MIT Sloan Management Review* (Spring 2001): 82.

16. Zipkin, "The Limits of Mass Customization"; and "A Long March," *The Economist*, 14 July 2001, 63–65.

17. Baxter International Inc., based in the United States, split into two separate entities. Baxter Healthcare in this example and the following ones became Allegiance Corporation in 1996. Allegiance Corporation merged with Cardinal Health, Inc., in February 1999, and is now known as Allegiance Corporation, a Cardinal Health company.

18. Michael V. Marn and Robert L. Rosiello, "Managing Price, Gaining Profit," *Harvard Business Review* (September–October 1992): 84–94.

19. Joseph Lampel and Henry Mintzberg, "Customizing Customization," *Sloan Management Review* (Fall 1996): 21–30.

20. We provide other company examples and discuss assessing customer value in detail in Chapter 2.

21. Robin Cooper and Robert S. Kaplan, "Profit Priorities from Activity-Based Costing," *Harvard Business Review* (May–June 1991): 130–137; and William Rotch, "Activity-Based Costing in Service Industries," *Cost Management* (Summer 1990): 4–14. For some work in this area, see Barry J. Brinker, ed., *Emerging Practices in Cost Management* (Boston: Warren, Gorham & Lamont, 1992).

22. William R. Benfield and Dale B. Christensen, *Keeping the Wholesaler's House in Order: How Attention to Returned Goods Processing Can Improve the Bottom Line* (Reston VA: National Wholesale Druggists' Association, 1993).

23. The power generation business of ABB was merged with the power generation business of ALSTOM in June 1999 to create a new Netherlands-based joint venture, ABB

Alstom Power, owned 50:50 by ABB and ALSTOM.

24. Philip Kotler, *Marketing Management*, 11th ed. (Upper Saddle River, NJ: Prentice Hall, 2003).

25. "The Price Is Wrong," *The Economist*, 25 May 2002, 59–60.

26. James C. Anderson and James A. Narus, "Selectively Pursuing More of Your Customer's Business," *MIT Sloan Management Review* (Spring 2003): 42–49.

27. James C. Anderson and Florent G. Carbonneau, "Exelon: Eco-Preferred® Power," Kellogg School of Management, Northwestern University, January 2003.

28. Mark Ingebretsen, "Mass Appeal: Ross Controls Builds Customers for Life with Mass Customization," *Business Marketing* (March 1997): 1, 14, 52; and Carol L. Karnes and Larry P. Karnes, "Ross Controls: A Case Study in Mass Customization," *Production & Inventory Management Journal* (Third Quarter 2000): 1–4.

29. Rangan, Moriarty and Swartz, "Segmenting Customers."

30. Hermann Simon, "Pricing Opportunities— And How to Exploit Them," *Sloan Management Review* (Winter 1992): 55–65.

31. Shantanu Dutta, Mark Bergen, Daniel Levy, Mark Ritson, and Mark Zbaracki, "Pricing as a Strategic Capability," *MIT Sloan Management Review* (Spring 2002): 61–66.

32. Elliot B. Ross, "Making Money with Proactive Pricing," *Harvard Business Review* (November–December 1984): 145–155; and Michael V. Marn and Robert L. Rosiello, "Managing Price, Gaining Profit," *Harvard Business Review* (September–October 1992): 84–94.

33. G. Dean Kortge and Patrick A. Okonkwo, "Perceived Value Approach to Pricing," *Industrial Marketing Management* (May 1993): 133–140.

34. Stuart U. Rich, "Price Leadership in the Paper Industry," *Industrial Marketing Management* (April 1983): 101–104.

35. Thus, although the adage by Publilius Syrus (first century, B.C.) that "Everything is worth what its purchaser will pay for it" is true in that an offering is worth *at least* that much, it is likely an underestimate of the actual value of the offering. Note also that when building customer value models as we advocate in Chapter 2, to make the task manageable, suppliers estimate $\Delta \text{Value}_{f,a}$ and so do not know the customer incentive to purchase Offering$_a$. This assessment does not matter in practice, though, since Supplier$_a$ is giving this value away, so too must Supplier$_f$. Thus, it is an unknown constant that does not affect purchase decisions between the two offerings.

36. For further discussion on these factors, see Simon, "Pricing Opportunities"; and Hermann Simon, *Price Management* (Amsterdam: Elsevier-North Holland, 1989), chap. 6.

37. Susan P. Douglas and C. Samuel Craig, "Evolution of Global Marketing Strategy: Scale, Scope and Synergy," *Columbia Journal of World Business* (Fall 1989): 47–59.

38. Douglas and Craig, "Evolution of Global Marketing," 51.

39. Douglas and Craig, "Evolution of Global Marketing," 54.

40. Douglas and Craig, "Evolution of Global Marketing," 56.

41. William Taylor, "The Logic of Global Business: An Interview with ABB's Percy Barnevik," *Harvard Business Review* (March–April 1991): 91–105.

42. Christopher A. Bartlett and Sumantra Ghoshal, "Organizing for Worldwide Effectiveness: The Transnational Solution," *California Management Review* (Fall 1988): 54–74.

43. Bartlett and Ghoshal, "Organizing for Worldwide Effectiveness," 71.

44. Kenichi Ohmae, "Managing in a Borderless World," *Harvard Business Review* (May–June 1989): 152–161.

45. Ohmae, "Management in a Borderless World," 155.

46. John A. Quelch and Edward J. Hoff, "Customizing Global Marketing," *Harvard Business Review* (May–June 1986): 59–68; "Outsourcing to India: Back Office to the World," *The Economist*, 5 May 2001, 59–62; Taylor, "The Logic of Global Business"; and Ohmae, "Managing in a Borderless World." ABB Asea Brown Boveri Ltd. refers to this process as creating a "multidomestic

enterprise," while Ohmae refers to this process as "insiderization."

47. As we noted in Chapter 4, most research and writing on brands and branding has been based on, and focuses on, consumer markets. This bias is perhaps even more the case for global branding. So, again, drawing on this work and our experience, we adapt it for application in business markets. In this section, we draw on David A. Aaker and Erich Joachimsthaler, "The Lure of Global Branding," *Harvard Business Review* (November–December 1999): 137–144; and Kevin Lane Keller, *Strategic Brand Management: Building, Measuring, and Managing Brand Equity*, 2nd ed. (Upper Saddle River, NJ: Prentice Hall, 2003), chap. 14.

48. Niraj Dawar and Tony Frost, "Competing with GIANTS: Survival Strategies for Local Companies in Emerging Markets," *Harvard Business Review* (March–April 1999): 119–129.

49. In some instances, the value of the firm's market offering may be lower than that of local alternatives. The firm still may enter the foreign market, offering a relatively lower price to maintain the inequality of equation 5.2, with the intent of competing in the "low end" of the market.

50. Because business ethics and legal systems vary across countries, in some country markets, managers in customer firms may expect bribes or other similar payments as additional incentive to change when they award their business to foreign suppliers. See Tina Rosenberg, "The Taint of the Greased Palm," *The New York Times Magazine*, 10 August 2003, 28–33; "The Worm That Never Dies," *The Economist*, 2 March 2002, 12; "The Short Arm of the Law," *The Economist*, 2 March 2002, 63–65; and Jean-Claude Usunier, *Marketing Across Cultures*, 2d ed. (London: Prentice Hall Europe, 1996), chap. 14.

51. "When the Walls Come Down," *The Economist*, July 5, 1997, 61–63.

Chapter 6

New Offering Realization

OVERVIEW

*T*he intent of a new market offering is to fulfill the requirements and preferences of target market segments and customers better than previous offerings of the supplier. Businesses *create value* with new offerings by increasing the difference between what these offerings are worth to target customers and the total costs to provide them. A new offering can create value in a number of ways: (1) it lowers the customer's total costs; (2) it provides superior performance in the customer's application; (3) it meets customer's changing requirements and needs; (4) or it lowers the supplier's own costs, which it wholly or partly passes on to customers in the form of lower prices. It is critical to marketplace success that a supplier's new offering also must be superior to the offerings of its competitors in one or more ways that target segments and customers value.[1]

New offering realization is the process of developing new core products or services, augmenting them to construct market offerings, and bringing them to market. Realization encompasses all the activities a supplier does to transform an idea into a market offering that it commercializes. New offering realization comprises understanding and implementing the means of consistently producing the core product or service, and the design and delivery of augmenting services, programs, and systems that enhance the value of the core product or service.[2] Firms strive to

Figure 6.1
New Offering
Realization

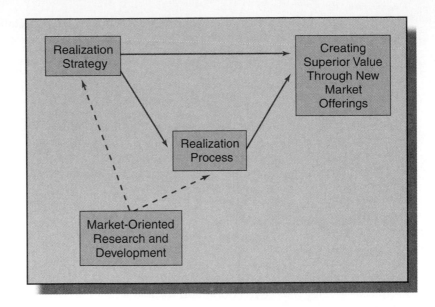

commercialize new market offerings with greater speed, lower total cost, and greater marketplace success than they have previously or than their competitors can.

To accomplish these goals, a firm needs a realization strategy that coordinates, prioritizes, and guides its various realization efforts. This chapter begins with an approach to realization strategy that suppliers can use to strengthen their realization performance. We next survey a number of realization process models that firms in different industries use to direct and manage individual realization projects. We then present a general realization process model and relate the firm models we survey to it. The last section of the chapter focuses on how firms can make new offering realization more market oriented. We depict new offering realization in Figure 6.1.

REALIZATION STRATEGY

New offering realization has the potential to provide significant outcomes in three areas: It can strengthen the firm's market position; it can improve the firm's resource utilization—enabling the firm to reuse product and process know-how—and it can be a vehicle for organizational enhancement and renewal.[3] Most firms, though, find that new offering realization all too seldom delivers these rewards. As examples, NeXT, Inc., spent $200 million of investment funds developing and marketing its sleek black NeXT desktop computer before discontinuing it in 1993, and FedEx lost $340 million on its Zapmail two-hour document delivery service before ending it in 1986.[4] Wheelwright and Clark, experts in product development, suggest the following causes for why new offering realization often falls short in practice: unanticipated shifts in technology or market requirements, mistaken expectations of other functional areas' performance, unexpected technical problems, problem-solving delays, and unresolved policy issues.[5]

To overcome or minimize these realization shortcomings, Wheelwright and Clark advocate that firms generate a **development** or **realization strategy** that encompasses the following:[6]

- Creating, defining, and selecting a set of development projects that will provide superior products and processes
- Integrating and coordinating functional tasks, technical tasks, and organizational units involved in development activities over time
- Managing development efforts so they converge to achieve business purposes as effectively as possible
- Creating and improving the capabilities needed to make development a competitive advantage over the long term

Wheelwright and Clark visually capture these activities in a development strategy framework, which we depict in Figure 6.2. The firm's technology strategy and market strategy serve to bound and focus the development strategy, although as the two-headed arrows in Figure 6.2 suggest, some interplay occurs between these strategies. The firm's **technology strategy** defines what knowledge and know-how resources the firm requires, how it will attain them, and how they will translate into market advantages for the firm. Market strategy, as we discussed in Chapter 4, defines the target market segments and customers and a course of action that the firm will pursue to deliver superior value to them. Note also at the end of the development "funnel" the presence of a Post-Project Learning and Improvement step, which then feeds back to both technology strategy and market strategy. Wheelwright, Clark, and others have stressed the need for firms to make learning a formal part of new development projects.[7] To accomplish this, firms should specify learning objectives in their new development project planning, have project leaders conduct a "learning audit" at the end of each project, and adopt a performance review system that monitors and rewards these activities.

Wheelwright and Clark added Development Goals and Objectives and the Aggregate Project Plan as crucial preproject mechanisms for generating and implementing realization strategy. They argue these mechanisms allow managers to resolve policy issues and concerns that run across multiple projects, and better coordinate and integrate the firm's development efforts. We next examine development goals and objectives, and the aggregate project plan in greater detail. We then discuss the contributions that concurrent engineering can make to realization performance. Finally, we consider the role of outside development relationships and networks in realization strategy.

Development Goals and Objectives

In defining its development goals and objectives, a business specifies what it is seeking to achieve in new offering realization. Obviously, it wants greater success, but defining what exactly "greater success" means is crucial. In doing so, management confronts conflicts that exist among the goals and objectives, and through debate and

Figure 6.2 Development Strategy Framework

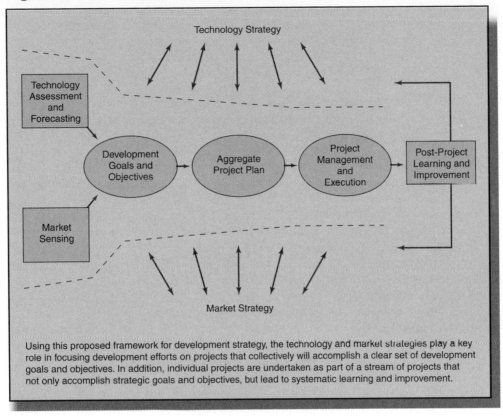

Using this proposed framework for development strategy, the technology and market strategies play a key role in focusing development efforts on projects that collectively will accomplish a clear set of development goals and objectives. In addition, individual projects are undertaken as part of a stream of projects that not only accomplish strategic goals and objectives, but lead to systematic learning and improvement.

Source: Adapted from Steven C. Wheelwright and Kim B. Clark, *Revolutionizing Product Development: Quantum Leaps in Speed, Efficiency, and Quality* (New York: The Free Press, 1992), p. 35.

discussion, makes the required trade-offs. Further, management needs to distinguish between goals for new offering realization as a whole and objectives for individual development projects.

Overall Development Goals

Because of different business strategies that they are pursuing, firms may vary in the overall goals they set for new offering realization. The overall goals of learning, efficiency, and speed-to-market should be of interest to management regardless of the business strategy the firm is pursuing, although the relative emphasis placed on each may vary depending on the business strategy.[8] **Learning** refers to gains in design and process knowledge and know-how, and is paramount for organizational enhancement and renewal to occur. To gain the most, a firm needs to manage learning across all realization efforts. Chaparral Steel, a steel minimill located in Texas, does three things that maximize its overall learning from its development efforts:

First, it requires every development project to advance the company's capabilities. Second, it carefully plans which series of projects to undertake and how to carry them out so that altogether they will strengthen the company's overall set of capabilities. And third, after each project has been completed, Chaparral analyzes it to find out what it achieved or failed to achieve so the organizational lessons—not flow charts and organization structures but the way people actually worked best together—can be passed on to subsequent projects.[9]

Efficiency concerns getting the most out of available resources. As with learning, to gain the most, a firm needs to manage efficiency across all realization efforts. For example, one measure that Hewlett-Packard uses to monitor its overall realization efficiency is "'project team change-over waste': the cost of time and resources spent between the end of the previous effort and the point at which all team members are again fully engaged in value-adding activity."[10]

Speed-to-market refers to the time it takes to complete a development cycle, and improving it has become almost a mantra for new offering realization in business markets. Yet, the firm must understand what advantage speed-to-market provides and how it gauges performance for this goal. As an example, the semiconductor company Analog Devices uses the concept of half-life to gauge its performance on speed-to-market: The time to complete a realization project should decrease by half for each constant period of time, such as every two years.[11] So, the time-to-market should decrease from 36 months to 18 months to 9 months over successive two-year periods. Analog Devices will need to revise how they gauge performance on this goal at some point, though, because becoming faster no longer will provide an advantage, suggesting that other goals will become predominant. Von Braun has cautioned firms about the harmful consequences of an acceleration trap, where technology-driven firms introduce and discontinue products faster and faster.[12]

Managing speed-to-market at the overall level can dramatically affect the speed-to-market of individual projects. Demands for the same resource from multiple projects, such as support technicians who perform testing of prototypes, can create bottlenecks that cause lengthy project delays. Adler, Mandelbaum, Nguyen, and Schwerer found that if firms lowered their planned usage of development resources from 90 percent to 80 percent of overall capacity, they could decrease development cycle times by 30 percent or more.[13] So, building in slack can reduce overall development times.

Defining the overall goals of new offering realization (and the measures that will assess their achievement) brings the conflicts that exist among these goals into sharper focus for management. The previous example illustrates a trade-off between efficiency and speed-to-market as overall new offering realization objectives. Similarly, learning as a goal will adversely affect speed-to-market and efficiency in that establishing learning goals and conducting learning audits takes time and other resources. The trade-off in favor of having learning as an overall goal is based upon the belief that it will eventually pay significant dividends in increasing the speed-to-market and efficiency of realization efforts as a whole. Management needs to validate such beliefs over time with internally generated data, just as it needs to validate market views with market data.

Finally, as an overall assessment of new offering realization performance, some firms use the sales or profits that new offerings generate. Medtronic, a leading medical device company, has as its stated policy that 70 percent of revenue should come from products launched within the past two years. DuPont Company recently promised that by 2005, one-third of its revenue will come from products introduced in the last five years, which would represent substantial improvement.[14]

Project Objectives

Individual development projects play different roles in a firm's realization efforts, as we discuss in the next section on aggregate project plans. Thus, the relative emphasis management places on specific objectives will vary across projects. Smith and Reinertsen, product development consultants, contend that firms must balance four key objectives in managing individual development projects:[15]

- *Development speed or time-to-market*, which is "the time between the first instant someone could have started working on a development program and the instant the final product was available to the customer"[16]
- *Product cost*, which is the total cost of the product to the supplier, including all costs it incurs in marketing, sales, and support services (that are part of the purchase price customers pay)
- *Product performance*, which is how well the product meets the requirements and preferences that target customers have specified
- *Development program expense*, which consists of all the one-time development costs a specific project incurs

Smith and Reinertsen observe that every development project will have to confront trade-offs among these four objectives, and making them correctly is paramount for project success. For example, outsourcing some part of a project adds to the development program expense, but it lowers the time to market. To guide managers in making these trade-off decisions, Smith and Reinertsen recommend comparing different cases using cumulative profits over the life of the product as the criterion measure. They advise managers to construct an economic model using spreadsheet software to explore the effects of trade-offs on cumulative profits. This kind of analysis can produce insights, but managers must be cautious about relying too much on the apparent certainty of quantification. The accuracy of the data used and the assumptions made in constructing the relationships among the variables are crucial in determining a model's practical worth. For example, although cumulative profits may be a worthwhile indicator of financial success, as we have seen, managers may want to consider other realization goals, such as learning, as well. Taking them into account will lead managers to make more complicated, qualitative judgments on trade-off decisions.

To understand the varying roles or contexts of individual projects, Dolan advocates that the firm use a **newness map** that has two dimensions: the newness of the developed product or service to the firm (low to high), and the newness to the market (low to high).[17] A firm can portray its portfolio of projects on this map to recognize what the paramount marketing issues will be for each project. As an example, when the anticipated outcome of a project is an offering that will be low to moderate in newness to the firm and newness to the market, cannibalization versus incremental sales is a paramount marketing issue. **Cannibalization** is when a new offering takes a portion of its sales from an existing offering of the firm. The firm may be willing to endure some cannibalization when its objective for the new offering is to blunt inroads made by a recently introduced competitor's offering. Alternatively, its objective may be to maximize cannibalization, as, for example, when the new offering has greater profitability than the existing offering. Thus, management sets the objectives for projects based on its understanding of their context.

What measures do firms use to assess the achievement of project objectives? To capture variation in project roles, Griffin and Page constructed six development scenarios that systematically vary along the two dimensions of the newness map.[18] Experienced practitioners judged which measures were most useful for evaluating the success of individual projects for each of these six scenarios. The set of measures that the practitioners evaluated comprised customer-based, financial, and technical performance measures of success. With *new-to-the-world projects* (high newness to the firm and to the market), practitioners regard marketplace reaction measures such as customer acceptance and customer satisfaction as most useful. For *line extensions* (moderate newness to the firm and to the market), meeting profit goals, competitive advantage, and market share are the most useful measures.

Best practice firms do not simply rely on post-project measures to evaluate project performance. They also devise measures that can be used *during* a project to provide early warning signals and suggest corrective actions. Recognizing and responding to development problems as they occur increases the rate of project success. "Therefore, smart innovators add leading in-process indicators that measure, for example, anticipated break-even time, quality of planning, conformance to best-practice, time spent with customers, timeliness of deliverables, thoroughness of early engineering analysis, and quality of resources."[19]

The Aggregate Project Plan

An **aggregate project plan** is a mechanism "to ensure that the collective set of projects will accomplish the development goals and objectives and build the organizational capabilities needed for ongoing development success." It allows management to think through in a systematic way how the firm can achieve realization performance that is greater than simply the sum of the projects done. Management should select, sequence, and manage individual development projects to create and leverage interdependence, synergy, and learning across the set of development projects. Three basic steps in constructing an aggregate project plan are: (1) mapping the varying kinds of development projects, (2) making capacity decisions, and (3) making provisions for gaining critical skills and capabilities.[20]

Mapping the Kinds of Development Projects
The first step in generating an aggregate project plan is to understand how the firm is allocating resources across varying kinds of development projects and look at the mix of projects that the firm is doing. Wheelwright and Clark advise creating a map having two dimensions: the extent of product change and the extent of process change. They find these two dimensions most useful for organizing projects because each determines the amount of realization resources a project requires. We reproduce the resulting development project map in Figure 6.3. Product change ranges from

Figure 6.3 Mapping the Five Types of Development Projects

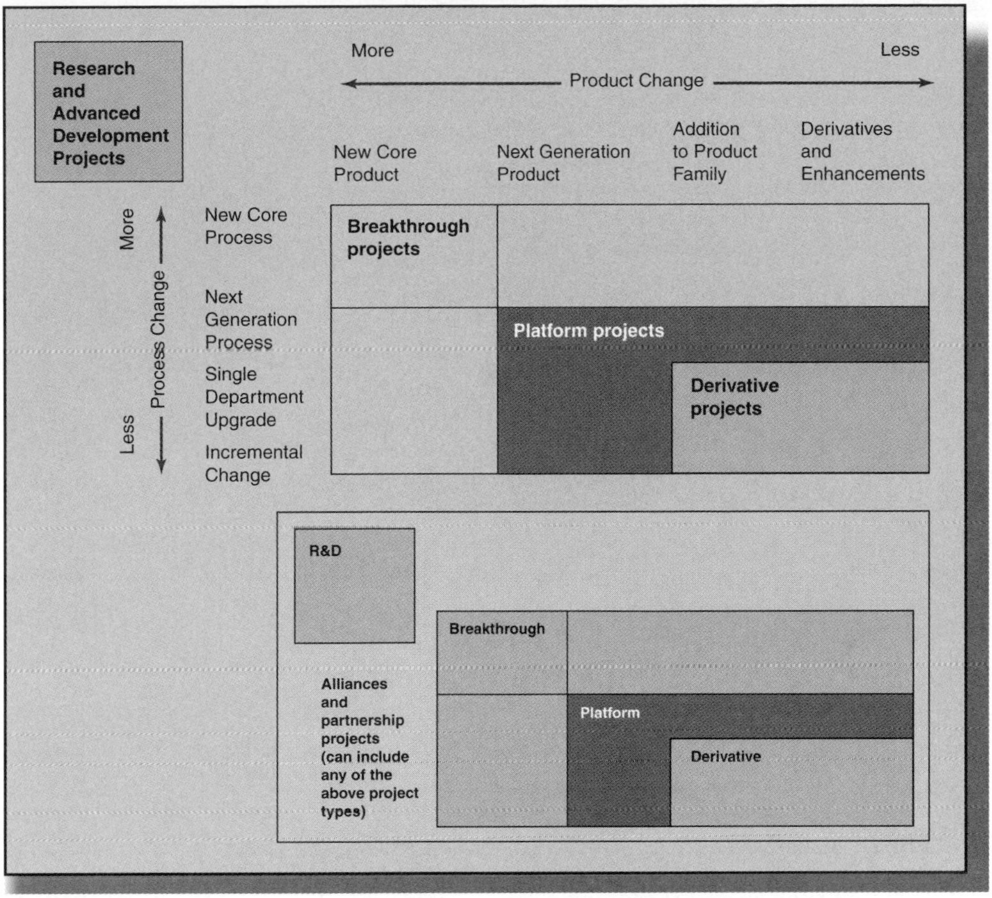

Source: Steven C. Wheelwright and Kim B. Clark, "Creating Project Plans to Focus Product Development," *Harvard Business Review* (March–April 1992): 74.

"derivatives and enhancements" to "new core products," whereas process change ranges from "incremental change" to "new core process." Wheelwright and Clark delineate five kinds of development projects that correspond to areas of the map. Management arranges the projects within these areas, based on each project's expected outputs.

Derivative projects are initiatives that realize small advances in the firm's current offerings or production processes, such as making cost reductions in existing products, providing product line extensions by adding or subtracting secondary features, and devising incremental improvements for an existing production process. Derivative projects have shorter time lengths and require relatively little management involvement or other realization resources. However, they can produce profitable products and enhance the firm's capabilities. As an example, we consider in Box 6.1 how ABN-AMRO Bank created letters of credit syndication (LCS) as a derivative

BOX 6.1
Derivative Product Realization: Letters of Credit Syndication at ABN-AMRO Bank

Letters of credit syndication (LCS) is a short-term, trade-related product whereby ABN-AMRO (AA) sells part of the risk it incurs in confirming an issuing bank's letter of credit (LC). AA retains all documentary risk and transactional risk (dealing with the beneficiary firm); the LCS participating bank takes on the risk that the issuing bank defaults (due to insolvency or illiquidity) or the country defaults (in the case of government-owned banks).

The steps that comprise an LCS are

1. The LCS Unit of AA receives an LC for a specified monetary amount from an issuing bank (e.g., Banco Do Brazil), asking for confirmation. A bank providing confirmation of an LC guarantees the beneficiary of the LC that the issuing bank will meet its obligations under the LC.

2. In accepting this business, AA reaches (or even exceeds) its established bank or country credit limits.

3. The LCS Unit sends an invitation specifying the details of the LC (e.g., amount, lifetime, pricing to syndicate participant) to targeted banks. To assist in this targeting, the Unit maintains a database on participant preferences for countries and banks, their appetite for participating, and their speed of response (e.g., within 10 minutes). The Unit prefers one participant bank per LCS deal whenever possible, although sometimes more than one is needed because of the size of the transaction.

4. After acceptance by return facsimile, formal documentation is exchanged, sent in duplicate with one signed copy returned.

5. The LCS Unit issues payment to the syndicate participant at the conclusion of the deal. The margin it retains between the fee it collects for the confirmation and the fee that it pays to the participant covers the costs of packaging the LCS, exposure to some residual risk in the participating bank, and profit.

What was the realization process for LCS at AA? The idea of LCS had been around for some time. AA had engaged in LCS over a number of years, such as when it sold down some risk in Iran during the 1980s. The process and pricing were not well defined, and considerable variability was involved in both.

In 1993, Otto Röell saw a market opportunity for a more structured, centrally coordinated LCS product. At the time, country limits were under pressure, forcing AA to decline some deals. So, a primary goal of LCS was to create more availability, especially for AA's corporate clients. Concurrent goals were to streamline the LCS process, and to have as much uniformity as possible in the documentation and pricing of LCS. Röell began to develop a structured LCS product and assessed its feasibility with three banks that had established country limits (lines of credit allocated to each country), but were not using them.

In 1994, the LCS Unit was formed with two people, Röell and his associate, Jan Hoogervorst. The Unit began a market introduction of LCS with 15 participating banks. These syndicate participants were either European branches of foreign banks or European banks with little foreign business but established country limits. By the end of 1995, the number of participating syndicate banks had grown to 60. Product sales of LCS grew tenfold over the three-year period.

product that provided a profitable product and significantly expanded its capacity to service its corporate clients.[21] Building upon the letters of credit (LC) platform product, the LCS project required incremental process changes and realization resources to provide a worthwhile addition to the LC product family.

At the opposite end of the development gamut, **breakthrough projects** generate new core products and processes that are fundamentally different from previous generations. Breakthrough products create new markets or are in response to nascent markets with unique requirements. As an example, we consider in Box 6.2 how Kleinwort Benson created *privatization* as a breakthrough product in response to changing government policy.

BOX 6.2
Breakthrough Project: Privatization at Kleinwort Benson

Privatization is the sale of a state-owned industry by a government to individual investors and institutions. In privatizing an industry, a government has five basic aims: (1) to increase efficiency through competition, deregulation, and other means; (2) to raise finance that can be used to reduce government borrowing or to reduce taxation; (3) to encourage employees to own shares in the company in which they work; (4) to deepen and broaden share ownership in the general economy; and (5) to strengthen the capital market. In 1981, the British government asked Kleinwort Benson (KB), a British investment bank now part of Dresdner Bank Group, to act as its principal advisor in the sale of British Aerospace and Cable & Wireless. Privatization as a financial service draws upon many of KB's conventional corporate finance skills, such as valuation and structural advice, and equity capital market capabilities, such as new issue structure and pricing. It also has some fundamentally different requirements, such as devising mechanisms to increase stock ownership by individuals versus institutions, and developing methods of valuation for government-owned firms that take into account their prior reliance on government subsidies and monopoly power. KB's experience as the principal advisor to the British government for the privatization of British Telecom (BT) in 1984, at the time the largest public flotation ever, provides an illustrative example.

Three aspects needed to be resolved in preparation for the flotation of BT. The first aspect was to devise a regulatory system that would provide oversight of BT's dominant position and prevent any abuse of BT monopoly powers. The second aspect was to determine an appropriate capital structure for BT that gave it the necessary financial strength to remain a major force within its home market and to compete successfully overseas. The third aspect was to specify the relationship between the government and BT after the flotation to ensure that the government distanced itself from the commercial operations of the company, while allowing for the government to ensure BT's independence and freedom from takeover.

The value of the shares to be sold was about £4 billion, some seven times bigger than that of any previous U.K. issue and also many times bigger than anything attempted in the United States. In addition to its traditional U.K. and overseas institutional markets, KB also targeted two new market segments: the U.K. general public and BT employees. Some KB and government innovations significantly raised the incentive to purchase shares for these latter segments. First, shares were offered on an installment basis. Only 50p of the 130p offer price was paid by investors at the time of allotment, with the balance being paid in two installments over 17 months, yet dividends were paid on the full value of the shares. Second, a small shareholder's bonus offered either 10 percent additional shares or credit vouchers for telephone bills to targeted small investors that held their shares for at least three years. Third, employees were given three incentives to purchase: Each employee would receive the first £70 of shares for free; they would receive two shares for each one

(continued)

BOX 6.2
Continued

they bought, up to £300 of shares; and they would receive a 10 percent discount on the third installment of shares purchased up to a maximum of 1,600 shares. Finally, KB created the Pathfinder Prospectus and the Mini Prospectus to convey the essential information about the BT offering in a nontechnical, understandable way to potential investors.

The results for the privatization of BT were outstanding. The offering was more than nine times oversubscribed. The final allocation for the four market segments was U.K. institutions, 47 percent; U.K. public, 34 percent; BT employees and pensioners, 5 percent; and overseas, 14 percent. Importantly, 96 percent of BT employees became shareholders.

Privatization has become a financial service for which KB is well known, and it remains a market leader in privatization.

Sources: Adapted from Timothy Barker, Vice Chairman, Kleinwort Benson Group PLC, speech delivered on 23 February 1994; and John Moore, "British Privatization—Taking Capitalism to the People," *Harvard Business Review* (January–February 1992): 115–124.

Platform projects "are in the middle of the development spectrum and are thus harder to define. They entail more product and/or process changes than derivatives do, but they don't introduce the untried new technologies or materials that breakthrough products do."[22] Platform products represent the natural starting point for the core product part of **flexible market offerings**.[23] Initially, the platform product is the "naked solution" for the product component for the target market segments and customers. The initial platform product provides little flexibility, offering few or no options that some, but not all, segment members value. Over time, derivative projects provide product options that some, but not all, members of initially targeted segments value. The value proposition could also be extended to other segments that the firm decides to target. We consider positioning for offerings from platform and derivative projects in Box 6.3.

As an example of a platform product, consider how Asea Brown Boveri (ABB) standardized its offering of power plants. Because the price of a power plant is several hundred million dollars, ABB had to provide some flexibility in the product part of the market offering. Yet, this requirement does not necessarily mean that each power plant must be a one-off, custom designed and built product. Rather, ABB's insight was to recognize where flexibility created significantly greater value for the customer than the incremental cost of ABB providing it. Figure 6.4 depicts which power plant subsystems to standardize, which to customize, and the "boundary" subsystems that needed to be negotiated, depending upon the customer's requirements. Having a reference power plant of modular construction, and repetition in building that power plant product were critical for gaining advantage for ABB. In return, ABB could provide these *reference power plants* at a significantly lower price to customers and, importantly, deliver the plant in a significantly shorter period of time, allowing the customer to begin earning revenue from the generated electricity.[24]

Two kinds of development projects management needs to include in the aggregate project plan appear outside the boundaries of the development map in Figure 6.3. **Research and advanced development projects** "aim at inventing new science or capturing new know-how so that required knowledge will be available for application in

BOX 6.3
Positioning Offerings from Platform and Derivative Projects

Conceptualizing development projects as breakthrough, platform, or derivative can also provide a meaningful way of *positioning* the resulting products to prospective customers. The platform product should emphasize the essential attributes to the target customers and provide the overarching value proposition. The firm subsequently positions derivative products relative to the platform product position. These derivative products might strengthen the value proposition for subsegments within the originally targeted market segments that come to have special requirements. Alternatively, derivative products might add attributes that are essential to other market segments, or might delete attributes from the platform product that other market segments regard as superfluous. In each case,

the derivative product strengthens the value proposition for the targeted segment.

The derivative product positioning to the prospective customers would communicate differences from the established meaning of the platform product, making it easier for them to understand. Moreover, whether attributes are added or deleted, the firm would frame the differences as gains in value for the target customers. As an example, Okuma America Corporation defeatured one of its state-of-the-art machining centers to gain entry into the small machine-shop segment and compete with lower-end Korean tool builders. Okuma positioned its Cadet™ line as performing the lathe machining functions that shop owners valued most, at a price they could afford.

specific development projects."[25] Wheelwright and Clark draw a sharp distinction between this kind of development project and commercial development projects, which consist of breakthrough, platform, and derivative projects. They stress separating invention from application, and that whenever possible, an invention's applied workability should be demonstrated prior to its use in a commercial development project. Yet, research and advanced development (RAD) projects and commercial projects must be part of the same plan because they compete for development resources, and management must provide mechanisms to ensure smooth exchange of knowledge back and forth between RAD and commercial projects.

Alliances and partnership projects are those done in conjunction with one or more outside firms. The projects may be RAD or commercial in nature, and the extent of involvement of the firm in the project can range from minimal oversight to extensive interaction and involvement. "Even when the partner company takes full responsibility for a project, the acquiring company must devote in-house resources to monitor the project, capture the new knowledge being created, and prepare for the manufacturing and sales of the new product."[26] We discuss the role of supplier relationships and networks in innovation in the next section.

Making Capacity Decisions

After understanding the number of proposed and current projects, and the mix of these projects, management must make some hard decisions about the number and mix of projects to start or complete with the resources they have. "When organizations overextend their resources, productivity declines, the number of projects 'in process' increases, projects take longer to complete, and the rate of project completions

Figure 6.4 Standardization of Combined Cycle Power Plants at ABB

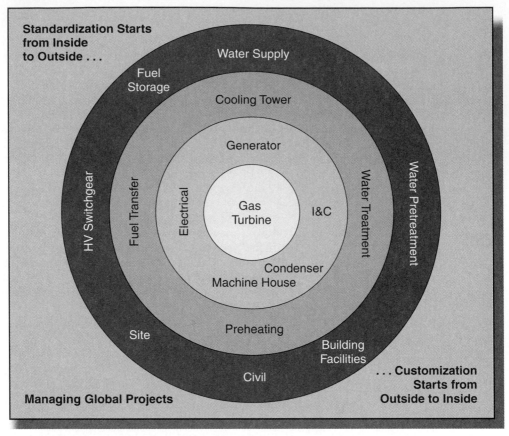

declines."[27] Wheelwright and Clark observe that it is not unusual for firms to find that their project commitments greatly exceed available development resources, sometimes by more than twice their capacity!

Management has several related capacity decisions to make. First, it likely needs to reduce the number of projects being done at any one time. Management must postpone some projects, and it needs to adroitly refuse or cancel others that do not appear promising. Second, it likely needs to resequence some projects to provide a better mix or flow of projects. For example, a particular sequence of projects may enable the firm to build upon its learning and knowledge in a way that reduces the overall time required to complete the sequenced set of projects. Taking projects out of the order of when individuals requested them may go against an implicit policy of "first-in, first-out" project scheduling and execution, and anger those whose projects are "bumped." Finally, management must decide upon a preferred level of development capacity utilization. This decision will depend, in part, on the mix of projects being done and the resource bottlenecks that are likely to occur. As we discussed earlier, building in slack can reduce overall development times.

Gaining Critical Skills and Capabilities

As a final step in constructing an aggregate project plan, management needs to consider how the set of candidate development projects will enable the firm to build or acquire the critical skills and capabilities it will need for future development and marketplace success. As Wheelwright and Clark contend, "Possibly the greatest value of an aggregate project plan over the long-term is its ability to shape and build development capabilities, both individual and organizational. It provides a vehicle for training development engineers, marketers, and manufacturing people in the different skill sets needed by the company."[28]

Three aspects to consider are building technical knowledge, cross-functional cooperation, and project leadership capability. Assignments to project teams should be made to build technical knowledge for the organization and in the individuals themselves. For example, a firm can use job rotation between the research and advanced development group and the commercial development group to alternately deepen and broaden individuals' technical knowledge and capability. Building and reinforcing cross-functional cooperation is paramount to technical and marketplace success. A study of commercialization by McKinsey & Company found that:

> High-performing companies emphasize a set of skills notably different from their less successful counterparts. They value cross-functional skills, while other companies pride themselves on their functional strengths. High performers boast, "We've got the best project managers in the world." Low performers say, "We've got the best circuit designers."[29]

Participating in cross-functional work teams for projects, training, and job rotation across functional areas builds cross-functional skills and appreciation for how each area contributes to marketplace success. Finally, the preceding quote also points to the critical importance of project leadership. To build this capability, individuals need to receive training on how to work in teams and have a series of project assignments with increasing responsibility. Project leadership would progress from derivative projects to platform projects to breakthrough projects.

Concurrent Engineering in Realization Strategy

To significantly improve speed-to-market and realization efficiency, a number of best practice firms make concurrent engineering a part of their realization strategies. **Concurrent engineering** is where firms work on the process for making a product while they are still in the process of designing it.[30] Firms that practice concurrent engineering purposely overlap stages of their development processes that have traditionally been strictly sequential. They form cross-functional teams composed of members from design, engineering, manufacturing, procurement, and marketing who are responsible for a realization project from its inception through its market launch. To facilitate communication and social interaction among team members, management often **collocates** the team; that is, it has them work together in a single place throughout the project.[31] Primary suppliers play a more active role in concurrent engineering and may even provide **resident engineers**—engineers a supplier temporarily assigns to the customer's location to work closely with the cross-functional project team.[32] We first look at point-based versus set-based approaches to concurrent engineering, then show a relationship between set-based concurrent engineering and flexible market offerings.

Point-Based versus Set-Based Approaches to Concurrent Engineering

In a point-based approach to concurrent engineering (CE), individuals responsible for the design of a product generate a number of alternatives and select what appears to be the most promising design solution. Then, they and their counterparts responsible for the process of making the product go back and forth with the design, making successive improvements until both groups arrive at a mutually satisfactory solution.[33] The CE practice of collocated, cross-functional teams accelerates this process. Yet, the process still has a sequential, though iterative, character. Obstacles that individuals responsible for making the product encounter require backtracking for reevaluations and modifications by the design team. This backtracking slows down the realization process, and those responsible for the process of making the product may wait until most or all of the design parameters are settled before proceeding with their work on the manufacturing process.

A set-based approach to CE offers a way around the shortcomings of point-based CE. **Set-based concurrent engineering** "refers to a deliberate effort to define, communicate about, and explore sets of possible solutions, rather than modifying a point solution—and in some cases, these sets may be deliberately more constrained than common industry practice."[34] A firm uses its accumulated knowledge about its design and manufacturing capabilities to specify what the feasible ranges are for design parameters (as well as noting problems that have occurred outside these ranges). Critically, research suggests that downstream engineering should pursue set-based concurrent engineering for those areas where upstream engineering understands the structure of the problem and the set of relevant variables, but is uncertain what the specific values of those variables will be. When there is ambiguity about the structure of the problem and what the relevant variables might be, iterative coordination and problem-solving are preferred.[35] Ward, Liker, Cristiano, and Sobek find that Toyota uses audit sheets to track deviations from designated constraints, organize communication between affected groups, and provide a mechanism for resolving problems:

> These sheets give the nature of the problem, a countermeasure suggested to alleviate the problem, the suggesting department, and a sign-off for the affected functional areas. Often the suggestions resolve the problem to all parties' satisfaction. However, if they are unable to find a common ground, a functional group (say, die design) may develop a new technology or process advance to make the design feasible, and then revise the lessons-learned book.[36]

Box 6.4 considers how set-based CE might have altered a point-based CE project failure at PWR Company.

Set-Based Concurrent Engineering and Flexible Market Offerings

We use Nippondenso, a world leader in radiators and alternators based in Japan, to show a relationship between set-based concurrent engineering and flexible market offerings. Through its participation in an early supplier involvement program with Toyota, Nippondenso learns about Toyota's upcoming requirements for all of its

BOX 6.4
New Product Development Programs—The Need for Set-Based Concurrent Engineering

PWR Company (a disguised name) is a manufacturer of uninterruptible power supplies (UPS), products that protect computers and other hardware from fluctuations in electric power quality. Recently, PWR initiated a new product development program, named 510, to significantly increase its sales to performance-oriented customers. The 510 program had a clear business objective: leverage existing technology to quickly deliver a reliable, modular product to the mid-range UPS market.

To help ensure the success of the 510 program, PWR embraced four key elements of concurrent engineering (CE): (1) establish a cross-functional team to achieve early simultaneous influence; (2) collocate team members; (3) use computer and information technology; and (4) implement in-process design controls. In spite of seemingly successful use of these elements, after six months, only the electrical engineering (EE) design group was working. Other engineering groups, as well as purchasing and product management, indicated that any further progress on their part was now dependent on EE decisions. Concurrent engineering had become sequential engineering with downstream resources waiting for upstream decisions. As a result, the 510 program made slow progress, and senior management canceled it in its eighth month. CE had failed.

Subsequent to the failure, one team member conducted an analysis to determine why success was not achieved. Although CE provided noticeable benefits early in the program,

the point-based approach to CE that PWR was practicing had devolved into an "over the wall," sequential design paradigm. If management had recognized the need to change this design paradigm to a set-based approach, the 510 program might have been saved.

For example, the EEs at PWR hesitated to communicate the circuit design options they were in the process of evaluating. Had they communicated the options, the team would have observed that each option required surface-mount technology to meet dimensional constraints. With this information, manufacturing engineering could have started evaluating equipment capable of handling surface-mount technology, which was currently beyond PWR's capability. With set-based CE, designers communicate to other team members those aspects of the design alternatives that they are considering that are constant across the set. Parallel development proceeds on the basis of what is known.

The PWR manufacturing engineers would not have known the exact surface-mount equipment specifications, but they could have anticipated the future demand for surface-mount capability and begun to research machine options. They could have learned enough even to make an equipment purchase decision without incurring prohibitive risk. With the information a set-based approach to CE provides, downstream team members can anticipate, act upon, and, with surprising consistency, meet program challenges before they adversely affect the development timeline.

Source: Contributed by Samuel Bachman,. Kellogg School of Management, Northwestern University.

prospective models. Armed with this knowledge and knowledge gained from its other customers, Nippondenso uses set-based CE to converge upon a single design concept that it uses to define a product family that collectively will satisfy the requirements for an entire set of automobiles. Significantly, it produces all the variants of the product family on the same line. Nippondenso refers to this approach of providing extensive product variety (e.g., more than 700 different alternators) while standardizing the production process as *standardized variety.* "For example, the development group will develop a modularized plan to standardize the various components of the alternator to meet all requirements. It might develop three different body types, nine different wire specifications, four different regulators, etc., all mutually compatible."[37]

Standardized variety is a means of providing flexibility at lower cost in the product component of the market offering. Notice that modularity (with compatibility) is a design constraint in set-based CE. It is a design imperative. In much the same way, senior management can make commonality of parts a design imperative, imposing it as a design constraint in set-based CE. This reduces the number of like parts across a product family that are uniquely different in ways that do not contribute value. Ford Motor Company's Expedition sport utility vehicle and F-150 truck share about half of their parts. This is a result of the company's Ford 2000 initiative, which had as one of its goals greater commonality of parts.[38] Modularity and commonality provide greater flexibility while lowering acquisition, manufacturing, and after-sales service costs.

Outside Development Relationships and Networks in Realization Strategy

In business markets, a crucial part of a firm's realization strategy is understanding what role outside development relationships will play. Firms may require resources that are technical, economic, social, or even political in nature for successful new offering realization. The latitude senior management has in deciding whether to develop the resource in-house or to seek it from outside sources will vary considerably, depending on the kind of project and the resource required. We discuss alternative development structures the firm might pursue, the various aims firms have for outside relationships, and factors that senior management should consider in making their decisions about outside development relationships and networks.

Alternative Development Structures

A firm can pursue a number of development structures to gain needed resources. The firm might outsource a technical resource—simply acquire it from an outside supplier that develops it for sale to the firm. The firm might license the technology, which involves gaining the intellectual property rights. In rapidly developing fields, such as semiconductors and electronics, firms often exchange intellectual property rights through cross-licensing arrangements, where any discrepancies in the value between the firms' respective patent portfolios are compensated for with royalty payments. Not only does this provide firms with greater intellectual property resources, it also provides them with freedom to design and operate without fear of patent infringement litigation.[39]

The firm might collaborate with an outside firm to codevelop a technical resource it needs. This outside relationship can be with another firm, such as a supplier or customer. The "outside" relationship even may be with a development group from another business unit, subsidiary, or division of the same firm. When Lockheed

Martin, the large defense and aerospace firm, bids for a new contract, it creates a "'virtual company,' a new unit that draws on several parts of the vast firm."[40]

The collaboration may be with two or more outside development partners; that is, a business network focused on research and advanced development, or commercial development. As an example, consider the development network that collectively realized a wood saw that sawmills could use to cut frozen timber, which we depict in Figure 6.5 and describe in Box 6.5. Notice how the technical requirements for the wood saw sparked development activities not only in the saw equipment producer's relationships with its suppliers and sawmill customers, but also in connected relationships, such as the saw blade producer's relationships with its suppliers.

The actors comprising the network can be suppliers, competitors, or customers to one another. As we saw in Chapter 1, the firms may have **multiplex relations**, taking on more than one role with respect to other actors. The actors in the network can all be outside firms or a mix of inside-the-firm and outside partners. For example, the Mercedes unit of Daimler-Benz is collaborating with Daimler's Dornier and MBB aerospace units, as well as an outside firm, Canada's Ballard Power Systems, to develop a vehicle powered by a fuel cell.[41]

BOX 6.5
Realization of New Wood Saw Equipment

A saw equipment producer required a series of cooperative developments in outside relationships to realize band saw equipment that sawmills could use to cut frozen timber, a necessity for the equipment to be used in Sweden. The saw equipment producer began by working with its components supplier to provide an initial, technical solution. The producer then collaborated with two customer firms to test this solution—a small sawmill located nearby with which it had worked on other projects and a large sawmill that it viewed as an opinion leader. The latter was interested because it had several large investment projects coming up. Working together with the small customer, the saw equipment producer successfully developed and tested the first prototype, a small band saw. But when the saw equipment producer transferred this solution to the larger customer, cracks developed in a bigger prototype, and there were even some serious breakdowns in which the whole band saw broke off.

The saw equipment producer and the large sawmill believed that weaknesses in the steel and especially in the welding seams of the band saws were the problems. So the large sawmill initiated technical cooperation with a saw blade producer in the belief that it would be possible to eliminate these problems by making changes in the saw blade producer's production process. However, these firms found that it was necessary for the saw blade producer to get adaptations in the steel it bought from a saw steel company as well as acquiring new equipment for the welding operation. These efforts were not wholly successful, so the saw equipment producer had to make further adaptations to its equipment. The total process took several years to accomplish but was, in the end, very successful.

Source: Adapted from James C. Anderson, Håkan Håkansson, and Jan Johanson, "Dyadic Business Relationships Within a Business Network Context," *Journal of Marketing* (October 1994): 1–15.

Figure 6.5
New Wood Saw Equipment Network

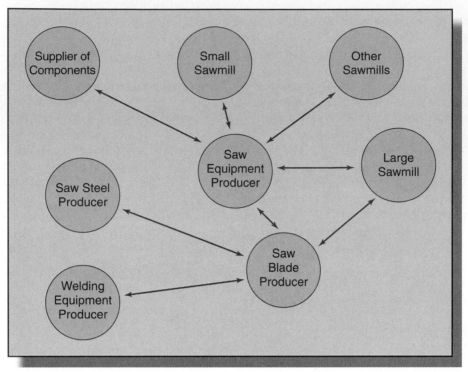

Source: James C. Anderson, Håkan Håkansson, and Jan Johanson, "Dyadic Relationships Within a Business Network Context," *Journal of Marketing* (October 1994): 3.

Aims of Development Relationships and Networks

What purposes do outside development relationships and networks serve that firms are not able—or choose not—to fulfill in-house? We can broadly group the aims as technical, economic, social, or political (a notable kind of social aim), and each can be present to varying extents in seeking outside relationships. Outside suppliers might have technical resources that the firm does not have, such as design expertise, process engineering know-how, or technological artifacts. The firm may view these resources as peripheral to its realization strategy or may recognize that developing them internally would significantly slow its speed-to-market. Box 6.6 recounts how PEG Company used an outside relationship to dramatically improve its speed-to-market.

Using the resources of an outside supplier can significantly lower development costs, as was the case with PEG's use of NXT. The outside supplier may have an advantage in a resource that would be prohibitively expensive to duplicate. Another economic aim is that by pooling resources, two or more firms leverage their respective technical capabilities while lowering the development costs to each. IBM, Toshiba, and Siemens are collaborating in the design and fabrication process for a 256-megabit memory chip, which will take about eight years and cost

BOX 6.6
Tapping the Strengths of Supplier Networks

In 1994, PEG Company (a disguised name) lagged the competition in offering hardware that would connect its products to computer networks. PEG needed to quickly produce an electronic device that would help customers better manage the PEG products installed on their business computer networks—ultimately improving reliability of these networks for the customer.

Top management at PEG recognized the need for quick-to-market product realization and appointed a task force of experienced marketing, engineering, and operations managers. This cross-functional task force established major new product development (NPD) program requirements, such as launch date, budget, differentiating features, and cost and price targets. Since the task force perceived product differentiation as the primary program requirement, it decided to contract with NXT Company (a disguised name)—an entrepreneurial start-up with specific expertise in the technology. The task force chose the NXT option over private-labeling another company's existing product or performing design and manufacture in-house. NXT had established credibility through its success in launching a similar product and through articles NXT management had written. The PEG task force contacted NXT management and, after several meetings, the two parties signed a development agreement.

Under the terms of the development agreement, NXT was responsible for design and manufacture of the product. PEG would provide sales, marketing, and technical service. Through its efforts in developing other products, NXT had established a network of suppliers and contacts. PEG viewed this network—which NXT had originally created to bring products to market in an entrepreneurial environment (i.e., quickly and inexpensively)—as an asset. The firms in the network had demonstrated both their capability and flexibility with programs in which Year 1 production would be fewer than 1,000 units.

The selection and involvement of NXT and its network early in the process allowed a broader group of professionals to influence the PEG product design. These suppliers were able to make product design decisions that leveraged the full benefit of their strengths and process capabilities. For example, one design engineer had extensive experience with a particular microprocessor. On a previous project, he had designed supporting circuity, programmed, and debugged this microprocessor chip set. Using this processor eliminated the risk and expense of learning to program a different chip set. As another example, the contract manufacturer recommended changing six specific parts because they were currently having difficulty sourcing them for another client.

Within 10 months, a fully functional preproduction unit was operating successfully in beta-site testing. The product featured several exclusive benefits and employed cutting-edge technology, making it less expensive and more effective for the customer. The 10-month development time represented a 25 percent improvement over a past PEG program of similar complexity. In order to minimize cost, people participated in the NPD program only as needed, which reduced the number of people billing 40+ hours to the project, and total labor cost came in 10 percent under budget. As an illustration, the project's two electronics engineers worked evenings and weekends while maintaining full-time employment with another company. Review meetings were scheduled accordingly. These engineers, paid as outside contractors, were former colleagues of one of the NPD team members, so the team knew the quality of their work and their experience in designing the specific circuitry.

Source: Contributed by Samuel Bachman, Kellogg School of Management, Northwestern University.

a daunting $1 billion.[42] In doing so, they also hope to forge an industry standard for these chips to speed market acceptance.

Another kind of economic aim is for two or more firms to collaborate on common design and technical specifications for products that do not provide any of them with an advantage. In this way, participating firms lower the costs of products that each purchases and also improve their efficiency. For example, General Motors, Ford Motor, and Chrysler are collaborating to reduce "more than 100 different wiring connectors to fewer than 10, which would be standard throughout the industry, lowering parts costs, reducing the difficulty of building cars, and making them easier to repair."[43]

A social aim of outside relationships and networks might be to have a number of firms commit to developing and using a particular technology. Adobe Systems has furnished programming tools such as software development kits and application programming interfaces to outside developers for free. In doing so, Adobe gains the support of these developers in upholding its Portable Document Format (PDF) as the dominant format, enhancing the value of its full-version Acrobat product.[44] Apart from these consensus-building effects on reducing risk, by pooling resources, outside relationships and networks also allow firms to reduce their risks through sharing the financial burden of development. Finally, firms may use outside relationships and networks for political aims to persuade industry associations, regulatory agencies, or governments to adopt standards that favor their developed technology over rival technologies.

Decision Considerations

Our discussion of the aims of outside relationships and networks has touched on some considerations for senior management to use in making decisions. Senior management will find that it must consider social as well as strategic factors. It also must understand the technology cycle and the resource demands of different kinds of development projects.

Eisenhardt and Schoonhoven studied product development alliances in the semiconductor industry over an eight-year period.[45] Their research sought to determine what strategic and social factors predict the formation of development relationships or alliances between firms. Firms with innovative technologies, that were competing in emergent markets, or that had larger numbers of competitors were significantly more likely to form alliances. Although these strategic factors are not so surprising, Eisenhardt and Schoonhoven also found that social factors related to top management characteristics were significant. "Firms with top management teams that were large, experienced, and well-connected through former employers and high-level previous jobs formed product development alliances at higher rates."[46]

Hamel, Doz, and Prahalad stress that firms considering outside relationships (with current or potential competitors) must delimit cooperation carefully and guard against competitive encroachment:

> A strategic alliance is a constantly evolving bargain whose real terms go beyond the legal agreement or the aims of top management. What information gets traded is determined day to day, often by engineers and operating managers. Successful companies inform employees at all levels about what skills and technologies are off-limits to the partner and monitor what the partner requests and receives.[47]

They also observe that firms that benefit most from outside relationships put in place practices and mechanisms to learn as much as possible from the partner, even in areas outside the formal agreement.

Drawing on a number of examples of technological evolution, Tushman and Rosenkopf propose a **technology cycle** consisting of four sequential stages: technological discontinuity, an era of ferment, the emergence of a dominant design, and an era of incremental change. Tushman and Rosenkopf stress that a firm must forge outside relationships and networks that serve social and political purposes for it to prevail in the latter three stages. For example, a firm must recognize that technical prowess or economic strength may be insufficient for it to bring about a **dominant design**, which is a single architecture that becomes the acknowledged standard in a product class. "Where technological discontinuities may be driven by random events or strokes of genius . . . dominant designs are driven by the visible hand of organizations interacting with other organizations and practitioner communities to shape dimensions of merit and industry standards to maximize local needs." In fact, superior interorganizational network skills can prevail over superior technology, as was the case for Matsushita's VHS format versus Sony's BETA format for videocassette recorders.[48]

REALIZATION PROCESS MODELS

One of the captivating aspects of business markets is their marvelous diversity. Examining a number of realization process models from different business markets provides some appreciation for this diversity. We also will see that some common characteristics emerge. We then present a general realization process model that has these characteristics, is market oriented, and emphasizes cross-functional coordination. We conclude by considering some next-generation changes in realization process models.

A Variety of Realization Process Models

We briefly examine the realization process models for SMALLFRY Industrial Design, AKZO NOBEL Coatings, Kleinwort Benson Investment Management, ABB Asea Brown Boveri Ltd. large system projects, and ABN-AMRO Bank Global Transaction Services. These models run the gamut from investment products to power plants. Each provides us with further understanding of the new offering realization process in practice.

SMALLFRY Industrial Design

SMALLFRY Industrial Design is a specialist industrial design consultancy based in England. Its success lies in closely supporting its clients' business objectives by applying a strategic approach to design projects. SMALLFRY's stated aims are to increase added value, improve product quality, and reduce manufacturing costs for its clients by carefully interpreting marketing, customer, and technical requirements into effective manufacturing solutions. Its capabilities cover all aspects of design realization, from seeking out new product opportunities and concept generation through to compiling full manufacturing specifications for a new product offering.

SMALLFRY acts as an external design resource for client companies with a wide range of design experience and product types. Consequently, its realization process needs to work alongside a variety of internal process models that client firms use. SMALLFRY has carefully developed its Product Development Flow Diagram, which we reproduce in Figure 6.6, to give a clear overview of the key design stages and highlight the critical activities under each stage. This overview ensures that

Figure 6.6 SMALLFRY's Product Development Flow Diagram

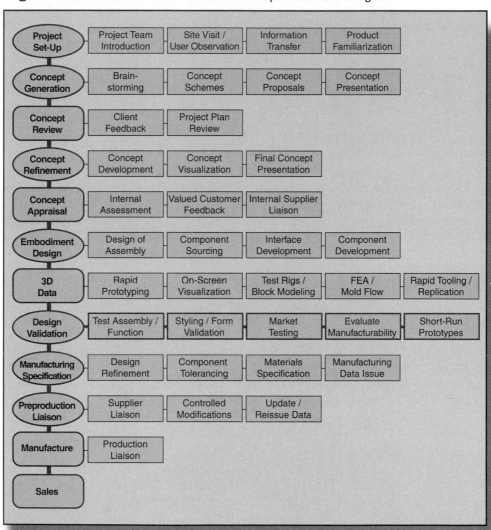

SMALLFRY's work ties in with the client's own process and activities and helps to prevent vital steps from being overlooked in the realization process. The flow diagram breaks down the process into 12 stages from project setup to final manufacture and marketplace sales. It is intended as a prompt for activities that need to be addressed throughout the realization process, clarifying the contribution that an external design resource can make and the major points of interaction with the client firm.

To accommodate the majority of scenarios, SMALLFRY's flow diagram assumes that the client has a clear understanding of the nature of the product it wishes to develop and has assembled information on the core factors governing the product's realization. As an aid to assembling this information, SMALLFRY offers a Product Design Specification Checklist, which we reproduce in Figure 6.7. This checklist highlights the critical aspects of marketing, technical performance, manufacturing, usage, maintenance, and contractual considerations that will directly affect the scope of the subsequent realization work.

By necessity, SMALLFRY's all-encompassing realization model is a simplified, linear version of a range of complex activities that often run concurrently. Still, it has proved of great benefit in describing the general process to client firms that are not experienced in running design realization projects or do not have a formalized process for these activities themselves. It also helps provide personnel from the cross-functional teams within an organization who only participate in certain stages of the process with a better understanding of where their contribution fits into the overall picture.

AKZO NOBEL Coatings

At AKZO NOBEL (AN) Coatings, Innovative Research, which is the research and advanced development unit, feeds into Product Development, which is the commercial development unit. Product Development has international and local country market product development responsibility, and it also has technical support responsibility for the local country markets. On the international side, new offering realization can be a joint Business Unit Coatings North and South (Europe) effort; an international brand initiative, such as for the Sikkens® professional line of coatings; or a multibrand initiative, in which the same technology underlies a product that has a different brand name in each country market. A local initiative is a product that is of interest to one country market.

We reproduce the AN Coatings realization process model in Figure 6.8. The process begins with an *idea phase*, in which anyone in the business unit can contribute a short idea paper. The business unit management team meets every three months to consider idea papers and project proposals, and to give approvals. Following idea approval, AN Coatings names a project manager and forms a project team, which has primary responsibility for the remaining phases of the realization process. A noteworthy aspect of the AN Coatings process is that it does not end at the completion of the *market introduction phase*; there is a subsequent *aftercare phase*. This phase takes place about 12 months after AN Coatings introduces the offering to the market, when AN coatings makes small improvements, if needed, based on customer remarks and feedback. AN Coatings has found that small technical adaptations can make a significant difference in the market acceptance of a new product.

Figure 6.7 SMALLFRY's Product Design Specification Checklist

1 Marketing
1.1   Product justification
1.2   Primary use
1.3   Secondary uses
1.4   Product features
1.5   Associated client products
1.6   Target market
1.7   Competitive situation
1.8   Projected introduction
1.9   Product life
1.10 Future developments
1.11 Pricing strategy
1.12 Visual precedents
1.13 Graphic identification
1.14 Corporate identity
1.15 Sales outlets
1.16 Sales distribution
1.17 Packaging

2 Technical Performance
2.1   How does the product work?
2.2   What elements does it consist of?
2.3   How are the elements related?
2.4   Performance requirements
2.5   Power supply—variations
2.6   Dimensional constraints
2.7   Ambient operating conditions
2.8   Applicable standards
2.9   Applicable regulations

3 Manufacturing
3.1   Available facilities
3.2   Preferred materials
3.3   Target production rate
3.4   Total production quantities
3.5   Proposed batch size
3.6   Packaging methods
3.7   Distribution method
3.8   Size/Weight restrictions
3.9   Tooling amortization policy

4 Usage
4.1   Storage means
4.2   Installation or preparation method
4.3   Environmental requirements
4.4   Product operation sequence
4.5   Operation duration and frequency
4.6   Where used?
4.7   Type of operator
4.8   Effects on other people

5 Maintenance
5.1   What maintenance required?
5.2   Frequency of maintenance
5.3   By whom?

6 Contractual
6.1   What is the patent situation?
6.2   Copyright
6.3   Confidentiality

Figure 6.8 The Realization Process Model at AKZO NOBEL Coatings

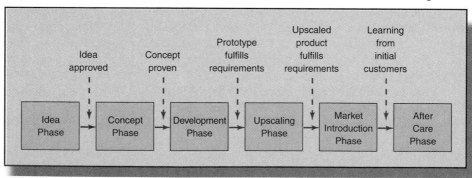

Kleinwort Benson Investment Management

Kleinwort Benson Investment Management (KBIM) is a unit of London-based Dresdner Kleinwort Benson, an investment bank.[49] Several years ago, KBIM had a sales orientation that led to a proliferation of mutual funds and other products for company pension funds and other institutions. The result was a large portfolio of marginally profitable products. These events led KBIM to create a Marketing Committee, which recognized the need for a more structured, new-product development process. Drawing on its own experience as well as those of some other banks, KBIM constructed the product development process that we reproduce in Figure 6.9. The purpose of the process was to ensure that individuals sponsoring a new product idea would consider the necessary elements of a new product's development in time scales appropriate to allow others to carry out other necessary work, while controlling the overall cost and risk to KBIM.

Four committees provide oversight and guidance in the new offering realization process:

1. *Marketing Committee* (MC), comprising 12 members selected from KBIM division heads, designed to be more imaginative, yet objective.
2. *Risk Management Committee*, comprising 6 to 8 members, focuses on credit limit approval and exposure to Kleinwort Benson. The head of the private bank serves on this committee, and the others are knowledgeable and experienced in finance and treasury.
3. *Investment Committee*, comprising 6 to 8 members, with the Chief Investment Officer as chair.
4. *Investment Management Executive Committee* (IMEC), which is an interlinking committee in that each member is on at least one of the other committees.

The sponsor of the initial idea forms a project group that goes through the process, beginning with initial product development and continuing through launch plan management. Notice that the project would go to either the Risk or Investment Committees (rarely would both need to sign off), depending upon whether it was a debt, equity, or bond product.

KBIM has worked hard to move project groups from viewing the MC as a hurdle to viewing it instead as a resource that adds value by offering "builds" on initial product ideas. For example, recently the MC suggested to a project group that rather than going to the market directly with a new investment product, they consider using Building Societies as strategic distribution partners that would take the marketing risk. Further, the MC gave a qualified, initial approval to the project subject to further research (which subsequently supported the reorientation to indirect participation).

KBIM recognizes the intent of its new offering realization process is not to enforce a rigid, bureaucratic process that stifles product development. Some flexibility is needed. One way the KBIM MC provides this flexibility is through *qualified project approvals,* subject to further research that will supply critical information needed for a decision. This allows other development activities to proceed while the specified research is done. Another way it provides flexibility is through a *fast-track option,* where an idea sponsor requiring rapid approval is permitted to call a meeting with at least two members of the MC who can approve the initiative if they both believe it to

Figure 6.9 Kleinwort Benson Investment Management's Product Development Process

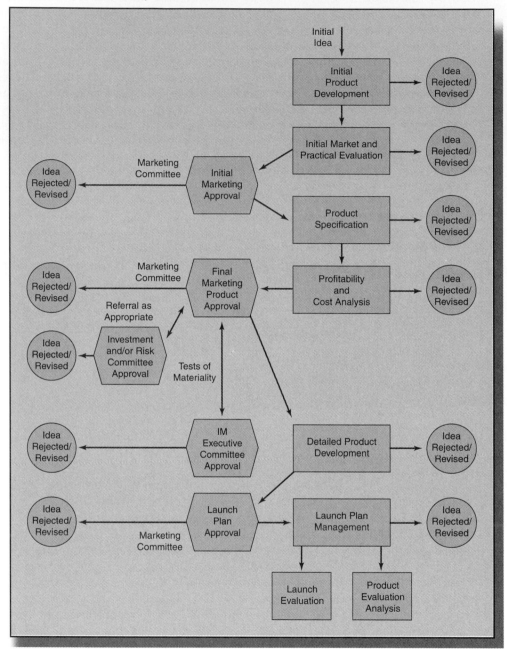

be in KBIM's overall interest. The idea sponsor can then present the project with supporting documentation at a later meeting of the full MC. This flexibility has proved to be important where a prospective client has initiated a request for KBIM to design a specific solution that is typically a deviation of an existing product.

ABB Asea Brown Boveri Large-System Projects

ABB Asea Brown Boveri (ABB) defines **large-system projects** as those priced at greater than $15 million. Power plants and paper and pulp mills are examples. Large systems projects are becoming an increasingly significant way of doing business for ABB in that they now account for about one-third of ABB's annual turnover. ABB has constructed a realization process model for large-system projects, which we reproduce in Figure 6.10. This model outlines a systematic process for ABB to understand which projects to pursue, to capture the projects it wants, to manage risk, and to lower the costs of executing the projects for customers.

We can use gas-fueled power station projects to illustrate several aspects of the realization process. Fifty percent of the cost per kilowatt produced is the fuel. ABB uses its design expertise and technical knowledge to increase the efficiency of the plant to lower this cost. Fifteen percent of the cost is financing. ABB uses predesign to accelerate completion of the project, thereby reducing finance cost and generating earlier revenues. Thirty percent of the cost is equipment. ABB has established linkages among participating ABB units to lower total costs through superior fit and process. An internal ABB consortium or network can supply all of the equipment for a power station. Finally, 5 percent of the cost is power plant operations and maintenance. ABB uses its knowledge and experience to do this at a lower cost, offering service contracts to customers.

Figure 6.10 ABB—How to Pursue the Business Opportunity

Development	Preacquisition	Acquisition	Execution
Opportunity Tracking	Customer Needs	Request for Proposal	Award
Relationship Building	Identification	Project Kick-Off	Project Plan
Customer Needs	Networking	Meeting	Reviewed
Assessment	Preliminary Strategy	Bid/No Bid Decision	Implementation
Probability	Competitive	Competitive	Team
Assessment	Assessment	Differentiation	Customer Service
Project Screening	Risk Assessment	Strategy	and Follow-Up
Pursue/No Pursue	Go/No Go Decision	ABB Matrix	
Decision	Specification	Risk Management	
Technical Positioning	Shaping	Pricing	
Prestudies	Capture Plan	Management Review	
		Tender Submission	
		Negotiation	

ABN-AMRO Bank Global Transaction Services

The Global Transaction Services (GTS) Unit of ABN-AMRO Bank (AA) has embedded its new offering realization process within its overall process for product management. We depict this process in Figure 6.11. The new offering realization process has four phases: idea filtering, product development, performance management, and close down.

A spark of inspiration from a member of the GTS organization often sets off the process. The *idea filtering* stage is an investigation into the consequences of pursuing an idea. It begins with secondary research, but proceeds to primary market research and initial logic designs. The business decides whether to pursue the idea based on the fit with other activity that is going on, current (or expected) capabilities, and how persuasive the evidence is that a sufficient return on investment is available. In the proposal subphase, the product manager must delineate the opportunity and convince the business that it is worth performing a fuller investigation of the feasibility and viability of the idea. In the justification subphase, the product manager must convince the business that the idea is worth committing the major resources necessary to develop the product. A significant part of this is that the initiative must have the commitment of all functional areas that would be involved in its development and support.

The purpose of the *product development* phase is to turn the idea into reality, and develop the product up to its market launch. As the subphases convey, the product development phase has a strong project-management orientation. In fact, a professional project manager is appointed to work with the product manager and formal project control is implemented. Multiple subprojects are likely, with at least one per functional area typical. It is also typical that each functional area appoints a subproject manager for the duration of development. However, the product manager does not take a "back seat." It remains the product manager's primary responsibility to see that resources are used efficiently; risks, assumptions and dependencies are controlled; and a market-ready product is made available on time and budget.

The purpose of the *performance management* phase is to realize the return on the initial and ongoing investment, and it encompasses the launch, growth, maturity, and decline of the product. As such, it calls on a wide range of skills from the product manager, who effectively acts as the managing director of the product, responsible for its profitability and continued competitiveness. In the market launch subphase, customers begin to use the product. The product manager courts early adopters whose usage will drive opinion in the marketplace. The market launch subphase is an intensive period of ironing out unanticipated bumps in the service that inevitably occur despite the best planning and testing. Once the product is in the market, it needs to be modified recurrently to fulfill (changing) requirements and preferences of customers, which is indicated by the enhancement and maintenance projects in Figure 6.11.

The purpose of the *close-down* phase is to make an orderly withdrawal from an unsustainable market position. The close-down stage is a delicate operation. Customers will be used to the product and there is likely to be resistance to change to a newer, replacement GTS product. Alternatively, customers may be switching rapidly to a competitor's product, while the existing product is being clung to internally at AA. Judged by its impact on the Bank, AA GTS considers withdrawal of a

Figure 6.11 Product Realization and Management at ABN-AMRO Bank Global Transaction Services

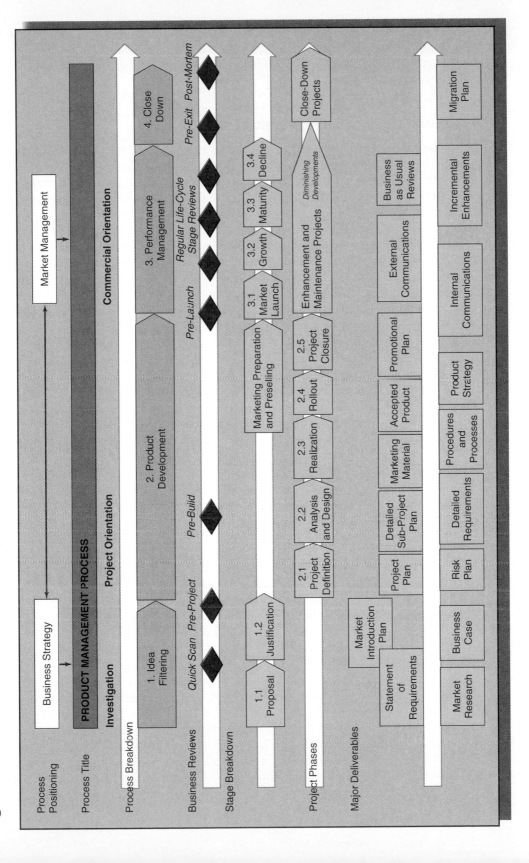

product from the market just as important as the launch of a new product. In fact, it believes that products should be designed with withdrawal in mind. Finally, the post-mortem enables AA GTS to capture and integrate its learnings from its entire experience with a product.

A General Realization Process Model

Given the diversity in the realization process models we have reviewed, is there a general realization process model that pulls together their common characteristics? A general realization process model that we prefer is one that Wheelwright and Clark provide, which we reproduce in Figure 6.12.[50] This model emphasizes cross-functional integration and provides the primary activities of engineering, marketing, and manufacturing for each development phase. Wheelwright and Clark broadly define these functional areas, intending marketing to include market research and sales, and manufacturing to include process development, manufacturing engineering, and plant operations. This model also specifies the key milestones and key decisions for each phase. Because approval acts a "gate" through which a project must pass to progress to the next development phase or "stage," this kind of model of the realization process is called a **stage-gate model**.

Wheelwright and Clark maintain that new offering realization requires more than cross-functional coordination; it requires **cross-functional integration**, which means that management or the project team add specific activities that support cross-functional work. "For example, engineering builds very early system prototypes in order to support marketing's desire to develop richer customer insight early in the process."[51] To reinforce this integration, Wheelwright and Clark express the milestones in Figure 6.12 to focus attention on how the different functional activities in each phase fit together. They recognize that cross-functional integration truly occurs when individuals from different functional areas work together to accomplish interdependent tasks. In so doing, those individuals gain appreciation and respect for what each functional area contributes to new offering realization. Not every development project requires cross-functional integration, though. When the project involves substantial continuity and experience from past realization efforts and marketplace change is methodical, cross-function coordination is sufficient.

Another aspect of the model that we find desirable is the inclusion of a market introduction phase. This phase encompasses all activities that are part of the market launch for the new offering and concludes with its demonstrated commercial viability. Often, firms mistakenly believe that their new product development process is finished at the end of the detailed design and development or commercial preparation phase. A market launch that is inadequate or poorly done is one of the leading causes of new product failure.[52]

We relate the various realization process models that we have examined to this general realization process model in Figure 6.13. Each of them is consistent with the general realization process model, with the variations reflecting each firm's unique strategy, circumstances, and marketplace. For example, SMALLFRY Industrial Design's model is more elaborate earlier in the realization process than later, in keeping with its focus as an industrial design consultant. Some of the process models appear simpler, but recall that each phase has a number of subphases that we did not

Figure 6.12 A General Realization Process Model

Functional Activities Under Cross-Functional Integration

| Functional Activities | Concept Development | Product Planning | Detailed Design and Development | | Commercial Preparation | Market Introduction |
			Phase I	Phase II		
Engineering	Propose new technologies; develop product ideas; build models; conduct simulations	Choose components and interact with suppliers; build early system prototypes; define product architecture	Do detailed design of product and interact with process; build full-scale prototypes; conduct prototype; testing	Refine details of product design; participate in building second-phase prototypes	Evaluate and test pilot units; solve problems	Evaluate field experience with product
Marketing	Provide market-based input; propose and investigate product concepts	Define target customer's parameters; develop estimates of sales and margins; conduct early interaction with customers	Conduct customer tests of prototypes; participate in prototyping evaluation	Conduct second-phase customer tests; evaluate prototypes; plan marketing rollout; establish distribution plan	Prepare for market rollout; train sales force and field service personnel; prepare order entry/process system	Fill distribution channels; sell and promote; interact with key customers
Manufacturing	Propose and investigate process concepts	Develop cost estimates; define process architecture; conduct process simulation; validate suppliers	Do detailed design of process, design and develop tooling and equipment; participate in building full-scale prototypes	Test and try out tooling and equipment; build second-phase prototypes; install equipment and bring up new procedures	Build pilot units in commercial process; refine process based on pilot experience; train personnel and verify supply channel	Ramp up plant to volume targets; meet targets for quality, yield, and cost
Key Milestones	• Concept for product and process defined	• Establish product and process architecture • Define program parameters	• Build and test complete prototypes • Verify product design	• Build and refine 2nd phase prototype • Verify process tools and design	• Produce pilot units • Operate and test complete commercial system	• Ramp up to volume production • Meet initial commercial objectives
Key Decisions	CONCEPT APPROVAL	PROGRAM APPROVAL	DETAILED DESIGN APPROVAL	JOINT PRODUCT AND PROCESS APPROVAL	APPROVAL FOR FIRST COMMERCIAL SALES	FULL COMMERCIAL APPROVAL

Phases at Development

Source: Steven C. Wheelwright and Kim B. Clark, *Revolutionizing Product Development: Quantum Leaps in Speed, Efficiency, and Quality* (New York: The Free Press, 1992), p. 173.

Figure 6.13 Relating the Various Realization Process Models to the General Realization Process Model

General Realization Process Model:	Concept Development	Product Planning	Detailed Design and Development	Commercial Preparation	Market Introduction	[Post Project Learning and Improvement]
SMALLFRY Industrial Design Model:	Project Set Up → Concept Appraisal	Embodiment Design	3D Data → Manufacturing Specification	Pre-Production Liaison; Manufacture	Sales	
AKZO NOBEL Coatings Model:	Idea Concept		Development	Upscaling	Market Introduction	After Care
Kleinwort Benson Investment Management Model:	Initial Product Development; Initial Market and Practical Evaluation	Product Specification; Profitability and Cost Analysis	Detailed Product Development	Launch Plan Management		Launch Evaluation; Product Evaluation/ Analysis
ABB Asea Brown Boveri Ltd Large System Projects Model:	Development	Pre-Acquisition	Acquisition	Execution		
ABN-AMRO Bank Global Transaction Services Model:	Idea Filtering		Product Development	Performance Management		Close Down

254

detail. The ABB Asea Brown Boveri Ltd. is an example. Finally, the formal inclusion of a phase following market introduction in the Kleinwort Benson Investment Management, AKZO NOBEL Coatings, and ABN AMRO Bank Global Transaction Services models is in keeping with the Post-Project Learning and Improvement phase depicted at the end of the development process "funnel" in Figure 6.2.

Augmenting Services in Realization Process Modelsm

We elaborate on this model by considering the planning, design, development, and delivery of the augmenting services, programs, and systems that enhance the new core product's or service's value. Planning for the augmenting services for the core product or service should begin in the *product planning* phase. Devising, designing, and prototyping these augmenting services should occur in the second phase of *detailed design and development*. The firm also should estimate the resource requirements and costs of providing the augmenting services. The firm should run pilot programs for the augmenting services during the *commercial preparation* phase with customers that are testing the new product, and make final refinements in the services, estimates of resource requirements and costs, and customer feedback mechanisms. At the *market introduction* phase, the firm is able to deliver the augmenting services at the requisite levels to support the market launch of the new offering.

"Next-Generation" Realization Process Models

New product development is an area of active inquiry, where academic researchers, consultants, and pundits continually suggest new developments and refinements in the new product development process. Cooper has proposed a next-generation product development process that he contends is fundamentally different from stage-gate models of the realization process in four ways[53]:

1. *Fluidity:* It is fluid and adaptable, with overlapping and fluid stages for greater speed.
2. *Fuzzy gates:* It features conditional Go decisions (rather than absolute ones), which are dependent on the situation.
3. *Focused:* It builds in prioritization methods that look at the entire portfolio of projects (rather than one project at a time) and focuses resources on the "best bets."
4. *Flexible:* It is not a rigid stage-and-gate system; each project is unique and has its own routing through the process.

Cooper recognizes that these characteristics also have the potential to produce more mistakes because the process becomes more unstructured, and it shifts some decision responsibility from senior management to project managers and teams. Adler, Mandelbaum, Nguyen, and Schwerer also advocate more fluidity and flexibility, and propose that firms construct *processing network models* that capture the overlap and simultaneous nature of development across functional areas.[54]

Supplier firms that compete in dynamic marketplaces, such as high-technology markets, take advantage of the greater agility that "next-generation" realization processes provide. By overlapping concept development and implementation phases, a firm can incorporate late-breaking changes into its product design without sacrificing overall speed-to-market, as measured from project start until market introduction. These changes may be in response to evolving customer requirements, technological advances, or new knowledge of competitors' products.[55]

Another "next-generation" variation in realization processes is to take a short hiatus in the middle of the development phase for a new platform product. Firms use this hiatus to define and initiate the realization processes for derivative products that will fill openings in the market that the new platform product will create. By purposively overlapping its realization processes in this way, the firm improves the speed-to-market of its derivative products and thwarts rapid-response competitors from beating them to market niches.[56]

We can see these next-generation characteristics reflected in the various realization process models that we considered. ABB's use of established linkages among participating ABB units in large-system projects provides fluidity. Indeed, the cross-functional integration of the Wheelwright and Clark realization process model strives to provide fluidity. KBIM's use of qualified project approvals is an instance of fuzzy gates, and its fast-track option provides flexibility in its realization process. Finally, the aggregate project plan of Wheelwright and Clark is a focus mechanism for prioritizing projects and allocating resources across a set of projects.

MARKET-ORIENTED REALIZATION

Firms in business markets should have the intent of being market oriented and customer focused in their realization efforts. Learning about the requirements and preferences of target market segments and customers early in the realization process, and collaborating with selected customers should increase speed-to-market, lower realization cost, and improve marketplace success. Yet, many firms have difficulty understanding what this means for them and how to accomplish it in practice. Moreover, it is comfortable for research and development groups (as well as other functional areas) that view themselves as largely removed from the marketplace to remain, or revert to being, inward looking.

We have discussed a realization strategy and a realization process that are market oriented. Here, we consider further how to make new offering realization market oriented and customer focused. We first suggest ways in which a firm's research and advanced development group can be market oriented. We then offer ways in which a firm's development process can be market oriented.

Market-Oriented Research

Research and advanced development (hereafter, simply Research) has a pioneering or scouting mission in most firms; it is responsible for generating new scientific and technical knowledge. It seeks to push back the knowledge frontiers in science and technology in ways that create value over the long term. The intent is that Research's work translates into technology that firms can commercialize in new offerings. In contrast, Commercial Development (hereafter, simply Development) has a more practical and short-term mission; it uses, adapts, or further develops known technologies to produce new core products or services for the firm to offer to the market. Research and Development (R&D) have a critical linkage; each is dependent upon the other, at least partly, for its own success within the firm. So, R&D must work together to translate generated knowledge resources into products for commercialization, and marketplace understanding into direction for future Research efforts.

Businesses are placing greater demands on Research to be market oriented.[57] R&D budgets are either stagnant or growing slowly at most firms. Firms appear to be placing more emphasis and spending on research than in recent years, restoring the balance compared with the proportion spent on development, but in return they are insisting that Research interact regularly with marketing and other executives from the business units. Each of these reflect senior management discontent with the marketplace results that Research has produced with their resources. Senior management increasingly wants Research to demonstrate how it is contributing to an advantage in the market.

To excel with limited resources, Research needs to focus its efforts and leverage its resources with outside relationships. Furthermore, Research needs to connect itself with the market. We briefly examine each of these in turn.

Creating Focused Research Centers

Research management in consultation with senior management needs to make choices about which basic areas of science and technology research the firm will pursue actively. As an example, General Electric has reduced the number of areas for long-term research from 20 to just five.[58] An organizational mechanism that a firm can use to focus its scientists and other resources on particular areas is the *research center*. AKZO NOBEL Coatings' Innovative Research unit focuses on six research areas: high solids, water-borne, color, powder, pigment dispersants, and new coating chemistry. It has created a research center for each of these areas. Innovative Research has also established a number of mechanisms to facilitate sharing information across research centers, such as having common raw material codes so each center knows what the others are using.

Scientists in focused research centers need to make decisions about how they can best leverage their allocated resources. What knowledge should they generate internally, what knowledge should they cogenerate through collaborative relationships and research networks, and what knowledge should they acquire from outside research sources? One concept that should influence these decisions is **sticky information**; that is, the extent to which it is costly to transfer knowledge or information from the place where it resides to another location and have it in a form the information seeker can use.[59] Information might be sticky due to its nature, such as being tacit rather than explicit. Alternatively, information might be sticky due to the amount a provider needs to send the seeker, because the seeker cannot specify in advance what parts will be germane.

A focused research center can pursue collaborative relationships with universities, government-funded laboratories, research institutes, or other firms' research units. Intel is supporting a number of small labs staffed by 20–30 researchers, that it terms *lablets*, which are located adjacent to leading universities. Each lablet is focusing on a nascent technology and is directed by a faculty member who has taken a temporary leave of absence. A focused research center also can participate in research networks that comprise a mix of outside partners. For instance, the pharmaceutical firm Pfizer has teamed up with academic researchers and small biotech firms at its Discovery Technology Center to develop computerized methods for screening thousands of potential drug molecules per day. This Center is located in Cambridge, Massachusetts, apart from its main R&D facility in Connecticut.[60]

As part of its activities, a research center should actively monitor science and technology developments both within and outside its industry. Kodama maintains that firms should engage in collaborative research with a variety of firms across many different industries. In doing so, the firms can gather intelligence on how existing technologies might be combined to create hybrid technologies, which he calls *technology fusion*.[61]

Finally, a research center should not overlook the potential benefits of having its scientists participate in social networks with academic scientists. Rather than having the commercial intent of a business network, a **social network** is "a collectivity of individuals among whom exchanges take place that are supported only by shared norms of trustworthy behavior." A study of two new biotechnology firms' use of social networks found that scientists at one firm collaborated with academic researchers at 144 different external institutions over a 10-year period, whereas scientists at the other firm collaborated with academic researchers at 147 different external institutions over a comparable 9-year period. Interestingly, although both firms were located in the United States, 29 percent of the collaborations for the first firm and 43 percent of the collaborations for the second firm were with researchers at institutions outside the United States. Commenting on their results, the researchers stated, "This evidence suggests that Firms X and Y continued to gain benefits from research collaborations during the period studied in terms of prospecting for innovations, reducing their direct R&D costs, accessing the knowledge of immobile external scientists, and attracting and retaining scientist-employees."[62]

Connecting Research with the Market

"Selling only on price. Where is the fun in it?" A director of a basic research unit made this to-the-point observation. He understands the role of Research is to add value in the marketplace. He recognizes that his business unit needs innovation so that when there is market pressure on price, the business has something different it can offer, something that provides greater value to its customers than the products of its competitors. How can other firms get their researchers as connected with the market as this director is?

Regular, scheduled interactions with the design engineering, manufacturing engineering, field engineering, and advanced marketing groups appear to be the best answer. These interactions should include a mix of one-on-one information exchanges and more-structured group-to-group exchanges. We recommend an alternating "home and away" schedule for these interactions, where participants take turns visiting and spending time at each other's location. General Electric built meeting and conference facilities at its Nishkayuna, New York, central research lab. Its head of global research and development has found that some of the best ideas come during off-hours, when employees from across the company are having a meal together or relaxing in the lounge.[63]

In one-on-one meetings, field engineers and marketers can relate to research scientists changes in customers' requirements, and advances in competitors' offerings. It is especially important to communicate to Research (and to Development) as early as possible new or anticipated entrants whose offerings use different technology. In meetings with design engineers and manufacturing engineers, researchers can communicate their progress on research projects as well as learn of difficulties that the developers are having in working with, adapting, and further developing new and existing technologies. Research should periodically put on research symposia or innovation fairs, where it presents recent research advances to design engineering, manufacturing engineering, field engineering, and advanced marketing groups. At these more-structured meetings, Research also can apprise symposium participants of technological advances that it sees occurring in other areas; speculate on their relevance, with further innovation, in the firm's markets; and gain valuable feedback for future research initiatives from the symposium participants. Finally, Research can participate in "home and away" research overviews with research units of strategic customers, where supplier development groups facilitate and also attend these meetings.

Market-Oriented Development

Predicting the applications of an innovation other than its initial one has proven extraordinarily difficult for companies. For example, Motorola initially saw cellular phones as replacement technology for its two-way radios in vehicles; at the time, it never envisioned that customers would use them outside of a vehicle! Tellis and Golder found that enduring market leadership is due not to being first to market, but instead to envisioning a larger potential market, managerial persistence, financial commitment, and relentless innovation (improvement of the invention). Robinson and Min found that first entrants in a new industrial market face the greatest market and technological uncertainties, but compensating for this, they benefit from first-mover advantages that might include introducing follow-on offerings that better meet the requirements and preferences of developing market segments. This research suggests how critical market-oriented development is to enduring market leadership.[64]

We consider four ways for the firm to be market oriented in its development of new offerings: (1) use positioning statements as a market-focusing mechanism; (2) research customer requirements and preferences and translate them into design specifications; (3) guide realization efforts with customer value assessment; and (4) tailor market introductions of new offerings.

Positioning Statements as a Market-Focusing Mechanism

Positioning statements can assist in focusing a project team on the market throughout the realization process. At each phase, senior management should require the project team to provide a positioning statement as part of its review materials. Each positioning statement would contain the three critical components we discussed in Chapter 4: target, offering concept, and value proposition. Although the team might state elements of the positioning statement in broad or coarse terms in the initial phases, senior management would expect to see refinement and greater specificity as the project moves through the realization process. This expectation pushes the team to think about the characteristics of target customers, the essential attributes of the offering for customers, and the worth of the new offering to the customer. To reach this specificity, the team would have to translate customer requirements and preferences into design specifications, and conduct value assessments with target customers.

Researching Market Requirements and Translating Them into Design Specifications

Simply put, there is no substitute for market research on the requirements and preferences of target customers to inform and guide realization efforts. Such research can take a number of forms, such as field qualitative research by a firm's development engineers or an outside engineering consulting firm, focus groups, and quantitative field survey research by an outside market research firm. Astute firms employ more than one method, seeking convergence in the results they obtain. Market research complements reports from the sales force and field engineering, which are also valuable sources of information about customer requirements and preferences, and how they are changing.

What customers are of particular interest for the firm to research? Customers that have knowledge or experience that can significantly contribute to a firm's realization efforts are of interest. These customers may be current users, prospective customers, or even customers that have recently switched to competitors' offerings. When Boeing Company began to design the 777 passenger jet in early 1990, for the first time, it invited a few airline customers, such as United Airlines, to participate in Japanese-style design build teams. The resulting aircraft better met the customers' requirements and preferences, such as widening the plane slightly to allow wider seat bottoms, and redesigning the overhead lamps so that burned-out bulbs could be easily replaced.[65]

Indeed, evidence shows that lead-user customers are often sources of innovation to supplier firms.[66] **Lead-users** are current or prospective customers who are experiencing problems or needs that will become widespread in the market in the foreseeable future. They would derive significant value immediately from an innovative solution. Such customers may have begun problem-solving activities themselves. Another kind of customer that is of interest to research is the **leap-frog customer**, which is a small aggressive firm, possibly a newer entrant, that is pursuing a riskier development strategy to gain market share.[67] Finally, the firm should seek to participate in early supplier involvement (ESI) programs of large strategic customers. We view these ESI collaborations as a kind of participant-observer research.

The kind of input about innovation that a supplier solicits from present or prospective customers can make a difference in how worthwhile that input turns out to be. Ulwick advises against asking customers what they want in an offering or to suggest solutions for problems they experience with current offerings, but instead solicit from them changes in the *outcomes* that they seek from an offering. "A well-formatted outcome contains both the type of improvement required (minimize, increase) and a unit of measure (time, number, frequency) so that the outcome statement can be used later in benchmarking, competitive analysis, and concept evaluation." Examples of outcome statements from a study of improvements for angioplasty balloons used to clear blocked arteries of cardiac patients are "Minimize restenosis (or the recurrence of a blockage)" and "Minimize the amount of force required to cross the lesion with the balloon." Ulwick recommends soliciting these outcomes from a diverse set of customers and not just lead-users, whose recommendations may have limited appeal to the broader market.[68]

Translating target customer requirements and preferences into design specifications is a crucial step in connecting the marketplace with realization efforts. Often, gaps occur between the way a customer expresses the performance it is seeking and the way a supplier specifies how it makes products. As an example, an appliance customer might want *formability* in a steel coil that allows it to perform a deep, reverse-draw operation to create the inner tub for a washing machine. The problem is that a steelmaker characterizes the products it produces in terms of *chemistry* and *metallurgy*. What specific chemistry and metallurgy will provide the desired formability? A firm can pursue several translation approaches: quality function deployment, prototyping, beta testing, and realizing flexible product components.

Quality function deployment (QFD) is a set of methods and tools for translating target customer requirements and preferences into internally understood engineering and manufacturing parameters. The *house of quality* is a prominent QFD methodology that brings together in a "house" configuration a list of customer attributes (CA) the firm generates from market research; a list of engineering characteristics (EC) that will likely affect the CA; the relationships between CA and EC; the relationships within EC; objectives measures of EC; and judgments of the technical difficulty, imputed importance, and costs of achieving target levels of EC. QFD can be a valuable methodology in the concept development and product planning phases of the realization process, and its use can extend to manufacturing process design. Further, Hauser and Griffin found that use of QFD led to greater communication among cross-functional team members and communication patterns that were more horizontal, rather than "up-over-down" through management. The downside was less communication with others in the firm outside the team.[69]

The project team should attempt to gain feedback on its translation as early as possible in the realization process. **Prototypes** are a research tool that allows selected customers to experience in a rough form the functionality or performance of a new offering and give feedback to the project team. Firms are looking for ways to lower the cost of prototypes, and some have turned to computer simulations rather than constructing physical prototypes. Boeing Company estimated that it saved $21 million during the engineering and manufacturing development phase of its realization process for the Osprey V-22 helicopter by eliminating physical mock-ups and instead relying on computer-simulated prototypes to verify clearances and accessibility.[70] Not only do computer-simulated prototypes reduce realization costs, they also speed up the realization process. "Millennium Pharmaceuticals in Cambridge, Massachusetts, for instance, incorporates new technologies such as genomics, bioinformatics, and combinatorial chemistry in its technology platform for conducting experiments. The platform enables factory-like automation that can generate and test drug candidates in minutes or seconds compared with the days or more that traditional methods require."[71]

Later in the realization process, a firm can use **alpha testing**, where individuals within the firm simulate the target customer's use of a nearly realized product. After making any necessary adjustments or refinements, the firm proceeds with **beta testing**, where the firm provides select customers with the new offering and gains feedback on it from the customers' experiences. The firm uses this feedback to make any final adjustments or refinements in the new offering before its market introduction. Dolan and Matthews conclude from their research on beta testing that "Beta-testing is most valuable when

1. users are heterogeneous;
2. potential applications of the product are not fully understood;
3. alpha testing is unable to guarantee a "bug-free" product;
4. product complexity limits the potential sample size in product-use tests;
5. the decision-making unit for a purchase is complex, so the opinions of a variety of people within an organization must be understood; and
6. opinion leadership phenomenon is operative.[72]

Finally, in certain cases, it is extraordinarily difficult to know the customer's application of a new offering; that is, the customer's application information is "sticky."[73] In such a case, a firm can respond with a product that provides flexibility through two components: one component that is standard across all applications, and a user-friendly component that enables customers to tailor the standard component to their own requirements. An example would be an integrated circuit supplier providing standard silicone wafers along with a CAD software package to its custom circuit users so that they can produce application-specific integrated circuits (APSIC). Another example is a software company providing a standard software package along with a user "tool kit" that enables customers to customize the program to their diverse applications.[74]

Firms mistakenly take shortcuts when they omit market research and product testing to speed up their realization efforts. As the accompanying Dilbert cartoon (Figure 6.14) humorously illustrates, such shortcuts often lead to bad results.

Guiding Realization Efforts with Customer Value Assessment

Although customer value assessment is a kind of market research, we discuss it separately because most market research that firms use to understand the requirements and preferences of target customers does not address the question, "If we accomplish this, what is it worth to the customer in its application?" Knowing that an improvement in some functionality is important does not tell a firm whether the customer is

Figure 6.14   Dilbert on Market Research and Product Testing in New Offering Realization

DILBERT reprinted by permission of United Feature Syndicate, Inc.

willing to pay what it will cost to provide that improved functionality. Value assessment provides this essential information to guide realization efforts.

In realization projects that are **technology push**, where the firm's new offering will introduce new technology into the market, it can use value assessment to persuasively demonstrate to prospective customers how the new technology provides greater value or lower cost to them. This demonstration is especially critical when the new technology gives the market offering a higher price than competitors' offerings using more established and familiar technologies. At the same time, the firm can learn how the value of its new technology varies across applications, customer capabilities, and usage situations. Box 6.7 provides an example of how Rohm & Haas used BioCompare© to demonstrate the value of an affinity chromatography resin it was developing.

BOX 6.7
BioCompare© Value Assessment Tool

Bette Acker, Business Development Manager for Specialty Materials at Rohm and Haas Company, developed BioCompare as a tool to persuasively demonstrate the value of an affinity chromatography resin under development at Rohm and Haas versus other bioprocessing options to produce high-purity, biologically active drugs. Producing target proteins of extraordinary purity (99.99%) is a painstaking undertaking, comprising a number of steps, the first of which is the preparation of a fermentation broth. As the fermentation proceeds, many materials are produced within the broth, and the isolation of the target protein or material of interest from the broth can require many sequential processes of isolation and purification.

Affinity chromatography is a special form of chromatography, which many pharmaceutical firms use. Affinity chromatography takes advantage of the unique affinity of one material for another material. Analogous to a lock and key being unique to each other, an affinity resin has a material chemically bound to a support resin that only will attract a target material in the fermentation broth that uniquely fits its "lock." The fermentation broth is poured into a column containing affinity resin at a specific step in the bioprocessing sequence, and the target protein is bound to the resin until it is removed in a subsequent step. Affinity resins can be expensive ($2,500/liter). In order for a prospective user to consider them in a bioprocessing scheme, their value must be clearly demonstrated versus other bioprocessing options, such as more traditional chromatography or membrane filtration.

BioCompare is a value-in-use program that enables the prospective user to compare up to five different bioproduction schemes for a target protein. Input prompts and built-in, pull-down menus enhance the Excel®- based program's ease of use. To start, the user completes a worksheet that pulls together the necessary input data. Once the input is entered, BioCompare can be used to calculate the costs and time associated with a specific bioproduction scheme, display alternative bioproduction schemes for a specific protein and compare their total values-in-use, and calculate the raw material costs associated with a specific step. Cost and value components, such as total protein, target protein concentration and purity, raw material cost, and labor costs, are generated for each step of each bioproduction scheme studied.

Although Rohm and Haas did not commercialize this affinity resin because of a change in business focus, BioCompare provided an essential tool in working with key development partners (pharmaceutical companies) to better understand the potential value of affinity chromatography in their own applications.

In realization projects that are **market pull**, where the firm is developing its new offering in response to customer requests or demands, it can use value assessment to provide guidance on what improvements are worthwhile for it to pursue, and the priority it should give to potential advances. The value assessment can examine the incremental value target customers would place on changes in the market offering from its present levels of functionality or performance to levels that represent short-term achievable development objectives. The firm can have managers in different functional areas of the customer firm respond to offering attributes for which they are primarily responsible. For example, a chemical pigment producer had customer firm managers in production and R&D perform a conjoint task for short-term achievable changes in technical attributes, such as gloss and dispersability. It also had general management and purchasing managers perform a conjoint task for short-term achievable changes in commercial attributes, such as delivery service and payment terms.

Tailoring Market Introductions of New Offerings

A firm should tailor its market introductions of new offerings, striving for commonality and consistency where it can, yet recognizing where it needs to remain flexible. This is particularly true where the firm is introducing the new offering into a number of country markets. AKZO NOBEL (AN) Coatings' market launch of Sikkens Cetol Novatech®, which we recount in Box 6.8, provides a noteworthy case study of market introduction.

AN Coatings management focuses on three critical activities in the market introduction phase of new offering realization:

1. *Know the local market*. For example, how important is drying time? Further, environmental concern is lower in some countries.
2. *Internal selling*. It is essential to gain the commitment of local country managers. Approach them in their local languages.
3. *Motivate channel partners*. Motivate the paint dealers to stock and market the product. Clearly communicate the economic advantages of the product to them in their local languages.

Notice that having downstream actors involved earlier (than the market introduction phase) in the realization process contributes to success in the preceding activities, as when AN Coatings had all the European country market managers participate in the decision to use Austria as the test market.

One other aspect of market introduction that we want to address is pricing new offerings. As we discussed in the Chapter 5, we strongly recommend value-based pricing. Pricing new offerings requires some elaboration on our earlier framework. Because a new offering ranges from low to high in "newness to the market," firms typically need to provide prospective customers with a larger **incentive to change**; that is, initially give an additional part of the offering's incremental value as monetary motivation to try something different. It is critical for the firm to think about this pricing tactic and manage it separately from the pricing strategy for the new offering.

Some firms mistakenly blur the two, introducing a new offering at a "low introductory price," with the intent of raising the price as the offering becomes established in the market. Customers view the fairness of prices relative to a reference point

BOX 6.8
AKZO NOBEL Coatings' Tailored Market Introduction of Sikkens Cetol Novatech®

Sikkens Cetol® is a translucent paint (wood stain) that is applied on wood as an external finish. AKZO NOBEL (AN) is the market leader in Europe. Recently, AN Coatings introduced a new high-solid coating, Sikkens Cetol Novatech, which lowered the organic solvent content to 35 percent from 65 percent. Traditional alkyd coatings have much greater solvent emission. Solvent is a transport media for paint, which means it keeps the paint in a liquid state. It serves no function in terms of protecting the painted surface per square foot per year, however. High-solid coatings have greater value because of environmental concern about depletion of the ozone layer, lower cost per coated square foot (because it contains less solvents), and lower toxicity, which results when the professional painter is exposed to volatile organic compounds.

AN Coatings selected Austria as a test market because it is a country where translucents are important; there are many natural wood chalets. In applying high-solid coatings, the painter moves from applying three layers to two layers to obtain the same coverage. So, although the price per liter is higher, when viewed as a paint system that produces coated walls, the total cost is less.

To demonstrate high-solid coatings' value and to encourage trial by professional painters, AN Coatings produced a paint kit that it provided free of charge. Along with a letter and leaflet explaining the advantages of high-solid coatings, the kit provided 1 liter of Novatech paint (worth $15–$20). One advantage of the new product was its longer "open" time—the amount of time after applying the coating where the painter could go back over the surface and touch up any imperfections. The corresponding disadvantage was slower drying, which presented a positioning issue for marketing communications.

All European country market managers were involved early in the product development and market introduction process, even participating in the decision to have Austria as the initial test market. The marketing communication strategy was to have as many common elements as possible in the advertisements across Europe, with the remaining elements tailored to local country considerations. For example, the ads for each country featured a wooden hand holding a paint brush to emphasize the application of coating natural wood. The ads appeared in trade magazines for painters and architects. AN Coatings uses architects to create "pull."

Although AN Coatings prefers to have an integrated launch across Europe, the local country organization can decide to delay introduction of a new coating if they are having local difficulties. The general manager for AN Decorative Coatings has the final say in resolving disputes between the international marketing managers and the local market manager. For example, the Cetol Novatech technology was introduced later in Spain as Procolor Novatech.

rather than in absolute terms.[75] By introducing at a low price, the firm establishes an expectation, or reference point, with the customer of what the price should be for the offering. When it attempts to raise price, customers react angrily because the firm is asking the customer to pay more than it expects for the offering, with no noticeable change in its value. Instead, the firm should introduce the new offering at the higher price that represents its pricing strategy, and then discount off this price with initial use discounts. An **initial use discount** is a pricing tactic that is an invoice reduction used to encourage prospective customers to try an offering that is new to them. The offering's actual price is listed on the invoice, then reduced by the incentive to change, with the notation "initial use discount." In this way, the firm establishes the reference point that represents the pricing strategy of the offering while it signals the incentive to change. Note that this initial use discount may be large, as much as 100 percent of the reference price in the case of trial samples, such as AN Coatings' paint kit.

Finally, marketing communication tools can influence the size of the incentive to change a firm needs to provide. When a firm can give prospective customers a low-cost, low-risk "experience" with the new offering, it may not need to offer as large an incentive to change. As an example, AN Coatings provides *Color Advice* as a value-added service, where it takes a photograph of a building, digitally scans it into a computer, and then uses proprietary software to show the building owner what the building would look like painted in various ways.

SUMMARY

New offering realization is the process of developing new core products or services, augmenting them to construct market offerings, and bringing them to market. Realization encompasses all the activities a firm does to transform an idea into a market offering that the firm commercializes. New offering realization has the potential to create value for the firm and its customers. It can strengthen a firm's market position, improve its resource utilization, and contribute to organizational enhancement and renewal. A firm generates a realization strategy as a means of accomplishing its realization objectives. As part of its realization strategy, a firm defines its goals and objectives for overall development efforts and for individual projects, and resolves conflicts that occur in pursuing them. It constructs an aggregate project plan that: maps the mix of derivative, breakthrough, and platform projects it is doing; enables it to make resource capacity decisions; and outlines how it will gain critical skills and abilities. As a final part of realization strategy, we considered what roles and purposes outside development relationships and networks can serve in the firm's realization efforts.

Realization process models delineate the phases and decision points through which development projects progress. The realization process models of SMALLFRY, AKZO NOBEL Coatings, Kleinwort Benson Investment Management, ABB Asea Brown Boveri Large-System Projects, and ABN-AMRO Bank Global Transaction Services convey the wonderful diversity of business markets, yet some common characteristics emerge. We presented a cross-functional, general realization process model that has five phases—concept development, product planning, detailed design and development, commercial preparation, and market introduction—and provides the key milestones and decisions for each.

Firms in business markets should have the intent of being market oriented and customer focused, yet many firms encounter difficulty understanding what this means for them and how to accomplish it in practice. Some ways for Research to be market-oriented are to create focused research centers that support the firm's long-term business strategy, and to connect itself with the market through regular, scheduled interactions with design engineering, manufacturing engineering, field engineering, advanced marketing groups, and research units of strategic customers. A firm can be market oriented in its development of new offerings by using positioning statements as a market-focusing mechanism; researching customer requirements and preferences, and translating them into design specifications; guiding realization efforts with customer value assessment; and tailoring market introductions of new offerings.

ENDNOTES

1. Robert G. Cooper, *Winning at New Products: Accelerating the Process from Idea to Launch*, 2nd ed. (Reading MA: Addison-Wesley Publishing Company, 1993).

2. George Stalk, Philip Evans, and Lawrence E. Schulman, "Competing on Capabilities: The New Rules of Corporate Strategy," *Harvard Business Review* (March–April 1992): 57–68. Because of the growing significance of augmenting services, programs, and systems to marketplace success, we prefer the term *new offering realization* to the traditional term *new product development*, where often augmentation of new products has been treated almost as an afterthought and considered just prior to their market introduction. In addition, some managers still narrowly view new product development as the activity of the research and development (R&D) department. New offering realization, in contrast, both emphasizes the critical nature of the design and delivery of the augmenting elements, and the cross-functional nature of transforming ideas to new market offerings. When we do use the term *development* in this chapter, it carries this broader meaning.

3. Steven C. Wheelwright and Kim B. Clark, *Revolutionizing Product Development: Quantum Leaps in Speed, Efficiency, and Quality* (New York: The Free Press, 1992).

4. Christopher Power et al., "Flops," *Business Week* 16 August 1993, 76–82; Herb Brody, "It Seemed Like a Good Idea at the Time," *High Technology Business* (October 1988): 38–41.

5. Wheelright and Clark, *Revolutionizing Product Development*, 29–31. In contrast, a recent meta-analysis of 24 predictors of new product performance found that product advantage, market potential, meeting customer needs, predevelopment task proficiencies, and dedicated resources have the strongest effects on new product success. See David H. Henard and David M. Szymanski, "Why Some New Products Are More Successful Than Others," *Journal of Marketing Research* (August 2001): 362–275.

6. Wheelright and Clark, *Revolutionizing Product Development*, 34.

7. H. Kent Bowen, Kim B. Clark, Charles A. Holloway, and Steven C. Wheelright, "Development Projects: The Engine of Renewal," *Harvard Business Review* (September–October 1994): 100–120.

8. Abbie Griffin and Albert L. Page, "The PDMA Success Measurement Project: Recommended Measures for Product Development Success and Failure," *Journal of Product Innovation Management* (November 1996): 482.

9. Bowen et al., "Development Projects," 119.

10. Herman J. Vantrappen and Philip D. Metz, "Measuring the Performance of the Innovation Process," *Prism* (Fourth Quarter 1994): 25–26.

11. Vantrappen and Metz, "Measuring the Performance."

12. Christoph-Friedrich von Braun, "The Acceleration Trap in the Real World," *Sloan Management Review* (Summer 1991): 43–52. See also George Stalk, Jr., and Alan M. Webber, "Japan's Dark Side of Time," *Harvard Business Review* (July–August 1993): 93–102.

13. Paul S. Adler, Avi Mandelbaum, Viên Nguyen, and Elizabeth Schwerer, "Getting the Most out of Your Product Development Process," *Harvard Business Review* (March–April 1996): 134–152.

14. "Devices and Desires," *The Economist*, 2 September 2002, 66; and Amy Barrett, "DuPont Tries to Unclog a Pipeline," *Business Week*, 27 January 2003, 103–104.

15. Preston G. Smith and Donald G. Reinertsen, *Developing Products in Half the Time* (New York: Van Nostrand Reinhold, 1995).

16. Smith and Reinertsen, *Developing Products*, 18.

17. Robert J. Dolan, *Managing the New Product Development Process* (Reading, MA: Addison-Wesley Publishing, 1993).

18. Griffin and Page, "The PDMA Success," Figure 2, 489.

19. Vantrappen and Metz, "Measuring the Performance," 26.

20. Wheelwright and Clark, *Revolutionizing Product Development*. The quote is drawn from p. 48.

21. As we discussed in Chapter 1, a documentary letter of credit (LC) is an irrevocable commitment made by an issuing bank on behalf of its corporate customer (e.g., the importer) to pay a specified monetary amount to a beneficiary (e.g., the supplier firm in an international trade transaction) when it is presented with the documents specified in the LC, provided all conditions in the documentary LC have been fully met.

22. Steven C. Wheelwright and Kim B. Clark, "Creating Project Plans to Focus Product Development," *Harvard Business Review* (March–April 1992): 73.

23. We focused primarily on the augmenting services, programs, and systems part of flexible market offerings in Chapter 5.

24. The power generation business of ABB was merged with the power generation business of ALSTOM in June 1999 to create a new Netherlands-based joint venture, ABB Alstom Power, owned 50:50 by ABB and ALSTOM.

25. Wheelwright and Clark, *Revolutionizing Product Development*, 49.

26. Wheelwright and Clark, "Creating Project Plans," 75.

27. Wheelwright and Clark, *Revolutionizing Product Development*, 50.

28. Wheelwright and Clark, "Creating Project Plans," 81.

29. T. Michael Nevens, Gregory L. Summe, and Bro Uttal, "Commercializing Technology: What the Best Companies Do," *Harvard Business Review* (May–June 1990): 162.

30. Jeffrey K. Liker et al., "Involving Suppliers in Product Development in the United States and Japan: Evidence for Set-Based Concurrent Engineering," *IEEE Transactions on Engineering Management* (May 1996): 165–178.

31. Allen Ward et al., "The Second Toyota Paradox: How Delaying Decisions Can Make Better Cars Faster," *Sloan Management Review* (Spring 1995): 43–61.

32. Jeffrey H. Dyer, "How Chrysler Created an American Keiretsu," *Harvard Business Review* (July–August 1996): 42–56.

33. Liker et al., "Involving Suppliers."

34. Ward et al., "The Second Toyota Paradox," 44.

35. Christian Terwiesch, Christoph H. Loch, and Arnoud De Meyer, "Exchanging Preliminary Information in Concurrent Engineering: Alternative Coordination Strategies," *Organization Science* (July–August 2002): 402–419.

36. Ward et al., "The Second Toyota Paradox," 52.

37. Ward et al., "The Second Toyota Paradox." The quote is taken from p. 55.

38. Marjorie Sorge, "Expedition Takes a Walk on the Wild Side: Ford Cuts Development Costs, Tries New Manufacturing Ideas with Its New SUV," *Automotive Industries* (August 1996): 49.

39. Peter C. Grindley and David J. Teece, "Managing Intellectual Capital: Licensing and Cross-Licensing in Semiconductors and Electronics," *California Management Review* (Winter 1997): 8–41.

40. "Missile to Queen's Rook Four," *The Economist*, 17 May 1997, 74.

41. "Electrifying," *The Economist*, 20 December 1997, 98–99; "New Power," *The Economist*, 30 August 1997, 17; and Peter Coy, with Neil Gross, Silvia Sansoni, and Kevin Kelly, "What's the Word in the Lab? Collaborate," *Business Week*, 27 June 1994, 78–80. For an interesting perspective on gaining new ideas for innovation from outsiders, see Darrell Rigby and Chris Zook, "Open-Market Innovation," *Harvard Business Review* (October 2002): 80–89.

42. Otis Port, with Richard Brandt, Neil Gross, and Jonathan B. Levine, "Talk About Your Dream Team," *Business Week*, 27 July 1992, 59.

43. Port, "Talk About Your Dream Team," 79.

44. "Trapeze Artists," *The Economist*, 14 December 2002, 22–23.

45. Kathleen M. Eisenhardt and Claudia Bird Schoonhoven, "Resource-Based View of Strategic Alliance Formation: Strategic and Social Effects in Entrepreneurial Firms," *Organization Science* (March–April 1996): 136–150.

46. Eisenhardt and Schoonhoven, "Resource-Based View," 146.

47. Gary Hamel, Yves L. Doz, and C.K. Prahalad, "Collaborate with Your Competitors—and Win," *Harvard Business Review* (January–February 1989): 134.

48. Michael L. Tushman and Lori Rosenkopf, "Organizational Determinants of Technological Change: Toward a Sociology of Technological Evolution," in *Research in Organizational Behavior*, vol. 14, B. Staw and L. Cummings, eds. (Greenwich, CT: JAI Press, 1992), 311–347. The quote is taken from p. 322.

49. Dresdner Bank, the corporate parent of Dresdner Kleinwort Benson, was acquired by Allianz AG in July 2001.

50. Wheelwright and Clark, *Revolutionizing Product Development*.

51. Wheelwright and Clark, *Revolutionizing Product Development*, 174.

52. Cooper, *Winning at New Products*.

53. Robert G. Cooper, "Third Generation New Product Processes," *Journal of Product Innovation Management* (January 1994): 9.

54. Adler et al., "Getting the Most."

55. Marco Iansiti and Alan MacCormack, "Developing Products on Internet Time," *Harvard Business Review* (September–October 1997): 108–117.

56. Behnam Tabrizi and Rick Walleigh, "Defining Next-Generation Products: An Inside Look," *Harvard Business Review* (November–December 1997): 116–124.

57. Peter Coy, "Research Labs Get Real. It's About Time," *Business Week*, 6 November 2000, 51; Barrett, "Dupont Tries to Unclog a Pipeline;" Michael Arndt, "3M: A Lab for Growth," *Business Week*, 21 January 2002, 50–51; Erika Jonietz, "Economic Bust, Patent Boom," *Technology Review* (May 2002): 71–72; and Rachel Emma Silverman, "GE Goes Back to the Future," *The Wall Street Journal*, 7 May 2002, B1, B4.

58. Silverman, "GE Goes Back to the Future."

59. Eric von Hippel, "'Sticky Information' and the Locus of Problem Solving: Implications for Innovation," *Management Science* (April 1994): 429–439.

60. Wade Roush, "Lean Mean R&D Machines," *Technology Review* (December 2001): 71–73.

61. Fumio Kodama, "Technology Fusion and the New R&D," *Harvard Business Review* (July–August 1992): 70–78.

62. Julia Porter Liebeskind et al., "Social Networks, Learning, and Flexibility: Sourcing Scientific Knowledge in New Biotechnology Firms," *Organization Science* (July–August 1996): 428–443. The first quote is taken from p. 430 and the second from p. 437.

63. Silverman, "GE Goes Back to the Future."

64. "The Shock of the Not Quite New," *The Economist*, 18 June 1994, 81; Gerard Tellis and Peter N. Golder, "First to Market, First to Fail? Real Causes of Enduring Market Leadership," *Sloan Management Review* (Winter 1996): 65–75 (additionally, Tellis and Golder found that a fifth factor, asset leverage, enables late entrants to gain market leadership through exploiting advantages that they possess, such as related technologies or established distribution channels); and William T. Robinson and Sungwook Min, "Is the First to Market the First to Fail? Empirical Evidence for

Industrial Goods Businesses," *Journal of Marketing Research* (February 2002): 120–128.

65. Michael J. Parks, "How Boeing Hatched Its Highest-Tech Bird," *Business Week*, 22 January 1996, 18; and Bill Richards, "Designed for Comfort: The New Boeing 777," *Hemisphere* (June 1995): 87–88.

66. Eric von Hippel, *The Sources of Innovation* (New York: Oxford University Press, 1988).

67. James C. Anderson and James A. Narus, "Partnering as a Focused Market Strategy," *California Management Review* (Spring 1991): 95–113.

68. Anthony W. Ulwick, "Turn Customer Input into Innovation," *Harvard Business Review* (January 2002): 91–97. The first quote is taken from p. 95 and the second from p. 97.

69. John R. Hauser and Don Clausing, "The House of Quality," *Harvard Business Review* (May–June 1988): 63–73; and Abbie Griffin and John R. Hauser, "Patterns of Communication Among Marketing, Engineering and Manufacturing—A

Comparison Between Two New Product Teams," *Management Science* (March 1992): 360–373.

70. Stanley W. Kandebo, "V-22 Modifications Focus on Cost, Producibility," *Aviation Week and Space Technology*, 22 May 1995, 35.

71. Stefan Thomke, "Enlightened Experimentation: The New Imperative for Innovation," *Harvard Business Review* (February 2001): 68.

72. Robert J. Dolan and John M. Matthews, "Maximizing the Utility of Customer Product Testing: Beta Test Design and Management," *Journal of Product Innovation Management* (September 1993): 318–330.

73. von Hippel, "Sticky Information."

74. von Hippel, "Sticky Information"; and Stefan Thomke and Eric von Hippel, "Customers as Innovators," *Harvard Business Review* (April 2002): 5–11.

75. Gerald E. Smith and Thomas T. Nagle, "Frames of Reference and Buyers' Perception of Price and Value," *California Management Review* (Fall 1995): 98–116.

Chapter 7

Business Channel Management

OVERVIEW

*E*merging information, logistics, and supply management technologies have reinvigorated business channel management thinking. Rather than just selecting from conventional direct and indirect channels, business marketers can now configure more novel value-adding networks. These channel networks combine elements of the supplier firm's direct sales forces, traditional reseller firms, pioneering online formats, and third-party service providers. Supplier firms are deploying multiple channels far more often to gain access to a broader array of segments. They are also using these channels interchangeably to provide seamless customer service across situations and applications. This new thinking has enabled firms to meet customer requirements and preferences in superior ways, but it has also created challenges, prompting managers to reformulate the process of business channel management.[1]

Coughlin, Anderson, Stern, and El-Ansary formally define **marketing channel** as "a set of interdependent organizations involved in the process of making a product or service available for consumption or use."[2] Building upon this definition and incorporating recent trends, we describe **business channel management** as the process of designing a set of marketing and distribution arrangements that create superior customer value for targeted market segments and customers, and executing those arrangements either directly through supplier firm sales forces and logistics systems or indirectly through resellers and third-party service providers. We diagram this process in Figure 7.1 and examine each step in detail in this chapter.[3]

Figure 7.1 Business Channel Management

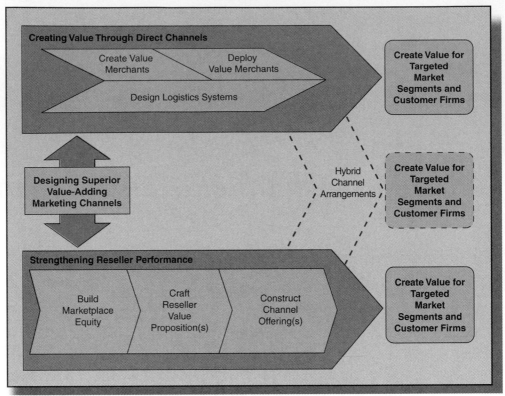

To begin, we present a framework for designing superior value-adding marketing channels. Pivoting on a thorough customer value assessment and the creation of tailored market offerings, the framework guides business market managers through the tasks of assembling a channel network and forging capabilities-sharing arrangements that enable the supplier firm to consistently and profitably meet customer requirements and preferences. In contrast to organizations that serve the consumer marketplace, firms in business markets are much more likely to do business directly with customers in some or all targeted market segments. Thus, in the second section, we discuss how firms add value through direct channels focusing on sales force and logistics systems issues.

In the final section, we turn our attention to situations where suppliers rely on a network of resellers and third-party service providers to add complementary value to their market offerings. When suppliers do so, they must devise programs and systems that encourage partners to contribute their capabilities and to aggressively market resulting offerings to customers. We contend that suppliers can and do elicit outstanding performance through a technique called channel positioning.

Designing Superior Value-Adding Marketing Channels

One of the most consequential changes in channel management thinking has been the recognition that channel selection takes on many of the characteristics of classic sourcing decisions that we depicted in Chapter 3. In essence, business market managers must decide whether to insource the provision to customers of some or all market offering elements or to outsource them to resellers or third-party service providers. As with other sourcing decisions, managers seek to generate the greatest customer value profitably by drawing upon the firm's core capabilities and competencies while leveraging the complementary resources of channel partner firms. A key difference between traditional sourcing and channel sourcing is that a contracted channel partner is likely to maintain the "face" before the customer. As such, issues concerning "ownership" of customers arise that are not of concern in more familiar outsourcing situations. We will examine them in detail later on in the chapter when we discuss building marketplace equity.

We now examine the five steps of designing superior value-adding marketing channels.

1. Assess the value of potential augmenting service offering elements to customers.
2. Envision a value proposition for each targeted market segment.
3. Reformulate the augmenting service offering for each targeted market segment.
4. Configure the channel network.
5. Finalize marketing and distribution arrangements.

Assess the Value of Potential Augmenting Service Offering Elements to Customers

Consistent with our overall approach to business market management, managers should begin the channel design process with a thorough customer value assessment. They use two central questions to guide their inquiries: (1) What augmenting products and services do customers want along with the supplier's core market offering? and (2) How much are they worth to customers? In Chapter 2, we explain a variety of value assessment techniques that managers can use to answer these two questions.

When conducting the value assessment, business market managers should focus on key service outputs their customers require because service is the principal value that channels provide.[4] In operational form, examples of service outputs are 95 percent on-time delivery, 24-hour availability of 50,000 stock-keeping units (SKUs), and $250 minimum order size. In particular, managers should pay attention to the importance of five services to customers—integrated supply, local customization, emergency delivery, technical support, and product standardization. These services will strongly indicate the type of channel network the supplier firm should adopt. For example, if integrated supply is an essential value driver, the supplier firm may require the assistance of a reseller to bundle the supplier's offering along with complementary products and services possibly from other vendors into a total solution.

On the other hand if local customization is key, the supplier firm may have to hire third-party service providers such as assemblers or value-added resellers to make final modifications in the product.

The key findings of the value assessment will be a prioritized list of value elements specified in terms of the service outputs that targeted customers require and an indication of the price they are willing to pay to receive them. By matching the customer value of the service outputs to estimates of the supplier costs that will be incurred to provide them, business market managers will be able to guage the profit potential of serving those customers.

Envision a Value Proposition for Each Targeted Market Segment

Business market managers adopt the customer firm's perspective asking, "Why should our firm want to purchase the supplier's market offering instead of a competitor's offering?" Using inputs from the customer value assessment, managers answer this question by envisioning a distinct value proposition for each targeted market segment. In Chapter 4, we covered the task of writing value propositions in business markets.

A value proposition promises a handful of superior benefits to prospective customers with particular attention directed to one convincing, "shattering value." Simultaneously, it often furnishes proof or a "reason to believe" those promises. Importantly, the customer value proposition serves as a beacon for all the supplier firm's channel network design efforts.

Reformulate the Augmenting Service Offering for Each Targeted Market Segment

For each targeted market segment, business market managers now ask "How should the augmenting service offering be reformulated to strengthen the envisioned value proposition?" In Chapter 5, we discussed an approach for building flexible market offerings, which provides the guidance and tools for answering this question. Managers add new products and services unearthed during the customer value assessment or enhance existing service outputs identified as significant value drivers. The output of this exercise will be reformulated market offerings, each of which more closely matches the requirements of a targeted segment.

If the supplier firm has been previously marketing an offering, business market managers should compare the existing offering to the reformulated version. Minor differences may indicate that only incremental channel improvements are necessary. Such improvements might entail bolstering technical service capabilities through reseller training programs, adding third-party service providers to enhance emergency delivery capabilities, or partnering with another supplier to secure complementary product lines for a total solution. On the other hand, major differences may point to the need for radical channel redesign. In this case, business market managers may have to develop an entirely new channel network model.

Configure the Channel Network

Entering the channel design phase, business market managers pose the question "What type of channel network will be needed to deliver the reformulated offering to targeted customers?" To answer this question, managers turn to the tools of supply network design that we covered in Chapter 3. In fact, pundits argue that channel network and supply network design actually address the same set of issues only from different organizational perspectives—the marketing and purchasing departments, respectively. Furthermore, they recommend that marketing and purchasing personnel work together to build a comprehensive network from the ultimate customer to third-tier suppliers. To do so, managers must think in terms of business processes and functions, consider streams of competition and plan lean enterprises, adopt a channel network strategy, and build a channel network model.

Think in Terms of Business Processes and Functions

Progressive business market managers conceptualize channel networks both vertically across all channel levels and horizontally within each channel level. When they consider a channel vertically, they see a set of **business processes**, such as facilitating exchange, providing market access, and augmenting the marketing offering. Significantly, channel members must coordinate activities across firms to complete a business process. On the other hand, when they view channels horizontally, business market managers see **functions**, or the tasks that a specific channel partner firm performs. These functions include buying, selling, breaking bulk, assembling the offering, providing credit, transportation, warehousing, and postsale servicing.[5]

As management consultants point out, the vertical or business process perspective is most appropriate when radical channel redesign is necessary. Through business process reengineering, the supplier firm is often able to eliminate resource and effort redundancies within the entire channel network, thus lowering total system costs, while strategically deploying channel members' capabilities to maximize the total value delivered. Such reengineering typically brings new types of channel partners and distribution arrangements.

On the other hand, when incremental channel improvements are needed, experts urge firms to focus on functions. Incremental improvements might entail the addition or termination of a specific reseller firm to increase sales in a given territory. Often, incremental channel improvements feature **functional spin-off** or **functional acquisition**, whereby a supplier firm and its resellers trade the performance of a channel task for increased sales or lower costs. For example, many chemical companies have spun off the drumming function to chemical distributors who perform the task more efficiently. Chemical distributors not only incur lower costs and investments associated with drumming but also they reap greater profits from the value-added service.[6]

Consider Streams of Competition and Plan Lean Enterprises

In years past, managers viewed competition in channels as horizontal in nature with suppliers competing against suppliers, resellers against resellers, and customers against customers. The Japanese revolutionized our view of competition with their strategic alliances known as *keiretsus*. As described in Box 7.1, keiretsus are networks of specialized organizations linked together with the purpose of serving a specific

BOX 7.1
Japanese Keiretsus

Three basic types of keiretsu are relevant to marketing channels. The first is referred to as a **horizontal keiretsu**. It is composed of a group or "wheel" of companies from a variety of industries. Typically, a major bank is at the center of the wheel to provide financing for members. A major trading company that handles domestic and international distribution of products provides the "glue" that binds participants. Member companies are linked by cross shareholding, interlocking directorates, and a president's club comprised of chief executives who meet periodically. The largest keiretsu is the Mitsubishi Group, which has more than 190 member companies, over 300 billion yen in sales, and more than 360,000 employees. Others include the Mitusui, Sumitomo, Fuji, DKB, and Sanwa Groups.

A **vertical keiretsu** represents a union among highly specialized manufacturers and service providers within a particular industry that spans significant portions of a value-added chain. They can include raw materials processors, primary materials manufacturers, resellers of various types, and original equipment manufacturers. Typically, a core manufacturer provides leadership and control over the affairs of other members. Often, this manufacturer assembles the components smaller members produce into finished products. The 12 big vertical keiretsus have combined annual sales of 10 trillion yen and employ more than 200,000 employees. The largest include Nippon Steel, Hitachi, Nissan, Toyota, Matsushita, Toshiba, Tokyu, and Seibu.

The third type of alliance is called a **distribution keiretsu**. It is comprised of a manufacturer and the various types of wholesalers, distributors, and retailers in its marketing channels. The purposes of distribution keiretsus are to achieve market access and coverage, build a uniform brand image, secure customer feedback, and enforce reseller price maintenance. Matsushita, Toshiba, and Toyota lead the largest distribution keiretsus. Given that these distribution keiretsus are dominated by a manufacturer, it is difficult for outside producers (especially from abroad) to obtain their services.

Source: Nakato Hirakubo, *An Analysis of the Japanese Market: Consumer, Distribution System, and Market Structure* (New York: Center for Applied Research, Pace University, 1992).

market or markets. Of particular interest are vertical keiretsus, which are organized around value-added chains. Competition here is vertical in nature. A keiretsu competes against another keiretsu at the customer level. Their rivalry is focused on delivering high-quality products and relevant augmenting services at the lowest total cost. At the same time, within a given keiretsu, firms work together closely and perform whatever tasks are necessary, even noncustomary ones, to meet customer requirements. We refer to this form of business market contention as **streams of competition**.[7]

We urge business market managers to configure channel networks in ways that create superior value relative to opposing streams of competition. To do so, managers should adopt the Womack and Jones concept of the lean enterprise when conceiving their channel network, planning channel strategy, and setting network objectives. A lean enterprise is a group of individuals, functions, and legally separate but operationally synchronized companies. In a lean enterprise, managers focus on improving business processes by allocating functions to the most capable channel partners, bolstering partner firms' ability to perform those tasks, coordinating and integrating the efforts of all firms in the lean enterprise, and eliminating unnecessary redundancies in efforts.[8]

Adopt a Channel Network Strategy

Bucklin's classic postponement and speculation strategies, which we mentioned in Chapter 3, furnish a sound foundation for channel network design. Although Bucklin's original treatise applies largely to manufactured goods, we can readily broaden its implications to services. When the key element in a supplier firm's proposed value proposition is local customization, a **postponement strategy** is appropriate. Here, the supplier delays final changes to an offering's form until the last possible moment through the use of third-party service providers or supplier-owned regional assembly facilities. For example, if physical modifications to products are necessary, the supplier firm might partner with local assemblers, fabricators, or value-added resellers. If integrated supply management or technical service tailored to local applications are key value drivers, the supplier might partner with resellers. These partner firms would be responsible for bundling products and services into total solutions and furnishing applications-specific technical support, respectively.[9]

When low price and product standardization are the key elements of the value proposition, a **speculation strategy** is recommended. In terms of physical products, a supplier firm speculates by manufacturing them in large lots, storing them in inventory in a central location in anticipation of orders, and shipping them in bulk directly to customer firms or to resellers for sale to other customer firms in small lots. To speculate with technical support service, the supplier might provide customer firms with self-help manuals or software, operate an Internet-based technical service site, or direct customer inquiries to a telephone support center.

Experts have added two intermediate strategies to Bucklin's approach. When the key element of the value proposition is emergency delivery, managers turn to **logistics speculation** whereby a vendor produces standardized products and either stocks inventory in supplier-owned local distribution centers or relies on overnight delivery services such as FedEx or UPS, to ship them from a centralized warehouse. When customers demand low price yet require minor adjustments to offerings managers draw upon **manufacturing speculation**. In the case of products, the vendor produces large quantities of modules or components and delays assembly until an order has been received. Dell's build-to-order supply network is a well-cited example of this strategy. As for the services portion of a total solution, a supplier firm might choose to distribute a standardized product to customer firms, and then rely on franchised service vendors to furnish a variety of predefined services such as installation, training, and troubleshooting to customer firms for a fee upon request.[10]

Build a Channel Network Model

A channel network model maps out the business processes and functions required to provide the reformulated augmenting service offering to targeted customer firms. The model also specifies whether the supplier firm, resellers, third-party service providers, or customer firms will complete these required processes and functions. There are two general network models—conventional channels and modular channels—plus a composite called hybrid channels. Naturally, when selecting a model, managers must weigh each alternative in terms of service delivery quality, operating costs, and profit potential while taking into account the resource limitations of the firm.

When diagrammed, **conventional channels** resemble linear pipelines. Various channel member firms appear as nodes in the pipelines. Products and services flow from a supplier firm either directly or indirectly through resellers to a market segment or customer firm. Along the way, each firm completes clusters of business functions. The unique group of functions performed distinguishes one type of channel member from another. For example, a manufacturer's agent primarily makes technical sales calls and takes orders for a supplier. On the other hand, a distributor purchases and takes title to the supplier's products in bulk, breaks bulk, stores local inventory, assembles assortments or total solutions for customer firms, makes promotional sales calls, takes orders, and provides financing, as well as furnishing a host of other services. Typically, one dominant firm serves as **channel captain**, managing and coordinating all distribution efforts and investing in and cultivating brand or reseller equity.[11]

In direct conventional channels, the supplier firm performs all the required business functions, maintains the "face" or contact with the customer firm, "owns" the customer relationship, and captures all resulting profits. In indirect conventional channels, business functions are allocated among the supplier firm and reseller firms. Both sets of firms work as partners, sharing profits through various discounts, commissions, and allowances. The reseller firm often manages the face before the customer and may even claim ownership of the customer relationship. In some indirect conventional channels the supplier firm may not know who the ultimate customers are or in which applications they use the supplier's product. In Figure 7.2, we illustrate a conventional channel for an agricultural chemical. The sequence of boxes and arrows captures the way that pundits traditionally diagram marketing channels.

Figure 7.2
Conventional
Channel for an
Agricultural Chemical

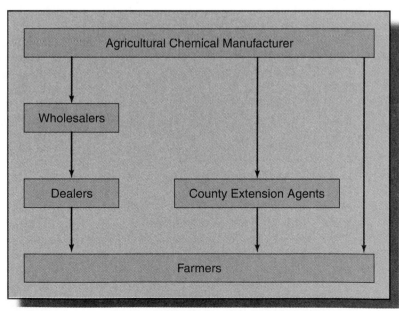

Emerging information and logistics technologies have given rise to **modular channels**, which appear on paper as complex networks of relationships among firms.[12] They too can be either direct or indirect channels. Business market managers from one firm act as the **system integrator**, envisioning the channel network, selecting participating firms, and managing ongoing relationships.[13]

The system integrator begins by **deconstructing** all the business processes required to provide the reformulated market offering down to individual functions or tasks.[14] Then, the manager determines which type of firm is best suited to perform each function. The system integrator hires the selected firms as subcontractors and compensates them on a fee-for-service or retainer basis. Importantly, the system integrator maintains the face before the customer, retains sole ownership of the customer relationship, manages the network, and promotes its own brand equity. Often, coordination and integration of all modular channel activities is done electronically via partner relationship management (PRM) systems, which we discuss in Chapter 9. In Box 7.2, we describe a modular channel from Monsanto's Animal Agriculture Business and diagram it in Figure 7.3.[15]

In a **hybrid channel**, business market managers combine features of both conventional and modular channels. For example, a supplier firm might choose to complement a conventional channel network with backup support from a modular channel. Let's say that a computer software producer distributes its programs through computer dealers and retailers. Because many of these resellers might not have technical service capabilities, the software producer may choose to create a network of

BOX 7.2
Monsanto's Animal Agriculture Business Develops an Innovative Modular Channel

Seeking to circumvent the often convoluted and inefficient reseller-based channels for agrichemicals in the United States (U.S.) Monsanto's Animal Agriculture Business (MAAB) built an innovative modular channel for its controversial bovine somatotropin, POSILAC®, in 1993. POSILAC increases the milk production of dairy cows. MAAB crafted this channel with a network of third-party information technology, logistics, and cash management suppliers.

Once MAAB received approval for POSILAC from the U.S. Food & Drug Administration (FDA), managers hired Marketing Technologies International Inc. (MTI) to design a marketing database. MTI maintains the industry-respected AGLIFE database, which contains a precise and up-to-date listing of more than 130,000 active dairy farmers in the United States, including their names, addresses, and telephone numbers. MTI helped MAAB to identify the 35,000 dairy farmers that they believed to be the top prospects for POSILAC. Next, MAAB requested that its advertising agency, Geile-Rexford, develop a product launch program. Geile-Rexford created and mailed a launch kit, featuring a video and collateral materials, to the 35,000 prospects identified by MTI.

MAAB asked FedEx Logistics Services (FLS) to build an integrated logistics system for POSILAC. The FLS system works as follows. Monsanto manufactures POSILAC at a subsidiary in the Netherlands. FLS packages the POSILAC in bulk containers and flies them to its Memphis hub. There, FLS employees

(continued)

BOX 7.2
Continued

transfer the liquid into dosage-size containers and store them in a refrigerated warehouse. FLS not only provides a toll-free telephone number for farmers to call, it runs an outgoing telemarketing group for MAAB. When a dairy farmer calls, FLS answers as "Monsanto" and takes orders for POSILAC. FLS personnel even help farmers obtain FDA approval to use POSILAC. If the farmer has a technical question or problem, FLS transfers the call to a bank of independent veterinarians in St. Louis. FLS order center and telemarketing personnel use their networked workstations to access MTI-managed database information on the number of cows the farmer has and the cows' prescribed POSILAC dosage. FLS warehouse people assemble the order and ship it to the farmer, often directly to the dairy barn, via FedEx. FedEx bills the farmer and collects receivables.

After the farmer administers the POSILAC, Browning Ferris Industries (BFI) gathers, recycles, or disposes of spent syringes. Moore Business Forms issues monthly statements to dairy farmers concerning their POSILAC usage. Bank of America furnishes cash management and financing services to the farmers. Finally, MTI collects information from its network partners concerning POSILAC orders, shipments, and payments, and then updates their respective databases.

MAAB managers claim that the service its channel provides for POSILAC is so seamless and reliable that many dairy farmers are unaware that they are not dealing directly with Monsanto most of the time. As of 2001, POSILAC is the largest-selling dairy animal pharmaceutical in the United States.

Sources: Albert Fried-Cassorla, "Launching POSILAC to Dairy Farmers," *AgriMarketing* (March 1994): 44–47; interviews with managers.

Figure 7.3
Monsanto's Modular
Channel for POSILAC®

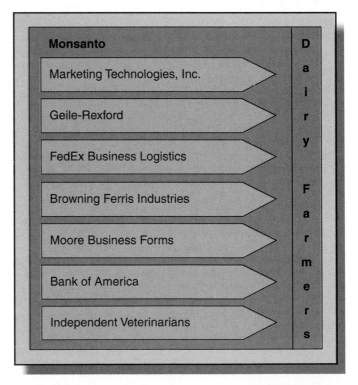

authorized technical support providers to work jointly with the resellers. The software producer might also take the lead and coordinate the efforts of resellers and support providers. In this way, the producer enhances the ability of resellers to furnish a total solution of software and value-adding services without forcing them to unnecessarily expand the scope of operations outside their core capabilities.[16]

Adaptive channels are a special hybrid in which suppliers, resellers, third-party service providers, and customer firms agree to share complementary capabilities for prespecified compensation to fulfill critical yet infrequent customer requirements. Because adaptive channels improve the effectiveness of channel partnerships, we discuss them in Chapter 9.

Finalize Marketing and Distribution Arrangements

With a channel network design in hand, business market managers ask the final questions, "Which firms will we ask to participate in the network and what will their roles be?" To resolve these issues, managers seek to balance exposure and coverage by determining what kind of and how many resellers to authorize in a given geographic region or trade area.[17] Mindful that channel partnerships require "gives & gets," business market managers then devise a feasible profit model for all proposed participants before assigning responsibilities. Next, they carefully choose channel partners, deliberately seeking out top-performing and forward-thinking resellers. Whenever appropriate, business market managers adopt supporting electronic business (e-business) and wireless technologies to bolster partner productivity and adapt international channels to local customs and established distribution practices. Finally, to reduce risk, managers place side bets on alternative marketing and distribution arrangements.

Balance Exposure and Coverage in Marketing Channels

Business market managers realize that to gain desired market access, channels must provide sufficient exposure and coverage. **Exposure** is the degree to which targeted customer firms are actually reached and served by selected resellers. It demands that managers match customer requirements and preferences with the abilities of alternate resellers to deliver superior value.

If a supplier firm is pursuing an undifferentiated marketing strategy, then business market managers are likely to rely on a **single-channel strategy** whereby all products are marketed either directly or through one type of reseller. Alternatively, if the supplier firm has adopted target marketing, business market managers may turn to a **multiple-channel strategy** and use a separate channel to reach each segment. For example, an electrical product supplier may have to use two different channels to reach the large-scale electrical contractor and "gypsy" electrical contractor segments. Large-scale contractors buy large quantities and assortments of electrical products and services and typically receive greater value from electrical distributors such as Graybar. In contrast, gypsy contractors work on small repair projects, often "out of the back of a pickup truck." For this reason, they purchase small quantities and limited assortments of products, and commonly get better service when they shop at a building supplies store, such as Home Depot.[18]

In recent years, the Internet has diluted the strategic intent of multiple channels. Rather than purchasing products from the same channel every transaction, managers routinely search the Internet for the best deal across all channels and resellers. The practice has given rise to more frequent channel conflicts and gray markets. To accommodate, if not capitalize on this trend, many supplier firms have adopted modular or hybrid channels that empower customers to select from different resellers or formats as their requirements change from transaction to transaction.

Coverage refers to the number of resellers authorized per geographic trade area. By adjusting the level of coverage, the supplier makes it more convenient for the customer to purchase an offering. Coverage entails a choice of **distribution intensity**: **exclusive**, where a supplier authorizes one reseller per trade area; **selective**, where it authorizes a limited number of resellers per trade area; or **intensive**, where it essentially authorizes all resellers that want to carry its line.[19]

Business market managers should ground their exposure and coverage decisions in reliable, accurate, and timely estimates of demand for each trade area. They must seek to gain a deep understanding of customer requirements, the target-market penetration capabilities of alternate channels, and the segments on which resellers are focusing. As part of this learning process, they conduct market research to estimate the market potential of their firm's offering in each segment and to determine with which resellers customers prefer to do business.

Armed with an appraisal of demand and segment preferences, managers determine the maximum number of customers to which a reseller can provide the desired levels of service outputs. Then, they estimate the number of resellers to authorize by dividing projected demand by reseller service capacity for each targeted trade area. In practice, the decision turns out to be more of an art than a science because of limited supplier knowledge and wide variation in number of customers that each available reseller can adequately service. Thus, firms often start with a minimum per trade area and add new resellers as they learn about unfulfilled demand.

One firm that has mastered exposure and coverage is the Parker Hannifin Corporation (PHC). Realizing that customers in the lumber, fishing, and aircraft industries in the Pacific Northwest purchase its line of pneumatics, PHC has designed a unique channel network. Rather than authorizing one or two industrial distributors, as it does in most of the United States and Canada, Parker Hannifin utilizes three separate channels there—forestry equipment distributors, marine distributors, and industrial distributors. PHC directs each channel at a separate target segment. In the Seattle area, two of these three types of distributors are located across the street from one another. Little conflict arises among the three distributors because they don't serve the same segments. As a result, PHC maximizes penetration in each of the three market segments.

Devise Profit Models

Before asking firms to join a channel network, business market managers must think through viable profit models not only for their own firm but also for prospective partners. As supplier expectations and requirements for channel network partners have changed so too have compensation methods. Traditionally, supplier managers set suggested resale prices and then provided resellers with a combination of trade discounts, volume discounts, rebates, and special incentives to entice full-service resellers to market their product lines. They intended that trade discounts would cover reseller costs and afford a reasonable profit. With rudimentary accounting tools at their disposal, supplier managers often used industry averages for reseller costs and profits when setting trade discounts. Noting that suppliers often kept trade discount amounts unchanged for years rather than adjusting them in parallel with rises in service costs, reseller managers have long disparaged the practice. As for resellers engaged primarily in selling tasks—manufacturer's representatives, agents, and brokers—supplier firms commonly offered commissions and bonuses based on realized sales.

In recent years, these longstanding models have begun to break down. Among full-service resellers, cutthroat competition has compelled many firms to price well below suggested resale prices. This practice trivializes trade discounts and has forced many reseller firms to earn a living off meager volume discounts, rebates, and incentives. Given the volatility of sales in some markets, manufacturer's representatives, agents, and brokers are increasingly requesting that a greater percentage of their compensation come in the form of guaranteed salaries or fees.

In response, business market managers have begun to experiment with alternative compensation schemes. For example, McKinsey & Company, Inc., developed a cost-to-serve (CTS) model, which it advocates that supplier firms use in place of traditional trade discount schemes. Under the McKinsey CTS model, participating wholesalers are compensated for each service they perform for a supplier. Payments cover the actual costs a specific wholesaler incurs plus a prespecified profit. Critics argue that the CTS model is more difficult and costly to implement. To participate, wholesalers have to create activity-based costing systems that monitor the ongoing costs of providing each service. They also have to enter into complex negotiations with suppliers over compensation for each service. However, McKinsey consultants counter that the CTS model not only serves as a strong incentive for superior wholesaler performance but also enhances supply chain efficiency.[20] In modular channels, where firms serve as subcontractors and perform prespecified tasks, CTS models or a "retainer contract" variant have become commonplace.

Realizing that resellers stand to gain far greater profits from providing services to customers than from merely selling products, supplier managers have also begun to create forward-thinking certification programs, franchising and licensing agreements through which resellers can charge service fees for such things as applications design, installation, maintenance, and consulting. Finally, as more and more resellers turn to e-business, supplier firms have shown them how to gain incremental profits from their Web sites through commissions on referrals, advertising charges, and syndication fees.

Carefully Select Channel Partners

Business market managers identify and then select existing or potential channel-partner firms that can best perform some or all the required channel functions. Of course, managers realize that their choice of channel partners is often constrained. To begin, they specify those channel capabilities the supplier firm seeks in terms of such things as technical competence, sales force deployment, warehouse and delivery capabilities, financial stability, and leadership. Next, business market managers internally generate a comprehensive list of candidates for each reseller type targeted or acquire them from governments, database marketing firms, or trade associations. For example, the U.S. Department of Commerce keeps track of resellers through its North American Industry Classification System, while the National Association of Wholesaler-Distributors monitors reseller firms in more than 105 industries. Suppliers also can gather general and financial information about these firms from public and commercial sources such as Dun & Bradstreet. Managers eliminate those resellers that do not meet screening requirements.[21]

Managers then conduct a market research survey to assess customer preferences for, and satisfaction with, specific reseller firms. As part of the survey, respondents evaluate reseller firms in terms of their abilities to deliver necessary service outputs to create a list of prospective reseller partners. Then, they reconcile this list with the one we described in the previous paragraph to create a list of prospective resellers. To validate the research, managers visit each prospective reseller, particularly those located outside of the firm's domestic market, to tour facilities, assess capabilities, and gauge management interest.

Business market managers now enter into partnership negotiations with preferred resellers. Following productive negotiations, the supplier and its resellers summarize the terms of their relationship in a sales agreement. The agreement will identify the responsibilities of all parties for completing business processes and the rewards that each will receive.

Consider E-Business and Wireless Technologies

Considerable debate surrounds the issue of whether evolving e-business and wireless technologies constitute new marketing channels or are merely computer and telecommunications-based tools that enable existing channels to function more efficiently. Regardless of the eventual outcome of that debate, managers should use the technologies wherever they stand to increase the value of the offerings that the channel network provides. In particular, they need to determine whether new types of resellers might complement or replace existing channel members and whether new transaction formats might augment modular and hybrid channels.[22]

The Internet has given rise to two new types of resellers: infomediaries and metamediaries. An **infomediary** is a broker that finds, retrieves, sorts, processes, and analyzes information from the World Wide Web. Infomediaries typically receive subscription or other fees from firms for conducting information searches, seeking buyers or sellers, aggregating orders, making referrals, and consulting. Internet portals and browsers, such as Yahoo!, AOL, Microsoft Network (MSN), and Google, are among the most successful. Another form of infomediary is the "comparison agent". It allows customers to search the Internet for sources of supply and to compare vendor prices. By paying infomediaries listing fees and charges for banner and pop-up advertisements, a supplier firm can further enhance market awareness of its offerings.[23]

Metamediaries are Web sites that furnish multivendor, multiproduct, and multiservice marketspace for customer firms. Suppliers commonly pay such firms in the form of commissions on sales. Grainger and Marshall Industries are two prominent metamediaries in business markets. Metamediaries are a particularly attractive option when a supplier firm needs to bundle its market offering with complementary products and services into a total solution.

According to consultants Friedman and Furey, e-business creates added value by helping customers learn, shop, buy, and get help. Four electronic transaction formats facilitate such added value: communities, catalogs, auctions, and exchanges. They are particularly useful in the case of modular and hybrid channels because managers can use these formats to improve the performance of specific channel functions. A **community** is a hosted, though unmoderated, cyber forum where users exchange information about a particular product or service, technology, or industry.

For example, in the software industry a common practice for suppliers is to set up and operate a Web site where users can come to find answers to pressing program problems. Volunteer programmers may even staff "for free" and solve user problems for the personal satisfaction it brings.[24]

With a **catalog** format, a firm posts detailed information about the company and its market offerings. In more advanced systems, customer firms have access to pricing information, use an "electronic shopping cart" to select items for purchase, configure more complex offerings, and are able to order products or services 24-hours a day, 7-days a week (24×7). Catalog sites are perhaps the most common because they are relatively easy to set up and operate, and customers are familiar with the practice from personal experiences.

In an **electronic auction**, one firm posts an offering and other parties submit bids. In a forward auction, a supplier firm lists products or services and potential customers bid for them, with the highest bidder winning. In Chapter 3, we addressed reverse auctions where a customer firm manages the process. Supplier firms tend to use forward auctions opportunistically and tactically to sell items of unknown value, perishable goods, surplus or discontinued items, and used equipment.

A business-to-business (B2B) **exchange** is an electronic forum where multiple buyers and sellers can make bids or accept offers for a variety of products and services. Buyers and sellers can accept any price offered at any time and either party can withdraw or revise a bid. In some exchanges, electronic bidding is followed up with face-to-face negotiations. Vertical exchanges are industry specific, such as for auto parts, chemicals, or steel; while horizontal exchanges are service specific, such as for advertisements, accounting services, or consulting. Suppliers, customers, or industry associations can sponsor exchanges. Much ballyhooed during the latter 1990s, exchanges have had limited success. Covisint, ChemConnect, eSteel, Elemica, and Exostar are among the more prosperous B2B exchanges.[25]

The convergence of wireless communications, mobile computing, and the Internet may have major implications for channel network design in the near future. These **wireless technologies** range in complexity from beepers to personal digital assistants to mobile telephones. Widely popular in the consumer arena, particularly in Europe and Japan, this evolving technology has already yielded two proven applications in business markets. The first is remote, 24×7 tracking of order, payment, and delivery status. Perhaps more promising, the second is contact management. This application is particularly useful in modular channels where personnel from several companies interact with customer firms. Functioning as a communications medium for PRM systems, text and instant messaging features of mobile phones or other wireless devices enable all contact personnel to have immediate access to sales leads, service requests, summaries of previous sales and service calls, and sensor readings, as well as to process invoices.[26]

In Box 7.3, we describe how Putnam Investments has embraced the Internet as a value-added service and prospecting tool for its government and institutional customers.

Build International Marketing Channels

Those firms that currently operate or are expanding internationally should anticipate longer business processes and additional functions in their marketing channels. They must cover additional geography and adhere to export and import regulations of each

BOX 7.3
Putnam Builds an Institutional Web Site

Based in Boston, Putnam Investments manages more than $300 billion in assets. In general, the institutional asset management industry has been slow to embrace the Internet as a value-added service and prospecting tool. The delayed response can be partially attributable to the personalized nature of the institutional business as well as the focus on the retail segment, which has proved to be much more tech-savvy than the institutional counterparts. As such, as the end of the twentieth century drew near, the institutional industry had a surprising lack of Internet service offerings.

Despite its size and success, Putnam Investments focused more on its retail Web site as the institutional segment remained quiet in its demands for such services. Putnam's focus shifted dramatically in late 1998, when a request for proposal (RFP) submitted by the Alaska Permanent Fund ("Alaska"), one of the largest plans in the country, explicitly required that respondents address their Internet capabilities. Alaska's circumstances were initially considered unique. However, as a lead-user, Alaska's demands for investment information via the Internet would prove to be a critical success factor in the institutional marketplace.

During the construction of the trans-Alaska oil pipeline in the 1970s, the state recognized that it would garner significant revenues from the pipeline. As a result, the state voted to develop the Permanent Fund so that all of Alaska would enjoy some benefit (in the form of a dividend) from the oil bubble. The Fund invests in equities and fixed income products offered by investment managers that were chosen by the Board of Trustees.

For ease of interpretation, the Fund aggregates all the performance of the underlying investment managers into one composite valuation. The composite valuation is posted on the Fund's Web site so that participants, located in varied remote areas of the state, can monitor the performance of the entire Fund and manage their expectations for their next dividend. If accessible electronically, Alaska can download the manager's returns, holdings, and trades, which in turn reduces the time required and the room for error to aggregate the information into one composite valuation.

The Web-based managers also enables Alaska to track the performance of its own personnel. For example, providing holdings and trades on a monthly basis enables Alaska to monitor the extent to which its managers are buying and selling stocks/bonds in accordance with the objectives set forth when the manager was selected. With access to the managers' holdings, Alaska can also conduct more sophisticated holdings-based analysis that is more accurate for evaluating the optimality of the plan's overall structure than a returns-based analysis.

As a lead-user in its application of the Internet, Alaska offered Putnam the specs required to meet its requirements and preferences, which served as a platform for satisfying all institutional clients. In response to the RFP, Putnam created a task force dedicated to designing an institutional Web site that met the needs of the most sophisticated plan sponsor (i.e., Alaska). Alaska's requests included daily pricing of holdings in their portfolio as well as an appraisal report at month-end listing the trades implemented and the market value of the portfolio. Beyond the specs requested, Putnam added a Webcast call feature whereby the portfolio manager would address all institutional clients with an update on the portfolio's performance, positioning, and his or her outlook for the future. With offices in Fairbanks, Alaska, the Fund considered the Webcast call a considerable value-added service because it decreased the time and travel required by the Trustees to meet with portfolio managers at their offices.

Putnam did recognize that its competitors would quickly follow suit as Alaska touts the value added by such offerings. To differentiate itself from the inevitable competition, the task force designed specs that not only met Alaska's requests, but that also could be customized so that each institutional client could

BOX 7.3
Continued

choose from a menu of information to access via the Web and have input into the look and feel of their individual site. By doing so, Putnam was able to attract plan sponsors that were frustrated with the Web as they struggled to find the information they most valued amongst the plethora of content and pictures.

Putnam's ability to customize the site based on the type of user also enabled it to increase the value of services it provided to investment consultants. Although hired for their intellectual capital, investment consultants struggle at quarter-end to produce a comprehensive performance evaluation report for their clients. The production costs can be significant as the consultants look to aggregate the information into one consistent format, easily interpreted by their clients (similar to the Alaska model).

Sensitive to the extent to which consultants value the accessibility of information, Putnam provided the consultants access to the client's site after receiving authorization from the client. In doing so, the production time required to produce a performance evaluation report is greatly reduced. Performance evaluation reports include a composite calculation of the client manager's performance on a quarterly, annual, three-year, and five-year basis. The report further includes written commentary explaining performance of each of the managers as well as a capital markets overview. Traditionally, an investment consultant would have to sift through all the quarterly letters written by the investment managers, looking for useful information to explain the manager's performance. To calculate composite performance, the consultant would have to manually enter each of the managers' performance numbers into their system. Via its Web site, Putnam enables the consultant to download performance and copy statements explaining performance, which reduces entry time and room for error. Putnam also has added a section of the Web site dedicated to white papers regarding capital market issues, which the consultant can use to counsel their clients more effectively and efficiently.

Since launching the institutional Web site in 1999, Putnam has been awarded the highest honors in Web development, specifically for the institutional market. Kasina, a strategic e-business consulting firm, evaluated the institutional Web sites available in the marketplace, rating their ease of use, depth and breadth of information content, including product, firm, and performance, and degree of customization. In their white paper, entitled "Impact of the Web on Institutional Asset Management," Kasina recognized Putnam's Web site as one of the top five in the industry.

More than 400 institutional clients use the Web site today, each with varying degrees of customization, but all with the same level of security. With client endorsements and industry honors, Putnam's sales managers often demo the Web site at final presentations or leave behind a CD with a tour of the Web site. With the prospect's name highlighted on the top of each page of the demo, Putnam is able to demonstrate its ability to provide customized value-added solutions.

Source: Contributed by Amy Walls, Kellogg School of Management, Northwestern University.

country market as well as its local culture and distribution practices. In addition, international business market managers should expect the division of functions among channel members to vary from region to region and from country to country.[27] We provide a brief description of the various types of international resellers in Box 7.4. In general, managers have four basic choices concerning international channels and resellers.[28]

BOX 7.4
Examples of International Marketing Channels and Resellers

I. Resellers Involved in International Marketing
   A. Domestic Reseller-Exporters
   - **Export management company (EMC):** An international sales organization that functions as the exclusive export department for a group of noncompeting manufacturers. An EMC handles the entire exporting operation for a client, functioning as the manufacturer in the eyes of international customers. They work under contract and are paid by salary, commission, or retainer plus commission.
   - **Manufacturer's export agent (MEA):** Operating within limited markets and under a short-term contract, an MEA acts as a firm's sales representative in an international marketplace. This type of firm offers far more limited services than an EMC and is paid on a commission basis.
   - **Commission agent (CA):** A CA represents international customers interested in buying domestic products. They are paid a commission by the international buying organization.
   - **Domestic trading company (DTC):** A domestic trading company provides a full range of exporting services for clients within its home country. These services can include international warehousing and physical distribution, financing, insurance, marketing research, market development, and selling. A DTC handles goods from numerous manufacturers.
   - **Export broker (EB):** Working on a commission basis, export brokers bring domestic manufacturers together with prospective international buyers. They do not take title or physical possession of goods.
   - **Cooperative exporter (CE):** A CE is another manufacturer that has an international marketing channel already established. Serving as either EMCs or CAs for manufacturers that lack international distribution, they market others' goods along with their own.

   B. International Reseller-Importers
   - **Import broker (IB):** Located abroad, this type of broker establishes contacts for a supplier with potential customers within the broker's home country.
   - **Managing agent (MA):** An MA serves as a manufacturer's agent in another country. It performs related selling activities.
   - **International trading company (ITC):** Headquartered in another country, an ITC performs similar functions to a DTC.
   - **Import jobber (IJ):** An IJ is a jobber located in another country that specializes in importing goods. It performs the typical array of wholesaling functions.

II. Countertrade Arrangements
   - **Barter:** In its simplest form, barter entails the exchange of products without the use of money.
   - **Clearing arrangement:** This is a type of barter in which a number of transactions are consolidated into a single contract to purchase a specified amount of goods and services. Credit is often involved in such agreements.
   - **Switch trading:** Switch trading is a triangular, barter arrangement in

BOX 7.4
Continued

which a third-party is brought into the deal to dispose of merchandise.

- **Buy-back:** Under this form of barter, an exporter agrees to set up and operate a plant in another country and contracts to buy a percentage of that plant's output for a set period of time.

- **Offset:** An agreement in which an exporter sells goods at a set price and is paid in currency. A reciprocal arrangement is made for that exporter to in turn buy a certain amount of goods from the client.

Sources: Subhash C. Jain, *International Marketing*, 6th ed. (Cincinnati, OH: South-Western College Publishing, 2000); and Anne T. Coughlin, Erin Anderson, Louis W. Stern, and Adel I. El-Ansari, *Marketing Channels*, 6th ed. (Upper Saddle River, NJ: Prentice Hall, 2001).

A firm can rely upon domestic reseller-exporters to handle international marketing functions. Domestic reseller-exporters operate within the supplier's home country and provide services from offices within that home country. Although specific responsibilities vary across nations, two general categories exist: agents and merchants. Agents, such as export management companies, a manufacturer's export agents, and domestic trading companies, largely perform selling activities without taking title to goods and are paid either a commission or a fee for service. Merchants such as export merchants, cooperative exporters, and export vendors, on the other hand, take title and physical possession of goods and perform other marketing functions. They make their profit from the resale of products in other countries.

A firm can choose to deal with international reseller-importers. These resellers are based in the country that managers target, and specialize in importing goods from abroad. Among these agents are brokers, managing agents, international trading companies, import jobbers, and national distributors and dealers. Like their domestic counterparts, international reseller-importers vary in terms of the marketing functions they perform, whether they take title to goods, and the manner in which they are compensated.

A supplier can decide to market directly in the targeted nation. It might establish an in-country sales and service office. Or the supplier might acquire or set up its own production facilities and develop a direct sales force for the nation or region. Some resource-rich suppliers may even choose to acquire a local distributor or dealer firm to handle channel functions. Although marketing directly may at first seem to be a high-risk and resource-intense strategy, international business market managers may find that they have no choice when penetrating certain markets. For example, in Japan where working relationships in vertical keiretsus are long running and close, access to the best channels and resellers may be blocked. Furthermore, where access is possible, resellers may give low priority to imported lines out of loyalty to traditional suppliers.[29]

Finally, a firm might engage in countertrade. Broadly defined, countertrade is the exchange of goods or services for the promise to reciprocate through the purchase of the other party's goods or services. The most common types of countertrade include barter, clearing arrangements, and switch trading. Countertrade partners often include governments and businesses, as well as individuals.

Business market managers often find international channels, especially those in emerging markets, to be particularly challenging. Not only must managers be imaginative and design new channels that meet unique local requirements, they must also be prepared to quickly alter their channel strategies whenever market conditions shift dramatically. In Box 7.5, we illustrate this challenge, recounting the difficulties that Acer Computer faced in penetrating the Russian computer market.

BOX 7.5
Acer Computers Serves the Russian Market from Finland

Headquartered in Singapore, Acer Computers is the world's fifth-largest personal computer (PC) manufacturer. As is the case with many global firms, Acer initially served the Russian market by importing its PCs from Asia via Western Europe and conducting marketing activities from a Russian sales office. Although Acer sales in Russia were growing rapidly, management decided in 1995 that they could grab a larger share of the market by "localizing" the assembly of its PCs. If they assembled locally, they reasoned that they would be able to price more competitively and shorten lead times.

However, Acer management quickly concluded that "setting up shop" in Russia would be extremely difficult, if not impossible. Russian tax codes include more than 4,000 documents. They are supposedly so contradictory and poorly drafted that it is almost impossible for any company to comply in full. Resulting fines for noncompliance routinely exceed a firm's gross sales. Russian bureaucrats have a reputation for creating roadblocks for foreign investors. They allegedly prey on such firms, routinely extracting significant bribes and kickbacks. As if dealing with the Russian government was not trying enough, Acer would also have to confront organized and disorganized crime. Reportedly ubiquitous in Russia, crime made it difficult for legitimate businesses to securely store inventory and to make safe and consistent deliveries. Rather than deal with these problems, Acer management decided to create an innovative business channel network.

Acer turned to a Finnish government agency, the Invest in Finland Bureau, for assistance. In addition to offering a highly developed infrastructure and a law-abiding business environment, Finland offered a special and simple customs regime for foreign firms that plan to import goods for reexport to Russia. The Finnish Bureau introduced Acer managers to Wilson Finland, a subsidiary of a Swedish-owned international freight firm that specializes in transporting goods between Finland and Russia. Wilson Finland helped Acer find an industrial park and establish an assembly facility in Lappeenranta, Finland, which is located near the Russian border. Acer configured the plant to produce 7,000 PCs per month, more than enough for the Russian market.

To avoid dealing with Russian bureaucrats and criminals, Acer planned to sell its PCs to six Russian distributors "at the factory gate." In effect, they would transfer title and physical possession of the PCs while they were still in Finland. The Russian distributors would have to cleverly overcome government procedures and criminal activities. In this way, Acer would be able to sustain its reputation for observing all laws and regulations in the countries where it operated. Wilson Finland, in turn, would provide delivery services to distributor locations.

Through these channel arrangements, Acer gained a secondary benefit. At the time, Russians perceived the value of PCs manufactured in Western Europe and North America to be greatest, those made in Asia to be second greatest, and those produced in Russia to be the lowest. By assembling their PCs in Finland rather than Asia, Acer would improve the perceived value of their products. Importantly,

BOX 7.5
Continued

Russians would pay a larger price premium for the PCs.

Although Acer's strategy succeeded initially, the firm encountered unanticipated difficulties at the end of 1996. A host of new Russian computer companies began operations. Although these firms had no alternative to assembling their PCs locally, they were more adept at working the Russian bureaucratic system. One of these firms, VIST, did an outstanding job of building its brand equity via heavy advertising and a network of first-rate service centers located across Russia. As a result, Russian customers began to trust PCs made in Russia and became less willing to pay a premium for those produced in Europe. By the end of 1996, Russian producers had gained a two-thirds market share.

Thus, the Acer example demonstrates that although firms intent on penetrating emerging markets must create innovative channel arrangements, they must be prepared to respond and adapt to sudden and unexpected changes in local conditions.

Source: "Laptops from Lapland," *The Economist*, 6 September 1997, 71–72.

If Possible, Place Side Bets

With growing market fragmentation, business market managers are not as confident as they were in their ability to select the one best channel structure. As a consequence, managers increasingly place **channel side bets.** Rather than invest all their resources in one channel, they simultaneously experiment with several parallel systems. Moreover, they allow the marketplace to select through sales transactions the marketing channels that create the greatest value. However, placing side bets requires additional resources and likely will generate conflict between the supplier's resellers in the parallel systems. In Box 7.6, we provide an example of how the alliance between Thomson Consumer Electronics and Hughes Electronics placed marketing channel side bets with its digital satellite system.

BOX 7.6
Placing Side Bets on Digital Satellite System Marketing Channels

An alliance between Thomson Consumer Electronics, its RCA-brand television systems unit, and Hughes Electronics Corporation launched the digital satellite system (DSS) in the United States in 1994. A DSS installation includes a satellite dish and translator along with Hughes Communications' DirecTV and/or Hubbard Broadcasting's USSB programming. The alliance developed DSS as a low-cost technological alternative to be positioned between standard satellite reception systems and the ballyhooed high-definition television systems (HDTV). Potential customers for DSS were in commercial, institutional, and consumer market segments. Because DSS was a new and untested technology, alliance partners were not sure which marketing channels and augmenting services these segments would prefer. Rather than launch DSS through one marketing channel, the partners decided to experiment and offer customers the choice of several alternative channels and service bundles.

(continued)

BOX 7.6
Continued

Assuming that customers would be familiar with existing satellite dealers and demand a high level of installation and repair services, the alliance began by authorizing RCA's existing satellite systems dealers to carry DSS. However, realizing that satellite dealers tend to operate in out-of-the-way locations, alliance managers decided to make DSS available in "high traffic" shopping malls. They also authorized Sears. Such a move would augment DSS with Sears' service network.

At the same time, alliance managers wondered whether customers would prefer buying DSS at an electronic products store. After all, a customer who just purchased a new television set might be convinced that DSS would improve reception quality. Alternatively, a customer who just acquired DSS might conclude a new television was needed to go along with better reception. Thus, the alliance authorized Circuit City and BrandSmart USA. Finally, given the popularity of home entertainment and home theater centers in the United States, alliance managers wondered whether consumers might want to renovate their family rooms once they purchased DDS. Therefore, they authorized Lowe's Building Supplies to carry DSS. As it turns out, Lowe's not only sells building supplies, it also markets televisions and other appliances and offers remodeling and room design assistance.

Sources: Margorie Costello, "Digital Satellite System," *Broadcast Engineering* (July 1995): 24–28; manager interviews.

CREATING VALUE THROUGH DIRECT CHANNELS

Firms in business markets are more likely to market their offerings directly to customer firms than their consumer market counterparts. Customer firms are far fewer in number. Furthermore, customers tend to purchase products in large quantities, require technical support, and prefer closer relationships with suppliers. Taken together, these factors provide a powerful economic incentive for supplier firms to serve customers directly. In addition, popular direct marketing tools such as catalogs, e-mail ordering systems, and e-business make direct channels both practical and cost effective. In Box 7.7, we discuss how Cisco Systems has built its entire business around a direct Internet-based channel.

When a supplier firm chooses to "go it alone," it faces unique implementation challenges. Among the most important of these issues are building and maintaining a sales force and a logistics system. In this section, we explore issues related to executing a direct channel network. Given that we advocate a value-based market management approach, we begin by discussing the training programs, sales tools, and compensation systems that suppliers use to develop a sales force of value merchants. Then we describe how suppliers deploy these value merchants among potential customers to maximize profits.

To physically deliver products or services to customers, supplier firms must create appropriate infrastructure, which often includes order entry and processing systems, inventory management systems, warehouses, and delivery vehicles. Thus, we

BOX 7.7
Cisco Systems Pioneers Business-to-Business Commerce on the Internet

With 2002 U.S. sales and net income exceeding $18.9 billion and $1.9 billion respectively, Silicon Valley-based Cisco Systems produces multiprotocol routers, digital switching devices, ethernet hubs and transceivers, frame relays, wireless networking systems, and Internetwork Operating System (IOS) software, among many other lines. Cisco products make the Internet function properly by linking together diversely configured and remotely located computer systems into an online communication network that can exchange data rapidly and accurately. Yet, Cisco doesn't just sell products for the Internet, it sells them *on* the Internet. In fact, more than 90 percent of its revenues and 38 percent of its purchasing orders in 2002 were transacted over the Internet, making Cisco one of the largest marketers and purchasers "on the Web."

Challenged to "practice what it preaches," Cisco management deployed what the firm touts as its Global Networked Business (GNB) model via IOS software on its Web site—*www.cisco.com*. Cisco's GNB model urges other firms to devise a strategy for generating sales and providing support via the Internet. Under this GNB model, firms provide all of their own customers 24-hour global access to service and support. Cisco's Web site provides different levels of detail and confidentiality as a function of user status—customers, reseller partners, prospects, suppliers, or employees.

For example, browsers have access to Cisco events calendar, online magazine, press releases, product catalog, brochures, and service and support information. Registered customers, on the other hand, can do all of their business with Cisco online. They can buy products, check order status, inspect prices, review network configurations, download software updates, obtain technical help, and download product and technical information. Customers also have the option to register for Cisco training seminars, read technical papers, download public software files, and buy promotional merchandise and Internet software.

In 2001, more than one-third of all Cisco's business functions were Internet-enabled and the firm seeks to convert the remaining two-thirds within five years. Laudibly, Cisco's e-business activities saved the firm more than $1.5 billion in 2001 through increased operational efficiency and cost avoidance. Finally, Cisco managers claim that their e-business capabilities expanded the firm's customer base more than 17 percent since their inception.

Sources: Mike Heller, "Global Networking," *Telephony* (May 1997): 26–27; Brent Schlender, "Computing's Next Superpower," *Fortune*, 12 May 1997, 88–100; and "Cisco Systems Profile," *Hoover's Online* [Internet], (Austin, TX: Hoover's Inc., cited May 2002), available at *http://www.hoovers.com*.

explore logistics systems and describe how supplier firms can draw upon emerging technologies to do so.

Creating a Sales Force of Value Merchants

In today's demanding business environment, a supplier's sales force must be comprised of highly skilled professionals. Each salesperson must be able to investigate customer requirements and preferences, demonstrate value, negotiate terms and conditions, and take the order. As if these tasks are not enough, the salesperson is increasingly responsible for the profitability of each customer account to the supplier firm. We contend that a supplier firm must create a sales force of value merchants to ensure that each of these demanding tasks is performed competently.

A **value merchant** recognizes the costs and value associated with each element of a market offering and seeks an equitable return for both the supplier firm and customer firm. The value merchant stands in stark contrast to the all-too-common **value spendthrift**, who either cuts price needlessly or gives away extra services "for free" to gain the next sale. To create value merchants, the supplier firm must instill a value philosophy, train the salesperson on value-selling techniques, and compensate the sales force as a function of value delivered.

Internally Promote a Value-Based Marketing Philosophy

To inspire value merchants, senior management needs to put a philosophy in place that the firm generates value with both its core offering and its augmenting services, and that the firm expects to receive an equitable return for this value. For instance, the Sonoco Products Company's corporate culture reinforces to each salesperson the preeminence of value in the firm's overall market strategy. From the day they are hired, sales representatives learn that Sonoco products are typically higher priced than those of competitors. They also quickly discover that Sonoco prospers because it provides value to its customers in the form of technologically superior products and outstanding services. From these lessons, salespersons readily conclude that if they are to succeed at Sonoco, they must sell value and not price. Moreover, the Sonoco "value story" is repeatedly reinforced through such things as annual reports, brochures, company newsletters, case histories presented at sales meetings, and sales tools.

Train Value Merchants

Giving value away is easy. Obtaining an equitable return on the value provided to customers is quite the opposite. A first step in countering the tendency to cut price is for senior management to provide salespersons with an adequate understanding not only of the value services provide, but also of their cost and profitability. Companies such as Angus Chemicals and Van Den Bergh Foods, for example, furnish salespersons with information about the costs to deliver each of their services. Management must also inform their salespersons about the relationship between sales volume and account profitability. Based on this information, the sales force focuses its efforts and those of service providers toward those accounts that have the greatest profit potential.

Knowledge of the value of services is not enough. Salespeople also need opportunities to practice value-based selling in a controlled situation to build up the requisite skill set. To create a breed of value merchants, Sonoco Products Company provides extensive training on how Sonoco products and services create customer value. As part of these value-selling programs, Sonoco trainers give salespeople experience in using case studies in the selling process. Based on market research and often including videotapes, these case histories demonstrate three benefits to customers: (1) Sonoco products provide lower costs to customers; (2) Sonoco products and services result in greater sales to customers; and (3) Sonoco products and services are more innovative than those of the competition. These value case studies enable Sonoco salespeople to demonstrate in a compelling way that it is in the customer's best interest to pay a premium for Sonoco market offerings.

In addition to "snapshot" value-based sales tools, experienced value merchants employ a complementary, value-accumulation tool that documents the value provided to a customer over time. Such a tool arms salespeople with a proactive response to customer questions of, "What have you done lately?" This question often arises in account reviews. Astute suppliers create this tool, train salespeople in its use, and compensate them for taking the time to keep score on the value created in the relationship, which tends to be forgotten.

Compensate Value Merchants Based on Profitability of Accounts

Value merchant compensation is based on short-term and long-term profitability. A reorganization at Sonoco Consumer Products Division provides a noteworthy example. Division accounts are now divided up on a market-by-market basis, and cross-functional teams of about five members are each responsible for a portfolio of accounts. Each team manages its own business. They develop market plans, prepare budgets, and initiate product and service improvements. Their compensation system reinforces salespeople for short- and long-term customer profitability. Each sales manager can earn up to 50 percent and each salesperson up to 25 percent of his or her salary in bonuses that are based on account sales and operating profit improvement, customer satisfaction, customer accounts receivable levels, and securing long-term, single-source supply contracts. Looking to the future, Sonoco executives see more and more sales force compensation being based on the long-term provision of value to customers.

More fine-grained criteria for value merchant compensation emerge when the supplier gains the capability of monitoring which products and services each customer uses. Senior management must guard against compensation schemes that reward salespeople for selling separately as many products and services as they can to the customer. Although this practice will most likely provide a short-term spike in customer contribution to profitability, long term it will undermine credibility with the customer and sacrifice future business. The challenge is for sales management to integrate short-term performance with long-term results. This goal suggests the need for an inclusive set of measures that captures how well the firm is meeting customers' present and envisioned requirements.[30] In Box 7.8, we discuss how the GLS Corporation uses its compensation system to create a sales force of value merchants.

Deploying Value Merchants

When staffed with a limited number of value merchants, supplier firms deploy them selectively among prospective customers to yield the greatest possible sales and profits. First, if necessary, suppliers create separate sales forces to serve distinct market segments. Second, they determine the number of value merchants needed to provide appropriate market coverage. Third, supplier firms designate individual areas of responsibility. Finally, they assign value merchants to specific areas of responsibility.[31]

Establish Necessary Sales Units

Recognizing differential sales and profit potential among targeted segments, suppliers increasingly divide the sales force into several units. Managers make this decision based on the the knowledge required to adequately market the offering and on the types of working relationships required in each targeted market segment. In Chapter 10, we explore relationship-building efforts in detail.

Shapiro identified four types of field sales forces. Each type has different responsibilities and organization. In a **transactional field sales force**, each salesperson is responsible for calling on customers in a defined territory. They perform traditional selling activities—making presentations, asking for orders, and making after-sale calls. Their efforts revolve around discrete exchanges or series of exchanges.[32]

BOX 7.8
The GLS Sales Force Incentive Program

The GLS Corporation, a major distributor of composite materials in the United States, obtains about twice the sales per sales representative as its nearest competitor. Steven Dehmlow, president of GLS, believes that his firm's sales force incentive program significantly motivates this superior performance. The incentive plan has three components: a competitive base salary, a quarterly incentive, and a *quality-of-margin multiplier.* GLS begins with a highly competitive base salary that sales managers continuously adjust to attract and retain the best sales representatives in the industry.

Next, GLS provides a quarterly incentive calculated as a percentage of the total gross margin dollars generated by the sales rep minus inbound freight charges. GLS managers prefer gross margin dollars because they feel that it is a relatively "clean" number that everyone understands. Moreover, gross margin is a financial number that the sales rep controls and drives. Seasoned GLS reps, for instance, have significant pricing authority. They can negotiate "support" in the form of price discounts from suppliers. Importantly, GLS managers share gross margin information on all products and services with sales representatives.

GLS managers use a quality-of-margin multiplier when determining quarterly bonuses. At the end of each quarter, sales managers calculate the total gross margin dollars each sales representative has earned. Then, the sales manager subtracts a set of costs from each representative's total gross margin dollars. The surplus above a pre-specified amount indicates the representative's *quality of margin.* GLS gives the representative a bonus in the form of a percentage of that surplus. The percentages or quality-of-margin multipliers are laid out in an increasing, stair-step fashion. With these multipliers, the best sales reps can readily double their base salary. Yet, the incentive plan also promotes responsible sales to accounts that will pay their bills; when the accounts receivable from a given customer exceed 60 days at the end of a quarter, the rep loses the bonus on that transaction.

The incentive system has had an impact on salesperson behaviors. Reps "manage the mix" of each transaction, seeking volume sales and promoting margin-enhancing bundles of products and services. They "hang tough" in negotiations with customers in order to gain a better price. And they selectively seek lower prices and support in competitive situations from GLS suppliers.

In a **systems sales force**, salespersons from several product groups or divisions within a company work together. They temporarily band together in a team, to sell a solution comprised of products or services from their respective groups. A team sales effort is appropriate in these situations because no one salesperson has the technical knowledge of all components of the system. Customers benefit from systems selling in that they don't have to listen to separate presentations from sales representatives from each group.

As the sales and profit potential of accounts grows, firms turn to dedicated sales teams. A **major account sales force** takes one of two forms. When important customers have multiple divisions located across the nation or world, suppliers often rely on contracts. A **major account contract** creates uniform pricing and coordinated servicing for all customer divisions. A major account manager is responsible for the account and spends much time calling on the national headquarters of the customer firm, because the customer firm's senior managers who sign the major account contract and then coordinate its implementation across divisions are typically located there. The major account manager also supervises those field sales representatives who call on customer plants within their territories. The selling team is comprised of all individuals who call on that customer. For larger and more collaborative relationships, firms turn to **major account programs**. Teams are comprised of cross-functional personnel charged with developing all aspects of the relationship. Cross-functional personnel serve several accounts at once.

For accounts with the greatest potential, suppliers use **strategic account management**. A strategic account team is comprised of cross-functional personnel who are permanently assigned to one customer. They may even maintain offices at the customer's facility. Their task is to manage the entire customer relationship. Strategic account management teams spend less time on sales and marketing, and more time on such tasks as joint research and development than their transactional field sales force counterparts.

In addition to these four types of field sales forces, supplier firms commonly have an inside sales force. Inside salespeople maintain relationships via telephone, fax, or other electronic media with customer firms that are too small or strategically insignificant to justify frequent field sales calls. Suppliers sometimes organize inside sales into three groups. A **telemarketing group** is responsible for making proactive and outgoing calls on customers to solicit orders. An **order center** takes incoming calls from customers and processes transactions. A **customer service group** provides technical problem-solving assistance over the telephone, by fax, or via the Internet.

Determine the Number of Value Merchants Needed

Managers routinely use one of two methods for estimating necessary sales force size. In the **breakdown method**, they begin by forecasting total annual sales in monetary units in the market. Then managers assess how much sales a single salesperson can generate annually acting alone or as part of a team. To determine how many representatives are needed, managers simply divide the annual sales forecast by the sales a single representative can generate.

Realizing that accounts frequently require different levels of service, that all geographic areas do not contain an equal number of prospects, and that salespersons have unique capabilities, progressive companies turn to the workload approach. With the **workload approach**, business market managers estimate the total efforts that sales personnel must undertake to serve the entire marketplace. They measure total efforts as a function of such things as number of accounts, calls needed per account in a given time period, the amount of time spent per call with each account, and the geographic distance to be covered. Managers then divide this estimate by the total amount of work a single salesperson can handle.

Designate Areas of Responsibility

Next, business market managers develop areas of responsibility or portfolios of accounts for sales representatives to manage. Their goal is to allocate accounts equitably in terms of sales potential and amount of work. By doing so, managers boost sales force morale, minimize disputes over fairness, and simplify the performance evaluation process. The nature of these portfolios or areas of responsibility varies by type of sales force. For example, in a strategic account program, the business market manager identifies all key accounts. Then, the manager assigns each key account to a separate strategic account team.

With a transactional sales force, managers design geographic territories. To do so, they first select the most appropriate geographic control unit. Among the units widely used are states or provinces, counties, trading areas, cities or metropolitan areas, and postal code zones. Then they estimate potential sales, number of accounts, and dispersion of accounts within potential territories. At this stage, managers perform a workload analysis and delineate tentative territories. More sophisticated firms utilize one of many sales force planning models that are currently available on interactive computer software. Two of the most popular of these models are CALLPLAN and MAPS. After reviewing the tentative territories and making modifications, managers formally map sales territories.[33]

Assign Value Merchants to Areas of Responsibility

Finally, the business market manager determines which value merchant or sales team should be assigned to each designated area of responsibility. Managers use their familiarity with each value merchant's capabilities, personality, and preferences to match each salesperson to an area of responsibility that is most likely to be productive. Customer feedback and preferences should also play a significant part in these assignment decisions.

Designing a Logistics System That Creates Value

According to Fuller, O'Connor, and Rawlinson, logistics systems represent a vast untapped arena for creating customer value. Although 10 percent of the typical manufacturing firm's operating costs are related to logistics few firms have applied the rigorous tools of total quality management and business process engineering to them. As customer firms increasingly consider acceptable quality and competitive price as "table stakes" in doing business, suppliers must create value and competitive advantage in the form of logistics-related services that provide customers with convenience, reliability, and support.[34]

In response, companies are implementing integrated logistics systems. **Integrated logistics systems** (ILS) entail the interfirm and cross-functional planning, implementation, and control of the flow and storage of raw materials, in-process inventories, finished goods, and related information from supplier firms to customer firms. They encompass three management activities: materials management, material flow systems, and physical distribution. ILS systems are closely linked to the firm's information technology (IT) systems. Often, third-party suppliers design and manage these ILS systems. Notable among these suppliers are FedEx Logistics Services, Roadway Express, CSL Logistics, USCO Logistics, GATX, and Caterpillar Logistics Services.[35]

When designing an ILS system, business market managers conduct the following tasks:

- Segment the market into logistically distinct businesses.
- Establish differential service standards for each market segment.

- Tailor unique logistics systems to deliver differential services.
- Exploit economies of scale among the different logistics systems.

Segment the Market into Logistically Distinct Businesses

As with other business market management tasks, senior managers charter a cross-functional team to design the ILS system. The team's first task is to group customers into segments that operations experts call logistically distinct businesses. A **logistically distinct business** (LDB) is a set of customers that have unique physical distribution service requirements. A supplier firm must build a separate logistics system and strategic business unit to serve each. In business markets, common LBDs include systems contracts, maintenance, repair, and operating supplies (MRO) replenishment, emergency orders, special orders for customized offerings, bulk shipments to stock, and items that have special handling requirements. These aspects correspond to the supply management models that we discussed in Chapter 3.[36]

Establish Differential Service Standards for Each Market Segment

For each LDB, the team specifies the firm's service standards. For example, in the case of systems orders, the team determines which product bundles to provide to each customer, which suppliers will provide complementary items or services, when and where to deliver products, and how to enter products into the customer's inventory system. When planning for emergency orders, the team identifies which items are highly critical to customers, how much inventory of each critical item to hold in reserve for crises, and how to provide immediate delivery. For special-handling situations, the team evaluates such things as packaging alternatives, transportation mode options, environmental control systems, and delivery procedures.

Tailor Unique Logistics Systems to Deliver Differential Services

The cross-functional team designs a logistics system for each LDB that creates superior value by meeting or exceeding service standards. Each system entails order receipt and processing, warehousing, materials handling, transportation, and control and tracking. When deciding on each component of a logistics system, the team considers the value each element creates for customers and its cost. They may decide to outsource some or all of the system elements.

Exploit Economies of Scale Among the Different Logistics Systems

Before implementing a separate logistics system for each LDB, team members determine whether they can achieve any cost economies by consolidating two or more of the proposed systems. For example, it may be possible for the firm to combine systems that deliver emergency orders, special orders for customized products, and items that have special handling requirements. Alternatively, the supplier may employ a single logistics system to handle systems contracts and MRO replenishment. When making the decision to consolidate LDBs, the team must trade off reductions in costs with lower service levels. Here, knowledge of the value that customers place on each service is essential.

STRENGTHENING RESELLER PERFORMANCE

An essential ingredient for executing an indirect channel network is a comprehensive program of reseller support. We contend that such an approach should be based on a simple concept—that the best way to ensure resellers deliver superior value to customers is for the supplier to create superior value for resellers. Channel positioning is a way to do so.[37]

Drawing on the bedrock marketing principles of segmentation, targeting, and positioning, we define **channel positioning** as the process of establishing and sustaining the supplier's reputation among targeted resellers for providing superior value. Several prerequisites and building blocks of channel positioning need to be addressed. Suppliers need to consider the reseller as a partner and to develop a working relationship that builds mutual self interest. With significant mutual self interest, both the supplier and the reseller recognize the importance of each other's contribution, and coordinate efforts to better satisfy the requirements of customers.[38]

The supplier must conceive a potent **reseller value proposition** and provide it through a distinctive bundle of core products, capability-building programs, and incentives that we refer to as the **channel offering**. The channel offering not only compensates resellers in part for their efforts, but also encourages them to contribute augmenting services to the market offering that they provide to customers. Then the supplier must gain a reputation or **channel position** among resellers for delivering superior value.

Channel positioning involves four steps:

1. Determine reseller performance expectations.
2. Assess the reseller value of channel offering elements.
3. Craft a reseller value proposition and channel offering.
4. Communicate the reseller value proposition.

We begin our discussion of channel positioning by introducing the concept of marketplace equity, which prompts managers to think strategically about the contributions that they and their resellers are making to provide value to targeted market segments.

Build Marketplace Equity

Equity is a concept that captures the past, present, and future value a market offering provides to a customer. When a supplier reaches customers through resellers, business market managers need to further elaborate the equity concept, decomposing marketplace equity into its constituent components: brand, reseller, and channel equities. Cultivating and sustaining each of these equities are central tasks of channel management.[39]

Decompose Marketplace Equity
Marketplace equity represents the value that a customer firm receives from acquiring a particular supplier's product or service through a particular reseller in its local

trade area. Marketplace equity is a joint result of reseller equity and brand equity. **Reseller equity** is the value of acquiring a supplier's offering from a particular reseller versus other authorized resellers in the local trade area, whereas **brand equity** is the value of acquiring a particular supplier's offering versus other competing suppliers' offerings. **Channel equity** captures the value a reseller receives from the channel offering a supplier provides. Significantly, channel equity may consequently contribute to reseller equity. We conceptually depict this decomposition in Figure 7.4 .

The relative contributions of brand equity and reseller equity to marketplace equity determine not only the nature of the partnership between a supplier firm and its reseller but also respective profit margins. Economist Robert Steiner explains the linkage in terms of two cross-elasticities of demand that can be illustrated via a hypothetical, purchasing "moment of truth." At some point in time, a customer manager contacts a reseller firm with the intention of buying a branded product. When the manager asks the reseller salesperson for the item, the salesperson responds that the product is out of stock. The customer manager has two choices and Steiner represents each as a cross-elasticity of demand. In scenario 1, the customer manager remains steadfast in his or her desire to purchase the branded product and contacts other reseller firms until he or she can secure it. In scenario 2, the salesperson convinces the customer manager to purchase a competitor's comparable product that is in stock.[40]

Figure 7.4
Decomposing
Marketplace Equity

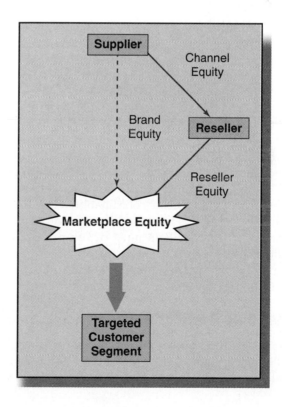

Brand equity is clearly superior to reseller equity in scenario 1. The supplier firm has a power advantage over resellers, directs overall marketing efforts, and takes the lion's share of profits the product generates. This scenario develops whenever the customer firm believes that the supplier provides the essential value through such things as innovation, product quality, and technical service. Conversely, reseller equity dominates brand equity in scenario 2 and the reseller has the advantage. This case arises when the customer firm believes that resellers furnish key value elements via such things as product availability, 24×7 delivery, and liberal credit policies. Of course, in a third scenario the customer managers believe that brand equity and reseller equity are equivalent. This is perhaps the preferred instance in that both firms recognize that they each significantly contribute to marketplace equity and must work together for mutual gain.

Cultivate Brand and Reseller Equity

Profound implications for both supplier and reseller managers arise in the management of marketplace equity. For supplier firms, we underscore the importance of developing and sustaining strong brand equity among targeted customers. Yet, too often supplier firms treat resellers as the "final customer," lose track of actual customers and their applications, and neglect to cultivate brand equity. For example, a supplier of recessed lighting that sells its products through mass merchants, such as Home Depot or Lowe's, should not focus its equity building efforts solely on the mass merchant. Instead, it should continue to reinforce brand equity with small electrical contractor customers through marketing communications and support services, such as a toll-free, installer assistance line that is staffed 18-hours a day, 7 days a week. Building equity with the customer is essential to create the "pull" necessary to avoid having mass merchants regard the supplier's products as "commodities."

Simultaneously, reseller firms must strive to keep their equity strong by customizing the mix of products and services that they offer to customer firms, by improving the quality of customer services such as on-time delivery, routine maintenance, and credit, and by aggressively promoting their firms to customers. For the reseller, building equity with the customers ensures long-term loyalty, yields continuous opportunities to cross-sell other products and services, and enables the firm to avoid intense price competition.

As supplier and reseller firms face significant "streams of competition," they must work together to build superior marketplace equity. Two channel management tasks ensure a high level of coordination. First, firms must select their partners wisely. Ideally, the supplier's brand equity should complement the partner's reseller equity. Second, the supplier firm must develop significant channel equity by providing resellers with superior value in the form of a channel offering. Such an offering must not only bolster any weaknesses in the reseller's customer-serving capabilities, but also encourage the reseller to enthusiastically promote the supplier's product lines.

Determine Reseller Performance Expectations

Channel positioning begins as supplier managers determine their expectations of reseller performance. Following candid discussions with resellers, supplier managers should summarize the supplier's expectations, taking into account both marketplace realities and the supplier's objectives. Suppliers that intend to target several market segments and to reach them through separate channels should develop expectations for each type of reseller they authorize. Managers formalize these expectations in oral or written sales agreements, policy statements, and annual objectives or quotas. They should communicate these expectations and explain specific points to all authorized resellers through personal contacts and correspondence.

It is essential that managers explicitly state expectations in terms of desired levels of market penetration, market offering augmentation, and management professionalism so they can design appropriate support programs. Suppliers state market penetration objectives in terms of territory sales to targeted market segments, market share, new accounts developed, sales calls made on potential customers, and changes from last year's sales levels. On the other hand, to ensure that market-offering augmentation is done properly, suppliers may require resellers to provide such things as facilities and personnel, technical and marketing expertise, and repair and service work. Finally, managers define reseller professionalism in terms of such things as the extent of strategic planning, financial management, operations management, and succession planning.

Assess the Reseller Value of Channel Offering Elements

As Figure 7.5 shows, channel offerings have three major components: channel core elements, capability-building programs, and incentive programs. **Channel core elements** are those basics that resellers must have from all their suppliers, such as adequate financial returns and strong brand equity for the supplier's line within the reseller's home country. **Capability-building programs** enable resellers to strengthen their own performance and to enhance the value they provide to customers. Examples are training programs, information-sharing systems, and collaborative policies. Given that competing suppliers often offer similar core elements, we find that capabilities programs represent the most potent, strategic means of differentiating a supplier's offerings. **Incentive programs** motivate short-term improvements in reseller and salesperson performance. These programs commonly entail bonuses for the supplier's salespeople, growth rebates for the reseller firm, and contests for reseller sales forces.

To gather input for the channel positioning process, supplier managers assess the reseller value of channel offering elements and construct a channel positioning matrix. In Chapter 2, we described a variety of techniques that business market managers can use to assess value. We urge managers to use a variety of qualitative and quantitative techniques to first gain a general understanding of reseller requirements and then to identify those handful of channel offering elements that create the greatest value. During the process, business market managers must be mindful of what elements competitors are providing resellers.

Construct a Channel Positioning Matrix

A **channel positioning matrix** refers to a detailed comparative analysis of what a supplier provides to its resellers, what its competitors provide, and what its resellers' requirements are. Business market managers should construct a separate channel positioning matrix for each type of authorized reseller. We present a channel positioning

Figure 7.5 The Channel Offering

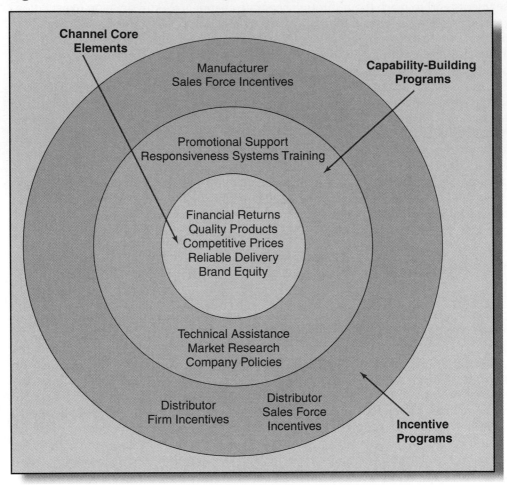

Source: James A. Narus and James C. Anderson, "Strengthen Distributor Performance Through Channel Positioning," *Sloan Management Review* (Winter 1988): 33.

matrix in Figure 7.6. As we see in the figure, managers begin by listing in the left-hand column the key elements of channel offerings common to the industry. In a second column, managers summarize the elements of the channel offering that resellers require. Next, they describe the supplier's current channel position and offering in the third column. Lastly, managers state the positions and offerings of relevant competitors in additional columns.

Some suppliers find it useful to add a column in which they construct a **best practice composite**. For each element, they list the supplier firm that provides the best program or system. It may be the supplier firm, one of its direct competitors, or a firm that markets a complementary line to the same resellers. Because it is unlikely that one firm will be the best at all elements, what results is a composite of the best practices of a number of competing suppliers. The logic for constructing a best practice composite is that resellers' experiences with all their suppliers shape their expectations of each

Figure 7.6 The Channel Positioning Matrix

	Distributors' Requirements	MicroChem Offering	CLT Equipment Offering
Channel Position	Not Applicable	Low Price Leader	Computer Networking Leader
Core Elements			
Functional Discount	32% off suggested resale price	32%	32%
Payment Discount	2/10/net 30	2/15/net 60	None/net 45
Quality Discount	3% on orders of 50–100 units	4% on orders of 50–100 units	3% on orders of 50–100 units
	5% on orders of 100+ units	7% on orders of 100+ units	5% on orders of 100+ units
Quality Measured in Life Cycle Costs*	$225	$250	$225
Suggested Resale Price Per Unit	$35	$25	$35
Completeness of Product Line (# of complementary products)	7 out of 12 items	6 out of 12 items	7 out of 12 items
Reliability of Delivery	90% of orders filled in one week	85% of orders filled in one week	95% of orders filled in one week
National Reputation Development	$1 million in annual national televising	$750,000 in annual national televising	$1.25 million in annual national televising
Capability-Building Programs			
Promotional Support	Product literature and catalogues	Product literature and catalogues	Product literature and catalogues
Responsiveness Systems	None	None	Computerized order entry expert systems
Training	One-week sales course	One-day sales course	One-week sales course plus videotapes
			Three-day course on computer systems
Technical Assistance	5–10 tech reps	2 tech reps	10 tech reps
			Portable problem-solving computers
Company Policies Distribution Selectivity	120 distributors for United States; few per trade area	250 distributors for United States; many per trade area	131 distributors for United States; few per trade area
Return Policies	10% of annual purchases	5% of purchases	10% of purchases
Incentive Programs			
Manufacturer's Sales Force Programs	Commission on sales to distributors	Commission on sales to distributors	Bonus on sales over quota to distributors
Distributor-Firms Programs	Rebates on purchases made prior to peak sales periods	Rebates	Rebates
			Price reductions in orders placed by computer
Distributor's Sales Force Programs	Spiffs Annual sales contests	Spiffs	Spiffs
			Monthly contest based on sales and computer utilization
			Blazers awarded to best salesperson of the year

*Life cycle cost refers to the total costs of using a product or service over its productive lifetime.

Source: Adapted from "Strengthening Distributor Performance Through Channel Positioning," James A. Narus and James C. Anderson, *Sloan Management Review* (Winter 1988): 38, by permission of publisher. Copyright © 1988 by Sloan Management Review Association. All rights reserved.

supplier's performance. Simply being the best within the set of direct competitors may not be enough. Business market managers can benchmark the best practices of noncompeting firms that market complementary lines. In exchange, managers allow these noncompeting firms to benchmark their own firm's best practices.

The results of the channel positioning matrix analysis suggest changes for the supplier to pursue that will contribute most to a reseller value proposition. Managers might decide to bolster competitive strengths, where the supplier already does a superior job in furnishing the offering elements that resellers value. They most often pursue unfulfilled requirements—where the reseller values an offering element, yet no one in the industry comes close to delivery of an acceptable version—as the source of a distinctive, reseller value proposition. The supplier might close other gaps as a matter of "defensive" channel positioning. Importantly, they also prune support programs that resellers do not value. The supplier might pass on cost savings from such program terminations to resellers in the form of discounts or rebates. Given the intense competition in most industries today, managers are likely to find only a handful of gaps. However, managers should remember that they can establish a potent reseller value proposition with only a few points of difference.

Craft a Reseller Value Proposition and Channel Offering

Based on the value assessment and channel positioning matrix, business market managers devise a reseller value proposition using the process that we described in Chapter 4. Ideally, the reseller value proposition should reinforce the envisioned customer value proposition. Suppliers that serve several market segments through different types of resellers may at this point choose to develop a distinct value proposition for each type of reseller. If so, managers should strive to create an umbrella value proposition position by establishing some common elements across all the propositions. The reseller value proposition outlined in each statement should be observable, distinctive, and communicable to resellers. Supplier managers must now reformulate their channel offering to bolster the reseller value proposition.

Devise and Pretest the Channel Offering

To reformulate a channel offering, business market managers identify key elements and determine the level that the firm is prepared to offer. Obviously, a reseller is likely to give extra effort toward the promotion of a line that brings it outstanding profits. When an industry is highly competitive in terms of core elements offered to resellers, capability-building programs are likely to be the most useful. As an example, companies such as DuPont and Parker-Hannifin have long relied on technical training programs and market research to provide their resellers with the specialized skills and sales leads necessary to take advantage of emerging market segments.[41] In Box 7.9, we present an example of how a supplier, Bruce Foods Corporation, used capability-building programs to improve reseller performance in Europe.

Incentive programs are least likely to result in a long-term value proposition because competitors can readily copy them. Managers should only consider them after they have completed the other two sections of the offering, and should use incentives sparingly to reinforce the more long-lasting changes they seek in the capability-building programs. Research suggests that of the three types of incentives, those

BOX 7.9
Bruce Foods Coaches European Distributors on How to Prepare Tacos

One of the challenges that managers at Bruce Foods Corporation (BFC) faced in their initial efforts at penetrating the European specialty foods market with their Casa Fiesta® line of Mexican foods was coaxing Europeans to try Mexican foods. Prior to the mid-1980s, most Europeans had limited knowledge of Mexico and its cuisine. Moreover, Western Europeans traditionally disliked spicy foods and preferred not to eat foods directly with their hands. BFC management concluded that in-store product tastings and cooking demonstrations would have to be a central component of their awareness- and interest-building efforts. Unfortunately, few specialty foods distributors and their retail counterparts knew how to prepare simple Mexican dishes, such as tacos.

To remedy the problem, BFC managers developed a two-day course on how to prepare Mexican food. They crisscrossed Europe, presenting the seminar for Casa Fiesta distributor sales representatives. BFC awarded each sales rep who successfully completed the course a "Master in Mexican Cooking" certificate. Reportedly, many reps proudly display the certificates in their offices to this day.

With distributor sales reps and retailers up to speed on Mexican food preparation, BFC began to develop recipes and cookbooks that could be distributed during in-store demonstrations. Although these cookbooks could be given out as premiums for free with the product in some countries, in other countries, such as Germany, BFC had to unbundle and sell the cookbooks for a nominal fee. BFC managers quickly learned to tailor their cookbooks and recipes to European tastes. Even though they often do eat ground beef or pork, Europeans generally prefer lighter versions of most Mexican dishes, which have more fresh ingredients and are lower in fat. So, BFC offered standard, easy-to-prepare recipes, but gave consumers the choice of substituting local ingredients, such as Parma ham in Italy and more fish in Scandinavian countries, to address differing European palates. Only when BFC had trained distributors and retailers on Mexican food preparation and developed localized recipes and cookbooks were they able to successfully sponsor demonstrations and taste tests. To further support Casa Fiesta distributors in the early days, BFC managers also engaged in public relations to promote the Casa Fiesta brand and the Mexican food category, gaining coverage in newspapers and magazines.

Today, many Europeans from Portugal to Lithuania are familiar with Mexican food, and the category is one of the fastest-growing ethnic cuisines in Europe.

directed toward the reseller firm are preferable to those targeted at reseller employees, mostly because reseller managers want to direct the activities and efforts of their own employees.

Having assembled a tentative channel offering, supplier managers should review and pretest it to be certain that it will be effective. One way to accomplish these tasks is to formally present the offering at the firm's reseller council meeting and solicit evaluations and suggested improvements. We discuss reseller advisory councils fully in Chapter 9.

Improve Reseller Target-Marketing Efforts via Tailored Channel Offerings

By carefully crafting channel offerings, supplier managers can significantly improve resellers' target marketing efforts, while reducing the likelihood of interchannel conflict. Consider the example of a manufacturer of three lines of power saws. The first is a basic line of saws that a supplier targets at small and gypsy contractors for use in home repairs and remodeling. The supplier markets the line through home improvement centers like Home Depot, Lowe's, and Builders' Square largely on the basis of competitive price. To ensure the performance of the home improvement centers, the supplier developed a channel offering featuring generous functional discounts that enable resellers to keep prices competitive, minimal stock-keeping units (SKUs) to reduce the resellers' inventory commitments, and instructive and eye-catching packaging that allows the product to sell itself.

The supplier sells a second line of professional saws that they target at larger contractors that specialize in building housing developments. They market the line through contractor supplies distributors. In this market segment, contractor customers require a broad line of professional saws and supplies for highly specialized applications. To support distributors, the firm created a wide range of SKUs, substantial quantity discounts that can be passed along to contractors that purchase a large number of saws annually, and cooperative advertising funds that can be used only in trade journals targeted at home builders.

For large-scale contractors that build offices and commercial buildings, the supplier markets a line of top-end saws that cut concrete and steel girders. They sell these saws exclusively through specialty cutting-tool distributors. Compared to the first two categories of resellers that make their profits primarily from the sale of products, these specialty distributors emphasize value-added services. Such services include construction-site layout design, materials processing systems planning, and recommendations on proper tool usage. For this reason, the supplier's channel offering among specialty cutting-tool distributors revolves around its distributor capability-building services. Thus, it provides a range of highly technical training programs for resellers' service engineers, joint sales calls and design assistance for key contractor customers, and a technical center staffed with engineers who can promptly answer a reseller's most difficult applications questions.

Communicate the Reseller Value Proposition

To secure the desired channel position, the supplier firm actively communicates the value proposition to resellers relying upon the full range of promotional tools available and appropriate to the industry. To sustain each value proposition, the supplier must deliver what it has promised. In addition, business market managers should reinforce the value proposition at every opportunity. Given that many of the most distinctive aspects of a channel offering are eventually duplicated by competitors, managers must constantly monitor the marketplace. They should record any competitive moves as adjustments to the channel positioning matrix. To track channel perceptions, managers should conduct reseller satisfaction studies at least annually. In Box 7.10, we present a disguised example of the process of channel positioning.

BOX 7.10
An Example of Channel Positioning

Chemparts, Inc. (a disguised name), manufactures a line of specialty repair parts for equipment used in one segment of the chemical process industry. The firm has an established marketplace position of technical excellence in the production of top-quality parts for use in highly acidic or caustic applications. The firm sells the lines exclusively to industrial distributors for resale.

Although Chemparts' line had distinct quality advantages, distributors' selling efforts were limited because the products required a difficult, technical sales approach. Distributors found it easier to sell less-complicated, better-known lines on price than to initiate discussions of value-in-use. For years, the firm made halfhearted efforts to improve distributor performance, relying on incentive programs. Results were mixed at best.

Then Chemparts' managers decided to take a strategic approach using channel positioning. Because the firm sold only to one segment, managers decided to establish one channel position and to provide a single channel offering to industrial distributors. The firm began the formal process by summarizing its expectations of distributors. These included selective penetration of its target market and augmentation of the products with technical design and problem-solving assistance. The firm also sought increased distributor professionalism in technical selling and marketing.

Second, Chemparts' managers reviewed reseller requirements of a channel offering. Using market research and sales force intelligence, the firm identified the channel offering elements of its two key rivals, MicroChem and CLT Equipment (also disguised names). They quickly discovered that their functional discount did not correspond to the required level of distributor competence and effort. Technical assistance and national advertising were also deficient. We summarize this information in Figure 7.6.

Managers identified gaps in the offerings and contrasted these with Chemparts' capabilities and reseller requirements. They decided that a value proposition could be built around technical support leadership: both end-users and distributors placed a high value on technical assistance; the position had been ignored by competitors; and the firm had strong technical capabilities. Chemparts' marketing managers wrote this value proposition: "Let Chemparts' unsurpassed technical support help make your firm the one customers call when they need critical design work and emergency service!"

Third, Chemparts' managers reformulated the channel offering, listing elements needed to meet distributor requirements and establish a technical support leadership position. They improved quality, including completeness of product line and new product development. Chemparts created technical design, selling, and technical-service training programs. They hired more technical reps and problem-solving specialists. The firm offered sales leads, market research, and joint sales call assistance. Managers pruned unnecessary incentive programs. We outline their revised channel offering in Figure 7.7.

Fourth, Chemparts communicated its value proposition to distributors through a series of advertisements in two leading distributor publications. Managers gave a presentation of the position at the annual distributor sales meeting. Chemparts' distributor-marketing manager made calls on each distributor. Also, Chemparts presented a policy manual in which the value proposition was articulated to all distributors.

As a result of its channel positioning efforts, Chemparts simplified and gained control of its distributor programs, created a reputation among distributors as the industry's technical support leader, improved distributor technical selling and assistance capabilities, and most important, strengthened the firm's presence in the final-customer marketplace. For three years following implementation, Chemparts' sales of the line grew at a rate significantly higher than that of its principal competitors, MicroChem and CLT Equipment.

(continued)

BOX 7.10
Continued

Figure 7.7 Revised Channel Offering for Chemparts, Inc.

Channel Position	Technical Support Leader
Core Elements	
Functional Discount	33% off suggested resale price
Payment Discount	2/10/net 30
Quantity Discount	3% on orders of 50–100 units
	5% on orders of 100+ units
Quality Measured in Life Cycle Costs*	$285
Suggested Resale Price Per Unit	$45
Completeness of Product Line (number of complementary products)	12 out of 12 items
Reliability of Delivery	95% of orders filled in one week
National Reputation Development	$1 million on national televising
Capability-Building Programs	
Promotional Support	Product literature and catalogues
	Sales leads and market research
	Demonstration kits
	Joint sales calls
Responsiveness Systems	800 for customer problem solving
	Well-trained order center personnel
Training	One-week technical sales course
	Three-day product applications course
	One-week technical design course
Company Policies	
Distribution Selectivity	80 distributors for the U.S.; exclusive trade areas
Return Policies	10% of annual purchases
	All defective parts
	All discontinued parts
Incentive Programs	
Manufacturer Sales Force Programs	Bonus paid on distributor sales to final customers
	Bonus for new customers developed with distributors
Distributor Firm Programs	Award given to top 10% of distributors for annual sales
Distributor Sales Force Programs	None

*Life cycle cost refers to the total costs of using a product or service over is productive lifetime.

Source: Adapted from "Strengthening Distributor Performance Through Channel Positioning," James A. Narus and James C. Anderson, *Sloan Management Review* (Winter 1988): 39; by permission of publisher. Copyright © 1988 by Sloan Management Review Association. All rights reserved.

SUMMARY

Progressive business market managers consider the marketing channel a network or web of capabilities embedded in an extended enterprise. As part of an extended enterprise, channel members selectively draw upon the capabilities of their partner firms to perform vital business processes and functions that fulfill customer requirements. Working together in this manner, the supplier, resellers, and third-party service providers create and share value far in excess of what they could acting alone.

Business channel management is the process of designing a set of marketing and distribution arrangements that fulfill the requirements and preferences of targeted segments and customers, and executing those arrangements either directly through supplier firm sales forces and logistics systems or indirectly through resellers and third-party service providers. To design superior value-adding channels, business market managers conduct a thorough customer value assessment and envision a superior value proposition. Using sourcing procedures, they reformulate their market offerings drawing upon supplier firm capabilities while leveraging the strengths of potential channel partners. Rather than just selecting from conventional direct and reseller channels, managers combine elements of the supplier firm's direct sales force, traditional resellers, innovative online formats, and third-party service providers, into more dynamic and flexible networks.

When a supplier firm chooses to serve the marketplace directly, it must furnish many of the capabilities, resources, and functions that reseller firms normally provide. To ensure that the direct channel creates the intended value, the supplier must build a sales force of value merchants. A value merchant recognizes the costs and value associated with each element of a market offering and seeks an equitable return for both the supplier firm and customer firm. To cultivate value merchants, suppliers must offer training programs, provide value-based sales tools, and construct compensation systems that reward personnel for providing value to customers. Once value merchants have been trained, suppliers deploy them to maximize profits. To physically deliver products or services to customers, supplier firms must construct an appropriate integrated logistics system with order entry and processing procedures, inventory management programs, warehouses, and delivery vehicles.

Suppliers turn to channel positioning to ensure that resellers will enthusiastically market their products and services. The approach calls for managers to identify a distinctive reseller value proposition and to devise a channel offering comprised of core elements, capability-building programs, and incentive programs. That offering provides resellers with the tools and incentives necessary to deliver complementary value to customers. Suppliers promote the reseller value proposition via advertising, sales presentations, and communications to the trade. When managers' efforts are successful, the supplier's brand equity combines with reseller equity to create competitive advantage in the form of marketplace equity. Marketplace equity represents the value that a customer firm receives from acquiring a particular supplier's product or service through a particular reseller in its local trade area.

1. For the sake of simplicity and consistency, we define key marketing channel members as follows. A *supplier firm* produces the core product or service of a marketplace offering. A *reseller firm* takes the core product or service, adds value to it with augmenting products and services, and then markets the enhanced offering. We see *reseller* as less confusing than terms such as *intermediary, middleman, distributor, wholesaler,* and *dealer,* which often have industry-specific meanings and usage. A *third-party service provider,* such as a trucking firm, public warehouse, or information system vendor, furnishes additional augmenting services on a fee basis to suppliers and resellers. Finally, a *customer firm* acquires a market offering from a supplier or reseller for the customer's own use, or for inclusion into the products or services it produces.

2. Anne T. Coughlin, Erin Anderson, Louis W. Stern, and Adel I. El-Ansary, *Marketing Channels,* 6th ed. (Upper Saddle River, NJ: Prentice Hall, 2001), 3.

3. In an *indirect channel,* the supplier firm employs reseller firms to market its products and services to customer firms. In a *direct channel,* the supplier firm markets those products and services to customer firms.

4. Louis W. Stern and Frederick D. Sturdivant, "Customer-Driven Distribution Systems," *Harvard Business Review* (July–August 1987): 34–41; and Louis W. Stern, Frederick D. Sturdivant, and Gary A. Getz, "Accomplishing Marketing Channel Change: Paths and Pitfalls," *European Management Journal* (March 1993): 1–8.

5. Michael Hammer and James Champy, *Reengineering the Corporation* (New York: HarperBusiness, 1993); and Bert Rosenbloom, *Marketing Functions* (Washington, DC: The Distribution Research & Education Foundation, 1987).

6. Bruce Mallen, *Principles of Marketing Channel Management* (Lexington, MA: Lexington Books, 1977).

7. Nakato Hirakubo, *An Analysis of the Japanese Market: Consumer, Distribution System, and Market Structure* (New York: Center for Applied Research, Pace University, 1992).

8. James P. Womack and Daniel T. Jones, "From Lean Production to the Lean Enterprise," *Harvard Business Review* (March–April 1994): 93–105.

9. Louis P. Bucklin, "Postponement, Speculation, and the Structure of Distribution Channels," *Journal of Marketing Research* (February 1965): 26–31.

10. Philip B. Schary and Tage Skjøtt-Larsen, *Managing the Global Supply Chain* (Copenhagen: Copenhagen Business School, 2001): 69.

11. Coughlin, Anderson, Stern, and El-Ansari, *Marketing Channels,* 16.

12. Modular channels are also referred to as *deconstructed channels, virtual channels, demand networks, value-engineered channels,* and *networked channels.*

13. Charles C. Snow, Raymond E. Miles, and Henry J. Coleman, Jr., "Managing 21st Century Network Organizations," *Organizational Dynamics* (Winter 1992): 5–19.

14. Lawrence G. Friedman and Timothy R. Furey, *The Channel Advantage* (Oxford, UK: Butterworth-Heinemann, 1999).

15. *Monsanto Corporation Annual Report 2001* (St. Louis, MO: Monsanto Corporation, 2002).

16. Frank V. Cespedes and E. Raymond Corey, "Managing Multiple Channels," *Business Horizons* (July–August 1990): 67–77; and R.T. Moriarty and Ursula Moran, "Managing Hybrid Marketing Systems," *Harvard Business Review* (November–December 1990): 146–157.

17. A *trade area* is the geographic area within which firms operate. Firms commonly specify their trade area as a function of the size of potential business and logistics or other resource constraints.

18. Philip Kotler, *Kotler on Marketing* (New York: The Free Press, 1999).

19. Coughlin, Anderson, Stern, and El-Ansary, *Marketing Channels;* and Gary L. Frazier and Walfried M. Lassar, "Determinants of

20. Distribution Intensity," *Journal of Marketing* (October 1996): 39–51.

20. "McKinsey Study Backs Cost-to-Serve Wholesale Model," *CM/Circulation Management* [Internet] (Overland Park, KS: PRIMEDIA Business Magazines Media Inc., cited January 2002), available at *http://www. circman.com.*

21. Arthur Andersen & Co., *Facing the Forces of Change 2000* (Washington, DC: Distribution Research & Education Foundation, 1992).

22. Kevin L. Webb, "Managing Channels of Distribution in the Age of Electronic Commerce," *Industrial Marketing Management* (April 2002): 95–102.

23. E-business definitions in this section are adopted from Steven Kaplan and Mohanbir Sawhney, "B2B Marketplaces," *Harvard Business Review* (May–June 2000): 97–103; Mohanbir Sawhney and Steven Kaplan, "Let's Get Vertical," *Business 2.0* (September 1999): 1–7; and Mohanbir Sawhney, "Making New Markets," *Business 2.0* (May 1999): 1–5.

24. Friedman and Furey, *The Channel Advantage.*

25. Eric Young, "Web Marketplaces that Really Work," *Fortune* (Winter 2002): 78–84.

26. Ravi Kalakota and Marcia Robinson, *M-Business: The Race to Mobility* (New York: McGraw-Hill, 2002).

27. David Arnold, "Seven Rules of International Distribution," *Harvard Business Review* (November–December 2000): 131–138.

28. International channel definitions adapted from Subhash C. Jain, *International Marketing*, 6th ed. (Cincinnati, OH: South-Western College Publishing, 2000); and Coughlin, Anderson, Stern, and El-Ansari, *Marketing Channels.*

29. Jack G. Kaikati, "Don't Crack the Japanese Distribution System—Just Circumvent It," *Columbia Journal of World Business* (Summer 1993): 34–45.

30. Robert S. Kaplan and David P. Norton, "Putting the Balanced Scorecard to Work," *Harvard Business Review* (September–October 1993): 134–149.

31. This discussion is based on Gilbert A. Churchill, Jr., Neil M. Ford, Orville C. Walker, Jr., Mark Johnston, and Greg Marshall, *Sales Force Management with Excel Spreadsheets*, 7th ed. (New York: McGraw-Hill/Irwin, 2003); and Andris A. Zoltners,

Prabhakant Sinha and Greggor A. Zoltners, *The Complete Guide to Accelerating Sales Force Performance* (New York: AMACOM, 2001).

32. Benson P. Shapiro, "Close Encounters of the Four Kinds: Managing Customers in a Rapidly Changing Environment," *HBS Note 9-589-015* (Boston, MA: Harvard Business School, 1988).

33. R. S. Howick and M. Pidd, "Sales Force Development Models," *European Journal of Operations Research* (October 1990): 295–310; Leonard M. Lodish, "CALLPLAN: An Interactive Salesman's Call Planning System," *Management Science* (December 1971): 25–40; and Zoltners, Sinha, and Zoltners, *The Complete Guide to Accelerating Sales Force Performance.*

34. This section draws on Joseph B. Fuller, James O'Connor, and Richard Rawlinson, "Tailored Logistics: The Next Advantage," *Harvard Business Review* (May–June 1993): 87–98; and Donald J. Bowersox, "The Strategic Benefits of Logistics Alliances," *Harvard Business Review* (July–August 1990): 36–45.

35. Bob Deirlein, "Fleet Speak," *Beverage World* (March 1997): 106–110; and "Integrated Logistics: Journey to the Ultimate Customer," *Materials Handling Engineering* (March 1996): 63–66.

36. Fuller, O'Connor, and Rawlinson, "Tailored Logistics."

37. This sections draws heavily from James A. Narus and James C. Anderson, "Strengthen Distributor Performance Through Channel Positioning," *Sloan Management Review* (Winter 1988): 31–40.

38. James A. Narus and James C. Anderson, "Turn Your Industrial Distributors into Partners," *Harvard Business Review* (March–April 1986): 66–71.

39. Kevin Lane Keller, *Strategic Brand Management*, 2nd ed. (Upper Saddle River, NJ: Prentice Hall, 2002).

40. Robert L. Steiner, "The Inverse Association Between the Margins of Manufacturers and Retailers," *Review of Industrial Organizations*, 8 (1993): 717–740.

41. Rajagopalan Sethuraman, James C. Anderson, and James A. Narus, "Partnership Advantage and Its Determinants in Manufacturer and Distributor Working Relationships," *Journal of Business Research* (December 1988): 327–347.

Section IV

Delivering Value

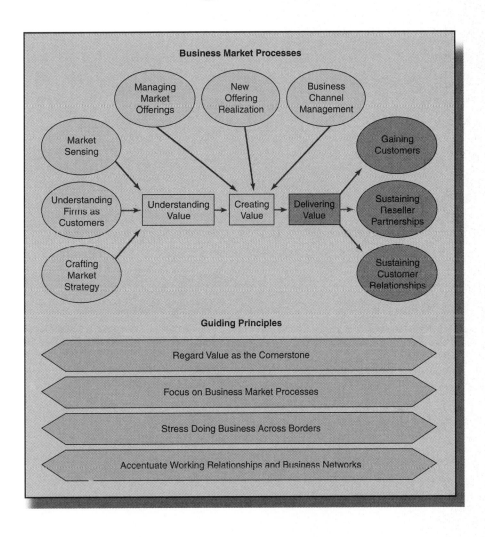

Chapter 8

Gaining Customers

OVERVIEW

*A*ccording to Professor Philip Kotler, "Marketing is the science and art of finding, keeping, and growing profitable customers."[1] In the final chapters of this book, we address these tasks through three related business market processes. Gaining customers focuses on finding and delivering value initially to new customers, whereas sustaining customer relationships concentrates on keeping and growing profitable customers. Sustaining reseller partnerships examines all three activities when a firm chooses to deliver value indirectly to customers through a channel network of resellers and third party service providers.

Gaining customers is the process of prospecting for new business relationships, assessing the mutual fit between prospective customer requirements and supplier offerings and priorities, making the initial sale, and fulfilling the initial order to the customer's complete satisfaction. We depict this business market process in Figure 8.1. Leading business market managers view gaining customers as a winnowing process in which a supplier firm begins with a large pool of potential customers, sequentially eliminates candidates where opportunities to deliver and share value are poor, and finishes with a significant number of profitable new customers.

In the first section of this chapter we explore methods of prospecting for new customers. We argue that business market managers must coordinate two distinct but related prospecting activities: generating leads via databases and prompting inquiries

Figure 8.1 Gaining Customers

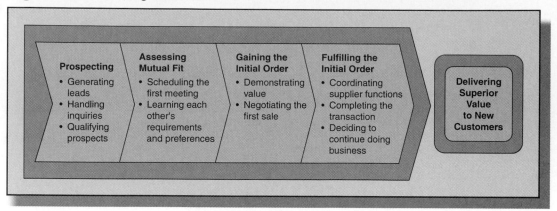

via integrated marketing communications. Further, we stress that suppliers must follow up and qualify leads and inquiries as viable prospects. In the second section, we discuss how supplier and prospective customer firms use early meetings to learn about each other's requirements and preferences, and to determine whether a match exists between their respective strategic goals. We urge business market managers to focus their efforts on prospects where mutual fit exists and have the discipline not to dilute their limited resources pursuing potential business that does not accomplish the firm's strategic ends.

In the third section, "Gaining the Initial Order," we discuss selling techniques. Through them, a sales representative tailors the value proposition and presentation style to unique prospect requirements and preferences. Moreover, the salesperson competently demonstrates the value of the offering and negotiates an equitable transaction with the customer firm. In the next section of the chapter, we strongly assert that progressive supplier firms must be concerned with fulfilling the initial order. Thus, we examine how supplier firms can better coordinate functions to seamlessly fulfill initial orders and provide complete customer satisfaction. Finally, we consider a major decision the supplier firm must make—whether to continue doing business with a newly gained customer. Consistent with guiding principles of business market management, firms should cultivate long-term relationships with customers where the supplier stands to deliver and equitably share the greatest value.

PROSPECTING FOR NEW BUSINESS RELATIONSHIPS

For discussion purposes, we distinguish between three types of potential customers that supplier firms isolate while prospecting. **Leads** are names of possible clients that business market managers generate from computer databases. **Inquiries**, on the other hand, are customer-initiated business contacts with the supplier firm. **Prospects** are leads and inquiries that the supplier firm has qualified as having significant sales and profit potential. Thus, **prospecting** entails the related activities of internally generating leads from databases, prompting and gathering inquiries externally from the marketplace, and qualifying leads and inquiries as significant prospects. As we illustrate via the dashed lines in the prospecting "funnel" in Figure 8.2, these related prospecting activities serve as ever finer "screens" through which only the highest potential customer firms pass.[2]

Although all prospecting efforts encompass these three activities, their nature varies as a function of the total number of potential customers, how readily the supplier firm can enumerate them, the type of market offering sold, and the firm's overall strategic intent in gaining customers. For example, an electronics company that seeks to market an innovative weather-tracking device for commercial airplanes will not have to use a computer database system to generate the names of major aircraft manufacturers. In other markets, readily identifiable potential customers may not

Figure 8.2 The Prospecting Funnel

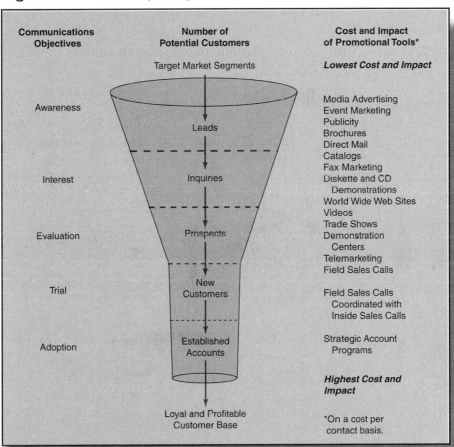

exist. The supplier firm will have to "create" customer firms before it can market offerings to them. As an example, Box 8.1 recounts how U.S.-based Bruce Foods Corporation developed the European commercial market for Mexican food products.

As for the supplier firm's strategic intent, we present four key options in the product market growth matrix in Figure 8.3. When **market penetration** is the primary goal, business market managers seek to increase the firm's share of business for an existing offering among current, former, and new customers within presently served markets. Alternatively, if **product development** is the objective, managers attempt to cross-sell a new product or service to current customers. On the other hand, if **market development** is the intent, they pursue new business for the firm's present offerings in previously untapped geographic territories or market segments. When pursuing **diversification**, business market managers enlarge the supplier firm's customer base, seeking new customers in unexplored markets for the new offerings. In each of these four instances, the business market manager's prospecting approach will differ slightly. In the coming sections, we discuss how generating leads, prompting inquiries, and training the sales force to pursue prospects differs under each of these strategic options. Finally, we point out another increasingly practiced approach to gaining new customers. Resource-rich companies can simply *acquire* competing firms that already serve customers in desirable market segments, territories, or nations.[3]

Generating Leads from Business Market Databases

Conceptually, the task of generating leads from databases is deceptively simple. As we discussed in Chapter 2, the business market manager first develops a profile of the key descriptors of firms or managers in each targeted market segment. Then, using a variety of statistical programs, the manager scans readily available databases and isolates company or manager names that closely match the target segment profile. As an example, consider A/E/C Systems International.

BOX 8.1

Bruce Foods Uses Marketing Channels to Develop the European Market for Mexican Food Products

Established in 1928, Bruce Foods Corporation (BFC) is one of the larger, privately owned food manufacturers in the United States. Among its most popular brands are "The Original" Louisiana Hot Sauce®, Louisiana Gold® Pepper Sauce, Bruce's® Yams, and Casa Fiesta® Mexican Foods. With the intent of piggybacking on the worldwide publicity created by the World Cup Soccer Tournament held in Mexico City in 1984 and the explosive growth of "Tex-Mex" restaurants in the United States, BFC management decided in the mid-1980s to introduce its Casa Fiesta Mexican Foods in Europe. Simultaneously, its two major rivals, Old El Paso® and Lawry's® businesses, announced their intentions of opening operations in Europe.

While Old El Paso and Lawry's adopted American-style entrance strategies featuring expensive mass media advertising campaigns, the much smaller BFC turned to a channels-based strategy. Realizing that most Europeans at the time were unfamiliar with Mexican cuisine, BFC managers began building primary

BOX 8.1
Continued

demand for Mexican foods. For starters, they went to major European beer producers and wholesalers and convinced them to provide nacho chip warmers to select bars and pubs. In return, BFC agreed to pay for these warmers. The idea was well received by producers and wholesalers as well as by bar and pub owners. The bar and pub owners received a high-margin and low-cost snack that prompted customers to buy more drinks. Producers and wholesalers, on the other hand, received the credit for providing this new revenue source for free. And BFC got its Casa Fiesta name displayed in many bars and pubs across Europe.

To further develop primary demand, BFC management worked closely with institutional food distributors to spur the opening of Mexican restaurants. BFC markets their products to restaurants through exclusive arrangements with one institutional food distributor per European country. Together, BFC and distributor managers targeted geographic areas populated by upscale and highly educated professionals for restaurant development. For example, one prime target market was German university towns. To aid in the development process, BFC developed a manual on how to open and operate a Mexican restaurant or take-out business. The firm also provides free restaurant management consulting assistance. One success story comes from Reykjavik, where BFC helped its Icelandic distributor open a Mexican restaurant.

Perhaps the most important component of the BFC strategy involved specialty food distributors that sell to the retail trade. Early on, BFC managers determined that distributor selection would be the key to success.

They carefully aligned the firm with one of the top two specialty foods distributors in each country. Each of these distributors provided market access to the leading retailers in their respective countries. Rather than burden distributors and retailers with too broad an assortment, BFC managers limited their initial efforts to complete, ready-to-prepare taco dinners. To get the distributors' attention and help them secure scarce retail shelf space, BFC provided retail gross margins in excess of 40 percent. This margin level contrasts favorably with the typical specialty food item that has a gross margin of about 11 percent. To complement these margins, BFC also provided distributors and retailers with significant cooperative funds for market development and high-quality promotional pieces.

Only after BFC had secured strategic shelf space across Europe, did BFC begin to advertise. Those advertisements used the theme "The Romance of Old Mexico" and promoted the growing popularity of Mexican foods. BFC competitors, on the other hand, turned to large-scale American-style advertising campaigns that focused on the merits of eating tacos in general. Unfortunately for them, when consumers went to grocery stores to buy taco mixes, they only found Casa Fiesta brands in stock. To make matters worse, research showed that consumers assumed Casa Fiesta had sponsored all of the print and television advertisements they had seen. Not only had BFC penetrated the European market, it gained the largest share of market in several countries. Its success in Europe led BFC to become one of the first U.S. specialty foods companies to build manufacturing facilities in Europe.

A/E/C Systems is a small firm that runs computer trade shows for the design and construction industries. Over the years, the firm has developed a database of more than 50,000 names and addresses of construction engineers and architects worldwide. The firm obtained these names from the registration lists of previous conferences and from commercial list vendors. Based on their experience and statistical

Figure 8.3
The Product Market Growth Matrix

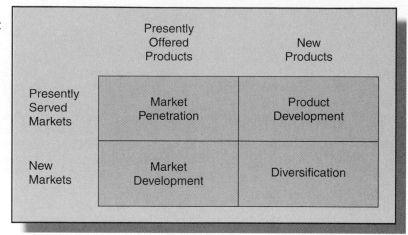

Source: These options are drawn from Igor Ansoff, "Strategies for Diversification," *Harvard Business Review* (September–October 1957): 113–124.

analyses of descriptive data from past conference participants, A/E/C Systems managers have identified 39 key attributes of potential customers that are most likely to attend seminars. These encompass such things as job title, employer sales and industry, geographic location, project specialization, and primary interests. Information on each of these 39 attributes appears in the database, along with the 50,000 names and addresses. When planning an upcoming conference, A/E/C Systems managers develop a profile of desired attendees and exhibitors from a subset of the 39 attributes. Then they search the 50,000 entries for matches with the profile. The firm mails each of these leads a conference announcement, a package of personalized information, and a registration form.[4]

However, as experienced managers know, when it comes to lead generation, actually doing it well is difficult. For starters, many firms have only a vague notion of their target market segments. As a result, they are never able to narrow their list of leads down to a manageable, high-potential group. Perhaps more troubling is the fact that many suppliers' databases are either hopelessly out of date or contain irrelevant data. In addition, many managers lack the statistical skills necessary to accurately probe the databases for leads. In fact, these problems have become so acute that many supplier firms outsource the entire lead-generation process to database marketing consultants.[5]

Increasingly supplier firms that choose to do the work internally rely on a **customer relationship management (CRM) system**, which is defined as ". . . the set of tools and processes a firm uses to identify, attract, and retain customers and to leverage its relationships with customers."[6] Within the CRM system, firms commonly maintain a reliable customer database and supplemental market databases. A **customer database** is the supplier firm's repository for all relevant information about past and present customers. For each customer, it should contain transaction prices and profits from past orders, costs to serve, an estimate of the supplier's share of the customer's business, a forecast of potential sales, important customer firm characteristics, the names of buying team members and their roles in purchase decisions, previous account call reports, product or service applications, and relevant buying practices, policies, and patterns. Firms should further supplement their customer database with research findings from value assessments and estimates of the lifetime value of each customer.[7]

A **market database**, on the other hand, contains key manager names and addresses plus limited descriptive information on each company in the defined market. Most often, supplier firms rent or acquire such databases in the form of industry lists from commercial list vendors. In the United States, Dun & Bradstreet, American Business Information, Database America, Trinet, R. L. Polk, and TRW are the leading list vendors. Once managers obtain these industry lists, they commonly merge them or run them in parallel with their in-house customer database to create a comprehensive database that reflects market potential. In doing so, they eliminate duplicate entries.[8]

When pursuing greater market penetration, progressive managers may have information on all potential customers already in the firm's CRM system. They develop a target segment profile based on the characteristics of the firm's most profitable and strategically desirable customers. Then, using statistical tools, managers examine the comprehensive database for firms that match the profile. Leads might represent firms that have similar characteristics, but simply purchase smaller amounts. Even though these accounts may not have been of interest in the past, the supplier might now reach these smaller volume accounts through alternate channels, such as direct marketing in conjunction with third-party order fulfillment.

With product development as the firm's stated goal, business market managers draw upon past research and experience to identify product or service applications, customer capabilities, and customer requirements for which the supplier firm's newly developed offering will create the greatest value. Turning to the CRM system, business market managers search for current customer firms that meet this target segment profile. Managers designate these firms as product development leads and direct cross-selling activities toward them.

To guide market development efforts, business market managers again develop a profile of high-profit customers from the firm's existing customer database. If the market is small in size or the supplier can readily enumerate potential customers, managers use internal databases. If they lack information on the new market, they rent a list of potential customers from a commercial vendor. In turn, managers analyze the list for matches with the high-profit customer profile. They use resulting company or manager names as market development leads. Finally, in the case of diversification, managers rely heavily on instinct, developing a "best-guess" profile of most-likely customers. Alternatively, many supplier firms hire consultants to develop a profile of most-likely potential customers. Then they rent lists of firms in those new markets they believe to be the most promising. As before, they match the profile with market database listings and isolate leads for diversification.

Prompting and Gathering Inquiries via Integrated Marketing Communications

Recent marketplace trends have altered the nature of prospecting, placing greater importance on prompting and gathering inquiries. Many customer firms have adopted a "reverse marketing" philosophy and now actively search for suppliers. The emergence and growth in popularity of Internet-based search engines make it increasingly feasible and cost effective for customers to do so. The bottom line for managers is to develop systems that enable potential customers to easily find the supplier firm. One way to accomplish this task is to link prospecting activities with an integrated marketing communications plan.[9]

Use Integrated Marketing Communications to Reach the Target Market

Within the context of business market management, **integrated marketing communications (IMC)** can be defined as

> a concept of marketing communications planning that recognizes the added value of a comprehensive plan. Such a plan evaluates the strategic role of a variety of communications disciplines—for example, general advertising, direct response, sales promotion, and public relations—and combines these disciplines to provide clarity, consistency, and maximum communications impact through the seamless integration of discrete messages.[10]

IMC entails four closely coordinated activities.

First, business market managers set sequential communications objectives, often relying on one of the many response hierarchy models to guide the process. **Response hierarchy models** describe the cognitive, affective, and behavioral stages that a customer goes through during the purchasing process. For example, Rogers' Diffusion-Adoption Model proposes five: awareness, interest, evaluation, trial, and adoption.[11]

Second, managers develop a complementary and cost-effective mix of promotional tools to achieve each communications objective. For example, industry magazine advertising is well suited for generating awareness, technical brochures generate interest, product samples and special discounts prompt trial, and the sales force can persuade customer managers to adopt the product as part of their firm's specifications. The manager's choice of specific promotional tools is tempered by cost considerations. Typically, tools with the lowest cost per contact such as mass media advertising have the least impact, whereas high-impact tools such as a sales call have high costs per contact. As Figure 8.2 indicates, when seeking new customers, managers are likely to begin with lower-cost and lower-impact promotions to generate inquiries and progress to higher-cost and -impact promotions targeted toward their best prospects.[12]

Third, as we discussed in Chapter 4, business market managers create a value proposition and communicate it through all promotions. Consider the case of Greif Incorporated. Greif produces fiber drums, plastic drums, and intermediate bulk containers for food products and chemicals manufacturers. Rather than competing on a price-per-container basis, Greif markets complete packaging systems. Greif's value proposition, *total cost-based packaging* (TCBP), promises that its systems can significantly reduce a customer's total costs of packaging. Greif account managers communicate TCBP via promotional brochures that highlight potential cost savings, videotapes that demonstrate how Greif containers save money, and presentations in which they report cost-of-use analysis findings. In Box 8.2, we discuss how Greif salespeople conduct research and use value assessment to quantify the value proposition for each customer.

BOX 8.2
Greif Incorporated Markets Total Cost-Based Packaging

Greif Incorporated manufactures fiber drums, plastic drums, and intermediate bulk containers (IBCs), which are plastic containers surrounded by a protective metal cage. Customers use all three forms of containers to store and transport liquids and solids, such as chemicals and food additives. Greif managers believe that IBCs provide the lowest total cost solution for customer requirements. The problem the division faces is explaining why customers should spend $150 on one IBC instead of $100 on five fiber drums to transport equivalent volumes of materials. This reasoning is particularly challenging in that other firms compete solely on low price.

In response, Greif managers developed a value proposition called *total cost-based packaging* (TCBP). Greif's strategic account managers proposed the proposition after noticing two major market trends. First, customers increasingly want to reduce their total packaging costs yet are not really sure what those expenses are. Second, customers desire packaging systems that enable them to customize market offerings for their own end-users. Through TCBP, Greif promises to develop a comprehensive packaging system for a customer firm that minimizes their total packaging costs. Each TCBP solution encompasses a standard offering of plastic drums and IBCs, reuse or recycling services, and optional services, such as handling systems redesign and drum cleaning.

To devise a TCBP solution, a Greif strategic account manager conducts detailed research side-by-side with customer managers. Greif managers use a comprehensive value model, or in Greif parlance, a *cost-of-use model*, to understand total costs. The Greif marketing group developed this model following a series of 20 case studies of the packaging cost structures of major customers. Key parameters include the costs associated with drum tracking, retrieval, paperwork creation and handling, cleaning and maintenance, recycled drum testing, and recertification and testing, among others. Following investigations at the customer's plant site, the account manager plugs identified costs into the cost-of-use model spreadsheet. Through scenario planning, he determines what steps can be taken to minimize the customer's total packaging costs. Then, the strategic account manager constructs several viable TCBP solutions and price structures from which the customer can choose.

With potential solutions in hand, the Greif strategic account manager, along with a team of Greif experts from logistics, handling systems, and computer services, gives a comprehensive presentation to the prospect's senior management at their headquarters. During the presentation, they discuss the merits of each TCBP solution and the associated prices. Following a successful sale, the Greif manager provides quarterly reviews to customer managers that document actual cost savings.

The final challenge of IMC is to synchronize the efforts of all marketing-related groups that will implement selected promotional tools. Although many companies now use contact management modules available in their CRM systems to do so, other firms such as Hewlett-Packard (HP) prefer periodic face-to-face group meetings. During the 1990s, senior management set about integrating the communications efforts of HP's field sales operations, product line teams, and geographic marketing operations across North America, Europe, and Asia, along with the corporate marketing division. Their intent was to ensure that each group communicates together and sends out a consistent message to customers.

To achieve this lofty goal, senior management established marketing councils within HP. Representatives of each of HP's marketing-related groups are members of the councils. During a three-day annual meeting and periodic teleconferences, the councils create a comprehensive communications strategy for both ongoing campaigns and new product launches. Marketing councils strive to communicate the latest technological advancements to sales representatives and changing customer requirements to research and development engineers. When they complete a new communications strategy, the marketing council turns it over to local marketing groups to implement. In turn, these marketing groups tailor global messages to the requirements of local customer segments.[13]

Encourage and Process Inquiries

When gaining customers is the goal, business market managers use a comprehensive IMC program to stimulate inquiries from various categories of potential clients. To cost-effectively reach the entire target market, business market managers place direct response advertisements in highly focused industry magazines. Direct response advertisements (DRA) are print promotions that feature a special offer and a request for the reader to contact the supplier for "further information." The supplier includes either a business reply card (BRC), a toll-free telephone number, or a Web site address to facilitate inquiries. The latest generation of virtual DRAs includes banner and "pop-up" advertisements on the Internet at business-to-business Web sites.[14]

Business market managers use direct mail in the form of newsletters and information packets to communicate with internally generated leads. For example, Panasonic's Factory Automation (PFA) Division produces two newsletters. *Automation Line* is a four-page, two-color newsletter it mails quarterly to leads identified from Panasonic's *market* database. The newsletter contains general-interest stories and basic information on Panasonic products. Panasonic managers use the newsletter to prompt inquiries via BRCs or toll-free numbers during market development and diversification initiatives. The PFA Division mails *The Panasert Technical Bulletin* to Panasonic customers that have made major capital investments in Panasonic factory automation technology. Managers base these mailings on the firm's *customer* database. In contrast to the first newsletter, the *Bulletin* contains detailed, technical information on the productive use of Panasonic products, changes in automation technology and processes, product and engineering developments at PFA, and new PFA products. PFA managers use the *Bulletin* to encourage inquiries during market penetration and product development efforts.[15]

IMC plans also rely on interactive media to stimulate inquiries. Trade shows and exhibitions, traditional favorites, provide suppliers with access to many potential customers in short periods of time. In Europe and Japan, trade shows and exhibitions commonly attract tens of thousands of active and informed businesspeople from all functions. They often last one or two weeks and feature technical demonstrations and educational sessions.[16]

The Internet and extranets afford supplier firms a myriad of opportunities to prompt inquiries from potential customer firms. Perhaps the simplest and least expensive means of doing so is through a content-only Web site. In business markets, content-only sites serve as an interactive "electronic trade show," where potential customers can enter at will, 24-hours a day, 7-days a week (24x7), from anywhere in the world, search and download company information and product specifications, read promotional materials and answers to frequently asked questions (FAQs), and perhaps even obtain price quotes. Often the site sponsor provides a toll-free telephone number for customers to call to speak with a salesperson or place orders.

Next in terms of sophistication are online catalog sites that contain not only product information and price lists but also provide interactive service and order entry systems to customers. As an example, review Box 7.6 on Cisco Systems. Catalog sites are effective in generating inquiries as well as orders for generic products. Forward auction sites that companies such as Grainger and GXS run as well as B2B exchanges such as Covisint, ChemConnect, and Exostar, similarly furnish opportunities for prospective customers to find suppliers and to acquire products and services online. They are often useful in marketing leverage and bottleneck items.[17]

Business market managers have even gained limited success through the use of the Internet's original "killer application," e-mail, to prompt inquiries. One emerging and promising approach is **HTML or XML e-mail** in which plain text is replaced with high resolution and multicolored graphics that have the look and feel of a Web site. HTML or XML e-mail can communicate more detailed information and reportedly yields higher response rates than traditional e-mail. Perhaps the greatest challenge to business market managers using e-mail campaigns is coping with recipients' aversion to "spam", or unsolicited promotional messages. One approach to overcoming this aversion is through **permission marketing** where managers ask prospects in advance whether they want to receive promotional e-mail messages.[18]

Many suppliers have problems processing inquiries because they tend to arrive at seemingly random intervals in large numbers. Often, no one keeps track of them, they get lost, or they sit for weeks in stacks in the mailroom. Fortunately, a number of third-party-provided services, supported by innovative CRM software modules, enable firms to do a better job of managing inquiries. For example, AT&T's Advanced Network Solutions Division (ANSD) created a service known as Prospecting Plus. It enables a supplier to gather inquiries, often in the form of information cards or brief questionnaires, from a variety of media—telephone, fax, mail, and the Web. At the heart of ANSD efforts is a software module, Electronic Commerce Services Transaction Platform, that collects the inquiries simultaneously from these media, transfers them into a single data file, and downloads them to the client twice per day. The key advantage of Prospecting Plus is that users get all inquiries in a uniform format in one place.[19]

Foster Strong Brands

Even though generating inquiries is an important short-term objective of IMC, business market managers should never lose sight of a more important strategic goal—bolstering brand equity. As we discussed in Chapter 4, brands play two critical roles in business markets. In the case of generics and leverage items, purchasing managers may limit their "choice set" in buying situations to well-known brands in order to reduce risk and time-related costs. In the case of criticals and bottleneck items, purchasing managers may use a brand name as a short-hand descriptor for previously demonstrated value. This practice saves them time and effort, in that they don't have to complete a value assessment each time they acquire an offering. Thus, a strong brand may be the most effective tool that the business market manager has to gain customers. As a result, supplier firms should use every IMC program to build awareness and to reinforce the value of their brands.[20]

Qualifying Leads and Inquiries as Prospects

In years past, business market managers would immediately pass along internally generated leads and externally gathered inquiries to the field sales force. However, with the average cost of today's sales call ranging from $250 to $500 and the average "yield" from leads hovering between 1 and 2 percent, companies increasingly first qualify leads and inquiries as prospects. To **qualify** a lead or inquiry, the supplier (or contracted third parties) contacts the potential customer via direct mail, fax, e-mail, or telephone, and asks a series of preliminary questions to confirm that the firm has significant sales and profit opportunity.[21]

At the center of qualifying efforts is a brief questionnaire. Experts urge suppliers to ask all prospective clients at least five questions: (1) Is the potential customer currently using a similar product or service? (2) Is the firm considering purchasing the offering? (3) When does the firm plan to execute the transaction? (4) Is the individual contacted the ultimate decision maker? and (5) Has funding been approved for the acquisition?[22]

A supplier has several options for distributing the qualifying questionnaire. Managers can embed it on direct-response advertisements or direct mail pieces within BRCs so that inquiries prequalify themselves when they request further information. To qualify Web browsers, the supplier can require all visitors to complete the questionnaire during "registration" as a prelude to gaining access to Web site information. Another approach that is gaining popularity is fax or e-mail qualification. Here, the supplier faxes or e-mails the questionnaire to the lead or inquiry, often along with a specification worksheet. In turn, the potential customer faxes or e-mails the forms back to the supplier. Perhaps the most common method, and definitely the preferred one for high-potential accounts, is telephone qualification. Using an automated script, a telemarketing rep prompts a potential customer through the questions and probes for additional information.

Over a period of time, market researchers from the supplier firm should evaluate questionnaire responses and develop a scheme for prioritizing prospects. Often, researchers rely on statistical tools such as discriminant analysis to sort accounts based on sales and profit potential and the opportunity for the supplier to deliver value. For example, Belden Wire & Cable Company, a U.S.-based specialty steel supplier with annual sales of approximately $750 million, devised a ranking matrix that rates prospects as "hot," "warm," or "cold." Each category is based upon the prospect's responses to a qualification questionnaire, past sales history with Belden, expected product usage, and current wire and cable purchases. Now when Belden marketing personnel qualify leads or inquiries, they designate them as hot, warm, or cold prospects based on ranking matrix criteria. Then they turn hot prospects over to the field sales force and warm prospects over to the telemarketing unit for follow-up.[23]

We conclude this section with an observation. Progressive business market managers encode all pertinent information they gain during lead generation, inquiry gathering, and prospect qualification in the firm's CRM databases. In this way, they upgrade and refine the databases and ensure that the firm's future prospecting efforts will be more productive.

Getting the Sales Force to Follow Up with Prospects

Experts contend that lack of follow-up is the key reason for the failure of many firms' prospecting efforts. Often, field sales representatives never contact most of the prospects that business market managers have spent time, effort, and resources to uncover. Clearly, to improve the yield from prospecting, suppliers must gain the commitment and support of the sales force. To do so, business market managers must create programs and systems for the sales force that deliver four critical elements: knowledge, motivation, experience, and sales support.[24]

Provide Knowledge to Create an Informed Sales Force

It goes almost without saying that sales representatives must possess sufficient product and market knowledge to be successful. This knowledge is particularly important when product development, market development, and diversification strategies call for reps to sell new products or penetrate new markets. Furthermore, sales reps may require cutting-edge selling skills to gain new customers. Logically, business market managers gain sales force commitment first and foremost by providing training on product and market knowledge as well as selling skills.

Sales personnel often attribute their failure to follow up with prospects to a lack of understanding of the role that it plays in overall company strategy. All too often, reps are left "out of the loop" when prospecting programs are introduced and explained. To remedy this problem, business market managers if not senior management must keep the sales force informed about how following up with prospects fits into the firm's goals and strategies. Some companies create sales advisory councils to do so. A sales advisory council is a cross-functional group comprised of respected salespeople, product managers, direct marketing personnel, advertising agency account representatives, and customer service personnel, as well as senior managers. The council meets periodically to discuss proposed company goals, strategies, and programs, and to suggest ways to integrate interdepartmental efforts. By participating in council meetings, sales personnel gain an appreciation for their role, contribute to the design of corporate plans, and commit to following up on leads and inquiries.[25]

Motivate Sales Representatives to Follow Up

Sales representatives, as well as other professionals, tend to complete tasks they are paid to do. Therefore, one of the strongest ways to motivate them to follow up on prospects is to link their compensation packages to new account development. To do so, business market managers devise a series of activity quotas linked to prospecting. These quotas might include such things as the number of sales calls on prospects to be made per quarter, number of new accounts to be gained, and sales or turnover to new accounts. In turn, managers tie performance to base salary increases or to bonuses. In general, the larger the salary component or bonus linked to the quota, the more time reps will devote to follow-up.[26]

To inspire sales force efforts, business market managers often involve salespeople in the planning and design processes for prospecting programs. For example, at Motorola, managers actively seek continuous two-way dialogue with all salespeople concerning lead generation and inquiry-gathering efforts. Before any new program is announced, managers contact all sales representatives by mail, by telephone, or in person. Sales reps learn the details of the program, its purpose, the target audience, timing, and how resulting prospects should be handled. More importantly, business market managers ask salespeople to share their thoughts on the proposal and to offer suggestions. Motorola managers make it a point to implement as many sales force recommendations as are feasible. Once programs have been introduced, Motorola managers maintain sales force enthusiasm by providing "extra" local support in the form of increased direct mail, advertising, and trade show coverage to sales reps who actively participate. Finally, Motorola gives the sales force "the credit" for prospecting program success, which serves as a potent social recognition or reward for outstanding efforts. To do so, managers publish case histories and success stories in company newsletters.[27]

Give Sales Representatives Experience Dealing with Prospects

Pundits claim that many salespeople fail to actively pursue prospects because they require "cold" calls. After all, few salespeople really like making cold calls. For business market managers, solving this problem demands that they remove the "cold" from the call. The obvious way is to qualify the prospect well in advance. Another is to give sales reps plenty of practice so that they feel at ease dealing with prospective new customers.[28]

A number of innovative training programs are useful here. To begin with, sales managers can create role-playing situations by having sales reps make prospecting calls on the firm's own purchasing department or on managers from cooperative customers. Some firms videotape such calls, using them to work with trainers to build and refine selling skills. Then salespeople meet as a group to critique one another and vote for the one they felt did the best. The sales manager reinforces the process by providing some reward, either social recognition or a small remuneration, to the winner.

Another proven training approach is to use field joint sales calls as a transition to field sales competency. The supplier has each field salesperson make calls with a technical specialist or a sales manager, who takes a less active and more supportive role as the calls progress, letting the field person work with a "technical safety net." Of course in both of these approaches, sales managers must provide constructive feedback on progress and coaching. In Chapter 9, we further discuss the importance of coaching to sales force and marketing channel performance.

Furnish Abundant Sales Support

A final way to gain sales force commitment is to provide reps with sales support that makes following up with prospects an easier task. Traditionally, such support came in the form of market research, collateral materials, and technical information. Emerging information technologies and communications media enhance not only the quality but also the availability of sales support.

Baan, the ERP software and Internet-enabled business solutions group of London-based Invensys, PLC (annual sales of more than €11 billion) furnishes its sales personnel with an online system, *Publish on Demand*, which enables them to customize brochures for prospects. Following preliminary discussions with a prospective client, a Baan salesperson can go online to a company-restricted Web site. There, the salesperson finds templates for solution-specific brochures along with an inventory of photographs and standardized paragraphs. Using his or her knowledge of customer requirements and preferences, the salesperson can electronically tailor a brochure by inserting and editing desirable paragraphs and photos on a template. As company policy requires that each brochure conclude with a value proposition, the salesperson can create a proposition specifically for a prospect. When the draft of the brochure is done, the salesperson electronically sends it to the director of marketing and communications for reviewing, editing, and printing. According to Baan managers, the final brochures are available in about two days. Now, when a Baan salesperson gives an important sales presentation to a prospect, he or she can distribute a customized brochure to listeners.

Suppliers not only use value models to inform and guide their own decision making, they also use the results to create value-based sales tools that better enable their sales forces to persuasively demonstrate the superior value their firms' offerings provide. **Value-in-use case histories** are written accounts that document the cost savings or added value a customer firm actually received from its use of a supplier's market offering. Sonoco Product Company's Protective Packaging Division (SPPD) maintains a database of its cost-of-use case studies, so that its salespeople can draw on them when making proposals to other prospects. These case studies enable SPPD salespeople to tangibly convey the cost savings that the prospects themselves would likely realize.

Getronics, an Amsterdam-based provider of information and communications technology solutions and services (annual sales greater than €4.1 billion), takes this one step further furnishing its sales representatives with a compact disk (CD) set entitled, "Plain Talk. Practical Solutions." The two-pack set contains a series of professionally produced videos with audio-tracks describing the company and its solutions, two presentations, and numerous case studies from major clients. When visiting a prospect, the sales rep can either mute the audio-track and give the presentation himself or herself or leave the CD set with the client to view at a more convenient time and place.

Other firms support sales efforts by creating an organization whose units complement and reinforce each other. IBM, for instance, created a Teleservices Center to work with its field sales representatives. Through the Teleservices Center concept, IBM management hopes to increase overall customer satisfaction with IBM services, reduce the cost of customer contacts, reduce the sales cycle, and ensure consistent and high-caliber account coverage for all sizes of customers. The Teleservices Center is organized into three operating groups. Telesales, Customer Service, and Direct Marketing/Lead Generation. The Telesales Group has sales and account management responsibilities for medium to low-end products. Telesales reps establish relationships with new customers, identify needs, propose solutions, and ask for orders. Customer Service resolves customer problems—from simple questions to complex technical issues—over the telephone. Lastly, the Direct Marketing/Lead Generation Group identifies and qualifies leads and participates in targeted promotional campaigns. Once the group qualifies leads, it turns them over to either the field sales force or telesales. With this support, IBM field sales reps have more time to devote to major accounts and hot prospects.[29]

Finally, progressive firms are using CRM systems to improve sales force productivity. The most popular and effective CRM modules address lead distribution, prospect sales cycle tracking, contact management, product configuration, pricing, call reporting, and territory management. When deployed effectively, these CRM modules allow all supplier employees who "touch" the prospective customer to know in real time what actions the firm has taken for each prospect, what further steps need to be taken, and what support and cooperation will be needed to land the account.[30]

ASSESSING MUTUAL FIT

After refining the list of qualified prospects to those that the supplier firm cannot serve exclusively via indirect means such as catalogs, direct mail, the Web, or resellers, the business market manager instructs either a field or inside salesperson to initiate direct contact, or "sales calls." Through these calls, the salesperson assesses the opportunity to deliver and equitably share value, and ideally, takes the first steps in building a long-term business relationship. In these initial contacts, the rep will likely find significant diversity in selling situations across the pool of prospects. These selling situations vary by industry and within an industry as a function of each prospect's philosophy of doing business, purchasing orientation, purchasing portfolio matrix category, technological sophistication, capabilities, and market offering usage and applications.[31]

Recognizing the variation in selling situations, sales professionals practice **adaptive selling**, or "the altering of sales behaviors during a customer interaction or across customer interactions based on perceived information about the nature of the selling situation."[32] Of these behavioral changes, modifying the sales approach is the most pertinent. Salespeople can also alter their communication style, for instance becoming more or less technical, to better match a purchasing manager's competence and personality. They can modify message content, perhaps varying emphasis placed on certain offering benefits. Lastly, salespeople can change their call strategy by deviating from the call plan.[33]

Consultants Rackham and DeVincentis distinguish between three sales approaches: transactional, consultative, and enterprise selling. **Transactional selling** focuses on gaining the order for a product or service as quickly as possible. In fact, advocates urge salespeople to structure the entire sales call as a prelude to closing or "asking for the order." With **consultative selling**, the sales representative becomes a long-term, trusted, and value-adding resource for a customer firm by gaining an in-depth understanding of its operations and by contributing analytical expertise to resolve pressing problems. Acting as a consultant, the rep crafts and recommends a total solution or bundle of products and services designed to precisely meet customer firm requirements and preferences. Seeking a strategic alliance or even a joint venture with an important customer to exploit a market opportunity, a supplier's senior management uses **enterprise selling** to convincingly elaborate the benefits of combining and sharing complementary competences and capabilities across firms. In enterprise selling, the offering is a partnership and not just products and services.[34]

As sales representatives routinely use both transactional and consultative selling while gaining customers for products and services, we will address them in detail in this chapter. Although experts have devised various consultative selling methods in recent years, we focus our attention on one, SPIN® selling.[35] We believe that SPIN selling is the most consistent with business market management's emphasis on value. In Figure 8.4, we contrast transactional selling with SPIN selling. Enterprise selling, on the other hand, is an approach for securing partnerships between firms. We will further examine it in Chapter 10.

Figure 8.4 Contrasting Transactional and SPIN® Approaches to Selling

Selling Stage	Traditional Selling	SPIN Selling
Planning the Call	Study call reports and files	Same
	Set call objectives	Same
	Prepare presentation	Same
	Review offering knowledge	Same
	Reflect on offering benefits	Review value elements
Opening the Call	Relate to buyer's personal interests	Get down to business quickly
	Complement, mystify, or intrigue buyer	Begin asking questions
	Make an opening benefit statement	Don't offer solutions too soon
Investigating Needs	Ask general open-ended questions to uncover customer problems	Uncover implied needs and develop them into explicit needs via situation, problem, implication, and need-payoff questions
Proposing Solutions	Sell benefits	Demonstrate capabilities
	Personalize benefits to unique customer needs	Show how offering meets explicit needs and articulate value
	Handle objections	Prevent objections
Gaining the Order	Close early and often	Obtain the right commitment in the form of advances and orders
		Make additional calls on the customer as needed
Following Up After the Sale	Check to be sure the offering has been delivered	Same
	Correct installation and start up problems	Same
	Ensure customer satisfaction	Same
		Ascertain the value promised has been delivered
		Seek new ways to add value

As we outlined in Figure 8.1, the first part of assessing mutual fit is the salesperson scheduling the first meeting with a prospect. After discussing this, we examine how the salesperson and prospect manager learn each other's requirements and preferences. Through these interactions, managers determine whether it is in the supplier and customer firm's best interests to do business together. ABN-AMRO Bank's approach to gaining new correspondent banking customers in the United States nicely illustrates assessing mutual fit. We describe this in Box 8.3 and return to it several times in this section. To account for the variation in selling situations, we contrast how assessing mutual fit differs in transactional and SPIN selling.

BOX 8.3
ABN-AMRO Gains Correspondent Banking Customers in the United States

John Eck, senior vice president for the Correspondent Banking Unit of ABN-AMRO (AA) Bank in the United States, has among his principal assignments gaining new correspondent banking business for AA within the U.S. marketplace. Importantly, AA prefers long-term alliances with a limited number of commercial banks where AA delivers superior value, rather than short-term transactional business with a multitude of banks. As a result, Eck must be selective in identifying and pursuing banks whose philosophy of doing business meshes with that of AA.

The most promising market segment for AA is banks with limited international networks. For these banks, AA delivers value via access to major currency clearing centers in Europe as well as to its international banking network, which has operations in more than 70 countries. By outsourcing some part of their international banking services to AA, these banks are able to offer global banking services without having to invest significantly in enabling information technology and in bricks and mortar abroad. Instead, they can focus on their core business of serving the domestic U.S. market.

Eck uses two related techniques to prospect for new customers: cold calls and conference roundtables. For example, he identified the Silicon Valley Bank (SVB) of California as a desirable prospect. SVB has $2 billion in assets and numerous high-technology business customers that do business internationally. In order to compete effectively with banks like Bank of America, SVB needed a global presence. Unfortunately, it lacked the resources to set up its own operations in other countries. Eck's first contact with the SVB came via a cold call. A European customer of AA asked for confirmation of a letter of credit (LC) issued by SVB. Responding to this request provided the opportunity for Eck to contact the bank. Capitalizing on this contact, he arranged a visit to the bank.

To continue the dialogue with Silicon Valley Bank as well as to cultivate other prospects, Eck decided to sponsor a luncheon and roundtable discussion at the annual Bankers' Association for Foreign Trade (BAFT) Convention. As it turns out, bankers responsible for foreign trade welcome the opportunity to discuss banking issues with counterparts at other institutions. Eck obtained a preregistration list of conference attendees and selected approximately 15 bank executives from U.S. banks. AA already had accounts at these banks, so the executives were familiar with Eck's bank. He carefully selected lunchtime during the second day of BAFT to avoid conflicts with other events.

Prior to the conference, Eck invited the 15 bankers to attend and requested topics for discussion. After receiving their responses, he prepared a final agenda for the meeting and sent it to them so that they could prepare their thoughts. A sample discussion topic was, "Our bank charges us too much for capital, so we have a hard time making money. How can we get our bank to lower its charges?" During

BOX 8.3
Continued

the roundtable, Eck served as moderator, guiding discussions. The roundtable was a success. Not only did attending bank executives gain insights from the discussions, they were able to network with colleagues at other banks.

Eck used the goodwill created to schedule follow-up meetings. For example, he set up a breakfast meeting at the BAFT Convention with the senior vice president of a prospective customer, Mellon Bank (MB) of Pittsburgh. MB has total assets greater than $40 billion, but only limited international presence. Rather than discussing the nitty-gritty of correspondent banking, Eck used the breakfast to learn more about the business philosophy of MB and to gain a better understanding of its operations. He also touched upon some recent AA initiatives, such as Global Transaction Service (GTS). In turn, the senior vice president expressed interest in AA's trade and cash management services, so Eck arranged for a follow-up visit to Pittsburgh with an AA team of specialists.

The meeting at MB focused on the impact of the European Monetary Union (EMU) on MB and its customers. To engage and inform MB, Eck arranged to have AA's chief economist and AA's head of Capital Markets Activities teleconference in from Amsterdam and discuss their areas of expertise. Also present in person at the meeting were AA experts on corporate cash management under the EMU and interbank trading and settlements. Lastly, Eck informed MB about legal risks to MB's customers due to the uncertain legal environment surrounding contracts denominated in currencies that will no longer exist under the EMU. A luncheon followed these discussions, which allowed more informal interaction between AA representatives and several senior executives of MB, with the intent of developing better cultural rapport between the institutions.

In time, AA gained both SVB and MB as customers.

Scheduling the First Meeting

In today's hectic workplace, salespeople frequently find making an initial appointment with a prospect to be a major challenge. With most managers' agendas overfilled with pressing work, few have time for "get acquainted" sessions. Technology often poses a barrier, as witnessed by the difficulties one encounters trying to get through a company's automated voice-mail system. How the sales representative arranges for that first meeting is a function of the selling situation.

Getting Started for Simple Sales

In a **simple sale**, the customer firm requires an offering of low importance and minimal risk such as a generic item. In general, customer managers fully understand the basic attributes and applications of the offering they require and do not need a technical explanation. Simple sales correspond to the **straight rebuy** or **modified rebuy** buying situations we discussed in Chapter 3. A purchasing manager typically has sole authority and can make the purchase immediately, often based on lowest price. Examples of simple sales are the acquisition of corrugated packaging materials and printing.

When confronted with a simple sale, sales representatives use the techniques of transactional selling. Here, "timing is everything" for the salesperson. The prospective customer commonly makes such purchases either when a problem arises unexpectedly within the firm or an existing vendor botches an order. Thus, the salesperson makes periodic and routine "cold" calls on prospects. The rep gains access to the purchasing manager by promising special "deals" or by making an attention-getting new claim about her product. If the purchasing manager has spare time or faces a crisis situation revolving around the product, he meets with the salesperson.

Initiating Dialogue for Complex Sales

In a **complex sale**, the customer seeks an offering of greater significance and associated risk such as a bottleneck or critical item. More than likely, customer managers are not fully aware of their firm's requirements or how those requirements might best be satisfied. Because of this lack of awareness, a **buying team** of customer managers will require detailed explanations about the performance of alternative market offerings. Complex sales correspond to the modified rebuy or **new task** buying situations we discussed in Chapter 3. Examples of a complex sale are a government's acquisition of a 300-megawatt power plant, or a firm's purchase of a pension plan for its employees.

In a complex sale, the customer firm conducts analyses of alternate offerings and requires a longer period of time to decide what to purchase. The buying team may demand multiple sales calls from cross-functional representatives of the supplier firm. Based on its analyses, the team recommends a purchase based on an offering's value or total cost to the customer firm. Importantly, the buying team will most likely make its decision when supplier representatives are not present. To handle a complex sale, representatives turn to a consultative selling approach, such as SPIN selling.

The example of ABN-AMRO (AA) gaining correspondent banking customers in the United States represents a complex sale. Eck does not walk into a prospective banking partner unannounced and begin to sell letters of credit to the first bank executive he meets. Instead, he needs to have a valid reason for a "cold" call. That reason must deliver some value to the prospect. In the case of Silicon Valley Bank (SVB), he used a request from a European customer to confirm a letter of credit as the reason to call on bank officials. SVB managers met with Eck because the letter of credit represented significant business for the bank. In the case of the roundtable at the Bankers' Association for Foreign Trade (BAFT) Convention, Eck used the opportunity to discuss banking issues with their peers to gain access to 15 bank executives.

Given that a buying team makes the decision in a complex sale, a salesperson must skillfully identify the team's **gatekeeper** and schedule the initial meeting with that person. The gatekeeper is the person who has principal responsibility for regulating the flow of information to and from the buying team as well as providing the sales rep with access to specific team members. Thus, in the case of Mellon Bank of Pittsburgh, Eck deliberately invited the senior vice president of Mellon Bank to attend the BAFT roundtable and used the goodwill it created to schedule a follow-up breakfast. At that breakfast, Eck touched on AA initiatives that were of interest to the senior vice president.

Learning Each Other's Requirements and Preferences

In most cases, a salesperson will spend a portion of the initial encounter with the prospect getting acquainted and learning about their requirements and preferences. However, in a simple sale, the prospect and the salesperson often are able to articulate the potential customer's requirements after a short period of interaction. As a result, experts in transactional selling instruct the sales representative to quickly close the sale, then negotiate the terms and conditions of the order.

In a complex sale, neither the prospect nor the sales representative may fully comprehend customer requirements. Because considerable risk is involved and both firms frequently seek a long-term relationship, both supplier and customer representatives are not in a hurry to consummate the deal. Thus, in a consultative selling approach, such as SPIN selling, the salesperson devotes several sales calls to surface and specify prospect requirements and preferences. Typically, the rep will uncover these requirements by calling on purchasing and other customer managers during visits. We now compare how learning differs between transactional and SPIN selling. As in Figure 8.4, we contend that the salesperson learns in three selling stages: planning the call, opening the call, and investigating needs.

Plan the Call

When using transactional selling, a salesperson selects a prospect for an upcoming call and develops a call plan. In a **call plan**, the representative briefly identifies key objectives to accomplish during the call, selects topics to discuss, formulates a presentation, and considers selling tactics. While preparing the call plan, the rep reviews call reports from previous encounters, if any, with the potential customer and examines customer files to glean information about possible customer needs. A rep will also study pertinent market offering information and major benefits.

The sales representative follows similar procedures under SPIN selling with a few minor differences. To begin with, the salesperson uses the call-planning period to become reacquainted with the specific value elements of the firm's market offerings. Most important, the representative's objectives are likely to be more detailed. In a simple sale, the salesperson may be able to get an order during the first meeting. Therefore, call objectives will likely revolve around closing. Because a complex sale often entails a long sales cycle, the rep may use the first call to learn about the prospect's business philosophy, mission and goals, and purchasing orientation. The salesperson's major objective during the first call on a prospect may be to get invited back. For example, John Eck of AA used a first encounter with a prospect to learn about their bank's philosophy of doing business and operations. Then, he made arrangements to visit the prospect's bank, meet with key executives, and give a formal presentation of AA's value-adding capabilities.

Open the Call

The salesperson arrives at the prospect firm, greets the purchasing manager, exchanges business cards, and engages in small talk for about 5 to 10 minutes. This scenario comprises the **opening** of the presentation.[36] In both transactional and SPIN selling, an important objective during the opening and initial portion of a sales call is to establish trust. **Trust** is "the firm's belief that another company will perform actions that will result in positive outcomes for the firm, as well as not take unexpected actions that would result in negative outcomes for the firm."[37] Consultants have identified five trust-builders that sales personnel use to establish trust between organizations: candor, dependability, competence, customer orientation, and likability. The rep demonstrates **candor** by speaking openly and honestly about the supplier's market offerings and their potential fit with customer requirements. The salesperson cultivates a reputation for **dependability** by fulfilling promises such as getting answers to a prospect's technical questions or delivering samples on time. He displays **competence** through a professional demeanor, command over relevant product and application knowledge, and problem-solving skills. A sales professional shows a **customer orientation** by learning more about customer requirements, empathizing with prospects' problems, and providing advice that helps customers resolve difficulties. Finally, the representative establishes **likability** by being courteous and polite, making efficient use of the customer manager's time, and finding points of commonality both as they relate to business and personal affairs.[38]

When utilizing transactional selling, the salesperson strives to find common personal interests during the opening. For instance, a rep who spots a football pennant on the wall talks about the local football team's latest match. When the salesperson has established rapport with the purchasing manager, it's time to grab the manager's attention by making an intriguing claim about the product, perhaps making a riveting benefit statement.

Although the opening is similar in SPIN selling, the rep does not try to contrive or force points of common personal interest. Furthermore, the salesperson does not make a benefit statement immediately. After all, a rep does not really understand the customer's requirements and preferences. Instead, the rep gets down to business quickly and moves on to the next critical stage of SPIN selling—investigating needs.

Investigate Requirements and Preferences

The salesperson devotes a significant part of the sales call to exploring the prospective customer firm's requirements and preferences. Gaining an understanding of a customer firm's requirements may seem relatively straightforward, yet understanding customer managers' preferences often is not. For example, the salesperson must attempt to discern the extent to which internal political considerations at the customer firm will positively or negatively affect prospects of doing business. The company culture also will often exert a subtle, though significant, influence on customer managers' preferences. Connected relationships with other firms that either the salesperson's firm has or the customer firm has also may influence the customer firm's willingness to do business with the salesperson's firm. So, although customer managers' preferences may not be apparent, at least initially, it is worth investigating them thoroughly. Accommodating them may be the deciding factor in purchase decisions.

In a simple sale, prospect requirements tend to be basic and straightforward, and the investigation phase tends to be brief. Here, advocates of transactional selling urge the salesperson to ask a series of general open-ended questions to encourage the purchasing manager to elaborate any current problems. When the purchasing manager describes a problem that the supplier's market offering can resolve, the representative launches into a formal sales presentation or "pitch."

As a consultant, the salesperson asks a series of focused SPIN questions during calls. Through these questions, the rep helps the customer manager uncover **implied needs**, which are vaguely defined areas of discontent, dissatisfaction, and discomfort with current operations, and to develop them into **explicit needs**, which are precise specifications of products and augmenting services that resolve the customer's problems. The sales representative uses **situation questions** to gather general background information about the customer firm. Experts suggest that salespeople use these sparingly because clever reps can and should obtain most background information from secondary sources during call planning. The rep should pose at least two situation questions: Who are the other members of the buying team? and What roles do buying team members play in the purchasing process?

Moving on as quickly as possible, the salesperson asks a series of **problem questions**, which seek to pinpoint the customer firm's difficulties and dissatisfactions. Most likely, customer managers will answer in generalities or with imprecise statements. Some examples of problem questions are Why are you dissatisfied with your current computer system? What happens to your production line during peak loads? How quickly does your current maintenance contractor respond to your equipment breakdowns and how long does it typically takes them to repair machines?

To this point, the questioning strategies of transactional and SPIN selling are similar. They begin to diverge when the salesperson as consultant poses **implication questions**, which require customer managers to fully articulate the consequences of not resolving the firm's difficulties. Importantly, the skilled sales rep prompts the prospect whenever possible to define both incurred costs and lost benefits in monetary terms. To structure implication questioning, sales representatives often turn to the total cost of ownership (TCO) analyses that we discussed in Chapter 3. For example, account representatives from major consulting and information technology firms routinely begin engagements with diagnostic TCO assessments. Through these TCO assessments, reps and purchasing managers jointly identify and quantify major "points of pain" or cost drivers for the prospect company that might not otherwise be apparent. Then they configure a total solution that dampens the impact of these cost drivers. In Box 8.4, we illustrate how representatives at Rockwell Automation use TCO analyses in consultative selling.[39]

The following are sample implication questions:

- You've pointed to a bottleneck in your main production line. How many sales have you lost during the past month because you could not get product out the door on time?
- You state that 10 percent of your MRO purchases are unplanned. What are your firm's total costs associated with an unplanned purchase?

The final phase of questioning is the most important because it yields arguments that each customer manager can use to sell the supplier's market offering to other members of the buying team when the sales representative is not present. **Need-payoff questions** help the customer manager assess the solution's worth that the supplier firm's market offering provides. Ideally, the skillful salesperson uses need-payoff questions to prompt the customer manager to specify the worth in monetary terms. Need-payoff questions take the following form:

- Suppose that you had a material that was 50 percent easier for your machine operators to use. How would that cut your current rejection rate? What would those cost savings be worth to your firm?
- How much would you be willing to pay per month if you could restrict long-distance calling privileges solely to authorized personnel?

To assist customer managers to quantify a solution's worth, sales representatives should use Internet-based or laptop computer-based value models or worksheets such as the BT Compass we discussed in Chapter 2.

BOX 8.4
Consultative Selling with Rockwell Automation's TCO Toolbox™

Rockwell Automation is a world-leading provider of industrial automation power, control, and information solutions that help customers meet their manufacturing productivity objectives. The company brings together leading brands in industrial automation for Complete Automation solutions, including ALLEN-BRADLEY® controls and engineered services and Rockwell Software® factory management software, DODGE® mechanical power transmission products, and Reliance Electric™ motors and drives.

With the intent of increasing the value that sales engineers deliver to customer firms, senior management at the Power Systems Group of Rockwell Automation challenged senior business analyst Joseph Razum to develop a sales tool based on the total cost of ownership (TCO) concept. The analytical procedures and software that resulted would come to be known as the TCO Toolbox. This innovative consultative selling tool would enable sales engineers to conduct a TCO appraisal of customer firms' manufacturing and maintenance processes. Based on the results of such analyses, sales engineers would propose a total solution comprised of Dodge and Reliance Electric TCO product and service solutions. Following several months of development, Rockwell Automation introduced the TCO Toolbox in 2001. In less than 6 months, sales engineers conducted more than 50 TCO appraisals documenting approximately $3.7 million in operating and maintenance costs savings to customer firms.

Food Industry Business Manager Mark McElhinny's experience with a major agricultural produce supplier exemplifies the TCO appraisal and solution-generation process. For years, a California-based grower and processor of vegetables (Processor) had made decisions on the acquisition of equipment and maintenance, repair, and operating (MRO) supplies based on the traditional approach of selecting the lowest bidder. By the turn of the millennium, cutthroat international competition

persuaded this customer's senior managers to seek collaborative relationships with suppliers in order to reduce total costs and identify revenue-enhancing opportunities. Intrigued by Rockwell Automation's new TCO approach, Processor management invited McElhinny to conduct a TCO appraisal at a major plant. Along with Razum, McElhinny spent a day at the California plant site evaluating Processor operations. Processor personnel cooperated fully in the research, furnishing detailed cost and technical data on plant operations.

Using TCO Appraisal™ procedures, McElhinny and Razum began by mapping the steps in the plant's vegetable processing operations. They quickly learned that three sizing tasks (i.e., vegetables are mechanically sorted by size and weight) contributed significant costs and served as potential logjams in operations (e.g., if sizing equipment failed the entire plant would be shut down until it was repaired). Next, they identified all the major cost drivers associated with the operation, including such things as equipment and component prices (e.g., bearings, gearboxes, drives, and motor prices), line inspection, maintenance, overhaul, and downtime costs. For each cost driver, McElhinny and Razum in turn charted the constituent tasks (e.g., inspection, removal of failed bearings and installation of new ones, lubrication, bearing recycling) that contributed expenses to the process. As they reviewed the results of the TCO Appraisal, the pair made an important discovery—all sizing equipment bearings failed within 6 months even though they were designed to last a full year and the costs associated with physically replacing those bearings vastly exceeded industry averages.

Rockwell Automation managers and their customer counterparts conducted an in-depth evaluation of all sizing equipment bearing costs. The customer firm used a total of 24 sizing machines in three separate vegetable processing steps. Each sizing machine used 30 standard bearings. Processor personnel

BOX 8.4
Continued

designed, manufactured, and maintained the sizing equipment. Investigations revealed that the first two sizing steps in the processing operation were the source of many problems. During these two steps, the sizing equipment removed soil, debris, and water from the vegetables. It seemed clear that these extraneous materials were jamming and wearing down the bearings at a rapid rate. The Rockwell Automation managers also uncovered redundancies and inefficiencies in the Processor's maintenance and bearing replacement procedures. Continuing on with the assessment, managers gathered relevant data on such things as the incumbent bearing prices, Processor labor rates, and maintenance procedure times. They also established values for such things as annual system downtime, opportunity cost of downtime, and the amount of scheduled versus unscheduled maintenance.

Based on their TCO Appraisal, McElhinny and Razum recommended that the Processor replace its incumbent bearings with Dodge EZ KLEEN® bearings and institute a revised maintenance and bearing replacement regimen. EZ KLEEN bearings would provide several key benefits. Not only did they have protective features that keep out contaminants, they are lubricated for life, which eliminates a relubrication maintenance activity, and come with a two-year warranty. Moreover, EZ KLEEN bearings can be replaced significantly

quicker and easier than the incumbent bearings. Inputting their data and assumptions into a TCO Toolbox software model, McElhinny and Razum estimated that although EZ KLEEN bearings have a price slightly higher than the incumbent bearings, they would reduce the Processor's total costs $60,000 annually. To validate the TCO Toolbox estimate, McElhinny and Razum proposed a one-year pilot test on one sizing machine. The Processor's senior management agreed to the pilot test.

Following the pilot test, Rockwell Automation managers used the TCO Toolbox to calculate actual cost savings attributed to the spherical, EZ KLEEN bearings. Not only had they reduced the sizing machine's TCO, they likely extended its useful lifetime. In addition, Rockwell Automation's solution reduced machine downtime, increased plant reliability, and freed up maintenance personnel to complete other value-added activities. For their part, Rockwell Automation not only gained an immediate sale, but also converted a transactional account into a collaborative partner. Meticulously saving all data and insights from the pilot test, Razum and McElhinny wrote a persuasive case study for Rockwell Automation sales engineers, recalibrated and fine-tuned TCO Toolbox formulas, and crafted a more precise value proposition for similar application segments.

GAINING THE INITIAL ORDER

At the close of the assessing mutual fit portion of the gaining customers process, the business market manager along with the salesperson determines whether it is in the best interests of the supplier firm to do business with the prospect. If the answer is an emphatic "yes," the sales representative takes deliberate steps to gain an initial order. If the answer is an unqualified "no," the salesperson directs her attention to another prospect firm.

In many instances, to proceed with gaining the initial order, the supplier must first gain approved-vendor status. By conveying **approved-vendor status**, purchasing managers indicate that they are confident the supplier firm will dependably deliver the value that its representatives promise, and formally recognize it as a potential supplier to their firm. To gain designation as an approved vendor, the salesperson, working together with other supplier personnel, provides product samples to the customer firm for testing, evidence of quality or conformance to ISO 9000 series standards, and proof of management capability and technical competence. Often, a cross-functional team from the customer firm will visit the supplier firm and tour its facilities as part of the process.

In this section, we discuss how the salesperson demonstrates the value of the supplier firm's market offering and convinces the prospect to acquire it. We conclude by examining how the salesperson negotiates for the order. As in the previous section of this chapter, we continue to contrast the nature of these activities within the context of transactional and SPIN selling.

Demonstrating and Documenting Value

Armed with a clear understanding of prospect needs, the salesperson practices adaptive selling, modifying the supplier's value proposition and market offering elements to better align them with customer requirements and preferences. In Box 8.5, we discuss how a sales representative for QUALCOMM, a manufacturer of satellite

BOX 8.5
QUALCOMM Introduces High Technology into a Low-Technology Industry

QUALCOMM markets transportation solutions in the form of satellite-based tracking systems to trucking firms that specialize in long hauls, less-than-truckload deliveries, and irregular or flexible routes. Its OmniTRACS® service represents the core service offering, which it augments with a number of optional services, such as SensorTRACS®. QUALCOMM OmniTRACS (OT) entails a satellite dish and an intelligent communications unit placed on board customer trucks, plus satellite time that enables customer firm managers to track and communicate with the truck driver while on the road in remote locations. OT helps the truck fleet customer gain better fleet utilization through increased load miles, and decreased out-of-route and empty "back haul" miles; it assists in lowering fuel costs, long-distance telephone charges, and maintenance costs; and it promotes lower driver turnover and higher dispatcher productivity.

SensorTRACS (ST) entails the placement of sensors on critical truck parts, such as the engine, odometer, or trailer. These sensors transmit information on driver and truck performance back to QUALCOMM and, in turn, the trucking firm. ST allows the trucking firm to provide driver bonuses based on reduced idling time, increased fuel efficiency, and lower truck maintenance charges. ST also monitors the status of special cargo. For example, ST can monitor the temperature of a refrigerated trailer and alert the driver if it rises to a dangerous level.

OT and ST are high-technology products that provide a comprehensive solution to trucking firms' scheduling and routing requirements. To gain customers for them, though, QUALCOMM managers must answer two recurring customer questions: (1) How will the new system contribute to the trucking firm's bottom line? and (2) How will the trucking firm pay for the system? QUALCOMM uses a value-based marketing approach to provide answers.

According to QUALCOMM managers, value-based marketing requires that the supplier "reach the customer's head, heart, and

BOX 8.5
Continued

stomach." To reach the customer's head, QUALCOMM developed a Cost/Benefit Analysis worksheet for its sales representatives. The sales rep and the customer sit down and work through the analysis to show customers where cost savings will come.

The worksheet contains 16 rows and 3 columns, where each row represents a benefit or cost category. In the far left column, QUALCOMM provides customers with dollar ranges of revenues, profits, or costs for each benefit or cost category based on its own research or American Trucking Association studies. Using these ranges as a guide, the potential customer provides its own estimate for each row, which the sales rep records in the extreme right column. Then, in the middle column, the sales rep estimates the dollar benefits and cost savings that the customer firm can expect to receive if it purchases QUAL-COMM services. Finally, the sales rep summarizes them as a total monthly benefit.

QUALCOMM sales reps use the worksheet to identify at least five items that make the value of OT and ST apparent to the customer. Moreover, they try to find one "shattering value" that makes the investment in the system immediately and unquestionably worthwhile to the customer. Although managers at large trucking firms typically demand detailed worksheet analyses, managers at smaller firms often find them bewildering. To sell value to these smaller yet important prospects, QUALCOMM sales reps revert to a basic PowerPoint® presentation that substitutes cartoon icons and clearly identified cost savings for detailed analyses.

To reach a prospect's heart and stomach, QUALCOMM demonstrates the value of its offerings and establishes trust. This is due to the fact that most customers can only appreciate some of the benefits and cost savings of OT and ST when they experience them. QUALCOMM provides this demonstration through side-by-side tests. QUALCOMM managers encourage prospects to test out OT or ST for a month simultaneously with a competitor's system. They help prospects to track benefits and cost savings during the trial. Prospects are often impressed by the superiority of OT and ST and order them immediately.

In those cases where QUALCOMM faces in-kind competition, managers turn to a finer-grained value analysis. For example, they might investigate the differential reliability of QUALCOMM versus competitor systems, using metrics such as percent of messages not delivered. Alternatively, they might evaluate the ability of competing systems to monitor idling costs. Finally, given that QUALCOMM services are more comprehensive, managers stress the cumulative benefits of their offerings.

tracking systems for trucks, uses a value model to evaluate the worth of these systems to prospective customers. During such analyses, a rep tries to identify five significant value elements and at least one "shattering value." A shattering value is an element that makes investment in the tracking system clearly worthwhile. Using these insights, the QUALCOMM salesperson customizes the firm's value proposition for the prospect.

As another example, in Box 8.6, we describe how account managers for Sonoco's Protective Packaging Division work with potential customer managers to research their current packaging costs, use a cost-of-use approach to design solutions that reduce those costs, and then incorporate the results of those analyses in sales presentations. As we have noted, Sonoco gets a second use from its value assessment efforts by documenting them in case studies so that account managers can use when marketing Sonoco solutions to other prospects.

The Sonoco Products Company's Protective Packaging Division (SPPD) converts company paper products into a variety of shapes, such as rods and cones for use in the packaging of major appliances and white goods. In the words of division managers, "SPPD creates customized shapes using common materials." Because SPPD products are often more expensive than competing packaging materials, division managers rely on a cost-of-use approach to guide marketing efforts. In SPPD parlance, *cost-of-use* encompasses a customer's total expenses incurred during the application of SPPD products. In essence, SPPD sells the total value it creates by lowering a customer's total packaging costs. These cost reductions come in the form of reduced product damage, less inventory, reduced packaging costs, more efficient packaging systems, and so on.

Through a series of sales calls with a prospective customer's senior managers, plant managers, and packaging specialists, SPPD representatives investigate the prospect's current packaging costs. They focus exclusively on "hard" costs that can be documented, such as those associated with package weight and the number of packaging components. SPPD reps avoid "soft" numbers, such as service-related costs, so that the customer cannot challenge their cost figures. With a better understanding of the customer's current costs, SPPD managers design a total packaging solution. Then they compare the cost of use associated the customer's current packaging system with that of SPPD's proposed solution. In turn, SPPD prices its packaging solution as a function of total cost reductions.

SPPD representatives present their proposals plus the results of their investigations to a prospect's senior management. During the formal presentation, SPPD reps provide detailed case studies of cost savings delivered to other customers. One year following the acceptance of a proposal, SPPD audits actual cost savings and reports findings to the customer. Furthermore, SPPD saves these findings in a file of cost-savings case studies. SPPD reps, in turn, draw on these case studies when making proposals to other prospects.

SPPD puts its cost-savings case studies to use in other important ways. To begin, SPPD engineers identify commonalities in packaging solutions delivered across customers. In this way, they drive toward product standardization in the SPPD product portfolio, thus reducing the division's manufacturing costs. SPPD management also makes a concerted effort to apply insights gained from customer case studies to its own operations, thus gaining process improvements and internal cost reductions. Finally, SPPD uses its findings in the new-product development process. For example, insights gained from case histories prompted the development of key line extensions including expanded polystyrene shapes and inner packs.

After selecting a market offering that meets prospect requirements, the salesperson enters the presentation stage of the interaction with the prospect. As in Figure 8.4, the rep must persuasively propose solutions and gain the order.

Propose Solutions

Again, how the salesperson approaches the presentation varies across transactional and SPIN selling. During transactional selling training programs, instructors counsel salespeople to personalize market offering benefits to customer needs via the FAB approach. It entails translating **features**, which are product characteristics or specifications, and **advantages**, which are functions that the supplier's product performs

Figure 8.5 Drilling Down to Worth with Value Mapping

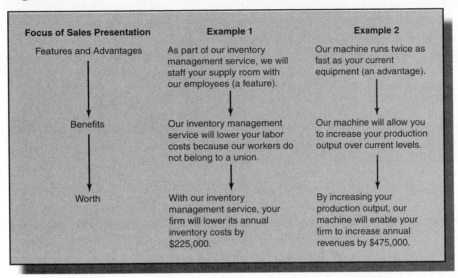

Focus of Sales Presentation	Example 1	Example 2
Features and Advantages	As part of our inventory management service, we will staff your supply room with our employees (a feature).	Our machine runs twice as fast as your current equipment (an advantage).
Benefits	Our inventory management service will lower your labor costs because our workers do not belong to a union.	Our machine will allow you to increase your production output over current levels.
Worth	With our inventory management service, your firm will lower its annual inventory costs by $225,000.	By increasing your production output, our machine will enable your firm to increase annual revenues by $475,000.

better than competitive models, into customer-specific **benefits**, which summarize how the product will help the prospect. In Figure 8.5, we provide two examples of how a salesperson converts a feature and an advantage into benefits.

In SPIN selling, the salesperson explains how the supplier firm's market offering meets the explicit needs of the customer firm. As illustrated in Figure 8.5, this goes beyond stating benefits to explicating the worth of the supplier firm's market offerings. Business market managers refer to this practice of translating features and advantages to benefits and ultimately to worth as **value mapping** or value stream mapping. Progressive suppliers often "explode" value maps backward to determine which internal business processes yield specific offering features and advantages. In this way, they can take deliberate steps to improve the value of their offerings by reengineering related business processes.[40]

Salespeople demonstrate the value of their market offerings in a variety of ways:

- **Customer value model**—As per our discussions in Chapter 2, the supplier firm should build a customer value model in which as many elements as possible have been stated in monetary terms.
- **Joint value assessment**—The sales representative and customer managers can work through the customer value model together, quantifying and specifying each element for the customer's own situation.
- **Side-by-side tests**—To overcome any skepticism over value estimates on the part of prospects, where possible, the sales representative should urge the customer to evaluate the supplier's offering versus a competitor's offering in rigorous comparative tests.
- **Value-in-use case studies**—The supplier firm should prepare and distribute value-in-use case studies from current customers. An outside auditing firm might even be hired to verify customer benefits and cost savings.

- **Placeholders**—In Chapter 2, we urged supplier firms to represent less tangible value elements within value models with a "value placeholder." These placeholder elements should draw a prospect's attention to viable and important sources of value.
- **Signaling criteria**—As we pointed out in Chapters 2 and 3, the supplier firm may not be able to quantify certain value elements. Here, the salesperson communicates value via signaling criteria that are nonmonetary representations of worth.

Box 8.7 recounts a noteworthy case on how the Swedish company SKF enables its salespeople, working along with customer managers, to measure the value of their offerings through the SKF Documented Solutions™ Program.

When proposing solutions, salespeople can expect to encounter objections from prospects. In transactional selling, experts view objections, or resistance to the sales message, as a sign of prospect interest. Salespeople handle objections by first listening carefully to objections and then answering each one thoroughly. Given that reps commonly hear the same objections across customers, managers advise them to prepare "canned responses" prior to the sales call.

Another key difference between transactional and SPIN selling is that advocates of SPIN selling urge sales reps to prevent objections rather than to just handle them. How does the salesperson prevent objections? First, the rep makes a greater effort at qualifying prospects and reduces the likelihood of calling on a firm that has no need for the supplier's offering. Second, the rep shrewdly uses implication and need-payoff questions to get purchasing managers to "sell it to themselves." Third, the salesperson who has a deeper understanding of the prospective customer's requirements and preferences can propose more tailored offering options that are worthy of serious consideration.

Gain the Order

Because it is possible for a salesperson to take an order on the first sales call with a prospect, the most important part of transactional selling is closing. According to traditional thinking, the sales rep must "always ask for the order" when making a sales call. In fact, sales courses routinely instruct salespeople to close early and often and at least five times during the call. To help reps with their closing techniques, pundits have written many books that summarize snappy and clever, if not high-pressure, closing lines. Among the classic closes are

- *Assumption Close*—Where do you want it delivered?
- *Alternative Close*—Do you want the 3-year or 4-year maintenance contract?
- *Standing-Room-Only Close*—If you don't order now, I'll have to sell it to another customer firm that has expressed an interest in it.
- *Last-Chance Close*—This special offer ends today. If you wait until tomorrow, you'll have to pay full price.
- *Order-Blank Close*—The salesperson begins to fill out the order form before the customer has agreed to the purchase.

Although closing is considered to be essential in SPIN selling, the ultimate goal is obtaining commitment from the customer. In Chapter 10, we discuss in detail the importance of commitment within customer and supplier working relationships.

BOX 8.7
SKF Gains and Grows Customers via Its Documented Solutions™ Program

Based in Göteborg, Sweden, AB SKF is the world's leading provider of bearings and seals. With annual turnover exceeding SEK42 billion (Swedish kronor), SKF is organized into five divisions: industrial, automotive, electrical, service, and aero & steel. Authorized resellers account for a significant portion of these sales. In recent years, SKF senior management has taken a broader perspective, positioning SKF as a solutions and profitability improvement company.

In March 2002, SKF USA Inc. launched its Documented Solutions Program (DSP). DSP features laptop software that enables a sales representative working with customer managers to conduct a value assessment and demonstrate the cost savings an SKF solution can provide. SKF recognized the need to support customers in managing their total cost of operations and where SKF can help them become more profitable. SKF drew on its vast industry-specific experience, investments in benchmarking studies, and its results working with customers to create an extensive database that serves as the knowledge bank of DSP. Importantly, DSP software is interactive, allowing customer managers to plug in their own numbers for materials, labor, downtime, and energy costs to calculate their own return on investment or break-even analysis. Alternatively, SKF sales representatives can use basic instruments such as amp meters and vibration sensors to calculate energy usage and forecast bearing life. Based on this research, they can diagnose root cause failure and propose changes that affect the customer's total cost of ownership. SKF is investing heavily throughout the world to support customers in their quest to become more efficient and profitable. In Figures 8.6 and 8.7, we reprint material promoting the Documented Solutions Program from SKF.

Depending on customer interest and subsequent negotiations, SKF is prepared to back up its predicted cost savings in a performance agreement. SKF and its customer agree on the key performance measurements that they will track to determine actual cost savings and enter into an Integrated Maintenance Solutions™ (IMS) contract. After a defined time period, these cost savings are audited. If SKF fails to provide the cost savings it predicted, as spelled out in the IMS contract, it would pay the customer the difference. If SKF exceeds the forecast, it would share in a portion of the documented cost savings.

SKF sales representatives successfully use DSP not only to gain new customers, but also to grow business with existing customers. For example, they routinely support their authorized reseller partners with joint sales calls on existing customers. While the reseller salesperson focuses his or her attention on process quantification (e.g., cost savings from 24x7 delivery, local inventory) during such calls, the SKF representative concentrates on more-demanding applications quantification, such as estimating possible increases in pump life. Such collaborations often lead to an irresistible value proposition for customer firms. In a recent case, SKF sales representatives used DSP to convince a major customer to avoid shifting its bearing purchases to reverse auctions as well as to persuade the customer to move a greater share of its business to SKF and its reseller. When SKF and the customer audited the cost savings produced after a prespecified period, they discovered that the realized cost savings significantly exceeded the total purchase price of the bearings acquired!

(continued)

Commitment "captures the perceived continuity or growth in a relationship between two firms."[41] According to research from the Dartnell Corporation, a leading sales management consulting firm, the typical sales professional makes an average of about four calls on a prospect to close a business sale.[42] For this reason, advocates of the

BOX 8.7
Continued

Figure 8.6 SKF Documented Solutions™ Program Promotional Brochure Cover

Source: Used by permission of SKF USA Inc.

SPIN selling approach urge salespeople to seek increasing customer commitment with each contact rather than to mindlessly try to close during every call. In fact, they argue that asking for the order too early and too often during the sales cycle may actually alienate and anger the prospect.

BOX 8.7
Continued

Figure 8.7 SKF Documented Solutions™ Program Description

How much can SKF save you?

Let's do the numbers.

Introducing SKF Documented Solutions.

SKF is probably not the first of your supplier partners to talk about "documented savings." But we are confident that no one else can match the new tool we've developed for predicting the real-world, annual net cost savings you could realize from SKF products and services. An extension of our global "Real Conditions/Real Solutions" strategy, SKF Documented Solutions can show you how to cut thousands, if not hundreds of thousands of dollars, from your total operating budget.

Explore options and calculate savings.

At the heart of the SKF Documented Solution Program is powerful new proprietary software that draws on years of industry-specific experience and real-world performance data to "prove" savings in advance. In about one hour with an SKF representative, you can see precisely how a particular SKF solution can reduce your total cost of operation. And because the program allows you to plug in your own numbers—for materials, labor, downtime, energy costs, etc.—you can have confidence in the forecasted savings.

Based on industry-specific successes.

With nearly 100 years of experience, SKF knows a lot about your industry—the technical challenges you face, and how they can affect productivity and profitability. The SKF Documented Solution Program uses SKF's significant experience in your industry to document the viability of specific savings solutions. You'll see the actual, bottom-line results of similar solutions implemented by other companies in your industry.

*Patents Pending. All rights reserved by SKF
© 2001 SKF

Source: Used by permission of SKF USA Inc.

As per adaptive selling, the salesperson must assess the events during a given call and seek an appropriate level of commitment from the prospect. SPIN selling divides possible commitments into two broad categories. **Advances** represent progress in the purchasing process, while **orders** are actual sales. Examples of advances include such things as making appointments with other members of the buying team, getting approval from the customer to deliver a sample product, and making definite plans for a follow-up sales call. To be successful, the salesperson pursues an appropriate advance from a prospect at each stage of the sales cycle, working up to the initial order.

Negotiating the First Sale

In business markets, a customer firm's tentative decision to buy prompts more detailed negotiations with the supplier firm. Three aspects that we single out for consideration are pricing the initial offering, negotiation approaches, and understanding the best alternative to a negotiated agreement (BATNA).

Pricing the Initial Offering

As a prelude to price discussions, the two firms must come to a preliminary agreement on the precise nature of the market offering the supplier will provide. Although supplier and customer may concur on the makeup of the naked solution, they may have different views as to which optional services are to be included at what total price. As per our discussions of managing market offerings in Chapter 5, supplier and customer representatives may be willing to trade product or service elements for price modifications. For example, in the case of defeaturing or cooperative pricing, the supplier firm may lower a product's price if the customer firm relaxes specifications that in turn allow the supplier to produce the offering at a lower cost.

Of course, supplier and customer must negotiate a final price. As part of this negotiation, the supplier might use the pricing tactic of an **initial use discount**, which appears as a price reduction on the invoice. The supplier may use this tactic as an additional inducement for change or as compensation for perceived or actual switching costs that the customer will incur. The initial use discount has the advantage of establishing in the customer's mind what the supplier believes is the equitable price for the value the offering provides, and one that the customer should expect to pay on subsequent purchase occasions. **Trade-in allowances**, another form of initial use discounts, are credits a customer firm receives from a new supplier in exchange for that customer's used equipment or unused supplies.

Suppliers also commonly use a number of other pricing tactics. **Early payment discounts** allow customers to deduct a percentage from the invoice for paying within a specified number of days. **Volume discounts** provide lower unit prices in return for larger-quantity orders. **Freight allowances** are invoice reductions that compensate customers for transportation and delivery charges. **Rebates** or **bonuses** cover a variety of schemes where suppliers provide money or additional products and services at no charge as a reward based on the amount of business a customer has done with the supplier during some time period.

Finally, once both sides have come to agreement on the final configuration of the market offering and its price, they must also finalize terms and conditions. These include such things as when and where deliveries are to be made, the nature of payment schedules, the particulars of return goods policies and warranties, and installation procedures. **Extended dating**, where the customer gets an unusually long period to pay for its purchase, serves as another pricing tactic.

Negotiation Approaches

As we mentioned in Chapter 3, the sales rep must be familiar with two approaches to bargaining. In **distributive negotiations**, the two sides assume that the value "pie" is fixed and haggle over one item, typically price. With this approach, each party views gains for one party as coming at the expense of the other, and acts accordingly. In **integrative negotiations**, the two sides first prioritize their own requirements and then trade off elements that are less important to their respective firms for those that are more important. With this approach, the two parties work together to find ways to expand the outcomes available, which they equitably share.

Naturally, as part of adaptive selling, the salesperson must select the bargaining approach that fits the situation. Typically, selling and bargaining approaches go "hand in hand." For example, when discussing price in a simple sale with a purchasing manager whose firm has a buying orientation, the salesperson will most likely draw on the techniques of transactional selling and distributive negotiations. On the other hand, when working out the final details of a market offering in a complex sale with a major account that adheres to a supply management orientation, the representative will likely utilize consultative selling and integrative bargaining.

Of course, even when a customer firm and supplier firm use integrative bargaining to expand the value pie, they ultimately must split the expanded value. So, a distributive bargaining phase follows integrative bargaining. Yet, firms typically find it easier to split an expanded pie, in part because they each recognize the greater present and future value that they can generate by preserving goodwill in their relationship.

Understanding BATNA

Regardless of the negotiation approach taken, the salesperson should develop what Fisher and Ury call a **best alternative to a negotiated agreement (BATNA)**. A BATNA is the most favorable option that the supplier can pursue if the supplier firm cannot reach an equitable agreement with a prospect. Thus, the BATNA is a standard for comparison during bargaining. If the terms of an agreement exceed the BATNA, the sales representative accepts the terms of the deal. On the other hand, if it falls below the BATNA, the rep declines and either makes a counteroffer or terminates the discussions.[43]

In business markets, a BATNA might entail seeking out another promising prospect or market segment if the prospect refuses to pay an equitable price for a highly augmented market offering. Alternatively, the supplier firm might choose to market new offerings if the firm couldn't make a profit from existing offerings. With a BATNA in mind, the salesperson is more objective in dealings with a prospect. Rather than caving in on price to gain the order, the salesperson knows the alternatives in advance. By understanding the BATNA, the rep has the confidence to say "no" to a bad deal. Lost orders are not necessarily failures. Sometimes it is better to let a competitor "win" a bad deal.

INITIAL ORDER FULFILLMENT

Contrary to what many sales and marketing experts apparently believe, the process of gaining customers does not end with the receipt of an order. Instead, we argue that business market managers must take deliberate steps to ensure that the offering is delivered as promised and meets prospect requirements to their complete satisfaction. We refer to these activities as **order fulfillment**. In all too many firms, though, order fulfillment falls short of being seamless and error free. Responsibilities for order fulfillment typically cut across many functional groups, and rarely does one person oversee and coordinate cross-functional activities. Furthermore, no one has a clear understanding of how order fulfillment works in its entirety. As a result, order fulfillment systems are often poorly coordinated and suffer from communications lapses, resulting in certain tasks going uncompleted and others suffering from duplication and redundancy in efforts across functional groups.

As outlined in Figure 8.1, we begin this final section of the chapter by recommending actions that supplier firms can take to coordinate cross-functional order fulfillment efforts. Next, we turn our attention to completing the initial transaction. Once the initial order has been fulfilled, the business market manager reflects on the process and makes another essential screening decision—whether to continue doing business with the customer.

Coordinating Supplier Functions

Managers and experts in the field of operations commonly embed order fulfillment within a larger order management cycle.[44] Depicted in the second column of Figure 8.8, the typical **order management cycle (OMC)** is a 10-step process from planning to postsales service that defines a company's business system.[45] As Shapiro, Rangan, and Sviokla illustrate in the chart, most firms divide responsibilities for performing each of these steps among diverse functional groups and rarely, if ever, put a single senior manager or function in charge. With many handoffs between functions, the likelihood customers will "fall through the cracks" and receive poor service increases dramatically. To fill in these cracks, Shapiro, Rangan, and Sviokla urge companies to coordinate the activities of diverse functions in several ways.

To begin with, they argue that senior management must promote internally a systems philosophy based on customer responsiveness. They do so by providing training to managers from all relevant functions about the importance of OMC and their group's role in it. To reinforce the systems philosophy, senior management simultaneously creates individual rewards based on cross-functional performance of OMC tasks. Obviously, when functional groups are compensated for working together, they develop better ways to handle customer order "handoffs." Next, working as a team, key managers from relevant functional areas use business process mapping to chart the firm's OMC. Then, drawing upon business process reengineering, they redesign the OMC to make it more responsive to customer needs. Reengineered OMC systems often use management information systems such as CRM and partner relationship management (PRM) to streamline order fulfillment and link functional groups. For example, in Box 8.8 we illustrate how Siebel Systems software helped Asyst Technologies to synchronize its cross-functional OMC activities.

To sustain the practice of interfunctional cooperation, Shapiro, Rangan, and Sviokla urge senior managers to periodically assign projects to these cross-functional teams associated with OMC issues. Finally, to ensure long-term cross-functional cooperation, progressive firms place a senior manager in charge of the overall OMC process. Armed with the appropriate authority, this manager resolves differences between groups and inspires the functions to work together.

Figure 8.8 The Order Management Cycle

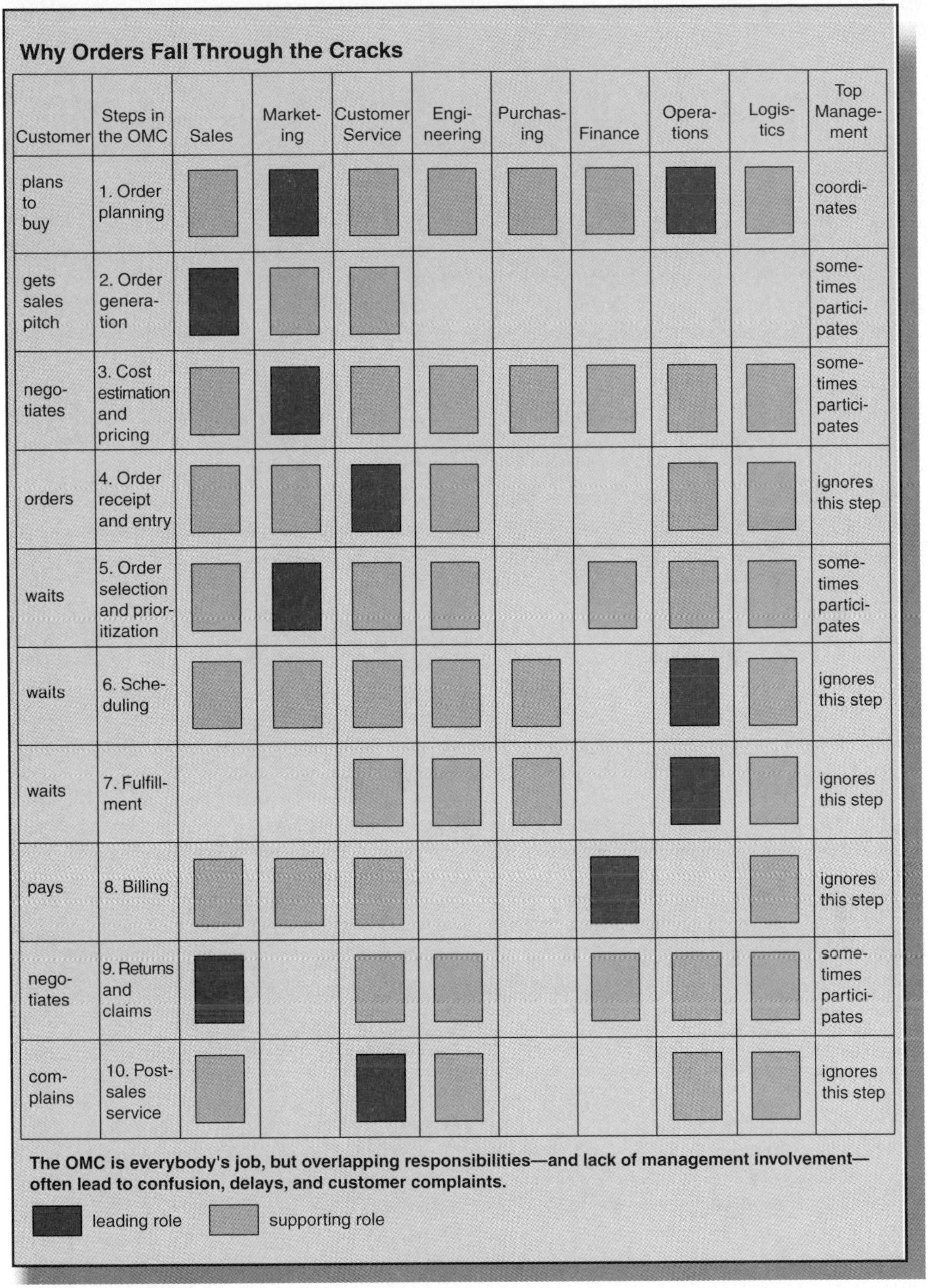

Why Orders Fall Through the Cracks

Customer	Steps in the OMC	Sales	Marketing	Customer Service	Engineering	Purchasing	Finance	Operations	Logistics	Top Management
plans to buy	1. Order planning	supporting	leading	supporting	supporting	supporting	supporting	leading	supporting	coordinates
gets sales pitch	2. Order generation	leading	supporting	supporting						sometimes participates
negotiates	3. Cost estimation and pricing	supporting	leading	supporting	supporting	supporting	supporting	supporting	supporting	sometimes participates
orders	4. Order receipt and entry	supporting	supporting	leading	supporting			supporting	supporting	ignores this step
waits	5. Order selection and prioritization	supporting	leading	supporting	supporting		supporting	supporting	supporting	sometimes participates
waits	6. Scheduling	supporting	supporting	supporting	supporting	supporting		leading	supporting	ignores this step
waits	7. Fulfillment			supporting	supporting	supporting		leading	supporting	ignores this step
pays	8. Billing			supporting	supporting		leading		supporting	ignores this step
negotiates	9. Returns and claims	leading		supporting	supporting		supporting	supporting	supporting	sometimes participates
complains	10. Post-sales service	supporting		leading	supporting			supporting	supporting	ignores this step

The OMC is everybody's job, but overlapping responsibilities—and lack of management involvement—often lead to confusion, delays, and customer complaints.

■ leading role   ▢ supporting role

Source: Benson P. Shapiro, V. Kasturi Rangan, and John J. Sviokla, "Staple Yourself to an Order," *Harvard Business Review* (July–August 1992): 118.

BOX 8.8
Siebel eBusiness Applications® Helps Asyst Technologies Improve Sales Forecasting and Product Configuration Capabilities

With annual sales exceeding $2 billion, Siebel Systems, Inc., is the world's leading provider of eBusiness applications software. Its integrated family of software solutions enables firms to deploy sales, marketing, and customer service systems across all sales channels including the Web, call centers, field sales forces, resellers, and dealer networks. By providing a centralized repository of customer data captured from all customer interactions across all channels and touch points, Siebel eBusiness Applications permit organizations to maintain an ongoing and seamless dialogue with customers regardless of when, where, or how the interaction occurs. They enable organizations to apply best practices in sales, marketing, and service, thereby enabling organizations to better understand, anticipate, and respond to customer needs. And, by providing real-time views of customer activity, Siebel eBusiness Applications give managers better visibility into market dynamics and customer demand. Siebel System's experiences with a client, Asyst Technologies, illustrate how its applications can improve sales forecasting and product configuration.

Based in Fremont, California, Asyst Technologies markets automation systems, materials, and controls that firms such as Intel, Motorola, and Texas Instruments use to manufacture semiconductor wafers and chips. Asyst annual sales exceed $500 million. For many years, Asyst managers cobbled together a monthly sales forecast from disparate sets of data supplied by four internal groups. Each group generated and used the data for its own purposes. One group estimated sales by part numbers, another predicted sales to specific customers, a third projected total dollar revenues, and yet another anticipated total shipments. A master scheduler reconciled the four sets of data in a decidedly unscientific manner into a single forecast. Unfortunately, the forecast was so inaccurate that the firm experienced significant problems with materials

orders, manufacturing schedules, inventory levels, incomplete shipments, and delivery timetables.

Forecasting problems were compounded by the fact that Asyst lacked a product configuration system. Asyst account managers would routinely write up orders for complex systems without specifying requisite parts or considering the technical feasibility or cost of their proposed solution. Instead, they would merely hand off the order to an applications engineer who would review the proposal, determine parts and process requirements, assess costs, and review prices. Understandably, the process frequently resulted in invalid product designs, costly rework, delivery delays, angry customers, and reduced profits.

To remedy these problems, Asyst management asked Siebel Systems and Siebel Alliance Partner and systems integrator PricewaterhouseCoopers (PwC) to develop and implement a solution. Seibel and PwC managers proposed a solution composed of Siebel Sales® and Siebel eConfigurator applications. Seibel Enterprise Integration Manager® (EIM) software would link these front-office applications to Asyst's back-office systems comprised of enterprise resource planning (ERP) software and various databases. Siebel Sales would permit Asyst managers to access in real time data on customer orders from the four internal groups as well as other sources, track the progress of all account managers in securing new business, synchronize and integrate all available data on future sales, and devise and circulate more reliable sales forecasts. Siebel eConfigurator would complement Siebel Sales. Drawing on Asyst engineering specifications and cost data, Siebel eConfigurator allowed account managers to work with customer managers online in real time to design complex offerings that are accurate, complete, technically valid, and profitable.

Drawing upon the expertise of Siebel and PwC personnel, Asyst implemented both

BOX 8.8
Continued

Siebel Sales and Siebel eConfigurator within six months. Asyst managers report that Siebel Sales has yielded a dramatic improvement in forecasting—materials forecasting is 50 percent more accurate, the time required to develop a reliable forecast has dropped from four weeks to one, and the company can now forecast by part number, region, account manager, product mix, and average sales price relative to cost. The forecasts in turn have enabled Asyst to better control materials orders and inventory and to project profitability.

Furthermore Asyst has seen a 50 percent drop in delayed deliveries and an improvement in delivery accuracy. With Siebel eConfigurator, Asyst account managers work with customers in real time to configure and price orders. As a result, reworking and unbilled product costs were largely eliminated, average order configuration time has dropped from 25 to 2 days, and applications engineers no longer have to review orders and instead direct their efforts toward new product development.

Completing the Transaction

In addition to cross-functional integration, Shapiro, Rangan, and Sviokla argue that customer-responsive order fulfillment hinges on order selection, prioritization, and scheduling, as well as cost estimation and pricing. These are steps 3, 5, and 6 in the OMC in Figure 8.8. In this section, we present the technique of revenue or yield management as a means of addressing these related issues. Then we examine the salesperson's task of following up to make certain that the final four steps of the OMC are executed to the customer's complete satisfaction.

Manage Revenue[46]

"**Revenue management** is the application of disciplined tactics that predict consumer [customer] behavior at the micromarket level and that optimize product availability and price to maximize revenue growth."[47] Widely practiced in the airline and hospitality industries, revenue management is applicable to market offerings that share some or all of certain characteristics. They include perishable products and opportunities, markets featuring seasonal or periodic demand, differential offering value across market segments, competition for offerings between small-quantity and short-term users and large-scale and long-term users, and frequent discounting to meet competition. In business markets, revenue management is particularly useful in such industries as business travel and lodging, and consulting and research. Managers in other settings might also consider applying it.

In Figure 8.9, we summarize the seven core concepts of revenue management. The central idea is that firms can optimize profits by balancing supply and demand at the microsegment level via price rather than at the mass-market level via capacity modifications. To do so, firms segment markets in terms of value and set prices as a function of those differential values rather than costs.

Often, time is a determinant of value, with time-sensitive customers willing to pay more for assurances that they will receive a service immediately when they require it. Critically, supplier firms reserve or restrict a certain portion of their products and services for these high-value and high-profit-potential customers. If the firm ever "stocks out," it is on low-value offerings targeted toward low profit-potential

Figure 8.9
The Seven Core
Concepts of
Revenue
Management

- Focus on price rather than costs when balancing supply and demand.
- Replace cost-based pricing with market-based pricing.
- Sell to segmented micromarkets, not mass markets.
- Reserve sufficient product for most valuable customers.
- Make decisions based on knowledge, not suppositions.
- Exploit each product's value cycle.
- Continually reevaluate revenue opportunities.

Source: Adapted from Robert G. Cross, "Launching the Revenue Rocket," *Cornell Hotel and Restaurant Administration Quarterly* (April 1997): 33.

customers. Thus, rental car companies always reserve a certain number of premium-priced cars for price-insensitive business travelers, who will drive them for several days, rather than to rent them at a discount to bargain-hunting vacationers, who will use them for just one day.

Another time-based concept that comes into play in revenue management is that of the value cycle, which we described in Chapter 3 and illustrated in Box 3.6. The **value cycle** captures ebb and flow of benefits and costs that accrue to a customer firm over time across an offering's activity cycle. Of particular importance in revenue management is the urgency with which segments require an offering after its commercialization and the price premium that each segment is willing to pay to acquire it as soon as possible after introduction. Armed with knowledge of an offering's value cycle, the business market manager can tactically adjust its price as a function of time from introduction in order to maximize profits.

In gaining new customers, the business market manager can use revenue management concepts to guide order selection, prioritization, and scheduling, as well as for cost estimation and pricing decisions. The supplier should target market segments and prospective customers within those segments that receive the greatest value from a market offering. Furthermore, it should focus its market or product development initiatives on them. In situations in which capacity is overbooked, inventory should be held in reserve for these segments. Importantly, managers should price the offering as a function of the value it creates for the segment. As for the remaining segments, their place in the order fulfillment queue is a function of their location in the value cycle and their profit potential for the supplier firm.[48]

Follow Up with Prospects After the Sale

As order fulfillment activities on the initial sale wind down, the salesperson makes follow-up calls to the new customer. As Figure 8.4 summarizes, the purpose is to ensure that the correct offering has been delivered in the appropriate amounts and that it is performing correctly. If problems have arisen, the sales representative resolves them. Postsales service may also be provided in the form of maintenance and repair work. In addition, the salesperson must be certain that the customer readily understands the invoice it received is accurate and pays promptly. In the rare cases when products are defective, the sales representative may be responsible for managing product returns and claims procedures.

Although these tasks are basically the same in transactional and SPIN selling, some important differences are noteworthy. When practicing SPIN selling, the salesperson must ascertain that the supplier has delivered on its value promise. For example, in high-tech markets salespeople commonly return to the customer firm after a reasonable period of time to perform a value audit. Using the value assessment techniques we described in Chapter 2, they assess the performance of the supplier's offering. Often, salespeople report these results in terms of **return on investment (ROI)**, comparing delivered benefits and cost savings to resources expended to acquire and operate the offering. Software producer Siebel Systems and the high-tech consulting firm The Gartner Group, among many others, have developed and market ROI models, programs, and services that enable both supplier and customer firms to perform and interpret such analyses.

Lastly, the salesperson should confirm that the customer is completely satisfied with its initial experience in doing business with the supplier. A part of this is actively probing for any areas of discontent. In the process, the salesperson constantly searches for new opportunities to add value to customer-specific offerings.

Deciding Whether to Continue Doing Business Together

At the conclusion of the first iteration of gaining a customer, business market managers perform one final screening task. They reflect back on the previous cycle of events and determine whether it is in the best interests of the supplier firm to continue serving the new account. In fact, it is the ideal time for managers to make such a determination because they have superior information for assessing mutual fit. Firms must recognize that even after careful screening, they still will not have perfect account selection, and some "false positive" selections are inevitable. To completely satisfy a new customer may require alterations in offerings or other commitments of resources that the supplier is unwilling to make.

In contrast, new customers that are attractive to the supplier represent a potentially valuable asset. Suppliers may provide extraordinary responsiveness to such customers to signal their interest in further developing the relationship. As we discussed in Chapter 2, the supplier should tailor the customer feedback it seeks from first-time customers. For example, how easy was it to do business with the supplier? Feedback is critical for making process improvements, because ease of doing business is critical for attracting new customers. Further, gaining immediate customer feedback enables the supplier to learn quickly of any problems or mistakes, giving the supplier an opportunity to remedy them and improve its chances of retaining the customer. Finally, gaining new customer feedback can suggest worthwhile market offering modifications.

SUMMARY

Gaining customers is the process of prospecting for new business relationships, assessing the mutual fit between prospective customer requirements and supplier offerings and priorities, making the initial sale, and fulfilling the initial order to the customer's complete satisfaction. Prospecting entails the related activities of generating leads internally from databases, prompting and gathering inquiries externally from the marketplace, and qualifying leads and inquiries as significant prospects. Although all prospecting efforts encompass these three activities, their nature varies as a function of the total number of potential customers, how readily the firm can enumerate these prospective customers, and the supplier firm's overall strategic intent in gaining customers. To improve the yield from prospecting, a supplier must gain the commitment and support of its sales force, which requires the provision of knowledge, motivation, experience, and sales support.

In assessing mutual fit, the salesperson schedules an initial meeting with a prospect, often followed by others, to learn each other's requirements and preferences. Through this interaction, managers determine whether it is in the supplier and customer firms' best interests to do business together. The variation in selling situations in business markets requires sales professionals to practice adaptive selling. For expositional clarity, we examined two fundamental approaches to selling: transactional selling and consultative selling, as embodied in the prominent SPIN selling process. Transactional selling focuses on gaining the immediate order as quickly as possible, whereas with consultative selling, the salesperson becomes a long-term, trusted, and value-adding resource for a customer by gaining a deep understanding of customer operations and offering problem-solving assistance.

To gain the initial order, the supplier firm demonstrates the value of its market offerings and convinces the prospect to acquire it. The supplier may demonstrate value in a variety of ways—a value model, joint value assessment, side-by-side tests, value-in-use case studies, placeholders, and signaling criteria. Following this demonstration, the salesperson negotiates the initial sale. Settling on the market offering that the supplier will provide and its pricing is critical to this step. The supplier and customer alternatively may use distributive or integrative bargaining in these negotiations. The supplier salespeople must recognize the best alternative to a negotiated agreement (BATNA) to avoid making deals that are not in the supplier's best interests.

After obtaining the initial order, the supplier firm strives to fulfill its promises. Yet, few firms have developed an integrated order management cycle (OMC) process to provide seamless, error-free order fulfillment. To coordinate participating OMC functions, progressive firms analyze their current system via business process mapping and seek a systems solution, cultivate a systems philosophy across the entire organization, reward all functions for working together, and place a senior manager in charge of the entire process. Rather than simply taking orders on a "first-come, first-served" basis, a supplier can use techniques of revenue management to focus efforts on high-value segments, price based on value, and give fulfillment preference to customers in high-value segments in overbooking situations. Once the initial transaction is completed, the salesperson follows up to ensure complete customer satisfaction. At the conclusion of the process, supplier managers decide whether it is in their firm's best interest to continue doing business with the new customer.

ENDNOTES

1. Philip Kotler, *Kotler on Marketing* (New York: The Free Press, 2001), 121.
2. Managers, pundits, and academics use the terms *leads*, *inquiries*, and *prospects* interchangeably. We use the following definitions to illustrate how suppliers screen firms during prospecting and to draw a managerially useful distinction between categories of potential customers.

3. These options are drawn from Igor Ansoff, "Strategies for Diversification," *Harvard Business Review* (September–October 1957): 113–124.

4. Anne Field, "State of the Art Precision Marketing," *Inc. Technology,* 2 (1996): 54–58.

5. Randy Bean, "Business-to-Business Direct Marketing: The Most Commonly Asked Questions," *Direct Marketing* (June 1995): 27–29, 78; and Kenneth M. Culpepper, "Database Maintenance Planning: Scheduling, Updates & Results," *Direct Marketing* (December 1996): 16–20.

6. Andris A. Zoltners, Prabhakant Sinha, and Greggor A. Zoltners, *The Complete Guide to Accelerating Sales Force Performance* (New York: AMACOM, 2001), 389.

7. Robert C. Blattberg, Gary Getz, and Jacquelyn S. Thomas, *Customer Equity* (Boston: Harvard Business School Press, 2001), 53.

8. Arnold Fishman, "List Industry Overview," *Direct Marketing* (August 1991): 46–47.

9. Micheil R. Leenders and David L. Blenkhorn, *Reverse Marketing* (New York: The Free Press, 1988).

10. Philip Kotler, *Marketing Management,* 11th ed. (Upper Saddle River, NJ: Prentice Hall, 2003), 583. Summarized from American Association of Advertising Agencies statement.

11. Everett M. Rogers, *Diffusion of Innovation,* 4th ed. (New York: The Free Press, 1995).

12. This discussion and the third column of Figure 8.2 are adapted from Benson P. Shapiro and John Wyman, "New Ways to Reach Your Customers," *Harvard Business Review* (July–August 1981): 103–110.

13. John F. Yarbrough, "Putting the Pieces Together," *Sales & Marketing Management* (September 1996): 69–77.

14. Jakki Mohr, *Marketing of High-Technology Products and Innovations* (Upper Saddle River, NJ: Prentice Hall, 2001).

15. Kent Hanson, "Working Customer Databases," *Business Marketing* (May 1993): 71.

16. Richard Strauss, "What It Costs to Penetrate the World's Largest Market," *Industrial Marketing Digest* (Fourth Quarter 1989): 37–45; and Amanda Burnside, "Taking the Stand," *Marketing,* 28 June 1990, 31–32.

17. Robert E. Hall, *Digital Dealing* (New York: W.W. Norton & Company, 2001).

18. Dana Blankenhorn, "Next Stop: HTML Mail," *Marketing News* (January 2002): 15; and Seth Godin, *Permission Marketing: Turning Strangers into Friends, and Friends into Customers* (New York: Simon & Schuster, 1999).

19. David Rohde, "Prospecting by Phone, Fax, and Internet for Sales Gold," *Network World,* 4 November 1996, 23.

20. David A. Aaker, *Building Strong Brands* (New York: The Free Press, 1996).

21. Philip Kotler, *Marketing Management;* and Tom Eisenhart, "Going the Integrated Route," *Business Marketing* (December 1990): 24–28.

22. Robyn Griggs, "Give Us Leads!" *Sales & Marketing Management* (July 1997): 66–72.

23. Griggs, "Give Us Leads!"

24. Jeff Abugel, "Ad Bust: Slowpoke Marketers Lose Billions," *Business Marketing* (May 1997): 1, 33; and Joyce K. McArdle, "How to Create New Business Prospects: A Telemarketing Guide for Economic Developers," *Economic Development Review* (Winter 1996): 57–59.

25. Eisenhart, "Going the Integrated Route."

26. Gilbert A. Churchill, Jr., Niel M. Ford, and Orville C. Walker, Jr., *Sales Force Management,* 5th ed. (Burr Ridge, IL: Irwin, 1997).

27. Libbie Bramson, "Make Sales a Partner in Lead Generation Programs," *Sales & Marketing Management* (July 1990): 94–96.

28. Tom Przybylski, "BtoB Direct," *Marketing Tools* (January–February 1995): 54–62.

29. Peggy Morelli, "Telemarketers Serve Clients," *Business Marketing* (April 1994): 27–29.

30. Howard Anderson, "Selling Will Never Be the Same," *Sales & Marketing Management* (March 1989): 48–53; Nikhil Hutheesing, "Speaking with One Voice," *Forbes,* 23 September 1996, 214–215; and Zoltners, Sinha, and Zoltners, *The Complete Guide to Accelerating Sales Force Performance.*

31. Although we use the phrase *sales representative* throughout the rest of the chapter, a supplier actually may have a sales team making the call and continuing the process. We discuss sales teams further in Chapters 7 and 10.

32. Barton A. Weitz, Harish Sujan, and Mita Sujan, "Knowledge, Motivation, and Adaptive Behavior: A Framework for Improving Selling Effectiveness," *Journal of Marketing* (October 1986): 175.

33. John F. Tanner, Jr., "Adaptive Selling at Trade Shows," *Journal of Personal Selling & Sales Management* (Spring 1994): 15–23.

34. Neil Rackham and John DeVencentis, *Rethinking the Sales Force* (New York: McGraw-Hill, Inc., 1999).

35. We base this discussion on Neil Rackham, *SPIN Selling* (New York: McGraw-Hill, 1988).

36. Pundits alternately refer to the opening as *the approach* or *the preliminaries* in the case of SPIN selling.

37. James C. Anderson and James A. Narus, "A Model of Distributor Firm and Manufacturer Firm Working Partnerships," *Journal of Marketing* (January 1990): 45.

38. Stephen X. Doyle and George Thomas Roth, "Selling and Sales Management in Action: The Use of Insight Coaching to Improve Relationship Selling," *Journal of Personal Selling & Sales Management* (Winter 1992): 59–64.

39. Marc Wouters, James C. Anderson, and Finn Wynstra, "The Adoption of Total Cost of Ownership for Sourcing Decisions—A Structural Equations Analysis," Eindhoven University of Technology Working Paper (August 2002).

40. R. Eric Reidenbach, Reginald W. Goeke, and Gordon McClung, *Dominating Markets with Value* (Morgantown, WV: Rhumb Line Publishing, 2002); Jonathan Gutman, "A Means-End Chain Model Based on Consumer Categorization Processes," *Journal of Marketing* (Spring 1982): 60–72; and Thomas J. Reynolds and Jonathan Gutman, "Laddering Theory, Method, Analysis, and Interpretation," *Journal of Advertising Research* (February–March 1988): 11–31.

41. James C. Anderson, Håkan Håkansson, and Jan Johanson, "Dyadic Business Relationships Within a Business Network Context," *Journal of Marketing* (October 1994): 10.

42. "It Takes 3.9 Calls to Close a Sale," *The American Salesman* (August 1995): 8–9.

43. Roger Fisher and William Ury, *Getting to Yes* (New York: Penguin Books, Ltd., 1981).

44. This discussion is based on Benson P. Shapiro, V. Kasturi Rangan, and John J. Sviokla, "Staple Yourself to an Order," *Harvard Business Review* (July–August 1992): 113–122.

45. Shapiro, Rangan, and Sviokla, "Staple Yourself to an Order."

46. This discussion is based on Robert G. Cross, *Revenue Management* (New York: Broadway Books, 1997); and Robert G. Cross, "Launching the Revenue Rocket," *Cornell Hotel and Restaurant Administration Quarterly* (April 1997): 32–43.

47. Cross, "Launching the Revenue Rocket," 33.

48. For a detailed description of procedures and mathematical models of revenue management, see Frederick H. Harris and Peter Peacock, "Hold My Place, Please," *Marketing Management* (Fall 1995): 34–46.

Chapter 9

Sustaining Reseller Partnerships

OVERVIEW

*I*n an indirect marketing channel, a supplier and its resellers must leverage their respective resources to find, keep, and grow jointly targeted customer firms. They must work together to deliver value to these customers firms and then share the rewards equitably. Over time, the supplier and select reseller firms commit to reseller partnerships and actively work to sustain them.[1]

A **reseller partnership** refers to "the extent to which there is mutual recognition and understanding that the success of each firm depends on the other firm, with each firm consequently taking actions so as to provide a coordinated effort focused on jointly satisfying the requirements of the customer marketplace."[2] Thus, we define **sustaining reseller partnerships** as the process of (1) a supplier and its resellers fulfilling commitments they have made to deliver value to customer firms, (2) strengthening this delivered value, and (3) working progressively together to continue to fulfill changing marketplace requirements. Figure 9.1 depicts this process of sustaining reseller partnerships.[3]

In this chapter, we explore the process of sustaining reseller partnerships. To begin, we consider how a supplier and its reseller firms fulfill commitments to one another. Next, we discuss actions that supplier and reseller firms take to strengthen the value they jointly deliver to customer firms. We conclude by

Figure 9.1 Sustaining Reseller Partnerships

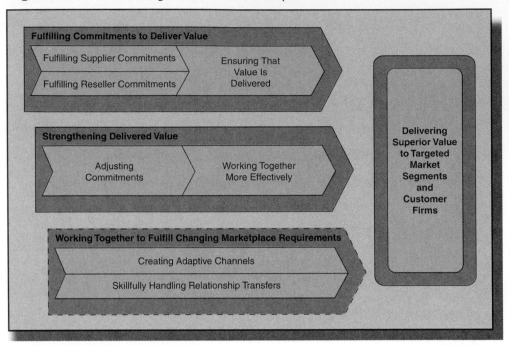

identifying situations in which marketplace requirements change significantly and by offering guidance on how a supplier and its resellers can continue to prosper by reformulating the way they deliver value to customers. Because not all firms confront these situations, we depict them within the dashed arrow in Figure 9.1.

FULFILLING COMMITMENTS TO DELIVER VALUE

In reseller partnerships, both the supplier and reseller firms make commitments to one another to assist in delivering value to customer firms. **Commitment** "captures the perceived continuity or growth in the relationship between two firms."[4] It entails a "desire to develop a stable relationship, a willingness to make short-term sacrifices to maintain the relationship, and a confidence in the stability of the relationship."[5] In essence, each firm formally or informally promises to invest certain resources and capabilities in the partnership, perform certain channel tasks, and share profits. Once they make such commitments, supplier and reseller firms must strive to consistently fulfill them.

Fulfilling Supplier Commitments to Deliver Value

Clearly, the greatest component of customer value the supplier firm contributes is its products and services. However, as we pointed out in Chapter 7, progressive business market managers think more broadly in terms of marketplace equity. When they do, managers realize they can ensure that superior value is delivered to customer firms by assisting reseller firms on tasks the resellers cannot efficiently complete by themselves. By so doing, they bolster not only the channel equity but also the reseller equity components of marketplace equity. Thus, supplier firms commonly make commitments to provide resellers with help in the form of responsive sales and marketing programs, pricing support in competitive situations, and operational and technical assistance.

Provide Responsive Sales and Marketing Programs

Some reseller firms do not have sufficient resources or capabilities to conduct periodic market research studies. As a result, they may have difficulty identifying emerging customer prospects or adapting their market offerings to better meet changing market preferences. Let's consider how the Parker Hannifin Corporation and Okuma America help resource-constrained distributors overcome these deficiencies.

Parker Hannifin Corporation (PH) supports distributor sales and marketing efforts through its Industrial Distribution Marketing System (IDMS). By contract, PH requires its distributors to forward copies of all customer invoices involving PH products to the manufacturer's market research department. Analysts code these invoices by customer and industry numbers and enter the sales data into the IDMS database. This database contains extensive profiles on existing and potential PH customers worldwide. Rather than using the invoices opportunistically, PH creates a marketing tool, Product-Market Sales Analysis reports (PMSA). Periodically, PH sends each distributor a customized PMSA report that analyzes the distributor's product line sales by geographic region, by market segment, and by customer firm. The report identifies prospects and forecasts sales. To aid with the selling process, PH furnishes contact information on these prospects to distributors and proposes a strategy for cultivating new business from existing and potential accounts. This strategy includes recommendations on how to customize offerings for local customers and how to cross-sell the full line of PH products.[6]

For years, Okuma America Corporation published a magazine called *Machining Today*. The magazine contained technical articles, such as how to increase machine tool productivity and how to manage a machine shop, and reports on news items concerning the industry. Okuma used the magazine to support its distributors. First, the magazine's printer created separate issues for each of Okuma's distributors. It did this by inserting advertisements for a particular distributor strategically inside the front and back covers as well as in the centerfold to create the impression that the distributor had produced the magazine. Second, Okuma mailed copies of the customized magazine to existing and prospective customers in each distributor's territory. To do so, Okuma assembled a database of customer companies across North and South America. Not only did the magazine create a favorable impression of Okuma distributors among customers, it yielded sales leads for distributors that they would not have gained acting alone. By 2001, the costs of printing and mailing the magazine became prohibitive. Rather than completely abondoning the program, Okuma and its distributors now send out shorter and more focused direct mail pieces to prospective customers.

Back Up Resellers with Pricing Support

When faced with cutthroat price competition, many reseller firms forgo well-conceived, value-based marketing strategies and slash prices indiscriminately. All too often, this response precipitates a downward price spiral within an industry and jeopardizes reseller profitability. To keep resellers focused on delivering value, leading supplier firms promise pricing support. For example, the Lincoln Electric Company, a manufacturer of welding equipment and supplies, devised what it calls the Guaranteed Cost Reduction Program to help its distributors cope with intense price competition from other welding product manufacturers. The program works as follows. Whenever a customer demands that a distributor lower prices on Lincoln supplies and equipment to meet those of competitors, Lincoln and that distributor guarantee in writing that they will find cost reductions in the customer's plant that meet or exceed the price difference. All the customer has to do is continue buying Lincoln Electric products from the distributor.[7]

If the customer agrees, a Lincoln sales rep and a distributor counterpart survey the customer's operations, identify possible cost reductions, and help to implement them. At the end of a prespecified time period, an agreed-upon third party independently audits performance. If the cost savings do not match those promised, Lincoln Electric and the distributor pay the customer the difference, with Lincoln contributing 70 percent. Since the program was initiated, Lincoln has only failed to deliver promised cost savings in only two instances![8]

On occasion the supplier adjusts its pricing so resellers can obtain customer business, in part, through lower price. In exchange for a large order, the reseller may offer a customer a price discount, and the supplier sometimes supports this lower price by reducing its invoice price to the reseller. These large-order price discounts are a pricing tactic that suppliers and resellers should use selectively to win business in pursuit of their market strategy. The supplier sometimes also supports its resellers in their efforts to gain new customers by providing additional gross margin to partially compensate the resellers for the initial-use discounts they give. Finally, a supplier and its reseller sometimes pass on the lower costs of a transaction to a customer in the form of a lower price. This is an instance of defeaturing or cooperative pricing, where the customer absorbs one or more functions that the supplier or its reseller normally would perform. An example would be a supplier drop shipping a large quantity to a single customer location. The customer either uses the large quantity at that location, or breaks bulk and further distributes it internally.

Furnish Operational and Technical Support

Increasingly, supplier firms gain economies of scale for an entire marketing channel by maintaining and providing operational and technical support in the form of inventory control, logistics, and customer service systems for other channel partners. By eliminating redundancies, the supplier firm enables reseller partners to offer a broader array of services at far lower costs than they could acting alone. The following examples demonstrate how suppliers help their resellers deliver value in these ways.

The Panduit Company, a manufacturer of electrical components, established a Vendor Managed Inventory (VMI) system to reduce the inventory investments and related warehousing costs of its distributors. Through its VMI system, Panduit continuously receives withdrawal and inventory balance information from its distributors via electronic data interchange and automatically replenishes those inventories to a predetermined level. Panduit sets these levels to yield the lowest total operating costs at a given customer service level for each distributor. Panduit then arranges shipments, consolidates loads, and schedules deliveries. It also provides electronic order acknowledgments, shipping notices, and invoices. Whenever Panduit's VMI system shows that distributors are maintaining too much stock of slow-moving items, Panduit generates a return order with no restocking charges and takes the inventory back. Distributors claim that the system has reduced their operating costs, enabled them to provide better service to customers, and minimized out-of-stock occurrences.[9]

Okuma has instituted *Okuma Care*, a 24-hour, seven-day-a-week (24 × 7) customer-service support program for its North American Market to improve its distributors' technical and service capabilities. Through Okuma Care, Okuma makes technical expertise and repair parts available to distributor service personnel. Whenever an Okuma distributor runs into a technical or service problem that its technicians cannot solve, the distributor can contact Okuma's Charlotte, North Carolina, headquarters for technical service counsel or parts, anytime of the day or week. Based upon the immediacy and severity of the problem, the distributor chooses from three levels of support. The distributor can use Okuma's online system, Okumalink, to download files on how to service machines. Alternatively, the distributor can telephone toll free to an answer line and speak to a service engineer. Finally, if the problem is critical, Okuma will dispatch a technical rep or team to the customer's site.

Pass the Critical Incident Test

To this point, we have focused on routine commitments that suppliers address through formal programs. At times though, crises will arise that demand an immediate and decisive response from the supplier. More often than not, the supplier will not have a formal policy or program in place to deal with the incident. Instead, managers must act intuitively with the partner's best interests in mind. Perhaps, even more than formal programs, successful resolution of such crises sends a strong message to distributors that the supplier is committed to the reseller partnership. We refer to such events as the **critical incident test**. The Dayco Products Company, a manufacturer of plastic tubing and parts, provides an excellent example. A number of years ago, an industrial distributor needed to place an emergency order but could not get through to Dayco's order center. He was, however, able to phone Dayco's chairman of the board because the chairman made it a point to be accessible to all the distributors. Rather than turn the distributor over to a subordinate, the chairman listened to the distributor carefully, worked up a three-page order, and later made sure that the order had been filled. Over time, Dayco managers and distributors have repeated this story. It sent a loud and clear message about the importance of distributors and the firm's overall intentions.[10]

Fulfilling Reseller Commitments to Deliver Value

Resellers too must meet commitments to deliver value to customer firms. Perhaps the most important way that resellers work to meet commitments is by consistently providing superior service to customer firms. However, reseller firms also promise to contribute to marketplace equity in other ways. They do so by innovating in the local marketplace and by actively participating in the supplier firm's new offering realization and quality improvement programs. In these ways, reseller firms not only boost their own reseller equity but also enhance the supplier's brand equity.

Provide Consistently Superior Service to Customer Firms

Resellers augment a supplier's market offering with a variety of value-added services. To be sure that they are providing excellent service, resellers are turning to techniques popularized by the quality movement. For example, customers sent Central States Industrial Supply (CSIS), a distributor of pipes, valves, and fittings, a "wake-up call" via a market research survey. According to survey results, CSIS provided no exceptional services to customers. Managers quickly discovered that customers believed the quality of CSIS's services was highly inconsistent.[11]

To ensure that CSIS consistently delivered service superior to its competitors as well as to eliminate work process redundancies in the company, CSIS management decided to pursue ISO 9002 registration. Senior managers appointed an ISO coordinator. She attended ISO training schools and joined a local network group of firms undergoing the ISO process. With the help of cross-functional employee teams, the ISO coordinator devised standard procedures for performing the firm's services and a quality management system. After testing the procedures and verifying that they worked properly, the firm implemented the system. Then the ISO coordinator documented those procedures for ISO registration purposes. Following detailed audits by ISO representatives, CSIS received its ISO 9002 registration. Today, CSIS management is confident that the firm delivers consistently superior services to its customers.

Innovate in the Local Marketplace

Because they are "closer" to the market, resellers are often in a better position to detect changes in local requirements and exploit them. For instance, as a new market segment emerges, a progressive reseller might customize existing supplier offerings with appropriate augmenting services and begin to develop new accounts. Alternatively, as technology evolves, a reseller may be able to put those developments to use for customer firms in the form of new support services. By acting promptly in both cases, the reseller firm strengthens marketplace equity, increases sales for the supplier and itself, and solidifies working relationships between channel members and customer firms. Boxes 9.1 and 9.2 provide outstanding examples of two reseller firms that have reputations for innovation, PSS World Medical Inc. and McKesson Corporation.[12]

Enhance the Supplier's Brand Equity

A reseller firm can help the supplier deliver superior value to customer firms by offering new product ideas and by participating in quality improvement efforts. For example, the Cameron & Barkley Company (Cambar) enthusiastically cooperates with suppliers in the new offering realization process. Cambar sales representatives routinely study customer applications for needs that current products do not meet. For example, Cambar reps learned that welders needed a welding shield that would fit on full-face respirators. They relayed this insight to a supplier that developed and then marketed the desired shield. Furthermore, the firm conducts an annual market research survey of customers to identify new product ideas, and summarizes major findings for its suppliers. When select supplier partners introduce new products, Cambar frequently tests prototypes at customer locations or participates in test markets. Often, Cambar ideas lead to innovative products. Working closely with Dalloz Safety Products, Cambar managers convinced the supplier's R&D group to design

BOX 9.1

PSS World Medical Inc. Pioneers the Alternate Sites Medical Supplies Marketplace

While many medical supplies distributors were content to exclusively serve large hospitals, PSS World Medical Inc. targeted the alternate sites market in the United States. Alternate sites are physician's offices, surgical centers, and clinics. During the early 1990s, revenues of alternate site medical providers skyrocketed due to government pressures to restrain medical cost increases. PSS managers recognized that the needs of this market were largely going unserved. To capitalize on this opportunity, PSS developed a new business concept—to provide next-day delivery of any common item to physician's offices and other alternate sites. Its mission was to become the first national physician supply distributor in the United States.

To implement the concept, PSS hired a new generation of technically competent salespersons, armed them with laptop computers, and created state-of-the art wireless sales automation, e-commerce, and logistics systems. With their laptops and a wireless Internet-based sales tool called Instant Customer Order Network (ICON), PSS sales representatives access sales and product usage information on customers, display manufacturers' electronic catalogs to customers, run cost analyses based on a physician's product usage rates, take product orders, and transmit and track those orders from client offices. A customer version, MyPSS Portal, empowers alternate sites to order directly from PSS via the Internet. PSS delivers orders with its own trucks or via UPS, either the same day during the afternoon or first thing the next morning. A final ingredient of success is PSS's incentive system—all employees receive bonuses based on profitability rather than on sales volume. As a result, personnel continuously strive to reduce operating costs while adding value to their offerings.

PSS efforts have benefited customers, suppliers, and PSS alike. Physician customers' office supplies, for instance, have been reduced from 10+ days of inventory to less than 2 days. Suppliers gained access to new markets. For example, Abbott Labs' sales of lab equipment to physicians increased dramatically. Perhaps most importantly, PSS sales and profits increased an average of 23 percent per year during the 1990s.

Sources: Nancy A. Helman, "PSS," *Incentive* (December 1996): 28–29; Curt Werner, "Distributors Find Big Opportunity in Alternate Site Sales," *Health Industry Today* (December 1996): 1–11; John Case, "The 10 Commandments of Hypergrowth," *Inc.* (October 1995): 33–44; and "PSS Launches Integrated Physician Supply Site," *Health Industry Today* (January 2001): 12.

---

safety goggles with frame colors and lens options that mirrored the styles of popular sunglasses young people wear. The result was a successful line of stylish safety goggles.[13]

Dealers are actively involved in Caterpillar's product quality, cost reduction, and manufacturing improvement efforts. The *Partners in Quality Program*, for example, links personnel responsible for building a particular machine with select dealers. These individuals meet quarterly as a team to discuss quality issues. Dealers also audit each Caterpillar machine they receive, and if anything is wrong, they feed that information back to the plant immediately so that corrections can be made. As an illustration, a dealer discovered that hoses in a new grader model had been installed incorrectly and immediately notified the factory. Caterpillar retrained the assembler, fixed the machines still in the factory, and notified other dealers to repair the machines in their inventories. In another instance, Caterpillar's dealer in Thailand

BOX 9.2
The McKesson Corporation Creatively Supports Its Pharmacy Customers

The McKesson Corporation, the multibillion-dollar wholesaler of pharmaceuticals, furnishes further examples of reseller innovations. McKesson consistently strives to deliver greater value to its pharmacy customers by helping them reduce their costs of operations, by enabling them to gain access to new customers, and by assisting them with the creation of better services. For example, McKesson was one of the first pharmaceutical distributors to equip delivery personnel with hand-held, Palm OS-Based, Symbol scanners. Prior to delivery, warehouse personnel load customer invoice files onto the scanners. At the point of delivery, personnel scan items and automatically compare them with the customer's invoice. As a result, McKesson has dramatically increased the level of accurate, on-time deliveries.

McKesson's Omnilink Program is an online software system that automatically performs pre- and postedits for pharmacies to ensure that they have properly submitted claim forms to insurance companies and government agencies. The edits check for errors in such things as dosage information, pricing, refill limits, and brand recommendations.

Given the stringent and unique requirements of third-party payers and the time required to process claims, Omnilink makes the pharmacist's job easier and less costly.

McKesson's CareMax Program is a provider network of pharmacies that can meet the standards of most third-party contracts. To qualify, pharmacies must meet a series of operational requirements. When they do, the pharmacies gain access to additional third-party contracts, which they could not serve previously. Finally, McKesson has teamed up with a software house, MedOutcomes Inc., to offer a pharmaceutical care training program for pharmacies. The program, called MedOutcomes, offers customers the training and software required for them to offer "pharmaceutical care" to consumers. Using a disease management approach, the program instructs the registered pharmacist on how to interview patients, conduct appropriate laboratory tests, instruct patients on drug usage and potential interactions, and track the patient's disease state. The program enables the pharmacist to offer superior outpatient care than was previously possible.

Sources: Debbie Epstein, "MedOutcomes Prepares R.Ph.s for Disease Management," *Drug Topics*, 2 September 1996, 32–35; Carol Ukens, "McKesson Programs Invest in Future for Clients," *Drug Topics*, 4 March 1996, 124; and Jay Werb and Paul Sereiko, "Electronic Proof of Delivery," *Frontline Solutions* (February 2002): 42–45.

concluded that a pump in a new line of hydraulic excavators was not durable enough to meet local working conditions. It persuaded Caterpillar to use a different pump on the machines until engineers could redesign the one in question.[14]

Pass the Critical Incident Test

To succeed, resellers, just as suppliers, must go beyond programs and practice a partnering philosophy. On a Thanksgiving holiday, a critical compressor failed at the plant of one of the major suppliers to Continental Glass, an industrial distributor. Because of the holiday, the supplier was unable to find a trucker willing to move a replacement compressor halfway across the country to the disabled plant. As a distributor that provided 24-hour service, Continental Glass was on call for emergency service that day and transported the needed compressor. As was the case with

Dayco, the Continental Glass story received widespread circulation within the firm and industry.[15]

Ensuring That Value Is Delivered

Periodically, supplier and reseller managers take stock of overall channel performance to determine whether they have fulfilled their commitments to deliver value to customer firms. They conduct market research to learn whether the value promised to customer firms has been delivered. In addition, supplier and reseller firms conduct financial analyses to determine whether they have received an equitable return on the value they have delivered. Supplier and reseller managers use the insights they gain from these evaluations to improve their value-delivery efforts.

Conduct Market Research

Using procedures we discussed in Chapter 2, business market managers perform both customer satisfaction and customer value assessment studies. For instance, drawing on customer firm names from its IDMS system that we described earlier, Parker Hannifin managers conduct an annual customer satisfaction study. The study assesses how well PH and its distributors meet customer expectations and identifies ways PH and its distributors can improve their market offerings. Best practice examples of value assessment in marketing channels are the SKF Documented Solutions Program, which we described in Chapter 8, and the Applied Industrial Technologies Documented Value-Added Reports, which we present in Chapter 10. In both cases, managers return to customer firms and conduct value-in-use studies to document benefits provided and costs saved.

Business market managers use the findings of these research projects in several ways. First, reseller and supplier managers reexamine what each contributes to the delivery of value to customers to determine whether a realignment of channel tasks and rewards is necessary. For example, they might eliminate products and services from their respective offerings that they find are value drains. Another result of the research might be that the supplier adapts its channel offering to better motivate and enable its resellers to serve customers. Finally, the research findings might also point to needed improvements in supplier and reseller firm coordination.

Getting an Equitable Return on Delivered Value

As a complement to customer satisfaction and value assessment studies, supplier and reseller managers routinely evaluate channel financial performance. They do so for two important reasons. First, they want to ascertain that the supplier and its reseller firms have realized the financial returns they expected. Obviously, partner firms are more motivated to continue delivering superior customer value if these expectations have been met or surpassed. Second, managers hope to find ways to improve productivity. For example, if they learn that the channel's delivery costs are out of line with industry standards, they would investigate how to strengthen their logistics system. Commonly, managers evaluate financial performance through diagnostic measures, profitability analyses, and return on investments assessments.

A diagnostic measure signals that a problem may exist with a channel. Traditionally, managerial accountants have relied upon ratio analyses as diagnostics.

The process runs as follows. First, managers calculate a given ratio for the firm's channels. A ratio contrasts two or more income statement or balance sheet items for a specific firm. Second, the manager compares it to industry averages. Trade associations and consulting firms commonly compile and publish these industry averages in **performance and activity reports (PAR)**. In theory, if a firm's ratio is close to the industry average, then it is doing acceptably well on that dimension. Third, managers use ratios to track performance over time, to compare relative performance of two firms, and to make cross-industry comparisons. Suppliers and resellers rely on different sets of performance ratios.

Suppliers frequently use distribution-related costs as channel performance diagnostics. In companies that sell exclusively through resellers, these distribution-related costs can exceed 40 percent of total revenues. The most readily available diagnostics are **expense-to-revenue (E/R) ratios**. Suppliers evaluate four categories—customer communications, paperwork flows, physical distribution, and financial risk assumptions. Suppliers use these ratios to learn whether certain costs are under control and to contrast the efficiency of one channel versus another.[16]

Resellers that stock inventory, such as wholesalers, distributors, and dealers, regard three diagnostics as critical. **Turns × earns** is the product of annual inventory turnover times average gross margin. Resellers evaluate it for the firm as a whole and for major product lines. Turns × earns captures two critical performance dimensions for resellers: how quickly they are turning inventory and how much gross profit they make on these sales. **Gross margin return on inventory (GMROI)** is average gross margin divided by average inventory. Managers use GMROI as a surrogate for return on assets. **Gross margin return on receivables (GMROR)**, on the other hand, is average gross margin divided by average account receivables. Receivables are resellers' second largest investment category. Because GMROI and GMROR are readily calculated, they provide "quick and dirty" measures of asset turnover.[17]

For resellers that do not carry inventory, managers evaluate activity measures rather than asset turnover. Thus, they spend greater time examining such things as return on equity, gross margin, and E/R ratios. Furthermore, managers review personnel productivity measures in great detail. These items include such things as the number of billable hours charged, the ratio of potential to charged billable hours, and E/R ratios related to employee activities.

Although performance diagnostics serve to flag potential problem areas, they frequently do not provide sufficient insight into the nature and cause of these difficulties. To gain such perspectives, managers turn to profitability analyses. Manning proposed an activity-based costing (ABC) approach for exploring distribution channel profitability from the supplier's perspective, called **strategic cost management (SCM)**. SCM recasts the direct costing income statement around distribution-related activities.[18]

The SCM approach has four steps. First, managers divide the organization's costs into activity costs, such as order processing and selling costs, and into nonactivity costs such as regional advertising or trade-show participation. At the same time, they estimate the amount of expenditures associated with activity and nonactivity costs. Second, managers subdivide and classify these costs as channel-related or specific reseller-related costs. Third, managers trace each cost back to individual channels or resellers. Tracing entails developing approximations of the cost required to perform a specific task. Fourth, managers either estimate revenues channels or resellers generate them, and then they construct direct costing income statements. With these analyses, managers can readily examine the profitability of channels or resellers.

In recent years, investors and senior managers have demanded that business market managers accomplish more with fewer resources. In response, more sophisticated business market managers have begun to evaluate reseller and channel performance and make related decisions based on metrics that take investments into account. Among these metrics are the traditional financial ratios of **return on assets (ROA)** and **return on investment (ROI)**, which are defined as net profits after taxes divided by total assets and shareholder equity, respectively. Naturally, when conducting distribution-related assessments, managers would focus on profits, assets, and investments associated with specific channels or reseller firms.

Criticizing weaknesses in accounting practices related to asset and investment valuations, financial experts increasingly recommend that firms consider more meaningful and practical metrics such as shareholder value added (SVA) and economic value added (EVA®) instead of ROA and ROI. **Shareholder value added** is the net present value of incremental cash flows arising from an investment minus the capital charges associated with the investment. **Economic value added** is incremental net operating profits after taxes derived from an investment minus related capital charges. Consultants contend that SVA provides superior insights into long-term performance while EVA yields better understanding of short-term results.[19]

Synchronizing Joint Fulfillment Efforts

As the use of modular and hybrid channels grows, business market managers must strive for the synchronization of channel partner efforts at fulfilling commitments. For example, a customer firm that requests a consultative sales call from a supplier firm, acquires that supplier's market offering from a distributor, and uses an authorized and independent technical service provider for repair work, may expect that all three firms maintain a shared record of its requirements, understand its evolving applications and problems, and coordinate all subsequent interactions. Partnership relationship management systems are a mechanism for seamlessly integrating these channel partner efforts.

Partner relationship management (PRM) is a business regimen that enhances the ability of a supplier firm, resellers, and third-party service providers to deliver superior customer value through synchronized operations, selling, marketing, and servicing efforts. PRM system functionality facilitates communication with partner firms, the provision of technical support, order processing and tracking, and the improvement of selling effectiveness. As with customer relationship management (CRM), PRM systems often entail Internet or extranet-based software. Typically, supplier firms create PRM software modules individually as applications arise. These modules are configured to draw upon accounting and operations data from the firm's enterprise resource planning (ERP) system.

As part of the PRM system, business market managers establish a Web site or online portal exclusively for the use of channel partners. Perhaps the easiest and often the first modules to be added to a PRM system seek to sychnronize communications between the supplier, resellers, and customer firms. For example, publish-on-demand capabilities enable resellers to download and print up-to-date product information, promotional materials, brochures, and manuals 24×7. These capabilities frequently empower resellers to customize standard documents to better meet the requirements of local customers. More advanced communications applications include contact management. Contact management modules keep sales, service, and operations personnel aware of the nature and content of all calls that supplier, reseller, and third-party providers make on each customer firm. With these modules a supplier can forward such information immediately to all relevant personnel via personal computers or mobile telephones.

Through its Web site, a supplier can furnish resellers with repair manuals and technical problem-solving search engines. Some suppliers even provide technical training exercises and simulations for reseller personnel to use. And, PRM software can route technical service requests immediately to an appropriate authorized service provider for resolution.

Another popular PRM application addresses order management concerns. For example, online order placement systems allow reseller managers to electronically scan available inventories, place orders, track deliveries, and review account billing records. Such modules not only reduce transaction costs but also improve the accuracy and timeliness of deliveries.

To improve the selling and marketing effectiveness of resellers, supplier firms increasingly distribute qualified sales leads through their PRM systems. Product configuration and proposal generation modules help resellers specify feasible offerings that better meet customer requirements and write more persuasive sales proposals. Pricing configurators that enable resellers to match proposed product and service specifications with their own firm's costs and profit rules can help ensure that resellers gain a reasonable return on their efforts. Finally, partner life cycle management modules empower suppliers to monitor ongoing reseller performance.

In Box 9.3, we describe how Acros Whirlpool uses a PRM system to synchronize the activities of its reseller sales forces and its authorized service providers across Latin America.

BOX 9.3
Acros Whirlpool Synchronizes Partner Sales and Service Efforts

Based in Mexico, Acros Whirlpool S.A. is a joint venture between Vitro S.A. and the Whirlpool Corporation. The company manufactures a wide range of branded home appliances including refrigerators, washing machines, dishwashers, air conditioning systems, and ovens. Acros Whirlpool markets these products through a network of distributors and repair service providers to customers across Latin America. In 2001, annual sales topped U.S. $629 million.

With a widely dispersed network of channel partners, Acros Whirlpool executives sought to synchronize and upgrade channel sales and service capabilities. Their goal was to improve partner revenues while lowering total costs. Acros Whirlpool executives turned to Siebel Systems for guidance in implementing a partner relationship management (PRM) system. Siebel Systems, Inc., is the world's leading provider of customer relationship management, employee relationship management,

BOX 9.3
Continued

and PRM solutions. Working with Deloitte Consulting, Siebel account managers recommended Siebel PRM and eCustomer software modules as the foundation for Acros Whirlpool's system. The applications would be available to channel partners 24x7 via the Internet through the Acros Whirlpool portal.

The portal provides important marketing and service functionality to Acros Whirlpool and its partners. To begin with, the system enables channel partners to view all historical sales information, compare current sale performance versus the competition, monitor credit status, and review all commercial agreements. Acros Whirlpool can review and coordinate all business communications with partners across diverse media including the Internet, e-mail, telephone, face-to-face, mail, and fax. Partner managers are able to search and download an extensive library of marketing collateral materials including brochures, pricing schedules, and technical documents whenever necessary. As for technical service assistance, both distributors and repair service providers can access an inventory of frequently asked questions and their solutions via the portal. More importantly, distributors can create repair service requests on behalf of their customers, which are automatically routed to Acros's support organization for resolution. Once the request has been logged, distributors can track problem resolution status, and review the details of any repairs.

Acros Whirlpool managers believe that the Siebel applications have improved customer satisfaction, enhanced the firm's ability to sell and service its products, and significantly reduced customer service costs. The firm is planning to implement additional PRM applications with the intent of improving selling effectiveness.

STRENGTHENING DELIVERED VALUE

As is the case with other aspects of business market management, complacency often brings the demise of reseller partnerships. For this reason, supplier and reseller managers must examine their partnerships and seek ways to strengthen the value they deliver to customer firms. In some cases, managers must adjust commitments by reformulating channel partners' gives & gets and by making changes in joint annual plans. In most others, they seek incremental process improvements by learning to work together more effectively.

Adjusting Commitments

Given the dynamic nature of the marketplace, partner firms occasionally need to adjust their commitments to the partnership. In this section, we discuss how firms make such adjustments. We begin by examining how firms realign the gives & gets of the partnership to restore equity. Then we describe how partner firms modify joint annual plans to account for changing market conditions.

Reformulate Channel Partners' Gives & Gets

To sustain or enhance high levels of channel performance, business market managers must periodically examine and adjust the balance in partner firms' gives & gets. **Gives** are the specific investments and resources a firm contributes, such as knowledge, personnel, fixed assets, and cash. **Gets**, on the other hand, are the specific gains a firm receives, such as greater expertise, enhanced capabilities, and additional profits. It is here that disconnects often occur; what one channel member thinks it is giving to a partner firm is significantly different from what that partner perceives it is getting.

Often, business market managers can trace inequities in gives & gets back to the vagaries of traditional channel compensation practices. In Box 9.4, we describe traditional discounts and allowances. Even though the traditional methods of reseller compensation are widely practiced, many managers question their practicality and equity. As we mention in Chapter 7, resellers complain that trade discounts, determined as a function of industry standards or average gross margins, underestimate the true costs they incur. And due to intense price competition, resellers rarely receive the suggested resale price on products and hence never gain the gross margins that trade discounts are supposed to provide. As a result, far too many resellers believe that they are not receiving adequate compensation for their efforts and investments.

How can progressive firms eliminate inequities? They begin by evaluating both their own gives & gets and those of their channel partner. At a joint management meeting, both reseller and supplier managers construct two sets of T-accounts, as in an accounting ledger, one for each firm. In one column, managers comprehensively

BOX 9.4
Traditional Reseller Discounts and Allowances

The **trade** or **functional discount**, stated as a percent reduction from the suggested resale price, ideally covers the reseller's costs of performing assigned tasks and provides the reseller with a reasonable profit. Suppliers derive trade discount amounts for specific products from one of three sources: historical industry discounts, industry gross margin averages, or turns × earns ratios.

Firms supplement the trade discount with a **quantity** or **volume discount**, designed to motivate resellers to buy in large quantities and store local inventory. Suppliers state quantity discounts either as a percent reduction from suggested resale price or from the reseller's net or invoice price. They commonly offer tiers of quantity discounts reflecting the supplier's economies of scale in production and logistics. For example, a supplier might offer a progressively higher discount to a reseller for buying a product in box loads, truckloads, and rail carloads.

Suppliers offer resellers a **payment discount** to encourage them to pay for goods immediately. The payment discount is stated as a percent reduction off the invoice price. Perhaps the most common payment discount, 2/10/net 30, is "a 2 percent reduction off invoice price if the reseller pays within 10 days. The net amount is due in 30 days." Shrewd suppliers periodically change this discount to reflect their current cost of capital.

An **allowance** is an extra payment designed to gain reseller participation in special programs. Cooperative advertising, merchandising, and delivery allowances are perhaps most common. Suppliers exercise their own discretion in selecting allowance amounts; however, they must make them available to all their resellers. They pay allowances through a reduction in invoice prices.

list the gives, while in the other column, the gets. Supplier and reseller managers then use these T-accounts to surface and discuss discrepancies in perceived gives & gets, and negotiate changes in the structure of gives & gets to attain equity. As we point out in Chapter 7, business market managers may need to rethink channel partners' profit models.

To better reflect channel partner gives & gets, some progressive suppliers have migrated toward a **functional allowance**. Here, the supplier pays a reseller a set percent off the reseller buy price for performing specific tasks. Several years ago, the GLS Corporation, a major distributor of composite materials and thermoplastic elastomers, agreed to become the exclusive supplier of Shell Chemical's Kraton® thermoplastic-rubber compounds for plastic molded goods applications in the United States. Kraton rubber is a versatile material and, in addition to plastics molding, has many substantial applications, such as adhesives, lubricants, asphalt, and polymer modification.

The plastics molding opportunities are smaller and fragmented. Shell wanted to apply more of its resources to develop sales in larger applications, so it turned to GLS for assistance. In response to this challenge, GLS created its own applications support laboratory and staffed it with two chemists and a materials engineer. Additionally, the firm hired sales engineers and trained them to provide product specification and applications assistance as well as to give technical sales presentations. For its efforts, GLS received a functional allowance for market development, which was paid as a percent reduction off the acquisition price of Kraton, plus sales growth bonuses.

Another innovative compensation approach that some suppliers use is paying resellers a **fee-for-service**. Under this arrangement, a supplier pays its reseller partners a prespecified amount for performing a particular function. Microsoft, for example, pays authorized support centers a fee for providing technical assistance to customers. The fee allows the support centers to cover the costs of personnel and equipment as well as to make a profit. LaBlond Makino, a Japanese-owned machine tool builder, has taken this approach one step further. It specifies the amount of technical service days or hours it expects its distributor partners to provide to customers. In essence, LaBlond Makino keeps distributors **on retainer** because they are paid whether or not they provide service.

Make Responsive Adjustments to the Joint Annual Plan

A supplier and its resellers most often put gives & gets and their respective objectives into practice through joint annual planning. Quite simply, when resellers participate in the planning process, they are more likely to view the plan as theirs and work hard to implement it. To reinforce these commitments, a supplier and its resellers conduct both planning and review sessions at least once a year, preferably at each reseller's home office. During these meetings, managers discuss the three fundamental questions for planning market strategy that we discussed in Chapter 4: (1) What do we know? (2) What do we want to accomplish? and (3) How will we do it?

After these individual sessions, the business market manager summarizes perspectives in an annual **reseller marketing plan**, both for each reseller partnership and for the channel network as a whole. Such plans typically begin with a situation analysis, which assesses strengths, weaknesses, opportunities, and threats for the supplier and reseller. The next section lists mutual objectives that the supplier and reseller commit to accomplishing. The next two sections are a basic requirements section that spells out the kinds of support that resellers will need, and an action program section that delineates the actions the supplier and reseller will take separately and together in the marketplace. The last section is implementation and control, which charts a timetable for program implementation, assigns responsibilities for execution, and defines performance measures and expectations. Supplier managers should meet with each reseller quarterly to review each firm's performance versus the plan and to initiate corrective actions.

Although reseller marketing plans provide a coordinated course of action to pursue, business market managers recognize the necessity of responding to market changes. Not only do market conditions change, but the supplier and its resellers also learn through implementing the plan, which may prompt them to make changes. Rather than waiting until the next formal planning session, progressive suppliers and resellers adjust the existing marketing plan when necessary. The following examples illustrate how two leading firms successfully adapt ongoing reseller marketing plans.

To further penetrate the mining and heavy construction industries, Caterpillar designed and introduced a revolutionary new tractor, the D9L. Caterpillar expressly created the D9L to deliver improved traction, reduced stress on the undercarriage and fast-wearing parts, easier and faster repairs, and improved productivity to mine operators and construction firms. Caterpillar priced the D9L significantly higher than traditional tractors and encouraged dealers to actively promote it in the United States and Middle East. Conditions changed soon after the marketing plan was implemented. Komatsu entered the marketplace with aggressively priced models. Perhaps more ominously, D9L models in the field began to fail after 2,500 hours of operation. It turned out that a variety of parts used in the new design were not durable enough to withstand severe operating environments. Clearly, Caterpillar and its dealers had to modify their marketing plans.[20]

Working as partners, Caterpillar and its dealers initiated both strategic and tactical remedial actions. To begin with, Caterpillar redesigned failing systems and rushed superior replacement parts to dealers. Dealers, in turn, implemented a comprehensive program for repairing equipment in the field, even replacing parts on machines that had not yet failed. Interfirm teams of mechanics flew to dealerships that were overwhelmed with repair calls and serviced crippled D9Ls. Looking to the future, Caterpillar repositioned the D9L to be more competitive with Komatsu models. As a result of these joint efforts, D9L downtime was minimized, customer dissatisfaction evaporated, and the D9L become a popular product in the mining and heavy construction industries.

When PSS World Medical Inc., the medical supplies distributor, began targeting physicians, the firm promised next-day delivery and charged premium prices for its services. By the mid-1990s, demands for heath-care reform in the United States and insurance company demands for lower costs prompted physicians to demand lower prices on supplies. In addition, a number of discounters entered the market, causing prices to deteriorate even further. Rather than clinging to the marketing plans PSS had forged with its suppliers, PSS management modified its strategies.

The firm began by dropping prices on 300 of its most popular items. PSS then initiated a buying club called *Network Plus* for physicians. PSS provided a lower price to participating physicians in exchange for contractual commitments for greater shares of customer business. Importantly, even though PSS shifted its strategy to be more price competitive, management did not abandon its profit-based incentive systems. This direction prompted employees to aggressively pursue cost reductions instead of just slashing prices. They also significantly lowered selling and administrative costs at PSS. As a result of the change in strategy and its profit-based incentives, PSS witnessed an increase in both market share and profit margin during a period in which most competitors suffered major losses in sales and profits.[21]

Working Together More Effectively

As with the practice of *kaizen*, supplier and reseller managers religiously pursue continuous channel improvements to strengthen the value they jointly deliver to customer firms. Establishing a reseller advisory council is one way to do so. Such councils enable them to pinpoint market opportunities and find creative solutions to mutual problems. Supplier and reseller firms also rely on training and coaching as mechanisms to improve each other's performance. Finally, partner firms strive to strengthen levels of interfirm coordination by communicating more effectively, by clarifying roles and responsibilities, and by resolving conflicts.

Establish a Reseller Advisory Council

A **reseller advisory council** is a consultative forum typically composed of key managers from a supplier firm and 10–15 of its reseller firms. The council typically meets once or twice a year for one to two days to discuss issues of common concern and to suggest improvements in product lines, supplier policies, marketing programs, market trends, and so on. The forum is not a legislative body, a bargaining unit, or a gripe session. Rather, it is an advisory group that offers counsel to the supplier.

Advisory councils function best as a means of incremental channel improvement. They share characteristics with other commonly used problem-solving teams, such as quality circles, labor-management committees, task forces, and focus groups. Run properly, councils improve market response, new product and service marketing, and channel management both domestically and internationally. Here are a few examples of how firms have used them.[22]

Toro, a major manufacturer of lawn mowers, relies on its reseller advisory council for local market intelligence. The firm and its resellers, in turn, use such intelligence to respond to competitive threats before they become acute. At one of its council meetings, for instance, Toro managers learned from a North Carolina dealer that a new German company had introduced a greens-cutting machine into the golf course market in the United States. Another council member verified that the competitor had entered the Florida market as well. More importantly, the Florida dealer explained how the firm's sales force successfully sold against the new product by highlighting the superior value of Toro's equipment and the dealer's repair services. From these discussions, Toro and reseller managers quickly devised a value-based training program for dealer salespeople and a cooperative merchandising program. Working together, Toro and its resellers launched a successful counterstrike.

Business market managers frequently use reseller advisory council meetings to brainstorm product line extensions and new customer services. For example, several years ago, Fort Howard Paper Company's council identified growing plastic plate usage among institutional food users. Resellers pointed to major "gaps" in Fort Howard's plastic plate line that prohibited them from capitalizing on this surging demand. Following council suggestions, Fort Howard acquired a plastic plate manufacturer whose lines filled those gaps. With a full line, Fort Howard resellers successfully penetrated the emerging segment.

Loctite, a subsidiary of The Henkel Group, manufactures specialty adhesives. At a reseller advisory council meeting in Europe, Loctite managers verified the need for a new label adhesive in the French marketplace. Because of "green" environmental regulations, the French recycle bottles often. For this reason, processors prefer adhesives that permit them to remove labels easily. Based on these insights, Loctite developed a label adhesive exclusively for the French market.

Train and Coach Partner Firms

Perhaps the most direct way to strengthen delivered value is through training and coaching. **Training** entails imparting knowledge and skills in a systematic manner through courses, seminars, and demonstrations. Increasingly, not only are supplier firms offering such programs for their resellers, but resellers also are providing them to supplier firms. While supplier training programs focus on such things as product knowledge, selling skills, and technical competence, reseller courses concentrate on such things as customer applications, changing customer needs, and operational procedures.

Training efforts commonly take two forms: certification programs and skills training. Through a certification program, one firm requires that personnel from its partner take a series of technical courses and demonstrate competence, often through an examination, before the partner firm is officially allowed to perform certain tasks or offer particular services. For instance, the Microsoft Corporation requires third-party service engineers to become certified to deliver value-added business solutions or technical support using Microsoft products. To become certified, technicians complete a series of courses and demonstrate proficiency with Microsoft programs through certification exams. When they pass these exams, individuals are formally recognized as Microsoft Certified Professionals. They can include this designation on their resumes and promote it to prospective customers.

Skills training entails courses on focused topics. For example, a supplier might offer reseller sales reps a course in how to sell to major accounts. Alternatively, a reseller firm might provide supplier operations and information systems personnel with a course on reseller-industry bar-coding standards. Whereas in the past, firms provided skills training largely in a classroom setting, they are increasingly using emerging technologies to enable personnel to study at their own convenience in locations of their own choosing. For example, the Mita Corporation, a supplier of photocopying equipment, created a CD-ROM–based sales training program for its dealers. Using their own personal computers, the sales reps walk through all the steps associated with selling copier equipment. Moreover, because the CD-ROM program is "interactive," the sales reps can participate in role-playing exercises. Via a keyboard, the sales rep "speaks" to a hypothetical customer, making a sales presentation, handling objections, and asking for the sale. At the end of the exercise, the program rates the rep and offers suggestions on how to improve.[23]

The Ford Motor Company created the satellite-based Fordstar Network, to beam training programs and technical information directly to its dealers in the United States, Canada, and Mexico. The first Fordstar Network program furnished training on how to repair onboard electronics on Ford vehicles. Service engineers at more than 6,000 dealer sites and 300 Ford locations participated. At the dealerships, these service engineers sat around conference tables and viewed an instructor on a monitor. An audio interaction feature of the network enabled the instructor to questions participants and listen to their responses. The instructor used computer programs, videotapes, and a laser disc player to perform mathematical calculations, demonstrate repair procedures, and convey technical information. Importantly, Ford reports that the network dramatically reduced training costs per students and cut by half the amount of time dealer personnel had to spend away from their dealerships for training.[24]

Research demonstrates that most participants forget more than 80 percent of what they learned within one month after attending a training program. Such findings indicate the importance of a second performance enhancement tool—coaching. **Coaching** entails the improvement and reinforcement of desired skills, behaviors, and performance through periodic assistance, counseling, and practice. Partner firms coach each other at both the strategic and skills levels.[25]

Senior or middle-level managers provide strategic coaching or conceptual guidance during the joint annual planning, implementation, and review processes. During those meetings, the coach shares the wisdom of experience with partner managers and helps them to craft a set of goals, strategies, and activities for the coming year. Skills coaching serves to strengthen the partner's behavior at the tactical level. For example, a supplier that conducts a technical selling training program for reseller salespersons might follow it up by having its field engineers make a series of joint sales calls with the salespersons. The field engineers provide advice and act as a technical "safety net," allowing the reseller salespersons to fearlessly practice their newly learned skills.

Strengthen Interfirm Coordination

Through **coordination**, the customer firm and supplier firm synchronize their activities, resources, and capabilities to accomplish a collective set of tasks. Firms achieve better coordination by improving communications, clarifying roles and responsibilities through agreements, and promptly resolving conflicts.[26]

Communication is "the formal and informal sharing of meaningful and timely information between firms."[27] Supplier and reseller managers use advances in information technology and bridging to improve interfirm communications. Okuma America Corporation provides an excellent example. Okuma managers have developed an online portal called *Okumalink*. Okumalink allows Okuma distributors to access the manufacturer's server. With Okumalink, distributors can check the firm's inventory of parts and equipment, examine product specifications, see engineering changes, scrutinize warranty requirements, and verify parts numbers. Distributors can use Okumalink to send e-mail messages to one another. Okuma has created a separate file where distributors post their accepted proposals for the sale of machine tools and service. Now, other distributors learn how to devise winning proposals and to sell to customers in new industries.

Bridging entails establishing and sustaining communications between partner firms across functions and management levels. The Dayco Products Company has long required that its president, distributor marketing managers, and key operations personnel call on distributors each year to demonstrate the importance of their partnership. Bridging should also be practiced across careers and generations. GLS Corporation has a policy of tracking the careers of all the supplier sales reps and marketing managers that they have dealt with over the years. Normally, this tracking entails occasional phone calls, letters, and holiday cards. By doing so, GLS has managed to maintain contacts at various organizational levels within their supplier partners. In the case of a multibillion-dollar chemical supplier, this continuous contact includes the chairman of the board of directors.[28]

Progressive companies improve channel coordination by writing more equitable sales agreements, policy manuals, and policy statements. Each of these documents has a special purpose. The sales agreement, in the form of a written contract, formally and legally specifies the benefits and responsibilities of both parties within the partnership. By specifying these key gives & gets of the relationships, the written sales agreement serves to sharpen expectations and direct the actions of both firms.

Although companies generally write sales agreements in broad, legal terms, they clarify those terms and conditions in policy manuals and policy statements. A policy manual contains far more detailed descriptions of tasks each member should perform, such as the layout of material data and safety sheets, handling procedures, and product labeling. It provides a summary of key supplier and resellers' policies. A policy statement is a detailed statement of changes and modifications in a specific policy. Key examples might include pricing sheets, payment terms, and product line specifications. The supplier issues these statements periodically to reflect changes in market conditions and company strategy.

Experienced business market managers understand that every reseller partnership has some conflict. By **conflict**, we mean "the overall level of disagreement in the working partnership. As such, conflict is determined by the frequency, intensity, and duration of disagreements."[29] By anticipating channel conflict and putting conflict resolution mechanisms in place, progressive managers turn potentially destructive disputes into opportunities for improvement. Box 9.5 describes some practical means for reducing and resolving reseller and supplier conflict. When implemented properly, these conflict resolution mechanisms enable channel partners to vent frustrations and create mutually acceptable solutions to common problems.

BOX 9.5
Resolving Reseller-Supplier Conflict

A low-cost, yet effective means to resolve reseller-supplier conflict is to train **boundary-spanning personnel**, or individuals who are in contact with the partner firm on a regular basis, to be sensitive to inherent trouble spots. For a supplier, boundary-spanning personnel are likely to be field sales reps and inside customer service reps, while for resellers, they are likely to be purchasing managers or general managers. These persons should learn to identify emerging problems and try to resolve them informally and immediately before they escalate into relationship-threatening crises.

BOX 9.5
Continued

An alternative is to establish a regular **employee exchange program**, in which firms assign personnel for periods of time to channel partner operations. In the first of two varieties of these programs, the employee spends several weeks at the partner firm, rotating through a variety of positions. In this way, the individual becomes familiar with the tasks and problems that the partner firm must address. Hopefully, this experience leads to empathy and better understanding of the partner's plight. In the second, the employee actually works on-site at the partner firm. For example, a staff member from the firm's order center might be assigned to the purchasing department of a particularly large reseller firm. At the reseller's establishment, the individual would take the reseller's orders, transmit them to the supplier, and oversee delivery.

Firms can better understand issues and concerns of channel partners through **trade association membership**. Many reseller associations, for example, offer associate memberships for suppliers. By attending conferences and receiving newsletters, both channel partners can learn how the other operates and what problems they must routinely address.

Finally, some suppliers have established the office of **ombudsman**. The ombudsman is typically a retired reseller manager or principal employed by the supplier, who has credibility with both parties. Serving as the "friend" of the reseller, the ombudsman listens to reseller concerns, draws on experience to assist the supplier in finding equitable solutions, and helps explain them to resellers.

Sources: Louis W. Stern, Brian Sternthal, and C. Samuel Craig, "Managing Conflict in Distribution Channels: A Laboratory Study," *Journal of Marketing Research* (May 1973): 169–179; and Bruce A. Jacobs, "Tell It to Bob," *Industry Week* (September 1982): 62–63.

WORKING TOGETHER TO FULFILL CHANGING MARKETPLACE REQUIREMENTS

To this point in the chapter, we examined the process of sustaining reseller partnerships under routine circumstances. What happens when marketplace or customer requirements change significantly? To continue to deliver superior value to targeted segments and customers, progressive firms create adaptive channels and transfer customer relationships.

Creating Adaptive Channels[30]

A handful of forward-looking companies are experimenting with their channel networks to make them more flexible and responsive. Although the scope of the experiments and the specifics vary widely, each embraces a concept we call **adaptive channels**. The managers whose innovations have given rise to this concept view their distribution channels as webs of capabilities embedded in an extended enterprise. They have realized that by sharing their resources and capabilities in novel ways and new situations, they can take advantage of profit-making opportunities that they could not exploit alone.

To act on this realization, these managers first identify infrequent yet critical customer requirements that they cannot routinely fulfill on their own. Then they make progressive, cooperative arrangements with other channel members for assistance that will enable them to meet those requirements. The partner firms define in advance the nature of such assistance, the procedures for providing it, and the appropriate remuneration. Often, PRM software furnishes the interfirm interfaces necessary to activate these prearranged agreements when appropriate

We divide adaptive channel initiatives into three broad categories. In the first, channel partners design arrangements that ensure they are routinely able to cope with unpredictable or unusual demands for products and services. In the second, adaptive channel arrangements focus on meeting customers' growing demands for broader market offerings—products and services that the channel member does not normally provide. In the third, the objective is to improve the quality of service throughout the distribution channel by substituting the superior capabilities of one member for the subpar capabilities of another.

Provide Support in Extraordinary Situations

Through **auxiliary support systems**, distribution channel members cope with unexpected or unusual demands for products and services by sharing inventories and support services in return for prespecified remuneration. What makes auxiliary support possible is information technology that monitors the availability of offerings and processes orders, as well integrated logistics systems that deliver those offerings rapidly from distant locations to customers' sites.

Firms use three variations of auxiliary support systems. In the first, the supplier shares its inventory with its network of resellers. In Box 9.6, we relate how Volvo Trucks and its dealers solved a vexing business problem in getting replacement parts to truck fleet customers in two different application segments. In the second, a supplier and its resellers share inventory with one another. In Box 9.7, we describe how Okuma America Corporation created a network that enables the firm and its distributors to exchange machine tools and repair parts when the need arises.

A third variation in auxiliary support systems is when firms use adaptive channel arrangements to provide services in extraordinary situations. Consider Microsoft's product-support approach. Microsoft delivers most of its technical problem-solving assistance to customers over the telephone. Although engineers at one of its U.S. support centers can handle most requests, the firm's goal of answering 90 percent of service calls within 60 seconds is severely put to the test during product launches.

To handle the overload during peak periods, Microsoft relies on a carefully selected network of authorized support centers and Microsoft service providers. Microsoft programs its telephone switching system with call arrival forecasts, goals for minimum waiting time, and estimates of support staff availability—its own and that of its partners. When Microsoft product service engineers cannot take a call during a prespecified interval, the switching system automatically transfers the call to a designated service provider, where an engineer takes it and resolves the customer's problem. Microsoft compensates the service providers on a per-call basis with a guaranteed number of calls per day. Fees paid to service providers reflect their investments in facilities, equipment, direct phone lines, and hiring and training of support engineers. Microsoft managers report that the system is so effective that it smoothly handled technical service calls following the most recent version of Windows.

BOX 9.6
Volvo Trucks and Its Dealers Respond to Emergency Repair Situations

Volvo Trucks sells commercial trucks and repair parts in the United States through a distribution channel that includes regional warehouses and commercial truck dealers. In the mid-1990s, the company's dealers had been reporting more and more stockouts on critical parts, even though inventory levels were soaring. Because they could not provide consistent, timely repairs, the dealers were losing a considerable amount of business that could have been a major growth opportunity.

Volvo managers knew that the problem was related to the dealers' inability to predict demand for parts and services accurately. Through careful market research, they learned why that was the case. Customers use replacement parts in two different situations: scheduled maintenance and emergency roadside repairs. In the first situation, Volvo's conventional distribution system was working well because customers' requirements varied little and the necessary parts could be ordered and delivered ahead of time. In the second, the system was extremely ineffective because the demand for emergency repairs could not be predicted. No matter how much inventory the company put into the channel, it seemed that the critical parts were not readily accessible. Little wonder that when owners learned how long they would have to wait to get their

trucks moving again, they located competing dealers that had substitute parts to make the repairs.

Once Volvo understood the problem, it could address it. Working with FedEx Business Logistics Services, the company set up a warehouse in Memphis, Tennessee, that would stock the full line of truck parts. Now, when a dealer needs parts for an emergency repair and that part is not available, the manager calls a toll-free number and the parts are shipped out by FedEx, often on an afternoon flight so they arrive that same night. Parts can be picked up at the airport by the dealer's personnel, delivered to the dealer's offices, or even dropped off at the roadside repair site. Volvo charges dealers for the delivery service, but the dealers do not mind because they can pass the charges on to the anxious customers who are willing to pay for prompt service.

Today, Volvo is losing less business because of stockouts, and dealers' revenues from emergency repairs have risen significantly. Moreover, Volvo eliminated three warehouses and reduced its total inventory by about 15 percent. Lower inventory and storage costs more than offset increases in the company's freight charges. Managers report that they have been overwhelmed with compliments from both dealers and customers.

Source: Adapted from "Rethinking Distribution: Adaptive Channels," James A. Narus and James C. Anderson, *Harvard Business Review* (July–August 1996): 112–130.

Responsively Broaden the Market Offering

Sophisticated companies are increasingly choosing to outsource their supply management function via integrated supply management (ISM) contracts to a single distributor to reduce their total transaction costs. Even though ISM contracts provide a tremendous opportunity for distributors to increase both sales and profits, fulfilling them requires a broader market offering as well. In addition, customers are likely to expect the reseller to handle their infrequent or emergency requests for unusual products and support services.

To capitalize on this opportunity, distributors are turning to **reseller alliances**. In these alliances, members agree to pool their resources and capabilities and broaden one another's market offerings. By joining forces, they can exploit opportunities that they could not on their own, and they can meet demands that fall outside their traditional

BOX 9.7
Okuma and Its Distributors Share Inventory Across Three Continents

Okuma America Corporation, a subsidiary of Japanese machine tool builder Okuma Corporation, provides an outstanding example of how distributors can routinely satisfy unexpected demands by sharing the burden of maintaining safety stocks and making emergency deliveries. The expense of stocking a full line of machine tools, which often cost more than $100,000 apiece, along with a complete assortment of repair parts, which number in the thousands, is prohibitive. Historically, it has hampered the ability of distributors to provide responsive service. To overcome the problem, Okuma created its own auxiliary support system.

Okuma requires each of its 46 distributor locations in North and South America to carry a minimal number of machine tools and select repair parts in inventory. The company tries to ensure that nearly all Okuma machines and parts are in stock either in its warehouse in Charlotte, North Carolina, or somewhere in the distribution channel. An online portal called Okumalink keeps distributors informed about the location and availability of machine tools, spare parts, and used equipment in Okuma warehouses in Charlotte and Japan.

When a customer orders a machine tool or part that the distributor does not have, the distributor checks Okumalink to determine whether the item is in stock at Okuma facilities. If it is available, the distributor can order it electronically. If it is not, the distributor can use Okumalink to scan other Okuma distributors' inventories or e-mail them directly to find the closest location where items are available. Then, the manager phones or e-mails a counterpart at the stocking site and arranges for delivery of the item directly to the customer's plant site. Both distributors, in turn, share the commission on the sale of the machine tool or parts. Okuma further supports the availability of repair parts with a 24-Hour Shipment Guarantee—if parts are not shipped within 24 hours of order receipt, the customer receives them for free.

The benefits of Okuma's auxiliary support system are significant. Investments and costs associated with stocking and handling inventory were reduced for the total channel system. Simultaneously, Okuma has created 48 potential pathways—its 46 distributors plus 2 company warehouses—for their products and services to reach each customer. As a result, the likelihood that a distributor will lose a sale because the needed item is out of stock has been dramatically lowered. Furthermore, customer satisfaction has increased because the superior service promised by Okuma is being consistently delivered.

Source: Adapted from "Rethinking Distribution: Adaptive Channels," James A. Narus and James C. Anderson, *Harvard Business Review* (July–August 1996): 112–130.

areas of specialization. In return for its contribution, each member shares the resulting sales and profits. In Box 9.8, we describe how Grainger Integrated Supply Operations (GISO) draws on a network of complementary firms to serve the emerging ISM market segment.

Whereas GISO relies on written contracts to bind members of its reseller alliance, other resellers achieve similar results through consortia. To form a consortium, resellers of complementary lines contribute equity and create a separate corporation. This new corporation markets the collective product lines and services of its members, primarily to ISM customers. Through the consortium, member firms can serve customers individually when they only want specialty products and technical service, or collectively when they want broader offerings. Consortium members can also draw on partner inventories when a traditional customer wants something out of the

BOX 9.8
Grainger Integrated Supply Operations Forges a Reseller Alliance

Grainger Integrated Supply Operations (GISO), a Grainger division established in 1995, shows how a reseller alliance works. GISO's goal is to handle the acquisition, materials management, and warehouse activities of major customers across as broad a range of products and services as is possible. To do so, GISO draws upon three groups of suppliers for support: Grainger's traditional MRO distribution business, Best-in-Class Suppliers (BICs), and a Sourcing Group. Products from these suppliers can be delivered separately to customers or consolidated into one shipment.

When GISO receives an order, it immediately goes online to see whether the items are available from Grainger's traditional distribution business. If Grainger cannot fulfill the order, GISO turns to its network of best-in-class suppliers—outstanding specialty distributors that carry complementary products. Written contracts with each supplier specify the products it will supply through GISO, and the suppliers set the prices of those products

themselves. GISO pays the supplier immediately on delivery, then collects the revenues or holds the accounts receivables itself. To participate, the suppliers pay an annual management fee, a minor transaction fee, and logistics costs.

When GISO gets an order that neither Grainger nor the independent suppliers can meet, it turns to its own sourcing group. The group routinely scours the world to satisfy requests for unusual products and services. For example, ARCO Alaska requested bear repellent for its pipeline workers. The repellent comes in a small can and is sprayed in a stream or fog at menacing grizzly bears. GISO managers tracked down a small business in a remote part of Alaska that manufactured the repellent. Then they determined whether spray or stream applicators would be most useful for oil pipeline workers and what size containers would be most economical. Once these decisions were made, GISO managers figured out how to get the repellent from the supplier to ARCO workers.

Source: Adapted from "Rethinking Distribution: Adaptive Channels," James A. Narus and James C. Anderson, *Harvard Business Review* (July–August 1996): 112–130.

ordinary. Participating reseller firms share consortium profits in the form of dividends, capital gains, or both. In Box 9.9, we present iPower Logistics's innovative approach for building reseller consortia.

As with the previous auxiliary support systems, a consortium can be based around the provision of services as well as products. Consider Intercore Group, a consortium of four U.S. machine tool distributors: Excel 2000 Machine Tools, Methods Machinery Company, Machine Tool Corporation, and Wing & Jabaay. Individually, each distributor had experienced difficulty providing timely, high-quality service; gaining large turnkey contracts from major customers; and reselling used equipment. Now when a consortium member spots an opportunity that it cannot handle alone or when it needs to provide technical assistance and does not have a service engineer available, its managers ask Intercore for assistance. Intercore also gives the distributors access to their partners' inventories of used equipment and enables them to make their used equipment available to a broader geographic market.

Based in independent offices in Indianapolis, Indiana, the consortium is largely an administrative operation. Each distributor has transferred one or two service engineers to Intercore, and an executive from one of the distributors serves as the head of operations. The consortium maintains relations with machine tools suppliers

BOX 9.9
The iPower Logistics LLC Approach to Reseller Consortia

iPower™ Logisitics LLC, now an independent company, franchises reseller consortia. Parker Hannifin Corporation (PH)—a manufacturer of fluid connectors, motion control systems, seals, and aircraft control systems—founded the iPower Distribution Group in 1994 as a wholly owned subsidiary. In the late 1980s, PH management became alarmed at the widespread consolidation of distributor firms and increasing customer demands for integrated supply management (ISM) contracts. Parker had long relied on eight types of smaller specialty distributors to market its products. Although these distributors were proficient at serving their traditional customer base, they did not have the breadth of lines to compete against giant distributors for the customers that wanted ISM contracts. To ensure that PH captured a share of the rapidly growing ISM market, managers had to devise a way to broaden the lines carried by their distributors without burdening them with excessive inventory.

Borrowing concepts from the successful Innovative Distribution Group in New England, PH management created a franchised business concept, the iPower™ Distribution Group, that is sold to distributors.

The franchise agreement requires that a group of specialty distributors from a geographic region form a consortium. Efforts must be made to ensure that each partner carries complementary lines and that the sum total of their lines meets the majority of product needs of major, local customers. In this way, the consortium can match the products and services provided by competing giants. iPower provides details on how to form the consortium, legal arrangements, operating procedures, and software for a shared information system to franchisees.

Today, iPower serves more than 165 large industrial customers through a network of 175 distributors. Managers claim that the consortium has allowed customer firms to reduce their procurement costs by 20 to 40 percent, while lowering their inventories by as much as 70 percent. In addition to offering a wide variety of industrial parts, electrical goods, power transmissions, and hydraulics and pneumatics systems, iPower furnishes numerous e-commerce services. These services include such things as iCustomer inventory management and delivery tracking software, iStorefront e-commerce Web sites, and the scanner-based iZap Bin Replenishment System.

Sources: Manager interviews and "Get the Power of iPower…", iPower Distribution Group [Internet] (Cleveland, OH: iPower Distribution Group, cited October 22, 2002), available from: *http://www. ipowerdg.com*.

and customers, markets technical service contracts, dispatches service engineers wherever needed, sends invoices to customers, and collects payments. Intercore distributes profits to its owners through dividends.

Share Capabilities with Other Channel Members
Ideally, every participant in the distribution channel should provide the same high-level service to every customer. In practice, of course, such consistency is virtually impossible because neither the supplier not any of its resellers is likely to excel at everything. Instead, companies tend to do an outstanding job with some services and a mediocre job with others. To overcome these discrepancies, suppliers and resellers are adopting **capabilities-sharing agreements**. Through such agreements, the superior service of one channel member substitutes for the subpar service of

another. In turn, channel members receive appropriate compensation for sharing their superior service capabilities.

SONEPAR, a €6.6 billion holding company based in France, has created centers of excellence among its European reseller subsidiaries to leverage their distinctive capabilities. We relate SONEPAR's experience in Box 9.10. Independently owned channel members can achieve similar gains through capabilities-sharing contracts with more resourceful partner firms. The technical problem-solving arrangement between Mori Seiki, the Japanese machine tool builder, and Landré Werkmetaal, a distributor based in the Netherlands, provides an outstanding illustration, which we recount in Box 9.11.

BOX 9.10
SONEPAR Establishes Centers of Excellence Within Its European Wholesaler Network

SONEPAR, a €6.6 billion holding company based in France, has more than 1,100 electrical wholesaler subsidiary locations scattered across Europe and the Americas. SONEPAR's wholesalers operate within an agreed-upon market focus. To improve the service capabilities of all its subsidiaries, SONEPAR managers identified and designated certain subsidiaries as centers of excellence. These centers possess superior knowledge or skill bases that can be transferred to other SONEPAR companies. For example, one wholesaler may provide outstanding point-of-sales materials, another may provide warehouse layouts, while still another may excel at electrical system design. Rather than duplicating efforts, SONEPAR managers encourage wholesalers that are experiencing problems to seek out assistance from an appropriate center of excellence.

An initial SONEPAR success story comes from Berantungsgessellschaft für Licht- und Elektrotechnik mbH (BLE), a center of excellence located in Soest, Germany, that has special expertise in lighting, data network technology, telecommunications, and office automation. BLE serves primarily as a training company for the employees and electrical contractor customers of SONEPAR subsidiaries. BLE runs these training programs either at its own facility or at locations of other SONEPAR subsidiaries. BLE also consolidates and translates technical documentation and training materials from electrical product suppliers. In doing so, BLE provides other SONEPAR distributors with superior technical materials and training programs than they could develop on their own, while eliminating redundant efforts and duplicated costs within all of SONEPAR.

BLE augments the capabilities not only of SONEPAR wholesalers but also of electrical products manufacturers. In the case of conventional electrical lines, BLE routinely consolidates technical materials from up to 15 suppliers for a given program. In this way, a training session in lighting might cover all major suppliers' products in an integrated way and address issues common to all vendors' lines, such as how to use software to calculate lighting levels in the design of a customer's lighting layouts. Such integrated programs are often more thorough and unbiased than those of suppliers. They also eliminate the need for each supplier to create and run separate and similar programs for each SONEPAR wholesaler. Not only does this approach save manufacturers money, it enables them to devote more attention to devising technical materials and running training programs for their own specialty lines.

Source: Adapted from "Rethinking Distribution: Adaptive Channels," James A. Narus and James C. Anderson, *Harvard Business Review* (July–August 1996): 112–130.

BOX 9.11
Landré Werkmetaal and Mori Seiki Leverage Technical Service Capabilities

Independently owned channel members can benefit from capabilities-sharing arrangements with more proficient partner firms. An outstanding illustration comes from technical problem-solving arrangement between Mori Seiki, the Japanese machine tool builder, and Landré Werkmetaal b.v., a distribution division of Geveke b.v., based in the Netherlands. Because of Mori Seiki's limited presence in Europe, the prohibitive costs of maintaining a large staff of service engineers, and occasional difficulties in dispatching service engineers from its Düsseldorf offices, the company found that it could not consistently guarantee customers prompt on-site technical problem-solving assistance. In addition, although Mori Seiki engineers were quite knowledgeable about their equipment's basic technology, they sometimes lacked the expertise to solve problems for customers who had unusual applications.

To help Mori Seiki overcome those challenges, Landré Werkmetaal's management proposed and implemented an arrangement with Mori Seiki called *rent-a-service-engineer*. Now, when Mori Seiki receives a request for service, it determines (a) whether it has required knowledge of the customer's application, (b) whether it has a competent service engineer available, and (c) whether that service engineer can reach the customer's plant site promptly. If the answer to each question is yes, Mori Seiki dispatches one of its own service engineers. On the other hand, if the answer to any or all of these questions is no, then Mori Seiki asks Landré Werkmetaal to send an engineer to the customer's plant site. Acting as a representative of Mori Seiki, the service engineer corrects the problem. Mori Seiki then pays Landré Werkmetaal a pre-specified per diem fee for the engineer's time plus travel expenses.

This arrangement has profound consequences for both Mori Seiki and Landré Werkmetaal. To begin with, Mori Seiki can forgo the high costs of hiring more service engineers and regularly dispatching them across Europe. At the same time, Mori Seiki does not have to request that the service engineers of all of its European distributors be skilled in solving every conceivable problem in every product application. Instead, it can confidently offer high quality and prompt on-site technical problem-solving assistance through this arrangement, due to Landré Werkmetaal's strategic location and technical competence. Landré Werkmetaal, in turn, makes more productive use of its service engineers' time and gains a higher yield on related expenditures. Furthermore, Landré Werkmetaal adds a profitable value-added service to its repertoire. In fact, it has been so successful that Landré Werkmetaal has created a similar arrangement in Europe with Dresser Industries, an American manufacturer that builds gas engines for power cogeneration systems.

Source: Adapted from "Rethinking Distribution: Adaptive Channels," James A. Narus and James C. Anderson, *Harvard Business Review* (July–August 1996): 112–130.

Overcome Implementation Problems

Although the idea of a more flexible and responsive distribution system is appealing, experienced managers recognize that significant hurdles stand between the idea and its implementation. To begin with, channel members are likely to be skeptical about the rewards of participation. That is particularly the case when the benefits of the new arrangement are conceptually different and more complex than those to which the distributors are accustomed, as when increased leverage or cash flow replaces a simple boost in gross margin.

Channel members are also likely to feel threatened by new cooperative arrangements because they stand to lose long-established functions, responsibilities, and relationships. To take one simple example, despite all the talk about "virtual" organizations, most distributors still feel more confident about their ability to provide first-rate customer service when they have a warehouse full of inventory than when they share supplies with another distributor 500 miles away.

To allay such fears and doubts, innovators must build trust and gain the commitment of potential channel members. For many organizations, pledges and guarantees are a good way to begin. By committing essential resources to the new system and guaranteeing its performance, most often with provisions for service recovery if the system fails, companies like Okuma have been able to overcome distributors' initial reservations. Then, as experience builds, the network of relationships within the distribution channel can be broadened and deepened. For instance, all of Okuma's distributors can post their inventory on Okumalink, enabling channel members to search for machine tool parts electronically. Box 9.12 provides an example of how Dunlop-Enerka used pledges and guarantees to implement an adaptive channel arrangement with selected European resellers.

Skillfully Handling Relationship Transfers

Changing marketplace or customer firm requirements may necessitate transferring customer relationships between a supplier and its resellers. For example, in the past, the principal working relationship was between a supplier and a customer firm. Now, to deliver the greatest value at the lowest total cost to the customer, the principal responsibility for the relationship needs to shift to one of the supplier's resellers. Successful relationship transfers require especially close coordination between the supplier firm and the reseller firm. For instance, they may make joint sales calls on the customer during a transition period. As time progresses, one of the partners (the reseller in our example) makes more and more of the contacts. The supplier should try to maintain some sort of relationship with the customer firm although it is significantly diminished.

To sustain the strength of the working relationship and to keep the customer's loyalty, business market managers must take steps to adroitly manage the transfer. As a prelude to relationship transfers, both reseller and supplier managers must agree on the conditions under which the principal responsibility for serving an account will shift from one firm to another. Then, they must spell out equitable compensation, if necessary, for transferring the relationships from one firm to the other.

Delineate Relationship Transfer Criteria

The breadth and depth of the market offering a customer account purchases and the account's service requirements are among the key indicators that a relationship transfer is needed. In general, the greater the volume and the more limited the assortments of products and services required, the more efficiently a supplier can serve the customer. This efficiency can be attributed to greater economies of scale in production and logistics, which translate into significant cost savings for the customer. In the reverse situation, the customer is often more efficiently served by a reseller because resellers are better able to exploit economies of scope by spreading out fixed transaction costs over a broader assortment.

BOX 9.12
Dunlop-Enerka Fosters Cooperation Among Its European Distributors

Dunlop-Enerka produces conveyor belts and markets them in Europe to mining and manufacturing companies. In general, Dunlop-Enerka sells conveyor belts directly to original equipment manufacturers. Distributors sell to the maintenance, repair, and operating supply (MRO) market segment. The nature of these markets and products has long posed a vexing problem for Dunlop-Enerka. About 80 percent of all orders entail cutting and splicing lengths of conveyor belts. Most MRO accounts, for instance, need customized replacement belts and installation service. In the past, Dunlop-Enerka's solution to this problem was to stock huge quantities of different-sized belts in different locations across Europe. The result was burdensome inventory costs.

As a remedy, Dunlop-Enerka devised an auxiliary support system. In order to secure initial distributor participation, the firm pledged essential resources. To begin with, Dunlop-Enerka unilaterally created a multilingual and internationally shared electronic data interchange system called DUNLOCOMM. Additionally, Dunlop-Enerka provided and installed computer monitors at participating distributor sites and trained distributor personnel how to use the system for free.

DUNLOCOMM electronically monitors the inventory stocked in its warehouses and those of a number of its Western European distributors on a daily basis. When a distributor immediately needs an out-of-stock conveyor belt, it uses DUNLOCOMM to scan those inventories to find the nearest firm location that has the belt in stock. The distributor then makes arrangements for next-day delivery by phone or fax.

To ensure the integrity of DUNLOCOMM, Dunlop-Enerka offered several guarantees. It guaranteed that all stocks listed on DUNLOCOMM were in fact available. If a distributor found that they were not present in a channel partner's warehouse as stated on DUNLOCOMM, Dunlop-Enerka customized the needed belt from the nearest larger belt size available in its own inventory. It further guaranteed that the customized belt would be delivered in 24 hours.

Dunlop-Enerka's pledges and guarantees succeeded in getting distributors to list their inventories on and to actively use DUNLOCOMM. Although DUNLOCOMM initially caused distributor inventories to drop precipitously and Dunlop-Enerka's stock to rise equivalently, as time has progressed, Dunlop-Enerka's inventory has dropped by 20 percent. With lower costs and faster inventory turnover, Dunlop-Enerka's profit margins increased by an average of 5 percent per product line. In addition, the company strategically invested inventory cost savings in new product development. This investment spawned several major product innovations that increased Dunlop-Enerka's total sales by 30 percent. It is also worth pointing out that as a result of Dunlop-Enerka's efforts, distributor inventories declined significantly while their ability to provide fast and reliable delivery of high-quality conveyor belts increased substantially. The consequences have been faster inventory turnover and greater profits for distributors and first-rate service for customers.

Source: Adapted from "Rethinking Distribution: Adaptive Channels," James A. Narus and James C. Anderson, *Harvard Business Review* (July–August 1996): 112–130.

The key for both channel partners is to identify the relevant sales breakpoint. For example, GLS and one of its plastics suppliers have specified the breakpoint as one truckload, or 40,000 pounds of resin, per month for an extended period of time. If GLS sales to a given account routinely exceed this amount, GLS transfers the account to the supplier. On the other hand, if a customer's purchases from the plastics supplier routinely drop below the breakpoint, the supplier transfers the account to GLS.

Changes in customer service requirements may also indicate the need to transfer relationships. For example, as customer requirements for technical assistance become more complex, direct sales by the supplier become more feasible because the supplier is often the best source of technical expertise for a particular product. Alternatively, as customers increasingly require integrated supply management contracts, the importance of the reseller increases because they offer one-stop shopping.

As an example, consider how Technische Unie, a Dutch electrical wholesaler owned by SONEPAR, and Draka, the cable manufacturer, handled the relationship transfer of PTT, the Dutch telephone company. Technische Unie markets integrated supply contracts to large customers and has established procedures for transferring accounts from suppliers. Several years ago, senior management at PTT demanded that its operations group reduce costs by 25 percent while increasing the availability of electrical equipment and parts to the firm's installers. At the time, only 70 percent of required supplies were available when needed. To capitalize on this opportunity, Technische Unie's managers went to Draka, a major supplier of PTT, and asked to supply all Draka cable and supplies to PTT. By offering Draka products along with those of other suppliers, Technische Unie would be able to provide an integrated supply contract to PTT. Draka agreed, and Technische Unie became the single-source supplier of electrical equipment and supplies to PTT. Within a short period of time, PTT gained access to 96 percent of its requirements in 24 hours and a reduction in costs that exceeded senior management's 25 percent goal.

Establish Equitable Compensation for Relationship Transfers

One of the best ways to ensure that relational transfers are made smoothly is to compensate the partner for loss of the customer. For example, GLS managers report that one supplier pays them a transfer fee and a 5 percent finder's fee for a transferred account for a period of six months to a year. Technische Unie demonstrates to suppliers how their infrastructure will be reduced through fewer warehouses, less inventory, and fewer employees following a relationship transfer. At the same time, Technische Unie furnishes suppliers with detailed market information on what the transferred customer is purchasing. Furthermore, Technische Unie encourages the supplier to continue sales and technical service calls on the customer.

SUMMARY

In this chapter, we examined the process of sustaining working partnerships within distribution channels. To sustain reseller partnerships, both supplier and reseller managers must consistently fulfill commitments to deliver value to customer firms. A series of best practice examples from leading supplier and reseller firms illustrated how they consistently and innovatively deliver on promises. We also showed how successful companies support their partners when unexpected crises arise, passing what we call the critical incident test.

Periodically, supplier and reseller managers take stock of overall channel performance by measuring customer satisfaction and the actual value customers receive. As a complement to this assessment, supplier and reseller firms conduct financial analyses to determine whether they have received an equitable return on the value they have delivered.

As is the case with other aspects of business market management, complacency often brings the demise of reseller partnerships. For this reason, supplier and reseller managers must examine their partnerships and seek ways to strengthen the value they deliver to customer firms. Toward this end, we described how managers occasionally adjust commitments by reformulating channel partners' gives & gets and by making changes in joint annual plans. In other situations, business market managers seek incremental process improvements by learning to work together more effectively. Firms can identify areas of improvement with reseller advisory councils and improve partner performance with training and coaching. To strengthen interfirm coordination, we provided recommendations on how firms can improve coordination, clarify roles and responsibilities through agreements, and resolve conflicts.

When marketplace requirements change, partner firms work together to find new ways to meet them. They create adaptive channels to address infrequent yet critical customer requirements by devising cooperative agreements with channel partners for assistance. Finally, they transfer customer relationships when necessary. To handle such transfers smoothly, channel partners identify conditions when channel arrangements must change, develop procedures for disengagement, and devise compensation systems to reward firms for transferring accounts.

ENDNOTES

1. As in Chapter 7, we use the following terms. In an *indirect channel*, a supplier firm employs reseller firms to market its offerings to customer firms. A *supplier firm* produces the core product or service of a marketplace offering. A *reseller firm* takes the core product or service, adds value to it with augmenting products and services, and then markets the enhanced offering. A *third-party service provider*, such as a trucking firm, public warehouse, or information system vendor, furnishes additional augmenting services on a fee basis to suppliers and resellers. Finally, a *customer firm* acquires a market offering from a supplier or reseller for the customer's own use, or for inclusion into the products or services it produces.
2. James C. Anderson and James A. Narus, "A Model of Distributor Firm and Manufacturer Firm Working Partnerships," *Journal of Marketing* (January 1990): 42.
3. Academics often refer to this process as *interorganizational governance*. To read more about governance issues, read Jan B. Heide, "Interorganizational Governance in Marketing Channels," *Journal of Marketing* (January 1994): 72.
4. James C. Anderson, Håkan Håkansson, and Jan Johanson, "Dyadic Business Relationships Within a Business Network Context," *Journal of Marketing* (October 1994): 10.
5. Erin Anderson and Barton Weitz, "The Use of Pledges to Build and Sustain Commitment in Distribution Channels," *Journal of Marketing Research* (February 1992): 19.
6. N. Mohan Reddy and Michael P. Marvin, "Developing a Manufacturer-Distributor Information Partnership," *Industrial Marketing Management* (1986): 157–163.
7. James A. Narus and James C. Anderson, "Turn Your Industrial Distributors into Partners," *Harvard Business Review* (March–April 1986): 66–71; and *Guaranteed Cost Reductions* (Cleveland, OH: Lincoln Electric Company, cited August 2003), available at *http://www.lincolnelectric.com*.

8. Anita Lienert, "A Dinosaur of a Different Color," *American Management Association Management Review* (February 1995): 29.

9. Arthur Hughes, "How Panduit Did It," *Marketing Tools* (March–April 1996): 4–7; and Tom Andel, "Manage Inventory, Own Information," *Transportation & Distribution* (May 1996): 55.

10. Narus and Anderson, "Turn Your Industrial Distributors."

11. Victoria Fraza, "Documented Success," *Industrial Distribution* (January 1997): 54–56.

12. Nancy A. Helman, "PSS," *Incentive* (December 1996): 28–29; Curt Werner, "Distributors Find Big Opportunity in Alternate Site Sales," *Health Industry Today* (December 1996): 1–11; John Case, "The 10 Commandments of Hypergrowth," *Inc.* (October 1995): 33–44; Debbie Epstein, "MedOutcomes Prepares R.Ph.s for Disease Management," *Drug Topics,* 2 September 1996, 32–35; and Carol Ukens, "McKesson Programs Invest in Future for Clients," *Drug Topics,* 4 March 1996, 124.

13. "Relationships Develop Products," *Industrial Distribution* (October 1996): S6–S8.

14. Donald V. Fites, "Make Your Dealers Your Partners," *Harvard Business Review* (March–April 1996): 88–89.

15. James A. Narus and James C. Anderson, "Distributor Contributions to Partnerships with Manufacturers," *Business Horizons* (September–October 1987): 34–42.

16. E. Raymond Corey, Frank V. Cespedes, and V. Kasturi Rangan, *Going to Market* (Boston: Harvard Business School Press, 1989).

17. Peter L. Mullins, *Effective Financial Management for Wholesaler-Distributors* (Washington, DC: National Association of Wholesaler-Distributors, 1979); and Peter L. Mullins, *Measuring Customer and Product Line Profitability: Beyond "Turn & Earn"* (Washington, DC: Distribution Research & Education Foundation, 1984).

18. Kenneth H. Manning, "Distribution Channel Profitability," *Management Accounting* (January 1995): 44–49.

19. Peter Doyle, *Value-Based Marketing* (Chichester, U.K.: John Wiley & Sons, 2000); and S. David Young and Stephen F. O'Bryne, *EVA® and Value-Based Management* (New York: McGraw-Hill, 2001).

20. Fites, "Make Your Dealers . . ."

21. Thayer C. Taylor, "Sales Automation Cuts the Cord," *Sales & Marketing Management* (July 1995): 110–115.

22. For a discussion on how to run a reseller advisory council, see James D. Hlavacek and James A. Narus, "Early Warnings in the Channel," *Marketing Management* 1, no. 4 (1993): 50–59.

23. Andy Cohen, "Dealer Training Goes Interactive," *Sales & Marketing Management* (December 1995): 31–32.

24. Larry Conley, "Head of the Class," *Satellite Communications* (October 1995): 26–34.

25. Neil Rackham and Richard Ruff, *Managing Major Sales* (New York: HarperBusiness, 1991).

26. Jakki Mohr and John R. Nevin, "Communication Strategies in Marketing Channels: A Theoretical Perspective," *Journal of Marketing* (October 1990): 36–51.

27. This quote is drawn from James C. Anderson and James A. Narus, "A Model of Distributor Firm and Manufacturer Firm Working Partnerships," *Journal of Marketing* (January 1990): 44.

28. Narus and Anderson, "Distributor Contributions."

29. This quote is drawn from Anderson and Narus, "A Model," 44.

30. This discussion is drawn from the article, James A. Narus and James C. Anderson, "Rethinking Distribution: Adaptive Channels," *Harvard Business Review* (July–August 1996): 112–120.

Chapter 10

Sustaining Customer Relationships

OVERVIEW

*I*ncreasingly, business market managers seek to maximize their firms' financial returns by balancing efforts to gain new customers with activities designed to retain and expand profitable share of business among existing customers. To do so, they build and sustain a portfolio of customer relationships. Some of these relationships will be collaborative and last many years, others will be short-lived and opportunistic. Some will be extensive in scope, others narrow. Some will be just beginning, others ending. Having discussed the process of gaining customers in Chapter 8, we turn our attention to those activities associated with keeping and growing profitable customer relationships.[1]

Sustaining customer relationships is the process of fulfilling mutually agreed-upon customer requirements in a superior way over time, and selectively pursuing continuity and growth through building mutual self-interest. This definition emphasizes that to deliver value, supplier and customer managers must reach a detailed understanding of customer requirements and preferences, and actively communicate with one another about how these requirements and preferences are changing. The supplier must anticipate and capably respond to these changes. By marketing tailored yet flexible offerings, the supplier strives to make itself indispensable to the customer. In exchange, the supplier retains and expands a profitable share of the customer's

Figure 10.1 Sustaining Customer Relationships

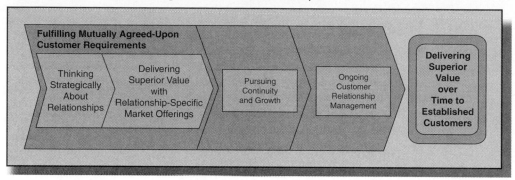

business that meets the goals of its market strategy. We sketch how to sustain customer relationships in Figure 10.1.

In this chapter, we address each aspect of sustaining customer relationships. We begin by providing a strategic foundation for relationship-building efforts. This foundation rests on the concepts of a relationship continuum and industry bandwidths, and the careful selection of customer partners. Next, we discuss how firms cultivate particular working relationships by delivering value in the form of relationship-specific market offerings. Then we turn our attention to the behavioral issues associated with working together by describing how firms promote open and honest communications, build trust and commitment, coordinate efforts, and anticipate and resolve conflicts. To grow profitable working relationships, progressive suppliers propose such innovative business arrangements as single-sourcing, facilities management, and outsourcing. We provide guidance on how a supplier firm can get the customer comfortable with these innovative ideas while ensuring an equitable sharing of the value they create through risk-sharing and gain-sharing agreements.

Firms formalize the ongoing administration of this process through a comprehensive system and set of procedures called customer relationship management (CRM). Market databases and activity-based costing systems provide the backbone for CRM and we explore how they are designed and implemented. Then, we examine how managers use CRM to evaluate customer relationships, propose changes to relationship-specific offerings, and if need be, recommend the reassignment or termination of accounts. We conclude by illustrating how a supplier firm can keep relationships vibrant by taking advantage of business networks.

FULFILLING MUTUALLY AGREED-UPON CUSTOMER REQUIREMENTS

As we argue in Chapter 4, managers must be selective in choosing which customers to serve and which requirements to fulfill. Rather than pursuing the same relationship with all customers, they must direct their resources to where they deliver the greatest value. To accomplish this goal, managers first think strategically about relationships, and then deliver superior value in the form of relationship-specific market offerings.

Thinking Strategically About Relationships[2]

All customer and supplier firms that do business together have some sort of working relationship. Jackson discussed a working relationship continuum along which industries fall.[3] We diagram this continuum in Figure 10.2. Purely **transactional relationships**, where the customer and the supplier focus on the timely exchange of basic products for highly competitive prices, anchor one end. Purely **collaborative relationships** anchor the other end. This latter kind of relationship comes about through **partnering**, which is a process where a customer firm and supplier firm form strong and extensive social, economic, service, and technical ties over time. The intent of partnering is to lower total costs or increase value, thereby achieving mutual benefit.[4]

Consider Industry Bandwidths

The nature of working relationships in business markets suggests that we need some further elaboration with respect to Jackson's rudimentary premise. Rather than occupying a single point on the continuum, each marketplace is better characterized as a range of relationships that are more collaborative or more transactional in nature relative to that marketplace's norm. We refer to this range as the **industry bandwidth of working relationships**. This bandwidth reflects the explicit or implicit relationship strategies that suppliers pursue in an industry. Firms either attempt to span the bandwidth with a portfolio of relationships, or treat all customers more or less alike, thereby having a narrower range of relationships than the industry bandwidth.

Figure 10.2 The Working Relationship Continuum and Industry Bandwidths

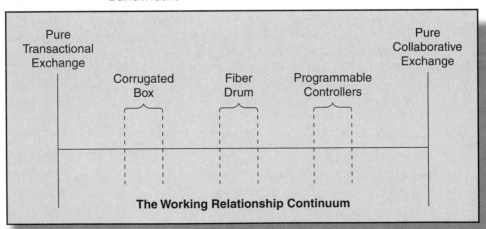

Source: Adapted from James C. Anderson and James A. Narus, "Partnering as a Focused Market Strategy," *California Management Review* (Spring 1991): 95–113.

Naturally, industry bandwidths for various markets fall along the entire continuum of working relationships. Even the most transactional relationship in one industry might be more collaborative in nature than the most collaborative relationship in another industry, and vice versa. For example, compare the corrugated box, fiber drum, and programmable controller industries that we depict in Figure 10.2. Because the underlying technology in the programmable controller industry is the most complicated and is still developing, collaborative relations in this industry can be all encompassing, ranging from codesign of manufacturing systems to installation, training, and maintenance. Collaborative relations in the fiber drum industry tend to be more circumscribed and focus on helping customers modify their systems and procedures in areas such as lifting and stacking fiber drums. Finally, because many customers consider corrugated boxes a commodity, long-term supply contracts and just-in-time inventory programs generally represent the extent of potential collaboration.

Partnering as a Focused Market Strategy

Business market managers recognize that not all customer firms want the same kind of relationship with a supplier, nor can the same kind of relationship deliver the same value to all customers. Instead, they draw on the bedrock marketing concepts of segmentation, targeting, and positioning (STP), which we discussed in Chapters 2 and 4, to formulate a relationship strategy. Business market managers first segment the marketplace, using progressive bases such as customer application, capabilities and business priorities, and usage situation. They then estimate the value of their offerings in these segments. Such information indicates how a supplier firm can enhance market offerings, if at all, through working relationships.

Next, managers target one or more segments for collaborative emphasis versus transaction emphasis. Specifically, they target segments where a firm's offering has superior value relative to the competition for collaborative emphasis and segments where its offering does not provide superior value for transaction emphasis. Segments where the firm has superior value represent natural places for the firm to allocate resources for relationship-building efforts. Customers in these segments are more likely to be receptive to such initiatives and may be proactive themselves in suggesting closer relations.

Having targeted specific segments, supplier managers then turn their attention to individual accounts. As Professor Narayandas aptly points out, managers must distinguish between customer selection and order selection. **Customer selection** is based on the supplier firm's mission and strategic intent and takes competencies and capabilities into consideration. **Order selection**, on the other hand, is tactical in nature and focuses on short-term resource utilization. Ideally, the supplier firm should deliberately seek out profitable orders from strategic customers. All too often, undisciplined firms take any order from any potential customer in order to make short-term sales quotas. Furthermore, managers frequently fail to discriminate between "bad orders from good customers" and "good orders from bad customers." Such short-sightedness reduces supplier profitability and diminishes its competitive advantage.[5]

In partnering as a focused market strategy, managers diligently concentrate on customer selection, identifying likely prospects for partnerships versus transactional relations. In doing so, a supplier develops selection criteria based on customer firm and marketplace characteristics. Among the more common are philosophy of doing business, the dependence of the supplier firm and the customer firm upon the relationship, and the technological edge a customer firm might contribute. Critically, managers determine how they will deal with accounts where the customer firm holds the power advantage.

Business market managers should target some firms in transaction-emphasis segments for collaborative efforts. Manufacturers of technology-based products should target lead-user accounts and leap-frog accounts for collaborative efforts as a strategy for improving the value of their market offering in presently designated transaction segments. Recall from Chapter 6 that a lead-user firm is one whose present requirements will reflect the segment's needs in future months or years, and one that is therefore positioned to benefit the most from collaborative solutions to those requirements. When competitors have already locked up lead-users in collaborative relationships, managers should pursue small, aggressive firms who have the ability to leap-frog the present segment leaders with new technology. Such leap-frog firms may be newer entrants that are willing to pursue a riskier development strategy to gain market share. By engaging in collaborative efforts, such as codesign, the supplier firm seeks to significantly improve the value of its future offerings in this application.[6]

We illustrate the activities of partnering as a focused market strategy through an example from Greif Incorporated in Box 10.1.

BOX 10.1
Greif Incorporated Sets Priorities for Serving Market Segments

Greif Incorporated manufactures lines of fiber and plastic drums as well as intermediate bulk containers (IBCs) that replace stainless steel drums in a multitude of industries ranging from cooking oil manufacturing to chemical production. Rather than attempting to serve all of these segments with all of its products at once, Greif uses a controlled migration strategy. Greif managers first prioritize segments based on the value its packaging systems provide in customer applications. They know that Greif systems create the greatest value in the following scenario:

- The disposal or reconditioning of drums or IBCs presents an environmental hazard.
- The cost of containers, and their transportation and handling, constitute a significant portion of the customer's total operating costs.
- Customers require odd-sized containers.

Then, they seek close collaborative relationships with customer firms in segments where Greif systems create the greatest value. As part of these collaborative relationships, Greif managers jointly conduct cost-of-use research with customer managers. As we discussed in Chapter 8, Greif managers use findings from such studies to construct total cost-based solutions. As a relationship becomes more collaborative, Greif managers persuade customer firms to trade up to higher-value Greif solutions. Thus, a customer's product usage often migrates from fiber drums to plastic drums to IBCs.

Over the years, Greif has reaped dividends from these collaborative relationships in the form of new product and service ideas. As time has progressed, Greif has moved down its priority list to serve segments with lower value potential. Greif pursues transactional relationships with these accounts and sells them primarily fiber drums and basic packaging systems.

Delivering Superior Value with Relationship-Specific Offerings

With segment and account targets in mind, business market managers construct and then implement relationship-specific offerings. Managers draw on the techniques of managing market offerings that we presented in Chapter 5. We add to that discussion in this section by describing a strategy for constructing relationship-specific offerings. Next, we describe how firms organize to deliver and sell relationship-specific offerings. Then, we suggest ways for business market managers to solve common relationship-offering implementation problems.

Construct Relationship-Specific Market Offerings

Business market managers configure a market offering to match the type of relationship pursued with a particular customer firm. In Chapter 3, we mentioned that the nature of the offering tends to expand from a single product or service in the case of a purely transactional relationship to a solution or bundle of products and services in a collaborative relationship to a partnership in a strategic alliance.[7] As a start in constructing the collaborative and transactional relationship offerings, the supplier firm does market research to determine the extent and intensity of collaborative and transactional efforts practiced in the industry. In other words, managers gain an understanding of the present industry bandwidth. At the same time, the supplier firm performs benchmark studies of other industries in an attempt to learn about collaborative and transactional practices that it might adopt or adapt into its current offerings. The supplier firm's strategy is then to extend the present industry bandwidth in both the collaborative as well as the transactional direction. By becoming more collaborative and more transactional in this manner, a supplier firm tries to gain a competitive advantage over other suppliers by better meeting customer requirements and preferences in both collaborative-emphasis and transaction-emphasis segments. We refer to this strategy as **flaring out from the industry bandwidth**.[8]

Managers modify the firm's market offering through flaring out by unbundling or flaring out with augmentation. To **flare out by unbundling**, business market managers either eliminate certain standard elements from the market offering entirely or transform them into options. In essence, the manager has moved the firm's market offering from *b* to *a* in Figure 10.3.

To **flare out with augmentation**, managers draw on the practices of more collaborative industries and add new programs and systems that collaborative accounts will value to the standard offering, or as options. Significantly, the supplier may not offer a number of these new programs and systems to transactional customers, even as options. In essence, business market managers move their firm's collaborative market offering from *c* to *d* in Figure 10.3.

As an example of augmentation, consider how Penske's Leaseway Auto Carriers flared out to create a collaborative offering in a market populated with transactional relationships. As part of its service to General Motors (GM), Leaseway hired operations researchers to build a model of GM's physical distribution requirements. Based on this model, Leaseway designed a program to help GM schedule shipping routes, select car models for shipping, and determine the optimal sequence for off-loading cars at GM dealers to minimize potential damage and delivery time. The computer model is highly interfaced with GM's in-house computer systems and can be utilized to troubleshoot emergency problems. Although Leaseway has only a 30-day contract

Figure 10.3 Flaring Out from the Industry Bandwidth

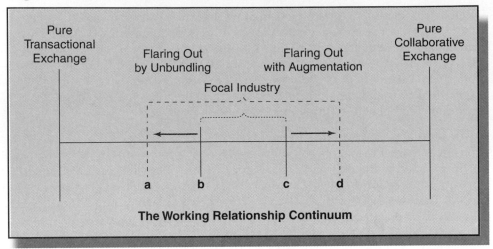

Source: Adapted from James C. Anderson and James A. Narus, "Partnering as a Focused Market Strategy," *California Management Review* (Spring 1991): 95–113.

with GM, that contract has been in effect continuously for over 35 years. Leaseway remains a major supplier of trucking services to GM.

Price Relationship-Specific Offerings

The relationship-specific pricing strategy and tactics reflect the underlying relationship strategy. For transactional relationships, business market managers lower the price for each service that is unbundled, but lower it less than the cost of presently performing the service, thereby improving the supplier's profit margin. The supplier firm markets its optional programs and services such as delivery, installation, training, maintenance, and technical service, in menu fashion, on an incremental price basis. A further feature of the pricing strategy for the transactional offering should be that the sum of the price increments for the entire set of unbundled services should be greater than any price premium granted for the collaborative offering. This pricing should reflect the economies of scope and scale that accrue from being a full-service supplier to a customer. Note that this pricing is market oriented in that it allows customer firms to choose the market offering and relationship that they perceive provides the greatest value.

The pricing strategy for collaborative market offerings takes an opposite tack. Because the only collaborative efforts undertaken are those that add value to or reduce the total cost of the exchange between firms, the supplier should seek a price premium in return for the collaborative offering. As an alternative, the supplier firm may seek a greater share of the customer's business, particularly when most potential cost savings occur in the customer firm's operation.

A mechanism for modifying the pricing of relationship offerings is **defeaturing**, a tactic we introduced in Chapter 3. For transactional customers that represent significant business, a supplier may defeature its offering and share the cost savings, at least in part, as lower price. Another tactic is to selectively inquire about the transactional customer's willingness to relax its stated specifications in return for a lower price.

In collaborative relationships, the customer and supplier firms work together to gain a deeper understanding of the customer's requirements and preferences. Collaboration allows the supplier to more fully use its expertise to propose modifications in the customer's specifications that will enable it to lower its price. At times, the supplier may even be able to redesign its offerings to provide greater functionality at the same price. Thus, defeaturing is a way for the supplier to modify and adapt its offerings so its prices are more in line with what transactional or collaborative customers are seeking. In each case, the supplier may retain a portion of the cost savings as incremental profit, and pass on the remainder to the customer as incentive to change.

Organize to Deliver Relationship-Specific Offerings

When a supplier firm decides to sustain a portfolio of diverse working relationships, it often establishes multiple sales forces. In Chapter 7, we described these alternative sales forces. Each of these sales forces provides a different level of service to targeted customer accounts.

Motorola's Semiconductor Products Sector provides an excellent example of how firms organize around relationships. The division has three field sales forces plus an inside sales force. Motorola's Strategic Market Sales Force is composed of teams of technical sales engineers, applications engineers, quality engineers, and service personnel, among others, that are assigned to strategic partnership accounts. It is the responsibility of these sales teams to deliver the technical and manufacturing know-how needed to make the partnerships successful.

Members of Motorola's Geographic Sales Force act individually, calling on the thousands of customers that buy Motorola products. They perform traditional selling tasks, such as making periodic customer visits, giving presentations, solving problems, and taking orders. Motorola's Distributor Sales Force represents Motorola to the trade. Member tasks include encouraging distributors to stock and sell Motorola products, coaching distributor sales personnel on merchandising techniques, and working with distributors to maintain sound working relationships with the smallest of Motorola customers. Finally, Motorola's Inside Sales Force makes outgoing telemarketing calls and takes incoming orders from transactional customers via the telephone and fax machines.

Sell Relationship-Specific Offerings

With multiple sales forces, business market managers must also reconsider the approaches the firm uses to sell relationship-specific offerings. In Chapter 8, we described and contrasted two such approaches: transactional and consultative selling. Transactional selling used in combination with direct marketing or e-commerce is most appropriate with transaction-emphasis accounts because it is focused and cost-effective. Consultative selling has its greatest utility with collaborative-emphasis customers as the salesperson diagnoses problems and opportunities the customer faces and proposes solutions in the form of a bundle of products and services. As firms become even more collaborative and seek strategic alliances such as joint ventures, syndication, and licensing agreements, they turn to a third approach: enterprise selling.

Enterprise selling is a set of skills, strategies, and processes that enable a supplier firm to identify and recruit a potential partner firm and then to work closely with that partner firm to create extraordinary value for end-users. Consultants Rackham and DeVincentis specify three general steps to the process: segmentation, value targeting, and value actioning. Enterprise selling begins as business market managers segment potential partner firms based on capabilities and business priorities. Then they assess prospective partner firms, determining for which the combined resources of the two companies are likely to yield offerings that create the greatest value for common end-users. They target the highest potential value-adding partner firms. The supplier's senior management, rather than its sales force, initiates contacts with a potential partner firm. Rather than selling a product or solution, senior managers stress the synergies that will result from sharing complementary competencies and capabilities such as proprietary technology and access to lucrative markets. They promote the significant financial returns both firms will gain from a close working relationship. Once a partnership is formed, cross-functional teams from both organizations work jointly to dissolve, redesign, and improve boundaries between the firms with the intent of creating the greatest possible end-user value.[9]

Solve Common Relationship-Offering Implementation Problems

When implementing relationship-specific market offerings, the supplier firm should expect to encounter some special cases or problems within certain relationships. Certain large accounts may not recognize the value of the market offering that they are presently receiving or are unwilling to pay a premium for it. The supplier firm should use marketing communications, supported by value case histories or other results gleaned from the earlier research, to persuasively demonstrate the superior value it provides. Greif Incorporated has centered its efforts around a dramatic set of videos. The videos convincingly show its intermediate bulk containers surpassing standards in a series of U.S. Department of Transportation tests.

Other large accounts that tacitly understand this greater value attempt to take advantage of the supplier. Each time the supplier firm offers some program or system that is designed to reduce cost or add value these accounts opportunistically demand all of the benefits, without granting some price premium in return. An alternate large-customer tactic is to "reward" the supplier with a larger share of the customer's business, but then request greater volume discounts. This scenario can be a "hollow bone" if it does not provide enough additional gross profit to cover the costs of the program or system. These opportunistic customers feel that they are "base-loading" the supplier's facility—they believe that they are enabling the supplier to surpass minimum capacity-utilization requirements and expect the supplier to make its profits on other, presumably smaller, customers' business.

During this critical moment of truth for the relationship, suppliers need to respond to such opportunistic accounts by "freezing" them at current levels of service and not offering them any new collaborative initiative, such as a codesign program. Should these accounts hear that the supplier has offered a new program to another customer and question the supplier as to why they have not been offered the program, supplier managers need to respond firmly. They should inform these customers that the supplier firm cannot afford to "give away for free" the value that such efforts produce, given their incremental cost. Furthermore, supplier managers should ask: If we undertook this collaborative effort and it produced the expected outcomes, what would it be worth to your firm? If the opportunistic customer responds by saying "Nothing" or some price or share of business increment less than the cost of the program, the supplier should respond that they cannot undertake the effort at that return. Supplier managers designate the offering for these opportunistic accounts as c in Figure 10.3.

In another troubling situation, certain large accounts may want the new, unbundled lower price, but the previous service level. Once again, the supplier firm faces a moment of truth. If these accounts are truly the ones that the supplier cannot afford to lose, some negotiation is needed. One compromise is to exchange a basic set of services, such as delivery and technical assistance, for a greater share of customers' profitable business and longer-term purchase commitments. Managers designate the market offering for these problematic accounts as *b* in Figure 10.3.

In Box 10.2, we present a detailed case study from Putnam Investments that illustrates the tasks of constructing, pricing, and selling relationship-specific offerings.

BOX 10.2
Putnam Builds Strategic Relationships

Putnam Investment's global investment business is headquartered in Boston, Massachusetts, with additional investment research analysts and sales staff located in London and Tokyo. Although Putnam's only business is investment management, its Strategic Relations Team (SRT) is a sign of its commitment to client service.

Putnam serves both institutional and individual clients. Institutional clients are particularly fee-sensitive and many firms are willing to negotiate fees to accommodate this segment. Putnam, however, has been able to successfully win placements despite its tough fee schedule. To shift the decision-making process away from price, Putnam communicates the benefits, beyond performance, that the prospects would enjoy should they select Putnam.

Many large corporate plans and endowments have an internal investment staff, dedicated to monitoring their roster of managers and conducting searches for new managers, thereby removing the need for an investment consultant. The dedicated staff, however, does not enjoy the knowledge base required to formulate opinions regarding capital market trends and their impact on the plan's portfolio; nor does their internal staff possess all the tools required to conduct a full asset allocation study.

As one of the largest global investment management firms, Putnam has access to all of the tools and information required to conduct these asset allocation studies. In addition, Putnam's staff of more than 40 global industry analysts, economists, and quantitative experts serves as a sophisticated resource to support research projects regarding capital market issues. With access to this resource, clients and prospects that require "investment consulting-type services" will value the Putnam product more than the alternative product that only delivers performance— something that cannot be guaranteed.

As a conduit for offering the value-added services, Putnam created the SRT. Given the consultant-type work carried out by the SRT—conducting asset allocation studies and writing research "white" papers—Putnam recognized that consultants could feel threatened by the SRT. Thus, when rolling out the SRT, Putnam met with largest investment consultants to explain the initiative. With a focus on the large corporate and large endowment segments of the market, which do not typically hire investment consultants, the threat was considered negligible.

To further nullify this threat, Putnam implemented a shared-expertise initiative with the consulting community. The SRT and the consultant enter an informal research partnership, whereby Putnam offers the consultants additional resources, including risk management software and economic forecasts. With access to these resources, investment consultants are able to offer their clients more value-added research and advice. For example, one of the largest consultanting firms was looking to write a white paper on the trend of style investing overseas as globalization was impacting diversification efforts. As a firm organized by

(continued)

BOX 10.2
Continued

global style—core, growth and value—Putnam provided the consultants with extensive analysis, including back-testing the correlations between international growth, international value, and domestic indices, which supported the use of style investing overseas. As the consultants were able to advise their clients about the benefits of style investing overseas, Putnam noticed an increase in the number of style-based searches, for which they submitted their style-oriented international product offerings.

On the other side of the relationship, Putnam enjoys access to the highest-profile investment consultants who can provide insights into what their clients are thinking, which in turn may lead to developing new offerings. For example, Putnam's ability to have frank and candid discussions with consultants indicated that demand for an international small cap offering was increasing. As a result, Putnam was one of the first firms to develop and offer a successful international small cap offering.

Beyond contributing to offering development, the consultant has a heightened awareness of the level of sophistication at Putnam. Such brand equity can translate into more invitations to bid for new business in the large public plan segment as well as the small- and medium-tier corporate and endowment segments of the market, which do employ investment consultants. With the shared expertise arrangement, the SRT not only increases the value of the product offering to large corporate and large endowment plans, but it also increases the value consultants derive from Putnam.

Competitive asset management firms offer similar services to strategic clients. Unlike its competitors, though, the SRT is integrated within the investment division at Putnam. Housed in the same building as the investment division, the SRT enjoys greater access to the source of information than its competitors. At competing firms, the strategic support group often represents an independent business unit, providing information to other end-users beyond purchasers of asset management products. For example, the strategic research group of a large financial intermediary provides the same generic research report to the investment banking clients of its investment-banking unit, to the high net worth clients of its private banking business, and to the institutional plan sponsors of its asset management group. In contrast, a Putnam SRT client enjoys research customized to its requirements.

The customized research the SRT conducts helped close new business opportunities at full fees. For example, a large prospect articulated to Putnam that it was revisiting its international equity structure. The prospect had a regional structure in place, with one international value manager, one European-only manager, and one Pacific Basin manager. The SRT conducted an analysis that demonstrated that as correlations between countries increased, the diversification benefits enjoyed by a regional structure decreased. Secondly, the SRT analyzed the prospect's international equity allocation on a securities level using the current holdings of its international value, European and Pacific Basin managers. The analysis revealed implicit style and cap biases that were not being diversified away by the regional structure. The SRT then demonstrated how the plan could eliminate these biases by restructuring the portfolio to include a Putnam international core and international large cap growth offering. The analysis the SRT conducted also highlighted the fact that the recommended allocation would have generated much higher returns with the same level of volatility than the current regional structure over the prior three years. This SRT work reduced the time and money the prospect's internal staff required to conduct the asset allocation study and to conduct a manager search. Impressed by the capabilities demonstrated, and supported by impressive performance numbers, the prospect hired Putnam to manage its international assets. Fees were not negotiated.

Source: Contributed by Amy Walls, Kellogg School of Management, Northwestern University.

PURSUING CONTINUITY AND GROWTH

Once the supplier firm has established a working relationship with a customer firm, business market managers pursue continuity and growth. By **continuity**, we mean that the supplier firm strives to retain the working relationship as long as it enables the both supplier and customer to each achieve their respective strategic objectives. As for **growth**, we mean that the supplier firm works to increase its profitable share of the customer's business and to become an irreplaceable partner. As we discussed in Chapter 1, relationship development progresses through a series of exchange episodes and interwoven business strands. Thus, the supplier firm pursues growth through broadening the scale and the scope of its business with the customer firm over time.

We begin this section by examining how firms manage the behavioral aspects of working together and foster continuity. Then we offer guidance on how firms can grow profitable working relationships by proposing and implementing such innovative business arrangements as single-sourcing, facilities management, outsourcing, and risk-sharing gain-sharing agreements. Finally, we explore CRM as a comprehensive system and set of procedures for finding, keeping, and growing profitable customers.

Working Together

To foster continuity in a working relationship with a customer firm, business market managers must address several ongoing behavioral issues. These issues include communication, trust and commitment, coordination, and conflict resolution. In addition, managers must develop and execute a robust plan for retaining key accounts.[10]

Promote Honest and Open Communication

Communication is "the formal and informal sharing of meaningful and timely information between firms."[11] Business market managers from progressive firms make it a point to meet with partner firm managers periodically in formal and informal settings to discuss market conditions. By doing so over many years, customer and supplier managers often develop personal relationships and become comfortable sharing critical information. In Box 10.3, we discuss how the Regional Unit Manager for Heineken Nederland B.V. uses this approach to sustain relationships within the Amsterdam horeca.

Bridging is the establishment of multiple levels of communications between firms, across functions, management levels, and business strands. Perhaps the most common entails the creation of cross-functional and interfirm teams. By giving the teams a variety of projects to work on and encouraging members to meet with regularity, business market managers give them a common point of interaction and set of mutual tasks. Often, these group activities go beyond the workday to include social activities, such as attending sporting events or participating in golf or tennis outings.

Bridging enables both the supplier and customer firms to minimize the detrimental effects of the untimely departure of a key employee. Often, such an individual possesses unique skills and personal relationships that are crucial; thus, his or her

BOX 10.3
Heineken Sustains Relationships with the Amsterdam Horeca

Horeca is a Dutch term for the food and beverage trade that includes pubs, cafes, grand cafes, hotels, and restaurants. To increase Heineken® beer sales among current horeca customers as well as to penetrate emerging "strategic sites" in the Amsterdam horeca, Fred Tromer, Regional Unit Manager for Heineken Nederland B.V., spends considerable time and effort sustaining close working relationships with entrepreneurs and developers. One such entrepreneur, Ron van Roekel, established more than 50 pubs, cafes, and grand cafes in Amsterdam over the past 20 years. His overall strategy is to acquire or lease a strategic site, develop a popular pub or cafe "concept" for that site, and then sell the pub or cafe after a year or two of successful operations. Typically, van Roekel owns two or three such developmental sites at a time. Tromer has worked with van Roekel for more than 15 years.

Heineken values its working relationship with van Roekel. For starters, he buys a lot of Heineken products. Perhaps more importantly, he routinely signs exclusive 10-year beer or 5-year beer and soft-drink supply contracts with Heineken for each establishment. Even after van Roekel sells the pub or cafe, Heineken retains the rights to sell beer and soft drinks for the remainder of the contract period. Finally, van Roekel provides Heineken with rapid access to emerging strategic sites within greater Amsterdam. Often, he has greater flexibility in acquiring properties and getting city permits because the Amsterdam City Council is more accommodating to the initiatives of an entrepreneur than to those of a major corporation.

Tromer meets with van Roekel regularly. They share information about developments in the market such as competitor activities, innovative restaurant concepts, and newly available strategic sites. Some of these meetings entail social as well as business activities. For example, Tromer invites van Roekel to attend the "Night of the Proms," which is a series of classical and pop concerts. Tromer also takes van Roekel to European Cup football matches or to the Davis Cup Tennis match when they are held in Europe.

With close working relationships such as the one with van Roekel, Tromer gets the chance to respond to competitive pricing threats. Furthermore, Heineken does not necessarily have to meet competitive price discounts. It might respond by offering something else of value. For example, Heineken might offer "free" advice by Heineken experts on interior design or feasibility studies. Heineken also might provide a pub with Heineken glassware for a "special" price or offer a special promotion, such as a music night or a karaoke show.

Van Roekel paid Tromer what is perhaps the ultimate tribute for their long and productive working relationship. Van Roekel named a grand cafe, Cafe Tromer, in honor of him.

loss might jeopardize the partnership. Professors Bendapudi and Leone recommend three steps that managers can take to ensure continuity in such situations. First, they advocate rotating staffs and using teams so that partners don't become attached to just one employee. Second, they argue that firms should develop other steady performers to work alongside essential personnel. Third, they urge firms to provide early notifications of personnel departures and to publicize transition plans to avoid catching the partner by surprise.[12]

Build Trust and Commitment

At the core of all successful working relationships are two essential behavioral characteristics: trust and commitment.[13] **Trust** in a working relationship is "the firm's belief that another company will perform actions that will result in positive outcomes for the firm, as well as not take unexpected actions that would result in negative outcomes for the firm. The strength of this belief may lead the firm to make a trusting response or action, whereby the firm commits itself to possible loss, depending upon the subsequent actions of the other company."[14] Professor Kumar argues that all firms build trust in three ways. First, the firm must demonstrate that it is dependable—it is reliable and honors its word. Second, the firm strives to act in the partner firm's best interests. Third, the firm cultivates a reputation for fairness.[15]

Leading firms demonstrate dependability over time. By starting on a small scale, perhaps through pilot projects, and then gradually increasing the scope of the alliance over exchange episodes, a firm shows that it can fulfill larger and larger promises. Moreover, as the two firms work together, managers gain a better understanding of their counterparts' goals, thought processes, corporate culture, and methods of operation. Rather than allow customer managers to draw conclusions about the firm's trustworthiness solely on intuition, some firms periodically verify relationship accomplishments. For example, in Box 10.4, we discuss how Applied Industrial Technologies (AIT) audits the value it delivers and reports those findings to customer firms. Through productive dealings with many companies over time, a supplier firm accumulates a track record and marketplace reputation for fairness.[16]

In doing business across borders, customer and supplier managers sometimes find it difficult to build trust, in part, because of their cultural differences. This difficulty is eased considerably when a customer firm and a supplier firm can have a collaborative relationship that extends across a number of country markets and cultures. Offering the capability of having a trustworthy relationship that extends across many country markets actually can be a distinctive supplier advantage, as the Cushman & Wakefield advertisement in Figure 10.4 conveys.[17]

Commitment, on the other hand, "captures the perceived continuity or growth in the relationship between two firms."[18] It entails a "desire to develop a stable relationship, a willingness to make short-term sacrifices to maintain the relationship, and a confidence in the stability of the relationship."[19] Business market managers further relationship commitment through unilateral pledges and guarantees. A pledge involves actions one firm takes that demonstrate good faith and bind it to the relationship. Pledges signal that the firm will not behave opportunistically in the relationship. To make a pledge, a firm typically invests nonredeployable assets, which are those resources and capabilities that it cannot divert to another relationship.[20]

Through a **guarantee**, one firm promises through a legally binding contract or warranty to absorb the risk and costs associated with unfulfilled promises made to a partner firm. Guarantees mitigate the risks and expenses of a partner in the unlikely event that a relational promise is not kept. For example, Okuma America Corporation offers a 24-hour shipment guarantee to its customers. According to this arrangement, Okuma promises that if a customer orders machine-tool repair parts and they are not shipped within 24 hours, the customer receives the parts for free.

Companies increasingly back guarantees with a service recovery system. A **service recovery system** entails the resources, procedures, and authority that empower and enable front-line personnel to resolve customer problems or compensate customers for unexpected lapses in service. Psychological methods of service recovery typically include an apology and an explanation of what went wrong. The

BOX 10.4
Applied Industrial Technologies Documents Value-Added Services Results

With annual sales exceeding $1.1 billion, Applied Industrial Technologies (AIT), formerly Bearings Inc., is one of the largest distributors of specialty replacement bearings, power transmission components, fluid power products, rubber products, and a large variety of specialty items in the United States. AIT primarily serves maintenance, repair, and operating supplies (MRO) markets within the primary metals, mining, pulp and paper, chemical processing, utilities, textiles, food processing, and agricultural industries. It operates more than 337 stocking branches across the United States.

In recent years, AIT management transformed the firm's overall mission. Whereas in the past, the firm pursued largely "parts-price" transactional business, it now actively seeks partnerships with targeted customers. Such partnerships deliver productivity-building and cost-reducing "total solutions" in six ways: through predictive maintenance, by eliminating duplicate inventories and streamlining storeroom operations, through technical support and training, by more efficient energy utilization, through lower transaction and procurement costs, and with continuous process improvement recommendations. The cornerstone of AIT's partnering efforts is its documented value-added program.

AIT defines documented value-added (DVA) as any cost-savings opportunity that AIT provides in addition to the product/services the customer purchases. As contrasted with other firms' cost-savings programs, DVA focuses on "hard" benefits, such as improved cycle times, that it can measure and validate with customers. AIT trains and rewards all of its employees from branch managers to field associates to delivery drivers to look for total cost savings solutions that can make each customer more productive and efficient.

To support employee DVA efforts, AIT developed a customized software program that calculates cost savings. A sales representative, for example, can run the program on a laptop while visiting a customer's plant site. Working with customer managers, the rep inputs data for a number of potential value-adding and cost-reduction variables. Importantly, AIT negotiates with each participating customer on which of these variables they will include. On either a monthly, quarterly, or semiannual basis, AIT presents each customer with reports that fully document the cost savings provided. In this way, customers can assess the value AIT has delivered relative to its promises.

AIT asks customers to sign and return copies of the cost-savings reports in order to establish the credibility of its numbers. Furthermore, managers ask select customers to provide testimonials that AIT uses in company advertisements and promotional materials. We provided examples of these in Figure 4.3. AIT keeps track of each cost-savings idea and aggregates DVA totals.

AIT is experimenting with the use of DVA assessments in value-based pricing. Whenever a competitor discounts price significantly below AIT's bid, AIT will make up the price differential by guaranteeing DVA cost savings. In this way, AIT hopes to shift the nature of competition away from price and toward the customer's total costs.

supplier firm designs them to diffuse anger and restore the customer's favorable perception of it. Tangible methods encompass monetary compensation for damages or inconvenience, immediate delivery of correct products or services ordered, and the resolution of customer problems. The supplier designs tangible service recovery to restore the customer's sense of equity in the business transaction. Shrewd business market managers monitor every service recovery event to better understand and bolster the weak links in their firm's service delivery processes.[21]

Figure 10.4 Cushman & Wakefield Offers a Trustworthy Relationship

TRUST. THE UNIVERSAL LANGUAGE FOR SUCCESSFUL PARTNERSHIPS.

The partnerships you formed in childhood have contributed to your success today. When you're exploring real estate opportunities 12 time zones away, global partnerships based on trust are crucial.

At Cushman & Wakefield, we're relationship-oriented, not just transaction-driven. That's why we've established a worldwide real estate services organization that offers the same standard of excellence on a global basis that distinguishes us in the U.S.

Today we provide real estate solutions tailored to our clients' specific needs in more than 30 countries, in the major business centers of the world.

Now that you're bigger, the world is even smaller. To put us to work for you call 1-800-346 6789.

CUSHMAN & WAKEFIELD.

Improving your place in the world.™

CUSHMAN & WAKEFIELD WORLDWIDE™

Source: Advertisement courtesy of Cushman & Wakefield.

Implement Coordination Mechanisms

By **coordination**, we mean the customer firm's and supplier firm's synchronization of activities, resources, and capabilities to accomplish a collective set of tasks. All working relationships require some degree of coordination. In some relationships, coordination tends to be mechanistic; that is, it is highly formalized and programmed, and is implemented through rules, policy statements, and rigid hierarchical control. As relationships become more collaborative, coordination becomes more organic. Organic coordination originates at the grassroots level of organizations, entails extensive information exchange, and is flexible, cooperative, and innovative in nature. As a result, business market managers create distinct coordination mechanisms as a function of the types of working relationship their firms seek and governance systems employed.[22]

In the most transactional working relationships, *the market* provides a high level of coordination between firms without the benefit of managerial intervention. The mechanism that achieves synchronization is **market-clearing price**, which balances supply and demand for a given offering. In this situation, a business market manager achieves coordination by allowing the price of the market offering to float to the market-clearing level. Although this approach runs counter to many managers' desire to exert control, in a number of industries—agricultural products, petroleum, and fasteners, among others—coordination is left largely to the market.[23]

When one partner firm is significantly less dependent upon that relationship than the other firm, that partner firm is likely to rely on power. By **power** we mean the ability of one firm to get its partner to undertake activities that the partner firm would not do on its own. Many managers believe that gaining and using power is the best way to achieve coordination. The use of power has serious drawbacks, though. Most firms dislike being "told what to do" and aggressively seek to "get even." Thus, managers should be prudent and sparing in their reliance on power. Scholars have identified six strategies for gaining and using power: information exchange, recommendations, promises, threats, legalistic pleas, and requests.[24]

A key question that often arises relative to power is: How can the weaker firm ensure that its more powerful partner will treat it fairly? The answer is through dependence-balancing operations, which are courses of action that the weaker firm pursues to equalize the importance of the relationship to both firms. For example, the weaker firm might make greater investments in the relationship until the resources both firms have committed are roughly the same. Alternatively, the weaker firm might seek out other partners. By doing so, the firm would reduce its dependence on the relationship. In a related move, the weaker firm might try to change nonredeployable assets into redeployable assets by finding new uses for them.[25]

In the most collaborative relationships, coordination based on cooperation becomes essential. **Cooperation** entails similar or complementary actions firms take in interdependent relationships to achieve mutual outcomes or singular outcomes with expected reciprocation over time. To encourage cooperation, business market managers promote shared norms concerning how to work together, how to jointly create value, and how to share benefits. They demonstrate to partner firms that cooperation is rewarded. Perhaps, most importantly, business market managers build mutual trust and commitment.[26]

Anticipate and Resolve Conflicts

Business market managers understand that every working relationship will eventually experience some sort of conflict. They know that it is just another part of doing business. By **conflict**, we mean "the overall level of disagreement in the working partnership. As such, conflict is determined by the frequency, intensity, and duration of disagreements."[27] Rather than glossing over or covering up disagreements, successful managers anticipate disputes and put into place mechanisms for immediately resolving them. By doing so, they avoid **pathological conflict** that serves to destroy, injure, or poison a relationship. Instead, they transform it into **functional conflict**. These productive discussions clear the air by ameliorating harmful tensions or ill will, and result in policy changes and procedures that add value or reduce costs within the partnership.[28]

Business market managers must gain an understanding of the underlying causes of conflict and determine when and how each are likely to manifest themselves in their industry. In general, managers trace disagreements to three primary sources. Goal incompatibility captures the fact that the mission, goals, and objectives of partner firms are disparate. At times, these differences create situations in which one partner can achieve its goals only at the expense of the other firm. The lack of agreement over responsibilities within the working relationship is domain "dissensus". Perhaps the most recurring disputes over domain relate to functions that each partner should perform, how partners should accomplish tasks, and the timing of efforts. Differing perceptions of reality similarly lead to disagreements. For example, differing perceptions of market trends, competitive threats, and emerging technologies often lead to conflicts between partners.[29]

With an understanding of potential sources of disagreements, business market managers create appropriate conflict resolution mechanisms. As we previously discussed, one way to prevent conflicts from escalating to major crises is to implement a service recovery system. A closely related and highly effective alternative is to train boundary-spanning personnel—individuals who are in contact with the partner firm on a regular basis—to be sensitive to inherent trouble spots. These persons should learn to identify emerging problems and to try to resolve them informally and immediately before they escalate into relationship-threatening crises. Alternately, the partners can designate individuals within their respective firms to resolve conflicts.

For intractable disputes, business market managers turn to mediation or arbitration. **Mediation** is the process in which a third party is brought in to help resolve a dispute by either refocusing discussion on key issues or suggesting viable solutions. In general, their role is to promote clear understanding of each firm's position and to encourage the open discussion of issues. Under **arbitration**, the firms legally agree to have a third party settle the disagreement. The decision of the third party, often a professional arbitrator, is final and legally binding. For these extreme conflict resolution mechanisms to function properly, firms need to agree ahead of time what types of concerns will trigger either mediation or arbitration and who can be brought in as an acceptable mediator or arbitrator.[30]

Customer Retention Planning[31]

While yesterday's marketers focused their efforts on landing new accounts, today's business market managers realize that keeping existing customers can dramatically boost a firm's profitability. To gain these benefits, business market managers develop formal **customer retention plans**. Although plans for all relationship categories follow the same general format, managers logically direct far greater resources and efforts at retaining collaborative customers.[32] In addition, whereas retention efforts for collaborative accounts focus on adding value and lowering total costs of a market offering, those for transactional accounts concentrate on reducing offering price.

During the customer retention planning process, the business market manager focuses on the following activities:

- Tracking customer retention
- Assessing the causes of customer defections
- Analyzing complaint and service data
- Establishing procedures for responding to defections
- Anticipating reformulation of the market offering

Business market managers must track customer retention on an ongoing basis. The best and most sensitive measure of customer retention is the **supplier's share of the customer's business**. This is the percentage of the customer's total purchase requirements for all offerings that the supplier firm would be able to provide. For each account, best practice managers monitor this measure, the total cost to serve the customer, and the customer's contribution to profitability because each one provides distinctive and useful feedback on how the supplier is doing in its working relationships. In Box 10.5, we discuss how Bank of America's® Global Corporate and Investment Bank measures its share of each customer's business.

Rather than allowing customers to drift away silently, business market managers track defectors and use them as a source of critical information about deficiencies in the firm's market offering. Periodically, astute managers contact lost customers and determine why those customers switched suppliers. At times, they are surprised to hear what the customer has to say.

At the same time, business market managers analyze complaint and service data. Instead of dismissing customer complaints as a nuisance, savvy business market managers use them for ideas on how to improve the firm's products and services. Managers also track the use of technical problem-solving services. Microsoft's AnswerPoint Unit provides technical problem-solving assistance to customers by phone. A technician who receives a call from a customer enters customer problems and recommended solutions into the firm's service usage system. The system monitors customer problems continuously. On a weekly basis, the system sends summaries of service patterns to both support service managers and to product development managers. Product-support service managers use the information to develop solutions for future callers and to plan for the availability of technicians. Product development managers use the information to eliminate recurring problems in the next upgrade of a software package.

When a pattern of defections appears, business market managers respond immediately. To do so effectively, they create procedures and systems ahead of time that allow them to act quickly when problems arise. In some cases, the procedures enable the supplier to redesign or modify existing products or services. In other instances, they allow the business market managers to hire additional personnel or provide better training.

Some firms forestall defections by building switching barriers. Switching barriers include such things as shared information systems, highly customized market offerings, and unique service. The more progressive firms exercise restraint when erecting such barriers. Most importantly, they do not use switching barriers to create hostages. Instead, they rely on switching barriers to provide them with the chance to respond to and rectify customer problems.

BOX 10.5
Bank of America® Measures Share of Customer's Business

With annual revenues exceeding $35 billion, total assets topping $622 billion, and deposits surpassing $374 billion, Bank of America Corporation (BAC) is one of the top three banks in the United States. Its Global Corporate and Investment Banking (GCIB) unit attains annual revenues greater than $9 billion and annual net operating profits of more than $1.9 billion, making it the largest corporate bank in the United States. GCIB is a full-service corporate and investment bank that provides creative, value-added capital-raising solutions, advisory services, derivatives capabilities, and equity and debt sales and trading, as well as traditional bank deposit and loan products, cash management, and payment services.

Relationship management teams from GCIB estimate and monitor the bank's share of customer's business for each strategic client. They triangulate on this measure, which GCIB refers to as *share of wallet*, in several ways. They begin by simply asking customer managers for an estimate. More often than not, these managers respond immediately and accurately.

For those customers that do not respond, GCIB managers analyze government and industry data. For example, based on annual reports, 10Ks, and other documents customers file with the U.S. Securities and Exchange Commission (SEC), managers determine the extent of capital acquisitions, business loans, and securities trading activities each account initiated during the past year. From these estimates, they can readily calculate interest payments and bank fees, among other payments, for each account. Dividing the actual amount of a customer's business with GCIB by the estimate of a customer's total banking business, managers reasonably approximate the bank's share of wallet.

They use a third source of information to confirm these approximations. As it turns out, the typical corporate customer uses 10 banks for major financial services. These banks fall into three tiers based on share of wallet and account profitability. The *lead bank* receives the bulk of the account's business and most importantly the high-profit business such as investment banking services. On the other hand, the five banks at the bottom tier receive the low profit margin, commodity product business such as risky corporate loans. By assessing what types of financial services the bank currently sells to an account, managers can predict in which of the three tiers their share of customer's business falls.

As part of the customer retention planning process, the supplier firm anticipates the reformation of its relationship-specific market offerings. In the case of collaborative accounts, the managers focus on adding value through such things as technical and application support during the initial stages of the product life cycle. As a product matures or customers gain extensive experience with it, managers modify the offering to emphasize ease of doing business. Ease of doing business refers to programs and systems that improve the efficiency of exchange, and/or make it more comfortable and effortless for customers' managers. For transactional accounts, managers continuously strive to lower the price of the market offering. They accomplish this by regularly unbundling or deleting unnecessary services.

Selectively Growing the Relationship[33]

As business market managers search for profitable growth, a natural place for them to look is doing more business with current customers. After all, it appears to be conventional wisdom that it is easier and less costly to gain incremental sales from loyal customers than from new ones. Yet, many suppliers lack sufficient knowledge to devise anything but the most simplistic growth strategies, such as "use cross-selling and upselling to get customers to buy more." Without a more fine-grained and disciplined approach, chasing incremental customer business with steeply discounted prices or closing deals through the provision of supplementary services "for free" may grow customer share but often wrecks a supplier's profits. Progressive suppliers practice a more nuanced and disciplined approach, answering the question: Which customer share growth prospects are worth pursuing and which are better left to competitors to fight over?

In this section, we provide guidance for resolving this question. We begin by discussing how firms can estimate and target share of customer's business. Then we examine several strategies that business marketers can use to selectively build share—focused share building, single-sourcing and multiple single-sourcing, working relationship broadening, and new profit models. Lastly, we emphasize the need for suppliers to put into place systems to document the profitability of share gains.

Estimate and Target Share of Customer's Business

To discover sources for profitable growth as well as to gauge progress in account strategies, a supplier must first gain an estimate of its share of each of its customer's business. To identify the best prospects, managers should drill down below the aggregate customer firm level to gauge share by such factors as offering category and customer firm location. Most firms begin the process of gathering share of customer business data by simply having their salespeople ask customers for the data or by examining secondary sources of information. Examples from Box 2.3 on Technische Unie and Box 10.5 on Bank of America illustrate these two approaches respectively.

Other companies supplement sales force data gathering with market research. Telindus, a leading network integrator for information technology (IT) and telecommunications solutions based in Belgium, is organized around eight competence centers, such as secure enterprise networks, e-business solutions, voice and video solutions, and IT systems management. Telindus account representatives estimate the firm's share of customer's business in each of these eight competence centers. As part of their consultative selling efforts among its top-20 accounts, Telindus sales representatives assist clients with the process of allocating their annual IT budget. Thus, these reps clearly understand Telindus's share by competence center of the top-20 accounts' IT budgets. To assess the remainder of its customer base, Telindus relies upon a multi-client study conducted by Computer Profile, a Belgian research company. Through a series of interviews with IT managers, Computer Profile estimates annual IT budgets and identifies major new IT projects for more than 600 actual and potential customer firms. In turn, Telindus uses Computer Profile research data to calculate its share of customers' business with each.

Armed with knowledge of their shares of customers' business, suppliers better understand the array of growth prospects with each customer. Taken together with knowledge of customer value for their offerings and the costs-to-serve each customer, progressive suppliers are able to accurately target the most profitable growth prospects. Further, managers can draw on this detailed knowledge of their customers to devise new ways of doing business that add value or reduce costs.[34]

Focused Share Building

SEGHERS Better Technology Group is a design, engineering, fabrication, and maintenance company that serves the petrochemical, power generation, and water treatment industries worldwide. Based in Mechelen, Belgium, SEGHERS specializes in high-pressure vessel repair and maintenance, and refinery shutdowns. SEGHERS relies on account profitability analysis to guide its efforts at building share of customer's business. Importantly, the company avoids pursuing large sales revenue, but marginally profitable, business in favor of becoming a **focused single-source provider** of a customer's purchase requirements. A focused single-source provider attempts to attain 100 percent of a customer's business in targeted offering categories while not pursuing other offering categories that it might supply to that customer.

For example, one of SEGHERS' key accounts recently built a plant next to an existing plant on the same property. While most competitors pursued service opportunities in the newer plant while shunning the older plant, SEGHERS did the reverse. Why? Because the older plant has a far greater need for profitable maintenance services, and knowing the older equipment well, SEGHERS possesses a distinctive capability to maintain it. At the same time, SEGHERS' profit analyses showed that the newer plant only required low-margin services, due in part to the fact that it contains new state-of-the art equipment, which does not require a lot of maintenance and overhaul work. Worse still, a number of competitors, which lack the discipline to refrain from chasing business with low prices, are capable of maintaining this equipment. Through diligent efforts SEGHERS gained 100 percent of the business in the older plant while leaving the relatively unattractive business at the newer plant for competitors to battle over.

In Box 10.6, we illustrate how Bank of America uses a client management approach to implement a focused share-building strategy among major corporate accounts.

BOX 10.6
Bank of America's Client Management Approach

Based in Charlotte, North Carolina, Bank of America Corporation's (BAC) Global Corporate and Investment Banking (GCIB) unit is the largest corporate bank in the United States. Instead of allowing representatives from each of BAC's divisions to independently sell services to each corporate customer, GCIB management carefully coordinates its efforts through two sets of teams: a relationship team and a deal team. The bank's stated goal is to provide superior customer value through teamwork, knowledge, skills, creativity, and product capabilities.

The process begins when GCIB senior managers assign a number of current and prospective strategic clients to a client manager. The client manager is an experienced banker whose role is that of advocate for those accounts. With the assistance of direct-report managers, the client manager assembles a **relationship team** comprised of product specialists from several bank divisions the customer is likely to patronize. The relationship team is a standing group that meets periodically with the client manager to evaluate business opportunities with each assigned customer account.

The first task that the relationship team completes is to prioritize accounts and set

(continued)

BOX 10.6
Continued

objectives. To do so, the team estimates the share of wallet and account profitability that GCIB currently has with each customer. Based on this assessment, the team sets priorities and targets specific potential accounts for prospecting, penetration, or relationship maintenance activities. Importantly, they direct their efforts and greatest resources toward the highest potential accounts in hopes of securing the greatest account profitability and share of wallet possible.

Next, the relationship team assesses each strategic client's requirements and proposes a customized package of banking services. Their strategy is to gain account penetration by right-selling the full range of financial products and services the customer needs. The client manager then coordinates team-selling efforts and formal presentations at the customer's headquarters. When a customer buys the solution, the team monitors delivery of those services and resolves any problems that might arise.

When the relationship team identifies a highly specialized opportunity that it cannot handle alone due to inadequate technical knowledge, the client manager calls on the services of an appropriate product specialist. The product specialist, in turn, assembles a deal team. The **deal team** is a temporary group, comprised of banking service experts, who create and sell a specialized financial solution to the customer.

For example, the client manager for a major energy corporation learned that his customer had acquired a company in Ireland and passed that information along to members of the relationship team. The team wondered whether that acquisition might create cross-border tax issues for the customer. They

called in a GCIB international banking expert to take a look. He assembled a deal team comprised of international, cross-border tax specialists. They proposed a tax saving, "sale and lease-back" arrangement for the assets the Irish subsidiary owned. The client approved the idea. When the transaction concluded, the deal team moved on to other projects while the client manager and the relationship team continued to search for new opportunities with the energy firm.

GCIB management evaluates client managers and product specialists in part on different criteria. While they assess client mangers on account profitability and share of wallet (see Box 10.5), they evaluate product specialists on share of market and product profitability. They obtain share of market for each product category primarily from *league tables* purchased from third-party consultants, such as Greenwich Associates or Prudential Financial Services. These divergent goals often create tension between client manager and product specialist. GCIB's senior management strives to reduce this tension in two ways. First, they instill across the bank the corporate values of doing what is in the best interest of the customer. Second, they monetarily reward and publicly recognize both for their teamwork.

Senior managers believe that the client management approach allows GCIB to address customer requirements simultaneously at the transaction and relationship level. As they see it, deal teams deliver superior value to a customer in a series of transactions that lead to a long-term collaborative relationship. By doing so, the relationship team gains greater access for GCIB to high-profit transactions in the future.

Pursue Single-Sourcing and Multiple Single-Sourcing

If a supplier continues to increase its share of a customer's business, it will ultimately end up in a single-sourcing arrangement. Given the traditional resistance of customer firms to single-sourcing, supplier firms must convince customer managers that such an arrangement will provide significant benefits and reduce risk. A long-standing concern of customers is that without competition, single-source suppliers will become complacent, causing product and service quality to decline. One way that Penske's Leaseway Auto Carriers mitigates this fear is through a 30-day cancellation clause in their automobile shipping agreements. As we mentioned earlier in this chapter, although they have such an agreement with General Motors, their collaborative relationship has remained vibrant for over 35 years. Another way to demonstrate unflagging interest in the relationship is to increase service levels periodically.

Multiple single-sourcing is a concept that enables customers and suppliers to reap the benefits of single-source arrangements while minimizing the potential drawbacks. Under a multiple single-sourcing arrangement, each plant in a customer's manufacturing network is single-sourced, yet the customer maintains at least two suppliers across the network. For example, a customer with ten manufacturing plants would have one single-source supplier at six of its plants and another single-source supplier at the other four plants, with each supplier serving as the backup to the other. As part of the arrangement, the customer might require each supplier to share process or product improvements with the other. The customer could then keep track of the improvements each supplier contributed and use that as a criterion for awarding future business.

Progressive suppliers often follow a two-step process for multiple single-sourcing: they first work with customers to persuade them on the value of being single-sourced at each location, regardless of which supplier is chosen. They then persuade those customers that selecting them as the single-source will deliver added value. Honeywell Fibers' experience supplying carpet mills provides an instructive case study. We recount it in Box 10.7.

Expand the Scope of Working Relationships

To gain a greater share of targeted customers' business, a supplier may decide to add expertise or a capability that it knows those customers would value. The supplier could then leverage that expertise or capability to provide a better solution to each of those customers—at a lower cost than any of them could replicate for themselves—in exchange for an incremental share of those customers' business.

For example, KLM Cargo, a unit of KLM Royal Dutch Airlines, has transformed its strategy from merely providing space on its airplanes to providing end-to-end supply-management solutions. When viewed simply as a space-provider, KLM Cargo was in danger of being relegated to the low-margin, commodity portion of point-to-point air cargo transportation while complementary service providers controlled the whole transaction and captured the more profitable portions of it. To reposition itself, KLM's Special Cargo (SC) business unit studied the requirements and preferences of selected customers and improvements in value and cost that could be achieved with a reconfigured end-to-end solution. Significantly, the customers it studied were not the intermediaries, such as freight forwarders and consolidators, to whom it was selling airplane cargo-container space, but the importers and large retailers that initiated the transactions and received perishable goods. KLM SC learned what problems these customers were experiencing, what percentage of spoilage was typical, and what price premium customers would be willing to pay for fresher products.

Under its *Fresh Partners* initiatives, KLM SC began to offer dedicated handling service that ensures an unbroken cool chain from producer to the point-of-delivery. The company now offers three levels of this cool handling service: fresh regular, fresh

BOX 10.7
Honeywell Fibers Practices Multiple Single-Sourcing

Tremendous customer consolidation in Honeywell Fibers' industry caused the company to focus its efforts on the carpet mills that it believed had the best chances of prospering. The largest carpet mill today is Shaw Industries, whose sales grew from $250 million to $4 billion in the last 15 years. Of Shaw's 100 manufacturing locations, 10–15 are yarn plants. Initially, Honeywell was supplying very little to Shaw. To become a strategic supplier, it developed an innovative product specifically designed to meet Shaw's demanding yarn and carpet manufacturing requirements.

Honeywell Fibers and Shaw then jointly created six-sigma teams to tackle some of Shaw's key challenges, such as achieving greater operating efficiencies, product aesthetics, and dye-ability. These joint studies revealed that using a single-source supplier for each Shaw plant would improve performance and lower costs. At each location, Shaw would be able to reduce the time it held inventory from one to two weeks down to three days. It could also limit the spinning equipment line changeovers by using a single fiber type as the source material for a variety of yarns of different construction, improve yield, and consolidate invoicing.

In the implementation, Shaw first made Honeywell Fibers the single-source supplier for one line at one plant, which represented about 25 percent of the plant's business. After demonstrating the viability of this move and the cost savings associated with it, Honeywell was made the single-source supplier on two lines at that plant and eventually for lines at other plants. Finally, Honeywell became the single-source supplier at one plant.

Now, Honeywell Fibers is single-sourced at several yarn plants and Shaw is one of its largest customers. Growth in their business together has been limited by mutual strategic considerations of how much business each wants a single supplier or customer to represent. Thus, Honeywell's strategy has been to shift its product mix to a more profitable one for both Shaw and itself, supplying fiber for the middle to the upper end of Shaw's carpet offerings. Interestingly, because of this focused share targeting, Honeywell no longer supplies the plant where it initially demonstrated the viability of the multiple single-sourcing concept.

Source: James C. Anderson and James A. Narus, "Selectively Pursuing More of Your Customer's Business," *MIT Sloan Management Review* (Spring 2003): 42–49.

cool, and fresh super cool. Each service guarantees the maintenance of a specific temperature throughout transport, from truck, to warehouse, to plane, to warehouse, to truck to the point-of-delivery.

KLM SC ensures cool transport of orchids, for example, from producer locations in Thailand to the world's largest flower market in Alsmeer, The Netherlands, and then on to the point-of-delivery in other countries. Customers such as U.S. Florimex, the largest flower trader in the world, are willing to pay the price premium for this cool transport service because *its* customers are willing to pay more for a fresher product and *it* gains more of *their* business. KLM SC also provides cool transport of salmon that are farm-raised in the fiords of Norway to destinations in Tokyo, Osaka, Sapporo, Hong Kong, and Beijing within 48 hours.

Through these Fresh Partners initiatives, KLM SC has become the single-source provider to its import-export customer for orchids and gained as large a share of the salmon producer's business as its capacity can handle. The former space-provider repositioned itself as a supply management provider of end-to-end solutions, provided itself with a more-profitable service offering and gained greater share of selected customers' business through strategically building the scope of its market.

Broaden Working Relationships

To grow its profitable share of a customer's business, many firms turn to a relationship migration strategy. Through a **relationship migration strategy**, the supplier firm seeks ever more collaborative dealings with a customer firm. As the relationship broadens, the supplier firm evolves from being a product vendor to a value-added supplier to a strategic partner and its offering expands from a product to a solution to a partnership. If done selectively and deliberately, the business market manager increases the customer's contribution to the supplier's profitability.[35]

Across South America, Lockheed Martin Global Telecommunications (COMSAT), the satellite transmission and telecommunications subsidiary of Lockheed Martin Corporation, uses what it calls a "pyramid strategy" to sequentially grow customer business. The pyramid contains four levels. First, COMSAT sells parts to a customer. These parts include switches, relays, routers, and links as well as satellite data-transmission time. Second, COMSAT tries to sell the existing customer the network or a total telecommunications solution featuring multiple suppliers of various systems components. Third, COMSAT tries to sell specialized, augmenting services. The most important is network management, which entails stationing people in a customer's plants and managing its telecommunications network. COMSAT also provides "certified repair services" for CISCO Systems and Motorola. Finally, COMSAT sells business solutions to customers. These consulting projects investigate nontechnical telecommunications-related business problems. For example, they might do a business process reengineering study to determine how to more efficiently use communications and data within the organization. In Box 10.8, we discuss how SEGHERS Better Technology Group has developed and implemented a similar strategy for growth through broadening collaborative relationships with important customers in Europe.

Adopt New Profit Models

In tandem with efforts to broaden working relationships and offerings to select customer accounts, business market managers strive to increase their yield on customer business by altering their firms' profit models. We discussed some of these new profit models in the context of marketing channels in Chapter 7. In transactional relationships, supplier firms focus on product sales and turnover and generate profits via full-cost pricing. As relationships become more collaborative and suppliers provide solutions, they often shift to variable-cost pricing and service fees to gain incremental revenues and profits. When they engage in the most collaborative of relationships or strategic alliances, business market managers turn to more unconventional and imaginative methods of garnering income such as licensing, syndication, and franchising agreements, agency and brokerage fees, referral fees, fees for service, percent of joint customer revenue, and joint promotional fees, among many others. One intriguing profit model is the risk-sharing, gain-sharing agreement.[36]

BOX 10.8
SEGHERS Relationship Growth Strategy

Because it must leverage limited resources, SEGHERS devised a growth strategy to expand its share of customers' business by progressively expanding its collaborative relationship with each. This strategy capitalizes on customers' increasing demands for one-stop shopping of industrial services and a trend toward greater outsourcing of plant maintenance. SEGHERS's strategy features a sequence of four business development steps.

First, when pursuing initial business with targeted accounts, the company focuses on providing one special service or activity where it has a distinctive capability, such as bolt tensioning, on-site machining, or value repair and overhaul. SEGHERS makes a concerted effort to furnish outstanding service during the initial encounter in order to build customer confidence in its capabilities.

Second, SEGHERS builds on this experience to propose a second level of services that it could profitably provide—ongoing plant maintenance. Again, it is important to note that SEGHERS does *not* pursue all maintenance business within a plant or refinery, but only those services in which it has distinctive capabilities and would garner significant profits. If a customer insists on a total maintenance

solution, SEGHERS selectively partners with another contractor that provides the required complementary services.

Major equipment overhaul serves as the third step in SEGHERS's account growth strategy. Senior managers use ongoing maintenance service to gain in-depth knowledge of a customer's requirements. SEGHERS technicians are trained to spot and report any service opportunities. For example, heat exchanger overhaul is a complicated and difficult operation for customers' maintenance staff to perform, yet it is a rather profitable service for SEGHERS.

When the customer becomes fully confident in SEGHERS's capabilities, SEGHERS's sales managers pursue the fourth level of desired business: total shutdown service, including planned and emergency shutdown. Total shutdown service is the most elaborate service SEGHERS offers, including piping repair and replacement, valve and pump overhaul, vessel overhaul and replacement, and control system maintenance. The work is expensive and may require an entire refinery to be shut down for a week or more. For SEGHERS, this service turns out to be demanding, yet much more profitable work.

Source: Adapted from James C. Anderson and James A. Narus, "Selectively Pursuing More of Your Customer's Business," *MIT Sloan Management Review* (Spring 2003): 42–49.

As we stressed at the beginning of this chapter, a supplier firm and customer firm engage in collaborative relationships and strategic alliances not because of altruism, but because of mutual self-interest. By mutual self-interest, we mean that both firms are motivated to work closely together because each firm reaps significant tangible and intangible benefits from doing so. **Risk-sharing, gain-sharing agreements** are mechanisms that partner firms can use to better align their self-interests. In these arrangements, a supplier assists its customers in becoming more profitable and exposes itself to potential or actual losses in accomplishing this. Common examples of risk-sharing agreements include warranties, guarantees, and joint investments. Gain-sharing agreements are another mechanism for aligning customer and supplier interests, and refer to arrangements where a supplier assists its customers in becoming more profitable and shares in the extent to which it accomplishes this goal. Increasingly, the two are combined into risk-sharing, gain-sharing arrangements.[37]

Under risk-sharing, gain-sharing arrangements, the customer and supplier work together with the intent of improving the customer's performance. In so doing, the supplier not only receives a prespecified portion of any success, it exposes itself to potential losses, should the cost savings it promised the customer not be realized. Allegiance Healthcare, a hospital supply company of Cardinal Health, provides an instructive example in its collaboration with a hospital system located in the Southwestern United States. Spurred on by a request for assistance from this hospital system, Allegiance dispatched a multidisciplinary team to gather data on-site over an eight-week period to identify all possible ways for the hospital system to reduce costs through improved resource management, process efficiencies, and distribution logistics.

Working with clinicians and managers at the hospital system, the team found areas where the greatest cost savings were possible, such as rational consumption of supplies, materials management, laundry and linen, and sterile processing. For each area, the team quantified the range of savings that could be achieved, based on the commitment of the customer to embrace the changes. Senior management of the hospital system and Allegiance reached an agreement and plan to tackle these cost savings opportunities together. To implement the agreement, a steering committee comprised of senior hospital managers and Allegiance account managers was formed to oversee the change efforts.

Under their five-year, risk-sharing, gain-sharing arrangement, Allegiance guaranteed cost savings of about $6 million per year, with a total, five-year guarantee of $28 million, taking into account the first-year implementation ramp-up. In return, Allegiance received 20 percent sales growth from the hospital system and 35 percent growth in Allegiance-manufactured products, which were demonstrated best value for their applications. These robust growth rates can be contrasted with the 3 percent sales growth, in general, in the health-care supplies market.

Document the Profitability of Greater Share

Gaining a greater share of a customer's business does a supplier little good when that incremental business comes at the expense of reduced profitability. Best practice suppliers have the discipline to accurately assess their total cost to serve each customer, including the costs of providing supplementary services, programs, and systems. Furthermore, they formally document how a greater share of a customer's business translated into greater profits. Profitability may come from lowered costs, a higher price paid by the customer, or a more-profitable mix of business with a customer. In turn, progressive firms use the knowledge gained to target customer firms for closer relationships and to tailor relationship-specific offerings during the upcoming year. In Box 10.9, we provide a detailed illustration of how Bank of America has selectively grown and documented its profitable share of customers' business.

BOX 10.9
Bank of America Selectively Grows Business via Integrated Banking

In early 2001, incoming chief executive officer, Kenneth D. Lewis, dramatically shifted the Bank of America's (BAC) overall strategy from rapid growth through aggressive bank acquisition to delivering superior shareholder value-added (SVA) through enhanced operating profits. To do so in business markets, BAC has implemented an **integrated banking model**, combining its corporate and Montgomery Securities units into its Global Corporate and Investment Bank (GCIB). In this way, GCIB will be able to provide its clients with a total financial solution comprised of both traditional corporate banking and investment banking services. BAC executives based this decision on a growing trend among major corporations to outsource a significant portion of their financial service requirements to a single bank and on the explosive growth in the highly profitable investment banking marketplace. However, this new model would place BAC in competition with well-established financial boutiques, such as Goldman Sachs, Morgan Stanley, Merrill Lynch, and Citigroup, which primarily offer investment banking services.

President of GCIB, Edward J. Brown III, is responsible for implementing the integrated banking model. In line with CEO Lewis's new strategy, Brown and his management team replaced GCIB objectives and employee performance measures based on *league table rankings* (i.e., market shares of specific product lines) with new ones based on *client profitability* and *share of wallet* (i.e., share of customer's business). Rather than pursuing revenue growth through cross-selling and up-selling any and all corporate accounts (i.e., corporations with sales in excess of $500 million), Brown and his team charted a focused strategy that pivots on what pundits call *right-selling* (i.e., profitably selling offerings that a customer truly requires) to select strategic clients. The strategy has several key elements.

Relative to other corporate banks, BAC has long maintained an unusually high level of market penetration among large corporations (e.g., 80 percent of the *Fortune* Global 500 and 95 percent of the *Fortune* Domestic 500). Instead of seeking greater sales across all of these companies, GCIB elected to focus on seven industry sectors—consumer product retailing, financial services, general industrial, health-care, media and telecommunications, natural resources, and real estate—developing industry expertise and highly customized offerings. Management targeted these sectors because of their attractiveness (i.e., profit and growth potential) and GCIB's ability to compete effectively (e.g., GCIB's core competencies, market expertise, and ability to meet client service requirements). Most importantly, GCIB managers believe that in these seven sectors, its client managers would have the greatest opportunity to leverage past corporate banking business to win highly profitable, investment banking business.

Even within these seven sectors, GCIB does not pursue all possible business. Senior managers have identified and targeted some 375 *strategic clients*. These strategic clients have either expressed an interest in or would most likely benefit from GCIB's integrated banking approach. Naturally, GCIB managers believe that these strategic clients offer the greatest profit potential. GCIB diligently seeks to become the *lead bank* for as many of these 375 strategic clients as is possible. Viewed as a trusted partner and financial advisor to a client's senior management, the lead bank gains the greatest share of wallet and profitable business from a given customer account.

GCIB altered its organization structure from one based on product lines and geography to one built around client-based teams. Each team has both corporate and investment banking expertise and can design and deliver total financial solutions across the entire equities and debt spectrum. In this way, GCIB management hopes to deepen its working relationships with each strategic client, tailor solutions that precisely meet customer

BOX 10.9
Continued

requirements, drive down the costs to serve each account, and increase the profitability of every customer firm.

GCIB teams strive to craft total financial solutions that not only meet client requirements but also yield a high level of profit for BAC. To help teams achieve these ends, GCIB management articulated a number of important directives. First, teams must strive to sustain profitable and highly stable fee-based global treasury and cash management business including funds collection and concentration, disbursements, investments, information reporting, and forecasting services. Second, teams must aggressively pursue a greater share of a client's highly profitable investment banking business such as equities, mergers and acquisitions, and risk management services. Third, teams must reduce, if not exit entirely, high-risk and low-profit loan business.

Within two years, GCIB's integrated banking model began to produce results. Even though GCIB revenues in 2002 declined

4 percent, operating profits increased 12 percent and SVA nearly doubled. Low-profit loan balances dropped from a peak of $99 billion in August 2000 to $67 billion in 2001 and are heading toward $50 billion. In the process, GCIB stepped back from many low-margin, primarily loan-based relationships with major corporations including Wal-Mart and IBM. Simultaneously, investment banking fees grew to account for more than 46 percent of GCIB revenues as GCIB vaulted from a virtual unknown in the business to become the 11th largest global investment bank. In 2001, GCIB gained lead bank status at 34 percent of its targeted strategic clients, up from 12 percent in 1999. More importantly, revenue per strategic client jumped 54 percent from 1999 levels. Finally, *Euromoney* magazine named Bank of America both the "World's Most Improved Bank" and the "Best U.S. Bank" in 2002. Magazine editors cited the progress GCIB made during the previous year as a major contributing factor.

Source: James C. Anderson and James A. Narus, "Selectively Pursuing More of Your Customer's Business," *MIT Sloan Management Review* (Spring 2003): 42–49.

Ongoing Customer Relationship Management

Throughout this book, we have articulated a vision of business market management that is data driven. Such data come from a variety of sources including the market, customers, accounting, and operations, among others. So, it is appropriate that we examine comprehensive data-driven systems and procedures that firms use to differentially and profitably relate to customer firms.

Customer relationship management (CRM) "is the bundling of customer strategy and processes, supported by relevant software, for the purpose of improving customer loyalty and, eventually, corporate profitability."[38] Consultants Rigby, Reichheld, and Schefter further argue that the imperatives of CRM are "acquiring the right customer, crafting the right value proposition, instituting the best processes, motivating employees, and learning to retain customers."[39] Endorsing the recommendation of pundits that a company should chart out its overall customer strategies, reformulate its business processes, and identify its information requirements before designing the system and acquiring software, we have deliberately addressed these issues in previous sections of the book before tackling CRM in earnest. And, we agree that the focus of CRM should be on systems and procedures rather than on technology and software. In fact, we find that many of the most productive CRM systems in use today are decidedly "low tech," relying upon a combination of manual procedures, telephone and fax machines, and rudimentary information technology networks.

In this section, we explore CRM. We begin by discussing systems needed to monitor, evaluate, and reassign accounts. These systems estimate customer equity, draw upon activity-based costing, and track transaction prices. Next, we review emerging CRM applications such as resource allocation, synchronization of marketing efforts, and updating value delivered. We conclude describing how business market managers can sustain customers through connected relationships.

Monitoring, Evaluating, and Reassigning Accounts

At the heart of a CRM system are databases and tools for monitoring and evaluating the status of working relationships with individual customer accounts. In Chapter 8, we discuss the market and customer databases that are part of CRM systems. To improve decision-making capabilities, business market managers must also incorporate financial data on each account. With a broader view of relationship performance, managers will be in a better position to reassign accounts and direct limited resources to efforts with the greatest payout. To do so, they need to estimate customer equity, implement activity-based costing, and monitor transaction prices.

Estimate Customer Equity

Customer equity is the sum of the lifetime values of all the firm's customers. The **lifetime value of a customer firm**, in turn, is the net present value of the total current and future revenues a given customer generates for a company minus all costs associated with acquiring and serving that customer. Ideally, customer equity should be the beacon that guides all business market management decisions. After all, with an understanding of customer equity, managers would be able to precisely allocate the firm's scarce resources to serving each customer account in proportion to its potential profitability.[40]

According to Blattberg, Getz, and Thomas, pursuing customer equity dramatically changes a firm's marketing efforts. These changes mirror the processes we advocate in this book. Most importantly, the firm's strategy, tactics, and execution become customer-driven rather than product- or brand-driven as managers strive to maximize customer profitability. The firm manages based on the customer life cycle rather than the product life cycle. In Chapter 8 and Figure 8.2, we described the **customer life cycle** in terms of the customer adoption process and the prospecting funnel. As we emphasized in Chapter 2, managers treat customers as a valuable asset to be cultivated and sustained and they link marketing efforts quantitatively to the financial worth of the firm. The company manages a portfolio of customer firms as in this chapter. Finally, the company organizes around the task of finding, keeping, and growing profitable customers.[41]

Although managing via customer equity has had reported successes in the direct marketing and retailing industries, we find few documented examples in business markets. In practice, few firms have the requisite financial reporting systems in place needed to generate data for the analyses. Moreover given dynamic market conditions and ever-changing costs-of-capital, future predictions of sales—let alone their net present values—are speculative at best. Until better data collection and forecasting procedures are developed, we urge managers to think strategically in terms of customer equity while making decisions based on rigorous analyses of customer contribution to profitability. This process requires a CRM system that taps activity-based costing data and monitors transaction prices for each customer account.

Implement Activity-Based Costing[42]

Rather than arbitrarily allocating expenses to individual units or customers, activity-based costing (ABC) matches expenses to activities that consume them. To apply ABC practices to customer firms, managers first identify customer cost categories and then determine the cost driver for each category.

Customer cost categories might include some or all of the following.[43]

- *Transaction-specific costs.* These expenses are associated with the processing and fulfillment of customer orders. They include such things as sales force commissions, order-processing costs, stock-picking expenses, and excise or value-added taxes.
- *Customer-specific costs.* Such costs reflect the customization of the market offering. The costs of optional services, codesign efforts, and sales calls are examples.
- *Customer segment costs.* These costs are directed at an entire market segment and cannot be traced to individual customers. Industry journal advertising, association membership, and trade show booths might fall in this category. Also, costs associated with a major-account sales team that has responsibility for several accounts are another example.
- *Support costs.* Support costs are those customer-sustaining expenditures that cannot be attributed to any specific account or segment. They include costs associated with such things as the division's staff personnel, senior managers, and offices. Corporate advertising that promotes an umbrella image or reputation for the firm is another example.

Cost-drivers are the specific factors that increase or decrease expenses in each of these categories. For example, customer-specific costs are likely to reflect customer capabilities and the complexity of the customer's applications. Importantly, the cost-drivers suggest ways to reduce resource consumption. A supplier firm, for instance, might target transactional customers that have extensive technical support capabilities or simple applications in order to minimize the firm's customer-specific costs.

Perhaps the most basic application of ABC analysis is to calculate the cost-to-serve a given customer. **Cost-to-serve** represents the total pre-sale, order-related, distribution, and post-sale service costs required to maintain an ongoing exchange relationship with a customer firm.[44] Firms with more sophisticated accounting systems use ABC information to develop a direct-costing income statement, which reflects the cost categories presented above and separates variable costs from fixed costs. This statement conveys four measures of profitability:

- Contribution margin is net sales minus direct labor, materials, and energy costs.
- Controllable margin is the contribution margin minus transaction- and customer-specific costs.

- Segment margin is the controllable margin minus customer-segment support costs and assigned corporate overhead.
- Net profit before taxes is the segment margin minus otherwise-unassigned corporate overhead.

It is important to note that a different manager might be responsible for each measure. A marketing manager might control the contribution margin, a relationship manager might be in charge of controllable margin, the division manager often handles segment margin, and the chief operating officer may have responsibility for net profits before taxes.

After a suitable period, business market managers use these ABC results to conduct an account variance analysis, which charts deviations from average performance on each measure. Business market managers begin by grouping all collaborative accounts together and all transactional accounts together and comparing their average results against the overall averages. Based on this review, managers might revise their targeting and resource allocation strategies. Next, managers compare each account's profitability measures to the relevant averages for its relationship segment. Thus, a business market manager would compare results for a collaborative account to the average for all collaborative accounts. In instances where measures such as controllable margin are negative, managers may decide to reassign the account, say from collaborative to transactional emphasis, raise its prices, or stop serving the customer altogether.

Monitor Transaction Prices

As a useful complement to ABC information, business market managers monitor **transaction pricing**, which focuses on realizing the greatest net price for each individual order. Managers learn from transaction prices the extent to which the firm's relationship-specific pricing strategies and tactics have been consistently applied. Underscoring the significance of managing transaction pricing, Marn and Rosiello contend that a 1 percent improvement in price, assuming no volume loss, increases a supplier firm's operating profits by 11 percent.[45]

To monitor transaction prices, business market managers apply three concepts. First, managers construct a "pocket-price waterfall," which refers to all terms, discounts, rebates, incentives, and bonuses that a customer firm receives for a given transaction. Managers then subtract these waterfall elements from list price to produce a pocket price, which refers to the revenue a supplier firm actually realizes from that transaction. Finally, for some relevant time period, managers construct a "pocket-price band," which is the distribution of all pocket prices the supplier realized from its customers for the offering. The width and shape of the distribution convey pricing consistency. Further analysis will reveal such things as which customer segments receive the greatest discounts, customers' willingness to pay, and how appropriately field salespersons are exercising their pricing authority.

As is the case with revenue management, which we discussed in Chapter 8, business market managers use information on the pocket-price band and waterfall to improve their firm's profitability. For starters, they drive sales and marketing efforts off the "tails" of the pocket-price band. They target customers at the high end of the band for more collaborative relationships. Specifically, they try to increase purchases within this desirable segment by offering these customers additional value-added services. Some suppliers devise and implement customer loyalty programs, where the suppliers share an additional portion of the value of each transaction with targeted customers to sustain and build relationships with them. Year-end rebates or bonuses tied to purchases or growth in purchases are examples. At the same time, managers try to get pocket prices at the low end of the band back under control by making relationships more transactional. For example, one company capped price exception discounts for customers at 5 percent and granted them only after managers completed specific volume and margin impact evaluations.[46]

As a final step, business market managers strive to reengineer the pocket-price waterfall. They do so by examining each pricing element's significance to individual customers and its impact on supplier firm profitability. In some cases, they might restructure the manner in which they present a price element to customers. For instance, they might subtract a promotional allowance from list price rather than from invoice price in order to create the illusion of lower prices. In another case, managers might shift funds from a price element that customers no longer value, such as a co-op advertising allowance, to one that is becoming increasingly important, such as a year-end rebate.

Evaluate Relationship Outcomes and Reassign Accounts

Sound CRM systems track cost-to-serve, transaction prices, and the contribution to profitability of each customer firm. Managers use this information to assess the results of their relationship-building efforts and take corrective actions such as reassigning accounts to different relational categories or redesigning relationship-specific offerings. Furthermore, as we discussed in Chapter 8, managers can build a profile of desirable prospective customer firms for use in future targeting decisions.

Professor Narayandas advocates evaluating the firm's portfolio of customers on a 2×2 grid, where average transaction price (high or low) functions as rows and cost-to-serve (high or low) as the columns. Naturally, the supplier firm needs to bolster collaboration with high price and low cost-to-serve customers because they are the most profitable. Conversely, unless some strategic reason dictates otherwise, supplier managers should consider not serving low price and high cost-to-serve customers. Rather than "firing customers," business market managers should reformulate their offerings and increase their prices to profitable levels. Then, customers can decide whether to pay the higher prices or to leave the relationship.[47]

The remaining two cells require more detailed evaluation. For example, some of the high cost-to-serve customers pay high enough prices to generate profits for the supplier. These collaborative-emphasis accounts should be retained and cultivated. However, those high cost-to-serve customers that do not pay high enough prices to yield a profit should be investigated. Their offerings too should be reformulated and their prices increased to profitable levels.

On the other hand, a number of low cost-to-serve customers firms pay sufficiently high enough prices to be profitable. These transactional-emphasis accounts should be actively pursued. Logically, accounts that pay low prices which do not cover their cost-to-serve should be abandoned. As with other portfolio models, Professor Narayandas argues that supplier firms alternatively can take steps to move customers to the profitable portion of the high price and high cost-to-serve cell and the low price and low cost-to-serve cell by taking steps to either lower costs or increase the value delivered and hopefully prices paid.

Professors Kaplan and Narayanan take these analyses one step further examining cumulative profitability of a firm's customer accounts over an extended period of time. They advise managers to create a "whale curve" of their portfolio by plotting cumulative profitability (i.e., percent of total firm profits) against specific customer accounts. In their research, they discovered that for the typical firm, the most profitable 20 percent of accounts generate between 150 percent and 300 percent of the firm's profits. The firm breaks even on the next 70 percent of customers and loses money on the rest. They recommend that suppliers strengthen relationships with the most profitable 20 percent of accounts, reduce cost-to-serve or increase prices paid by the middle group, and consider not serving the bottom 10 percent of customers.[48]

In their research on customer loyalty, Professors Reinartz and Kumar have provided controversial findings that challenge major assumptions about the profitability of long-term relationships.[49] For example they contend that in certain industries the most loyal customers may not be the most profitable because they expect and in fact pay lower prices because of their continued loyalty. Often, it is one-time transactional customers who pay the highest prices and are the most profitable. For the purpose of analyses, Reinartz and Kumar suggest creating a different 2×2 matrix by plotting cumulative profitability (i.e., high or low) against length of relationship (i.e., short-term or long-term customer) and then assigning each customer firm to one of four cells. They define "true friends" as highly profitable, long-term customers and advise suppliers to delight them with extraordinary levels of service. "Butterflies," on the other hand, are highly profitable short-term customers, and Reinartz and Kumar suggest that supplier firms actively seek them out and provide them with satisfying transactions. They advise supplier to pay little heed to "strangers" that are low profit, short-term customers. Finally, they recommend either cross-selling or up-selling or reducing the cost-to-serve for "barnacles" or low-profit, long-term customers.[50]

Business market managers should not limit the evaluation of relationships to quantitative, activity-based costing data and transaction price data. Given that the purpose of partnering is often learning, managers should consider qualitative measures, such as new product ideas contributed and amount of technology transferred. At times, these qualitative measures will be more revealing than those derived from accounting data.

Motorola's Semiconductor Sector provides an instructive example of relationship evaluation procedures. Several years ago, when Motorola began partnering in earnest, senior management devised a one-page Statement of Partnership Goals, which summarized what Motorola expected to achieve for both itself and key customers from the partnership process. We paraphrase the key objectives from this statement as follows:

- All partnership programs such as codesign or joint development will result in profits for both Motorola and its partner firm.
- Motorola's sales to the partner firm will be substantial or exhibit significant growth potential.
- Motorola should have a significant, if not exclusive, share of the partner's business.

- The partnership should contribute to the achievement of Motorola's technology roadmap goals.

Periodically, senior management compares outputs from each of the Semiconductor Sector's approximately 60 partnerships to the goals specified in the partnership statement. They consider such things as changes in sales and profits as well as the mix of complementary products sold to the partner firms. In order to gauge the benefits of the partnership to the customer firm, managers examine results of Motorola's annual customer satisfaction survey. The survey summarizes Motorola's performance from the perspective of partner firms' managers in such functional areas as manufacturing, engineering, purchasing, and R&D.

Following consultation with customer managers, Motorola downgrades partnerships that do not meet objectives. They accomplish this distancing in two ways. First, managers transfer the responsibility for a downgraded account from the Strategic Market or Segment Sales Force to the Geographic Sales Force. Second, Motorola disengages itself from partnership programs, such as joint product development. Conversely, Motorola upgrades promising geographic accounts to partnerships.

Emerging CRM Applications

Conventional CRM applications focus on account targeting, sales force automation, offering configuration and pricing, and information exchange. Evolving CRM uses include allocating resources, synchronizing marketing efforts, and updating delivered value.

Allocating Resources for Customer Acquisition, Retention, and Growth

As we mentioned previously, Blattberg, Getz, and Thomas urge companies to allocate marketing resources to the distinct tasks of customer acquisition, retention, and growth in proportion to their profit potential. A sound CRM system containing customer-specific longitudinal measures of requirements and preferences, customer value, cost-to-serve, transaction prices, and customer contribution to profitability enables managers to allocate marketing resources accordingly. For example, if managers discover that their firm serves primarily transactional-emphasis accounts, they may conclude that the likelihood of account retention and growth is meager. In this case, they would devote most of their marketing budget to finding new accounts. Conversely, if they learn that the number of potential accounts is limited and the cost of acquiring new customers is prohibitive, they would direct resources to customer retention and growth activities.[51]

Synchronizing Marketing Efforts

As marketing organizations become more complex, customer portfolios become more varied, and channels become more modular, supplier firms need to do more to synchronize operations, marketing, and service activities. CRM provides a means for ensuring that all managers who "touch the customer" are working in unison. In Box 10.10 we provide an example of how enterprise software from Siebel Systems helped CNT to synchronize its sales and service efforts.

BOX 10.10
Siebel Systems Helps CNT Synchronize Sales and Service Efforts

Based in San Mateo, California, Siebel Systems, Inc., is the world's leading provider of *e*Business applications software. Founded in 1993, Siebel Systems has been unrelenting in its efforts to innovate, grow, and improve the value of its software offerings. Initially, Siebel Systems focused on sales force automation applications, which provided functionality in the areas of contact management, opportunity management, and revenue forecasting. During the mid-1990s, Siebel Systems began to offer an integrated suite of sales, service, and marketing applications that enabled organizations to maintain a seamless, uninterrupted dialogue with customers at all points in the customer relationship. Late in the 1990s, Siebel Systems capitalized on emerging Internet technologies to develop applications that enabled organizations to also integrate their Web sites, partners, and resellers into their sales, marketing, and customer service systems. Siebel System's experiences with a client, CNT, demonstrate how its applications can be used to synchronize a firm's sales and service efforts.

With annual sales in excess of $175 million, CNT is a global provider of storage networking solutions to the data centers of leading financial services organizations, utilities, governments, and communications companies. A key component of CNT's overall value proposition is a high level of customer service pivoting on remote diagnostics, the 24×7 availability of competent telephone-based technical service, and prompt on-site support for repairs, maintenance, and upgrades. Importantly, delivery of CNT offerings requires the close coordination of its salespeople, telephone call center personnel, and field service engineers.

Yet by 1998, CNT managers recognized that the three groups were operating independently of one another, rarely sharing critical customer information in a timely manner. They attributed part of the problem to the fact that each group used its own customized software applications and databases. A lack of integration among these solutions inhibited the flow of information across groups and retarded the delivery of high-quality service. For example, it was not uncommon for a salesperson to walk into a customer facility unaware that the customer system was experiencing technical problems and that a CNT service engineer was also on-site. In addition, call center personnel might receive a telephone call from a customer and not know what applications they had purchased, what level of technical support they have specified in their service contract, what technical service problems had been encountered previously, or which field service engineers could be dispatched promptly to the customer's offices. It seemed as though each CNT sales or serviceperson had to rebuild knowledge of past dealings with a given customer at the onset of every encounter.

CNT management turned to Siebel Systems for an integrated, multichannel solution. Siebel managers recommended a suite of *e*Business Applications including Siebel Call Center, Siebel Field Service, and Siebel Sales. Working with the help of Deloitte Consulting and PricewaterhouseCoopers (PwC), Siebel personnel implemented the solution on time and on budget. The Siebel Call Center application would enable CNT to manage, synchronize, and distribute all customer contact information to all three service and sales channels. It would also provide a platform from which call center personnel could accurately diagnose technical problems and recommend appropriate remedies. Siebel Field Service would help CNT better manage service parts inventories and schedule service calls, provide technical information and repair procedures to field service engineers working on-site, and keep detailed records of all emergency and preventative maintenance incidents. Finally, Siebel Field Sales would allow CNT salespeople to share customer contact information with the other groups,

BOX 10.10
Continued

prepare quotes and proposals, circulate contract details, and schedule after-sales service and support.

According to CNT senior managers, Siebel *e*Business Applications streamlined overall business, service, and sales processes, saving the firm more than $1.7 million in operating costs. Call center agents now resolve 60 percent of technical service queries on the first call, compared to 20–30 percent under the old system. With detailed records of previous service incidents, field service engineers found that they didn't have to solve the same problems over and over again. Managers estimate that they saved more than 22,000 hours of call center personnel time and 1,800 hours of field service engineer time as a result. As for the CNT sales force, Siebel Sales has enabled salespeople to better manage the lead generation process, develop more effective sales campaigns, and prepare more accurate sales forecasts.

Updating Customer Value

To ensure the vitality of their working relationships, progressive firms periodically update the value of their relationship-specific market offerings. At times, business market managers draw on their firm's CRM system information to assist with this process. To do so adroitly, these managers constantly search for significant changes in customer requirements. When a critical trend emerges, they respond quickly. For example, they might add new services or product modifications that customers now need, while eliminating or unbundling offering elements that customers no longer value. Rather than reacting haphazardly each time customer requirements change, progressive firms devise procedures ahead of time for handling these eventualities.

Supplier managers must try to avoid complacency, an insidious relationship killer. They must continuously ask questions in a way that encourages customers to relate problems and shortcomings. The question, "What have we not done lately?" should be periodically addressed to each customer.[52] This question's wording is significant in two respects. First, it is phrased in a manner so as to encourage the voicing of problems, rather than simply soliciting a socially desirable response, such as "Fine." Second, the inclusion of "lately" recognizes the natural inertia that occurs in relationships and that leads to complacency. Most unhappy customers never complain.[53]

Sustaining Customers Through Connected Relationships

Up to this point in the chapter, we focused on managing dyadic relationships between a supplier firm and a customer firm. Yet to fully understand and capitalize on the nature of a dyadic relationships, business market managers must also consider the **business network** or interconnections among relevant people and organizations within which each dyadic relationship is embedded. Given the increasingly interconnected nature of commerce, suppliers must learn and implement a set of business network management skills. In fact, we already discussed some of these skills as they relate to supply and channel networks in Chapters 3, 7, and 9. In this section, we turn our attention to two more capabilities: managing within a business network context and adding value through business networks.[54]

Managing Within a Business Network Context

The pioneering work of the International Marketing & Purchasing Group (IMP) emphasizes the importance of gaining an in-depth understanding of the business network within which a firm operates. IMP scholars evaluate business networks in terms of actors, activities, and resources. **Actors** are individuals, organizations, and institutions connected through personal or business relationships. Business market managers need to identify key actors, assess the strength of their bonds, and map their interactions. **Activities** are the tasks that the actors perform that create value. Supplier managers should learn how activities are clustered within firms into sets, how activities between actors are linked, and how they are assembled into processes or patterns. Finally, **resources** are competencies and capabilities embedded in the network. Managers must catalog the resources of the network, evaluate links among them, and determine how they can use the constellation of network resources to create value.[55]

Knowledge of the business network enables managers to craft superior strategies and tactics. To sustain a working relationship with one customer, for example, the supplier firm may have to secure changes in other connected relationships. Alternatively, the supplier may have to coordinate the activities of several partners to maintain the integrity of value it provides to the customer. Scholars suggest a framework for crafting strategies based on describing, evaluating, and interpreting networks. Managers begin by describing the strategic situation the supplier firm faces and identifying the set of actors involved. Then, they create and evaluate an interdependence matrix that specifies the pattern of linkages among the actors. Next, managers interpret the portfolio of interdependencies assessing the resources and activities each network actor contributes. Finally, managers craft a network strategy for resolving the strategic situation. The resulting network strategy will pivot on intensifying, preparing, controlling, or neglecting working relationships with each actor in order to maximize the value created.[56]

To underscore the importance of managing the business network context, we present the Danprint Company case study in Box 10.11 and depict its business network in Figure 10.5. In Chapter 1, we presented additional concepts for analyzing and understanding business networks. We apply them here to draw insights about the relationship between Danprint and Softdrink, and what was occurring in other connected relationships.[57]

Considering its network identity, Danprint's relationship with the foreign paper mill had, to some extent, both constructive and harmful effects on its relationship with the Danish papermaker. Beyond this one instance, its collaborations with others had constructive effects on its network identity. The cooperative activities between Danprint and the equipment supplier to uphold the fill-rate guarantee for Softdrink illustrate activity complementarity, as did Danprint and the ink supplier working together on the printing quality. Danprint's collaborations in these connected relationships were clearly due to its relationship with Softdrink. In its efforts, Danprint also was signaling to other prospective large customers its availability and willingness to enter into relationships with them and make extraordinary efforts to sustain them. Thus, the relationship with the well-known and prestigious Softdrink was a central element in Danprint's network identity.

BOX 10.11
The Danprint Company Uses Connected Relationships to Solve a Vexing Problem

Danprint is a small Danish printer that supplied labels to a big Danish soft drink producer, Softdrink, for many years. The firm printed labels on a simple paper produced by a Danish paper mill. Although simple, the paper was quite special in some respects. It had a certain yellow shade that was strongly associated with Softdrink's image among its customers and distributors. Due to its wood content, the paper was also well adapted to Softdrink's equipment for cleaning and filling return bottles.

One day, the papermaker announced that it was going to stop producing the label paper. The reason was that Danprint was only a marginal purchaser of the product in comparison with journal printers, who were changing to other, more elegant, paper qualities. After some searching and several attempts with different potential suppliers, Danprint—and Softdrink—accepted one of the papermaker's other products that had the same wood content and color, but was more expensive.

Some years later, the papermaker announced that it was going to close the mill where it produced Danprint's paper. After further search, Danprint found a foreign paper mill, which, after some cooperation, could produce a paper with almost the same yellow color as the original paper. The new paper was more expensive than the old, but rather than taking the risk of relaunching the drink with a new label, Softdrink accepted the higher price.

But when Danprint used the foreign mill's paper, new problems occurred. The guarantee of Softdrink's filling equipment supplier concerning speed and function of its equipment was not valid unless it too found the paper acceptable. Consequently, Danprint and the equipment supplier started some cooperative activities on this in anticipation that it would lead to outcomes complementary to their relationships with the large, prestigious Softdrink. At the same time, Danprint also engaged in cooperation with its ink supplier to print on the new paper to the satisfaction of Softdrink and, of course, to its connected distributors and customers.

Finally, the effects of cooperation with the foreign supplier had two contrary effects on the relationship with the Danish papermaker. At first, cooperation with the competing foreign supplier had a negative impact. This effect appears, however, to have been offset later on by a positive transfer of knowledge to Danprint's relationship with the Danish papermaker. It turned out, whether it was planned or not, that Danprint succeeded in learning from its cooperation with the foreign mill the exact prescription of and procedure for testing their quality product. On the basis of this new know-how, Danprint returned to their old Danish papermaker in a stronger position and could induce this supplier to produce the paper at a much lower price.

Source: James C. Anderson, Håkan Håkansson, and Jan Johanson, "Dyadic Business Relationships Within a Business Network Context," *Journal of Marketing* (October 1994): 1–15.

The case study also shows that connections among firms in a business network cannot simply be seen as positive or negative. Rather, a relation may, in different ways, be both positively and negatively connected with another relationship at the same time. Danprint's relation with the foreign paper mill was, to some extent, negatively and positively connected to its relation with the Danish papermaker. And, apart from this, even though some connections are rather easy to estimate quantitatively,

Figure 10.5   Danprint Business Network

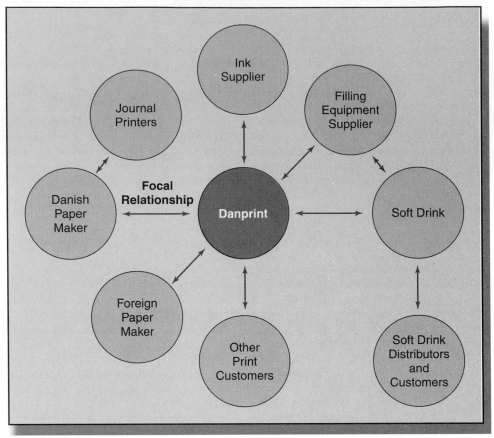

Source: Adapted from James C. Anderson, Håkan Håkansson, and Jan Johanson, "Dyadic Business Relationships Within a Business Network Context," *Journal of Marketing* (October 1994): 1–15.

others are entirely a matter of perceptual judgment or interpretations. Finally, the case also stresses the importance of time dependence in the analysis of business networks and the connections between dyadic relationships. The dyadic relationships develop over time within a network context, which is also evolving as time goes by.

Adding Value Through Business Networks

Research suggests that in some cases the total value of a solution is a function not only of a supplier's offering but also of the compatibility, accessibility, and quality of the networks within which it is embedded. These networks include the user network, the complements network, and the producer network. For example, in the case of high-technology products, the greater the installed base for an offering, the broader the variety of complementary products such as compatible software modules, and the more producers utilizing common standards, the greater is the value of an offering. As evidence, researchers cite studies demonstrating that although purchasing managers rate Unix operating systems as technically superior to Windows NT®, they are overwhelmingly more likely to acquire Windows NT for their companies because of the strength of Microsoft's user, complements, and producer networks. They recommend that business market managers make a concerted effort to strengthen these business networks. By cultivating potent networks, a supplier firm, even if it produces comparable products, may be able to dominate a market.[58]

A Final Thought on Sustaining Relationships

Working relationships with customer firms are a significant asset of any supplier's business. Through partnerships, a supplier can leverage its limited resources through joint efforts with customers, gain the benefits of customer ideas and experience, and garner higher profit margins from value-added services and larger shares of customers' business. On the other hand, transactional relationships offer the supplier the opportunity to prune elements of the market offering that customers regard as superfluous, yielding a more competitively priced offering. At the same time, this eases pressure on the supplier's profit margin.

To cultivate and sustain these disparate types of working relationships, managers must devise a coherent strategic approach. The relationship-sustaining approach that we have advocated has customer value as its cornerstone and adopts the basic premise that not all market segments, or customer firms, want the same working relationship—or value it the same. As we discussed, supplier managers must systematically decide which customer firms are in their firm's best interests to develop collaborative relationships, and then, actively work to keep them completely satisfied.

Finally, supplier firms must clearly understand the distinction between completely satisfying customer requirements and preferences, and "delighting" customers. Suppliers create delight when they provide outcomes that significantly exceed, rather than simply meet, customer expectations. Supplier managers must be aware, though, that when they provide exemplary service in one period, that level of service tends to become the customer's expectation for subsequent periods. As a result, business market managers may inadvertently create a game in which they must constantly try to top themselves at ever-increasing costs in order to retain every customer. Instead, forward-thinking suppliers employ delight selectively to achieve a strategic purpose, such as to reward trailblazing efforts with collaborative accounts. At the same time, they make certain that their firm completely satisfies all other collaborative accounts.

SUMMARY

In this chapter, we examined those activities associated with keeping and growing profitable customer relationships. We began by defining sustaining customer relationships as the process of fulfilling mutually agreed-upon customer requirements in a superior way over time and pursuing a targeted share of customers' business through building mutual self-interest. The foundations of this process are the concepts of a relationship continuum and industry bandwidths, and a strategic approach we refer to as "partnering as a focused market strategy." That approach is based on the fundamental marketing concepts of segmentation, targeting, and positioning. Among its key premises is the belief that close, collaborative relationships are not for every firm. Instead, business market managers strive to cultivate a portfolio of working relationships.

Because the various customer firms in a supplier's relationship portfolio have different requirements, business market managers will deliver value in the form of relationship-specific offerings. As customer firms become more collaborative, managers will craft more elaborate market offerings. Conversely, as customer firms become more transactional, the supplier firm will sell the most basic offering with few options. Flaring out from the industry bandwidth is a strategy that business marketers can use to configure imaginative relationship-specific offerings.

Although most managers readily grasp the concept of partnering, they have a much harder time understanding how to retain a portfolio of profitable customer relationships. Thus, we explored the behavioral issues that managers must be prepared to address when working together with customer firms including promoting open and honest communications, building trust and commitment, selecting coordination mechanisms, and resolving conflicts. By handling each behavioral issue in a superior way over time, business market managers make it advantageous for customers to engage in subsequent exchange episodes and to begin new business strands. To sustain relationships in a systematic manner, supplier firms often devise formal customer retention plans. As part of these plans, the business market manager tracks retention rates, assesses customer defections, analyzes complaints, responds immediately to thwart defections, and reformulates relationship-specific offerings.

To grow their share of profitable customer business, progressive suppliers propose such innovative business arrangements as single-sourcing, multiple single-sourcing, facilities management, and outsourcing. We provide guidance on how a supplier firm can get the customer comfortable with these innovative ideas while ensuring an equitable distribution of the value they create through new profit models such as risk-sharing, gain-sharing agreements. Collaborative risk-sharing, gaining-sharing agreements refer to arrangements in which a customer and supplier work together to improve the customer's performance, and in doing so, the supplier exposes itself to potential losses, yet also receives a prespecified portion of any success.

CRM is a comprehensive set of systems and procedures that firms use to differentially and profitably relate to customer firms. Market databases and activity-based costing systems provide the backbone for CRM. CRM systems empower business market managers to monitor, evaluate, and reassign customer accounts. Perhaps more importantly, CRM systems help managers to better allocate scarce marketing resources, synchronize operations, marketing, and service efforts, and update the value of relationship-specific market offerings. We concluded this chapter arguing that a supplier must keep relationships vibrant by using business networks.

ENDNOTES

1. Philip Kotler, *Kotler on Marketing* (New York: The Free Press, 2001), 121.
2. This discussion is based on the article, James C. Anderson and James A. Narus, "Partnering as a Focused Market Strategy," *California Management Review* (Spring 1991): 95–113.
3. Academics argue that relationships also vary in terms of interdependence and uncertainty. For a detailed description of

other types of relationships, read Joseph P. Cannon and William D. Perreault, Jr., "Buyer-Seller Relationships in Business Markets," *Journal of Marketing* (November 1999): 439–460; Oliver E. Williamson, *Markets and Hierarchies* (New York: The Free Press, 1975); Jan B. Heide, "Interorganizational Governance in Marketing Channels," *Journal of Marketing* (January 1994): 71–85; and Thomas Palay, "Comparative Institutional Economics: The Governance of Rail Freight Contracting," *Journal of Legal Studies* (June 1984): 265–288.

4. Barbara B. Jackson, *Winning & Keeping Industrial Customers* (Lexington, MA: Lexington Books, 1985).

5. Das Narayandas, *Note on Customer Management* (Boston, MA: Harvard Business School Press, 2002).

6. Eric von Hippel, "Lead Users: A Source of Novel Product Concepts," *Management Science* (July 1986): 791–805. We also discuss the lead-user concept in Chapter 6.

7. Neil Rackham and John DeVincentis, *Rethinking the Sales Force* (New York: McGraw-Hill, 1999).

8. Frances Gaither Tucker, Seymour M. Zivan, and Robert C. Camp, "How to Measure Yourself Against the Best," *Harvard Business Review* (January–February 1987): 8–10.

9. Rackham and DeVincentis, *Rethinking the Sales Force.*

10. F. Robert Dwyer, Paul H. Schurr, and Sejo Oh, "Developing Buyer-Seller Relationships," *Journal of Marketing* (April 1987): 11–27.

11. James C. Anderson and James A. Narus, "A Model of Distributor Firm and Manufacturer Firm Working Partnerships," *Journal of Marketing* (January 1990): 44.

12. Neeli Bendapudi and Robert P. Leone, "Managing Business-to-Business Customer Relationships Following Key Contact Employee Turnover in a Vendor Firm," *Journal of Marketing* (April 2002): 83–101; and Neeli Bendapudi and Robert P. Leone, "How to Lose Your Star Performer Without Losing Customers, Too," *Harvard Business Review* (November 2001): 104–112.

13. Robert M. Morgan and Shelby D. Hunt, "The Commitment-Trust Theory of Relationship Marketing," *Journal of Marketing* (July 1994): 20–38.

14. James C. Anderson and James A. Narus, "Toward a Better Understanding of Distribution Channel Working Relationships," in *Industrial Marketing: A German-American Perspective*, ed. K. Backhaus and D. Wilson (Berlin: Springer-Verlag, 1986), 326; and Denise M. Rousseau, Sim B. Sitkin, Ronald S. Burt, and Colin Camerer, "Not So Different After All: A Cross-Discipline View of Trust," *Academy of Management Review* (July 1998): 393–404.

15. Nirmalya Kumar, "The Power of Trust in Manufacturer-Retailer Relationships," *Harvard Business Review* (November–December 1996): 92–106.

16. Patricia M. Doney and Joseph P. Cannon, "An Examination of the Nature of Trust in Buyer-Seller Relationships," *Journal of Marketing* (April 1997): 35–51; Michael F. Wolff, "Building Trust in Alliances," *Research Technology Management*, (May–June 1994): 12–15.

17. Patricia M. Doney, Joseph P. Cannon, and Michael R. Mullen, "Understanding the Influence of National Culture on the Development of Trust," *Academy of Management Review* (July 1988): 601–620.

18. James C. Anderson, Håkan Håkansson, and Jan Johanson, "Dyadic Business Relationships Within a Business Network Context," *Journal of Marketing* (October 1994): 10.

19. Erin Anderson and Barton Weitz, "The Use of Pledges to Build and Sustain Commitment in Distribution Channels," *Journal of Marketing Research* (February 1992): 19.

20. Gregory T. Gundlach, Ravi S. Achrol, and John T. Mentzer, "The Structure of Commitment in Exchange," *Journal of Marketing* (January 1995): 78–92; and Anderson and Weitz, "The Use of Pledges," 18–34.

21. Christopher W. L. Hart, James L. Heskett, and W. Earl Sasser, Jr., "The Profitable Art of Service Recover," *Harvard Business Review* (July–August 1990): 148–156; and Sharon B. Schweikhard, Stephen Strasser, and Melissa R. Kennedy, "Service Recovery in Health Service Organizations," *Hospital & Health Services Administration* (Spring 1993): 3–21.

22. Jakki Mohr and John R. Nevin, "Communication Strategies in Marketing

Channels: A Theoretical Perspective," *Journal of Marketing* (October 1990): 36–51; T. Burns and G. M. Stalker, *The Management of Innovation* (London: Tavistock Publications, 1961); and Heide, "Interorganizational Governance in Marketing Channels."

23. Paul Milgrom and John Roberts, *Economics, Organization, and Management* (Upper Saddle River, NJ: Prentice Hall, 1995).

24. Anne T. Coughlan, Erin Anderson, Louis W. Stern, and Adel I. El-Ansary, *Marketing Channels*, 6th Edition (Upper Saddle River, NJ: Prentice Hall, 2001); Gary L. Frazier, "Interorganizational Exchange Behavior in Marketing Channels: A Broadened Perspective," *Journal of Marketing* (Fall 1983): 68–78; Gary L. Frazier and John O. Summers, "Interfirm Influence Strategies and Their Application Within Distribution Channels," *Journal of Marketing* (Summer 1984): 43–55; and Gary L. Frazier and Jagdish N. Sheth, "An Attitude-Behavior Framework for Distribution Channel Management," *Journal of Marketing* (Summer 1984): 43–55.

25. Jan B. Heide and George John, "The Role of Dependence Balancing in Safeguarding Transaction-Specific Assets in Conventional Channels," *Journal of Marketing* (May 1988): 20–35.

26. Anderson and Narus, "A Model"; and Heide and John, "The Role."

27. Anderson and Narus, "A Model," 44.

28. Coughlan, Anderson, Stern, and El-Ansari, *Marketing Channels*.

29. Larry J. Rosenberg and Louis W. Stern, "Toward the Analysis of Conflict in Distribution Channels: A Descriptive Model," *Journal of Marketing* (October 1970): 40–46; and Larry J. Rosenberg and Louis W. Stern, "Conflict Measurement in the Distribution Channel," *Journal of Marketing Research* (November 1971): 437–442.

30. Roy J. Lewicki and Joseph A. Litterer, *Negotiation* (Burr Ridge, IL: Irwin, 1985).

31. This discussion is based on the article: Glen De Souza, "Designing a Customer Retention Plan," *Journal of Business Strategy* (March–April 1992): 24–28.

32. Frederick F. Reichheld and W. Earl Sasser, Jr., "Zero Defections: Quality Comes to Services," *Harvard Business Review* (September–October 1990): 105–111.

33. This discussion is based on the article, James C. Anderson and James A. Narus, "Selectively Pursuing More of Your Customer's Business," *MIT Sloan Management Review* (Spring 2003): 40–49.

34. Robert S. Kaplan and V. G. Narayanan, "Measuring and Managing Customer Profitability," *Journal of Cost Management* (September–October 2001): 5–15; and Roland T. Rust, Christine Moorman, and Peter R. Dickson, "Getting Return on Quality: Revenue Expansion, Cost Reduction, or Both?" *Journal of Marketing* (October 2002): 7–24.

35. Narayandas, *Note on Customer Management*; and Rackham and DeVincentis, *Rethinking the Sales Force*.

36. Sandy D. Jap, "Pie Sharing in Complex Collaboration Contexts," *Journal of Marketing Research* (February 2001): 86–99.

37. James B. L. Thomson and James C. Anderson, "Pursuing Risk-Sharing, Gain-Sharing Arrangements," *Marketing Management* (Summer 2000): 40–47.

38. Darrell K. Rigby, Frederick F. Reichheld, and Phil Schefter, "Avoid the Four Perils of CRM," *Harvard Business Review* (February 2002): 102.

39. Rigby, Reichheld, and Schefter, "Avoid the Four Perils of CRM," 106.

40. Roland T. Rust, Valarie A. Zeithaml, and Katherine N. Lemon, *Driving Customer Equity* (New York: The Free Press, 2000).

41. Robert C. Blattberg, Gary Getz, and Jacquelyn S. Thomas, *Customer Equity* (Boston, MA: Harvard Business School Press, 2001).

42. Robin Cooper and Robert S. Kaplan, "Profit Priorities from Activity-Based Costing," *Harvard Business Review* (May–June 1991): 130–135.

43. George Foster and Mahendra Gupta, "Marketing, Cost Management, and Management Accounting," *Journal of Management Accounting Research* (Fall 1994): 43–77.

44. Narayandas, *Note on Customer Management*.

45. We base this discussion on the following article, Michael V. Marn and Robert L.

Rosiello, "Managing Price, Gaining Profit," *Harvard Business Review* (September–October 1992): 84–94.

46. Louise O'Brien and Charles Jones, "Do Rewards Really Create Loyalty?" *Harvard Business Review* (May–June 1995): 75–82.

47. Narayandas, *Note on Customer Management*.

48. Robert S. Kaplan and V. G. Narayanan, "Measuring and Managing Customer Profitability," *Journal of Cost Management* (September–October 2001): 5–15; and Robert S. Kaplan, *Using ABC to Manage Customer Mix and Relationships* (Boston, MA: Harvard Business School Press, 1997).

49. The criticisms arise from the authors' substitution of measures of tenure for loyalty in their statistical analyses and their failure to examine customer profitability over a sufficiently long period of time.

50. Werner J. Reinartz and V. Kumar, "The Impact of Customer Relationship Characteristics on Profitable Lifetime Duration," *Journal of Marketing* (January 2003): 77–99; and Werner J. Reinartz and V. Kumar, "The Mismanagement of Customer Loyalty," *Harvard Business Review* (July 2002): 86–94.

51. Blattberg, Getz, and Thomas, *Customer Equity*.

52. Theodore Levitt, "After the Sale Is Over," *Harvard Business Review* (September–October 1983): 87–93.

53. Reichheld and Sasser, "Zero Defections."

54. Judy K. Frels, Tasadduq Shervani, and Rajendra K. Srivastava, "The Integrated Networks Model: Explaining Resource Allocations in Network Markets," *Journal of Marketing* (January 2003): 29–45.

55. Håkan Håkansson and Ivan Snehota (eds.), *Developing Relationships in Business Networks* (London: Routledge, 1995); and David Ford, *Understanding Business Markets*, 2nd ed. (London: The Dryden Press, 1997).

56. Uta Jüttner and Lutz E. Schlange, "A Network Approach to Strategy," *International Journal of Research in Marketing*, 13 (1996): 479–494.

57. This discussion is drawn from the article, Anderson, Håkansson, and Johanson, "Dyadic Business Relationships," 1–15. The company names are disguised.

58. Frels, Shervani, and Srivastava, "The Integrated Networks Model.

INDEX

A

ABC. *See* Activity-based costing (ABC)
ABN-AMRO (AA) (Dutch bank)
    correspondent banking, 21, 32
    correspondent banking group (CBG), 21, 32
    correspondent banking units (CBUs), 21
    letters of credit syndication, 229, 230
    mutual fit, assessing, 334–335, 336
    realization process model of, 250–252, 254
Accounts, reassignment of, 427–429
Acer Computer, 290–291
Acquisition costs, 98
Acquisition, functional, 275
Acros Whirlpool, 372, 373
ACSI. *See* American Customer Satisfaction Index (ACSI)
Action plan, market strategy, 162–163
Activities, business network model, 30, 432
Activity-based costing (ABC), 98, 190, 425–426
Activity cycle, 120–122, 123
Actors, business network model, 30, 432
Adaptive channels, 281, 381–389
    auxiliary support systems, 382–383
    capabilities-sharing agreements, 386–387
    implementation problems, 387–389, 390
    integrated supply management (ISM), 383–384
    reseller alliances and consortia, 383–385
    sharing capabilities with channel members, 386–387
Adaptive selling, 332, 401
Adjusting commitments, partnership, 372–377
    gives & gets, reformulating, 373–375
    joint annual plan adjustments, 375–377
Advanced development projects, 232–233
Advanced intelligent network services, 62
Advances, 349
Advantages, product, 344–345
Advertisements, 324, 326
Advisory councils, reseller, 377–378
Advisory panel (CAP), customer, 165–166
A/E/C Systems, leads from business market databases by, 322
Affinity chromatography, 263
Aftercare phase, realization process model, 245
Agents, 289
Aggregate project plan, 228–235
    capacity decisions and, 233–234
    critical skills and capabilities, identifying, 235
    mapping of development projects, 228–233
        alliances and partnership projects, 233
        breakthrough projects, 231–232
        derivative projects, 229–230
        platform projects, 232
        research and development projects, 232–233
AGLIFE Database, 280
Agrichemicals, channels for, 278–279, 280

Airbourne Express, customer intimacy strategy, 141
Air France, 139
AKZO NOBEL (AN) Coatings
    creating value by adding new services, 194
    implementation of new market offerings, 202–203, 264, 265
    payoff from value assessments, 189, 190
    realization process model of, 245–246, 254
    research centers, 257
ALCOA, 142
Allaire, Xerox's, 9
Allegiance Healthcare, 181, 421
Alliances
    alliance networks, 27, 28
    alliances and partnership projects, 233
    Joint Strike Fighter (JSF) network, 27, 28, 29–30
    reseller alliances, 383–385
    strategic alliances, 25
Allocation skills, 163
Allowances, 374
Alpha testing, 261
Alternative close, 346
Alternative development structures, 238–239
Alternative marketing channels, 279–281
American Arbitration Association, 20
American Business Information, 323
American Customer Satisfaction Index (ACSI), 81–82
AMP, 216–217
Analog Devices, 226
Anderson, Eugene, 82
Anderson, James C., 28, 80
Angus Chemicals, 294
Annual plan, adjusting joint, 375–377
AOL, 284
Apple Computing, 196
Application, market segmentation based on, 47
Applied Industrial Technologies (AIT), 157, 158, 369, 407, 408
Appropriability, resource, 134
Approved-vendor status, 341
Arbitration, 20, 25, 411
Arcelor, 205
Architect, network roles and, 32
Areas of responsibility, sales representative, 297–298
Argentina, 17
Ariba, 96
Asea Brown Boveri (ABB), 232, 249, 254
    power transformers, 195
Assessment, value. *See* Value assessment
Association of German Engineers (VDI Zentrum Wertanalyse), 112
Assumptions, competitor analysis and, 56
Assumptive close, 346
AT&T, 118–119, 327
A. T. Kearney, 59
Auctions, electronic, 95–96, 285, 327

compensation of based on profitability, 295, 296
demonstrating and documenting value to prospects by, 342–349
follow up with prospects after the sale by, 356–357
motivating to follow up on prospects, 329–330
sales support for, 330–332
training to deal with prospects, 330
Sales support, 330–332
Sasser, W. Earl, 82–83
Scenario analysis, 151–152
Scenarios, constructing market, 151–152
SCM. *See* Strategic cost management (SCM)
Scope, expanding working relationship, 417–419
Scorecard, balanced, 154
Seesaw effect, 98
SEGHERS Better Technology Group, 415, 420
Segmentation. *See* Market segmentation
Segmentation, targeting, and positioning (STP), 14, 397
Seibu, 276
Selective intensity, 282
Self-explicated approach, assessment of customer value, 64
Selling
adaptive, 332
consultative, 332–333, 339, 340–341, 401
enterprise, 332, 333, 401–402
of relationship-specific offerings, 401–402
scheduling the first meeting, 335–336
SPIN approach. *See* SPIN selling
transactional, 332–333, 401
See also Sales calls
Sensing, market. *See* Market sensing
Sensitivity analyses, 74
Service costs, 188–189
Service recovery system, 407–408
Services
augmented, 176, 183, 255
characteristics unique to, 182
as core market offering, 182–183
flexible market offerings and
building flexibility into new, 193–195
pricing of, 195–196
reevaluation of standard services, 190–193
reexamination of optional services, 193
See also Market offerings
Service standards, differential for each market segment, 299
Set-based concurrent engineering, 236–238
SFK Documented Solutions Program, 346, 347
Share-building
adoption of new profit models and, 419–421
by Bank of America, 415, 416–417
broadening of working relationships and, 419, 420
documenting profitability of greater share, 421–423
estimating and targeting customer shares, 414
expanding working relationship scope, 417–419
focused, 415
single-sourcing and multiple single-sourcing and, 415–417
Shareholder value, 10
Shareholder value added (SVA), 371
Share of customer's business, 53
Bank of America measures of, 413
customer intimacy and, 142
customer retention and, 412
differentiation of commodities and, 180

estimating and targeting for profitable growth, 414
market segmentation and, 53
MASER LTDA research into, 149–150
as proxy for customer loyalty, 83
researching, 148
sales and profit forecasting and, 53
satisfaction measurements and, 82–83
Technische Unie's determination of, 54–55
Share of wallet, 422
Sharia law, 19
Shell International, 110, 111, 112, 375
Shopping bots, 95
Side bets, channel, 291, 292
Side-by-side tests, 345
Siebel, 354–355, 429, 430–431
Siemens, 43, 240
Siemens Malaysia, 44
Signaling criteria, 346
Simple sales, 335–336
Single-channel strategy, 281
Single-source provider, focused, 415
Single-sourcing, 94, 415
Single subjective index, supplier performance and, 125
Situation assessment, 150
Situation questions, 338–339
SKF Documented Solutions Program, 369
Skills training, 378–379
Skimming pricing strategy, 207
SMALLFRY Industrial Design, 243–245, 246, 254
Snow, Charles C., 31
Social networks, market-oriented research and, 258
Software, competitor analysis with, 58–59
Sole-sourcing, 94
SONEPAR, 386–387, 391
Sonoco Products Company, 75, 197–198, 294, 295, 331, 343, 344
Sourcing strategy, 102–104, 133
e-sourcing, 95–96
global sourcing, 95
multiple single-sourcing, 415, 417, 418
multisourcing, 94
outsourcing, 102
single-sourcing, 94, 415
sole-sourcing, 94
Spam, 327
Specifications, 97
Speculation strategy, 104, 277
Speed-to-market, 226
SPI. *See* Supplier performance index (SPI)
Spin-offs, 85, 275
SPIN selling, 333
call plans and, 337
commitment in customer and supplier relationships and, 346–349
demonstrating and documenting value to prospects and, 345–346
follow up after the sale, 356–357
investigation of prospects needs and requirements, 338–339
opening the sales call, 337–338
SPIN questions asked, 338–339
transactional selling vs., 333
Sprint Business, 49, 50–51
Standard Chartered, 31
Standardization, 101